Masterin
Financial Statements
Volume 1

Ryan Kraut

JUTA

Mastering Group Financial Statements Volume 1

First published 2019

Juta and Company (Pty) Ltd
First floor, Sunclare building, 21 Dreyer street, Claremont 7708
PO Box 14373, Lansdowne 7779, Cape Town, South Africa
www.juta.co.za

© 2019 Juta and Company (Pty) Ltd

ISBN 978 1 48511 189 4

Project manager: Carlyn Bartlett-Cronje
Editor: Lilane Joubert
Cover designer: Adam Rumball
Typesetter: Henry Daniels

Typeset in Sabon LT Std 10 on 12 pt

Contents

Preface

Mastering Group Financial Statements seeks to assist accounting students and practitioners in understanding and applying the concepts and principles of the following International Financial Reporting Standards (IFRSs) as they pertain to group accounting:

- IAS 7 *Statement of Cash Flows*;

- IAS 12 *Income Taxes*;

- IAS 21 *The Effects of Changes in Foreign Exchange Rates*;

- IAS 27 *Separate Financial Statements*;

- IAS 28 *Investments in Associates and Joint Ventures*;

- IAS 38 *Intangible Assets*;

- IFRS 3 *Business Combinations*;

- IFRS 5 *Non-current Assets Held for Sale and Discontinued Operations*;

- IFRS 9 *Financial Instruments*;

- IFRS 10 *Consolidated Financial Statements*;

- IFRS 11 *Joint Arrangements*; and

- IFRS 12 *Disclosure of interests in Other Entities*.

Mastering Group Financial Statements Volume 1 provides extensive practical guidance in applying the principles of control under IFRS 10, addresses the key disclosure requirements of group financial statements as per IFRS 12, explains the basic concepts of business combinations in accordance with IFRS 3 and covers in detail the principles and procedures for consolidating subsidiaries in all manner of scenarios.

This publication is designed to assist the needs of the following:

- Undergraduate and post graduate university students, enrolled in financial accounting courses. This includes students studying on a distance learning basis.

- Members and students of professional accounting bodies such as the South African Institute of Chartered Accountants, the South African Institute of Professional Accountants and the Institute of Certified Professional Accountants.

- Accounting practitioners and preparers of group financial statements.

About the author

Ryan Kraut CA (SA) M Com (Tax), is a Chartered Accountant with many years' experience in lecturing and tutoring financial accounting, from first-year to fourth-year (honours) level at two of the largest private tertiary educational institutions in South Africa.

A good deal of his financial accounting lecturing and tutoring, has focused on accounting for groups, which has enabled him to comprehend fully the difficulties students typically encounter in this area.

Setting and marking group accounting student exams has given him tremendous insight into the way students conceptualise and answer group accounting exam questions. This has informed his approach to creating a group accounting textbook that truly addresses students' needs and facilitates a fundamental understanding of underlying group accounting concepts.

Ryan currently works as an IFRS technical consultant and has also worked as a group accountant. This has provided him with considerable real-world group accounting and IFRS experience, which further enhances the technically sound and practical approach used in *Mastering Group Financial Statements Volume 1*.

Key features of the publication

LEARNING OBJECTIVES

Learning objectives are included at the beginning of each chapter. Students can use these to view the key topics covered in each chapter.

ILLUSTRATIVE DIAGRAMS

Illustrative diagrams, such as tables, decision trees and conceptual flowcharts, serve as a valuable learning aid by visually reinforcing the main text and by clearly connecting ideas and concepts.

WORKED EXAMPLES

Worked examples illustrate and explain in detail the preparation of group financial statements in accordance with IFRS. In doing so, the worked examples make use of both an analysis of equity and pro forma journal entries. In addition, consolidation worksheets are included, clearly showing how the pro forma journals that have been passed, result in the final amounts reported in the group financial statements. Extensive explanations in the worked example solutions enhance the understanding of group accounting concepts and principles.

SUMMARIES

Summaries at the end of each chapter provide a concise overview of the key concepts covered in each chapter.

END-OF-CHAPTER QUESTIONS

Comprehensive self-study questions are designed to test students' understanding of the concepts covered in a particular chapter and highlight possible areas where further work is required.

SUPPORT MATERIAL

Students

The following resources are freely available to students:

- *Integrated case study problems* – These problems are excellent preparation for tests and exams since they require students to apply their knowledge and understanding of a number of group accounting concepts and principles to a complex scenario. Fully worked solutions are provided.

- *Worked examples illustrating the pro forma journal entries* passed relating to subsidiaries, associates/joint ventures and joint operations, when depreciable property, plant and equipment, non-depreciable property plant and equipment as well as inventory is sold intragroup. Furthermore, an *extensive pro forma journal entries template* shows the pro forma journal entries passed in respect of subsidiaries, associates/joint ventures and joint operations, in multiple scenarios, when preparing group financial statements. These are valuable learning and revision tools for tests and exams.

Lecturers

- *Editable PowerPoint® slides*, organised by chapter.
- *An extensive bank of more than 30 questions with solutions*, covering second-year to fourth-year (honours) level, which lecturers can use/adapt as test and exam questions; tutorial questions; and additional class examples. A comprehensive index for these questions is supplied showing which chapters the question covers, the level of difficulty (basic, intermediate or advanced), the suggested year of study and the key issues covered in each question.
- *Solutions* to end of chapter questions in the textbook.

List of abbreviations

CSCIE	Consolidated statement of changes in equity
CSOPL_OCI	Consolidated statement of profit or loss and other comprehensive income
CU	Currency unit
IASB	International Accounting Standards Board
IFRS	International Financial Reporting Standards
OCI	Other comprehensive income
P/L	Profit or loss
RUL	Remaining useful life
SCIE	Statement of changes in equity
SFP	Statement of financial position
SOPL_OCI	Statement of profit or loss and other comprehensive income

AN INTRODUCTION TO GROUP ACCOUNTING

LEARNING OBJECTIVES

After studying this chapter, you should be able to:

- understand what group financial statements are;

- understand why we prepare group financial statements;

- identify a group of entities;

- know the different degrees of influence that an investor can exert over an investee and how this impacts on the accounting treatment of the investee in the group financial statements;

- define what is meant by control and explain each of the elements of control;

- critically analyse various investment structures to determine whether or not an investor has control over an investee;

- understand what consolidated financial statements are, when they need to be prepared and the basic accounting and financial reporting principles that underlie their preparation;

- know the requirements for classification of an entity as an investment entity as well as the accounting treatment of an investment entity in the consolidated financial statements;

- understand what a direct and an indirect controlling interest in a subsidiary is;

- know and apply the different accounting treatments for an investment in a subsidiary, an associate and a joint venture in the separate financial statements of the parent/investor;

- know the disclosure requirements in the separate financial statements of a parent that is exempt from presenting consolidated financial statements;

- know the disclosure requirements in the separate financial statements of:
  - a parent that prepares consolidated financial statements; and
  - an investor with joint control of, or significant influence over, an investee; and

- know the disclosure requirements of IFRS 12 Disclosure of Interests in Other Entities.

TOPIC LIST

Introduction

Entities invest (acquire equity interests) in other entities for a variety of reasons, for example:

- to obtain access to the necessary manpower, skills or resources;
- to assist entry into new or foreign markets by investing in companies already operating in such markets;
- to increase their market share by investing in competitors and other suitable entities; and
- to reduce costs through economies of scale or through investing in suppliers.

It is important for us to understand the **nature of the relationship** that arises when one entity (the investor) obtains an equity interest in another entity (the investee). More particularly, we need to establish the **degree of influence** that the investor has over the investee's **net assets** and **financial and operating activities** upon acquiring the equity interest.

1.1   The concept of group financial statements

In circumstances where an investor that is a separate reporting entity acquires control, joint control or significant influence upon acquisition of an equity interest in an investee, there arises a **combination of different entities** that together are known as a **group**.

Further, the **additional set of financial statements** that then needs to be prepared and that **combines the individual financial statements** of the entities to reflect the financial position, financial performance and cash flows of the group of entities as if they are a **single economic entity** is referred to as the **group financial statements**.

Group financial statements provide more decision-useful information to financial statement users than do the individual financial statements of the investor. This is because the investor's separate financial statements reflect investments in other entities simply at cost or fair value, with any dividends paid by the investee being recognised as income of the investor. This accounting treatment fails to reflect the decision-making power of the investor over the group entities, which is reflected in group financial statements by showing the appropriate portion (based on the degree of influence) of the net assets and results of the group as a whole. The group financial statements therefore enable the financial statement user properly to assess and form a complete picture of group resources controlled and group profits earned, and to understand the relative exposure of the investor to the risks and rewards inherent in the various group companies.

1.2   Understanding the degrees of influence

How a particular investee is accounted for in the group financial statements depends on the degree of influence that the investor exerts over the investee.

1.2.1 Control

Control represents the **strongest degree of influence** that an investor can exert over an investee. IFRS 10 *Consolidated Financial Statements* requires that when an investor, known as the **parent, controls** an investee, called a **subsidiary,** the parent is required – subject to limited exceptions – to prepare **consolidated financial statements.**

An investor **controls** an investee when it is **exposed,** or has **rights,** to **variable returns** from its involvement with the investee and has the **ability to affect those returns** through its **power over the investee** (IFRS 10.6).

Consolidated financial statements are the financial statements of **a group** in which the **assets, liabilities, equity, income, expenses** and **cash flows** of the **parent** and its **subsidiaries** are presented as those of a **single economic entity** (IFRS10 Appendix A).

The process of preparing consolidated financial statements is explained in detail in Volume 1 Chapters 3 to 8 and Volume 2 Chapters 1 and 7.

1.2.2 Significant influence

Significant influence is defined in IAS 28 *Investments in Associates and Joint Ventures* as the power to **participate in the financial and operating policy decisions** of the investee but is *not* control or joint control of those policies. Where there is **significant influence,** the investee is known as an **associate** and the **equity method,** as described by IAS 28, is used to account for the associate in, among others, the group financial statements. Broadly speaking, application of the equity method recognises the investor's share of any changes in the equity of the investee, after acquisition, in the financial reporting periods when such changes arise instead of when the investor receives dividends from its investee. The application of the equity method, under IAS 28, is covered in Volume 2 Chapter 2.

1.2.3 Joint control

Joint control is defined in IFRS 11 *Joint Arrangements* as the **contractually agreed sharing of control** of an **arrangement,** which exists only when **decisions** about the **relevant activities** require the **unanimous consent** of the **parties sharing control.**

Joint arrangements can either be classified as:

- a **joint venture,** which is a **joint arrangement** whereby the parties that have joint control of the arrangement have **rights to the net assets** of the arrangement; or

- a **joint operation,** which is **joint arrangement** whereby the parties that have joint control of the arrangement have **rights to the assets,** and **obligations** for the **liabilities,** relating to the arrangement.

In the case of a joint venture, the joint venturer (being the party to the joint venture with joint control thereof) is required to apply the equity method under IAS 28 – as discussed under Section 1.2.2 – to its investment in the joint venture in, among others, the group financial statements. Application of the equity method, under IAS 28, to joint ventures, is also dealt with in Volume 2 Chapter 2.

A joint operator (being a party to a joint operation that has joint control of that joint operation) is required to account for its share of the assets, liabilities, revenues and expenses relating to its interest in a joint operation in accordance with the IFRSs applicable to the particular assets, liabilities, revenues and expenses. IFRS 11, which regulates the accounting for joint operations, is covered in Volume 2 Chapter 3.

1.2.4 Simple share investments

Where there is **less than significant influence**, the investment, which is an investment in an **equity instrument** (i.e., ordinary shares), simply needs to be accounted for in the investor's **individual financial statements** in terms of IFRS 9 *Financial Instruments* as a **financial asset**, measured:

- at **fair value through profit or loss**; or
- at **fair value through other comprehensive income**.

This represents the **weakest form of influence** that an investor can exert over an investee.

1.3 Understanding control

Under IFRS 10, **control** determines which entities an investor (the parent) is required to **consolidate**. In this regard, an investor, irrespective of its relationship with an investee, should assess whether it is a **parent** by considering if it **controls the investee**. An investor controls an investee if and only if the investor has *all* of the following (IFRS 10.7):

- **power** over the investee;
- **exposure or rights to variable returns** from its involvement with the investee; and
- the ability to **use its power** over the investee to **affect the amount** of the investor's returns.

An investor should consider all facts and circumstances when assessing whether or not it controls an investee. Should facts and circumstances indicate that any of the three elements of control (as listed above) have changed, the investor should then reassess whether it still controls the investee (IFRS 10.8).

The means by which control is assessed in terms of IFRS 10 are illustrated in Figure 1.1.

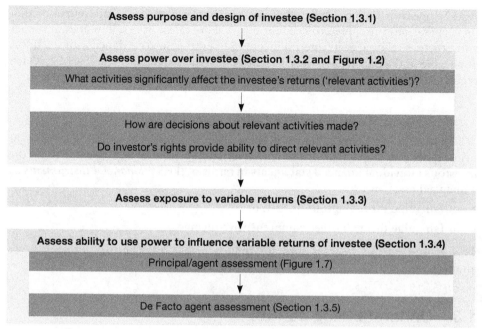

Source: PWC Practical Guide 19 – Consolidated Financial Statements – redefining control

Figure 1.1: *Framework for assessment of control*

1.3.1 Understanding the purpose and design of an investee

IFRS 10 requires an investor to consider the purpose and design of the investee when assessing control in order to (IFRS 10.B5):

- identify what the relevant activities of the investee are;
- establish how decisions about the relevant activities are made;
- determine who has the current ability to direct the relevant activities; and
- ascertain who receives returns from those activities.

By considering the purpose and design of the investee, it may be clear that the investee is controlled by **voting rights** attached to **ordinary shares** held in the investee. In such a case, in the **absence of any additional arrangements** that affect **decision-making rights**, if an investor **controls the majority of the voting rights** of an investee, it **controls** the investee (IFRS 10.B6).

Alternatively, the design of the investee may be such that voting rights are *not* the dominant factor in deciding control of the investee, such as when any voting rights pertain to **administrative tasks only**, and the relevant activities are directed by means of **contractual arrangements**. In those cases, the following should be considered in assessing the investee's purpose and design (IFRS 10.B8):

- risks and potential gains to which the investee was designed to be exposed;
- risks and potential gains which the investee was designed to pass on to parties involved with the investee; and
- whether the investor is exposed to all or some of these risks and potential gains.

1.3.2 Power over an investee

The first requirement to have control is **power**. An investor has power over an investee when (IFRS 10.10):

- it has **existing rights**
- that give it the **current ability**
- to direct the **relevant activities** (i.e., those activities that significantly affect the investee's returns).

Determining whether an investor has power depends on the relevant activities, the way decisions about the relevant activities are made and the rights that the investor and other parties have in relation to the investee (IFRS 10.B10).

Figure 1.2 summarises the considerations involved in the assessment of power, which are then discussed in the sections that follow.

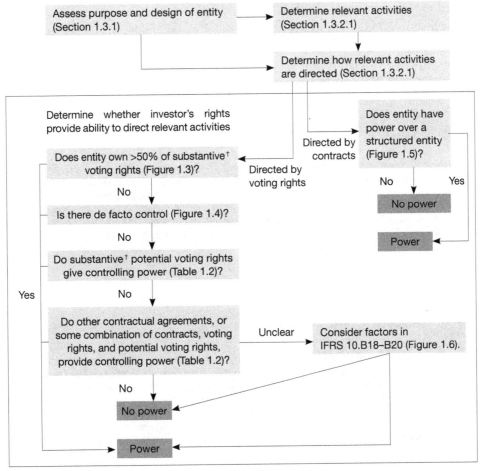

† Whether rights are substantive is dealt with in Table 1.1

Source: PWC Practical Guide 19 – Consolidated Financial Statements – redefining control

Figure 1.2: *Conceptual flowchart for assessment of power*

1.3.2.1 Relevant activities and direction of relevant activities

In terms of IFRS 10, relevant activities are those activities of the investee that **significantly affect the investee's returns.** In this regard, the Standard notes that a variety of operating and financing activities could potentially have a significant effect on the returns of an investee. Some examples include (IFRS 10.B11):

- selling and purchasing of goods and services;
- managing financial assets during their life and/or upon default;
- selecting, acquiring or disposing of assets (such as property, plant and equipment or investment property);
- researching and developing new products or processes; and
- determining a funding structure or obtaining funding (such as deciding whether to use debt or equity funding and the relative amounts thereof).

Decisions about relevant activities that an investor may make include, but are not limited to, decisions about (IFRS 10.B12):

- the investee's long-term strategy (e.g., through capital budgets) and tactical plans (e.g., through operational budgets); and
- the appointment, remuneration and termination of key service providers or key management of the investee.

Example 1.1: Relevant activities

Dynamic Engineering Ltd designs and manufactures a brand of the latest jet propulsion engines for the aerospace industry. Approximately 30% of its costs are currently attributable to research and development of a range of new highly advanced engines. Approximately 60% of its expenditures are for the manufacture of the new engines. The remaining 10% of expenditures pertains to administration and marketing. P Ltd acquired all the shares in and control over S Ltd on 1 January 20X8. This is the beginning of the financial year for both P Ltd and S Ltd.

Required
What are Dynamic Engineering's relevant activities?

Solution 1.1: Relevant activities

In this scenario the relevant activities appear to be the research and development and the manufacturing activities. While administration and marketing certainly form an integral function of the business, it would seem unlikely that they are the primary drivers of the investee's returns. It is important to note, however, that the key consideration is whether or not the activity significantly affects the investee's returns, rather than the total expenditure on each activity. If the competitive nature of the aerospace industry meant that brand awareness and exposure were instrumental to the company's success, marketing activities could well be 'relevant activities'.

It may be that activities both before and after a particular set of circumstances arises or event occurs, are relevant activities. Therefore, when two or more investors have the concurrent ability to direct relevant activities and those relevant activities occur at different times, it must be determined which investor is able to direct the activities that **most significantly** affect the investee's returns, which is then the investor with power over the investee (IFRS 10.B13).

 Example 1.2: Significance of relevant activities

X and Y form an investee to develop and market a medical product. X has full responsibility and the unilateral ability to make all decisions regarding product development and to obtain regulatory approval. Once the regulator has approved the product, Y has full responsibility and unilateral ability to make all manufacturing and marketing decisions.

Source: Example 1, IFRS 10 *Application guidance* (adapted)

Required
Which investor has power over the investee?

 Solution 1.2: Significance of relevant activities

All the activities (developing the product and obtaining regulatory approval as well as manufacturing and marketing) appear to be relevant activities. Thus, each investor needs to determine whether it is able to direct the activities that most significantly affect the investee's returns. That is, whether developing and obtaining regulatory approval, or whether manufacturing and marketing, are the most significant activities.

To make this determination each investor would need to consider:

- the purpose and design of the investee;
- the factors that determine the profit margin, revenue and value of the investee as well as the value of the medical product;
- the effect on the investee's returns resulting from each investor's decision-making authority with respect to the factors listed in the previous point; and
- its exposure to variability of returns.

Additional considerations specific to this example would be:

- the uncertainty of, and effort required in, obtaining regulatory approval (considering the investor's record of successfully developing and obtaining regulatory approval of medical products); and
- which investor controls the medical product once the development phase is successful.

1.3.2.2 Existing rights

For an entity to have power over another, the first requirement is for the investor to have **existing rights** at the **date** when the **assessment of power is made**. IFRS 10 notes that the rights that may give an investor power can differ between investees. Per the

Standard, examples of rights that, either individually or in combination, can give an investor power include but are not limited to (IFRS 10.B15):

- **actual** and **potential voting rights;**
- the right to **appoint, reassign** or **remove members** of the **investee's key management personnel** who **direct relevant activities;**
- the right to **appoint or remove another entity** (e.g., a service provider) that **directs the relevant activities;**
- the right to direct the investee to **enter into transactions that would benefit the investor** or veto (i.e., reject) any **changes to such transactions;** and
- **other rights** (e.g., contractual rights) that give the investor the **current ability** to **direct the relevant activities.**

Generally, when decision-making in relation to relevant activities is required on a **continuous basis** and a **range of operating and financing activities significantly affect returns, voting** or **similar rights** will provide **power.** In other cases, voting rights alone are insufficient to have power over an investee (e.g., when voting rights do not relate to relevant activities). In these circumstances it may be necessary for the investor to consider **contractual arrangements relating to the investee** – in addition to voting rights – before concluding that it has power over the investee (IFRS 10.B16–B17).

Substantive rights (IFRS 10.B22–B25)

In assessing whether it has **power,** an investor must consider only **substantive rights** in respect of an investee (held by the **investor** and by **other parties**). 'Substantive' means that the holder of the right must have the **practical ability to exercise that right** (IFRS 10.B22). To be substantive, rights must also be exercisable when decisions about the direction of the investee's relevant activities need to be made (IFRS 10.B24).

Further, substantive rights exercisable by **other parties** may prevent an investor from obtaining control, even if such rights holders are unable to initiate decisions. Substantive rights held by other parties may therefore prevent the investor from controlling the investee even if the rights give the holders only the current ability to **approve or block decisions that relate to the relevant activities** (IFRS 10.B25).

Whether rights are substantive depends on the facts and circumstances described in Table 1.1.

Table 1.1: *Factors to consider in assessing whether a right is substantive (IFRS 10.B.23–B.24)*

Factors	Examples
• Are there barriers (economic or otherwise) that would prevent (or deter) the holder from exercising its rights?	• Financial penalties or incentives. • High exercise or conversion price that deters conversion/exercise of rights. • Limited period in which to exercise/convert rights. • Absence of a suitable mechanism to allow exercise/conversion of rights (either in the investee's founding documents or in applicable law/regulation). • Inability of the holder to obtain information necessary for it to exercise/convert its rights. • Operational barriers or incentives (e.g., the absence of alternative competent managers to replace existing management after gaining control). • Legal or regulatory barriers that prevent the holder from exercising its rights (e.g., where a foreign investor is prohibited from exercising its rights).
• Do the holders have the practical ability to exercise their rights collectively, when the exercise of rights requires agreement by more than one party?	• The more parties required to agree to exercise their rights, the less likely the rights are substantive. • The lack of a suitable mechanism that provides these parties with the practical ability to exercise their rights collectively is an indicator that these rights are not substantive. • An independent board of directors may serve as a mechanism for a number of investors to act collectively in exercising their rights and would point to rights that may be exercised in this manner being substantive rights.

• Would the party holding the rights benefit from the exercise of the rights?	• Potential voting rights (discussed below) are more likely to be substantive if:
	  ■ Potential voting rights are in the money (e.g., option exercise price less than current market value of share)
	  ■ An investor would obtain other benefits from the exercise or conversion (e.g., by realising synergies between the investor and the investee) of the potential voting rights.

• Are the rights exercisable when decisions about the relevant activities need to be made?	• Ordinarily this means that voting rights should be currently exercisable, but this is not necessarily the case. For instance, a notice period for directors' or shareholders' meetings would not necessarily prevent majority voting rights (exercisable at the relevant meeting) from being substantive. Provided all significant decisions relating to the relevant activities must be made at such a meeting, the voting rights are substantive from the date of acquiring them.

Protective rights (IFRS 10.B26–B28)

As discussed above, **only substantive rights** are taken into account when considering existing rights for the purposes of **assessing power**. In contrast to substantive rights, **protective rights** are designed to **protect the interests** of their holder **without giving that party power** over the investee to which those rights relate. Consequently, an investor that holds only protective rights **cannot have power** and **cannot prevent** another party from having power over an investee (IFRS 10.B27).

Protective rights relate to **fundamental changes to the activities of an investee** that the holder does not agree with, or apply in **exceptional circumstances** (i.e., upon the happening of a contingent event). Note, however, that not all rights that apply in exceptional circumstances or are contingent on events are protective (see 'Structured entities' on p 19). Protective rights include (IFRS 10.B28):

- a lender's right to restrict a borrower's activities that adversely affect the borrower's credit risk to the lender's detriment (e.g., a loan agreement may place restrictions on new borrowings or the payment of dividends);
- rights of a non-controlling shareholder in an investee to approve:
  - capital expenditure greater than required in the ordinary course of business;
  - the issue of equity and debt instruments;
- rights of a lender to seize the assets of the investee upon default.

 Example 1.3: Protective rights

H holds 30% of the share capital of S. The remaining share capital is held by a financial institution. Per an operating contract entered into between H and the financial institution, H has the current ability to direct all the manufacturing, administration and marketing activities of S. Decisions to issue additional share capital and to obtain additional loan funding require the pre-approval of the financial institution.

Required
Which party has power over S?

 Solution 1.3: Protective rights

Although H holds only 30% of the share capital of S, per a contractual agreement it has the current ability to direct the relevant activities of S and therefore has power over S. The pre-approval for financing of S by the financial institution is a protective right that cannot prevent H from having power over S.

Franchises (IFRS 10.B29–B33)

Typically, franchise agreements give the franchisor rights that are designed to protect the franchise brand but that also give the franchisor certain decision-making rights with respect to the operations of the franchisee. The Standard requires that the **current ability** to **make decisions that significantly affect the franchisee's returns (i.e., substantive rights)** be **distinguished** from having the ability to **make decisions that protect the franchise brand** (i.e., **protective rights**). This results in the franchisor *not* having power over the franchisee if **other parties** have **existing rights** that give them the **current ability** to **direct the franchisee's relevant activities** (IFRS 10.B31).

The Standard further determines that the **lower the level of financial support provided by the franchisor** and the **lower the franchisor's exposure to variability** of returns from the franchisee, the **more likely** it is that the **franchisor** has **only protective rights** (IFRS 10.B33).

Voting rights (IFRS 10.B34–B50)

Most often the activities of an investee are directed through voting rights. Where the relevant activities of an investee are directed through voting rights, IFRS 10 provides guidance on matters to consider, which are discussed in the sections that follow.

Power with a majority of the voting rights (IFRS 10.B35)

An investor that holds more than half of the voting rights of an investee has power over that investee when the conditions illustrated in Figure 1.3 are satisfied.

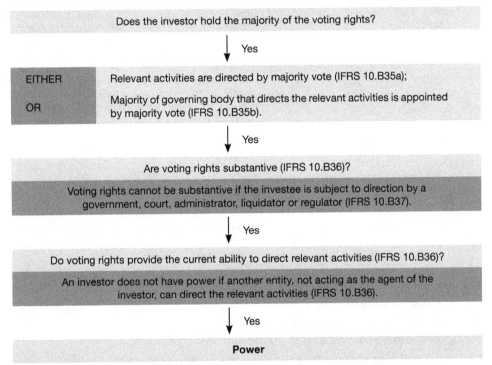

Source: PWC Practical Guide 19 – Consolidated Financial Statements – redefining control

Figure 1.3: *Flowchart for assessing whether voting rights provide power*

Power without a majority of the voting rights (IFRS 10.B38–B40)

An investor can have power even if it holds less than a majority of the voting rights of the investee. This is discussed in Table 1.2.

Table 1.2: *Power with less than a majority of the voting rights held*

Scenario	Explanation
• A contractual arrangement between the investor and other vote holders	• By entering into a contractual arrangement with other vote holders, the investor may be able to direct enough other vote holders on how to vote to enable the investor to make decisions about the relevant activities and thereby obtain power over the investee (IFRS 10.B39).
• Rights from other contractual arrangements	• Other decision-making rights, in combination with voting rights, may give an investor the current ability to direct the relevant activities. For example, a contractual arrangement in combination with voting rights may be sufficient to give the investor the current ability to direct the investee's manufacturing process or to direct other operating or financing activities of the investee that significantly affect the investee's returns (IFRS 10.B40).
• Potential voting rights	• This is discussed in detail in the section 'Potential voting rights'.
• The nature of and the circumstances surrounding the investor's voting rights	• This is discussed in detail in the section 'De facto control'.
• A combination of the above	• For example, a combination of 40% voting rights and 20% potential voting rights may give the investor power (IFRS 10.B50).

Potential voting rights (IFRS 10.B47–B50)

When determining power, an investor is required to consider **its potential voting rights** as well the **potential voting rights held by other parties**. Potential voting rights are **rights to obtain voting rights** in an investee, such as:

- options and forward contracts (on shares with voting rights) held by the investor or by another party; and

- financial instruments (e.g., convertible debentures or loans) that can be converted into shares with voting rights, held by the investor or by another party.

It is important to note that potential voting rights are considered **only if they are substantive.** That is, the holder must have the **practical ability to exercise these rights.** Common factors to consider when evaluating whether potential voting rights are substantive include:

- exercise price or conversion price compared to the instrument's market value;
- the ability of the holder to pay the exercise or conversion price; and
- the timing and length of the exercise or conversion period.

Furthermore, the Standard explains that if the investor also has **existing voting or other decision-making rights, such rights** must be **assessed together** with the **investor's potential voting rights** in determining whether the investor has **power** over an investee.

Example 1.4: Potential voting rights – Case 1

H Ltd holds 35% of the voting rights in S Ltd, whose relevant activities are directed through voting rights. In addition, H Ltd holds a currently exercisable in the money option to acquire an additional 20% of the voting rights of B Ltd.

Required
Does H Ltd have power over the investee (S Ltd)?

 Solution 1.4: Potential voting rights – Case 1

As the option is in the money, the exercise of the option is to the benefit of H Ltd. In addition, as the option is currently exercisable and there are no other barriers preventing H Ltd from exercising its option, the potential voting rights in S Ltd are substantive. H Ltd considers its current voting rights of 35% in combination with the potential voting rights that it can acquire in terms of the option (an additional 20%) to determine that it controls a majority (35% + 20% = 55%) of the investee's voting rights. Therefore H Ltd has power over the investee.

 Example 1.5: Potential voting rights – Case 2

H Ltd holds 25% of the voting rights in S Ltd, whose relevant activities are directed through voting rights. In addition, H Ltd enters into a forward contract whereby it is obligated to acquire ordinary shares carrying an additional 40% of voting rights in S Ltd. The forward contract will be settled in 25 days' time. Assume that all significant decisions that direct the relevant activities of S Ltd are required to be taken at a shareholders' meeting. Notice of 60 days is required by law to call a shareholders' meeting.

Required

(a) Does H Ltd have power over the investee (S Ltd)?

(b) If the facts were the same as in (a), except that the shareholders' meeting was convened 5 days after H Ltd entered into the forward contract, would H Ltd still have power over S Ltd?

 Solution 1.5: Potential voting rights – Case 2

(a) The voting rights under the forward contract are substantive from the date that H Ltd entered into the forward contract, given that they will be exercisable on the first date that decisions regulating the investee's relevant activities may be taken (effectively the date of next shareholders' meeting). Therefore H Ltd has power over S Ltd as it has substantive voting rights of 65% (25% + 40%), giving it the majority of voting rights.

(b) In this scenario H Ltd will acquire substantive rights under the forward contract immediately after the close of the shareholders' meeting in question only. This is so because the voting rights will be exercisable only at subsequent shareholders' meetings. Accordingly H Ltd would not have the current ability to direct the relevant activities and accordingly would not have power over S Ltd.

De facto control (IFRS 10.B41–B46)

An investor with **less than a majority of the voting rights** may still have the **practical ability** to direct the investee's **relevant activities unilaterally** (i.e., by itself) and thereby have **power** over the investee. In this way, provided the other criteria for control are met, the investor may have **de facto control** over the investee.

Typically, an investor will have de facto control over an investee when it has **less than a majority of the voting rights** but nonetheless holds the **largest block of voting rights**, with the **remaining voting rights** being **widely held** by a number of different investors. In such a scenario the investor would ordinarily have power, being able unilaterally to direct the investee's relevant activities, unless **a sufficient number of dispersed investors act together to oppose the influential investor**. In this case, as the collective action of a large number of unrelated investors is required, it would likely be difficult to organise such a concerted effort. Figure 1.4 summarises the considerations for the assessment of de facto control.

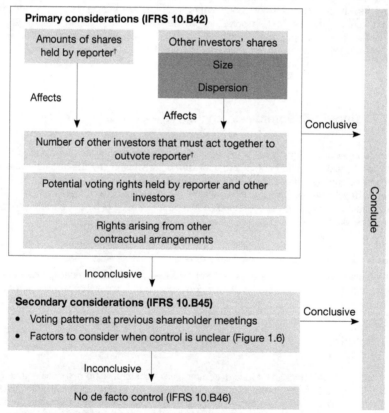

† 'Reporter' is used to refer to the reporting entity performing the assessment for de facto control over the investee.

Source: PWC Practical Guide 19 – Consolidated Financial Statements –redefining control

Figure 1.4: *Assessment of de facto control*

Example 1.6: Size and dispersion of voting rights – Case 1

H Ltd holds 45% of the voting rights in S Ltd, whose relevant activities are directed through voting rights. The remaining 55% of voting rights are widely held by thousands of individual shareholders (none of whom holds more than 1% of the voting rights). Further, no shareholders have collective voting arrangements.

Required
Does H Ltd have power over S Ltd?

 ## Solution 1.6: Size and dispersion of voting rights – Case 1

In this instance, H Ltd has a voting interest that is sufficiently dominant, taking into account the absolute size of its shareholding as well as the size of its shareholding relative to the highly dispersed other shareholders. Therefore, H Ltd can conclude that it has power over S Ltd. No further consideration of evidence of additional power is required in this scenario.

 ## Example 1.7: Size and dispersion of voting rights – Case 2

H Ltd holds 40% of the voting rights in S Ltd, whose relevant activities are directed through voting rights. Two other shareholders each hold 28% of the voting rights, while the remaining voting rights are widely dispersed among various shareholders, who do not individually hold more than 1% of the voting rights. Further, no shareholders have collective voting arrangements.

Required
Does H Ltd have power over S Ltd?

 ## Solution 1.7: Size and dispersion of voting rights – Case 2

As only two shareholders would need to co-operate in order to prevent H Ltd from directing the relevant activities of S Ltd, H Ltd does not have power over S Ltd.

 ## Example 1.8: Size and dispersion of voting rights – Case 3

H Ltd holds 42% of the voting rights in S Ltd, whose relevant activities are directed through voting rights. The remaining voting rights are widely dispersed among shareholders, none of whom holds more than 1% of the voting rights. The majority of these shareholders have a collective voting agreement in terms of which their votes are cast together by a nominated representative. The aggregate of these voting rights represents 56% of the voting rights in S Ltd.

Required
Does H Ltd have power over S Ltd?

Solution 1.8: Size and dispersion of voting rights – Case 3

Although in this example the remaining voting rights are widely dispersed, through the collective voting agreement the other shareholders have a mechanism to vote as an organised group of voters. As this organised group of voters controls 56% of the voting rights in H Ltd, they are able to prevent H Ltd from directing the relevant activities of the investee, S Ltd. Consequently, H Ltd does not have power over S Ltd, despite it being the single largest shareholder in H Ltd.

 Example 1.9: Past voter participation rates

H Ltd holds 40% of the voting rights in S Ltd, whose relevant activities are directed through voting rights. Three other shareholders each hold 5% of the voting rights while the remaining 45% of voting rights are widely dispersed among shareholders who do not individually hold more than 1% of the voting rights. No shareholders have collective voting arrangements. Decisions about the investee's relevant activities require the approval of the majority of votes cast at a relevant shareholders' meeting. An analysis of past shareholders' meetings shows that since the incorporation of S Ltd, no more than 70% of the voting rights have ever been represented, including H Ltd.

Required
Does H Ltd have power over S Ltd?

 Solution 1.9: Past voter participation rates

H Ltd does have power over S Ltd. This is because H Ltd has the practical ability unilaterally (i.e., by itself) to direct the relevant activities of S Ltd as it holds the 57% (40%/70%) majority of voting rights likely to be cast at a shareholders meeting.

Structured entities

In terms of IFRS 12 *Disclosure of Interests in Other Entities*, a **structured entity** is an entity that has been designed so that **voting or similar rights are not the dominant factor** in deciding which party **controls the entity,** such as when any voting rights relate to **administrative tasks only** and the **relevant activities** are directed by means of **contractual arrangements** (IFRS 12.B21). An investor, in assessing whether it has power over a structured entity, should consider the factors detailed in Figure 1.5.

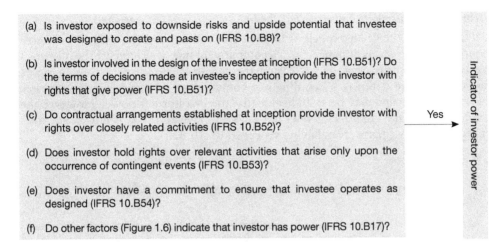

(a) Is investor exposed to downside risks and upside potential that investee was designed to create and pass on (IFRS 10.B8)?

(b) Is investor involved in the design of the investee at inception (IFRS 10.B51)? Do the terms of decisions made at investee's inception provide the investor with rights that give power (IFRS 10.B51)?

(c) Do contractual arrangements established at inception provide investor with rights over closely related activities (IFRS 10.B52)?

(d) Does investor hold rights over relevant activities that arise only upon the occurrence of contingent events (IFRS 10.B53)?

(e) Does investor have a commitment to ensure that investee operates as designed (IFRS 10.B54)?

(f) Do other factors (Figure 1.6) indicate that investor has power (IFRS 10.B17)?

Source: PWC Practical Guide 19 – Consolidated Financial Statements –redefining control

Figure 1.5: *Considerations in assessing power over a structured entity*

Items (b) to (e) in Figure 1.5 are discussed in further detail below.

Item (b): Involvement and decisions made at the investee's inception as part of its design

An investor should consider its involvement and decisions made at the investee's inception as part of the investee's design and should evaluate whether the transaction terms and features of its involvement provide it with rights sufficient to give it power. The Standard notes that being involved in the investee's design, by itself, is not sufficient to give an investor control. Nevertheless, involvement in the design may indicate that the investor had the opportunity to obtain rights sufficient to give it power over the investee (IFRS 10.B51).

Item (c): Contractual arrangements established at the investee's inception

Contractual arrangements to consider include call, put and liquidation rights established at the investee's inception. When these contractual arrangements involve activities that are closely related to the investee, they are considered relevant activities. This is the case even if these activities do not take place within the structured entity itself but in another entity (IFRS 10.B52).

Item (d): Right to direct relevant activities that arise upon the occurrence of certain events

The investee may be designed with an 'auto-pilot' feature, that is, the direction of the investee's activities and its returns are predetermined and cannot be changed by the investors. When the 'auto-pilot' feature comes to an end, when certain circumstances arise or events occur, activities that arise as a result are relevant activities of the investee. The investor that has decision-making rights when those circumstances arise or events occur, has power over the investee, even if such events or circumstances have not yet occurred/arisen. As was noted earlier, the fact that the right to make decisions is contingent does not, in itself, make such rights protective (IFRS 10.B53).

Item (e): Commitment to ensure that the investee operates as designed

An investor may have an explicit or implicit commitment to ensure that an investee continues to operate as designed. Such a commitment may well increase the investor's exposure to returns, thereby increasing the investor's incentive to obtain rights sufficient to give it power. Accordingly, a commitment to ensure that an investee operates as designed may be an indicator that the investor has power. However, the existence of such commitments does not, by itself, give an investor power, nor does it prevent another party from having power (IFRS 10.B54).

 Example 1.10: Power when voting rights are not dominant

An investee's only business activity, as specified in its founding documents, is to purchase receivables and to service them on a day-to-day basis for its investors. Servicing the receivables involves the collection and passing on of principal and interest payments as they fall due. Upon default of a receivable, the investee automatically sells the receivable to investor H Ltd as agreed separately in a sale agreement between H Ltd and the investee.

Source: Example 11, IFRS 10 *Application Guidance* (adapted)

Required
Does H Ltd have power over the investee?

 Solution 1.10: Power when voting rights are not dominant

The only relevant activity is managing the receivables upon default because it is the only relevant activity that can significantly affect the investee's returns. Servicing the receivables before default is not a relevant activity. This is because it does not require substantive decisions to be made that could significantly affect the investee's returns; the activities before default are predetermined and amount only to collecting cash flows as they fall due and passing them on to investors.

Therefore, only investor H Ltd's right to manage the receivables upon default should be considered when assessing the overall activities of the investee that significantly affect the investee's returns. In this example the investee's design ensures that the investor has decision-making authority over the activities that significantly affect the returns at the only time that such decision-making authority is required. The terms of the sale agreement are fundamental to the overall transaction and the establishment of the investee. Consequently, the terms of the sale agreement together with the founding documents of the investee mean that the investor, H Ltd, has power over the investee. This is the case even though the investor, H Ltd, takes ownership of the receivables only upon default and manages these receivables outside the legal boundaries of the investee.

Additional factors to consider in difficult circumstances (IFRS 10.B18–B20)

IFRS 10 recognises that in some circumstances it may be difficult to determine whether an investor's rights are sufficient to give it power over an investee. In such circumstances, the Standard provides guidance in the form of **primary** and **secondary** indicators of power, which are shown in Figure 1.6.

Primary indicators
Indicators of the practical ability to direct the investee (IFRS 10.B18)

- Non-contractual ability to appoint investee's key management personnel who have the ability to direct the relevant activities
- Non-contractual ability to direct investee to enter into significant transactions or to veto any changes to significant transactions for the benefit of the investor
- Ability to dominate the nomination of members to the investee's governing body or obtain proxies from other vote-holders
- Investee's key management personnel, or majority of governing body, are related parties of the investor (e.g., investee and investor share the same CEO)

Secondary indicators

Special relationship indicators of control (IFRS 10.B19)

Investees' key management personnel are current or ex-employees of the investor	**Exposure to variability of returns (IFRS 10.B20)** • Greater exposure, or rights, to variability of returns provides greater incentive to obtain power • Extent of exposure, in itself, is not determinative
Economic dependence on investor • Funding • Guarantees • Critical services • Technology • Supplies or raw materials • Licences or trademarks • Key management personnel • Specialised knowledge • Other critical assets Economic dependence alone does not lead to power (IFRS 10.B40).	
Investees' activities either involve or are conducted on behalf of investor	
Disproportionate exposure Exposure, or rights, to returns from involvement with investee is disproportionately greater than voting or similar rights. For example, >50% exposure but <50% votes.	

Source: PWC Practical Guide 19 – Consolidated Financial Statements – redefining control

Figure 1.6: *Factors to consider when the assessment of control remains uncertain*

It is important to note that the **primary** and **secondary indicators of power** illustrated in **Figure 1.6** must be considered **together with** an investor's **existing rights**. Furthermore, the indicators of power, as illustrated in Figure 1.6, must be considered only when the determination of power is **difficult**, that is, after considering the factors discussed in earlier sections of this chapter, it is **still not clear** whether an investor has power over a particular investee.

1.3.3 Exposure (or rights) to variable returns of an investee (IFRS 10.B55–B57)

An investor is **exposed, or has rights,** to **variable returns** from its involvement with an investee, when the **investor's returns from its investee** have the **potential to vary according to the investee's performance.** Investee returns can be positive (for example, profits earned), negative (e.g., financial losses incurred) or both positive and negative. IFRS 10 requires an investor to assess whether returns from an investee are variable and how variable those returns are based on the **substance** of the arrangement, ignoring the legal form thereof.

For example, an investor may hold a bond with contractually fixed interest payments so that in legal form the returns are fixed. In substance, however, because the realisation of the returns (i.e., the interest payments) depends on the credit risk of the issuer, the bond investor is exposed to variable returns. The greater the credit risk of the issuer, the greater the potential variability in the returns. Similarly, fixed performance fees from managing an investee's assets are, in substance, variable returns since the investor is exposed to the performance risk of the investee. The amount of variability depends on the investee's ability to generate sufficient profit to pay the fees (IFRS 10.B56).

Examples of exposures to variable returns include (IFRS 10.B57):
- dividends;
- other investee distributions of economic benefits (e.g., interest);
- changes in the fair value of the investor's investment in the investee (including credit losses);
- remuneration for servicing an investee's assets or liabilities;
- fees and exposure to losses from providing credit support (such as guarantees);
- residual interests in investee net assets upon liquidation; and
- returns that are not available to other interest holders (e.g., synergies between the operations of the investor or investee).

Although only **one investor** can control an investee at one particular time, **more than one party can participate in the returns of the investee** (IFRS 10.16). Consequently, although several parties may be exposed to variable returns (e.g., equity and debt holders or controlling and non-controlling interests), control can be vested in only **one of them.** Therefore an assessment of all the components of control is required to determine which of the investors controls the investee.

1.3.4 The link between power and returns (IFRS 10.17–18)

For an investor to have control it must not only have power over the investee and exposure to, or rights to, variable returns from its involvement with the investee, but must also have the **ability to use its power** to **affect its returns** from its involvement with the investee.

1.3.4.1 Delegated power: Principals and agents (IFRS 10.B58–B72)

The Standard requires that when an investor with decision-making rights assesses whether it controls an investee, it must determine whether it is a **principal** or an **agent**. An agent does *not* control an investee when it exercises the decision-making rights **delegated to it** as it is primarily engaged to act **on behalf of,** and **for the benefit** of, its **principal(s)** (IFRS 10.B58).

Therefore, sometimes a **principal's power** may be **held and exercisable** by an **agent,** but **on behalf** of the **principal.** This means that when assessing control, the **decision-making rights of the agent** must be treated as being held by the **principal directly** – power over the investee is held by the **principal,** rather than by the agent (IFRS 10.B59).

IFRS 10 sets out a number of factors to consider in order to determine whether a decision-maker is an agent or a principal. Several of these factors are determinative, but the majority are judgemental and **need to be considered together** in assessing whether the decision-maker is acting in the capacity of agent or principal. These factors are illustrated in Figure 1.7.

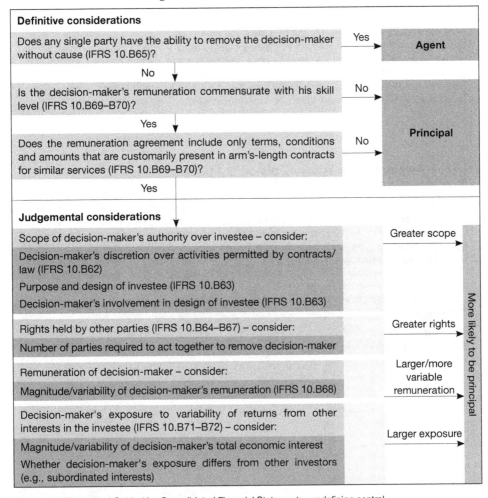

Source: PWC Practical Guide 19 – Consolidated Financial Statements – redefining control

Figure 1.7: *Assessment of whether a decision-maker is a principal or an agent*

Example 1.11: Agent vs principal – Case 1

H Ltd invests in an investment fund managed by a fund manager. The fund manager has decision-making rights that give it the current ability to direct all the relevant activities of the fund, within the parameters of the fund's founding document. The fund manager receives market-related compensation for its services of 1% of the net asset value of the fund.

H Ltd holds a 4% interest in the fund. Furthermore, H Ltd has the right to terminate the services of the fund manager at any time, without consulting any other parties, and does not need to show just cause for the termination.

Required
Is the fund manager an agent of H Ltd?

 Solution 1.11: Agent vs principal – Case 1

As H Ltd holds a removal right that it may exercise on its own, and the fund manager, which is the decision-maker, can direct all the relevant activities of the fund, the fund manager is automatically an agent of H Ltd and no other factors need to be considered to reach this conclusion. H Ltd will combine the fund manager's decision-making rights with its own in determining whether or not it controls the investment fund. Given that the fund manager is an agent of another party, it cannot control the investment fund.

 Example 1.12: Agent vs principal – Case 2

A fund manager establishes, markets and manages a fund that provides investment opportunities to a number of investors. The fund manager has decision-making rights that provide it with the current ability to direct all the relevant activities of the fund within the parameters of the fund's founding document. The fund manager receives market-based remuneration for its services of 1% of the net asset value of the fund, together with a market-related performance fee and holds 20% of the fund. In addition, the fund manager guarantees all the liabilities of the fund to parties other than the fund investors. The fund investors have the collective right to remove the fund manager by majority vote. There are 8 000 individual investors who hold the remaining 80% in equal portions.

Required
Is the fund manager an agent?

Solution 1.12: Agent vs principal – Case 2

The fund manager has the ability to direct all the relevant activities of the fund, for which it receives a market-based remuneration. Because the removal rights held by the other investors are so widely dispersed, little weight is placed on this factor. The fund manager has other interests in the investee, namely a substantial 20% interest in the fund, and provides a guarantee for fund liabilities over and above the remuneration that it receives for fund management services. Consequently, because of the fund manager's large economic interest in the investee (i.e., the fund) together with the fact that the variability of the fund manager's returns, attributable to the guarantee given by it, is most likely different from that of other investors, it may be concluded that the fund manager is not an agent. The fund manager will determine whether its rights are sufficient to give it control over the investment fund.

1.3.5 Relationship with other parties (IFRS 10.B73–B75)

When an investor assesses control, the Standard requires that the investor consider the **nature of its relationship with other parties** and whether those **other parties** are in fact **acting on the investor's behalf**, that is, as its 'de facto agents'. Not only the nature of the relationship is considered but also **how such parties interact** with **each other** and the **investor** (IFRS 10.B73).

Notably, an agent **need not be bound to the principal by a contract.** Per IFRS 10, a party is a de facto agent when the investor is, or those that direct the investor's activities, are **able to direct the party to act on the investor's behalf,** even when there is no contractual arrangement in place (IFRS 10.B74). Where an investor determines that another party is its de facto agent, this has important implications for assessing control. This is because in such circumstances the investor considers **its de facto agent's decision-making rights** and its **indirect exposure, or rights,** to **variable returns through the de facto agent** together with its **own,** when assessing **control** of an investee.

The Standard provides the following examples of such other parties that might act as de facto agents of the investor based on the nature of their relationship (IFRS 10.B75):

- the investor's **related parties;**
- a **party** that received its **interest in the investee** as a **contribution or loan** from the **investor;**
- a **party** that **agreed not to sell, transfer** or **encumber its interests** in the **investee without** the investor's prior consent;
- a party that **cannot finance its operations without subordinated financial support** from the **investor;**
- an **investee** for which the **majority of the members** of its **governing body** or for which its **key management personnel** are the **same** as that of the **investor;** and
- a **party** with a **close business relationship with the investor.**

1.3.6 Control of specified assets (silos) (IFRS 10.B76–B79)

IFRS 10 contains guidance that requires an investor to consider whether it should treat a **portion** of an investee as a **deemed separate entity**. Having made this determination, the investor then considers whether or not it **controls** and **should** therefore **consolidate** the **deemed separate entity** (IFRS 10.B76). Consequently, a situation may arise where an entity does not control an investee in its entirety, but controls the deemed separate entity.

A portion of an investee is treated as a deemed separate entity only if **both** of the following conditions are met (IFRS 10.B77):

- **Specified assets** of the **investee** (together with any related credit enhancements) are the **only source** of **payment** for **specified liabilities** of, or **specified other interests in**, the **investee**.

- **Parties, other than those with specified liability**, do not have **rights or obligations** related to the **specified assets** or to the **residual cash flows from those assets**. This implies:
  - that in substance none of the returns from the specified assets can be used by the remaining investee and none of the remaining liabilities of the deemed separate entity are payable from the assets of the remaining investee; and
  - that in substance all the assets, liabilities and equity of the deemed separate entity are ring fenced from the overall investee.

Such a deemed separate entity is often called a 'silo'. If the conditions set out above are satisfied, the investor considers whether it controls the deemed separate entity by considering the **same control criteria as apply to other entities**. This means that the investor must identify if it has **exposure or rights to variable returns** from its **involvement** in the **deemed separate legal entity** and the **ability to use its power over this entity** to **affect its returns** (IFRS 10.B78).

Should an investor determine that it **controls** the **deemed separate legal entity**, it must **consolidate that portion of the investee**. The **other party (or parties)** that have interest(s) in the investee **exclude** that **portion (i.e., the siloed portion) of the investee** when **assessing control** of, and in **consolidating**, the **investee** (IFRS 10.B79).

1.3.7 Continuous assessment (IFRS 10.B80–B85)

An investor must reassess whether it controls an investee if facts and circumstances indicate that there are changes to one or more of the three elements of control. Any of the elements of control may be affected by a change in facts and circumstances, as follows:

- **There may be a change in how power over an investee can be exercised.** For example, changes to decision-making rights may mean that voting rights no longer direct the relevant activities; instead such activities are directed by way of contract. Furthermore, an event may cause an investor to gain or lose power over an investee without the investor's involvement. For example, an investor may gain power over an investee because the contractual decision-making rights of another party have lapsed (IFRS 10.B81–B82).

- **There may be changes to an investor's exposure (or rights) to variable returns.** For example, an investor may lose control of an investee if it ceases to be entitled to receive returns or to be exposed to obligations. This could occur, for example, if a performance-based fees contract is cancelled (IFRS 10.B83).

- **The link between power and returns may have changed.** Changes in the overall relationship between the investor and other parties may mean that an investor no longer acts as an agent and vice versa. For example, if changes to the rights of the investor or of other parties occur, the investor may need to reconsider its status as a principal or an agent (IFRS 10.B84).

Ordinarily, an investor's initial assessment of control or of its status as a principal or an agent would not change simply because of a change in market conditions. If, however, a change in market conditions affects one or more of the three elements of control or changes the overall relationship between a principal and an agent, this could lead to a reassessment of control (IFRS 10.B85).

1.4 Consolidations – basic principles

1.4.1 Overview

As was explained in Section 1.2, once an investor has established that it **controls** an investee, IFRS 10 requires that the **investee (the subsidiary)** be **consolidated** into the **parent** to produce the **consolidated financial statements** of the parent group. More particularly, in terms of IFRS 10, **consolidation** of a subsidiary **commences** from the date that the parent **obtains control** of the subsidiary. Notably, the accounting requirements and their effect on consolidation, when control of a subsidiary is **first acquired** must be determined by IFRS 3 *Business Combinations* (see Volume 1 Chapter 2 and Volume 2 Chapter 1, which deal with business combinations). The IFRS 10 consolidation principles and procedures apply to the consolidation of subsidiaries **after the acquisition date.**

The principles, process and accounting methods used to prepare consolidated financial statements are dealt with in detail in Volume 1 Chapters 3 to 8 and Volume 2 Chapters 1 and 7. Here we will explain and discuss in broad terms the accounting requirements for consolidated financial statements in terms of IFRS 10.

1.4.2 Scope of IFRS 10

An entity that is a parent must present consolidated financial statements that meet the requirements of IFRS 10, with the exception of:

- A parent that meets all of the following conditions (IFRS 10.4(a)):
  - the parent itself is a wholly owned subsidiary, or, if a partially owned subsidiary, all the other owners of the parent (including those not otherwise entitled to vote) have been informed about and do not object to the parent not presenting consolidated financial statements;
  - the parent's debt or equity instruments are not traded in a public market;
  - the parent did not file, nor is it in the process of filing, its financial statements with a securities commission or other regulatory organisation for the purpose of issuing any class of instruments in a public market; and
  - the ultimate or any intermediate parent of the parent produces consolidated financial statements available for public use that comply with IFRSs, in which

subsidiaries are consolidated or are measured at fair value through profit or loss in accordance with IFRS 10.

- Post-employment benefit plans or other long-term employee benefit plans to which IAS 19 *Employee Benefits* applies (IFRS 10.4A).

- A parent which is as an investment entity in terms of IFRS10.27 if it is required in terms of IFRS 10.31 to measure all its subsidiaries at fair value through profit or loss (IFRS 10.4B). Investment entities are discussed in detail in Section 1.4.3 below.

1.4.3 Investment entities

Certain types of entities acquire investments in subsidiaries for reasons other than holding the subsidiary as a long-term investment. Such entities, which IFRS 10 refers to as 'investment entities', invest in other entities with the main purpose of **receiving dividend income** and **benefiting from increases in the fair value** of such investments (i.e., to benefit from capital appreciation of the investments). The intention of the investment entity is not to acquire a controlling interest in the operations and activities of the other entity.

Consequently, it would not make sense to consolidate the individual assets and liabilities of subsidiaries held by these investment entities. Instead, subject to limited exceptions discussed below, the subsidiaries of investment entities are measured at fair value through profit or loss, which provides more relevant information about the fair value of the investment entity's investments in subsidiaries.

1.4.3.1 Definition of investment entity

IFRS 10.27 defines an investment entity as an entity that:

- **obtains funds** from **one or more investors** for the purpose of providing those investors with **investment management services;**

- commits to its investors that its **business purpose** is to **invest funds solely for returns** from **capital appreciation, investment income,** or **both;** and

- **measures** and **evaluates** the **performance of substantially all of its investments** on a **fair value basis.**

The three key elements of the definition, namely investment management services, business purpose and fair value basis, are considered further below.

Investment management services

One of the essential activities of an investment entity is to obtain funds from investors in order to provide such investors with investment management services. It is this provision of investment management services that differentiates investment entities from other entities. For this reason the definition of an investment entity includes the fact that the investment entity obtains funds from one or more investor(s) and provides the investor(s) with investment management services (IFRS 10.BC237).

Business purpose

In establishing whether an entity invests solely for capital appreciation or for investment income, or both, the business purpose of the entity needs to be considered. Evidence of the entity's investment business purpose will typically be provided by the entity's corporate documents, publications and the manner in which it presents itself to other parties (IFRS 10.B85B).

An investment entity or its subsidiaries may provide investment-related services (e.g., investment advisory services, investment management, investment support and administrative services) either directly or through a subsidiary to third parties as well as to its investors, even if these activities form a substantial part of the activities of the entity (IFRS 10.B85C). Furthermore, an investment entity may participate in investment-related activities, such as the provision of management services, strategic advice and financial support (e.g., loan financing, capital commitments or a guarantee) to its investee provided that these investment-related activities are (IFRS 10B.85D):

- undertaken to maximise the capital appreciation of and/or investment income from the investee; and
- not a separate substantial business activity or a separate substantial source of income to the investment entity.

Where an investment entity has a **subsidiary that is not itself an investment entity, and whose main purpose is to provide investment-related services or activities,** as discussed in the paragraph above, to the investment entity itself or to other parties, the subsidiary **must be consolidated** and will *not* be measured at fair value through profit or loss (IFRS 10.32). This exception applies only to the particular subsidiary providing the investment-related service or activity; all the other subsidiaries of the investment entity will still be measured at fair value through profit or loss.

In addition, an investment entity does **not plan to hold its investments indefinitely** and should therefore have exit strategies for its investments (both equity and non-financial asset investments). The Standard does not consider exit mechanisms that have been put in place for default events, such as a breach of contract or non-performance, to be exit strategies (IFRS 10.B85F). An exception to this scenario arises where an investment entity has an investment in another investment entity that is formed in connection with the parent investment entity for legal, tax, regulatory or similar business purposes. In this instance the Standard explains that the parent investment entity **does not require an exit strategy** for its investment in the subsidiary investment entity, provided that the subsidiary investment entity has appropriate exit strategies for its **own investments** (IFRS 10.B85H).

IFRS 10 further explains that an entity is not investing solely for capital appreciation, investment income, or both, if the entity or another member of its group obtains benefits, or is planning to obtain benefits, from its investments that are not available to other parties, which are unrelated to the investee. Such benefits include (IFRS 10.B85I):

- rights to acquire, use, exchange or exploit processes, assets or technology of an investee;
- joint agreements or other agreements between the entity (or another group member) and an investee to develop, produce, market, or provide products or services;
- the investee providing financial guarantees or assets to serve as collateral for the borrowings of the entity (or another group member);
- an option held by a related party of the entity to purchase an ownership interest in the investee from the entity (or another group member); and

- transactions between the entity (or another group entity) and the investee which are on terms not available to unrelated parties, or are not at fair value, or which represent a substantial portion of the investee's or the entity's business activity. It is important to note, however, that an entity's strategy may be to invest in various investees in the same industry, market or geographical area in order to benefit from synergies which increase the capital appreciation and/or investment income from those investees. Should this be the case, then the entity will still be classified as an investment entity, even though such investees may trade with one another (IFRS 10.B85J).

Fair value basis

Fair value information is the primary driver of the decision-making processes both of the management of and investors in investment entities. Both management and investors evaluate the performance of an investment entity based on the fair value of its investments (IFRS 10.BC249). Consequently, an essential element of the definition of an investment entity is that it measures and evaluates the performance of substantially all of its investments on a fair value basis, which results in more relevant information than consolidating its subsidiaries. To demonstrate that an entity meets this requirement, an investment entity provides investors with fair value information and reports fair value information internally to its key management personnel to evaluate performance and to make investment decisions (IFRS 10.B85K).

In order to meet the fair value reporting and measurement requirements, an investment entity must (IFRS 10.B85L):

- elect to measure investment property at fair value in terms of IAS 40 *Investment Property*;
- elect the exemption from applying the equity method in IAS 28 for its investments in associates and joint ventures; and
- measure its financial assets at fair value in terms of IFRS 9.

Note that although an investment entity is required to measure investment assets at fair value, non-investment assets (e.g., head office property and related equipment) or liabilities of the investment entity do not need to be measured at fair value.

1.4.3.2 *Typical characteristics of an investment entity*

In determining whether an entity meets the definition of an investment entity, as discussed above, the entity must also consider whether it has the following typical characteristics of an investment entity (IFRS 10.28):

- more than one investment;
- more than one investor;
- investors that are *not* related parties of the entity; and
- ownership interests in the form of equity or similar interests.

Note that the absence of any of these typical characteristics does not necessarily disqualify an entity from being classified as an investment entity, but additional disclosures are then required in terms of IFRS 12 *Disclosure of Interests in Other Entities*.

More than one investment (IFRS 10.B85O–B85P)

In most cases an investment entity holds more than one investment in order to diversify its risk and maximise its returns. Holding a single investment, however, does not necessarily prevent an entity from meeting the investment entity definition – examples of this are when the entity:

- is in a start-up period and still needs to identify suitable investments;
- has not yet replaced investments that it has disposed of;
- has been established by a pool of investors to invest in an investment which would not be obtainable by individual investors (e.g., when the required minimum investment is too high for an individual investor); or
- is in the process of liquidation.

More than one investor (IFRS 10.B85Q–B85S)

Typically, an investment entity would have several investors who pool their funds, enabling access to investment management services and investment opportunities that they otherwise might not have had access to individually. Having several investors would make it less likely that the entity would obtain benefits other than capital appreciation or investment income. Nevertheless, an investment entity may be formed for a single investor that represents the interests of a wider group of investors (e.g., a pension fund, government investment fund or a family trust). It may also happen that an investment entity temporarily has a single investor, for example when the entity:

- is within its initial offering period;
- has not yet identified suitable investors to replace others; or
- is in the process of liquidation.

Unrelated investors (IFRS 10.B85T–B85U)

Typically an investment entity has several investors that are not related parties, as per IAS 24 *Related Party Disclosures*, of the entity or other members of the group containing the entity. The more unrelated investors an entity has, the less likely it is that the entity (or other group members) would obtain benefits other than capital appreciation or investment income. However, an entity may still qualify as an investment entity even though its investors are related; for example, an investment entity may, for the benefit of a group of its employees, set up a parallel fund that mirrors the investments of the entity's main investment fund. This parallel fund would likely also qualify as an investment entity even though all its investors are related parties.

Ownership interests (IFRS 10.B85V–B85W)

Ownership interests in an investment entity are typically in the form of equity or similar interests to which proportionate shares of the net assets of the investment entity are attributed. However, having different classes of investors, some of which have rights only to a specific investment or which have different proportionate shares of the net assets, does not prevent an entity from being an investment entity. Furthermore, an entity that has ownership interests in the form of debt may also qualify as an investment entity, provided that the debt holders are exposed to variable returns from changes in the fair value of the entity's net assets.

1.4.3.3 Investment Entities: exception to consolidation (IFRS 10.31–33)

As discussed above, if an entity is classified as an investment entity (subject to the exception noted above for a subsidiary that provides investment-related services or activities), that entity does not consolidate any of its investments in subsidiaries. Instead, all these investments are measured at fair value through profit or loss in accordance with IFRS 9.

In addition, the parent of an investment entity that is not itself an investment entity must consolidate its investment entity subsidiary as well as all of the subsidiaries of its investment entity subsidiary. Differently put, the parent of an investment entity must consolidate all the entities that it controls, including those controlled through an investment entity subsidiary, unless the parent itself is an investment entity.

1.4.3.4 Change in classification (IFRS 10.B100–B101)

Facts and circumstances may change, with the result that an entity may become an investment entity or it may cease to be an investment entity. In the event that this occurs, an entity is required to account for this change in its classification prospectively from the date of the change.

If an entity **becomes an investment entity**, then it must cease to consolidate its subsidiaries at the date of change in classification. Furthermore, the change is accounted for as a 'deemed disposal' or 'loss of control' of a subsidiary, where the fair value of the subsidiary at the date of change is deemed to be the consideration received for the 'deemed disposal' of the subsidiary.

If an entity **ceases to be an investment entity**, all subsidiaries (previously recognised at fair value through profit or loss) are consolidated from the date of change in classification. In addition, the date of change in classification is the deemed acquisition date of the subsidiary, where the fair value of the subsidiary at the date of change is deemed to be the consideration transferred in accordance with IFRS 3. Acquisitions and disposals of subsidiaries are dealt with in detail in Volume 2 Chapters 4 and 5.

 Example 1.13: Investment entity

Investment Corporation Ltd (IC Ltd) was established for the sole purpose of managing the retirement funds of various public sector pension funds with the objective of providing its investors with inflation-beating returns. The company has two main investors, the Public Sector Pension Fund and the National Mineworkers Union Pension Fund, each of which owns 50% of IC Ltd's ordinary share capital. IC Ltd's founding documents state that its purpose is to invest in equity investments with high growth potential, with the objective of realising capital appreciation over their life. IC Ltd's investments consist of equity investments in six technology companies, four of which are listed on the local securities exchange and two of which are private companies.

IC Ltd measures and evaluates its investments on a fair value basis. IC Ltd prepares quarterly reports, which are sent to investors and are used internally by the key management personnel of IC Ltd to measure performance. These reports typically include information about the return on investment and movements in the fair value of the investments made by IC Ltd.

IC Ltd has documented plans to dispose of its interests in each of its investees over an eight- to ten-year period. Such disposals include the outright sale for cash, the distribution of marketable equity securities to investors following the successful public offering of the investees' securities and the disposal of investments to the public or other related entities.

One of these investments, ABC Ltd, in respect of which IC Ltd holds a 65% controlling shareholding, is a subsidiary of IC Ltd.

Required
Discuss with reasons how IC Ltd should account for its investment in ABC Ltd.

Solution 1.13: Investment entity

For an entity to be classified as an investment entity it must meet all the elements of the definition of an investment entity, as discussed below:

- *The entity obtains funds from one or more investors for the purpose of providing those investors with investment management services (IFRS 10.27a).*

    IC Ltd obtains investment funds from two pension funds and provides these investors with investment management services.

- *The entity commits to its investors that its business purpose is to invest funds solely for returns from capital appreciation, investment income, or both.*

    IC Ltd's only investment activity is that of acquiring equity interests in companies with the purpose of realising capital appreciation of such investments over an eight- to ten-year period. Furthermore, IC Ltd has identified and documented exit strategies for its investments, all of which are equity investments.

- *The entity measures and evaluates the performance of substantially all of its investments on a fair value basis.*

    IC Ltd measures and evaluates its investments on a fair value basis and reports this information to its investors.

In addition, IC Ltd also displays the following typical characteristics of an investment entity (IFRS 10.28):

- it has more than one investor (two investors);
- these investors do not appear to be related parties;
- it has more than one investment (six investments); and
- ownership of IC Ltd is in the form of equity interests (the ordinary shares of IC Ltd are acquired), to which proportionate shares of the net assets of IC Ltd are attributed.

IC Ltd therefore meets the definition of an investment entity. Consequently, IC Ltd will not consolidate its subsidiary ABC Ltd or apply IFRS 3 *Business Combinations* thereto, but will instead measure the investment in ABC Ltd at fair value through profit or loss in accordance with IFRS 9.

1.4.4 Nature of consolidated financial statements

Consolidated financial statements are the **financial statements of a group** in which the **assets, liabilities, equity, income, expenses and cash flows** of the **parent** and its **subsidiaries** are presented as those of a **single economic entity** (IFRS 10 Appendix A).

As the definition of a subsidiary requires that the entity be controlled by the investor (which is then a parent), the implication is that the consolidated financial statements include the results of **all the operations controlled by the parent entity,** irrespective of the **separate entity in which those operations are conducted**. For this reason consolidated financial statements should produce the same results as if the subsidiaries' activities had been performed in a branch or division of the parent.

1.4.5 Consolidation procedures (IFRS 10.B86)

In order to achieve the objective of disclosing the results of a group as though they were those of a single economic entity, consolidated financial statements are prepared by:

- **Combining** the **financial statements** of the **parent** and **its subsidiaries line by line.** This is achieved by adding together like items of assets, liabilities, equity, income, expenses and cash flows of the parent with those of its subsidiaries.

- **Offsetting (eliminating)** the **carrying amount of the parent's investment** in each **subsidiary against** the **parent's portion of equity of each subsidiary** (IFRS 3 explains how to account for any related goodwill or gain on bargain purchase – see Volume 1 Chapter 2).

- **Eliminating, in full, intragroup assets** and **liabilities, equity, income, expenses** and **cash flows** relating to **transactions between entities of the group** (profits or losses resulting from intragroup transactions that are recognised in assets, such as inventory and fixed assets, are eliminated in full). Intragroup losses may be an indication of impairment that is required to be recognised in the consolidated financial statements (i.e., the loss is not eliminated). In addition, IAS 12 *Income Taxes* applies to temporary differences that arise because of the elimination of intragroup profits and losses. (The elimination of intragroup profits and losses is comprehensively dealt with in Volume 1 Chapter 6.)

1.4.6 Reporting date (IFRS 10.B92–B93)

The financial statements of the parent and its subsidiaries that are used in preparing the consolidated financial statements must have the **same reporting dates.** Where these dates differ, the subsidiary prepares **for consolidation purposes only,** additional financial information as of the **same date** as the **financial statements of the parent,** unless it is **impracticable** to do so. If it is **impracticable to do so,** the **most recent financial statements of the subsidiary** are **adjusted** for the effects of **significant transactions or events** that occur **between the date of those financial statements** and the **date of the consolidated financial statements.**

Further, the **difference** between the **subsidiary's reporting date** and that of the **parent cannot be more than three months,** while the **length of the reporting periods** and any **difference** between **the dates of the financial statements** must be the **same from period to period.** These concepts are discussed in further detail in Volume 1 Chapter 4.

1.4.7 Uniform accounting policies – parent and subsidiaries (IFRS 10.19 and IFRS 10.B87)

A parent must prepare consolidated financial statements using **uniform (i.e. the same) accounting policies** for **like transactions** and **other events in similar circumstances.** This implies that if a member of the group uses accounting policies **other than those** adopted in the **consolidated financial statements** for like transactions and events in similar circumstances, **appropriate adjustments** are made to that **group member's financial statements** in preparing the consolidated financial statements to ensure **conformity with the group's accounting policies** (see Volume 1 Chapter 4, where this concept is illustrated in Example 4.10).

1.4.8 Consolidation period and measurement basis (IFRS 10.20 and IFRS 10.B88)

Consolidation of a **subsidiary commences** from the **acquisition date**, being the date that the **parent obtains control** over it. With effect from this **acquisition date all income** and **expenses** of the **subsidiary** are **included in the consolidated financial statements** and are **based on the acquisition date values** of the **assets and liabilities** of the **subsidiary**, recognised in terms of **IFRS 3**. For example, the depreciation expense recognised in the consolidated statement of comprehensive income, after acquisition date of the subsidiary, is based on the fair values of the related depreciable assets of the subsidiary recognised in the consolidated financial statements, in terms of IFRS 3, at acquisition date (see Volume 1 Chapter 5 and Volume 2 Chapter 1, where these concepts are dealt with comprehensively). **Consolidation of the subsidiary ceases** when the **parent loses control** over the subsidiary (this is covered in detail in Volume 2 Chapters 4 and 5, which deal, among other things, with changes in ownership interests in subsidiaries).

1.4.9 Non-controlling interest

The non-controlling interest represents the **equity in a subsidiary** that is *not* **attributable directly** or **indirectly** to a parent. A parent presents the non-controlling interest in the **consolidated statement of financial position within equity, separately** from the **equity of the owners of the parent** (IFRS 10.22).

In addition, the **non-controlling interest's share** in the **profit or loss** and **in the total comprehensive income** of the **group,** is presented **separately** from that attributable to the **equity holders of the parent** in the, **consolidated statement of profit or loss and other comprehensive income** (IAS 1.81B). The treatment and disclosure of the non-controlling interest in the consolidated financial statements is dealt with in Volume 1 Chapter 4.

1.4.10 Direct and indirect controlling interests in subsidiaries

Where a parent **itself** acquires a controlling interest in a subsidiary (i.e., the parent owns subsidiary shares itself), the parent has a **direct controlling interest** in this subsidiary. An **indirect controlling interest** arises when a parent has a direct controlling interest in a subsidiary ('the first subsidiary'), which subsidiary, in turn, controls another subsidiary ('the second subsidiary'). As the parent **controls the first subsidiary**, it is able to **control this subsidiary's investment in the second subsidiary.** This implies that the **second subsidiary** is also a **subsidiary of the parent,** in addition to being a subsidiary of the first subsidiary. The parent therefore has an **indirect controlling interest** in the **second subsidiary,** held through its directly controlled interest in the first subsidiary.

Depending on the particular group structure, a parent could obtain control over a subsidiary by:

- holding a direct controlling interest in the subsidiary;
- holding an indirect controlling interest in the subsidiary; or
- holding a combination of a direct interest and an indirect interest in a subsidiary

This is best explained in the example that follows.

 Example 1.14: Direct and indirect controlling interests

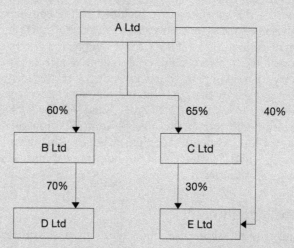

The diagram shows a number of companies and the percentage shareholding (being ordinary shares) each has in various other companies. Each share entitles the shareholder to one vote. Further, control of each company is determined solely by majority vote.

Required
Based on the diagram above, determine, giving reasons, which companies (if any) are controlled by A Ltd.

 Solution 1.14: Direct and indirect controlling interests

1. A Ltd controls both B Ltd and C Ltd. This is because A Ltd holds directly 60% and 65% of the voting rights in each company respectively (i.e., a majority – in excess of 50% – of the voting rights of B Ltd and C Ltd are held by A Ltd).

2. B Ltd controls D Ltd as it holds directly 70% (a majority) of the voting rights in D Ltd. As A Ltd controls B Ltd, A Ltd in turn controls 70% of the voting rights of D Ltd indirectly. Accordingly A Ltd controls D Ltd.

3. C Ltd owns 30% of the voting rights of E Ltd and A Ltd owns 40% of the voting rights of E Ltd. A Ltd therefore has control of E Ltd by virtue of its direct ownership of 40% of the voting rights of E Ltd plus its control, via C Ltd, of an additional 30% of the voting rights of E Ltd, which it controls indirectly. In total A Ltd has control over 70% (40% + 30%) – a majority – of the voting rights of E Ltd.

1.5 Separate financial statements (IAS 27)

1.5.1 Overview

In group financial statements, as discussed, we account for investments in subsidiaries, joint ventures and associates on the basis of such entities' reported results and net assets. In contrast, in its separate financial statements, the parent/investor accounts for its investment in subsidiaries, joint ventures and associates on the basis of its direct equity interest in the investee. (This is subject to the exception where the parent/investor elects to account for its investment in a subsidiary/associate/joint venture in its separate financial statements using the equity method in terms of IAS 28. This is discussed in Section 1.5.3.2.)

IAS 27 *Separate Financial Statements* outlines the accounting and disclosure requirements for 'separate financial statements', which are those presented by an entity in which the entity can elect to account for its investments in subsidiaries, joint ventures or associates either at cost, in accordance with IFRS 9, or using the equity method as per IAS 28 (IAS 27.4).

IAS 27 also prescribes the accounting treatment, in the separate financial statements of a parent or investor, for dividends received/accrued from its investments in subsidiaries and joint ventures or associates, and contains a number of disclosure requirements.

1.5.2 Objective and scope of IAS 27

IAS 27 should be applied in accounting for investments in subsidiaries, joint ventures and associates in the separate financial statements of a parent or investor where the parent or investor elects, or is required by local regulations, to present separate financial statements (IAS 27.2).

1.5.3 Preparation of separate financial statements

1.5.3.1 Requirement for separate financial statements

The Standard does *not* make compulsory which entities must produce separate financial statements available for public use. It applies when an entity prepares separate financial statements that comply with International Financial Reporting Standards (IAS 27.3).

Under IFRS 10, subject to limited exceptions discussed below, separate financial statements are presented in addition to (IFRS 10.6):

- consolidated financial statements; or
- the financial statements of an investor that does not have investments in subsidiaries, but has investments in associates or joint ventures that are required to be equity accounted in terms of IAS 28 (hereafter referred to as 'equity accounted financial statements').

If an entity has *no* interests in subsidiaries, joint ventures or associates, its financial statements are *not* separate financial statements (IAS 27.7). Further, should an investor be exempted in terms IFRS 10.4(a) (see Section 1.4.2) from preparing consolidated financial statements or from applying the equity method in terms of

IAS 28 (see Volume 2 Chapter 2), it may present **separate financial statements as its only financial statements** (IFRS 10.8).

In addition, an investment entity, discussed in Section 1.4.3, that is required, throughout the current period and all comparative periods presented, to **apply the exception to consolidation for all of its subsidiaries** in accordance with IFRS 10.31, prepares **separate financial statements as its only financial statements** (IAS 27.8A).

1.5.3.2 Preparation of separate financial statements

Separate financial statements are prepared in accordance with all the requirements of applicable IFRSs, *except* as regards the accounting for investments in subsidiaries, associates and joint ventures held by the parent/investor. Investments in subsidiaries, associates and joint ventures represent financial instruments, which would normally be accounted for in terms of IFRS 9. However, IAS 27 gives an entity a **choice of accounting methods** to apply in its separate financial statements in respect of these investments. An entity may elect to carry these investments (IAS 27.10):

- at **cost**;
- in accordance with **IFRS 9**, as **financial assets, subsequently measured** either at **fair value through profit or loss** or at **fair value through other comprehensive income**; or
- using the **equity method** as described in **IAS 28**.

Importantly, the choice of accounting treatment needs to be applied consistently to each *category* of investment. For example, if an entity has elected that a subsidiary should be carried at fair value in its separate financial statements, all subsidiaries must be carried at fair value in its separate financial statements.

Table 1.3 summarises the different accounting treatments as permitted by IAS 27 for investments in subsidiaries, joint ventures and associates, both at initial recognition and then subsequently in the separate financial statements of a parent/investor.

Table 1.3: *Different accounting treatment options available to a parent/investor in respect of investments in subsidiaries, joint ventures and associates, in its separate financial statements*

	Investment at cost	Investment at fair value through profit or loss in terms of IFRS 9	Investment at fair value through other comprehensive income in terms of IFRS 9	Equity method in terms of IAS 28
Measurement at initial recognition	• Recognised at cost, being the fair value of the consideration given. • Transaction costs are *included* in the investment cost.	• Investment recognised at cost, being the fair value of the consideration given. • Transaction costs that are directly attributable to the acquisition of the financial asset (investment) are *expensed*.	• Recognised at cost, being the fair value of the consideration given. • Transaction costs that are directly attributable to the acquisition of the financial asset (investment) are *included* in the investment cost.	• At cost, which comprises the *purchase price* of the investment and *directly attributable expenditure* necessary to acquire the investment.
Subsequent measurement	• Investment retained at cost. • Investment may need to be impaired (reduced in value) in terms of IAS 36 *Impairment of Assets*. Impairment of the investment results in a write-down of the investment to its recoverable amount (in terms of IAS 36, the recoverable amount of an asset is the higher of its fair value less costs of disposal and its value in use – the investment is impaired if its carrying amount, which is its cost, exceeds its recoverable amount) and the immediate recognition of an impairment loss in profit or loss.	• Investment remeasured to fair value at each reporting period end. • Fair value adjustments (gains and losses) included in profit or loss each year and closed off to retained earnings at year end.	• Investment remeasured to fair value at each reporting period end. • Fair value adjustments (gains and losses) included in 'other comprehensive income' each year and closed off to a mark to market reserve (component of equity) at year end.	• At cost, adjusted for the post-acquisition change in the investor's share of the investee's net assets (IAS 28.3). • The application of the equity method is dealt with comprehensively in Volume 2 Chapter 2.

In addition, if investments in subsidiaries, associates and joint ventures are **classified as held for sale or for distribution (or included in a disposal group classified as held for sale or for distribution)** in terms of IFRS 5 *Non-current Assets Held for Sale and Discontinued Operations*, the accounting treatment in the separate financial statements of the parent/investor is as follows (IAS27.10):

- investments accounted for at **cost** or using the **equity method** will be measured at **the lower of their carrying amounts and fair value less cost to sell** in accordance with IFRS 5; and

- investments already accounted for at **fair value** in terms of IFRS 9 will **continue to be measured at fair value in terms of IFRS 9** even after classification as held for sale. This is because the measurement requirements of IFRS 5 do not apply to financial assets that fall within the scope of IFRS 9.

Under IAS 28, when an investment in an associate or a joint venture is held by, or indirectly through, an entity that is a **venture capital organisation, a mutual fund, a unit trust, or a similar organisation,** then the **entity may choose** to measure its investment in the associate or joint venture at **fair value through profit or loss,** in terms of IFRS 9 (as opposed to equity accounting the investment, which is the normal treatment) in the consolidated or equity accounted financial statements (IAS 28.18) (see Volume 2 Chapter 2, dealing with associates and joint ventures, where this election is discussed in more detail).

Where an entity elects to account for its associate or joint venture investment at **fair value through profit or loss in its consolidated or equity accounted financial statements,** IAS 27 requires the entity also to account for these investments at **fair value through profit or loss in its separate financial statements** (IAS 10.11).

As discussed in Section 1.4.3, ordinarily a parent investment entity is required by IFRS 10 to account for its investments in subsidiaries at fair value through profit or loss in accordance with IFRS 9 in its consolidated financial statements (where consolidation of these investments is the normal treatment). In terms of IAS 27, where a parent investment entity accounts for its investment in a subsidiary at **fair value through profit or loss in its consolidated financial statements,** it is also required to account for its investment in a subsidiary at **fair value through profit or loss in its separate financial statements** (IAS 27.11A).

1.5.3.3 Recognition of dividends (IAS 27.12)

Dividends from **subsidiaries, joint ventures** or **associates** are recognised in the parent's/investor's **separate financial statements** when the parent's/investor's **right to receive the dividend is established.** The dividend is recognised in **profit or loss** of the parent/investor, **unless** the parent/investor elects to use the **equity method** under IAS 28, in which case the dividend is recognised as a **reduction in the carrying amount of the investment.**

Example 1.16: Accounting for an investment in a subsidiary in the parent's separate financial statements

Parent Ltd acquired 20 000 ordinary shares (out of a total of 30 000 issued shares) in Sub Ltd for CU 250 000 on 1 January 20x1, thereby obtaining control of Sub Ltd.

On 1 January 20x1 payment for the shares was made in cash and transaction costs of CU 12 000 were incurred and paid. At financial year end 31 December 20x1 the shares were trading at CU 18 each. On 31 October 20x1 the directors of Sub Ltd declared and paid a dividend of CU 1.20 a share.

Ignore taxation for the purposes of this example.

Required

Based on the above information, provide the journal entries that would be processed by Parent Ltd in its own records to account for its investment in Sub Ltd for the financial year ended 31 December 20x1, assuming that Parent Ltd:

(a) measures the investment in Sub Ltd at cost in its separate financial statements;

(b) measures the investment in Sub Ltd at fair value through profit or loss in its separate financial statements;

(c) measures the investment in Sub Ltd at fair value through other comprehensive income in its separate financial statements.

 Solution 1.16: Accounting for an investment in a subsidiary in the parent's separate financial statements

Part (a): Investment in Sub Ltd accounted for at cost

	Debit	Credit
1 January 20x1	CU	CU
Investment in Sub Ltd (SFP) (250 000 + 12 000)	262 000	
Bank (SFP)		262 000
Acquisition of investment in Sub Ltd		

	Debit	Credit
31 October 20x1	CU	CU
Bank (SFP) (1.20 Dividend per share × 20 000 Shares)	24 000	
Dividend income (P/L)		24 000
Recognition of dividend received from Sub Ltd		

Comments: Journals

- The transaction costs are capitalised (added) to the cost of the investment.
- The investment will be carried at cost in the statement of financial position of Parent Ltd at financial year end and at each subsequent reporting date until such time as it is sold or impaired.
- The dividend is recognised as income in the current financial year as the right to receive the dividend was established in the current year (on 31 October 20x1).

➠

Part (b): Investment in Sub Ltd measured at fair value through profit or loss

1 January 20x1	Debit CU	Credit CU
Other expenses (transaction costs) (P/L)	12 000	
Investment in Sub Ltd (SFP)	250 000	
Bank (12 000 + 250 000)		262 000
Acquisition of investment in Sub Ltd and recognition of transaction costs		

31 October 20x1	Debit CU	Credit CU
Bank (SFP) (1.20 Dividend per share × 20 000 Shares)	24 000	
Dividend income (P/L)		24 000
Recognition of dividend received from Sub Ltd		

31 December 20x1	Debit CU	Credit CU
Investment in Sub Ltd (SFP) [(20 000 Shares × 18 Fair value per share) – 250 000 Initial cost]	110 000	
Fair value gain (P/L)		110 000
Fair value gain on investment recognised		

Comments: Journals

- The transaction costs are expensed.
- Under IFRS 9, the investment will be remeasured to fair value at financial year end and each subsequent reporting date. Any fair value adjustments are recognised in profit or loss each financial year, which profit or loss is closed off to retained earnings at each financial year end.
- The dividend is recognised as income in the current financial year as the right to receive the dividend was established in the current year (on 31 October 20x1).

Part (c): Investment in Sub Ltd measured at fair value through other comprehensive income

1 January 20x1	Debit CU	Credit CU
Investment in Sub Ltd (SFP) (250 000 + 12 000)	262 000	
Bank (SFP)		262 000
Acquisition of investment in Sub Ltd		

31 October 20x1	Debit CU	Credit CU
Bank (SFP) (1.20 Dividend per share × 20 000 Shares)	24 000	
Dividend income (P/L)		24 000
Recognition of dividend received from Sub Ltd		

	Debit	Credit
31 December 20x1	CU	CU
Investment in Sub Ltd (SFP)		
[(20 000 Shares × 18 Fair value per share) – 262 000 Original cost]	98 000	
Fair value gain (OCI)		98 000
Fair value gain on investment recognised		

Comments: Journals

- The transaction costs are capitalised.
- Under IFRS 9, the investment will be remeasured to fair value at financial year end and each subsequent reporting date. Any remeasurement gains or losses are recognised in other comprehensive income each financial year, which is closed off to the mark to market reserve (a component of equity) at each financial year end.
- The dividend is recognised as income in the current financial year as the right to receive the dividend was established in the current year (on 31 October 20x1).

Deferred tax effects of fair value adjustments to investments in subsidiaries, joint ventures and associates in the separate financial statements of the parent/investor

Where a parent/investor accounts for its investments in subsidiaries, joint ventures or associates in its separate financial statements in terms of IFRS 9, by **recognising movements in the fair value of these investments** year on year, **deferred tax consequences** will arise in the separate financial statements.

This is because fair value adjustments to these investments, recognised in the parent's/ investor's separate financial statements each reporting period, result in **changes** to the **investments' carrying amounts,** *without* any **corresponding change** in the **investments' tax bases.** The tax bases remain unchanged as the revenue authority does *not* recognise these fair value adjustments for tax purposes. This implies that under IAS 12 temporary differences will arise each financial year end since the investments' carrying amounts – which include the year end fair value adjustments – will differ from their unchanged tax bases. In accordance with IAS 12, these temporary differences will, in turn, give rise to **deferred tax effects each financial year.**

Under IAS 12, the measurement of deferred tax liabilities and deferred tax assets should reflect the tax consequences that would follow from the manner in which the entity expects, at the end of the reporting period, to recover or settle the carrying amount of its assets and liabilities (IAS 12.51). Consequently, the manner in which the parent/investor expects, at reporting date, to recover the carrying amount of its investments in subsidiaries, joint ventures and associates, must be determined.

For purposes of this publication, it is assumed that the carrying amounts of these investments will be **recovered by way of sale.** It is further assumed for purposes of this publication, that the parent/investor is *not* a share dealer for income tax purposes. This implies that these investments, when sold in future periods, will be subject to **capital gains tax.** Therefore, deferred tax resulting from fair value adjustments made to these investments, will be calculated using the **effective capital gains tax rate.** For purposes of this publication it is assumed that **80% of all capital gains** are included in taxable income which is subject to **income tax** at the **rate of 28%.** This results in an **effective capital gains tax rate** of **22.4%** (100% × 80% Inclusion rate × 28% Income tax rate).

In addition, under IAS 12, deferred tax should be recognised as income or an expense and included in **profit or loss** for the period *except* to the extent that the tax arises from a transaction or event which is recognised, in the same or a different period, **outside profit or loss,** either in **other comprehensive income or directly in equity** (IAS 12.58).

Applied to investments in subsidiaries, associates or joint ventures carried at fair value, under IFRS 9, in the separate financial statements of the parent/investor:

- where the parent/investor recognises fair value remeasurement gains/losses in respect of these investments in **profit or loss,** any related **deferred tax effects will also be included in profit or loss** and will be closed off at financial year end to **retained earnings** in the statement of changes in equity of the parent/investor; and

- where the parent/investor recognises fair value gains/losses, upon remeasurement of these investments, in **other comprehensive income,** any **related deferred tax effects will also be included in other comprehensive income,** which is closed off at financial year end to a **mark to market reserve,** which is reflected as another component of equity in the statement of changes in equity of the parent/investor.

These concepts are illustrated in Example 1.17 that follows below.

Example 1.17: Accounting for deferred tax effects of investment in subsidiary fair value adjustments in the parent's separate financial statements

At the beginning of financial year 20x1, Parent acquired 100% of the ordinary shares of Sub, thereby obtaining control of Sub for cash of CU 1 200 000.

The fair value of Parent's shareholding in Sub at financial year end 20x1 and 20x2 was CU 1 800 000 and CU 1 450 000 respectively.

Ignore any transaction costs.

Parent is not a sharedealer for income tax purposes.

Required
Provide all the journal entries necessary to account for the above information in the separate financial statements of Parent for the financial years ended 20x1 and 20x2 assuming that Parent:

(a) measures the investment in Sub, under IFRS 9, at fair value through profit or loss;

(b) measures the investment in Sub, under IFRS 9, at fair value through other comprehensive income.

Solution 1.17: Accounting for deferred tax effects of investment in subsidiary fair value adjustments in the parent's separate financial statements

Part (a): Investment in subsidiary accounted for at fair value through profit or loss

Journal 1	Debit	Credit
20x1 – Beginning of the year	CU	CU
Investment in Sub (SFP)	1 200 000	
Bank (SFP)		1 200 000
Acquisition of investment in Sub		

Journal 2		Debit	Credit
20x1 – End of the year		CU	CU
Investment in Sub (SFP) (1 800 000 – 1 200 000)		600 000	
Fair value gain (P/L)			600 000

Fair value gain on investment recognised in profit or loss

Journal 3		Debit	Credit
20x1 – End of the year		CU	CU
Income tax expense (P/L) (600 000 (J2) × 22.4%)		134 400	
Deferred tax (SFP)			134 400

Deferred tax effects of fair value gain recognised in profit or loss

Explanation: Journal 3

	Carrying amount	Tax base	Temporary difference	Deferred tax asset/ (liability) at 22.4%	
	CU	CU	CU	CU	
Investment					
Beginning of year 1:					
Balance	1 200 000	1 200 000	–	Nil	
Movement for year 1:					134 400
Fair value gain	600 000				Profit or
temporary difference			600 000	(134 400)	loss **e**
End of year 1: Balance	1 800 000 **a**	1 200 000 **b**	600 000 **c**	(134 400) **d**	

Comments: Journal 3

a The carrying amount of the investment in Sub, which will be recovered by way of sale, has increased by CU 600 000 in year 1 because of the year end fair value adjustment processed for accounting purposes in Parent's separate financial statements.

b The tax base of the asset 'investment in Sub' is the amount that will be deductible for tax purposes against any taxable economic benefits that will flow to Parent, when it recovers the carrying amount of this investment, by way of sale. The tax base equals the initial cost of the investment in Sub of CU 1 200 000. Because the revenue authority does not recognise any accounting fair value adjustments to this investment for tax purposes, the tax base of this investment in Sub remains unchanged at CU 1 200 000.

c The increased carrying amount of CU 600 000 for the investment in Sub, which has an unchanged tax base, gives rise to a taxable temporary difference of CU 600 000. This is because the CU 1 800 000 carrying amount of the asset (the investment in Sub), which represents future taxable economic benefits, is CU 600 000 greater than its CU 1 200 000 tax base, the amount that is deductible for tax purposes against these future taxable economic benefits.

d The taxable temporary difference of CU 600 000, discussed in **c** above, gives rise to a deferred tax liability of Parent, at the capital gains tax rate, of CU 134 400. This is recognised by crediting deferred tax in the statement of financial position as per journal 3.

e As the fair value gain per journal 2 was recognised in profit or loss, so too must the deferred tax effects of this fair value gain be recognised in profit or loss. This is the debit entry in respect of deferred tax, which increases Parent's income tax expense by CU 134 400 in journal 3.

Journal 4	Debit	Credit
20x2 – End of the year	CU	CU
Fair value loss (P/L) (1 800 000 – 1 450 000)	350 000	
Investment in Sub (SFP)		350 000

Fair value loss on investment recognised in profit or loss

Journal 5	Debit	Credit
20x2 – End of the year	CU	CU
Deferred tax (SFP) (350 000 (J4) × 22.4%)	78 400	
Income tax expense (P/L)		78 400

Deferred tax effects of fair value loss recognised in profit or loss

Explanation: Journal 5

	Carrying amount	Tax base	Temporary difference	Deferred tax asset/ (liability) at 22.4%	
	CU	CU	CU	CU	
Investment					
Beginning of year 2: Balance	1 800 000	1 200 000	600 000	(134 400)	
Movement for year 2: Fair value loss temporary difference	(350 000) **a**	–	(350 000) **a**	78 400	78 400 **c** Profit or loss **d**
End of year 2: Balance	1 450 000 **b**	1 200 000	250 000	(56 000)	

Comments: Journal 5

a In year 2, the CU 350 000 decrease in the value of Parent's investment in Sub (i.e., the year 2 fair value loss) reduces the CU 600 000 taxable temporary difference that originated in year 1 by CU 350 000. This is because the year 2 fair value loss, which is recognised for accounting purposes, is not recognised for tax purposes. That is, in year 2, the carrying amount of the investment reduces by CU 350 000 with no corresponding reduction in its tax base.

b The carrying amount of the investment in Sub, which will be recovered by way of sale, has decreased by CU 350 000 because of the year-end fair value adjustment, processed for accounting purposes in Parent's separate financial statements.

c At the end of year 2, the CU 1 450 000 carrying amount of the investment in Sub has an unchanged (original) tax base of CU 1 200 000 which gives rise to a taxable temporary difference of CU 250 000. The deferred tax liability balance arising from this taxable temporary difference at the end of year 2 of CU 56 000 is, however, less than the CU 134 400 deferred tax liability calculated at the end of year 1, given – as discussed in **a** above – that the value of the investment in Sub has declined in year 2. The result is a year-on-year reduction in the deferred tax liability of CU 78 400 (CU 134 400 Balance beginning of the year – CU 56 000 Balance end of the year), which is the debit entry of CU 78 400 to the deferred tax liability as per journal 5 above.

d As the fair value loss per journal 4 was recognised in profit or loss, so too must the deferred tax effects of this fair value loss also be recognised in profit or loss. This is the credit entry in respect of deferred tax, which decrease's Parent's income tax expense by CU 78 400 in journal 5.

Part (b): Investment in Sub accounted for at fair value through other comprehensive income

Journal 1	Debit	Credit
20x1 – Beginning of the year	CU	CU
Investment in Sub (SFP)	1 200 000	
Bank (SFP)		1 200 000

Acquisition of investment in Sub

Journal 2	Debit	Credit
20x1 – End of the year	CU	CU
Investment in Sub (SFP) (1 800 000 – 1 200 000)	600 000	
Fair value gain (OCI)		600 000

Fair value gain on investment recognised in other comprehensive income

Journal 3	Debit	Credit
20x1 – End of the year	CU	CU
Income tax expense (OCI) (600 000 × 22.4%)	134 400	
Deferred tax (SFP)		134 400

Deferred tax effects of fair value gain recognised in other comprehensive income

Journal 4	Debit	Credit
20x2 – End of the year	CU	CU
Fair value loss (OCI) (1 800 000 – 1 450 000)	350 000	
Investment in Sub (SFP)		350 000

Fair value loss on investment recognised in other comprehensive income

Journal 5	Debit	Credit
20x2 – End of the year	CU	CU
Deferred tax (SFP) (350 000 × 22.4%)	78 400	
Income tax expense (OCI)		78 400

Deferred tax effects of fair value loss recognised in other comprehensive income

Comments: Journals

- The calculation and the explanation of the deferred tax effects of the fair value remeasurement gains and losses is almost exactly the same as for Part (a), the only difference being that deferred tax is recognised as an expense in year 1 and then an income in year 2 in **other comprehensive income** as opposed to profit or loss, as is the case in Part (a). This is because the underlying fair value adjustments in Part (b) are recognised in **other comprehensive income** – see journals 2 and 4.
- The fair value adjustments and the related deferred tax effects thereof, which are reflected in other comprehensive income, are closed off at year end to a mark to market reserve (being another component of equity) in the separate financial statements of Parent.

1.5.4 IAS 27 Disclosure requirements

When providing disclosures in its separate financial statements, an entity must apply all applicable IFRSs (IAS 27.15). Furthermore, the Standard lays down specific additional disclosure requirements for parents and investors that hold investments in subsidiaries, associates and joint ventures, which are discussed in the sections that follow.

1.5.4.1 Parent chooses not to present consolidated financial statements

IAS 27 requires the following disclosures in the **separate financial statements** of a parent that elects *not* to present consolidated financial statements in accordance with paragraph 4(a) of IFRS 10 (see Section 1.4.2) (IAS 27.16):

- the fact that the financial statements are separate financial statements;
- the fact that the exemption from consolidation has been used;
- the name and principal place of business (and country of incorporation if different) of the entity whose consolidated financial statements that comply with IFRS have been produced for public use and the address where those consolidated financial statements can be obtained;
- a list of significant investments in subsidiaries, joint ventures and associates, including:
  - the names of those investees;
  - the principal places of business (and countries of incorporation if different) of those investees; and
  - the proportion of ownership interest held and, if different, the proportion of voting rights held in those investees.
- a description of the method used to account for investments in subsidiaries, joint ventures and associates (e.g., at cost, fair value through profit or loss etc.).

When an investment entity that is a parent (other than a parent covered by the circumstances above) prepares separate financial statements as its only financial statements, the following disclosures are required (IFRS 10.16A):

- the fact that the parent's financial statements are separate financial statements, which are its only financial statements and the fact that the entity (i.e., the parent) is an investment entity; and
- the disclosures relating to investment entities as required by IFRS 12.

1.5.4.2 All other parents and investors in associates and joint ventures

When a parent, other than a parent covered by the circumstances discussed in Section 1.5.4.1 (i.e., a parent that **also presents consolidated financial statements**) or an investor with joint control of, or significant influence over, an investee prepares separate financial statements, the parent or investor must identify the financial statements prepared in accordance with IFRS 10, IFRS 11 or IAS 28 to which they relate.

In addition, the parent or investor must disclose in its separate financial statements (IAS 27.17):

- the fact that the statements are separate financial statements and the reasons why those statements are prepared if not required by law;
- a list of significant investments in subsidiaries, joint ventures, and associates, including:
  - the names of those investees;
  - the principal places of business (and countries of incorporation if different) of those investees; and
  - the proportion of ownership interest held and, if different, the proportion of voting rights held in those investees.
- a description of the method used to account for investments in subsidiaries, joint ventures and associates.

1.6 Disclosure of interests in other entities (IFRS 12)

IFRS 12 *Disclosure of Interests in Other Entities*, is a **disclosure** standard that requires a wide range of disclosures about an entity's **interests in subsidiaries, joint arrangements, associates** as well as in **consolidated and unconsolidated structured entities.**

IFRS 12 sets out an overall objective, which is to require an entity to disclose information that enables users of its financial statements to evaluate (IFRS 12.1):

- the **nature of, and risks associated with,** its interests in other entities; and
- the **effects of those interests** on its **financial position, financial performance, and cash flows.**

The disclosures required by IFRS 12 cover the following principal areas:

- **significant judgements and assumptions** made by an entity in determining, among other things, whether it controls, jointly controls or has significant influence over another entity;
- interests in **subsidiaries;**
- interests in **unconsolidated subsidiaries–investment entities;**
- interests in **unconsolidated structured entities; and**
- interests in **associates and joint arrangements.**

The IFRS 12 detailed disclosures required for **each of the principle disclosure areas** noted in the **first four bullet points** immediately above, are comprehensively dealt with in the Chapter 1 supplementary material, which may be accessed online from the JUTA website. The IFRS 12 detailed disclosures required for **the principle disclosure area noted in the last bullet point** immediately above, namely **interests in associates and joint arrangements,** are covered in detail in **Volume 2 Chapters 2 and 3.**

Summary

This chapter first explained the nature of group financial statements, why they are prepared and how the different degrees of influence exerted over an investee (i.e., control, joint control and significant influence) impact on the investee's accounting treatment in the group financial statements. Control, the strongest degree of influence, was addressed.

Under IFRS 10, when an investor (parent) **controls** an investee (subsidiary), the parent must prepare consolidated financial statements. Since the IFRS 10 requirement to consolidate operates on the existence of control, and the consolidation process is addressed in the next eight chapters, an in-depth discussion and explanation of the concept of control was provided. The following key learning points are important:

- An investor controls an investee if it has **power** over the investee, **exposure or rights to variable returns** from its involvement with the investee and the ability to **use its power** over the investee to **affect the amount** of the investor's returns. **Power** is defined as existing rights that give an investor the current ability to direct the investee's relevant activities (i.e., activities that significantly affect the investee's returns). Power arises from rights – voting rights (either majority or less than a majority), potential voting rights, other contractual arrangements, or a combination thereof.

- Only **substantive rights** (i.e., rights that can be practically exercised) held by the investor and by other parties are considered in assessing power.

- An investor has power over an investee when it holds a **majority of the voting rights** of an investee and the relevant activities are **directed by voting rights,** or a **majority** of the members of the **investee's governing body** is **appointed** by **votes** of the **holder** of the **majority of the voting rights.**

- In assessing power over an investee, an investor must consider **its substantive potential voting rights** as well as the substantive **potential voting rights held by other parties.** Furthermore, if the investor also has existing voting or other decision-making rights, such rights must be **assessed together** with the investor's potential voting rights.

- An investor has **exposure, or rights, to variable returns** from its involvement with an investee when the investor's returns from its investee have the potential to vary (positive, negative or both) according to the investee's performance.

- In assessing its **ability to use its power** to **affect its returns** from its involvement with the investee, the investor must determine whether it acts as agent or principal.

The next section of the chapter discussed what **consolidated financial statements** are, when they must be prepared and the basic accounting principles and procedures that underlie their preparation. This lays the groundwork necessary for you to understand the actual detailed mechanics of the consolidation process, dealt with in later chapters. The key aspects of this section are as follows:

- **Consolidated financial statements** are the **financial statements of a group** in which the **assets, liabilities, equity, income, expenses and cash flows** of the **parent** and **its subsidiaries** are presented as those of **a single economic entity.**

- A parent that is as an **investment entity,** however, does *not* consolidate its subsidiaries; rather, all its subsidiaries, subject to limited exceptions, are measured at **fair value through profit or loss.**
- When preparing consolidated financial statements:
  - combine line by line, like items of assets, liabilities, equity, income, expenses and cash flows of the parent with those of its subsidiaries;
  - offset (eliminate) the carrying amount of the parent's investment in each subsidiary against the parent's portion of equity of each subsidiary; and
  - eliminate in full intragroup assets and liabilities, equity, income, expenses and cash flows relating to transactions between entities of the group.
- The non-controlling interest represents the equity in a subsidiary that is not attributable directly or indirectly to a parent. The non-controlling interest is presented in the consolidated statement of financial position within equity separately from the equity of the owners of the parent. Additionally, the non-controlling interest's share in the group's profit or loss and total comprehensive income is presented separately from that attributable to the owners of the parent in the consolidated statement of profit and loss and other comprehensive income.

The chapter concluded by discussing, and explaining through two comprehensive worked examples, the manner in which an entity accounts for its investments in subsidiaries, associates and joint ventures in its own financial statements – called 'separate financial statements'– namely:

- at **cost;**
- at **fair value;** or
- using the **equity method.**

Knowing how a parent/investor accounts for investments in subsidiaries, associates and joint ventures in its separate financial statements will in future assist you in making the necessary adjustments required to account for these investments in the group financial statements.

In Volume 1 Chapter 2, we address the basic concepts in IFRS3, which deals with the accounting for all business combination transactions where control is obtained over another business.

QUESTIONS

Question 1.1

This question deals with unrelated Cases 1 to 5. Each case must be answered separately.

Case 1

Quality Roses Ltd owns and operates a rose farm that supplies a number of nurseries with a variety of rose types. In order to expand operations, Quality Roses Ltd purchased a 48% shareholding (each share entitles a shareholder to one vote) in Vanity Roses Ltd, a company that owns rose farms throughout the country.

In terms of the purchase agreement, Quality Roses Ltd will have the right to select the rose varieties to be grown and cultivated on the various farms of Vanity Roses Ltd. In addition, Quality Roses Ltd will also have the right to select the nurseries that will be supplied and to appoint staff and key management personnel for the various farms of Vanity Roses Ltd.

Required

Discuss, giving reasons for your conclusion, whether Vanity Roses Ltd is a subsidiary of Quality Roses Ltd.

Case 2

The ordinary shares in Blue Ltd on 31 December 20x5, its financial year end, are held 60% by Yellow Ltd and 40% by Green Ltd (each share entitles a shareholder to one vote). Decisions about Blue Ltd's relevant activities require the approval of the majority of votes cast at the annual general meeting (AGM). The next AGM of shareholders is scheduled for 1 March 20x6.

Since Blue Ltd's incorporation, Green Ltd has held preference shares in Blue Ltd. These preference shares are mandatorily convertible into 150 000 ordinary shares on 30 June 20x6. The shares are not convertible prior to that date. In addition, the holder of the preference shares does not have voting rights except on matters that directly affect its rights. At financial year end 31 December 20x5 Blue Ltd had 500 000 ordinary shares in issue.

Required

Discuss whether Green Ltd has power over Blue Ltd as at 31 December 20x5.

Case 3

Melon Ltd acquired 20% of the ordinary shares of Pear Ltd as well as an option to acquire an additional 40% of the ordinary shares (each share entitles a shareholder to one vote). There are no barriers to exercise of the option, which may be exercised at any time. Decisions about Pear Ltd's relevant activities are determined solely by voting rights.

Required

Discuss whether Melon Ltd controls Pear Ltd.

Case 4

Gamma Ltd has 2 500 000 ordinary shares in issue, of which Delta Ltd acquired 1 100 000 shares (each share entitles a shareholder to one vote). In addition, Delta subscribed for 1 000 000 debentures that were issued to it by Gamma Ltd and that are currently convertible into ordinary shares in the ratio of one ordinary share for every two debentures held. Furthermore, Gamma Ltd issued 1 500 000 options to shareholders other than Delta Ltd, which are currently exercisable. Decisions about Gamma Ltd's relevant activities are determined solely by voting rights.

Required

Determine, giving reasons for your finding, whether Delta Ltd controls Gamma Ltd.

Case 5

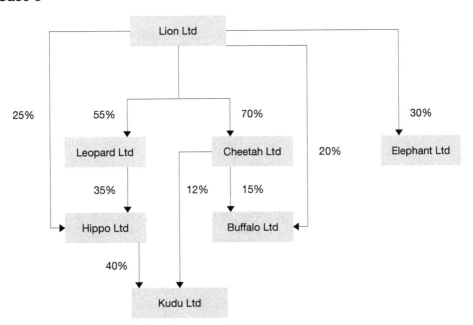

The diagram for Case 5 shows a number of companies and the percentage shareholding (being ordinary shares) each has in various other companies. Each share entitles the shareholder to one vote. Further, control of each company is determined solely by a majority of voting rights, with the exception of Elephant Ltd where, based on a contractual arrangement, Lion Ltd has the right to appoint the majority of the board of directors of this company.

Required

Based on the diagram, determine, giving reasons for your answer, which companies (if any) are controlled by Lion Ltd.

References

IAS 12 *Income Taxes*

IAS 27 *Separate Financial Statements*

IAS 28 *Investments in Associates and Joint Ventures*

IAS 36 *Impairment of Assets*

IFRS 5 *Non-currrent Assets Held for Sale and Discontinued Operations*

IFRS 9 *Financial Instruments*

IFRS 10 *Consolidated Financial Statements*

IFRS 11 *Joint Arrangements*

IFRS 12 *Disclosure of Interests in Other Entities*

PWC *Practical Guide 19 Consolidated Financial Statements – redefining Control*

IFRS 3 *BUSINESS COMBINATIONS* – BASIC CONCEPTS

LEARNING OBJECTIVES

After studying this chapter, you should be able to:

- know which transactions are excluded from the scope of IFRS 3;

- understand what constitutes a business in terms of IFRS 3;

- understand what is meant by a business combination as per IFRS 3;

- know how to apply the IFRS 3 acquisition method in accounting for a business combination, more specifically, be able to:

  - identify the acquirer;

  - determine the acquisition date;

  - recognise and measure the identifiable assets acquired and liabilities assumed;

  - recognise and measure any non-controlling interest in the acquiree;

  - measure the consideration transferred; and

  - recognise and measure goodwill or a gain from a bargain purchase.

- know the differences in accounting for an IFRS 3 business combination where an acquiree's net assets are directly acquired compared to an IFRS 3 business combination where the shares in an acquiree are purchased; and

- provide the disclosures required by IFRS 3 for a business combination that occurs in the current year.

TOPIC LIST

Introduction

A business combination arises when an **acquirer** obtains **control** of one or more **businesses**. IFRS 3 *Business Combinations* seeks to enhance the relevance, reliability and comparability of information provided by an entity in its financial statements about a business combination (e.g., acquisitions and mergers) and its effects. The Standard does this by establishing principles and requirements as to how an acquirer:

- recognises and measures the **acquiree's assets** and **liabilities** acquired and any **non-controlling interest** in the acquiree;
- recognises and measures **goodwill** acquired in a business combination or a **gain on a bargain purchase**; and
- determines what information to **disclose** to enable financial statement users to evaluate the **nature** and **financial effects** of the **business combination**.

The aim of this chapter is to provide a solid understanding of the fundamental IFRS 3 accounting and financial reporting concepts and principles that an entity needs to apply when it undertakes a business combination. Certain of the more complex aspects of IFRS 3, such as dealing with exceptions to the general recognition and/ or measurement criteria of the Standard, contingent consideration transferred in a business combination and the adjustments required when the business combination accounting is determined provisionally, are dealt with in Volume 2 Chapter 1.

2.1 The scope of IFRS 3 (IFRS 3.2, IFRS 3.2A and IFRS 3.3)

IFRS 3 must be applied when accounting for **any business combination**, *except* for the following:

- The **formation of a joint arrangement** in the financial statements of the **joint arrangement itself**. It is important to note that this exclusion applies only to the accounting by the joint arrangement itself in its own financial statements and *not* to the accounting by the parties to the joint arrangement in respect of their interests in the joint arrangement (IFRS 3.2(a)).
- The acquisition of an **asset or group of assets** that is *not* a business (see Section 2.2.2) as defined in terms of IFRS 3 (IFRS 3.2(b)).
- Combinations of entities or businesses under **common control** (IFRS 3.2(c)). This is a business combination in which all of the combining entities or businesses are ultimately controlled by the **same party or parties** both **before and after the business combination**, and that control is **not temporary** (IFRS 3.B1). For example, if H Ltd holds a 100% shareholding, which is a controlling interest, in A Ltd and B Ltd, and then sells its interest in B Ltd to A Ltd, this will result in a business combination involving entities under common control. Subsequent to the business combination, H Ltd controls A Ltd, which in turn controls B Ltd. Consequently, as H Ltd ultimately still controls both A Ltd and B Ltd after the business combination, IFRS 3 will not apply to this combination, provided that B Ltd's control of A Ltd is not temporary.
- The acquisition by an **investment entity** of a **subsidiary** that is required to be measured at **fair value through profit or loss** under IFRS 10 *Consolidated Financial Statements* (see Volume 1 Chapter 1) (IFRS 3.2A).

2.2 Determining whether a transaction is a business combination

Appendix A of IFRS 3 defines a business combination as a transaction or other event in which an **acquirer** obtains **control** of one or more **businesses**. The result of most business combinations is that one entity, the acquirer, obtains control over one or more other businesses, referred to as the acquiree.

A business combination may for legal, taxation or other reasons be structured in a variety of ways, which include but are not limited to (IFRS 3.B6):

- the purchase by an acquirer of the equity (shares) of the acquiree (i.e., the acquiree becomes a subsidiary of the acquirer parent entity);
- the purchase by the acquirer of all the net assets (rather than shares) of the acquiree;
- one combining entity transfers its net assets, or its owners transfer their equity interests, to another combining entity or its owners;
- all the combining entities transfer their net assets, or the owners of those entities transfer their equity interests to a newly formed entity; or
- a group of former owners of one of the combining entities obtains control of the combined entity.

As noted above, there are two critical elements – 'control' and 'business' – that must be present for a transaction or event to qualify as a business combination. These elements are discussed below.

2.2.1 Control

Control was discussed in detail in Volume 1 Chapter 1, but to repeat: control exists when an investor is **exposed, or has rights**, to **variable returns** from its involvement with the investee, and has the **ability to affect the amount of those returns** through its **power** over the **investee**. All the principles explained in Volume 1 Chapter 1 regarding the determination of when control exists must be applied in determining whether a transaction results in a business combination.

In a business combination an acquirer might obtain control over an acquiree in a number of different ways, for example (IFRS 3.B5):

- by transferring cash, cash equivalents or other assets to the sellers of the acquiree;
- by incurring liabilities, for example, where the consideration is paid in instalments to the sellers of the acquiree;
- by issuing equity interests, for example, when ordinary shares of the acquirer are issued as consideration to the sellers of the acquiree;
- by providing more than one type of consideration, for example issuing shares and transferring cash; and
- without transferring consideration, for example, if control is exercised by contract alone.

2.2.2 Business

A transaction or event is only a business combination if, among other things, the **assets acquired** and the **liabilities assumed** constitute a **business**. Appendix A of IFRS 3 defines a business as:

- an **integrated set** of **activities and assets,**
- that is capable of being **conducted and managed** for the **purpose** of **providing a return,**
- in the form of **dividends, lower costs** or **other economic benefits** directly to **investors, owners, members** or **participants.**

Furthermore, IFRS 3 notes that a business consists of **inputs** and **processes applied** to those inputs that have the ability to create **outputs**. The Standard defines these three elements of a business – namely inputs, processes and outputs – as follows (IFRS 3.B7):

- **Inputs** are economic resources that create, or have the ability to create, outputs when one or more processes are applied to it. Examples include non-current assets, intellectual property, the ability to obtain access to necessary materials or rights and employees.
- **Processes** are systems, standards, protocols, conventions or rules that, when applied to inputs, create or have the ability to create outputs. Examples would include strategic management and operational and resource management processes. Accounting, billing, payroll and similar administrative systems typically are *not* processes used to create outputs.
- **Outputs** are the result of inputs and processes applied to those inputs that provide, or have the ability to provide a return in the form of dividends, lower costs or other economic benefits directly to investors or other owners, members or participants.

The Standard explains that **outputs** are *not* **required** for an integrated set of activities and assets to qualify as a business. **Inputs and processes applied to those inputs** are, however, required in order for these activities and assets to be capable of being conducted and managed for the purposes of providing a return. In addition, a business does *not* have to include all the inputs or processes that the seller used in operating that business, provided that market participants are capable of acquiring the business and continuing to produce outputs, for example, by combining the business with their own inputs and processes (IFRS 3.B8).

A set of integrated activities and assets in its **development stage** may not have outputs. If not, the acquirer should consider other factors to determine if the set is a business, such as whether the set (IFRS 3.B10):

- has begun planned principal activities;
- has employees, intellectual property and other inputs and processes that could be applied to those inputs;
- is pursuing a plan to produce outputs; and
- will be able to obtain access to customers that will produce the outputs.

The assessment whether a particular set of assets and activities is a business is made based on whether the integrated set is capable of being **conducted and managed as a business** by a **market participant**. It is irrelevant whether the seller operated the set as a business or whether the acquirer intends to operate the set as a business (IFRS 3.B11).

In the absence of evidence to the contrary, a particular set of assets and activities, in which **goodwill is present,** is **presumed to be a business** (see Section 2.3.6.1 for a detailed discussion about goodwill recognition and measurement). However, a business need not have goodwill (IFRS 3.B12).

Should the assets acquired and liabilities assumed *not* constitute a business, then the acquirer must (IFRS 3.2(b)):

- identify and recognise the **individual identifiable assets acquired** in terms of the **relevant IFRSs** (e.g., IAS 16 *Property Plant and Equipment* and IAS 38 *Intangible Assets*) and liabilities assumed; and
- allocate the **total cost of the group** to the **individual identifiable assets** and **liabilities** based on their relative **fair values** at date of purchase. In addition, such a transaction does *not* give rise to goodwill.

Example 2.1: Does it qualify as a business combination? – Cases 1 and 2

Required
For each of the two separate cases below, determine, giving a motivation for your answer, whether the transactions qualify as a business combination in terms of IFRS 3.

Case 1
Meditech Ltd develops anti-venom medications to treat highly venomous snake bites, which it sells to various clinics. A few years ago it developed and patented a new anti-venom medication to treat the bite of a highly venomous sea snake. Recently, Meditech Ltd began manufacturing and marketing the medication on a commercial scale. Shortly thereafter Pharma Ltd acquired an 80% controlling interest in Meditech Ltd, and immediately and indefinitely suspended the manufacture of the medication and all of Meditech Ltd's operations in order to protect the market for its own snake bite remedies.

Case 2
Jet Ltd purchased the following in the current year:

- 30% of the voting rights of Turbine Ltd, a company which manufactures and sells engines for light commercial aircraft – this 30% shareholding acquired enables Jet Ltd to exercise significant influence over the financing and operating activities of Turbine Ltd; and
- a warehouse building to store components to be used in the manufacture of aircraft engines.

Solution 2.1: Does it qualify as a business combination? – Cases 1 and 2

Case 1
The acquisition of Meditech Ltd by Pharma is a business combination in terms of IFRS 3

- Meditech is a business, it has inputs (pre-existing intellectual property, staff and property, plant and equipment) in a managed production process to develop and manufacture medication for sale. This provides evidence that the integrated set of activities and assets that is Meditech's operations is clearly capable of being conducted and managed as a business by a market participant.In the evaluation of whether Meditech's activities and assets comprise a business, it is not relevant that Pharma does not intend to operate the set of activities and assets acquired as a business. Furthermore, as Pharma acquired a controlling interest in Meditech Ltd, control exists and the acquisition is thus a business combination.

Case 2
The acquisition of Turbine Ltd is *not* a business combination in terms of IFRS 3

- Clearly Turbine Ltd is a business as it has inputs (being raw materials to make aircraft engines) and processes in place to convert this input into an output (being the finished goods aircraft engines). However, as Jet Ltd has only significant influence over Turbine Ltd, control does not exist and therefore this is not a business combination.

The acquisition of the warehouse is *not* a business combination in terms of IFRS 3

- The warehouse building does not consist of any process that, when applied to inputs, could produce outputs. All of the inputs and processes would need to be provided by Jet Ltd. Consequently, the warehouse building on its own is not capable of being conducted and managed as a business by a market participant. This would be a simple asset acquisition in terms of IAS 16.

 Example 2.2: Acquisition of a group of assets that is not a business

H Ltd acquired the following assets of A Ltd on 1 January 20x6 for CU 3 500 000:

	Carrying amount in the records of A Ltd	Fair value on 1 January 20x6
	CU	CU
Property plant and equipment	750 000	1 100 000
Inventory	550 000	620 000
Investment property	1 200 000	1 500 000
Trade receivables	200 000	250 000
	2 700 000	3 470 000

Upon analysis of the acquisition transaction, H Ltd established that the acquisition does not meet the definition of a business.

Required
Prepare the journal entry in the records of H Ltd on 1 January 20x6 to record the acquisition of the assets acquired from A Ltd.

 Solution 2.2: Acquisition of a group of assets that is not a business

H Ltd will put through the following journal entry on 1 January 20x6:

Journal	Dr CU	Cr CU
Property plant and equipment (SFP) (3 500 000 × ^{Wkg1†}32%)	1 120 000	
Inventory (SFP) (3 500 000 × ^{Wkg1‡}18%)	630 000	
Investment property (SFP) (3 500 000 × $^{Wkg1#}$43%)	1 505 000	
Trade receivables (SFP) (3 500 000 × $^{Wkg1#}$7%)	245 000	
Bank (SFP) (given)		3 500 000
Accounting for the acquisition of assets		

Comments: Journal entry

- As H Ltd has not acquired a business from A Ltd, no business combination has occurred in terms of IFRS 3. Rather, there has simply been an asset acquisition.
- The purchase price of the group of assets acquired by H Ltd is allocated among the individual, identifiable assets based on their relative fair values as at date of purchase. No goodwill on acquisition is recognised since this is not a business combination.

Working: Journal entry

Working 1

	Fair value on 1 January 20x6	Allocation %	
	CU	CU	
Property plant and equipment	1 100 000	32%	†
Inventory	620 000	18%	‡
Investment property	1 500 000	43%	∓
Trade receivables	250 000	7%	∓
	3 470 000	100%	

† (1 100 000 / 3 470 000) × 100%   ∓ (1 500 000 / 3 470 000) × 100%
‡ (620 000 / 3 470 000) × 100%   ∓ (250 000 / 3 470 000) × 100%

2.3 Application of the acquisition method of accounting

In terms of IFRS 3, *all* business combinations need to be accounted for by applying the **acquisition method** , which views the business combination from the perspective of the entity that has **acquired control (i.e., the acquirer)** of **another entity (i.e., the acquiree).**

The steps involved in applying the acquisition method are as follows:

Step 1: Identify an **acquirer** (Section 2.3.1).

Step 2: Determine the **acquisition date** (Section 2.3.2).

Step 3: Recognise and measure the **identifiable assets acquired** and **liabilities assumed** (Section 2.3.3).

Step 4: Recognise any **non-controlling interest** in the acquiree (Section 2.3.4).

Step 5: Measure the **consideration transferred** (Section 2.3.5).

Step 6: Recognise and measure **goodwill** or a **gain from a bargain purchase** (Section 2.3.6).

Each of these steps is explained in detail in the sections that follow.

2.3.1 Identify an acquirer

IFRS 3 requires an acquirer to be identified for all business combinations as each business combination is viewed from the perspective of the acquirer. It is the **combining entity** that **obtains control** over the **acquiree** that IFRS 3 defines as the acquirer (IFRS 3 Appendix A). The guidance provided in IFRS 10 to determine control (as discussed in

Volume 1 Chapter 1) should be applied. In instances where application of this guidance does not clearly indicate which of the combining entities is the acquirer (i.e., in situations where it is unclear which entity acquired control over the activities of another entity), IFRS 3 requires that we consider the following factors in making a determination:

- Where a business combination is brought about mainly by transferring **cash** or **other assets,** or by **incurring liabilities,** the acquirer is usually the entity that **transfers the cash or other assets** (IFRS 3.B14).

- Where a business combination is brought about **mainly by exchanging equity instruments** (e.g., shares) the acquirer is – with a limited exception for reverse acquisitions (reverse acquisitions[1] are business combinations in which the acquirer is the entity whose equity instruments are being acquired and the entity issuing the equity instruments is the acquiree) – usually the entity that **issues its equity instruments as payment** for the net assets acquired. However, the following facts and circumstances should also be considered in identifying the acquirer in a business combination brought about by the exchange of equity instruments (IFRS 3.B15):
  - The acquirer is usually the combining entity whose owners as a group receive or **retain the largest portion of the voting rights** in the **combined entity.**
  - Should there be a substantial minority voting interest, without any individually significant voting interests, the acquirer is usually the combining entity whose single or organised group of owners holds the **largest minority voting interest** in the **combined entity.**
  - The acquirer is usually the combining entity whose owners have the ability to **appoint or remove a majority of the members of the governing body** of the **combined entity.**
  - The acquirer is usually the combining entity whose **(former) management dominates** the **management of the combined entity.**
  - The acquirer is usually the combining entity that **pays a premium over the pre-combination fair value** of the equity interests of the other combining entity or entities.

- Should the **size (assets, revenue, earnings)** of one of the combining entities be **significantly greater** than that of the other combining entity or entities, **the entity with greater size is usually the acquirer** (IFRS 3.B16).

- Where a business combination involves **more than two entities,** it needs to be considered which of the combining entities **initiated the combination** as well as the **relative size** of the combining entities in order to determine the acquirer (IFRS 3.B17).

It should be noted that if a **new entity is formed** that **issues equity instruments** to **bring about a business combination, that entity** is *not* the acquirer. Rather, **one of the combining entities** that **existed before the business combination** must be identified as the **acquirer** by applying the guidance above relating to which entity obtained control (IFRS 3.B18). To illustrate: If a newly incorporated Company A issues ordinary shares to the owners of Company B and Company C, in order to acquire all the shares in Companies B and C, then either Company B or Company C will be the acquirer. If the

---

1   The accounting, under IFRS 3, for business combinations that are reverse acquisitions, is beyond the scope of this publication.

former owners of Company B now own, because of Company A's share issue, a 70% interest in Company A, while the former owners of Company C own the remaining 30% interest in Company A, this could indicate that Company B is the acquirer.

However, if a new entity transfers **cash or other assets, or incurs liabilities** as **consideration,** to bring about the business combination, that entity may be the acquirer (IFRS 3.B18).

2.3.2 Determine the acquisition date

Once we have determined who the acquirer is, the acquirer must establish the **acquisition date** for the business combination. This is the date on which the acquirer obtains **control** of the acquiree (IFRS 3.8). Generally speaking, the date on which control is obtained is the date on which the acquirer **legally transfers** the **consideration (the purchase price), acquires the assets and assumes the liabilities** of the **acquiree** – this is known as the **closing date** (IFR 3.9).

However, in certain instances, the acquirer may obtain control on a date that is either **earlier or later** than the closing date (i.e., control can pass before a transaction is legally finalised). For example, the acquisition date would precede the closing date should a **written agreement** specifically provide that the acquirer **obtains control** of the acquiree on a date **before closing date** (IFRS 3.9).

In addition, it is important to note that if there are **suspensive conditions** attached to the business combination transaction (e.g., the approval of competition authorities is required), then control is not deemed to be transferred from the seller to the acquirer **until all suspensive conditions have been satisfied.**

The acquisition date is important for two purposes:

- It is the date on which the **consideration transferred, assets, liabilities, non-controlling interest** and **goodwill** are **measured.**
- It is the date from which the **results of the acquiree are included** in the **consolidated financial statements** of the acquirer (this is explained and illustrated from Volume 1 Chapter 3 onwards).

 Example 2.3: Acquisition date

Life Ltd is a long-term insurance company listed on the stock exchange. During its financial year ending on 31 December 20x5, Life Ltd acquired 90% of the shares and voting rights in Livelong Ltd, which is also a long-term insurer and a direct competitor to Life Ltd. The relevant activities of Livelong Ltd are directed by voting rights and the transaction qualifies as a business combination in terms of IFRS 3.

The heads of agreement for the acquisition of the shares by Life Ltd was signed on 30 March 20x5. The full agreement was signed on 14 June 20x5. According to the agreement, the effective date of acquisition was determined as 28 February 20x5. Approval by the Competition Commission was the last suspensive condition to be fulfilled. This approval was received on 18 July 20x5.

Required
Advise, fully motivating your answer, when the date of acquisition occurs for this business combination.

Solution 2.3: Acquisition date

- IFRS 3 defines the date of acquisition as the date on which the acquirer obtains control of the acquiree.
- Control is not deemed to have been transferred to Life Ltd until all suspensive conditions necessary to protect the parties involved have been satisfied.
- The fact that the agreement specifies an effective date does not necessarily make that date the date of acquisition.
- The acquisition only became unconditional on 18 July 20x5, when the final suspensive condition was met, with the Competition Commission granting its approval.
- The acquisition date for the purposes of this business combination is therefore 18 July 20x5.

2.3.3 Recognise and measure the identifiable assets acquired and liabilities assumed

As of the acquisition date, the acquirer must recognise, **separately from goodwill** (see Section 2.3.6), the **identifiable assets acquired, the liabilities assumed and any non-controlling interest** in the acquiree.

In order for the identifiable assets and liabilities of the acquiree to be recognised in a business combination (IFRS 3.11–3.12):

- they must **meet the definition of an asset or liability** in the *Framework for the Preparation and Presentation of Financial Statements* (Conceptual Framework) at the acquisition date; and
- they **must be part** of what the **acquirer** and the **acquiree (or its former owners)** **exchanged** in the business combination transaction, rather than being the result of **separate transactions**.

Furthermore, subject to limited exceptions, the acquirer must measure the identifiable assets acquired and liabilities assumed at their **fair values** at the **acquisition date** (IFRS 3.18).

2.3.3.1 Recognition conditions

Compliance with the Conceptual Framework definitions of assets and liabilities

As noted above, in order to obtain recognition in a business combination, the acquiree's identifiable assets acquired and liabilities assumed must comply with the definition of assets and liabilities in the Conceptual Framework. For example, post-acquisition reorganisation costs that the acquirer expects but is not obliged to incur in the future to discontinue operations of an acquiree do not meet the Conceptual Framework definition of a liability and are therefore not recognised as part of the accounting for the business combination.

Notably, IFRS 3 makes no reference to the general recognition criteria for assets and liabilities, as per the Conceptual Framework, namely of probability of an inflow/outflow of economic benefits and of reliable measurement. Consequently, IFRS 3 requires the acquirer to recognise identifiable assets acquired and liabilities assumed regardless of the probability of an inflow or outflow of economic benefits. The reason why these Conceptual Framework recognition criteria do not apply is because assets and liabilities acquired in terms of a business combination are measured at fair value, which fair value measurement already takes into account the probability of the inflow or outflow of economic benefits.

It is also important to note that the assets and liabilities that the acquirer recognises in accounting for the business combination may include certain assets and liabilities that the acquiree **had not previously recognised** in its **own financial statements**. For example, the acquirer may recognise acquired identifiable intangible assets (e.g., brand names, patents or customer relationships) that the acquiree did not recognise in its financial statements because it developed them internally and expensed the related costs.

The recognition of additional assets and liabilities in a business combination, not previously recognised by the acquiree, is examined in detail in Volume 2 Chapter 1. Also see Volume 1 Chapter 4, which deals with the recognition, at acquisition date, in terms of a business combination, of a deferred tax asset in the consolidated financial statements, in respect of the tax loss of a subsidiary at acquisition, where the subsidiary did not recognise the deferred tax asset in its own records.

Identifiable assets and liabilities must be part of the business combination exchange transaction

In addition to the requirement that the identifiable assets and liabilities must meet the definition of assets and liabilities as per the Conceptual Framework, the identifiable assets and liabilities must also be **part of what the acquirer** and the **acquiree (or its former owners) exchanged in the business combination transaction,** rather than being the result of **separate transactions**. This implies that the acquirer must recognise as part of applying the acquisition method (IFRS 3.51):

- only the consideration transferred **for the acquiree;** and
- only the assets acquired and liabilities assumed **in exchange for the acquiree.**

Separate transactions must be accounted for in accordance with the **relevant IFRSs.**

Thus, a transaction entered into by, or on behalf of the acquirer, primarily for the benefit of the acquirer or the combined entity rather than primarily for the benefit of the acquiree (or its former owners) before the business combination, would likely be a separate transaction (IFRS 3.52).

Furthermore, the following are examples of separate transactions that must *not* be included when applying the acquisition method (IFRS 3.52):

- a transaction that settles a pre-existing relationship between the acquirer and the acquiree;
- a transaction that remunerates employees or former owners of the acquiree for future services; and
- a transaction that reimburses the acquiree or its former owners for paying the acquirer's acquisition-related costs.

The manner in which we need to account for the three separate transactions listed above, in a business combination, is explained in detail in Volume 2 Chapter 1.

Example 2.4: Separate transaction not part of business combination

A potential acquiree has recognised an asset (Damages Receivable) relating to a lawsuit in respect of an unsettled claim against a potential acquirer. Accordingly, there is a pre-existing relationship between the two parties. The acquirer and the acquiree's owners agree to settle the claim as part of an agreement to sell the acquiree to the acquirer in a transaction that qualifies as a business combination. When the acquirer makes a lump-sum payment to the seller of the acquiree, part of the payment is to settle the legal claim and consequently is not part of the consideration transferred to acquire the business. The portion of the payment relating to the claim settlement must be excluded from the accounting for the business combination and accounted for separately.

In effect the acquiree relinquishes its claim (Damages Receivable) against the acquirer by transferring it (as a dividend) to the seller of the acquiree. Therefore, at the acquisition date, the acquiree has no receivable (asset) to be acquired as part of the business combination, and the acquirer would account for its settlement payment separately. This is an example of a transaction that settles a pre-existing relationship between acquirer and acquiree.

2.3.3.2 Measurement principles – assets and liabilities

As discussed above, in terms of IFRS 3, the acquirer is ordinarily required to measure the identifiable assets acquired and liabilities assumed in a business combination at **their fair values** at acquisition date.

'Fair value' is defined in Appendix A of the Standard as:

- the price that would be received to sell an asset or paid to transfer a liability;
- in an orderly transaction;
- between market participants at the measurement date.

When the acquirer determines that the **fair value** of an **asset or liability differs from** its **carrying amount**, as reflected in the books of the acquiree, the acquirer must **adjust the item's carrying amount to its fair value** in establishing the **fair value of the net assets acquired** in the business combination. For example, assume that at acquisition date an item of equipment with a carrying amount in the books of the acquiree of CU 300 000, has a fair value of CU 500 000. The acquirer would adjust the value of this equipment upwards by CU 200 000 in determining the fair value of the net assets acquired in the business combination.

Deferred tax effects of fair value adjustments at acquisition date

Under IFRS 3, the acquirer must **recognise** and **measure** the **deferred tax effects** of any **fair value adjustments**, at acquisition date, to the **acquiree assets acquired** and **liabilities assumed** in a **business combination**, in terms of **IAS 12** *Income Taxes* (IFRS 3.24). Note that the measurement of deferred tax assets and liabilities in terms of IAS 12 is an **exception** to the general requirement of IFRS 3 to measure assets and liabilities at fair value. This is because deferred tax assets and liabilities are measured at undiscounted amounts (i.e., the time value of money is not taken into account when measuring a deferred tax asset or liability) in accordance with IAS 12.

When a business combination results in a **parent–subsidiary** relationship (i.e., the business combination represents the acquisition of a controlling **shareholding** in a subsidiary by a parent), at acquisition IFRS 3 fair value adjustments to the subsidiary's assets and liabilities will give rise to **deferred tax effects** in the **consolidated financial statements**. In contrast, when an acquirer buys the acquiree's **net assets directly** in a business combination, at acquisition IFRS 3 fair value adjustments to the acquiree's assets and liabilities will *not* have deferred tax implications in the acquirer's own financial statements. These concepts are discussed below.

Deferred tax effects of fair value adjustments: Parent–subsidiary relationship arises from business combination

When, pursuant to a business combination, a parent obtains a controlling shareholding in a subsidiary, the subsidiary acquired is a **separate legal entity** to the parent. For this reason the tax authority – unless within a jurisdiction where group taxation applies[2] – will *not* recognise for tax purposes, any at acquisition fair value adjustments to the subsidiary's assets and liabilities recognised under IFRS 3, and which exist only in the consolidated financial statements of the group.

The result is that the at acquisition tax bases of the subsidiary's assets and liabilities remain unchanged, while for group purposes, the carrying amounts of these assets and liabilities are adjusted (either increased or decreased) to their at acquisition date fair values. At group level this creates at acquisition temporary differences, in terms of IAS 12, of the subsidiary (i.e., at acquisition carrying amounts of subsidiary assets and liabilities, which have been adjusted to fair value, are now greater or lesser than their unchanged tax bases) and the **recognition of a deferred tax asset or liability** of the subsidiary at acquisition date. More particularly, at group level, at acquisition IFRS 3 fair value adjustments to subsidiary assets and liabilities:

- that give rise to at acquisition **taxable temporary differences**, result in the at acquisition recognition of a **deferred tax liability** of the subsidiary, which liability **reduces** the net asset value (i.e., the equity) of the subsidiary acquired; and

- that give rise to **deductible temporary differences** result in the at acquisition recognition of a **deferred tax asset** of the subsidiary, which asset **increases** the net asset value (i.e., the equity) of the subsidiary acquired. Note that in accordance with IAS 12, a deferred tax asset may be recognised in respect of these deductible temporary differences **only to the extent** that it is **probable** that **taxable profit will be available** against which these **deductible temporary differences can be utilised** (IAS 12.24).

Recall from Volume 1 Chapter 1 that under IAS 12, the measurement of deferred tax liabilities and deferred tax assets should reflect the tax consequences that would follow from the manner in which the entity expects to recover or settle the carrying amount of its assets and liabilities (IAS 12.51). Consequently, the appropriate tax rate[3] used to measure the deferred tax effects of at acquisition fair value adjustments to subsidiary assets and liabilities must be determined by establishing the manner in

---

2   For purposes of this publication, it is assumed that group taxation **does *not* apply** in the jurisdiction(s) in which the group operates.

3   For purposes of this publication – except for foreign operations dealt with in Volume 2 Chapter 6 – it must be assumed that the group concerned operates in a jurisdiction which levies income tax at the rate of 28% and capital gains tax at the effective rate of 22.4% (100% × 80% Inclusion rate × 28% Income tax rate).

which the group expects – at acquisition date – to recover the carrying amount of these assets, and to settle these liabilities. For example:

- The carrying amount of an entity's **depreciable** property plant and equipment is expected to be recovered through use. Recovery through use generates taxable income taxed at the income tax rate of 28%. Consequently, deferred tax in respect of at acquisition fair value adjustments to a subsidiary's depreciable property, plant and equipment must be calculated using the income tax rate of 28%.

- The carrying amount of an entity's **non-depreciable** property plant and equipment (land) is expected to be recovered through sale. Recovery through sale results in capital gains tax being levied at the effective rate of 22.4%. Consequently, deferred tax in respect of at acquisition fair value adjustments to a subsidiary's non-depreciable property, plant and equipment must be calculated using the effective capital gains tax rate of 22.4%.

- The carrying amount of an entity's **inventory** is expected to be recovered through **sale**. Recovery through sale results generates **taxable income** taxed at the **income tax rate of 28%**. Consequently, deferred tax in respect of at acquisition fair value adjustments to a subsidiary's inventory must be calculated using the income tax rate of 28%.

The at acquisition deferred tax liability or asset, recognised at group level in respect of at acquisition fair value adjustments to subsidiary assets and liabilities, will **reverse** in subsequent periods as the assets are used, sold or impaired, and as the liabilities are settled. The effects, in the consolidated financial statements, of the post-acquisition reversals of these deferred tax assets and liabilities, are covered in detail in Volume 1 Chapter 5 and in Volume 2 Chapter 1.

Furthermore, any **additional assets and liabilities** of the subsidiary recognised as part of the business combination (that is, those assets and liabilities that the subsidiary did not recognise in its own financial statements, as discussed in Section 2.3.3.1) will also **give rise to deferred tax consequences**. This is because the revenue authority does not recognise these assets and liabilities for tax purposes; they exist only for accounting purposes in the consolidated financial statements of the group.

This means that these assets and liabilities of the subsidiary acquired, recognised as part of the business combination, will have **a tax base of NIL** and a **carrying amount** equal to their at **acquisition fair values**, which gives rise to **temporary differences** and therefore **deferred tax at acquisition date**. Taxable temporary differences will give rise to the recognition of a **deferred tax liability**, while **deductible temporary differences** will give rise to the recognition of a **deferred tax asset** at acquisition date, which will **affect the fair net asset value of the subsidiary acquired**, as discussed above. The deferred tax consequences of recognising additional assets and liabilities of a subsidiary, when accounting for a business combination, are dealt with in further detail in Chapter 9.

Deferred tax effects of fair value adjustments: Direct acquisition of net assets of acquiree in a business combination

Fair value adjustments to the assets and liabilities of an acquiree at acquisition date in a business combination where the **net assets** of the acquiree are **directly acquired** are *not* likely to have deferred tax implications. This is because the revenue authority would ordinarily **accept the fair values** of these assets and liabilities, being the values recognised by the acquirer for **accounting purposes**, for **tax purposes**. Accordingly, the **tax bases** of the **assets and liabilities** that are **acquired directly** – pursuant to the business combination – will be **equal** to the **carrying amounts** (which have been re-measured to fair value) thereof. The result is that *no* temporary differences will arise and consequently there will be *no* deferred tax implications.

Example 2.5: At acquisition fair value adjustments to assets of subsidiary, recognition of additional intangible asset of subsidiary and associated deferred tax effects

On 31 December 20x5 P Ltd acquired 100% of the share capital of S Ltd in a business combination transaction. Control was obtained as defined in IFRS 10 *Consolidated Financial Statements*. The statement of financial position of S Ltd that follows was presented at the acquisition date. The associated fair values as determined at acquisition date, in terms of IFRS 3, are provided.

Assume an income tax rate of 28% and a capital gains tax inclusion rate of 80%.

STATEMENT OF FINANCIAL POSITION OF S LTD AT 31 DECEMBER 20x5

	Carrying amounts CU	Fair values CU	Notes
Assets			
Property plant and equipment	800 000	1 300 000	Note 1
Land	500 000	750 000	
Trademark	200 000	315 000	Note 2
Trade receivables	420 000	385 000	
	1 920 000		

	Carrying amounts CU	Fair values CU
Equity and reserves		
Share capital	1 000 000	n/a
Retained earnings	740 000	n/a
Shareholders' equity	1 740 000	
Trade payables	180 000	180 000
	1 920 000	

Additional information

- Note 1: S Ltd accounts for all its property, plant and equipment using the historical cost model in terms of IAS 16 *Property, Plant and Equipment*.
- Note 2: This relates to a trademark purchased two years ago, which is carried at amortised cost in terms of IAS 38 *Intangible Assets*.
- Note 3: An independent valuator provided a fair value of CU 230 000 at acquisition date for an internally generated brand of S Ltd. This brand has not been recognised by S Ltd in its own financial statements. The estimated useful life of the brand was 15 years at acquisition date.

Required

Calculate the fair value of the identifiable net assets of S Ltd, acquired by P Ltd at acquisition date, in terms of IFRS 3.

Note: In arriving at your answer, you need to take into account any tax implications of:

- the fair value adjustments to the assets and liabilities of S Ltd; and
- any additional assets or liabilities of S Ltd recognised as part of the business combination.

Solution 2.5: At acquisition fair value adjustments to assets of subsidiary, recognition of additional intangible asset of subsidiary and associated deferred tax effects

	CU
Property, plant and equipment at fair value	1 300 000
Land at fair value	750 000
Trademark (purchased) at fair value	315 000
Brand (internally generated) at fair value	230 000
Trade receivables at fair value	385 000
Trade payables at fair value	(180 000)
Subtotal	2 800 000
Deferred tax adjustments – NET EFFECT **deferred tax liability** (see Calc 1 below)	(282 800)
Fair value of net assets (equity) acquired	2 517 200

Calculation 1: Tax effects of fair value adjustments and recognition of additional intangible asset of subsidiary

Item	Carrying amounts = IFRS 3 Fair values	Tax base	Temporary difference	Deferred tax asset/ (liability)	Calculation
Property, plant and equipment	1 300 000	800 000	500 000	(140 000)	[500 000 × 28%]
Land	750 000	500 000	250 000	(56 000)	[250 000 × 22.4%]
Trademark (purchased)	315 000	200 000	115 000	(32 200)	[115 000 × 28%]
Brand (internally generated)	230 000	NIL	230 000	(64 400)	[230 000 × 28%]
Trade receivables	385 000	420 000	(35 000)	9 800	[35 000 × 28%]
			TOTAL	**(282 800)**	

Note: Unlike S Ltd's other assets, the carrying amounts of which are recovered through use, the carrying amount of S Ltd's land is recovered through sale. The future sale of S Ltd's land will result in capital gains tax consequences. Accordingly, deferred tax on the remeasurement of S Ltd's land to fair value, is calculated using the effective capital gains tax rate of 22.4% (80% × 28%).

2.3.4 Recognise any non-controlling interest in the acquiree

As discussed above, business combinations can take the form of either the acquisition of the net assets of a business or the acquisition of a controlling interest in the equity (shares) of an acquiree. In the latter instance a parent–subsidiary relationship is created and consolidated financial statements must then be prepared in terms of IFRS 10.

The parent may acquire **all** the issued shares of the subsidiary, in which case the subsidiary is called a **wholly owned subsidiary.** Alternatively, should the parent acquire only **part** of the subsidiary's shares, the subsidiary would be referred to as a **partly owned subsidiary.** The non-controlling interest represents the **equity interest** in the **partly held subsidiary** that was *not* acquired by the **parent.**

IFRS 3 allows the acquirer a choice, available for each business combination, to measure the non-controlling interest at acquisition date, either (IFRS 3.19):

- at its **fair value;** or
- at its **proportionate share of the acquiree's identifiable net assets,** which have been fairly valued in terms of IFRS 3.

Note that this choice is available only if the non-controlling interests concerned are **present ownership interests** that entitle their holders to a **proportionate share** of the subsidiary's net assets in the event of liquidation of the subsidiary. A non-controlling interest in the **ordinary shares** of a subsidiary would meet these criteria, allowing the acquirer a choice between measurement of the non-controlling interest **either** at its **fair value** or at its **proportionate share** of the **acquiree's identifiable net assets.**

On the other hand, components of non-controlling interests that are *not* present ownership interests and *do not* entitle their holders to a proportionate share of the subsidiary's net assets upon liquidation of the subsidiary must be measured at **fair value** at acquisition date, unless IFRS requires another measurement basis. These components of non-controlling interests will include, for example, certain **preference shares** issued by a subsidiary. We measure these components of non-controlling interest at fair value because measurement at the proportionate share of the subsidiary's identifiable net assets may result in a value of zero, given that these instruments (such as certain preference shares) do not entitle their holders to a proportionate share of the subsidiary's net assets in the event of a liquidation. See Volume 1 Chapter 8 for further details regarding the recognition and measurement of the non-controlling interest in the preference shares issued by a subsidiary.

The **fair value** of the non-controlling interest may be measured based on **quoted prices in an active market for those shares not held by the acquirer.** In circumstances where quoted prices in an active market are **not available** (e.g., because the shares are not publicly traded), **other valuation techniques** may be used by the acquirer to determine the fair value of the non-controlling interest.

Example 2.6: Measurement of the non-controlling interest

On 31 December 20x5 the issued share capital of Stone Ltd, a company listed on a stock exchange, consisted of 120 000 ordinary shares. On this date Pebble Ltd acquired a 70% shareholding in Stone Ltd, giving Pebble Ltd control over Stone Ltd. The 70% shareholding in Stone Ltd was acquired at a cost of CU 2 000 000. The fair value of the net assets of Stone Ltd at acquisition date was CU 2 300 000. Furthermore, at acquisition date, each ordinary share in Stone Ltd was trading on the stock exchange at CU 20 per share.

Required

(a) Determine at what value the non-controlling interest of Stone Ltd will be measured at acquisition date if the non-controlling interest is measured at its proportionate share of the acquiree's identifiable net assets.

(b) Determine at what value the non-controlling interest of Stone Ltd will be measured at acquisition date if the non-controlling interest is measured at its fair value.

 Solution 2.6: Measurement of the non-controlling interest

(a) As Pebble Ltd acquired 70% of Stone Ltd, the non-controlling interest would have acquired the remaining 30% shareholding. Therefore, the non-controlling interest would be measured at CU 690 000, being 30% of the fair value of Stone Ltd's identifiable net assets of CU 2 300 000.

(b) The non-controlling interest would be measured at fair value based on the stock exchange share price at acquisition date, of CU 20 per share, as this is a quoted price in an active market. As the non-controlling interest holds a 30% shareholding, it acquired 36 000 (120 000 shares × 30%) of the issued shares of the subsidiary, Stone Ltd. Therefore, the non-controlling interest is measured at CU 720 000 (36 000 shares × CU 20 per share).

2.3.5 Measure the consideration transferred (IFRS 3.37 and IFRS 3.38)

The consideration transferred by the acquirer in a business combination is another term that describes:

- the acquirer's **purchase price** for the acquiree; or
- the **cost** of the acquiree to the acquirer.

The consideration transferred by the acquirer in a business combination must be measured at **fair value** at the **acquisition date** (with an exception for any portion of the acquirer's share-based payment awards exchanged for awards held by the acquiree's employees that is included in consideration transferred – see Volume 2 Chapter 1). The consideration transferred is calculated as the **sum of** the **fair values** of (IFRS 3.37):

- the **assets transferred** by the acquirer (e.g., cash, property, plant and equipment, intangible assets, investments, a business, or a subsidiary of the acquirer);
- the **liabilities incurred** by the acquirer to the former owners of the acquiree (e.g., borrowings incurred by the acquirer to use as consideration); and
- **equity instruments issued** by the acquirer (e.g., ordinary shares, preference shares and options).

When settlement of the purchase price is deferred and such deferral period is considered material, the present value of the amount payable – being the fair value of the consideration at acquisition date – must be determined by discounting the future payment due using the acquirer's incremental borrowing rate. For example, if a cash consideration of CU 1 000 000 is payable one year after acquisition date, and the interest rate (being the acquirer's incremental borrowing rate) is 5% per annum, then the present value of the cash consideration at acquisition date, of CU 952 381 (CU 1 000 000 / 1.05), will be the fair value of the consideration transferred, and the cost of acquisition.

The consideration transferred may include assets or liabilities of the acquirer that have carrying amounts that differ from their fair values at acquisition date (e.g., property, plant and equipment). If this is the case, then the acquirer must **remeasure** the transferred assets or liabilities to **fair value at acquisition date** and recognise any resulting **gains or losses** in its **profit or loss** (IFRS 3.38).

If, however, the transferred assets or liabilities remain **within the combined entity/group** after the business combination (e.g., property, plant and equipment is transferred directly to the acquiree rather than to the former owners of the acquiree), then the acquirer **retains control** of them. It follows that the acquirer would then measure these assets and liabilities at their **carrying amounts** immediately before acquisition date, with *no* gain or loss recognised, as these assets and liabilities are controlled by the acquirer both before and after the acquisition (IFRS 3.38). This will happen, for example, if the acquirer obtains its interest in the acquiree directly from that acquiree instead of from the acquiree's shareholders (i.e., the acquiree issues shares to the acquirer in exchange for assets).

Where consideration is in the form of **equity instruments** (e.g., the acquirer issues its own shares as consideration), the **fair value** of these equity instruments must be measured at the **acquisition date**, irrespective of when the equity instruments are actually issued.

 Example 2.7: Measurement of the consideration transferred

On 1 January 20x5 Pillow Ltd acquired a 100% interest in Slip Ltd. Pillow Ltd acquired the shares from Duvet Ltd, the former owner.

From that date Pillow Ltd had control over Slip Ltd. The consideration was settled as follows:

- A cash payment of CU 1 000 000.

- Transfer of land to Duvet Ltd. The land has a carrying amount of CU 250 000. The fair value of the land was CU 300 000 on 1 January 20x5 and CU 350 000 on 15 March 20x5, when transfer of the land was formally registered.

- Pillow Ltd issued 5 000 ordinary shares to Duvet Ltd on 20 January 20x5. Pillow Ltd's shares had a market price of CU 15 and CU 17 on 1 January 20x5 and 20 January 20x5 respectively.

Required
Provide the journal entry to account for the acquisition of Slip Ltd in the separate financial statements of Pillow Ltd.

Solution 2.7: Measurement of the consideration transferred

	Dr CU	Cr CU
1 January 20x5		
Investment in Slip Ltd (balancing figure) (SFP)	1 375 000	
Bank (SFP)		1 000 000
Land (at carrying amount) (SFP)		250 000
Gain on transfer of land (P/L)		Wkg1 50 000
Share capital (SCIE)		Wkg2 75 000
Recognising the acquisition of Slip Ltd		

Workings: Journal

Working 1:
300 000 Fair value – 250 000 Carrying amount

Working 2:
5 000 Shares × CU 15 Per share

Comments: Journal entry
- Note that the fair value of the land and the shares must be determined on acquisition date, being 1 January 20x5.
- As the land was transferred to the previous owners of Slip Ltd, namely Duvet Ltd, and not to Slip Ltd itself, we need to establish the fair value for the land and compare that to the land's carrying amount to determine any profit or loss on transfer to be recognised by Pillow Ltd (the acquirer).

2.3.5.1 Acquisition-related costs (IFRS 3.53)

Acquisition-related costs are transaction costs that an acquirer incurs when bringing about a business combination. These costs typically include:
- finder's fees;
- professional or consulting fees (e.g., costs for the services of lawyers, investment bankers, accountants, valuation experts and other third parties);
- general administrative costs (including costs of maintaining an internal acquisitions department); and
- costs of issuing and registering debt and equity securities (e.g., share issue costs).

As the above-mentioned costs are *not* part of the fair value exchange between the buyer and seller, they are accounted for as a **separate transaction** in which payments are made for services received, and will generally be **expensed to profit or loss** in the period in which the costs are incurred and the services are received. The costs to issue debt or equity securities must, however, be recognised in accordance with IAS 32 *Financial Instruments: Presentation* and IFRS 9 *Financial Instruments*.

In this respect, the costs incurred in:

- issuing a **debt instrument** must be **included in the value of the instrument** initially recognised (this will affect the amortised cost at which the debt instrument is carried); and

- issuing an **equity instrument** (e.g., shares) must be **deducted from equity** (e.g., deducted from share capital).

 Example 2.8: Acquisition-related costs

On 1 January 20x5 Abba Ltd acquired a 100% interest in Queen Ltd. From that date Abba Ltd had control over Queen Ltd. The purchase price was settled as follows:

- a cash payment of CU 1 000 000;
- issuing 20 000 shares to the seller with a fair value of CU 180 000; and
- issuing debentures to the seller for an amount of CU 420 000.

In addition to the above, legal and accounting costs of CU 60 000 were paid in relation to the acquisition of the shares in Queen Ltd. Also, costs of CU 8000 and CU 12 000 were incurred and paid in issuing the shares and debentures respectively.

Required
Provide the journal entries to account for the above-mentioned information in the separate financial statements of Abba Ltd.

 Solution 2.8: Acquisition-related costs

	Dr	Cr
Journal 1 (J1)	CU	CU
1 January 20x5		
Investment in Queen Ltd (balancing figure) (SFP)	1 600 000	
Bank (SFP) (given)		1 000 000
Share capital (SCIE) (given)		180 000
Debentures (financial liability) (SFP) (given)		420 000
Recognising the acquisition of Queen Ltd		

	Dr	Cr
Journal 2 (J2)	CU	CU
1 January 20x5		
Other expenses (P/L) (given)	60 000	
Share capital (SCIE) (given)	8 000	
Debentures (financial liability) (SFP) (given)	12 000	
Bank (SFP) (given)		80 000
Recognising the acquisition-related costs for the Queen Ltd business combination		

Comments: Journal 2
- The debenture issue costs do not form part of the consideration transferred in terms of the business combination; rather these costs are debited to the debenture account (it will therefore affect the amortised cost at which the debentures will be carried).
- In similar fashion, the share issue costs also do not form part of the consideration transferred in terms of the business combination; instead, these costs are debited directly to equity, reducing the share capital account.

2.3.6 Recognise and measure goodwill or a gain from a bargain purchase

2.3.6.1 Recognition and measurement of goodwill

Goodwill is an asset representing the payment made by the acquirer for the future economic benefits arising from other assets acquired in a business combination that are not capable of being individually identified and separately recognised (IFRS 3 Appendix A).

The future economic benefits embodied in goodwill may result from:
- various intangible assets not recognised at acquisition date (e.g., the acquiree's established customer base, dedicated employees and market share); and
- the benefits of synergy that arise in the business combination (e.g., economies of scale).

In addition, an acquirer may pay more than the fair value of the acquiree's net assets because it is obtaining the valuable right to control the acquiree (i.e., the payment for goodwill is a control premium paid).

Goodwill is measured at the acquisition date as shown in Figure 2.1.

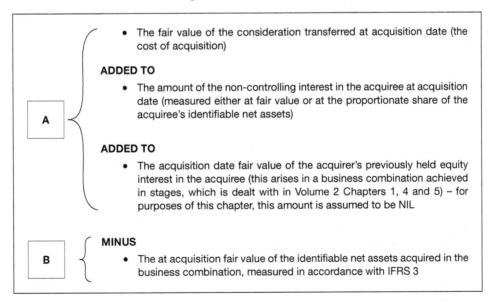

Figure 2.1: *Goodwill calculation (IFRS 3.32)*

Goodwill is then calculated as a **residual amount,** being the **excess** of **A** over **B.**

In a business combination in which the acquirer and the acquiree (or its former owners) **exchange only equity instruments,** the acquisition date fair value of the acquiree's equity interests may be more reliably measurable than the acquisition date fair value of the acquirer's equity interests. If this is the case, the acquirer must determine the amount of goodwill by using the **acquisition date fair value of the acquiree's equity instruments** instead of the acquisition date fair value of the equity instruments transferred by it (IFRS 3.33).

At acquisition date, goodwill is recognised by the acquirer as a **non-current asset,** measured at **cost. Subsequently,** in accordance with IAS 36 *Impairment of Assets,* goodwill is measured at **cost less any accumulated impairment losses.** Furthermore, goodwill must be **tested every year** for **possible impairment.** When goodwill is recognised in a business combination **during a particular year** it needs to be tested for impairment **before** the **end of that year.**

Any **impairment losses** in respect of **goodwill** are recognised as an **expense** in **profit or loss.** In addition, it is important to note that the **impairment of goodwill** may **never be reversed.** The accounting treatment for goodwill in the consolidated financial statements, both at acquisition date and subsequently, is comprehensively dealt with in Volume 1 Chapters 3 to 8 and Volume 2 Chapter 1.

Non-controlling interest and goodwill measurement

As discussed in Section 2.3.4, the non-controlling interest may be measured at acquisition date either at its fair value or at its proportionate share of the identifiable net assets of the acquiree. As was shown in Example 2.6, the particular method used to measure the non-controlling interest results in different values calculated for it. This, in turn, affects the amount of goodwill recognised, as goodwill is measured as a residual amount.

Partial goodwill method

Where the non-controlling interest is measured at its **proportionate share** of the **acquiree's (subsidiary's) net asset value,** any goodwill that arises on acquisition is **wholly attributable to the parent's investment.** Consequently, *no* goodwill will be attributed to the non-controlling interest. When goodwill is calculated this way, we refer to it as the **partial goodwill method.**

Full goodwill method

If the non-controlling interest is measured at **its fair value,** then goodwill relating to **all of the subsidiary's equity** is recognised. More particularly, the goodwill calculated is allocated **both to the parent and to the non-controlling interest.** The goodwill allocated to the non-controlling interest is calculated as the **excess of the non-controlling interest's fair value at acquisition date** over its **proportionate share** of the **acquiree's (subsidiary's) identifiable net assets at acquisition date.** When goodwill is calculated this way, we call it the **full goodwill method.**

Example 2.9: Goodwill measured at acquisition and measurement of the non-controlling interest

This example is a continuation of Example 2.6: Measurement of the non-controlling interest.

On 31 December 20x5 the issued share capital of Stone Ltd, a company listed on a stock exchange, consists of 120 000 ordinary shares. On this date Pebble Ltd acquired a 70% shareholding in Stone Ltd, giving Pebble Ltd control over Stone Ltd. The 70% shareholding in Stone Ltd was acquired at a cost of CU 2 000 000. The fair value of the identifiable net assets of Stone Ltd at acquisition date was CU 2 300 000.

Furthermore, at acquisition date, each ordinary share in Stone Ltd was trading on the stock exchange at CU 20 per share.

Required

(a) Determine the total amount of goodwill arising from this business combination, assuming that Pebble Ltd measures the non-controlling interest at its proportionate share of the identifiable net assets of Stone Ltd, an amount of CU 690 000.

(b) Determine the total amount of goodwill arising from this business combination, assuming that Pebble Ltd measures the non-controlling interest at its fair value, being CU 720 000.

(c) Determine the amount of goodwill attributable to Pebble Ltd and to the non-controlling interest respectively, assuming that Pebble Ltd measures the non-controlling interest at its fair value, being CU 720 000.

 Solution 2.9: Goodwill measured at acquisition and measurement of the non-controlling interest

	Part (a): NCI at proportionate share	Part (b): NCI at fair value
	CU	CU
Consideration transferred	2 000 000	2 000 000
Add: Non-controlling interest	690 000	720 000
Add: Fair value of previously held equity interest	–	–
Subtotal	2 690 000	2 720 000
Minus: Fair value of identifiable net assets of Stone Ltd at acquisition	(2 300 000)	(2 300 000)
Goodwill	**390 000**	**420 000**

Part (c): Goodwill attributable to Pebble Ltd and to the non-controlling interest

	Total equity	Pebble Ltd 70%	NCI 30%
	CU	CU	CU
Identifiable net assets of Stone Ltd at acquisition	2 300 000	1 610 000	690 000
Equity represented by goodwill – Pebble Ltd	**390 000**	**390 000**	**–**
Equity represented by goodwill – NCI	**30 000**	**–**	**30 000**
Consideration **plus** NCI at fair value	2 720 000	2 000 000	720 000

Example 2.10: Goodwill determination: Acquirer and acquiree exchange only equity instruments

On 31 December 20x6 the issued share capital of Jaguar Ltd consists of 100 000 ordinary shares. On this date Lion Ltd acquired a 75% controlling interest in Jaguar Ltd by issuing an additional 25 000 of its shares, with a market value of CU 20 per share. Due to the thinness of the market, however, this market price is not considered to reflect fair value. At 31 December 20x6 (acquisition date) the market value of Jaguar Ltd's shares was CU 9 per share, which was considered to reflect a fair value. The fair value of the identifiable net assets of Jaguar Ltd at acquisition date was CU 852 000.

Required
Determine the total amount of goodwill arising from this business combination, assuming that Lion Ltd measures the non-controlling interest at its proportionate share of the identifiable net assets of Jaguar Ltd.

 Solution 2.10: Goodwill determination: Acquirer and acquiree exchange only equity instruments

	CU
Consideration transferred	
(100 000 Shares of Jaguar Ltd × 75% Interest × CU 9 Per share)	675 000
Add: Non-controlling interest (852 000 Net asset value × 25%)	213 000
Add: Fair value of previously held equity interest	–
Subtotal	888 000
Minus: Fair value of identifiable net assets of Jaguar Ltd	(852 000)
Goodwill	36 000

Comment

- Because this is a business combination in which the acquirer and acquiree exchange only equity instruments and the acquisition date fair value of Jaguar Ltd's shares is more reliably measurable than that of Lion Ltd, the consideration transferred must be measured at CU 675 000 (100 000 Jaguar Ltd shares × 75% Interest × CU 9 Market value per share) instead of at CU 500 000 (25 000 Lion Ltd shares × CU 20 Market value per share).

2.3.6.2 Recognition and measurement of a gain on a bargain purchase

In terms of IFRS 3.34 a bargain purchase gain is recognised as the **excess of B over A** in Figure 2.1. That is, the **excess** of the **fair value of the acquiree's identifiable net assets** at acquisition date, over the **total of:**

- the **value of the consideration transferred;**
- the **non-controlling interest** in the **acquiree; and**
- the **fair value** of any **previously held equity interest** in the **acquiree.**

The gain is attributed **in full** to the **acquirer** – it is *not* allocated to the non-controlling interest (IFRS 3.34).

A bargain purchase may occur, for example, in a business combination where the seller is forced to sell because of specific circumstances such as financial distress or, for example, because of the acquirer's excellent negotiation skills.

Before recognising the gain – which is effectively a discount on the purchase price paid – in **profit or loss** of the **acquirer**, it is crucial first to establish that it is in fact a gain and not an error made:

- in the identification and/or measurement of the acquiree's identifiable net assets;
- in the measurement of the non-controlling interest in the acquiree (if any); and
- in the measurement of the cost of the business combination.

Accordingly, the acquirer must (IFRS 3.36):

- reassess whether it has correctly identified all the assets acquired and all the liabilities assumed (and, if necessary, recognise any additional assets or liabilities identified in this review); and
- review the procedures used to measure the following:
  - the identifiable assets acquired and liabilities assumed;
  - the non-controlling interest, if any;
  - for a business combination achieved in stages, the acquirer's previously held equity interest in the acquiree; and
  - the consideration transferred.

The objective of this review is to ensure that all available information at acquisition date was taken into account in measuring the amounts used.

Once a bargain purchase is **confirmed**, the **gain** is recognised immediately in **profit or loss of the acquirer**.

 Example 2.11: Measuring the gain on a bargain purchase

On 1 January 20x5 Copper Ltd acquired 80% of Gold (Pty) Ltd for CU 3 200 000, giving Copper Ltd control over Gold (Pty) Ltd. The fair value of the identifiable net assets of Gold (Pty) Ltd is correctly measured at CU 4 275 000.

Required

(a) Determine the bargain purchase gain that arises at acquisition date if the non-controlling interest is measured at its proportionate share of the identifiable net assets of Gold (Pty) Ltd.

(b) Determine the bargain purchase gain that arises at acquisition date if the non-controlling interest is measured at its fair value of CU 905 000.

S Solution 2.11: Measuring the gain on a bargain purchase

	Part (a): NCI at proportionate share	Part (b): NCI at fair value
	CU	CU
Consideration transferred	3 200 000	3 200 000
Add: Non-controlling interest	Wkg1855 000	905 000
Add: Fair value of previously held equity interest	–	–
Subtotal	4 055 000	4 105 000
Minus: Fair value of identifiable net assets of Gold (Pty) Ltd	(4 275 000)	(4 275 000)
Gain on bargain purchase (attributable only to Copper Ltd)	**(220 000)**	**(170 000)**

Workings: Gain on bargain purchase

Working 1:

4 275 000 Net asset value × 20%

2.4 Comparing the direct acquisition of the net assets of an acquiree, and the acquisition of the equity of an acquiree, in a business combination

IFRS 3 applies to all business combination transactions where control is obtained over another business. Typically, this occurs either:

- through the **direct** acquisition of assets and the assumption of liabilities of another entity (the acquiree), which constitute a business; or
- by the **indirect** acquisition of assets and assumption of liabilities of another entity through investment in the **equity** (i.e., **shares**) of another entity (the acquiree), that is, by acquiring a **controlling shareholding** in the acquiree.

If the business combination involves the purchase of the acquiree's **equity** (i.e., **shares**), this will result in a **parent–subsidiary relationship** where the acquirer is the parent and the acquiree is the subsidiary (i.e., an entity which is controlled by another entity). In such circumstances the acquirer:

- applies **IFRS 3** in its **consolidated financial statements** in dealing with the **initial accounting treatment** of the subsidiary on the **date of acquisition**; IFRS 10 then deals with the **consolidation process** and **procedures** that occur **after acquisition date**. (The preparation of consolidated financial statements, where IFRS 3 is applied at acquisition date and IFRS 10 is applied thereafter, is covered in detail in Volume 1 Chapters 3 to 8 and Volume 2 Chapter 1.)
- in terms of IAS 27, recognises its interest in the acquiree in its **separate financial statements** as an **investment in a subsidiary**, either at **cost**, at **fair value** in terms of IFRS 9, or by applying the **equity method** as per IAS 28 (see Volume 1 Chapter 1).

Where a business combination takes the form of the **direct purchase of the acquiree's net assets,** as opposed to the purchase of the equity of the acquiree, this does *not* result in a parent–subsidiary relationship. Consequently, consolidated financial statements are *not* prepared in these circumstances. Instead, the acquirer **applies IFRS 3** in its **separate or individual financial statements** in accounting for the **consideration transferred** and the **assets acquired** and **liabilities assumed,** including **goodwill** or a **bargain purchase gain.** Note that there is **no non-controlling interest** because the net assets of the acquiree are all owned by the **acquirer.** After the business combination, the acquirer will account for the **acquired assets and liabilities** in terms of the **applicable IFRSs** in its separate or individual financial statements.

 Example 2.12: Direct acquisition of the net assets of an acquiree

Guns Ltd decided to take over the assets and liabilities of Roses Ltd on 31 December 20x6 (the acquisition date) in a transaction qualifying as a business combination in terms of IFRS 3. The purchase consideration consisted of the following:

- CU 3 500 000 was paid in cash immediately on 31 December 20x6;
- 100 000 of Gun Ltd's shares with a market price of CU 12 per share on 31 December 20x6 were issued as consideration on 15 January 20x7, when the market price was CU 13 per share; and
- Land with a carrying amount of CU 220 000 and a fair value of CU 445 000 was transferred to the **sellers of the net assets of Roses Ltd on** 31 December 20x6.

Roses Ltd recognised the following assets and liabilities in its financial statements on 31 December 20x6:

	Carrying amount	Fair value
	CU	CU
Property, plant and equipment	1 200 000	1 500 000
Investment property	760 000	980 000
Inventory	1 900 000	2 100 000
Trade and other receivables	1 700 000	1 600 000
Trade and other payables	(780 000)	(780 000)
Long-term loan	(690 000)	(690 000)

Additional information
- The revenue authority accepted the transfer values of the above assets and liabilities for tax purposes.

Required
Prepare the journal entries required in the accounting records of Guns Ltd for the takeover of Roses Ltd's assets and liabilities on 31 December 20x6.

➨

Solution 2.12: Direct acquisition of the net assets of an acquiree

	Dr CU	Cr CU
Property, plant and equipment (SFP) (given: at fair value)	1 500 000	
Investment property (SFP) (given: at fair value)	980 000	
Inventory (SFP) (given: at fair value)	2 100 000	
Trade and other receivables (SFP) (given: at fair value)	1 600 000	
Trade and other payables (SFP) (given: at fair value)		780 000
Long-term loan (SFP) (given: at fair value)		690 000
Bank (SFP) (given)		3 500 000
Land (SFP) (at carrying amount: given)		220 000
Profit on disposal of land (P/L)		[Wkg1] 225 000
Share capital (SCIE)		[Wkg2] 1 200 000
Goodwill (SFP) (balancing figure)	435 000	
Acquisition of assets and liabilities in business combination on 31 December 20x6		

Workings: Journal

Working 1:
445 000 Fair value – 220 000 Carrying amount

Working 2:
100 000 Shares × CU 12 Per share

Comments: Journal entry

- As the business of Rose Ltd has been acquired, over which Gun Ltd has control, it qualifies as a business combination in terms of IFRS 3. Consequently, in terms of IFRS 3, all the identifiable assets acquired and liabilities assumed of the acquiree, namely Rose Ltd, must be measured at fair value at acquisition date, as must the consideration transferred by the acquirer, Gun Ltd.

- Goodwill of CU 435 000 is recognised by Gun Ltd, the acquirer. This is because the total consideration transferred, amounting to CU 5 145 000, exceeds by CU 435 000 the CU 4 710 000 at acquisition value of the identifiable net assets of the acquiree, Rose Ltd.

- Because the revenue authority has accepted the fair value transfer values of Rose Ltd's assets and liabilities for tax purposes, the carrying amounts of these assets and liabilities, recognised by Gun Ltd, pursuant to the business combination, equal their respective tax bases. Consequently, no temporary differences arise, which means that there is no deferred tax.

2.5 Disclosure of information about current business combinations (IFRS 3.59 and IFRS 3.B64)

In terms of paragraph 59 of IFRS 3, the acquirer must provide disclosures that enable users of its financial statements to assess the nature and financial effects of:

- business combinations that occur during the current reporting period; and
- business combinations that occur after the end of the reporting period but before the financial statements are approved for issue.

To enable users to assess the nature and financial effects of a business combination as required by paragraph 59 of the Standard, the following disclosures should be made for each business combination that occurs during the reporting period (IFRS 3.B64):

- the name and a description of the acquiree;
- the acquisition date;
- the percentage of voting equity interests acquired;
- the primary reasons for the business combination and a description of how the acquirer obtained control of the acquiree;
- a qualitative description of the factors that make up the goodwill recognised, for example, expected synergies from the business combination, or intangible assets that did not qualify for separate recognition;
- the acquisition date fair value of the total consideration transferred and the acquisition date fair value of each major class of consideration (e.g., cash, tangible or intangible assets, liabilities incurred and equity interests issued by the acquirer);
- for equity interests issued as consideration by the acquirer, both the number of instruments issued and the method used to value these instruments must be disclosed;
- full details (amounts, descriptions, estimated outcomes) of contingent consideration arrangements and indemnification assets (covered in Volume 2 Chapter 1);
- for acquired receivables, the following must be disclosed, by major class:
  - the fair value thereof;
  - the gross contractual amounts receivable; and
  - the best estimate at acquisition date of contractual cash flows, not expected to be collected.
- the amounts recognised as of the acquisition date for each major class of asset acquired and liabilities assumed;
- the disclosure in terms of IAS 37 *Provisions, Contingent Liabilities and Contingent Assets* for all contingent liabilities; for contingent liabilities not recognised, the reasons why the contingent liability could not be measured reliably (contingent liabilities in the context of business combinations are dealt with in Volume 2 Chapter 1);
- the total amount of goodwill that is expected to be tax deductible;
- full details about transactions that are recognised separately from the business combination, including details of acquisition-related costs;
- for a gain arising from a bargain purchase:
  - the reasons why the transaction resulted in a gain; and
  - the amount of any gain recognised and the line item in the statement of comprehensive income in which the gain was included.
- for each business combination in which the acquirer holds less than 100% of the equity interest at acquisition date:
  - the amount of the non-controlling interest in the acquiree, recognised at acquisition date; and
  - the basis of measurement of the non-controlling interest.

- full details about a business combination achieved in stages (this is addressed in Volume 2 Chapter 1);
- the following information about the acquiree's revenue and profit or loss:
  - the amounts of revenue and profit or loss of the acquiree included in the acquirer's consolidated statement of comprehensive income for the reporting period; and
  - the amounts of revenue and profit or loss of the combined entity on an annual basis, as if all business combinations for the year occurred at the beginning of the year.

Disclosure in aggregate of most of the information as listed above is required for individually immaterial business combinations, occurring during the reporting period, that are material collectively (IFRS 3.B65).

If the acquisition date for the business combination is after the end of the reporting period but before the financial statements are authorised for issue, the acquirer must disclose the information above, unless the initial accounting for the business combination is incomplete at the time that the financial statements are authorised for issue. In that situation, the acquirer must describe which disclosures could not be made and the reasons why they cannot be made (IFRS 3.B66).

In addition, a number of further disclosures are required to provide details of adjustments recognised in the current reporting period and that relate to business combinations that occurred in the period or in previous reporting periods. These are dealt with in Volume 2 Chapter 1.

Summary

This chapter covered the basic principles in IFRS 3. IFRS 3 deals with the accounting for a **business combination,** which is a transaction or event in which an acquirer obtains **control** over one or more **businesses.** The following key learning points are important:

- A business is an integrated combination of activities and assets that is capable of being conducted or managed to provide a return to investors in the form of dividends, lower costs or other economic benefits.
- A business consists of inputs and processes applied to those inputs that are capable of producing outputs. Whether a set of assets and activities is a business, is determined based on whether the integrated set is capable of being managed as a business by a market participant.

IFRS 3 requires that all business combinations be accounted for using the acquisition method. Application of the acquisition method involves the following steps:

Step 1: Identify the **acquirer.** This is the entity that **obtains control** over the acquiree.

Step 2: Determine the **acquisition date.** This is the date on which the **acquirer obtains control** of the acquiree.

Step 3: Recognise the **identifiable assets** acquired and **liabilities assumed** in the business combination. To qualify for recognition, the assets and liabilities:

- must meet the definitions in the **Conceptual Framework**; and
- must be **part of what is exchanged** in the business combination, i.e. they must *not* be the result of **separate transactions**.

The assets and liabilities recognised by the acquirer in terms of the business combination may include certain assets and liabilities not recognised by the acquiree in its own financial statements, for example internally developed intangible assets such as brand names, patents and customer relationships. Furthermore, recognition of these additional acquiree assets and liabilities in a business combination which results in a **parent subsidiary relationship** will result in **deferred tax effects** in the **consolidated financial statements**. This is because these assets and liabilities will have a carrying amount at acquisition date, with a corresponding nil tax base.

Step 4: Measure assets acquired and **liabilities assumed** at their **acquisition date fair values**. The remeasurement of acquiree assets and liabilities to fair value in a business combination which results in a **parent subsidiary relationship** will result in **deferred tax effects** in the **consolidated financial statements** because the assets acquired and liabilities assumed are adjusted to fair value, while their respective tax bases remain unchanged.

Step 5: Recognise and measure the **non-controlling interest** in the acquiree at:

- its **fair value** at acquisition date; or
- its **proportionate share** of the **at acquisition fair value** of the acquiree's **identifiable net assets**.

Step 6: Measure the **consideration transferred** at **fair value on acquisition date.** Consideration includes:

- assets transferred by the acquirer (e.g., cash, property, plant and equipment intangible assets, investments);
- liabilities incurred by the acquirer to the acquiree's former owners (e.g., a loan to fund the purchase consideration); and
- equity instruments issued by the acquirer (e.g., ordinary shares, preference shares, options).

Step 7: Recognise and **measure goodwill** or a **bargain purchase gain.**

- **Goodwill** is measured as the **excess** of:
  - the aggregate of the consideration transferred, the amount of any non-controlling interest in the acquiree, and in a business combination achieved in stages, the acquisition date fair value of the acquirer's previously held equity interest in the acquiree

  OVER
  - the fair value of the acquiree's at acquisition identifiable net assets acquired.

- Goodwill is recognised as a **non-current asset** and represents the **future economic benefits** arising from **other assets** acquired in a business combination that are *not* **individually identifiable** and **separately recognised. Goodwill is tested annually for impairment.**
- A bargain purchase gain arises when the **fair value of the at acquisition date identifiable net assets** of the acquiree **exceed** the sum of:
  - the acquisition date fair value of the consideration transferred;
  - the amount of any non-controlling interest in the acquiree; and
  - in a business combination achieved in stages, the acquisition date fair value of the acquirer's previously held equity interest in the acquiree.
- A bargain purchase gain is recognised in **profit or loss** of the **acquirer** at acquisition date.

A business combination involving the purchase of the acquiree's equity (i.e., shares) results in a **parent–subsidiary** relationship where the **acquirer** is the **parent** and the **acquiree** is the **subsidiary** (i.e., an entity which is controlled by another entity). In such circumstances the acquirer **applies IFRS 3 in its consolidated financial statements** in dealing with the **initial accounting treatment** of the **subsidiary** on the **acquisition date.** Volume 1 Chapter 2 provided you with fundamental IFRS 3 knowledge that you will learn to apply in Volume 1 Chapters 3 to 8 to account for subsidiaries at acquisition date for consolidation purposes.

In Volume 1 Chapter 3 we begin our detailed study of the mechanics of the consolidation process by learning how to prepare the consolidated financial statements of a parent and its wholly owned subsidiary.

QUESTIONS

Question 2.1

High Ltd acquired a 80% controlling interest in Tech Ltd on 1 June 20x5. High Ltd agreed to pay the following as consideration:

- High Ltd issued 120 000 ordinary shares to the previous shareholders of Tech Ltd. High Ltd and Tech Ltd agreed that the shares would be issued at CU 20 per share, but the shares traded on the stock exchange at CU 25 per share on 1 June 20x5.

- High Ltd will make a cash payment to the value of CU 6 000 000. This amount will be settled in three equal annual instalments, with the first instalment being paid on 1 June 20x6. The sale of shares agreement specifically stated that no interest is charged on this amount. High Ltd's incremental borrowing rate is 12% per annum.

- High Ltd agreed to transfer land to the previous Tech Ltd shareholders. The land had a carrying amount of CU 1 200 000 and a fair value of CU 1 700 000 on 1 June 20x5. On 18 June 20x5, when transfer of the land was formally registered, its fair value was CU 1 780 000.

- High Ltd undertook to deliver 80 of its new range of 3D flat screen television units, which it had manufactured (obtained from its finished goods stock) as part of the purchase price to the previous Tech Ltd shareholders as follows:

Date	Number of units delivered	Fair value per unit on delivery date
1 June 20x5	45 units	CU 25 000
1 September 20x5	35 units	CU 19 000

The cost of manufacture of each television unit was CU 16 000.

In relation to the acquisition of Tech Ltd, High Ltd paid share issue costs of CU 85 000 on 1 June 20x5.

In addition, on 1 June 20x5 the statement of financial position of Tech Ltd was as follows:

Assets	CU	Comments
Plant and equipment	2 300 000	• Fair value was CU 2 700 000 and asset recovered through use
Land	1 850 000	• Fair value was CU 2 320 000 and asset recovered through sale
Intangible assets	1 100 000	• Fair value was CU 1 325 000 and assets recovered through use
Investment	3 270 000	• Tech Ltd held 100 000 shares in a stock exchange listed company. These shares were trading at CU 36 per share on the stock exchange on 1 June 20x5
Inventory	1 190 000	• Fair value equals carrying amount
Trade receivables	700 000	• Fair value was CU 600 000
Bank	2 500 000	• Fair value equals carrying amount
Equity and liabilities		
Share capital and reserves	12 545 000	• n/a
Deferred tax	210 000	• Fair value equals carrying amount
Trade and other payables	205 000	• Fair value equals carrying amount

Additional information

- The income tax rate is 28% and 80% of capital gains are included in taxable income.
- Tech Ltd is not a sharedealer for income tax purposes.

Required

(a) Calculate the consideration transferred by High Ltd in acquiring Tech Ltd on 1 June 20x5.

(b) Prepare the journal entries that would have been passed in the financial records of High Ltd on 1 June 20x5 to record the acquisition of Tech Ltd.

(c) Calculate the goodwill or gain on bargain purchase price arising on the acquisition of Tech Ltd. Assume that High Ltd applies the partial goodwill method.

(d) Calculate the goodwill or gain on bargain purchase price arising on the acquisition of Tech Ltd. Assume that High Ltd applies the full goodwill method and that the fair value of the non-controlling interest was CU 2 825 000 at acquisition date.

Question 2.2

Calvin Ltd decided to take over the assets and liabilities of Prada Ltd on 31 December 20x5 (the acquisition date) in a transaction qualifying as a business combination in terms of IFRS 3 *Business Combinations*. The purchase consideration consisted of the following:

- CU 5 500 000 was paid in cash immediately on 31 December 20x5.
- 150 000 of Calvin Ltd's shares with a market price of CU 10 per share on 31 December 20x5 were issued as consideration on 2 February 20x6, when the market price was CU 9.50 per share.

- A final once-off cash payment of CU 1 995 000 was paid on 31 December 20x6. In terms of the sale of business agreement, no interest was charged on this amount. Calvin Ltd's incremental borrowing rate was 14% per annum.

Prada Ltd recognised the following assets and liabilities in its financial statements on 31 December 20x5:

	Carrying amount CU	Fair value CU
Property, plant and equipment	2 100 000	2 450 000
Investment property	1 600 000	1 800 000
Inventory	2 715 000	2 980 000
Trade and other receivables	2 212 000	2 050 000
Long-term loan	(1 100 000)	(1 100 000)
Deferred tax liability	(390 000)	(390 000)
	7 137 000	7 790 000

Further information

1. Prada owned certain trademarks with an indefinite useful life that it had not recognised. The fair value of these trademarks was estimated to be CU 875 000 on 31 December 20x5.
2. The revenue authority accepted the transfer values of the above assets and liabilities for tax purposes (including the trademarks at their fair value of CU 875 000).

Required

Prepare the journal entries required in the accounting records of Calvin Ltd for the takeover of Prada Ltd's assets and liabilities on 31 December 20x5 and the subsequent payment of the balance of the purchase consideration on 31 December 20x6.

References

Conceptual Framework for Financial Reporting

IAS 12 *Income Taxes*

IAS 16 *Property, plant and equipment*

IAS 27 *Separate Financial Statements*

IAS 28 *Investments in Associates and Joint Ventures*

IAS 32 *Financial Instruments: Presentation*

IAS 36 *Impairment of Assets*

IAS 37 *Provisions, Contingent Liabilities and Contingent Assets*

IAS 38 *Intangible Assets*

IAS 40 *Investment Property*

IFRS 3 *Business Combinations*

IFRS 9 *Financial Instruments*

IFRS 10 *Consolidated Financial Statements*

CHAPTER 3

CONSOLIDATION OF A WHOLLY OWNED SUBSIDIARY

LEARNING OBJECTIVES

After studying this chapter, you should be able to:

- know the basic consolidation principles for a parent with a wholly owned subsidiary;

- understand what the consolidation worksheet is and how it is used to prepare consolidated financial statements;

- explain what pro forma consolidation journals are and why they are processed;

- understand what the analysis of equity is and how it is used in preparing consolidated financial statements for a parent and its wholly owned subsidiary;

- identify and process the consolidation adjustments required at acquisition date to eliminate the investment in the subsidiary as well as the equity of the subsidiary and to recognise any goodwill or bargain purchase gain;

- prepare a consolidated statement of financial position for a parent and its wholly owned subsidiary at acquisition date;

- identify and process the consolidating pro forma journal entries to eliminate the effects of intragroup dividends;

- prepare consolidated financial statements for a parent and its wholly owned subsidiary for reporting periods after acquisition date;

- prepare consolidated financial statements for a parent and its wholly owned subsidiary acquired during a reporting period; and

- identify and process the consolidating pro forma journals to reverse fair value adjustments and the tax effects thereof for a parent's investment in a subsidiary in the parent's separate financial statements.

TOPIC LIST

Introduction

As you already know from Volume 1 Chapter 1, when one entity (the parent) obtains **control** over another entity (the subsidiary) the parent must – subject to limited exceptions – prepare **consolidated financial statements**. You will recall that **consolidated financial statements** are the **financial statements of a group** in which the **assets, liabilities, equity, income and expenses** and **cash flows** of the **parent** and its **subsidiaries** are presented as those of a **single economic entity**. A subsidiary must be consolidated from the date that **control is obtained** to the date that **control is lost**. The concept of control and the exceptions to consolidating a subsidiary have already been explained in detail in Volume 1 Chapter 1.

This chapter, as well as Volume 1 Chapters 4 to 8 and Volume 2 Chapter 1 that follow, will explain the way in which information in the financial statements of each of the entities within a group is combined to produce consolidated financial statements.[4]

This chapter focuses on the principles and procedures to consolidate the **wholly owned subsidiary** of a parent, first at date of acquisition, where only a consolidated statement of financial position is prepared, and then in subsequent reporting periods, where a consolidated statement of profit or loss and other comprehensive income and a consolidated statement of changes in equity are also prepared.

To keep things simple, the following aspects of consolidations are not covered in this chapter:
- consolidations of partly owned subsidiaries (i.e., where a non-controlling interest arises) – this is dealt with in Volume 1 Chapter 4;
- the implications of IFRS 3 fair value adjustments to the subsidiary's identifiable net assets at acquisition and the subsequent effects thereof in the consolidated financial statements – this is covered comprehensively in Volume 1 Chapter 5 and Volume 2 Chapter 1;
- aside from intragroup dividends, the treatment of intragroup transactions and balances in the consolidated financial statements, which are dealt with in Volume 1 Chapter 6;
- preparing consolidated financial statements for complex groups, for example, for a group where the parent has a subsidiary and this subsidiary, in turn, has a subsidiary of its own – this is addressed in Volume 1 Chapter 7;
- preparing consolidated financial statements where the subsidiary acquired has issued preference shares, which is dealt with in Volume 1 Chapter 8; and
- the implications in the consolidated financial statements of applying advanced IFRS 3 business combination concepts, which are covered in Volume 2 Chapter 1.

3.1 The consolidation process

The process of consolidation involves the **combining** of the **financial information** of a **parent** and its **subsidiaries** in a manner that presents these **separate legal entities** as **one economic entity**.

---

4   Note: The consolidated financial statements dealt with in Volume 1 Chapters 3 to 8 and Volume 2 Chapter 1 are (1) the consolidated statement of profit or loss and other comprehensive income, (2) the consolidated statement of changes in equity, and (3) the consolidated statement of financial position. The consolidated statement of cash flows is dealt with in Volume 2 Chapter 7.

To achieve this objective – as discussed in Volume 1 Chapter 1 – IFRS 10 sets out, in broad terms, the following consolidation procedures that should be applied (IFRS 10.B86):

- combine line by line, like items of assets, liabilities, equity, income and expenses of the parent with those of its subsidiaries;
- offset (eliminate) the carrying amount of the parent's investment in each subsidiary and the parent's portion of equity of each subsidiary and recognise, in terms of IFRS 3:
  - any goodwill that may arise; or
  - any gain on bargain purchase price that may arise.
- eliminate, in full, intragroup assets and liabilities, equity, income, expenses and cash flows relating to transactions between entities of the group.

Based on the list above, the consolidation process:

- begins by **combining** the assets, liability, equity, income and expense line items as per the **separate financial statements** of the **parent** with asset, liability, equity, income and expense line items as per the individual financial statements of its **subsidiary(ies),**
- then processing certain **adjustments and eliminations** as required to **eliminate common and intragroup items,**
- which then results in **consolidated financial statements** being produced as the **end product.**

It is important to note that a separate set of consolidated records is *not* maintained. That is to say, the separate general ledgers (from which the trial balances are extracted and the financial statements are produced) of the parent company and its subsidiaries remain **unaffected** by the consolidation process and procedures.

The implication of this is that the **consolidation procedures** must be **repeated for every reporting period** that **consolidated financial statements are produced.**

3.1.1 Consolidation methods

3.1.1.1 *The consolidation worksheet and pro forma journal entries*

There are several methods for performing a consolidation. One such method is the use of a consolidation worksheet. The consolidation worksheet (normally an Excel spreadsheet) first **aggregates (combines)** the **individual trial balances** of the **parent** and its **subsidiary(ies)** to produce a **pre-adjustment trial balance.** Thereafter, **eliminations** and **appropriate adjustments** (as required by IFRS 10, as discussed above) are made to the **pre-adjustment trial balance** by processing adjusting consolidation journal entries, known as **pro forma journals,** in the worksheet. The **end result** is now a new **single post-adjustment trial balance** reflecting **consolidated figures,** which make up the amounts to be **included in the consolidated financial statements** of the group.

It is important to note the following regarding pro forma journal entries:

- Unlike the journal entries you are familiar with, pro forma journals may affect the trial balance of **two separate entities** at the **same time** (e.g., a ledger account of the parent may be debited with a corresponding credit to the ledger account of the subsidiary).

- Unlike the journal entries you would have processed so far in your studies, pro forma journals are *not* processed in the individual general ledgers of either the parent or the subsidiary. Therefore the **individual trial balances** and the **financial statements** of the **parent** and **subsidiary remain unaffected.**

- Pro forma journals are required **solely for purposes of consolidation each reporting period** and, as discussed in the previous point, they are processed **outside of** the **general ledgers** of **both parent and subsidiary.** This means that pro forma journal entries need to be **repeated each year.** In other words, the trial balances of the parent and subsidiary, extracted each year, from which we prepare the consolidated financial statements *do not* include the pro forma adjustments that were passed when the consolidated financial statements of the prior year were prepared.

3.1.1.2 *The analysis of equity method*

This is an alternative, often shorter, method of setting out the workings required in arriving at certain of the amounts to be included in the consolidated financial statements. More particularly, this method involves **analysing the equity of the subsidiary** at **specific points** in time in a worksheet format as follows:

- at **acquisition date,** when:
  - the fair net asset value of the subsidiary is calculated;
  - any goodwill or gain on bargain purchase is determined; and
  - any non-controlling interest in the subsidiary's equity is established.
- at the **beginning of the current year,** when:
  - the movement in reserves (e.g., retained earnings) of the subsidiary since acquisition date to the beginning of the current year (after adjusting for any intragroup transactions and the subsequent effects of any at acquisition fair value adjustments to the subsidiary's net assets) is determined;
  - the amount of these reserves attributable to any non-controlling interest is established; and
  - the amount of these reserves attributable to the parent is calculated.
- at the **end of the current year,** when:
  - current year profit or loss and other comprehensive income of the subsidiary (after adjusting for any intragroup transactions and the subsequent effects of any at acquisition fair value adjustments to the subsidiary's net assets) is calculated;
  - the amounts thereof attributable to the non-controlling interest are established; and
  - the amounts thereof attributable to the parent are determined.

The manner in which to use the analysis of equity in preparing consolidated financial statements for a parent and its wholly owned subsidiary, at acquisition date and for subsequent reporting periods, is explained in this chapter, while in Volume 1 Chapters 4 to 8 and Volume 2 Chapter 1 the use of the analysis of equity is illustrated:

- when preparing consolidated financial statements for a parent and its partly owned subsidiary;

- when preparing consolidated financial statements that include consolidation adjustments for at acquisition remeasurements to fair value, in terms of IFRS 3, of assets and liabilities of the subsidiary;
- when preparing consolidated financial statements that include consolidation adjustments for intragroup transactions and balances;
- when preparing the consolidated financial statements of a complex group; and
- when consolidating a subsidiary that has issued preference shares.

3.1.2 Application of consolidation methods

In this publication, a comprehensive method is adopted to explain and illustrate the preparation of consolidated financial statements, which is covered in Volume 1 Chapters 3 to 8 and Volume 2 Chapter 1. For this reason, you will notice that in the majority of the worked examples in these chapters, more than one consolidation method is used. More specifically, use is made of:

- the **analysis of equity** of the subsidiary; and
- **pro forma consolidation entries.**

In light of this comprehensive approach, most often, the consolidated financial statements (or extracts thereof) in the worked examples of the above-mentioned chapters are compiled using both pro forma journals and an analysis of equity of the subsidiary. More precisely, most of the worked examples will require you to prepare an analysis of equity followed by pro forma journals and then finally the consolidated financial statements (or extracts thereof). Consequently, in these worked examples, you will notice that most of the workings for the figures included in the consolidated financial statements will refer both to particular pro forma journal entries and to specific amounts obtained from the analysis of equity of the subsidiary concerned. The purpose for using both methods in most of the worked examples is to enable you to develop the ability – for test and exam purposes – to prepare consolidated financial statements using either method, depending on the type of test or exam question.

Test and exam consolidation questions often require that you **first prepare all the pro forma journals** and **thereafter the consolidated financial statements (or extracts thereof).** For such questions, it would make sense to obtain the relevant totals and balances to be presented in the consolidated financial statements (or extracts thereof) by:

- first adding together the individual equity, asset, liability, income and expense line item amounts of the parent and its subsidiary (or subsidiaries), which you would obtain from the parent and subsidiary trial balances or financial statements (usually abridged) given in the question; and
- then adjusting these amounts, as appropriate, for the effects of the pro forma journals that you would have already provided in the first part of the question. Obviously for these types of questions it would not make sense to draw up and use an analysis of equity when compiling the consolidated financial statements.

Note that certain line items (e.g., goodwill or a bargain purchase gain) included in the consolidated financial statements will not have existed in the individual financial statements of the parent or its subsidiary and come about only on consolidation. Such items will then simply be obtained directly from the relevant pro forma journal passed, as opposed to being determined by adjusting the sum of individual line items in the financial statements or trial balances of the parent and its subsidiary (or subsidiaries).

For test and exam questions where pro forma journals are *not* required, it may well be preferable to use the **analysis of equity in conjunction with the parent and subsidiary trial balances or financial statements (usually abridged)**, as provided in the question, to compile the consolidated financial statements or extracts thereof. Alternatively, a **hybrid method** could be applied, which makes use of:

- **pro forma journal workings** for IFRS 3 at acquisition fair value adjustments (to subsidiary assets and liabilities and the knock-on effects of these adjustments in the post- acquisition period), and for the elimination and subsequent recognition of intragroup profits and losses, which then feed into

- **an analysis of equity of the subsidiary** used to calculate the post-acquisition equity of the subsidiary that is attributable to the non-controlling interest and to the parent respectively.

Furthermore, when test and exam questions require you to provide **specific amounts and balances** that would appear in the consolidated financial statements, for example, the closing consolidated retained earnings balance, goodwill, the consolidated profit attributable to the non-controlling interest etc., often the best method is to **calculate these figures directly** *without* the use of pro forma journals or an analysis of equity.

Do not be alarmed if all these methods appear somewhat confusing at this stage. All will become clear as you work through the comprehensive worked examples in this publication, the self-assessment questions at the end of each chapter and the case study questions which are accessible from the JUTA website.

As regards using the consolidation worksheet in tests and exams, it is likely to be far too time consuming to complete. However, a number of the worked examples in this publication include a consolidation worksheet, which serves as a valuable learning tool as it illustrates the full consolidation process from start to finish and clearly shows how the various amounts in the consolidated financial statements have been arrived at after adjusting for the effects of the pro forma journals. This too will become clear as you progress through the chapters.

3.2 Components of consolidated financial statements

Consolidated financial statements comprise the following:

- consolidated statement of financial position;
- consolidated statement of profit or loss and other comprehensive income;
- consolidated statement of changes in equity;
- consolidated statement of cash flows (dealt with in Volume 2 Chapter 7); and
- notes to the consolidated financial statements.

The layout of consolidated financial statements is very much the same as that used in individual financial statements that you would have prepared. The main differences relate to **partly owned subsidiaries**, where there is a **non-controlling interest element**. Volume 1 Chapter 4 illustrates the additional disclosures required on the face of the consolidated statement of financial position, the consolidated statement of changes in equity, as well as on the face of the consolidated statement of profit or loss and other comprehensive income, to reflect the non-controlling interest in the equity, reserves, and total comprehensive income of the group.

3.3 Consolidation of a wholly owned subsidiary at date of acquisition

As you will recall from Volume 1 Chapter 2, the **date of acquisition** in a business combination is – in accordance with IFRS 3 – the date when the acquirer obtains **control** over the acquiree. As discussed in Volume 1 Chapter 2, in a group context (i.e., when a controlling interest in the equity of another entity is acquired) the **acquirer is the parent entity** and the **acquiree is the subsidiary**. Furthermore, as was discussed in Volume 1 Chapter 2, the **consolidation** of a subsidiary **commences** from the **date of its acquisition by the parent**.

At **acquisition date** we are able to prepare **only a consolidated statement of financial position**, since there is no reporting period in respect of which a consolidated statement of profit or loss and other comprehensive income, and a consolidated statement of changes in equity, could be prepared for the subsidiary acquired. This is because any profits earned by the subsidiary **prior to acquisition date** belong to the **former owners** of the subsidiary. As such, they **cannot** be reflected as profits and reserves (e.g., retained earnings) of the group as they represent 'purchased profits' acquired as part of the equity of the subsidiary on acquisition date.

In preparing the at acquisition date consolidated statement of financial position, we:

• eliminate **common items** and recognise any goodwill arising on the acquisition of the subsidiary; and
• combine, **line by line**, the **remaining like items of assets, liabilities and equity** of the **parent** and its **subsidiary(ies)** at acquisition date.

The consolidation adjustments and eliminations required for a wholly owned subsidiary are discussed below.

3.3.1 Assets and liabilities of the subsidiary remeasured to fair value at acquisition date

As you will recall from Volume 1 Chapter 2, IFRS 3 requires that the subsidiary's identifiable net assets at acquisition date be measured at fair value. In circumstances where the fair value of assets and liabilities of the subsidiary at acquisition date differ from their carrying amounts, adjustments need to be processed, via pro forma journals, on consolidation:

• to adjust the carrying amounts of these assets and liabilities to fair value at acquisition date;
• to record, at acquisition date, the deferred tax effects of such fair value adjustments; and
• to ensure that the income and expenses of the subsidiary, recognised in the consolidated financial statements, are based on the fair values of these assets and liabilities at acquisition date. For example, depreciation expense recognised in the consolidated statement of comprehensive income after acquisition date must be based on the IFRS 3 fair values of the related depreciable assets recognised at acquisition.

99

The accounting treatment in the consolidated financial statements of these IFRS 3 fair value adjustments – both at and subsequent to acquisition date – is covered in detail in Volume 1 Chapter 5 and Volume 2 Chapter 1.

3.3.2 Elimination of common items

When the respective statements of financial position of a parent and its subsidiary (or subsidiaries) are combined to create a single consolidated statement of financial position that reflects a single reporting entity (i.e., the group), there are two **common items** that need to be eliminated:

- the line item '**investment in subsidiary**', an **asset** on the statement of financial position of the **parent**; and
- the portion of the **equity of the subsidiary acquired by the parent** (in this chapter 100% of subsidiary equity is acquired as a wholly owned subsidiary is acquired) reflected on the statement of financial position of the **subsidiary**.

The reason why we eliminate the parent's investment in its subsidiary on consolidation is because the consolidated financial statements show the group (parent and subsidiary) as one economic entity. Were we not to eliminate the parent's investment in its subsidiary, then from a group perspective we would be reflecting an **investment** made by the group in its **own equity**, which clearly is incorrect and non-sensical.

In addition, on consolidation we eliminate the equity of the subsidiary acquired by the parent, as the consolidated financial statements represent **one single economic entity**. It therefore would not make sense to reflect the equity of **two entities**. Accordingly, only the **parent's equity** should be presented. Put differently, we need to ask ourselves which equity we would need to acquire to buy into the group; clearly this would be the equity **only of the parent**.

 Example 3.1: Wholly owned subsidiary acquired at fair value of identifiable net assets

The purpose of this example is to illustrate the consolidation process for a wholly owned subsidiary at acquisition date. Neither goodwill nor a bargain purchase arises on acquisition. The elimination of the common items at acquisition date is shown.

P Ltd acquired all the shares in and control over S Ltd on 1 January 20x8. This is the beginning of the financial year for both P Ltd and S Ltd.

The condensed statements of financial position of P Ltd and S Ltd on 1 January 20x8 are as follows:

	P Ltd CU	S Ltd CU
Debits		
Property, plant and equipment	320 000	260 000
Investment in S Ltd	300 000	–
Trade receivables	150 000	120 000
	770 000	**380 000**

	P Ltd CU	S Ltd CU
Credits		
Share capital	320 000	140 000
Retained earnings	400 000	160 000
Trade and other payables	50 000	80 000
	770 000	**380 000**

Additional information

- P Ltd considered all the identifiable assets and liabilities of S Ltd to be fairly valued at acquisition date.
- P Ltd recognised the investment in S Ltd in its separate financial statements at cost price.

Required

(a) Prepare the analysis of equity of S Ltd at acquisition date.

(b) Prepare the at acquisition pro forma journal to eliminate the subsidiary's equity and the parent's investment in the subsidiary.

(c) Prepare the consolidated statement of financial position for the P Ltd group as at 1 January 20x8.

 Solution 3.1: Wholly owned subsidiary acquired at fair value of identifiable net assets

Part (a): Analysis of equity of S Ltd at acquisition

	Total equity CU	P Ltd (100%) CU
At acquisition date (1 January 20x8)		
Share capital	140 000	140 000
Retained earnings	160 000	160 000
Fair value of net assets of S Ltd	300 000	300 000
Goodwill	–	–
Investment in S Ltd (Consideration paid)	300 000	(300 000)

Comments: Analysis of equity

- The amount of consideration transferred by P Ltd to acquire its subsidiary S Ltd (which equals the cost of the investment in S Ltd) is the same value as the identifiable net assets of S Ltd at acquisition. Therefore no goodwill or gain on bargain purchase arises in this example.

Proof of calculation of purchase difference of S Ltd in terms of IFRS 3.32

Consideration transferred	300 000
Add: Non-controlling interest	–
Subtotal	300 000
Minus: Identifiable net assets	(300 000)
Goodwill/(Bargain purchase gain)	0

Part (b): Pro forma journal entry at acquisition date

Pro forma journal 1 (J1)	Dr CU	Cr CU
1 January 20x8		
Share capital (S Ltd) (SCIE) (given)	140 000[1]	
Retained earnings (S Ltd) (SCIE) (given)	160 000[2]	
Investment in S Ltd (P Ltd) (SFP) (given)		300 000[3]
Elimination of equity of S Ltd against investment in S Ltd		

Note: The numbers 1 to 3 next to each of the amounts in the pro forma journal above cross-references each of these amounts to the consolidation worksheet below. This system of cross-referencing the pro forma journal amounts to the corresponding consolidation worksheet applies throughout this chapter.

Comments: Pro forma journal 1

- Note how the subsidiary's (i.e., S Ltd's) share capital is eliminated (debited). This is because this share capital forms part of S Ltd's at acquisition equity which was purchased by the parent, P Ltd. The result is that it is only the parent's (i.e., P Ltd's) share capital that is recognised in the consolidated financial statements.

- Note how S Ltd's retained earnings balance at acquisition is eliminated (debited). This is because this reserve was accumulated by S Ltd before acquisition date and was therefore not earned by the group (i.e., it represents prior year earnings of S Ltd, purchased by P Ltd, which forms part of S Ltd's at acquisition equity) and therefore cannot be included in the group's retained earnings.

- As the at acquisition fair value of S Ltd's identifiable net assets (i.e., S Ltd's at acquisition equity) of CU 300 000 equals the cost of P Ltd's investment in S Ltd, as reflected in P Ltd's separate financial statements, both sides of the journal balance. We therefore know that there is no goodwill or bargain purchase gain to be recognised. That is, P Ltd paid fair net asset value when it acquired S Ltd.

The pro forma journal above can be illustrated as follows:

S Ltd's total (100%) fair value = CU 300 000			
Identifiable net assets of S Ltd (equity of S Ltd)	CU 300 000	CU 300 000	Investment in S Ltd

The full effects of the pro forma journal above on the consolidated statement of financial position of the P Ltd group are shown in the consolidation worksheet as at 1 January 20x8 below.

	P Ltd Dr/(Cr) CU	S Ltd Dr/(Cr) CU	Pro forma journals Dr/(Cr) CU J1	Con- solidated Dr/(Cr) CU
ASSETS				
Property, plant & equipment	320 000	260 000		580 000
Investment in S Ltd	300 000		(300 000)[3]	–
Trade receivables	150 000	120 000		270 000
EQUITY AND LIABILITIES				
Share capital	(320 000)	(140 000)	140 000[1]	(320 000)
Retained earnings	(400 000)	(160 000)	160 000[2]	(400 000)
Trade and other payables	(50 000)	(80 000)		(130 000)
	0	0	0	0

Note: Numbers 1 to 3 next to each of the amounts in the pro forma journals column of the consolidation worksheet above cross-reference each of these amounts to pro forma journal 1. This system of cross-referencing amounts in the consolidation worksheet to the corresponding pro forma journal(s) applies throughout this chapter.

Comments: Consolidation worksheet
- As illustrated in the consolidation worksheet above, once the common items have been eliminated, the like items as per the separate trial balances of P Ltd and S Ltd are added together line by line to arrive at the end point, being the consolidated figures.

Part (c): Consolidated statement of financial position at acquisition date

P LTD GROUP: CONSOLIDATED STATEMENT OF FINANCIAL POSITION AS AT 1 JANUARY 20x8	
	CU
Assets	
Non-current assets	
Property, plant and equipment (320 000 (P Ltd) + 260 000 (S Ltd))	580 000
Current assets	
Trade receivables (150 000 (P Ltd) + 120 000 (S Ltd))	270 000
Total assets	850 000
Equity and liabilities	
Share capital	320 000
Retained earnings	400 000
Equity attributable to owners of the parent	720 000
Current liabilities	
Trade and other payables (50 000 (P Ltd) + 80 000 (S Ltd))	130 000
Total equity and liabilities	850 000

Comments: Consolidated statement of financial position
- As there is no non-controlling interest, the total equity of the group is held exclusively by the owners of P Ltd the parent.

Example 3.2: Wholly owned subsidiary acquired and goodwill arises

The purpose of this example is to illustrate the consolidation process for a wholly owned subsidiary at the acquisition date where goodwill arises on acquisition.

The facts are exactly the same as in Example 3.1, except that P Ltd paid CU 350 000 for a 100% controlling interest in S Ltd.

The condensed statements of financial position of P Ltd and S Ltd on 1 January 20x8 are as follows:

	P Ltd	S Ltd
	CU	CU
Debits		
Property, plant and equipment	320 000	260 000
Investment in S Ltd	350 000	–
Trade receivables	150 000	120 000
	820 000	**380 000**
Credits		
Share capital	320 000	140 000
Retained earnings	400 000	160 000
Trade and other payables	100 000	80 000
	820 000	**380 000**

Required

(a) Prepare the analysis of equity of S Ltd at acquisition date.

(b) Prepare the at acquisition pro forma journal to eliminate the subsidiary's equity and the parent's investment in the subsidiary.

(c) Prepare the consolidated statement of financial position for the P Ltd group as at 1 January 20x8.

 Solution 3.2: Wholly owned subsidiary acquired and goodwill arises

Part (a): Analysis of equity (AOE) of S Ltd at acquisition

	Total equity	P Ltd (100%)
	CU	CU
At acquisition date (1 Jan 20x8)		
Share capital	140 000	140 000
Retained earnings	160 000	160 000
Fair value of net assets of S Ltd	300 000	300 000
Goodwill	50 000	50 000 **a**
Investment in S Ltd (Consideration paid)	350 000	50 000

Note: Throughout this publication, the letters adjacent to the amounts in the analysis of equity (in this example, the letter 'a' next to the goodwill figure) cross-reference these amounts to the consolidated financial statements which follow.

Explanatory notes: Analysis of equity

- Goodwill arises in this example as P Ltd paid an amount in excess of the fair value of the subsidiary's identifiable net assets at acquisition date.

Proof of calculation of purchase difference of S Ltd in terms of IFRS 3.32

Consideration transferred	350 000
Add: Non-controlling interest	–
Subtotal	350 000
Minus: Identifiable net assets	(300 000)
Goodwill/(Bargain purchase gain)	**50 000**

Part (b): Pro forma journal entry at acquisition date

Pro forma journal 1 (J1)	Dr CU	Cr CU
1 January 20x8		
Share capital (S Ltd) (SCIE) (given)	140 000[1]	
Retained earnings (S Ltd) (SCIE) (given)	160 000[2]	
Goodwill (SFP) (balancing figure)	50 000[3]	
Investment in S Ltd (P Ltd) (SFP) (given)		350 000[4]
Elimination of equity of S Ltd against investment in S Ltd and recognition of goodwill		

Comments: Pro forma journal 1

- The fair value of the identifiable net assets of S Ltd (i.e., the equity of S Ltd) at acquisition date amounts to CU 300 000. Because the consideration paid by P Ltd for this equity (which is the same as the cost of P Ltd's investment in S Ltd, as reflected in P Ltd's separate financial statements) was CU 350 000, the excess amount paid of CU 50 000 represents goodwill.

- Because the two common items (i.e., the investment in S Ltd and the equity of S Ltd at acquisition date) that we are eliminating against each other on consolidation have different values, for the pro forma journal entry to balance we require an additional entry. As the credit side (elimination of the cost of investment) exceeds the debit side (elimination of the equity of S Ltd at acquisition), an additional debit entry recognising goodwill is made. It therefore follows that goodwill can be calculated as the balancing figure in the pro forma journal per above.

The pro forma journal above can be illustrated as follows:

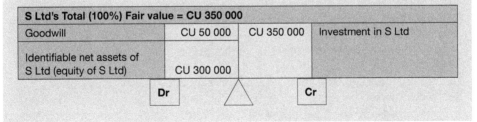

The full effects of the pro forma journal above on the consolidated statement of financial position of the P Ltd group are shown in the consolidation worksheet as at 1 January 20x8 below.

	P Ltd Dr/(Cr) CU	S Ltd Dr/(Cr) CU	Pro forma journals Dr/(Cr) CU	Consolidated Dr/(Cr) CU
ASSETS			J1	
Property, plant and equipment	320 000	260 000		580 000
Investment in S Ltd	350 000		(350 000)[4]	–
Trade receivables	150 000	120 000		270 000
Goodwill			50 000[3]	50 000
EQUITY AND LIABILITIES				
Share capital	(320 000)	(140 000)	140 000[1]	(320 000)
Retained earnings	(400 000)	(160 000)	160 000[2]	(400 000)
Trade and other payables	(100 000)	(80 000)		(180 000)
	0	0	0	0

Part (c): Consolidated statement of financial position at acquisition date

P LTD GROUP: CONSOLIDATED STATEMENT OF FINANCIAL POSITION AS AT 1 JANUARY 20x8	
	CU
Assets	
Non-current assets	
Property, plant and equipment (320 000 (P Ltd) + 260 000 (S Ltd))	580 000
Goodwill (see AOE **a OR** (J1))[†]	50 000
Current assets	
Trade receivables (150 000 (P Ltd) + 120 000 (S Ltd))	270 000
Total assets	900 000
Equity and liabilities	
Equity attributable to owners of the parent	
Share capital	320 000
Retained earnings	400 000
Total equity	720 000
Current liabilities	
Trade and other payables (100 000 (P Ltd) + 80 000 (S Ltd))	180 000
Total equity and liabilities	900 000

Explanatory notes

† As discussed in Section 3.1.2, most of the consolidated figures can be obtained either from the analysis of equity (AOE) or from the pro forma journal(s) passed.

Comments: Statement of financial position

- As was discussed in Volume 1 Chapter 2, goodwill is an asset of the subsidiary that represents the future economic benefits arising from assets that are not capable of being individually identified and separately recognised.

- As is illustrated in the above consolidated statement of financial position, the goodwill that arose on acquisition of S Ltd is recognised as a non-current asset at initial cost. Goodwill – as you will also recall from Volume 1 Chapter 2 – is then tested for impairment subsequent to acquisition date and is subsequently measured at cost minus any accumulated impairment losses. The subsequent impairment of goodwill is dealt with in Volume 1 Chapter 4.

 ## Example 3.3: Wholly owned subsidiary acquired and gain on bargain purchase recognised

The purpose of this example is to illustrate the consolidation process for a wholly owned subsidiary at the acquisition date where a gain on bargain purchase arises on acquisition.

The facts are exactly the same as in Example 3.1, except that P Ltd paid CU 270 000 for a 100% controlling interest in S Ltd.

The condensed statements of financial position of P Ltd and S Ltd on 1 January 20x8 are as follows:

	P Ltd	S Ltd
	CU	CU
Debits		
Property, plant and equipment	320 000	260 000
Investment in S Ltd	270 000	–
Trade receivables	150 000	120 000
	740 000	**380 000**
Credits		
Share capital	320 000	140 000
Retained earnings	400 000	160 000
Trade and other payables	20 000	80 000
	740 000	**380 000**

Required

(a) Prepare the analysis of equity of S Ltd at acquisition date.

(b) Prepare the at acquisition pro forma journal to eliminate the subsidiary's equity and the parent's investment in the subsidiary.

(c) Prepare the consolidated statement of financial position for the P Ltd group as at 1 January 20x8.

Solution 3.3: Wholly owned subsidiary acquired and gain on bargain purchase recognised

Part (a): Analysis of equity (AOE) of S Ltd at acquisition

	Total equity	P Ltd (100%)
At acquisition date (1 Jan 20x8)	CU	CU
Share capital	140 000	140 000
Retained earnings	160 000	160 000
Fair value of net assets of S Ltd	300 000	300 000
Gain on bargain purchase	(30 000)[1]	(30 000) a
Investment in S Ltd (Consideration paid)	270 000	270 000

Explanatory notes: Analysis of equity

[1] A CU 30 000 gain on bargain purchases arises in this example because the amount paid by P Ltd for subsidiary S Ltd is CU 30 000 less than the at acquisition fair value of the net assets of S Ltd.

Proof of calculation of purchase difference of S Ltd in terms of IFRS 3.32

Consideration transferred	270 000
Add: Non-controlling interest	–
Subtotal	270 000
Minus: Identifiable net assets	(300 000)
Goodwill/(Bargain purchase gain)	**(30 000)**

Part (b): Pro forma journal entry at acquisition date

Pro forma journal 1 (J1) 1 January 20x8	Dr CU	Cr CU
Share capital (S Ltd) (SCIE) (given)	140 000[1]	
Retained earnings (S Ltd) (SCIE) (given)	160 000[2]	
Gain on bargain purchase (P Ltd) (P/L) (balancing figure)		30 000[3]
Investment in S Ltd (P Ltd) (SFP) (given)		270 000[4]
Elimination of equity of S Ltd against investment in S Ltd and recognition of bargain purchase gain		

Comments: Pro forma journal 1

- As the at acquisition identifiable net assets of S Ltd (i.e., the at acquisition equity of S Ltd) of CU 300 000 was acquired by P Ltd for only CU 270 000, the difference represents a gain on bargain purchase (effectively a discount) of CU 30 000, which per IFRS 3 is recognised at acquisition date as income of the acquirer P Ltd.

- As was the case in Example 3.2, because we are eliminating two common items, each with a different value, against each other, for the pro forma journal entry to balance we require an additional entry. In this case, as the debit side (elimination of the at acquisition equity of S Ltd) exceeds the credit side (elimination of the investment in S Ltd), an additional credit entry recognising a gain on bargain purchase is made. Therefore, like goodwill, the gain on bargain purchase can be calculated as the balancing figure in the pro forma journal.

Pro forma journal 1 can be illustrated as follows:

S Ltd's total (100%) fair value = CU 300 000			
Identifiable net assets of S Ltd (equity of S Ltd)	CU 300 000	CU 30 000	Bargain purchase gain
		CU 270 000	Investment in S Ltd

Dr ⟋⟍ Cr

The full effects of the preceding pro forma journal on the consolidated statement of financial position of the P Ltd group are shown in the following consolidation worksheet as at 1 January 20x8.

	P Ltd Dr/(Cr) CU	S Ltd Dr/(Cr) CU	Pro forma journals Dr/(Cr) CU J1	Con-solidated Dr/(Cr) CU
ASSETS				
Property, plant and equipment	320 000	260 000		580 000
Investment in S Ltd	270 000		(270 000)[4]	–
Trade receivables	150 000	120 000		270 000
EQUITY AND LIABILITIES				
Share capital	(320 000)	(140 000)	140 000[1]	(320 000)
Retained earnings	(400 000)	(160 000)	160 000[2]	(400 000)
Gain on bargain purchase			(30 000)[3]	(30 000)
Trade and other payables	(20 000)	(80 000)		(100 000)
	0	0	0	0

Part (c): Consolidated statement of financial position at acquisition date

P LTD GROUP: CONSOLIDATED STATEMENT OF FINANCIAL POSITION AS AT 1 JANUARY 20x8	
	CU
Assets	
Non-current assets	
Property, plant and equipment (320 000 (P Ltd) + 260 000 (S Ltd))	580 000
Current assets	
Trade receivables (150 000 (P Ltd) + 120 000 (S Ltd))	270 000
Total assets	850 000
Equity and liabilities	
Equity attributable to owners of the parent	
Share capital	320 000
Retained earnings (P Ltd: 400 00 + 30 000 (AOE **a OR** (J1)) Gain on bargain purchase)	430 000
Total equity	750 000
Current liabilities	
Trade and other payables (20 000 (P Ltd) + 80 000 (S Ltd))	100 000
Total equity and liabilities	850 000

> **Comments: Consolidated statement of financial position**
> - As you will recall from Volume 1 Chapter 2, per IFRS 3, the gain that arises when an interest in a subsidiary is acquired for less than the fair value of the acquiree's identifiable net assets (which is known as a bargain purchase) is recognised in profit or loss of the acquirer on acquisition date. In this example, as we are not preparing a consolidated statement of profit or loss and other comprehensive income, the amount of the gain is added to retained earnings at the beginning of the year.

3.4 Consolidation of a wholly owned subsidiary for reporting periods after acquisition date

In the previous section we dealt only with the consolidation procedures to prepare a consolidated statement of financial position for a wholly owned subsidiary at acquisition date. The most important procedures were:

- the **elimination of common items**, that is the **elimination of the cost** of the **investment in the subsidiary against** the **at acquisition equity** of the **subsidiary**;
- the recognition of **goodwill** or **a gain on bargain purchase** in circumstances where the two common items had **different** at acquisition values; and
- the **adding together, line by line, of like items** of **assets, liabilities** and **equity** of the **parent** and **subsidiary** to generate the consolidated figures to be included in the consolidated statement of financial position.

In this section we will deal with the compilation of consolidated financial statements for any financial reporting date occurring after the acquisition of a wholly owned subsidiary. We still perform the same basic consolidation procedures as those followed with consolidations performed at acquisition date, namely:

- eliminate common items; and
- consolidate the remaining items on a line-by-line basis.

3.4.1 Preparation of consolidated financial statements post acquisition date for a parent and its wholly owned subsidiary

There are a number of further aspects to understand when preparing consolidated financial statements for periods after the date of acquisition, which are discussed below.

3.4.1.1 Repetition of pro forma consolidation journals

As was discussed in Section 3.1.1, a consolidation is effectively performed 'from scratch' **every reporting period end** after initial acquisition. The general ledgers and consequently the trial balances and the separate/individual financial statements of the parent and its subsidiary(ies) remain **completely unaffected** by any consolidation procedures that are performed for any given reporting period. To repeat, this is because the consolidation adjustments and eliminations are done by means of **pro forma journal entries** passed each year, which journals are processed **outside** of the general ledgers of the parent and subsidiary. The result is that a number of the pro forma journals passed in the **prior year(s), once again need to be passed** when preparing consolidated financial statements for the **current year.**

For purposes of this chapter the 'repeat pro forma journal' that is passed again each subsequent year is the pro forma journal that **eliminates the cost of the investment in the subsidiary against the at acquisition equity of the subsidiary**. This is because:

- the **subsidiary's trial balance** that we extract each year and from which we prepare its **individual financial statements** remains **unaffected** by the **prior year pro forma journals** passed and will therefore **continue** to reflect its **own equity**; and
- the **parent's trial balance** that we extract each year and from which we prepare its **separate financial statements** remains **unaffected** by the **prior year pro forma journals** and will therefore **continue** to reflect the **cost of its investment in the subsidiary**.

3.4.1.2 Preparation of the consolidated statement of profit or loss and other comprehensive income for a parent and its wholly owned subsidiary

The wholly owned subsidiary's current year profit or loss and other comprehensive income, that arises in the period after acquisition date, is part of the group's current year earnings and accordingly must be included in the consolidated statement of profit or loss and other comprehensive income.

More specifically, the consolidated statement of profit or loss and other comprehensive income for a parent and its wholly owned subsidiary is prepared as follows:

- Combine the **individual items** of **post-acquisition income and expenditure** of the subsidiary **line by line** with **like items of income and expenditure** of the parent. The **net result** of this combination is the *consolidated profit or loss for the year*. Since we are consolidating a wholly owned subsidiary, **all of this** *consolidated profit or loss* is attributed to the **owners (i.e., shareholders) of the parent**.
- Combine the **individual items** of **post-acquisition other comprehensive income** (e.g., property, plant and equipment revaluation gain) of the subsidiary **line by line** with **like items of other comprehensive income** of the parent. The **net result** of this combination is the *consolidated other comprehensive income* for the year. Since we are consolidating a **wholly owned** subsidiary, **the entire** *consolidated other comprehensive income* is attributable to the **owners of the parent**.
- **Add** the **consolidated profit or loss** for the year to the **consolidated other comprehensive income** for the year to obtain the *consolidated total comprehensive income* for the year. Since we are consolidating a **wholly owned** subsidiary, **the entire** *consolidated total comprehensive income* is attributable to the **owners of the parent**.

For purposes of this chapter, the process of eliminating intragroup dividends, which impacts on the preparation of the consolidated statement of profit or loss and other comprehensive income, is dealt with in Section 3.4.1.5.

3.4.1.3 Preparation of the consolidated statement of changes in equity for a parent and its wholly owned subsidiary

The consolidated statement of changes in equity consists of the following:

- **Share capital.** Only the share capital of the **parent** will be reflected in the consolidated statement of changes in equity. This is because, as was explained in Section 3.3.2, the share capital of the subsidiary, which forms part of the subsidiary's at acquisition equity, represents purchased equity, which is eliminated at acquisition date.

- **Consolidated retained earnings: beginning of the year**. This will be made up of the following:
  - the **retained earnings** balance of the **parent** at the **beginning** of the **financial year**

    PLUS/MINUS
  - the parent's 100% share of the increase (or decrease) in the retained earnings balance of the subsidiary from acquisition date to the beginning of the current financial year. It will be recalled that the at acquisition retained earnings of the subsidiary represents purchased equity and is therefore eliminated on consolidation.
- **Consolidated other reserve(s): beginning of the year.** As was the case with retained earnings, this will be made up of the following:
  - the **other reserve(s) balance(s)** of the **parent** at the beginning of the current financial year

    PLUS/MINUS
  - the parent's 100% share of the increase/(decrease) in the other reserve(s) balance(s) of the subsidiary arising in the period after acquisition date to the beginning of the current financial year. Common examples of 'other reserves' are the revaluation surplus and the mark to market reserve. Again, any 'other reserves' of the subsidiary at acquisition date represent purchased reserves, which are eliminated on consolidation.
- **Consolidated profit or loss.** This amount will be **added to (or deducted from if a loss)** the **opening balance** of the **consolidated retained earnings** and is obtained from the profit or loss section of the consolidated statement of profit or loss and other comprehensive income for the relevant reporting period concerned.
- **Consolidated other comprehensive income.** These amounts will be **added to, if positive amounts, or deducted from, if negative amounts,** the relevant **consolidated opening other reserves balances.** For example, a current year consolidated revaluation gain will be added to the opening consolidated revaluation surplus balance. These amounts are obtained from the other comprehensive income section of the consolidated statement of profit or loss and other comprehensive income for the relevant reporting period concerned.
- **Dividends declared/paid.** These amounts will be **deducted** from **consolidated retained earnings** and represent the dividends declared and/or paid **only to the shareholders of the parent.** Dividends declared/paid by the **subsidiary to the parent** are an intragroup transaction that is **eliminated** on consolidation. Intragroup dividends are discussed in Section 3.4.1.5.

3.4.1.4 Preparation of the consolidated statement of financial position for a parent and its wholly owned subsidiary

Each reporting period post acquisition, the consolidated statement of financial position for a parent and its wholly owned subsidiary is prepared as follows:

- Each reporting period end, all the **like items** of **assets, liabilities, equity, income** and **expenses** of the **wholly owned subsidiary** are **added line by line** to those of the **parent.**

- Pro forma journals are passed:
    - at acquisition, to **eliminate the parent's investment in the wholly owned subsidiary** against the **subsidiary's at acquisition equity** and to recognise any **goodwill or bargain purchase gain;** and
    - after acquisition date, to **eliminate intragroup transactions and balances** (e.g., intragroup dividends – discussed in Section 3.4.1.5).
- After the procedures in the bullet points immediately above have been performed, the consolidated statement of financial position each reporting date post acquisition will reflect:
    - aside from the parent's investment in the wholly owned subsidiary (eliminated at acquisition) and any intragroup receivables and payables (e.g., intragroup dividend payable and receivable which are eliminated against each other – discussed in Section 3.4.1.5), **100% of the assets and liabilities** of **both** the **parent** and the **wholly owned subsidiary;**
    - **goodwill, as a non-current asset,** in circumstances where the consideration transferred by the parent exceeds the fair value of the wholly owned subsidiary's at acquisition identifiable net assets; and
    - **equity attributable to the owners of the parent,** comprising:
        - ○ **the parent's equity** at reporting period end (increased by any bargain purchase gain recognised at acquisition in circumstances where the fair value of the wholly owned subsidiary's at acquisition identifiable net assets exceeds the consideration transferred by the parent)
        PLUS
        - ○ **the parent's 100% share** of the **wholly owned subsidiary's post-acquisition equity** (e.g., the parent's 100% share of subsidiary's post-acquisition retained earnings and revaluation surplus).

Note that the **equity** reported on the consolidated statement of financial position each reporting period end, comprises the **closing share capital, retained earnings, other reserve(s) balance(s)** as per the **consolidated statement of changes in equity.**

3.4.1.5 Intragroup dividends paid/payable

As has been discussed, IFRS 10 requires the **elimination** of **all intragroup transactions** and **balances on consolidation.** A very common intragroup transaction dealt with in this chapter is intragroup dividends declared and/or paid by a subsidiary to its parent company. All the other intragroup transactions are dealt with in Volume 1 Chapter 6.

As you will know from your previous studies, a dividend paid/payable representing a distribution of company profits to the shareholders of the company. Accordingly, it is *not* an expense and is therefore included in the statement of changes in equity, as a **deduction from equity** (normally retained earnings), rather than being included in the statement of profit or loss and other comprehensive income of the company declaring and paying the dividend. The dividend **received or receivable** is **income** in the hands of the shareholder, however, and is therefore recorded in the shareholder's **profit or loss.**

Suppose that a wholly owned subsidiary, Sub Co, declared a dividend of CU 100 000 to its parent, Parent Co, on 31 December 20x9, being its year end, and the year end of the group. The journal entries that will be recorded in the separate records of Sub Co and Parent Co on 31 December 20x9 will be as follows:

Records of Sub Co

	Dr CU	Cr CU
31 December 20x9		
Dividend declared (SCIE)	100 000	
Dividend payable (SFP)		100 000
Recognition of dividend declared by Sub Co		

Records of Parent Co

	Dr CU	Cr CU
31 December 20x9		
Dividend receivable (SFP)	100 000	
Dividend income (P/L)		100 000
Dividend declaration from Sub Co recognised as income		

The consolidation pro forma entries to eliminate the dividend transaction and the intra-group balances are then as follows:

Pro forma journal 1 (J1) 31 December 20x9	Dr CU	Cr CU
Dividend income (Parent Co) (P/L)	100 000	
Dividend declared (Sub Co) (SCIE)		100 000
Elimination of intragroup dividend on consolidation		

Comments: Pro forma journal 1

The reasons for eliminating the dividend transaction as shown in pro forma journal 1 are as follows:

- **Elimination of the dividend income.** On consolidation 100% of the 'pre-dividend' profits of the subsidiary are combined line-by-line with those of the parent. We eliminate the dividend income of the parent so that we do not duplicate the profits of the subsidiary that are included in the consolidated statement of profit or loss and other comprehensive income.

- **Elimination of the dividend declared/paid.** Dividends included in the consolidated statement of changes in equity should be only those declared/paid by the **parent company to its shareholders.** This is because the share capital of the subsidiary is eliminated on acquisition, as it is part of the at acquisition equity of the subsidiary which is set off against the cost of investment in the subsidiary, as discussed in Section 3.3.2. It follows that it would not make sense to reflect a dividend declared/paid, that is, a distribution of equity, to owners of the equity (the parent) when the equity that gives rise to the dividend does not exist from a group perspective.

In other words, the share capital from a group perspective (which is reflected in the consolidated statement of changes in equity) is **only that of the parent.** Therefore the dividends declared/paid that should be shown in the consolidated statement of changes in equity should only be in respect of dividends declared/paid to the owners of **that share capital,** which owners are the **shareholders of the parent.**

Pro forma journal 2 (J2) 31 December 20x9	Dr CU	Cr CU
Dividend payable (Sub Co) (SFP)	100 000	
Dividend receivable (Parent Co) (SFP)		100 000
Elimination of intragroup balances on consolidation		

Comments: Pro forma journal 2

In pro forma journal 2, we eliminate the dividend receivable (an asset) balance against the dividends payable (a liability) balance, as these two amounts arise from an internal transaction between two group companies. We cannot show an asset and corresponding liability in the consolidated statement of financial position as from a group perspective the group cannot be its own debtor and creditor. Therefore, elimination of these intragroup balances is required. This ensures that the consolidated financial statements are not misleading and that the financial position of the group is fairly presented.

3.4.1.6 Using the analysis of equity of the subsidiary to prepare consolidated financial statements of a wholly owned subsidiary

As was discussed in Section 3.1.1.2, the analysis of equity is a quick and effective tool to analyse the equity of a subsidiary acquired, from the group's perspective. The use of the analysis of the subsidiary's equity has already been illustrated at acquisition date – see Examples 3.1 to 3.3.

When dealing with the consolidation of a wholly owned subsidiary for a reporting period after acquisition date, the analysis of equity is extended and divided into three parts, as illustrated and explained in Table 3.1.

Table 3.1: *Format of analysis of equity – consolidation of wholly owned subsidiary at and after acquisition date*

	100%	P Ltd 100%	
	Total	At acquisition	Since acquisition
Part 1 – At acquisition Analyse subsidiary's equity at acquisition date (CSFP)	xxx	xxx	
Part 2 – Since acquisition to BOY Analyse all movements in subsidiary's equity between acquisition date and beginning of the current year (CSCIE)	xxx		xxx
Part 3 – Current year Analyse subsidiary's current year profit or loss and other comprehensive income (CSOPL_OCI)	xxx		xxx

Explanation: Part 1 of analysis of equity

At the **date of acquisition** we use the analysis of equity to:

- determine the **fair value** of the **identifiable net assets** of the **subsidiary;**
- establish the **equity of the subsidiary at acquisition** that must be **eliminated;** and
- **quantify** any **goodwill** or **bargain purchase gain** that must be recognised in the consolidated financial statements.

Explanation: Part 2 of analysis of equity

Here we analyse the **movement in the reserves of the subsidiary** between **date of acquisition** and the **beginning of the current year**. More particularly:

- The **movement** in the **retained earnings** of the **subsidiary** is analysed to establish the **parent's share** of the **subsidiary's post-acquisition profit or loss** to the **beginning of the current year** that has been closed off to retained earnings. Such profits or losses (included in retained earnings) represent post-acquisition equity that was not purchased by the parent; rather, it was earned by the group and is therefore not eliminated on consolidation.

- The movement in **other reserves of the subsidiary** (most commonly the revaluation surplus and the mark to market reserve) is analysed to establish the **parent's share** of the **subsidiary's other comprehensive income** that has been closed off to **other reserves** and that arose in the period **since acquisition to the beginning** of the **current financial year**. As with retained earnings, these other reserves represent post-acquisition equity of the subsidiary that is not purchased and that consequently is not eliminated on consolidation.

- When performing a consolidation of a wholly owned subsidiary, we simply add 100% of the **subsidiary's post-acquisition retained earnings** and **other reserves amounts**, obtained from the analysis of equity, to the **parent's opening balances for retained earnings and other reserves respectively**, to determine the **consolidated opening balances** for **retained earnings** and **other reserves** for the relevant reporting period. These opening balances appear in the consolidated statement of changes in equity.

Explanation: Part 3 of analysis of equity

Here we analyse the **profit or loss** as well as **other comprehensive income** of the **subsidiary** that has arisen in the **current financial year**. These amounts are then **added** to the **profit or loss** and to the **other comprehensive income** of the **parent** to obtain the **consolidated profit or loss** and **other comprehensive income** for the relevant reporting period, **all of which** is attributable to the **owners of the parent** (i.e. in the case of a wholly owned subsidiary there is no non-controlling interest to share in the profit and other comprehensive income of the subsidiary) which is **reported** in the **consolidated statement of profit or loss and other comprehensive income**.

 Example 3.4: Consolidation of a wholly owned subsidiary – reporting periods after acquisition date

The purpose of this example is to illustrate the consolidation process for a wholly owned subsidiary for a reporting period in the year of acquisition of the subsidiary as well as for a reporting period in the year after acquisition (i.e., two years after acquisition date), where goodwill arises and there are intragroup dividends paid.

P Ltd, a company with a 31 December year end, obtained control over S Ltd by purchasing 100% of the ordinary share capital of S Ltd on 1 January 20x8 for CU 660 000. At acquisition date the identifiable assets acquired and liabilities assumed were considered by P Ltd to be fairly valued. P Ltd recognises its investment in S Ltd in its separate financial statements using the cost price method. The following are the trial balances of P Ltd and S Ltd at 31 December 20x8 and 31 December 20x9:

Trial balance at 31 December 20x8	P Ltd Dr/(Cr) CU	S Ltd Dr/(Cr) CU
Share capital	(250 000)	(100 000)
Retained earnings (1 Jan 20x8)	(750 000)	(520 000)
Revenue	(460 000)	(508 000)
Cost of sales	290 000	240 000
Other expenses	85 000	18 000
Income tax	60 000	40 000
Trade and other payables	(38 000)	(25 000)
Bank	105 000	150 000
Trade and other receivables	126 000	243 000
Property, plant and equipment	172 000	462 000
Investment in S Ltd	660 000	–

Trial balance at 31 December 20x9	P Ltd Dr/(Cr) CU	S Ltd Dr/(Cr) CU
Share capital	(250 000)	(100 000)
Retained earnings (1 Jan 20x9)	(775 000)	(730 000)
Dividend paid	25 000	45 000
Revenue	(530 000)	(558 800)
Cost of sales	305 000	264 000
Other income	(55 000)	–
Other expenses	91 000	22 000
Income tax expense	64 500	45 000
Trade and other payables	(63 700)	(27 500)
Bank	191 000	160 000
Trade and other receivables	131 500	31 000
Property, plant and equipment	205 700	849 300
Investment in S Ltd	660 000	–

Note: The other income of P Ltd in 20x9 includes the dividend received from S Ltd.

Required

(a) Prepare the analysis of equity of S Ltd as at 31 December 20x8.

(b) Provide all the pro forma journal entries necessary to prepare the consolidated financial statements of the P Ltd group for the financial year ended 31 December 20x8.

(c) Prepare the consolidated financial statements of the P Ltd group for the year ended 31 December 20x8.

(d) Prepare the analysis of equity of S Ltd as at 31 December 20x9.

(e) Provide all the pro forma journal entries necessary to prepare the consolidated financial statements of the P Ltd group for the financial year ended 31 December 20x9.

(f) Prepare the consolidated financial statements of the P Ltd group for the year ended 31 December 20x9.

Solution 3.4: Consolidation of a wholly owned subsidiary – reporting periods after acquisition date

Part (a): Analysis of equity (AOE) of S Ltd at 31 December 20x8

		P Ltd 100%	
	Total equity	At acquisition	Since acquisition
At acquisition date (1 January 20x8)	CU	CU	CU
Share capital	100 000	100 000	
Retained earnings	520 000	520 000	
Fair value of net assets of S Ltd	620 000	620 000	
Goodwill	40 000	40 000a	
Investment in S Ltd (Consideration paid)	660 000	660 000	
Since acquisition			
• To beginning of current year:			
n/a	–		
• Current year:			
Profit for the year	Wkg1 210 000		210 000

Workings: Analyis of equity

Working 1

(508 000 – 240 000 – 18 000 – 40 000)

Explanatory notes: Analysis of equity

• P Ltd paid more than fair value of the net assets of S Ltd at acquisition date, resulting in goodwill being recognised.

• The period since acquisition to the beginning of the current year falls away as consolidated financial statements are being prepared for the **first reporting period** following the acquisition date. Put differently, the post-acquisition equity of S Ltd attributable to P Ltd consists entirely of S Ltd's current year profit. S Ltd's prior years' profits represent retained earnings of CU 520 000, which were purchased by P Ltd as part of the at acquisition equity of S Ltd and are therefore eliminated on consolidation (see pro forma journal 1).

Part (b): Pro forma journal entry

AT ACQUISITION

Pro forma journal 1 (J1) 1 January 20x8	Dr CU	Cr CU
Share capital (S Ltd) (SCIE) (given)	100 000[1]	
Retained earnings (S Ltd) (SCIE) (given)	520 000[2]	
Goodwill (SFP) (balancing figure)	40 000[3]	
Investment in S Ltd (P Ltd) (SFP) (given)		660 000[4]
Elimination of equity of S Ltd against investment in S Ltd and recognition of goodwill		

The full effects of the preceding pro forma journal on the consolidated financial statements of the P Ltd group are shown in the following consolidation worksheet as at 31 December 20x8.

	P Ltd Dr/(Cr) CU	S Ltd Dr/(Cr) CU	Pro forma journals Dr/(Cr) CU J1	Con-solidated Dr/(Cr) CU
Equity				
Share capital	(250 000)	(100 000)	100 000[1]	(250 000)
Retained earnings (BOY)	(750 000)	(520 000)	520 000[2]	(750 000)
Net profit	(25 000)	(210 000)		(235 000)
Retained earnings (EOY)	(775 000)	(730 000)		(985 000)
Total equity	**(1 025 000)**	**(830 000)**		**(1 235 000)**
Liabilities				
Trade and other payables	(38 000)	(25 000)		(63 000)
Total liabilities	**(38 000)**	**(25 000)**		**(63 000)**
Total equity & liabilities	**(1 063 000)**	**(855 000)**		**(1 298 000)**
Assets				
Bank	105 000	150 000		255 000
Trade and other receivables	126 000	243 000		369 000
Property, plant and equipment	172 000	462 000		634 000
Investment in S Ltd	660 000		(660 000)[4]	–
Goodwill			40 000[3]	40 000
Total assets	**1 063 000**	**855 000**		**1 298 000**
Profit or loss				
Revenue	(460 000)	(508 000)		(968 000)
Cost of sales	290 000	240 000		530 000
Other expenses	85 000	18 000		103 000
Taxation	60 000	40 000		100 000
Net profit	**(25 000)**	**(210 000)**		**(235 000)**

Part (c): Consolidated financial statements for the 20x8 financial year

P LTD GROUP: CONSOLIDATED STATEMENT OF PROFIT OR LOSS AND OTHER COMPREHENSIVE INCOME FOR THE YEAR ENDED 31 DECEMBER 20x8	
	CU
Revenue (460 000 (P Ltd) + 508 000 (S Ltd))	968 000
Cost of sales (290 000 (P Ltd) + 240 000 (S Ltd))	(530 000)
Gross profit	438 000
Other expenses (85 000 (P Ltd) + 18 000 (S Ltd))	(103 000)
Income tax expense (60 000 (P Ltd) + 40 000 (S Ltd))	(100 000)
PROFIT FOR THE YEAR	**235 000**
Attributable to:	
Owners of the parent	[†]235 000

Explanatory notes

† As this is a wholly owned subsidiary, all of the consolidated profit is attributable to the owners of the parent (i.e. there is no non-controlling interest to share in this consolidated profit).

P LTD GROUP: CONSOLIDATED STATEMENT OF CHANGES IN EQUITY FOR THE YEAR ENDED 31 DECEMBER 20x8	Share capital CU	Retained earnings CU	Total CU
Opening balance at 1 Jan 20x8	‡250 000	ǂ750 000	1000 000
Total comprehensive income:			
Net profit (from CSOPL–OCI)	–	235 000	235 000
Closing balance at 31 Dec 20x8	250 000	985 000	1 235 000

Explanatory notes

‡ Share capital is only that of the parent.

ǂ Retained earnings beginning of the year is only that of the parent.

P LTD GROUP: CONSOLIDATED STATEMENT OF FINANCIAL POSITION AS AT 31 DECEMBER 20x8	CU
Assets	
Non-current assets	
Property, plant and equipment (172 000 (P Ltd) + 462 000 (S Ltd))	634 000
Goodwill (see AOE **a OR** (J1))	40 000
Current assets	
Bank (105 000 (P Ltd) + 150 000 (S Ltd))	255 000
Trade and other receivables (126 000 (P Ltd) + 243 000 (S Ltd))	369 000
Total assets	1 298 000
Equity and liabilities	
Equity attributable to owners of the parent	
Share capital (from CSCIE)	250 000
Retained earnings (from CSCIE)	985 000
Total equity	ǂ1 235 000
Current liabilities	
Trade and other payables (38 000 (P Ltd) + 25 000 (S Ltd))	63 000
Total equity and liabilities	1 298 000

Explanatory notes

ǂ As we are dealing with a wholly owned subsidiary, the full equity of the group is owned solely by the parent's shareholders (i.e. there is no non-controlling interest).

Part (d): Analysis of equity (AOE) of S Ltd at 31 December 20x9

		P Ltd 100%	
	Total equity	At acquisition	Since acquisition
At acquisition date (1 January 20x8)	CU	CU	CU
Share capital	100 000	100 000	–
Retained earnings	520 000	520 000	
Fair value of net assets of S Ltd	620 000	620 000	
Goodwill	40 000	40 000a	
Investment in S Ltd (Consideration paid)	660 000	660 000	
Since acquisition			
• To beginning of current year:			
Retained earnings	Wkg1 210 000		†210 000b
• Current year:			
Profit for the year	Wkg2 227 800		227 800
	1 097 800		437 800

Workings: Analysis of equity

Working 1

730 000 – 520 000

Working 2

558 800 – 264 000 – 22 000 – 45 000

Explanatory notes

† This amount is S Ltd's prior year profit from Part (a) that was closed off to retained earnings at the end of the prior year. This prior year profit was earned AFTER the acquisition of S Ltd and accordingly forms part of group retained earnings.

Part (d): Pro forma journal entries for the 20x9 financial year

AT ACQUISITION

Pro forma journal 1 (J1)	Dr CU	Cr CU
Share capital (S Ltd) (SCIE) (given)	100 000[1]	
Retained earnings (S Ltd) (SCIE) (given)	520 000[2]	
Goodwill (SFP) (balancing figure)	40 000[3]	
Investment in S Ltd (P Ltd) (SFP) (given)		660 000[4]
Elimination of equity of S Ltd against investment in S Ltd and recognition of goodwill		

Comments: Pro forma journal 1

• As pro forma journals do not affect the separate accounting records of either S Ltd or P Ltd, the elimination of common items (and the recognition of any goodwill or gain on bargain purchase) needs to be processed every reporting period that consolidated financial statements are prepared.

CURRENT YEAR

Pro forma journal 2 (J2)	Dr CU	Cr CU
Other income (P Ltd) (P/L) (balancing figure)	45 000[5]	
Dividend paid (S Ltd) (SCIE) (given)		45 000[6]
Elimination of intragroup dividends		

Comments: Pro forma journal 2

- The debit in this journal eliminates the intragroup dividend received by P Ltd from S Ltd.
- The credit in this journal eliminates the dividend paid by S Ltd so that the consolidated statement of changes in equity reflects only the dividend paid by P Ltd to its shareholders.

The full effects of the preceding pro forma journals on the consolidated financial statements of the P Ltd group are shown in the following consolidation worksheet as at 31 December 20x9.

	Dr/(Cr) CU	Dr/(Cr) CU	Pro forma journals At acquisition Dr/(Cr) CU J1	Pro forma journals Since acquisition Dr/(Cr) CU J2	Con- solidated Dr/(Cr) CU
Equity					
Share capital	(250 000)	(100 000)	100 000[1]		(250 000)
Retained earnings (BOY)	(775 000)	(730 000)	520 000[2]		(985 000)
Net profit	(124 500)	(227 800)			[†](307 300)
Dividend paid	25 000	45 000		(45 000)[6]	25 000
Retained earnings (EOY)	(874 500)	(912 800)			(1 267 300)
Total equity	**(1 124 500)**	**(1 012 800)**			**(1 517 300)**
Liabilities					
Trade and other payables	(63 700)	(27 500)			(91 200)
Total liabilities	**(63 700)**	**(27 500)**			**(91 200)**
Total equity & liabilities	**(1 188 200)**	**(1 040 300)**			**(1 608 500)**
Assets					
Bank	191 000	160 000			351 000
Trade and other receivables	131 500	31 000			162 500
Property, plant and equipment	205 700	849 300			1 055 000
Investment in S Ltd	660 000		(660 000)[4]		–
Goodwill	–		40 000[3]		40 000
Total assets	**1 188 200**	**1 040 300**			**1 608 500**

Explanatory notes

† This amount has been brought forward from the second part of the consolidation worksheet on page 123.

	Dr/(Cr) CU	Dr/(Cr) CU	Pro forma journals At acquisition Dr/(Cr) CU J1	Pro forma journals Since acquisition Dr/(Cr) CU J2	Con- solidated Dr/(Cr) CU
Profit or loss					
Revenue	(530 000)	(558 800)			(1 088 800)
Cost of sales	305 000	264 000			569 000
Other income	(55 000)	–		45 000⁵	(10 000)
Other expenses	91 000	22 000			113 000
Taxation	64 500	45 000			109 500
Net profit	**(124 500)**	**(227 800)**			**‡(307 300)**

Explanatory notes

‡ This amount has been carried forward to the first part of the consolidation worksheet on page 122.

Part (e): Consolidated financial statements for the 20x9 financial year

P LTD GROUP: CONSOLIDATED STATEMENT OF PROFIT OR LOSS AND OTHER COMPREHENSIVE INCOME FOR THE YEAR ENDED 31 DECEMBER 20x9	
	CU
Revenue (530 000 (P Ltd) + 558 800 (S Ltd))	1088 800
Cost of sales (305 000 (P Ltd) + 264 000 (S Ltd))	(569 000)
Gross profit	519 800
Other income (P Ltd: 55 000 – 45 000 (J2) Elimination of intragroup dividend)	10 000
Other expenses (91 000 (P Ltd) + 22 000 (S Ltd))	(113 000)
Income tax expense (64 500 (P Ltd) + 45 000 (S Ltd))	(109 500)
PROFIT FOR THE YEAR	**307 300**
Attributable to:	
Owners of the parent	307 300

P LTD GROUP: CONSOLIDATED STATEMENT OF CHANGES IN EQUITY FOR THE YEAR ENDED 31 DECEMBER 20x9			
	Share capital CU	Retained earnings CU	Total CU
Opening balance at 1 Jan 20x9	250 000	†985 000	1 235 000
Total comprehensive income:			
Net profit (from CSOPL–OCI)		307 300	307 300
Dividend		‡(25 000)	
Closing balance at 31 Dec 20x9	250 000	1 267 300	1 517 300

Made up as follows:

† P Ltd: Opening Balance 775 000 + (S Ltd: 210 000 (see AOE **b**) P Ltd's 100% post-acquisition share of S Ltd retained earnings to BOY)

  OR

  P Ltd: 775 000 Opening balance + (S Ltd: 730 000 Opening balance – 520 000 (J1) Balance at acquisition)

  Note: S Ltd's at acquisition retained earnings of 520 000 was 'purchased' when S Ltd was acquired. Consequently it was not earned by the group and is eliminated on consolidation.

‡ This amount is the dividend paid to P Ltd's shareholders only. The dividend paid from S Ltd to P Ltd is intragroup and is therefore eliminated on consolidation (see (J2)).

P LTD GROUP: CONSOLIDATED STATEMENT OF FINANCIAL POSITION AS AT 31 DECEMBER 20x9	
	CU
Assets	
Non-current assets	
Property, plant and equipment (205 700 (P Ltd) + 849 300 (S Ltd))	1 055 000
Current assets	
Bank (191 000 (P Ltd) + 160 000 (S Ltd))	351 000
Trade and other receivables (131 500 (P Ltd) + 31 000 (S Ltd))	162 500
Goodwill (see AOE **a OR** (J1))	40 000
Total assets	1 608 500
Equity and liabilities	
Equity attributable to owners of the parent	
Share capital (from CSCIE)	250 000
Retained earnings (from CSCIE)	1 267 300
Total equity	1 517 300
Current liabilities	
Trade and other payables (63 700 (P Ltd) + 27 500 (S Ltd))	91 200
Total equity and liabilities	1 608 500

3.4.1.7 Parent acquires a subsidiary during a reporting period

It may happen that there is an interim acquisition of a subsidiary by a parent. In an interim acquisition, a parent acquires a subsidiary at a date that is later than the first day of the subsidiary's and the group's current reporting period (e.g., where a subsidiary is acquired on 1 September and both the subsidiary's and group's reporting period end is 31 December).

As you now know, when preparing consolidated financial statements, we first need to establish the at acquisition equity of the subsidiary acquired. Up until now, in all the examples in this chapter, the subsidiary's at acquisition equity consisted of its at acquisition share capital balance and retained earnings balance.

When an interim acquisition of a subsidiary (whether wholly owned or partly owned) occurs, the subsidiary would have earned a profit or incurred a loss for the period after its previous reporting date until the acquisition date. Because this profit (or loss) was earned (or incurred) before the subsidiary became part of the group, it constitutes pre-acquisition profit or loss that forms part of the subsidiary's at acquisition date equity. This implies the following:

- The at acquisition pro forma elimination journal must remove, from consolidated profit or loss, the subsidiary's current year profit or loss items that have accumulated from the beginning of the current year to date of acquisition.

- The subsidiary's current year profit or loss items that have arisen after acquisition date represent post-acquisition profit or loss of the group, and are therefore *not* eliminated.

Ordinarily, the parent will require the subsidiary to prepare financial statements as at the acquisition date. In such a case, the pre-acquisition profit or loss items can easily be determined and eliminated on consolidation. Should the subsidiary be unable to provide this information at acquisition date, the subsidiary's current year profit or loss would then need to be allocated to the pre-acquisition period and to the post-acquisition period based on the specific nature of each of the income and expense items making up this current year profit or loss.

This implies that each of the subsidiary's income and expense items must be carefully scrutinised to determine the appropriate basis on which each item should be apportioned between the pre- and post-acquisition periods. Certain items, such as depreciation and amortisation, tend to accumulate evenly over the reporting period. Other items, such as gains or losses on the disposal of property, plant and equipment, would ordinarily arise on a specific date, while other income and expense items may accrue during the reporting period at different rates. For example:

- Sales, cost of sales and gross profit may accrue unevenly over the reporting period because of seasonal trading.
- Salaries and wages may change over the reporting period because of appointments, retrenchments, resignations and bonus payments.
- Interest charges may fluctuate because of new loans raised, existing loans being repaid and/or floating interest rate loans.
- The subsidiary's current year income tax charge should be apportioned in the ratio of its taxable income for the periods before and since acquisition date.

Furthermore, items recognised in the subsidiary's other comprehensive income are allocated to the period before and after acquisition as follows:

- Fair value gains or losses recognised on financial assets at fair value through other comprehensive income are allocated to the period when the financial asset was adjusted to fair value. Ordinarily, this would be the acquisition date or at reporting period end.
- Revaluation gains recognised on property, plant and equipment and intangible assets are allocated to the period in which the revaluation was performed. Typically, this would be at acquisition date or at reporting period end.

The subsidiary's profit or loss for any reporting period, will, if impracticable to apportion based on the nature of the income and expense items making up this profit or loss, be treated as if it accrued evenly over the full reporting period, and be apportioned accordingly (i.e., allocated to the pre-acquisition and post-acquisition period pro rata based on months per annum).

Example 3.5: Consolidation of a wholly owned subsidiary acquired during a reporting period

The purpose of this example is to illustrate the consolidation process for a wholly owned subsidiary acquired during a reporting period and will show how profits of the subsidiary pre acquisition and post acquisition date are dealt with in the consolidated financial statements. The reporting period covers the financial year in which the subsidiary was acquired. In addition, goodwill arises on acquisition.

P Ltd, an entity with a 31 December financial year end, purchased 100% of the ordinary shares of S Ltd on 1 September 20x9 for CU 792 000. At that date all of S Ltd's assets and liabilities were considered to be fairly valued. P Ltd recognises its investment in S Ltd in its separate financial statements using the cost price method.

The trial balance for subsidiary S Ltd at 30 September 20x9, as well as the trial balances for P Ltd and S Ltd at 31 December 20x9 (financial year end) were as follows:

Trial balance at 1 September 20x9	S Ltd Dr/(Cr) CU
Share capital	(100 000)
Retained earnings (1 Jan 20x9)	(470 000)
Revenue	(335 280)
Cost of sales	158 400
Interest income	(33 000)
Other expenses	19 200
Income tax expense	33 600
Trade and other payables	(30 000)
Loan receivable	165 000
Trade and other receivables	152 780
Property, plant and equipment	439 300

Trial balance at 31 December 20x9	P Ltd Dr/(Cr) CU	S Ltd Dr/(Cr) CU
Share capital	(400 000)	(100 000)
Retained earnings (1 Jan 20x9)	(895 000)	(470 000)
Revenue	(1 200 000)	(558 800)
Cost of sales	612 000	264 000
Interest income	(240 000)	(55 000)
Other expenses	118 300	32 000
Income tax expense	83 850	56 000
Trade and other payables	(56 810)	(27 500)
Loan receivable	385 900	165 000
Trade and other receivables	508 950	165 000
Property, plant and equipment	290 810	529 300
Investment in S Ltd	792 000	–

Required

(a) Prepare the analysis of equity of S Ltd for the reporting period ended 31 December 20x9.

(b) Provide the pro forma journal entry required to prepare the consolidated financial statements of the P Ltd group for the year ended 31 December 20x9.

(c) Prepare the consolidated financial statements of the P Ltd group for the year ended 31 December 20x9.

 Solution 3.5 Consolidation of a wholly owned subsidiary acquired during a reporting period

Part (a): Analysis of equity (AOE) of S Ltd as at 31 December 20x9

	Total of S Ltd's equity 100%	P Ltd 100%	
		At acquisition	Since acquisition
At acquisition date (1 September 20x9)	CU	CU	CU
Share capital	100 000	100 000	
Retained earnings	470 000	470 000	
Pre- acquisition profit	Wkg1 157 080	157 080	
Fair value of net assets of S Ltd	727 080	727 080	
Goodwill – Parent (balancing figure)	64 920	64 920 a	
Consideration transferred	792 000	792 000	
Since acquisition			
• Current year:			
Profit for the year	Wkg2 104 720		104 720 b
	896 720		**104 720**

Workings: Analysis of equity

Working 1
Pre-acquisition profit

Revenue	335 280
Cost of sales	(158 400)
Interest income	33 000
Other expenses	(19 200)
Income tax expense	(33 600)
Profit: 1 Jan to 1 Sep 20x9	†157 080

Working 2
Post-acquisition profit

Revenue	558 800
Cost of sales	(264 000)
Interest income	55 000
Other expenses	(32 000)
Income tax expense	(56 000)
Profit for full year	261 800
Less: Pre- acquisition profit (Working 1)	(157 080)
Profit: 1 Sep to 31 Dec 20x9	‡104 720

Explanatory notes:

† This pre-acquisition profit of S Ltd is purchased profit and is added to the CU 570 000 net asset value (equity) of S Ltd at the beginning of the year to obtain the at acquisition net asset value (equity) of S Ltd of CU 727 080 (157 080 + 570 000).

‡ As this profit was earned after acquisition of S Ltd it represents profit earned by the group and must be included in calculating the consolidated profit for the year.

Part (b): Pro forma journal entry for the 20x9 financial year
AT ACQUISITION

Pro forma journal 1 (J1)	Dr CU	Cr CU
Share capital (S Ltd) (SCIE) (given)	100 000[1]	
Retained earnings (S Ltd) (SCIE) (given)	470 000[2]	
Revenue (S Ltd) (P/L) (given)	335 280[3]	
Cost of sales (S Ltd) (P/L) (given)		158 400[4]
Interest income (S Ltd) (P/L) (given)	33 000[5]	
Other expenses (S Ltd) (P/L) (given)		19 200[6]
Income tax expense (S Ltd) (P/L) (given)		33 600[7]
Investment in S Ltd (P Ltd) (SFP) (given)		792 000[8]
Goodwill (balancing figure)	64 920[9]	
Elimination of at acquisition equity and cost of investment, and recognition of goodwill		

Comments: Pro forma journal 1

- As the acquisition of the subsidiary occurred during a reporting period, we need to determine the pre-acquisition profit or loss of the subsidiary from its last reporting period to acquisition date, that is, for the eight-month period from 1 January to 1 September. A net profit of CU 157 080 (see Part (a)) was earned during this period.

- As this profit was earned by S Ltd before the acquisition date, it was not earned by the group and consequently it cannot be recognised as profit of the group. Rather, it represents purchased profits of S Ltd which increase S Ltd's equity acquired at acquisition by CU 157 080 and which must be eliminated on consolidation together with S Ltd's other at acquisition equity, which is made up of share capital and retained earnings.

- More particularly, the specific income amounts earned and expenses incurred by the subsidiary to date of acquisition are reversed as per this pro forma journal in order to:
  - remove the resulting pre-acquisition profit from the consolidated profit for the year; and
  - to reallocate it to at acquisition equity of the subsidiary.

The full effects of the preceding pro forma journal on the consolidated financial statements of the P Ltd group are shown in the following consolidation worksheet as at 31 December 20x9.

	P Ltd	S Ltd	Pro forma journals	Con-solidated
			At acquisition	
	Dr/(Cr)	Dr/(Cr)	Dr/(Cr)	Dr/(Cr)
	CU	CU	CU	CU
Equity				
Share capital	(400 000)	(100 000)	100 000[1]	(400 000)
Retained earnings (BOY)	(895 000)	(470 000)	470 000[2]	(895 000)
Net profit	(625 850)	(261 800)		(730 570)
Retained earnings (EOY)	(1 520 850)	(731 800)		(1 625 570)
Total equity	(1 920 850)	(831 800)		(2 025 570)
Liabilities				
Trade and other payables	(56 810)	(27 500)		(84 310)
Total liabilities	(56 810)	(27 500)		(84 310)
Total equity & liabilities	(1 977 660)	(859 300)		(2 109 880)
Assets				
Loan receivable	385 900	165 000		550 900
Trade and other receivables	508 950	165 000		673 950
Property, plant and equipment	290 810	529 300		820 110
Investment in S Ltd	792 000	–	(792 000)[8]	–
Goodwill			64 920[9]	64 920
Total assets	1 977 660	859 300		2 109 880
Profit or loss				
Revenue	(1 200 000)	(558 800)	335 280[3]	(1 423 520)
Cost of sales	612 000	264 000	(158 400)[4]	717 600
Interest income	(240 000)	(55 000)	33 000[5]	(262 000)
Other expenses	118 300	32 000	(19 200)[6]	131 100
Income tax expense	83 850	56 000	(33 600)[7]	106 250
Net profit	(625 850)	(261 800)		(730 570)

Part (c): Consolidated financial statements for the 20x9 financial year

P LTD GROUP: CONSOLIDATED STATEMENT OF PROFIT OR LOSS AND OTHER COMPREHENSIVE INCOME FOR THE YEAR ENDED 31 DECEMBER 20x9	
	CU
Revenue (1 200 000 (P Ltd) + (S Ltd: 558 800 – 335 280 Pre acquisition (J1)))	1 423 520
Cost of sales (612 000 (P Ltd) + (S Ltd: 264 000 – 158 400 Pre acquisition (J1)))	(717 600)
Gross profit	705 920
Other income (240 000 (P Ltd) + (S Ltd: 55 000 – 33 000 Pre acquisition (J1)))	262 000
Other expenses (118 300 (P Ltd) + (S Ltd: 32 000 – 19 200 Pre acquisition (J1)))	(131 100)
Income tax expense (83 850 (P Ltd) + (S Ltd: 56 000 – 33 600 Pre acquisition (J1)))	(106 250)
NET PROFIT FOR THE YEAR	†**730 570**
Attributable to	
Owners of the parent	730 570

Explanatory notes:

† This amount is the net profit of P Ltd for the full year of CU 625 850 added to the post-acquisition profit of S Ltd of CU 104 720 (see AOE **b**) for the four-month period from 1 September to 31 December 20x9.

P LTD GROUP: CONSOLIDATED STATEMENT OF CHANGES IN EQUITY FOR THE YEAR ENDED 31 DECEMBER 20x9			
	Share capital	Retained earnings	Total
	CU	CU	CU
Opening balance at 1 Jan 20x9	400 000	895 000	1 295 000
Total comprehensive income:			
Net profit (from CSOPL–OCI)	–	730 570	730 570
Closing balance at 31 Dec 20x9	400 000	1 625 570	2 025 570

P LTD GROUP: CONSOLIDATED STATEMENT OF FINANCIAL POSITION AS AT 31 DECEMBER 20x9	
	CU
Assets	
Non-current assets	
Loan receivable (385 900 (P Ltd) + 165 000 (S Ltd))	550 900
Property, plant and equipment (290 810 (P Ltd) + 529 300 (S Ltd))	820 110
Goodwill (see AOE **a OR** (J1))	64 920
Current assets	
Trade and other receivables (508 950 (P Ltd) + 165 000 (S Ltd))	673 950
Total assets	2 109 880

P LTD GROUP: CONSOLIDATED STATEMENT OF FINANCIAL POSITION AS AT 31 DECEMBER 20x9 (continued)	
	CU
Equity and liabilities	
Share capital (from CSCIE)	400 000
Retained earnings (from CSCIE)	1 625 570
Total equity attributable to owners of parent	2 025 570
Current liabilities	
Trade and other payables (56 810 (P Ltd) + 27 500 (S Ltd))	84 310
Total equity and liabilities	2 109 880

3.5 Consolidation adjustments: Investment in subsidiary carried at fair value in the separate financial statements of the parent

As was explained in Volume 1 Chapters 1 and 2, when a parent initially acquires an interest in a subsidiary, the consideration transferred must, subject to limited exceptions, be measured at acquisition date fair value. This **consideration transferred** is then the **initial cost of the investment in the subsidiary** when it is initially recognised in the parent's separate financial statements. It is **this cost of investment** that is then eliminated on consolidation against the at acquisition equity of the subsidiary acquired, as discussed above.

In Volume 1 Chapter 1 it was also explained that under IAS27 *Separate Financial Statements*, the parent has a choice of various methods for subsequently measuring its investment in a subsidiary in its separate financial statements. Among other methods, the parent may elect, in accordance with IFRS 9 Financial Instruments, to **remeasure** its investment in a subsidiary to its **fair value** at each subsequent reporting date, with the changes in fair value being recognised either:

- in **profit or loss**; or
- in **other comprehensive income.**

Where the parent, in its separate financial statements, elects to remeasure its investment in its subsidiary at fair value, **pro forma journals** must be processed **on consolidation:**

- to **reverse** the fair value adjustments made to the **investment in the subsidiary** in the **statement of financial position of the parent;**
- to **reverse** the **deferred tax effects** of these fair value adjustments in the statement of **financial position** of the parent;
- for current year fair value adjustments, to reverse the after tax effect of the fair value gains or losses recognised:
  - in the parent's **profit or loss** if the investment in the subsidiary is measured subsequently at **fair value through profit or loss**; or

- in the parent's **other comprehensive income** if the investment in the subsidiary is measured subsequently at **fair value through other comprehensive income;**
- to reverse, for fair value adjustments made by the parent to the investment in the subsidiary in **prior years,** the **after tax effect** of these **adjustments** against:
  - the parent's **retained earnings** if the investment in the subsidiary is measured subsequently **at fair value through profit or loss;** or
  - the parent's **mark to market reserve** if the investment in the subsidiary is measured subsequently **at fair value through other comprehensive income.**

After the above-mentioned pro forma journals have been processed, the investment in subsidiary will be restored to its **initial at acquisition cost.** We can then process, for consolidation purposes, the routine at acquisition elimination of the cost of the investment in the subsidiary against the subsidiary's at acquisition equity. In addition, the effects of these fair value adjustments (including tax effects) on the parent's **profit or loss, other comprehensive income, retained earnings,** or the **mark to market reserve,** as the case may be, will have been **reversed on consolidation.** These concepts are best illustrated in the following example.

Example 3.6: Consolidation of wholly owned subsidiary: Parent accounts for investment in subsidiary at fair value through other comprehensive income

On 1 January 20x5 P Ltd acquired 100% of the ordinary shares of S Ltd, thereby obtaining control of S Ltd for cash of CU 1 200 000.

At that date the equity of S Ltd comprised:
- share capital CU 200 000; and
- retained earnings CU 1 000 000.

At acquisition date P Ltd considered the carrying amount of the identifiable net assets of S Ltd to be equal to their at acquisition fair values.

P Ltd chose to measure its investment in S Ltd in accordance with IFRS 9, at fair value through other comprehensive income in its separate financial statements.

The income tax rate is 28% and 80% of capital gains tax included in taxable income.

P Ltd is not a sharedealer for income tax purposes.

The abridged trial balances of P Ltd and its subsidiary S Ltd at 31 December 20x5 and 31 December 20x6 are shown below.

Abridged trial balance at 31 December 20x5	P Ltd Dr/(Cr) CU	S Ltd Dr/(Cr) CU
Share capital	(350 000)	(200 000)
Retained earnings (1 Jan 20x5)	(870 000)	(1 000 000)
Trade and other payables	(119 100)	(103 012)
Deferred tax	(134 400)	–

	P Ltd Dr/(Cr)	S Ltd Dr/(Cr)
Abridged trial balance at 31 December 20x5 (continued)	CU	CU
Trade and other receivables	197 600	956 000
Inventory	152 000	489 000
Investment in S Ltd (at fair value)	1 800 000	–
Profit for period before tax	(290 000)	(188 888)
Income tax expense	79 500	46 900
Fair value gain: Shares (OCI)	(600 000)	–
Tax expense: Fair value gain (OCI)	134 400	–

	P Ltd Dr/(Cr)	S Ltd Dr/(Cr)
Abridged trial balance at 31 December 20x6	CU	CU
Share capital	(350 000)	(200 000)
Retained earnings (1 Jan 20x6)	(1 080 500)	(1 141 988)
Mark to market reserve (1 Jan 20x6)	(465 600)	–
Trade and other payables	(43 700)	(171 512)
Deferred tax	(56 000)	–
Trade and other receivables	245 285	1 119 300
Inventory	290 165	537 550
Investment in S Ltd (at fair value)	1 450 000	–
Profit for period before tax	(360 000)	(195 000)
Income tax expense	98 750	51 650
Fair value loss: Shares (OCI)	350 000	–
Tax expense: Fair value loss (OCI)	(78 400)	–

Required

(a) Provide the journal entries, including tax effects, that P Ltd would have processed in its separate financial statements for the 20x5 financial year in respect of the acquisition of the investment in S Ltd and the fair value adjustments thereto.

(b) Provide all the pro forma journal entries necessary to prepare the consolidated financial statements of the P Ltd group for the financial year ended 31 December 20x5.

(c) Provide all the journal entries that P Ltd would have recognised in its separate financial statements for the 20x6 financial year in respect of the fair value adjustment to its investment in S Ltd, including tax effects.

(d) Provide all the pro forma journal entries necessary to prepare the consolidated financial statements of the P Ltd group for the financial year ended 31 December 20x6.

Solution 3.6: Consolidation of a wholly owned subsidiary: Parent accounts for investment in subsidiary at fair value through other comprehensive income

Part (a): Journal entries in separate records of P Ltd for 20x5

Journal 1 (J1)	Dr CU	Cr CU
Investment in S Ltd (SFP) (given)	1 200 000	
Bank (SFP) (given)		1 200 000
Acquisition of investment in subsidiary S Ltd		

Journal 2 (J2)	Dr CU	Cr CU
Investment in S Ltd (SFP)	Wkg1600 000	
Fair value gain (OCI)		Wkg1600 000
Fair value gain recognised in respect of investment in S Ltd		

Workings: Journals in separate records of P Ltd

Working 1

1 800 000 Fair value EOY – 1 200 000 Initial cost

Journal 3 (J3)	Dr CU	Cr CU
Income tax expense (OCI)	Wkg2134 400	
Deferred tax (SFP)		Wkg2134 400
Deferred tax effects of fair value adjustment to investment in S Ltd		

Workings: Journals in separate records of P Ltd

Working 2

600 000 (J1) × 22.4% (80% × 28%) Effective capital gains tax rate

Part (b): Pro forma journal entries for 20x5

Pro forma Journal 1 (J1) Reverses Journal 2 in Part (a)	Dr CU	Cr CU
Fair value gain (P Ltd) (OCI)	600 000	
Investment in S Ltd (P Ltd) (SFP)		600 000
Reversal of fair value adjustment to investment in S Ltd		

Comments: Pro forma journal 1

- We debit the fair value gain of CU 600 000 in respect of the investment in S Ltd, recorded in other comprehensive income in the separate financial statements of P Ltd, in order to eliminate this gain on consolidation. This is because we do *not* recognise any changes to the fair value of the investment in the subsidiary in the consolidated financial statements.

- We credit the investment in S Ltd, recorded in the separate records of P Ltd, with CU 600 000 in order to reduce the investment to its initial at acquisition cost of CU 1 200 000. This cost is then eliminated against the at acquisition equity of S Ltd in a further pro forma journal entry (see pro forma journal 3).

- Note that, had P Ltd measured its investment in S Ltd at **fair value through profit or loss** in its separate **financial statements**, then:
  - we would have debited the fair value gain in **profit or loss** of P Ltd, that is, the **profit or loss** of P Ltd would have been reduced by CU 600 000 instead of reducing the other comprehensive income of P Ltd by this amount; and
  - the entry crediting investment in S Ltd would remain the same.

Pro forma journal 2 (J2) *Reverses Journal 3 in Part (a)*	Dr CU	Cr CU
Deferred tax (P Ltd) (SFP)	134 400	
Income tax expense (P Ltd) (OCI)		134 400
Reversal of deferred tax effects of fair value adjustment to investment in S Ltd		

Comments: Pro forma journal 2

- Because we reverse the fair value gain on consolidation in pro forma journal 1, we also need to reverse the deferred tax effects of this gain in the consolidated financial statements. This is achieved by:
  - debiting and so reversing the deferred tax liability, which was recognised in P Ltd's separate records; and
  - crediting and so reversing the income tax expense in other comprehensive income, recognised by P Ltd in its separate records.
- Note that had P Ltd measured its investment in S Ltd at **fair value through profit or loss in its separate financial statements**, then:
  - the entry debiting deferred tax in the statement of financial position would have remained the same; and
  - we would have credited the income tax expense in **profit or loss** of P Ltd. That is, the **profit or loss** of P Ltd would have been increased by CU 134 400 instead of increasing the other comprehensive income of P Ltd by this amount.

Pro forma journal 3 (J3)	Dr CU	Cr CU
Share capital (S Ltd) (SCIE) (given)	200 000	
Retained earnings (S Ltd) (SCIE) (given)	1 000 000	
Investment in S Ltd (P Ltd) (SFP) (given)		1 200 000
Elimination of common items at acquisition		

The full effects of the three preceding pro forma journals on the 20x5 consolidated financial statements of the P Ltd group are shown in the following consolidation worksheet as at 31 December 20x5.

	P Ltd Dr/(Cr) CU	S Ltd Dr/(Cr) CU	Pro forma journals Dr/(Cr) CU	Jour-nal ref	Con-solidated Dr/(Cr) CU
Equity					
Share capital	(350 000)	(200 000)	200 000	J3	(350 000)
Retained earnings (BOY)	(870 000)	(1 000 000)	1 000 000	J3	(870 000)
Net profit for the period	(210 500)	(141 988)			(352 488)
Retained earnings (EOY)	(1 080 500)	(1 141 988)			(1 222 488)
Mark to market reserve (BOY)	–	–	–		–
Other comprehensive income	(465 600)	–			–
Mark to market reserve (EOY)	(465 600)	–			–
Total equity	**(1 896 100)**	**(1 341 988)**			**(1 572 488)**
Liabilities					
Trade and other payables	(119 100)	(103 012)			(222 112)
Deferred tax	(134 400)	–	134 400	J2	–
Total liabilities	**(253 500)**	**(103 012)**			**(222 112)**
Total equity & liabilities	**(2 149 600)**	**(1 445 000)**			**(1 794 600)**
Assets					
Trade and other receivables	197 600	956 000			1 153 600
Inventory	152 000	489 000			641 000
Investment in S Ltd	1 800 000	–	(600 000)	J1	–
			(1 200 000)	J3	
Total assets	**2 149 600**	**1 445 000**			**1 794 600**
Profit or loss					
Profit before tax	(290 000)	(188 888)			(478 888)
Taxation	79 500	46 900			126 400
Net profit	(210 500)	(141 988)			(352 488)
Other comprehensive income					
Fair value gain shares (OCI)	(600 000)	–	600 000	J1	–
Taxation (OCI)	134 400	–	(134 400)	J2	–
Other comprehensive income	(465 600)	–			–

Part (c): Journal entries in the separate records of P Ltd for 20x6

Journal 1 (J1)	Dr CU	Cr CU
Fair value loss (OCI)	Wkg1350 000	
Investment in S Ltd (P Ltd) (SFP)		Wkg1350 000
Recognition of current year fair value loss on investment in S Ltd		

Workings: Journals in separate records of P Ltd

Working 1

1 450 000 Fair value EOY – 1 800 000 Fair value BOY

Journal 2 (J2)	Dr CU	Cr CU
Deferred tax (SFP)	Wkg2 78 400	
Income tax expense (OCI)		Wkg2 78 400
Recognition of deferred tax effects of current year fair value loss on investment in S Ltd		

Working 2

350 000 (J1) × 22.4% Effective capital gains tax rate

Part (d): Pro forma journal entries for 20x6

Pro forma journal 1 (J1)	Dr CU	Cr CU
Mark to market reserve (P Ltd) (SCIE)	Wkg1 600 000	
Investment in S Ltd (P Ltd) (SFP)		Wkg1 600 000
Reversal of fair value adjustment to investment in S Ltd in pior year		

Workings: Pro forma Journals

Working 1

1 800 000 Fair value BOY – 1 200 000 Initial cost

Pro forma journal 2 (J2)	Dr CU	Cr CU
Deferred tax (P Ltd) (SFP)	Wkg2 134 400	
Mark to market reserve (P Ltd) (SCIE)		Wkg2 134 400
Reversal of prior year deferred tax effects of prior year fair value adjustment to investment in S Ltd		

Working 2

600 000 Prior year fair value gain × 22.4% Effective capital gains tax rate

Comments: Pro forma journals 1 and 2

- In the prior year (i.e., 20x5) P Ltd, in its separate records, recognised the fair value gain and the deferred tax effects thereof in other comprehensive income, which was closed off to P Ltd's market to market reserve at prior year end. Consequently, in the current year (i.e., 20x6) the effects of the prior year fair value adjustment, net of deferred tax, will automatically be included in the opening balance of the mark to market reserve in P Ltd's separate records. For this reason, on consolidation we reverse P Ltd's prior year fair value adjustment and its associated deferred tax effects by adjusting P Ltd's mark to market reserve.

- The effect of pro forma journals 1 and 2 is to:
  - eliminate P Ltd's CU 465 600 (600 000 × 77.6%) mark to market reserve opening balance;
  - reverse the CU 134 400 deferred tax liability recognised by P Ltd in the prior year, attributable to the prior year fair value gain that P Ltd recorded; and
  - reverse the CU 600 000 prior year increase in the value of P Ltd's investment in S Ltd, attributable to the prior year fair value gain that P Ltd recorded.

- Note that had P Ltd measured its investment in S Ltd at **fair value through profit or loss**, then pro forma journals 1 and 2 above would have been the same, except for the fact that on consolidation we would have adjusted (decreased) P Ltd's opening **retained earnings** balance rather than a mark to market reserve, with the after tax effect of the prior year fair value gain. This is because both the prior year fair value gain and its related deferred tax effects would have been recognised in P Ltd's prior year **profit or loss**, which would have been closed off to P Ltd's retained earnings balance at prior year end. Consequently, the after tax effects of the prior year fair value gain, which would need to be reversed on consolidation, would have been included in P Ltd's opening retained earnings balance in the current year.

Note that we can combine pro forma journals 1 and 2 above into the following single pro forma journal:

Combined Pro forma (J1 and J2)	Dr CU	Cr CU
Deferred tax (P Ltd) (SFP)	Wkg1134 400	
Mark to market reserve (P Ltd) (SCIE)	Wkg2465 600	
Investment in S Ltd (P Ltd) (SFP)		Wkg3600 000
Reversal of after tax effects of prior year fair value adjustment to investment in S Ltd		

Workings: Combined Pro forma Journals 1 and 2

Working 1

600 000 Prior year fair value gain × 22.4%

Working 2

600 000 × 77.6% (100% − 22.4%) after tax OR Balancing figure

Working 3

1 800 000 Fair value BOY − 1 200 000 Initial cost

Pro forma journal 3 (J3) *Reversal of J1 of Part (c)*	Dr CU	Cr CU
Investment in S Ltd (P Ltd) (SFP)	350 000	
Fair value loss (P Ltd) (OCI)		350 000
Reversal of current year fair value loss recognised in respect of investment in S Ltd		

Pro forma journal 4 (J4) *Reversal of J2 of Part (c)*	Dr CU	Cr CU
Income tax expense (P Ltd) (OCI)	78 400	
Deferred tax (P Ltd) (SFP)		78 400
Reversal of deferred tax effects of current year fair value loss recognised in resprect of investment in S Ltd		

Pro forma journal 5 (J5)	Dr CU	Cr CU
Share capital (S Ltd) (SCIE) (given)	200 000	
Retained earnings (S Ltd) (SCIE) (given)	1 000 000	
Investment in S Ltd (P Ltd) (SFP) (given)		1 200 000
Elimination of common items at acquisition		

Comments: Pro forma journal 5

- The net effect of pro forma journals 1 and 3 is to reverse the net increase, of CU 250 000 (CU 600 000 Fair value gain in 20x5 − CU 350 000 Fair value loss in 20x6), in the carrying amount of P Ltd's investment in S Ltd in the period since S Ltd's acquisition up until current year end. Having passed pro forma journals 1 and 3, the carrying amount of the investment in S Ltd is reduced to its at acquisition cost of CU 1 200 000, which cost is then eliminated against the at acquisition equity of S Ltd in this pro forma journal 5.

The full effects of the preceding pro forma journals on the 20x6 consolidated financial statements of the P Ltd group are shown in the following consolidation worksheet as at 31 December 20x6.

	P Ltd Dr/(Cr) CU	S Ltd Dr/(Cr) CU	Pro forma journals Dr/(Cr) CU	Jour-nal ref	Con-solidated Dr/(Cr) CU
Equity					
Share capital	(350 000)	(200 000)	200 000	J5	(350 000)
Retained earnings (BOY)	(1 080 500)	(1 141 988)	1 000 000	J5	(1 222 488)
Net profit for the period	(261 250)	(143 350)			(404 600)
Retained earnings (EOY)	(1 341 750)	(1 285 338)			(1 627 088)
Mark to market reserve (BOY)	(465 600)	–	600 000	J1	–
			(134 400)	J2	
Other comprehensive income	271 600	–			–
Mark to market reserve (EOY)	(194 000)	–			–
Total equity	**(1 885 750)**	**(1 485 338)**			**(1 977 088)**
Liabilities					
Trade and other payables	(43 700)	(171 512)			(215 212)
Deferred tax	(56 000)	–	134 400	J2	–
			(78 400)	J4	
Total liabilities	**(99 700)**	**(171 512)**			**(215 212)**
Total equity & liabilities	**(1 985 450)**	**(1 656 850)**			**(2 192 300)**
Assets					
Trade and other receivables	245 285	1 119 300			1 364 585
Inventory	290 165	537 550			827 715
Investment in S Ltd	1 450 000	–	(600 000)	J1	–
			350 000	J3	
			(1 200 000)	J5	
Total assets	**1 985 450**	**1 656 850**			**2 192 300**
Profit or loss					
Profit before tax	(360 000)	(195 000)			(555 000)
Taxation	98 750	51 650			150 400
Net profit	(261 250)	(143 350)			(404 600)
Other comprehensive income					
Fair value loss shares (OCI)	350 000	–	(350 000)	J3	–
Taxation (OCI)	(78 400)	–	78 400	J4	–
Other comprehensive income	271 600	–			–

Summary

This chapter explained the principles and procedures necessary to **consolidate wholly owned subsidiaries,** first at acquisition date, where only a consolidated statement of financial position is prepared, and then in subsequent reporting periods, where a consolidated statement of profit or loss and other comprehensive income and a consolidated statement of changes in equity are also prepared.

In preparing the consolidated financial statements, consolidation adjustments, as required to **eliminate common and intragroup items,** are processed through **pro forma journal entries.** Pro forma journal entries are prepared for consolidation purposes only and are *not* recognised in the separate records of either the parent or the subsidiary. Thus, pro forma journals must be repeated each year when preparing consolidated financial statements.

Consolidation of a wholly owned subsidiary requires that the following procedures be performed:

- Like items of assets, liabilities, equity, income, expenses and cash flows of the parent are added **line by line** with those of its wholly owned subsidiary.
- At acquisition date, **common items** are eliminated by passing a pro forma journal in which:
  - the **'investment in subsidiary',** an asset in the parent's consolidated statement of financial position, is eliminated against the at acquisition equity (i.e., share capital, retained earnings and other reserves) of the wholly owned subsidiary acquired; and
  - **goodwill** is recognised under IFRS 3 in the consolidated statement of financial position as the excess of the cost of the investment in the subsidiary over the value of the wholly owned subsidiary's at acquisition equity; or
  - a **bargain purchase gain** is recognised under IFRS 3 in the parent's profit or loss in the consolidated statement of profit or loss and other comprehensive income as the excess of the wholly owned subsidiary's at acquisition equity over the cost of the investment in the wholly owned subsidiary.
- Where the investment in the wholly owned subsidiary is recognised at **fair value** (through profit or loss or through other comprehensive income) in the **parent's separate financial statements,** pro forma journals are processed to **reverse** the fair value adjustments and associated tax effects recognised in the parent's separate financial statements, both in respect of current and prior years.
- **Intragroup dividends** are **eliminated** by pro forma journals in which:
  - dividend income of the parent is eliminated against the dividend paid/declared by its wholly owned subsidiary; and
  - the dividend receivable of the parent is eliminated against the dividend payable of its wholly owned subsidiary.

The consolidated financial statements for a wholly owned subsidiary comprise:

- a consolidated statement of profit or loss and other comprehensive income consisting of the line by line combination, from acquisition date, of the:

- income and expenses of the parent and its wholly owned subsidiary; and
- other comprehensive income line items of the parent and its subsidiary.

Since the subsidiary is wholly owned there is *no* non-controlling interest. Accordingly, total comprehensive income each reporting period is always **wholly attributable to the owners of the parent.**

- a consolidated statement of changes in equity consisting of:
  - share capital of the parent only;
  - retained earnings made up of:
    - the **parent's opening retained earnings** balance **plus the parent's 100% share** of the subsidiary's **since acquisition retained earnings to the beginning of the current financial year**
    PLUS/MINUS
    - **total consolidated profit/(loss)**
    MINUS
    - **dividends** declared/paid to the **shareholders of the parent.**
  - other reserve(s) made up of:
    - the **parent's opening other reserve(s) balance(s) plus the parent's 100% share** of the subsidiary's **other reserve(s) since acquisition to the beginning of the current financial year**
    PLUS/MINUS
    - total consolidated **other comprehensive income**
- A consolidated statement of financial position, consisting of the **combination, line by line,** at financial year end, of the **assets, liabilities, and equity (net of at acquisition eliminations)** of the **parent** and its **wholly owned subsidiary.** Since there is no non-controlling interest, **100% of the group's equity** reflected on the consolidated statement of financial position is attributable to the **owners of the parent.**

Where a subsidiary whether wholly or partly owned is acquired **during a reporting period:**

- aside from the subsidiary's share capital, retained earnings and other reserves at the beginning of the year, the at acquisition pro forma elimination journal must **also eliminate** the subsidiary's **profit or loss and other comprehensive income** arising from the **beginning of the current year to date of acquisition;** and
- the subsidiary's **profit or loss and other comprehensive income** arising **after acquisition date** represents **post-acquisition** earnings (or losses) of the group and is therefore *not* eliminated.

This chapter has provided you with a firm grasp of the procedures necessary to consolidate a wholly owned subsidiary. You are now well equipped to tackle the consolidation of **partly owned subsidiaries** and to deal with **sundry consolidation aspects,** which are addressed in Volume 1 Chapter 4.

QUESTIONS

Question 3.1

The abridged trial balances of P Ltd and its subsidiary S Ltd at 31 December 20x6 are shown below.

Abridged trial balances at 31 December 20x6	P Ltd Dr/(Cr) CU	S Ltd Dr/(Cr) CU
Share capital	(550 000)	(150 000)
Retained earnings (1 Jan 20x6)	(470 000)	(482 000)
Dividend paid	110 000	76 000
Mark to market reserve (1 Jan 20x6)	(54 320)	–
Revaluation surplus (1 Jan 20x6)	–	(187 154)
Trade and other payables	(43 700)	(43 500)
Deferred tax	(37 900)	(85 066)
Trade and other receivables	391 500	439 300
Property, plant and equipment	277 200	558 298
Investment in S Ltd (at fair value)	740 000	–
Profit before tax	(529 000)	(114 750)
Income tax expense	189 500	30 000
Fair value gain: Investment in S Ltd (OCI)	(30 000)	–
Income tax expense (OCI) – Fair value gain	6 720	–
Revaluation gain: Land (OCI)	–	(53 000)
Income tax expense (OCI) revaluation gain land	–	11 872

Further information

1. On 1 January 20x5, P Ltd acquired a 100% controlling interest in subsidiary, S Ltd, for CU 640 000. At that date the equity of S Ltd comprised:
   - share capital CU 150 000;
   - retained earnings CU 410 000; and
   - revaluation surplus CU 120 000.

2. At acquisition date, P Ltd considered the carrying amount of the identifiable net assets of S Ltd to be equal to their at acquisition fair values. Furthermore, no additional assets, liabilities or contingent liabilities of S Ltd were identified at this date.

3. P Ltd accounted for its investment in S Ltd in its separate financial statements at fair value through other comprehensive income in accordance with IFRS 9.

4. The income tax rate is 28% and an effective capital gains tax rate of 22.4% applies.

5. P Ltd is not a share dealer for income tax purposes.

Required

(a) Calculate the goodwill or gain on bargain purchase arising on the acquisition of S Ltd.

(b) Prepare the pro forma journal entries required to prepare the consolidated financial statements of the P Ltd group for the year ended 31 December 20x6.

(c) Prepare the condensed consolidated statement of profit and loss and other comprehensive income as well as the consolidated statement of changes in equity for the P Ltd group for the year ended 31 December 20x6.

(d) Calculate the deferred tax balance, indicating whether it is an asset or a liability, that will appear in the consolidated statement of financial position the P Ltd group for the year ended 31 December 20x6.

Question 3.2

P Ltd acquired a 100% controlling interest in subsidiary S Ltd on 1 June 20x5 for CU 590 000.

At that date, the trial balance of S Ltd was as follows:

Trial balance at 1 June 20x5	S Ltd Dr/(Cr) CU
Share capital	(150 000)
Retained earnings (1 Jan 20x5)	(275 000)
Mark to market reserve (1 Jan 20x5)	(80 000)
Trade and other payables	(27 372)
Deferred tax	(10 773)
Trade and other receivables	107 465
Financial assets (at fair value through OCI)	490 000
Sales	(300 000)
Cost of sales	165 000
Income tax expense	38 000
Fair value loss: Financial asset (OCI)	55 000
Income tax expense fair value loss (OCI)	(12 320)

The trial balances of P Ltd and S Ltd as at 31 December 20x5, the financial year end of the group, were as follows:

Trial balances at 31 December 20x5	P Ltd Dr/(Cr) CU	S Ltd Dr/(Cr) CU
Share capital	(550 000)	(150 000)
Retained earnings (1 Jan 20x5)	(470 000)	(275 000)
Dividends paid	110 000	–
Mark to market reserve (1 Jan 20x5)	(56 931)	(80 000)
Trade and other payables	(40 335)	(36 272)
Deferred tax	(23 154)	(8 533)
Trade and other receivables	391 500	230 365
Financial assets (at fair value through OCI)	152 200	480 000
Investment in S Ltd (at cost)	590 000	–
Sales	(529 000)	(650 000)
Cost of sales	415 000	358 000
Income tax expense	34 000	81 000
Fair value (gain)/loss financial assets (OCI)	(30 000)	65 000
Income tax expense fair value gain/loss (OCI)	6 720	(14 560)

Further information

1. At acquisition date, P Ltd considered the carrying amount of the identifiable net assets of S Ltd to be equal to their at acquisition fair values. Furthermore, no additional assets, liabilities or contingent liabilities of S Ltd were identified at this date.

2. In accordance with IAS 27.10(a), P Ltd recognised the investment in S Ltd at cost.

3. The income tax rate is 28% and an effective capital gains tax rate of 22.4% applies.

Required

(a) Provide the pro forma journal entry required to prepare the consolidated financial statements for the P Ltd group for the financial year ended 31 December 20x5.

(b) Prepare the consolidated statement of profit and loss and other comprehensive income and the consolidated statement of financial position for the P Ltd group for the year ended 31 December 20x5.

(c) Provide only the at acquisition pro forma journal required in respect of the financial year ended 31 December 20x6.

References

IAS 12 *Income Taxes*

IFRS 3 *Business Combinations*

IFRS 9 *Financial Instruments*

IFRS 10 *Consolidated Financial Statements*

CONSOLIDATION OF A PARTLY OWNED SUBSIDIARY AND SUNDRY CONSOLIDATION ASPECTS

CHAPTER

4

LEARNING OBJECTIVES

After studying this chapter, you should be able to:

- understand what the non-controlling interest is and how it is brought to account in the consolidated financial statements;

- know how to apply the two options for measuring non-controlling interest at acquisition date in the consolidated financial statements;

- identify and process the pro forma journal entries at acquisition in order to eliminate the investment in subsidiary, recognise goodwill or a gain on bargain purchase and allocate the equity of the subsidiary to the non-controlling interest;

- prepare a consolidated statement of financial position at acquisition date for a parent and its partly owned subsidiary;

- identify and process consolidating pro forma journal entries to eliminate the effects of intragroup dividends and to allocate the appropriate portion of the dividend to the non-controlling interest;

- prepare consolidated financial statements for a parent and its partly owned subsidiary for reporting periods after acquisition date;

- deal with the impairment of goodwill in the consolidated financial statements; and

- prepare consolidated financial statements where:
  - the subsidiary has an accumulated loss at acquisition date or is insolvent;
  - the subsidiary incurs losses after acquisition date;
  - the subsidiary has a reporting date different to the reporting date of the group; and
  - the subsidiary has an accounting policy that is not the same as that of the group for a similar transaction and event.

TOPIC LIST

Introduction

In Volume 1 Chapter 3 we dealt with the preparation of consolidated financial statements for a wholly owned subsidiary, both at acquisition date and for reporting periods subsequent to acquisition date. In this chapter we do the same, but for **partly owned** subsidiaries.

You will recall from Volume 1 Chapter 2 that when a parent does *not* own all the shares in a subsidiary that it has acquired the acquired entity is known as **a partly owned subsidiary**. The **portion of the equity** of such a subsidiary **owned** by shareholders **other than the parent** is in turn referred to as the **non-controlling interest**.

The basic consolidation process and procedures for consolidating a wholly owned subsidiary (as explained in Volume 1 Chapter 3) are equally applicable when consolidating a partly owned subsidiary. The difference is that when consolidating a partly owned subsidiary, additional consolidation procedures are required to **recognise the non-controlling interest's share** in:

- the **net assets** of the **subsidiary**; and
- the **profit or loss** and **other comprehensive income** of the **subsidiary**

at **acquisition date** and in **subsequent reporting periods**. Accordingly, this chapter will discuss and explain these additional procedures.

Furthermore, the parent has a choice – as was explained in Volume 1 Chapter 2 – as to how the non-controlling interest may be measured at acquisition date: either measurement at the non-controlling interest's proportionate share of the fair value of the subsidiary's identifiable net assets, or measurement at the fair value of the non-controlling interest. The method chosen for measuring the non-controlling interest at acquisition, it will be recalled, affects the amount of goodwill recognised and whether goodwill recognised is solely that of the parent (the partial goodwill method) or is attributable to both the parent and the non-controlling interest (the full goodwill method). The measurement basis for the non-controlling interest may also affect the amount of any gain on a bargain purchase that arises. The **application** of the **full** and **partial goodwill methods** in the **consolidated financial statements** will be addressed in this chapter.

Other aspects relating to consolidations that will be dealt with later in this chapter include:

- the subsequent impairment of goodwill;
- the consolidation implications of a subsidiary:
  - that is insolvent on acquisition;
  - that has an accumulated loss on acquisition (including recognising a deferred tax asset at acquisition in respect of a corresponding tax loss); or
  - that incurs losses subsequent to acquisition.
- the situation where a subsidiary has a different reporting period to the group; and
- the implications for consolidation of a subsidiary that has an accounting policy for a like event or transaction that is inconsistent with the group's accounting policy.

4.1 Consolidation of a partly owned subsidiary at acquisition date

As has been discussed, a parent may obtain control over another company (which is then a subsidiary of the parent) **without** owning **all** the shares in the subsidiary. The implication of acquiring this partly owned subsidiary is that there will be **a non-controlling interest** (i.e., a shareholding in the subsidiary acquired by investors other than the parent) in the **net assets (i.e., equity)** and in the **profit or loss** and **other comprehensive income** of the **subsidiary**, that needs to be **identified** and **recognised** in the **consolidated financial statements.**

We begin this chapter by dealing with consolidation issues that arise and the additional consolidation procedures performed in order to prepare consolidated financial statements for a parent and its partly owned subsidiary at the **acquisition date.**

4.1.1 Preparation of the consolidated statement of financial position and consolidated statement of changes in equity for a parent and its partly owned subsidiary at acquisition date

As was shown in Volume 1 Chapter 3, when consolidating a subsidiary at acquisition date, whether wholly owned or partly owned, it would make little sense to prepare a consolidated statement of profit or loss and other comprehensive income at acquisition date as the subsidiary's equity on acquisition is, from the group's perspective, bought (and thus eliminated) as opposed to earned. Consequently, a consolidated statement of profit or loss and other comprehensive income would comprise only the parent's profit or loss and other comprehensive income.

We are, however, able to prepare at acquisition date both a consolidated statement of financial position and a consolidated statement of changes in equity for a parent and its partly owned subsidiary, as discussed in the sections that follow.

4.1.1.1 Consolidated statement of financial position at acquisition: partly owned subsidiary

The consolidated statement of financial position for a parent and its partly owned subsidiary at acquisition date is prepared as follows:

- **At acquisition date,** all the **like items** of **assets, liabilities** and **equity** of the partly owned subsidiary are **added line by line** to those of the **parent.**
- Pro forma journals are passed at acquisition date (see Section 4.1.1.4):
  - to **eliminate** the parent's **investment in the partly owned subsidiary;**
  - to eliminate the **partly owned subsidiary's at acquisition equity;**
  - to recognise the **non-controlling interest** in the **partly owned subsidiary;**
  - to recognise any **goodwill or bargain purchase gain.**

After the procedures in the bullet points immediately above have been performed, the consolidated statement of financial position at acquisition date will reflect:

- aside from the parent's investment in the partly owned subsidiary (eliminated at acquisition), **100%** of the **assets and liabilities** of **both the parent and the** partly owned subsidiary at acquisition date – this reflects the fact that the parent controls 100% of the subsidiary's net assets (equity).

- **goodwill, as a non-current asset,** in circumstances where the consideration transferred by the parent plus the non-controlling interest at acquisition, exceeds the fair value of the partly owned subsidiary's at acquisition identifiable net assets; and

- **an equity section** which **discloses separately** the **equity attributable to the owners (i.e., shareholders) of the parent** and the **equity attributable to the non-controlling interest** (IFRS 10.22 and IAS 1.54). This disclosure reflects the fact that there are **different owners** of the subsidiary's net assets (equity).

The equity attributable to the **owners of the parent** will consist **solely** of the **parent's equity at acquisition date** (increased by any bargain purchase recognised at acquisition in circumstances where the fair value of the partly owned subsidiary's at acquisition identifiable net assets exceeds the total of the consideration transferred by the parent and the at acquisition non-controlling interest). This is because the **partly owned subsidiary's at acquisition equity** is **eliminated** on consolidation.

The **equity attributable to the non-controlling interest** will be the **non-controlling interest's share** of the **at acquisition equity** of the partly owned subsidiary. Recall that the non-controlling interest recognised at acquisition may be **measured** either at its **at acquisition date fair value** or at its **proportionate share of the fair value of the partly owned subsidiary's identifiable net assets at acquisition date.**

The format of, and disclosures required, in the equity section of the consolidated statement of financial position of a parent and its partly owned subsidiary are shown in Figure 4.1.

	CU
Equity	
Share capital	xxx
Retained earnings	xxx
Other reserves	xxx
Equity attributable to owners of the parent	xxx
Non-controlling interest	xxx
Total equity	xxx

Figure 4.1: *Extract of the consolidated statement of financial position of a parent and its partly owned subsidiary: Equity section*

4.1.1.2 Consolidated statement of changes in equity: Partly owned subsidiary at acquisition

When the acquisition date of a partly owned subsidiary is the last day of the reporting period of the group, the consolidated statement of changes in equity prepared for that reporting period would include **an additional column** to reflect the **non-controlling interest** (which is a separate category of equity) in the **at acquisition equity** of the subsidiary acquired. **All other amounts** in this consolidated statement of changes in equity would pertain to the **equity of the parent** since the equity of the partly owned subsidiary would have been eliminated at acquisition date, which date is also the reporting period end for the group.

4.1.1.3 Recognition and measurement of the non-controlling interest and goodwill

As was explained in Volume 1 Chapter 2, on acquisition of a partly owned subsidiary, a parent may **choose** between the following **two alternatives** for **measuring** the **non-controlling interest** in terms of IFRS 3 Business *Combinations*:

- The non-controlling interest may be measured at its **proportionate share** of the **fair value of the subsidiary's identifiable net assets at acquisition date**. In this case, any **goodwill** recognised on acquisition of the subsidiary relates **only** to the **portion of the subsidiary's equity** acquired by the **parent**. Consequently, **all of this goodwill** is allocated **to the parent**. As will be recalled from Volume 1 Chapter 2, we refer to this method of calculating goodwill as the **partial goodwill method**.

- The non-controlling interest may be measured at its **fair value at acquisition date**. In this instance, any goodwill recognised on acquisition of the subsidiary relates to **all** of the **subsidiary's equity** acquired. Consequently, this goodwill is allocated **both** to the **parent** and to the **non-controlling interest**. As will be recalled from Volume 1 Chapter 2, we refer to this method of calculating goodwill as the **full goodwill method**.

Note, as discussed in Volume 1 Chapter 2, that this choice of two methods for measuring the non-controlling interest is only available if the non-controlling interests concerned are **present ownership interests** that entitle their holders to a **proportionate share** of the **subsidiary's net assets** in the event of **liquidation of the subsidiary**. For purposes of this chapter and the remaining chapters, with the exception of Volume 1 Chapter 8 – dealing with preference shares issued by a subsidiary – this choice is always available. This is because in these chapters, the non-controlling interest always represents a present ownership interest in the **ordinary shares** of the subsidiary, entitling the non-controlling shareholders to a proportionate share of the subsidiary's net assets in the event of a liquidation.

4.1.1.4 Preparing the pro forma journals at acquisition date

Volume 1 Chapter 3 explained that when processing the **at acquisition date pro forma journals** for a **wholly owned subsidiary** we were required to:

- **eliminate common items**, namely the **at acquisition equity** of the **subsidiary** was **eliminated** against the **parent's investment in the subsidiary**; and

- **recognise any goodwill** or **bargain purchase gain** that arose on acquisition as the balancing figure.

These consolidation principles apply equally to partly owned subsidiaries. When consolidating a partly owned subsidiary, however, we are further required to recognise the **non-controlling interest's share of the subsidiary's at acquisition equity**.

The at acquisition pro forma elimination journal for a partly held subsidiary is as follows:

	Dr CU	Cr CU
Equity (subsidiary) (SCIE)	xxx[1]	
Investment in Subsidiary (parent) (SFP)		xxx[2]
Non-controlling interest (SFP)		xxx[3]
Goodwill (SFP) (balancing figure)	xxx[4]	
OR		
Gain on bargain purchase (Parent) (P/L) (balancing figure)		xxx[5]
Elimination of common items and recognition of non-controlling interest and goodwill (or gain on bargain purchase)		

Explanation: Pro forma journal entry

Note: For purposes of the explanation that follows, assume that the above pro forma journal relates to an 80% partly owned subsidiary – that is, the non-controlling interest owns 20% of the equity of the subsidiary.

[1] This debit is the elimination of **100% of the equity** (i.e., share capital, retained earnings and other reserves) of the subsidiary at acquisition date.

[2] This credit is the elimination of the parent's cost of investment in the subsidiary which is the consideration transferred by the parent to acquire 80% of the subsidiary's at acquisition equity.

[3] This credit recognises the portion of the subsidiary's at acquisition equity that belongs to the non-controlling interest. The amount recognised depends on the method elected by the parent to recognise and measure the non-controlling interest at acquisition date as follows:

- If the non-controlling interest is measured at its proportionate share of the at acquisition net asset value (equity) of the subsidiary, then it is calculated as 20% of the at acquisition net asset value equity of the subsidiary with *no* goodwill being attributed to the non-controlling interest.

- If the non-controlling interest is measured at its fair value, then the amount credited to non-controlling interest on acquisition will equal this fair value. In such a case, to the extent that this fair value exceeds 20% of the subsidiary's at acquisition net asset value (equity), this excess is goodwill that is attributable to the non-controlling interest.

[4] This debit recognises goodwill in the consolidated financial statements. As is clear from the above pro forma journal, irrespective of whether or not we are consolidating a wholly or partly owned subsidiary, goodwill is always calculated as a **residual amount** and is consequently the **balancing figure** for this pro forma journal entry.

In addition, as was discussed in note 3 above, the amount of goodwill recognised, and whether or not goodwill is also attributable to the non-controlling interest, depends on the method chosen by the parent to measure the non-controlling interest at acquisition date.

[5] This credit recognises a bargain purchase gain as income of the parent. It will be recalled from Volume 1 Chapter 2 that when dealing with a partly owned

subsidiary, a bargain purchase gain represents the excess of the fair value of the subsidiary's identifiable net assets at acquisition date, over the total of:

- the value of the consideration transferred by the parent; and
- the non-controlling interest in the subsidiary at acquisition date.

As with goodwill, a bargain purchase gain is calculated as a residual amount and is therefore a balancing figure in the pro forma journal.

Example 4.1: Partly owned subsidiary acquired, partial goodwill method applies – consolidation at acquisition date

The purpose of this example is to illustrate the consolidation process for a partly owned subsidiary at the acquisition date where goodwill arises on acquisition and the partial goodwill method applies.

P Ltd acquired 80% of the ordinary share capital of S Ltd on 1 January 20x8 and obtained control over S Ltd on this date. This is the beginning of the financial year for both P Ltd and S Ltd. P Ltd paid CU 280 000 to acquire its 80% shareholding in S Ltd on 1 January 20x8.

P Ltd measures the non-controlling interest at its proportionate share of the identifiable net assets of S Ltd at acquisition date.

Also, at acquisition date, P Ltd considered the net assets of S Ltd to be fairly valued.

The condensed statements of financial position of P Ltd and S Ltd on 1 January 20x8 are as follows:

	P Ltd CU	S Ltd CU
Debits		
Property, plant and equipment	390 000	260 000
Investment in S Ltd (at cost)	280 000	–
Trade receivables	150 000	120 000
	820 000	**380 000**
Credits		
Share capital	320 000	140 000
Retained earnings	400 000	160 000
Trade and other payables	100 000	80 000
	820 000	**380 000**

Required

(a) Prepare the analysis of equity of S Ltd at acquisition date.

(b) Prepare the at acquisition pro forma journal.

(c) Prepare the consolidated statement of financial position for the P Ltd group as at 1 January 20x8.

Solution 4.1: Partly owned subsidiary acquired, partial goodwill method applies – consolidation at acquisition date

Part (a): Analysis of equity (AOE) of S Ltd at acquisition date

At acquisition date (1 January 20x8)	Total of S Ltd's equity 100% CU	P Ltd at acquisition 80% CU	Non-controlling interest 20% CU
Share capital	140 000	112 000	28 000
Retained earnings	160 000	128 000	32 000
Fair value of net assets of S Ltd	300 000	240 000	60 000
Goodwill – Parent (balancing figure)	[†]40 000	[†]40 000 a	[‡]–
Consideration and non-controlling interest	340 000	280 000	[‡]60 000 b

Explanatory notes

† These amounts are the same because the partial goodwill method is applied and therefore all the goodwill that arises belongs to the parent.

‡ As the partial goodwill method is used, no goodwill is attributed to the non-controlling interest.

‡ This amount represents the non-controlling interest's at acquisition share of the subsidiary's equity, which is calculated as the non-controlling interest's 20% proportionate share of the subsidiary's at acquisition identifiable net assets.

Calculation: 20% × 300 000 = CU 60 000

As we are now dealing with another category of equity, namely the non-controlling interest, the analysis of equity is extended to include an additional column to calculate and keep track of the non-controlling interest's share of the subsidiary's equity.

CHECK: IFRS 3.32 – Goodwill calculation

Consideration transferred	280 000
Add: Non-controlling interest	60 000
Subtotal	340 000
Minus: Identifiable net assets	(300 000)
Goodwill	**40 000**

Part (b): Pro forma consolidation entry at acquisition date

Pro forma journal 1 (J1)	Dr CU	Cr CU
Share capital (S Ltd) (SCIE) (given)	140 000[1]	
Retained earnings (S Ltd) (SCIE) (given)	160 000[2]	
Goodwill (SFP) (balancing figure)	40 000[3]	
Investment in S Ltd (P Ltd) (SFP) (given)		280 000[4]
Non-controlling interest (SFP)		[Wkg1]60 000[5]
Elimination of common items and recognition of non-controlling interest and goodwill		

Workings: Pro forma journals

Working 1

(140 000 + 160 000) × 20% NCI Share

Note: For purposes of this chapter, the numbers adjacent to the amounts in the pro forma journal cross-reference these amounts to the corresponding consolidation worksheet.

The full effects of the preceding pro forma journal on the consolidated statement of financial position of the P Ltd group are shown in the following consolidation worksheet as at 1 January 20x8.

	P Ltd Dr/(Cr) CU	S Ltd Dr/(Cr) CU	Pro forma journals Dr/(Cr) CU J1	Con-solidated Dr/(Cr) CU
ASSETS				
Property, plant and equipment	390 000	260 000		650 000
Investment in S Ltd	280 000		(280 000)[4]	–
Trade receivables	150 000	120 000		270 000
Goodwill			40 000[3]	40 000
EQUITY AND LIABILITIES				
Share capital	(320 000)	(140 000)	140 000[1]	(320 000)
Retained earnings	(400 000)	(160 000)	160 000[2]	(400 000)
Non-controlling interest			(60 000)[5]	(60 000)
Trade and other payables	(100 000)	(80 000)		(180 000)
	0	0	0	0

Part (c): Consolidated statement of financial position at acquisition date

P LTD GROUP: CONSOLIDATED STATEMENT OF FINANCIAL POSITION AS AT 1 JANUARY 20x8	
	CU
Assets	
Non-current assets	
Property, plant and equipment (390 000 (P Ltd) + 260 000 (S Ltd))	650 000
Goodwill (see AOE **a OR** (J1))	40 000
Current assets	
Trade receivables (150 000 (P Ltd) + 120 000 (S Ltd))	270 000
Total assets	960 000
Equity and liabilities	
Share capital	320 000
Retained earnings	400 000
Equity attributable to owners of the parent	720 000
Non-controlling interest (see AOE **b OR** (J1))	60 000
Total equity	780 000
Current liabilities	
Trade and other payables (100 000 (P Ltd) + 80 000 (S Ltd))	180 000
Total equity and liabilities	960 000

Example 4.2: Partly owned subsidiary acquired, full goodwill method applies

The purpose of this example is to illustrate the consolidation process for a partly owned subsidiary at the acquisition date where goodwill arises on acquisition and the full goodwill method applies.

This example is exactly the same as Example 4.1 except that P Ltd measures the non-controlling interest at its at acquisition date fair value of CU 75 000.

The condensed statements of financial position of P Ltd and S Ltd on 1 January 20x8 are as follows:

	P Ltd	S Ltd
	CU	CU
Debits		
Property, plant and equipment	390 000	260 000
Investment in S Ltd	280 000	–
Trade receivables	150 000	120 000
	820 000	**380 000**
Credits		
Share capital	320 000	140 000
Retained earnings	400 000	160 000
Trade and other payables	100 000	80 000
	820 000	**380 000**

Required

(a) Prepare the analysis of equity of S Ltd at acquisition date.

(b) Prepare the at acquisition pro forma journal.

(c) Prepare the consolidated statement of financial position for the P Ltd group as at 1 January 20x8.

Solution 4.2: Partly owned subsidiary acquired, full goodwill method applies

Part (a): Analysis of equity (AOE) of S Ltd at acquisition date

	Total of S Ltd's equity 100%	P Ltd at acquisition 80%	Non-controlling interest 20%
At acquisition date (1 January 20x8)	CU	CU	CU
Share capital	140 000	112 000	28 000
Retained earnings	160 000	128 000	32 000
Fair value of net assets of S Ltd	300 000	240 000	†60 000
Goodwill – Parent (balancing figure)	40 000	40 000 a	–
Goodwill – Non-controlling interest (balancing figure)	15 000		†15 000 b
Consideration and non-controlling interest	355 000	280 000	†75 000 c

Explanatory note

† We are measuring the non-controlling interest at its fair value of CU 75 000, which exceeds by CU 15 000 the non-controlling interest's 20% share of the subsidiary's net assets, which is an amount of CU 60 000. This excess of CU 15 000 is goodwill attributable to the non-controlling interest.

CHECK: IFRS 3.32 – Goodwill calculation

Consideration transferred	280 000
Add: Non-controlling interest	75 000
Subtotal	355 000
Minus: Identifiable net assets	(300 000)
Goodwill	**55 000**

Part (b): Pro forma consolidation entry at acquisition date

Pro forma journal 1 (J1)	Dr CU	Cr CU
Share capital (S Ltd) (SCIE) (given)	140 000[1]	
Retained earnings (S Ltd) (SCIE) (given)	160 000[2]	
Goodwill (SFP) (balancing figure)	55 000[3]	
Investment in S Ltd (P Ltd) (SFP) (given)		280 000[4]
Non-controlling interest (SFP) (given)		75 000[5]
Elimination of common items and recognition of non-controlling interest and goodwill		

The full effects of the above pro forma journal on the consolidated statement of financial position of the P Ltd group are shown in the consolidation worksheet as at 1 January 20x8 below.

	P Ltd Dr/(Cr) CU	S Ltd Dr/(Cr) CU	Pro forma journals Dr/(Cr) CU J1	Con- solidated Dr/(Cr) CU
ASSETS				
Property, plant and equipment	390 000	260 000		650 000
Investment in S Ltd	280 000		(280 000)[4]	–
Trade receivables	150 000	120 000		270 000
Goodwill			55 000[3]	55 000
EQUITY AND LIABILITIES				
Share capital	(320 000)	(140 000)	140 000[1]	(320 000)
Retained earnings	(400 000)	(160 000)	160 000[2]	(400 000)
Non-controlling interest			(75 000)[5]	(75 000)
Trade and other payables	(100 000)	(80 000)		(180 000)
	0	0	0	0

Part (c): Consolidated statement of financial position at acquisition date

P LTD GROUP: CONSOLIDATED STATEMENT OF FINANCIAL POSITION AS AT 1 JANUARY 20x8	
	CU
Assets	
Non-current assets	
Property, plant and equipment (390 000 (P Ltd) + 260 000 (S Ltd))	650 000
Goodwill (40 000 (see AOE **a**) + 15 000 (see AOE **b**)) **OR** (J1))	55 000
Current assets	
Trade receivables (150 000 (P Ltd) + 120 000 (S Ltd))	270 000
Total assets	975 000
Equity and liabilities	
Equity attributable to owners of the parent	
Share capital	320 000
Retained earnings	400 000
Equity attributable to owners of the parent	720 000
Non-controlling interest (see AOE **c OR** (J1))	75 000
Total equity	795 000
Current liabilities	
Trade and other payables (100 000 (P Ltd) + 80 000 (S Ltd))	180 000
Total equity and liabilities	975 000

4.2 Consolidation of a partly owned subsidiary after acquisition date

When consolidating a partly owned subsidiary for reporting periods post acquisition date, preparation of the following is now required each reporting period[4]:

- a consolidated statement of profit or loss and other comprehensive income;
- a consolidated statement of changes in equity; and
- a consolidated statement of financial position.

Key to the consolidation of a partly owned subsidiary for reporting periods post acquisition date is determining the **share of the non-controlling interest in**:

- the **profit or loss** and **other comprehensive income** of the partly owned subsidiary; and
- the **post-acquisition reserves** of the partly owned subsidiary to the beginning of the current reporting period.

---

4   Note that the preparation of a **consolidated statement of cash flows** for a group that has partly owned subsidiaries is dealt with in Volume 2 Chapter 7.

The additional consolidation procedures required to recognise the non-controlling interest's share in the post-acquisition equity of the partly owned subsidiary and the consequent preparation of the consolidated financial statements each reporting period after acquisition date, are dealt with in this section.

4.2.1 Preparation of the consolidated statement of profit or loss and other comprehensive income for a parent and its partly owned subsidiary: post acquisition

The preparation of a consolidated statement of profit or loss and other comprehensive income for a parent and its partly owned subsidiary consists of two main steps.

Step 1: As was explained in Volume 1 Chapter 3:

- **Combine** the individual items of **post-acquisition income and expenditure** of the **subsidiary line by line** with **like items of income and expenditure** of the **parent.** The net result of this combination is the consolidated profit or loss for the year.

- Combine the **individual post-acquisition items** of **other comprehensive income** (e.g., property, plant and equipment revaluation gain) of the **subsidiary line by line** with **like items of other comprehensive income** of the **parent.** The net result of this combination is the consolidated other comprehensive income for the year.

- Add the consolidated profit or loss for the year to the consolidated other comprehensive income for the year to determine the consolidated total comprehensive income for the year.

Step 2: To comply with the disclosure requirements of IFRS 10.B94, perform the following attributions:

- Attribute the consolidated profit or loss for the year – from Step 1 – to the **owners (i.e., shareholders) of the parent** and to the **non-controlling interest.**

   The consolidated profit or loss attributable to the owners of the parent is determined by adding the **current year profit or loss of the parent** to the **parent's share of the current year profit or loss of the subsidiary.**

   The consolidated profit or loss attributable to the non-controlling interest is determined as the **non-controlling interest's share of the subsidiary's current year profit or loss.**

- Attribute the consolidated total comprehensive income – from Step 1 – to the **owners of the parent** and to the **non-controlling interest.**

   The consolidated total comprehensive income attributable to the owners of the parent is determined in the following manner:

   - consolidated profit or loss attributable to the owners of the parent
      PLUS
   - **parent's other comprehensive income** for the current year
      PLUS
   - **parent's share of other comprehensive income of the subsidiary** for the current year.

The consolidated total comprehensive income attributable to the non-controlling interest is determined by adding the consolidated profit or loss attributable to the non-controlling interest to the **non-controlling interest's share** of the **subsidiary's current year other comprehensive income.**

Generally speaking, the **proportion of profit or loss and changes in equity (i.e., other comprehensive income and post-acquisition reserves) allocated** to the **parent** and the **non-controlling interest** in preparing consolidated financial statements, is determined solely based on **existing ownership interests** (IFRS 10.B89). That is, according to the **percentage shareholdings** in the subsidiary held by **the parent** and by **the non-controlling interest respectively.**

For example, where a subsidiary has a post-acquisition current year profit of CU 150 000 and the parent has a 75% ownership interest (i.e., a 75% shareholding) in the subsidiary, CU 112 500 (150 000 × Parent's shareholding of 75%) of this profit will be allocated to the parent while the remaining CU 37 500 (150 000 × 25% Shareholding of the non-controlling interest) will be allocated to the non-controlling interest.

However, an **exception** to the general rule of consolidating **only existing** ownership interests applies in certain circumstances where IFRS 10 requires that **both existing and** *potential* ownership interests be taken into account.

This is the case for an entity that has **in substance** an existing ownership interest as a result of a transaction that currently gives the entity access to the returns associated with an ownership interest. In such circumstances, the proportion of the subsidiary's profit or loss and changes in equity allocated to the parent and non-controlling interest in preparing the consolidated financial statements is determined by taking into account the **eventual exercise of those potential voting rights** and **other derivatives** that currently give the entity access to the returns (IFRS 10.B90).

In light of the above discussion, the disclosures required on the face of the consolidated statement of profit or loss and other comprehensive income are illustrated in Figure 4.2.

	CU
Profit for the year	xxx
Other comprehensive income	xxx
Total comprehensive income for the year	xxx
Profit attributable to:	
Owners of the parent	xxx
Non-controlling interest	xxx
Total comprehensive income attributable to:	
Owners of the parent	xxx
Non-controlling interest	xxx

Figure 4.2: *Extract from the consolidated statement of profit or loss and other comprehensive income*

The allocation of the appropriate share of the subsidiary's total comprehensive income to the non-controlling interest is made by passing the following pro forma journal entries (pro-forma journals that allocate post-acquisition losses to the non-controlling interest are illustrated in Example 4.8):

Pro forma journal 1 (J1)	Dr CU	Cr CU
NCI – Share of profit or loss (P/L)	xxx	
NCI – Equity (SFP)		xxx
Allocating the non-controlling interest its share of the subsidiary's profit for the year		

Pro forma journal 2 (J2)	Dr CU	Cr CU
NCI – Share of other comprehensive income (OCI)	xxx	
NCI – Equity (SFP)		xxx
Allocating the non-controlling interest its share of the other comprehensive income of the subsidiary for the year		

In the two pro forma journals above:

- We debit **profit allocation accounts** rather than debiting consolidated profit or loss and consolidated other comprehensive income **directly**. This is because for disclosure purposes, in the consolidated statement of profit or loss and other comprehensive income:
  - We are required to present the total consolidated profit or loss and the consolidated total of each component of other comprehensive income **before** any allocations thereof to the owners of the parent and to the non-controlling interest (see Figure 4.2).
  - We are also required to present (see Figure 4.2):
    - the share of the owners of the parent in the consolidated profit or loss and in the total consolidated comprehensive income for the year; and
    - the non-controlling interest's share of the consolidated profit or loss and of the total consolidated comprehensive income for the year.

  If we had debited consolidated profit or loss and consolidated other comprehensive income **directly,** then the disclosures provided in the consolidated statement of profit or loss and other comprehensive income would be incorrect as this would result in only a **net amount** (i.e., after deducting the non-controlling interest's share) being presented for consolidated profit or loss and for consolidated other comprehensive income for the period. In addition the non-controlling interest's share of these amounts would *not* be disclosed.

- The subsidiary's total comprehensive income earned increases the equity value of the subsidiary. Furthermore, the non-controlling interest–equity balance, presented on the face of the consolidated statement of financial position, constitutes the non-controlling interest's share in the total equity of the subsidiary at reporting period end. Accordingly, by allocating a portion of the subsidiary's total comprehensive income to the non-controlling interest, the non-controlling interest now shares in the subsidiary's larger equity value, causing its balance to increase. For this reason, the corresponding credit entry in pro forma journals 1 and 2 above is made to record the increased non-controlling interest–equity balance in the consolidated statement of financial position.

4.2.2 Non-controlling interest's share in the post-acquisition reserves of a subsidiary

Aside from sharing in the subsidiary's current year profit or loss and other comprehensive income, the non-controlling interest is also allocated its **share** of the **movement in the subsidiary's reserves** that arose in the period since **acquisition, up to the beginning of the current financial year.**

This implies that the parent is allocated the movement in the subsidiary's post-acquisition reserves up to the beginning of the current year, as **reduced by** the movement in these reserves **allocated to the non-controlling interest.**

For example, if the retained earnings of an 80% held subsidiary has increased by CU 100 000 since acquisition to the beginning of the year, then the parent's post-acquisition share thereof will be CU 80 000 (100 000 × 80%), with the remaining CU 20 000 being allocated to the non-controlling interest. This CU 80 000 will be added to the opening retained earnings balance of parent itself to determine the opening consolidated retained earnings balance for the group.

The allocation of the non-controlling interest's share of the movement in the subsidiary's post-acquisition reserves up to the beginning of the current year is made by passing the following pro forma journal entry:

Pro forma journal	Dr CU	Cr CU
Retained earnings/Revaluation surplus/Mark to market reserve (Subsidiary) (SCIE)	xxx	
NCI – Equity (SFP)		xxx
Allocating the non-controlling interest its share of the subsidiary's post-acquisition retained earnings/revaluation surplus/mark to market reserve to the beginning of the year		

In this pro forma journal the fact that the non-controlling interest is allocated a share in the post-acquisition growth in the subsidiary's reserves (as per the debit side of the pro forma journal) means that its equity interest in the subsidiary must increase. This is achieved by crediting the non-controlling interest equity account. The pro forma journal passed when there is a reduction/(increase) in the subsidiary's retained earnings/(accumulated loss) since acquisition to the beginning of the current year is dealt with in Section 4.2.6.

4.2.3 Preparation of the consolidated statement of changes in equity for a parent and its partly owned subsidiary post acquisition

In accordance with IAS 1 *Presentation of Financial Statements*, the consolidated statement of changes in equity must include the **total comprehensive income** for the period, showing **separately** the total amounts attributable to **owners of the parent** and to the **non-controlling interest** (IAS 1.106(a)). The implication of this disclosure requirement is that the consolidated statement of changes in equity prepared must include two new columns, which present:

- the **total equity** that **belongs to the parent;** and
- the **total equity** that belongs to the **non-controlling interest.**

In addition, as the non-controlling interest is a component of equity, the consolidated statement of changes in equity must disclose a **reconciliation** between the **non-controlling interest balance** at the **beginning** and at the **end** of the financial year (IAS 1.106(d)).

Finally, as we are presenting the financial statements of a group (which combine the parent and subsidiary into one single economic entity), one last column which presents the **total equity** of the group (being the sum of the equity of the subsidiary and the parent) must be added. The format of a consolidated statement of changes in equity for a parent and its partly owned subsidiary is provided in Table 4.1. Explanations then follow as to how various amounts (numbered 1 to 12) included in the consolidated statement of changes in equity in Table 4.1 are arrived at.

Table 4.1: *Format of the consolidated statement of changes in equity: Partly owned subsidiary*

	Share capital	Retained earnings	Revaluation surplus	Total parent equity	Non-controlling interest	Total equity of the group
Balance beginning of the year	xxx[1]	xxx[2]	xxx[3]	xxx	xxx[4]	xxx
Total comprehensive income:						
Profit for the year		xxx[5]		xxx	xxx[6]	xxx
Other comprehensive income			xxx[7]	xxx	xxx[8]	xxx
Dividends declared/paid		(xxx)[9]		(xxx)	(xxx)[10]	(xxx)
Balance end of the year	xxx	xxx	xxx	xxx	xxx[11]	xxx

Note: For explanatory purposes, assume that we are dealing with an 80% owned subsidiary, i.e., the non-controlling interest is 20%. Furthermore, assume that in the period since acquisition to the beginning of the year, the retained earnings and revaluation surplus of both the parent and the subsidiary have increased.

Explanatory notes: Table 4.1

[1] This amount is the share capital of the **parent only**. Remember that the share capital of the subsidiary is pre- acquisition equity, which is eliminated on consolidation.

[2] This amount is comprised of the following:
- the retained earnings balance of the parent at the beginning of the year
  PLUS
- the parent's 80% share of the increase in the retained earnings balance of the subsidiary since acquisition to the beginning of the current financial year.

[3] This amount is comprised of the following:
- the revaluation surplus balance of the parent at the beginning of the year

> **PLUS**
> - the parent's 80% share of the increase in the revaluation surplus balance of the subsidiary since acquisition to the beginning of the current financial year.

[4] The opening balance for the non-controlling interest consists of the following:
   - the non-controlling interest's share of the at acquisition equity of the subsidiary, measured either:
     - at its 20% share of the fair value of the subsidiary's identifiable net assets at acquisition; or
     - at its fair value at acquisition.

   PLUS
   - the non-controlling interest's 20% share of the increase in the subsidiary's retained earnings and revaluation surplus balances since acquisition up to the beginning of the current year.

[5] This amount is the parent's current year profit, plus 80% of the subsidiary's current year profit. This figure is the line item 'Profit for the year attributable to the owners of the parent', obtained from the consolidated statement of profit or loss and other comprehensive income.

[6] This amount is the 20% of the current year profit of the subsidiary allocated to the non-controlling interest. This figure is the line item 'Profit for the year attributable to the non-controlling interest', obtained from the consolidated statement of profit or loss and other comprehensive income.

[7] This amount is the parent's other comprehensive income for the current year, plus 80% of the current year other comprehensive income of the subsidiary.

[8] This amount is the 20% of the current year other comprehensive income of the subsidiary allocated to the non-controlling interest.

[9] This amount is the dividend declared/paid by the parent to its shareholders.

[10] This amount is the dividend paid/declared by the subsidiary to the non-controlling interest (and will be 20% of the total dividend declared/paid by the subsidiary). The accounting treatment of intragroup dividends where there is a non-controlling interest is discussed in Section 4.2.4.

[11] This amount represents the interest that non-controlling shareholders own in the year end equity value of the parent's subsidiary. It is also the non-controlling interest amount that is presented on the face of the consolidated statement of financial position at reporting period end.

Note: All the closing balances per the consolidated statement of changes in equity above are the closing balances that appear in the equity section of the consolidated statement of financial position of the group at reporting period end.

4.2.4 The effect of intragroup dividends on the non-controlling interest

In Volume 1 Chapter 3 it was explained that dividends paid or declared that are reported in the consolidated financial statements should only be those that have been paid or declared to the **shareholders of the parent**. Similarly, dividend income recognised in the consolidated financial statements should only be in respect of dividends received/receivable from **parties outside the group**. Accordingly, as was explained in Volume 1 Chapter 3, dividends declared/paid by a subsidiary to its parent are an intragroup transaction that needs to be eliminated on consolidation by passing the following pro forma entry:

Dr dividend income (Parent) (P/L)

    Cr dividend paid/declared (Subsidiary) (SCIE)

Where the company paying or declaring the dividend is a partly owned subsidiary, a portion of the dividend will be paid or declared to the parent, and a portion to the non-controlling interest. It is important to understand that the portion of the dividend paid or declared by the subsidiary to the **non-controlling interest is** *not* **an intra-group transaction** – rather, it represents **a distribution of the subsidiary's equity** that **reduces** the **non-controlling interest's equity interest** in the subsidiary. In order to recognise this **reduction** in the non-controlling interest's share of the subsidiary's equity, we **debit** the **non-controlling interest equity balance** in the pro forma journal passed. In other words, we set off the dividend paid/declared by the subsidiary to the non-controlling investors against the non-controlling interest equity balance. Therefore, the following pro forma entry is passed:

Pro forma journal	Dr CU	Cr CU
Dividend income (Parent) (P/L)	xxx	
Non controlling interest – Equity (SFP)	xxx	
Dividends paid/declared (Subsidiary) (SCIE)		xxx
Elimination of intragroup dividend and recognition of non-controlling interest in the dividend		

For this reason, in the consolidated statement of changes in equity – as is illustrated in Table 4.1 – of the total dividend paid or declared by the 80% partly owned subsidiary, **20% of this dividend**, which belongs to the **non-controlling interest**, will appear as a **deduction** in the **non-controlling interest column**.

In addition, if there are any unpaid dividends outstanding at the reporting period end, the unpaid portion relating to the non-controlling interest does *not* constitute an intragroup balance that must be eliminated. Instead it represents an **external obligation of the group to be disclosed as a liability on the consolidated statement of financial position** at reporting period end. Stated differently, of the **total dividend payable** recorded by the **subsidiary**, only the portion that is **due to the parent** is **eliminated against the dividend receivable** as recorded by the **parent**. This leaves the **remaining dividend payable** to the **non-controlling interest** to be presented as a **liability** of the group at reporting period end. To illustrate, suppose a 70% held subsidiary declares a total dividend at year end of CU 100, of which CU 70 is to its parent and the remaining CU 30 is to the non-controlling interest. The subsidiary will record a dividend payable of CU 100, while the parent will record a dividend receivable of CU 70.

The following pro forma journal will be passed on consolidation to eliminate the intragroup dividend and to recognise the effect of the portion of the dividend declared to the non-controlling interest on the non-controlling interest equity balance.

Pro forma journal 1 (J1)	Dr CU	Cr CU
Dividend income (Parent) (P/L) (given)	70	
Non-controlling interest – Equity (SFP) (given)	30	
Dividend declared (Subsidiary) (SCIE) (given)		100
Elimination of intragroup dividend and recognition of non-controlling interest in dividend		

The following pro forma journal will be passed on consolidation to eliminate the intragroup balances, which, as discussed above, relate only to the dividend due to the parent.

Pro forma journal 2 (J2)	Dr CU	Cr CU
Dividend payable (Subsidiary) (SFP) (given)	70	
Dividend receivable (Parent) (SFP) (given)		70
Elimination of intragroup balances		

4.2.5 Preparation of the consolidated statement of financial position for a parent and its partly owned subsidiary post acquisition date

Each reporting period post acquisition, the consolidated statement of financial position for a parent and its partly owned subsidiary is prepared as follows:

- at reporting period end, all the **like items** of **assets, liabilities, equity, income and expenses** of the **partly owned subsidiary** are **added line by line** to those of the **parent.**
- Pro forma journals are passed:
  - **at acquisition,** to (1) eliminate the parent's investment in the partly owned subsidiary; (2) eliminate the subsidiary's at acquisition equity; and (3) to recognise the non-controlling interest as well as any goodwill or bargain purchase gain; and
  - **subsequent to acquisition date,** to eliminate intragroup transactions and balances (e.g., intragroup dividends) and to allocate the non-controlling interest it appropriate share of the partly owned subsidiary's post-acquisition equity.

After the procedures in the bullet points immediately above have been performed, the consolidated statement of financial position each reporting date post acquisition will reflect:

- aside from the parent's investment in the partly owned subsidiary (eliminated at acquisition) and any intragroup receivables and payables (e.g., intragroup dividend payable and receivable which are eliminated against each other), **100% of the assets and liabilities** of **both** the **parent and the partly owned subsidiary.**
- **goodwill, as a non-current asset,** in circumstances where the consideration transferred by the parent plus the non-controlling interest at acquisition, exceeds the fair value of the partly owned subsidiary's identifiable net assets at acquisition.

- **Equity attributable to the owners of the parent,** comprising:
  - the **parent's equity** at reporting period end (increased by any bargain purchase gain that arose at acquisition in circumstances where the fair value of the partly owned subsidiary's at acquisition identifiable net assets exceeded the total of (1) the consideration transferred by the parent; and (2) the at acquisition non-controlling interest)

    PLUS
  - the **parent's share** of the partly owned subsidiary's **post-acquisition equity** (e.g., post-acquisition retained earnings and revaluation surplus).
- The **non-controlling interest** at reporting period end, comprising:
  - the **non-controlling interest** in the partly owned subsidiary's **at acquisition equity** (measured either at its proportionate share of the fair value of the subsidiary's at acquisition identifiable net assets, or at the non-controlling interest's at acquisition fair value)

    PLUS
  - the **non-controlling interest's share** of the partly owned subsidiary's **post-acquisition equity** (e.g., post-acquisition retained earnings and revaluation surplus).

Note that the **equity** reported on the consolidated statement of financial position each reporting period end, comprises the **closing share capital, retained earnings, other reserve(s) balance(s) and non-controlling interest balance** as per the consolidated statement of changes in equity.

Example 4.3: Partly owned subsidiary acquired, partial goodwill method applies – consolidation after acquisition date

The following are the condensed financial statements of P Ltd and its subsidiary, S Ltd, which is partially owned, two years after P Ltd acquired a portion of the ordinary share capital of S Ltd.

STATEMENTS OF FINANCIAL POSITION AS AT 31 DECEMBER 20x8	P Ltd CU	S Ltd CU
Assets		
Property, plant and equipment	41 500	70 000
Investment in S Ltd: 64 000 ordinary shares – at cost	95 000	–
Trade receivables	143 500	71 700
Total assets	**280 000**	**141 700**
Equity and liabilities		
Share capital (P Ltd 100 000 Shares / S Ltd 80 000 Shares)	100 000	80 000
Retained earnings	45 000	30 000
Revaluation surplus	18 000	12 000
Trade and other payables	117 000	19 700
Total equity and liabilities	**280 000**	**141 700**

EXTRACT: STATEMENTS OF PROFIT OR LOSS AND OTHER COMPREHENSIVE INCOME FOR THE YEAR ENDED 31 DECEMBER 20x8		
	P Ltd CU	S Ltd CU
Profit	15 180	15 950
Dividend received from subsidiary	4 000	–
Profit before tax	19 180	15 950
Income tax expense	(7 700)	(5 500)
Profit for the year	11 480	10 450
Other comprehensive income:		
Revaluation gain property, plant and equipment	5 000	3 000
Other comprehensive income for the year, net of tax	5 000	3 000
Total comprehensive income for the year	16 480	13 450

EXTRACT: STATEMENTS OF CHANGES IN EQUITY FOR THE YEAR ENDED 31 DECEMBER 20x8				
	Retained earnings		Revaluation surplus	
	P Ltd CU	S Ltd CU	P Ltd CU	S Ltd CU
Balance at 1 Jan 20x8	42 020	24 550	13 000	9 000
Total comprehensive income:				
Profit for the year	11 480	10 450		–
Other comprehensive income	–	–	5 000	3 000
Dividend	(8 500)	(5 000)		
Balance at 31 Dec 20x8	45 000	30 000	18 000	12 000

On 1 January 20x7, the acquisition date of S Ltd, S Ltd's equity consisted of the following:

• share capital of CU 80 000;
• retained earnings of CU 13 800; and
• revaluation surplus of CU 4 800.

S Ltd's net assets were considered to be fairly valued at acquisition date and P Ltd measures the non-controlling interest at its proportionate share of S Ltd's identifiable net assets. Further, P Ltd measures its investment in S Ltd at cost price.

Required

(a) Prepare the analysis of equity of S Ltd as at 31 December 20x8.

(b) Provide all the pro forma journal entries necessary to prepare the consolidated financial statements of the P Ltd group for the financial year ended 31 December 20x8.

(c) Prepare the consolidated financial statements of the P Ltd group for the year ended 31 December 20x8.

Solution 4.3: Partly owned subsidiary acquired, partial goodwill method applies – consolidation after acquisition date

Part (a): Analysis of equity (AOE) of S Ltd as at 31 December 20x8

CHECK: IFRS 3.32 – Goodwill calculation

Consideration transferred	95 000
Add: Non-controlling interest	19 720
Subtotal	114 720
Minus: Identifiable net assets	(98 600)
Goodwill	**16 120**

		P Ltd ^{Wkg1} 80%		
	Total of S Ltd's equity 100%	At acquisi-tion	Since acquisi-tion	Non-controlling interest 20%
At acquisition date (1 January 20x7)	CU	CU	CU	CU
Share capital	80 000	64 000	–	16 000
Retained earnings	13 800	11 040		2 760
Revaluation surplus	4 800	3 840		960
Fair value of net assets of S Ltd	98 600	78 880		19 720
Goodwill – Parent (balancing figure)	16 120 a	16 120		–
Consideration and NCI	114 720	95 000		19 720[1]
Since acquisition				
• To beginning of current year:				
Retained earnings (24 550 – 13 800)	10 750		8 600[2] b	2 150[3] c
Revaluation surplus (9 000 – 4 800)	4 200		3 360[4] d	840[5] e
				22 710[6] f
• Current year:				
Profit for the year	10 450		8 360[7] g	2 090[8] h
Other comprehensive income	3 000		2 400[9] i	600[10] j
Less: Dividends	(5 000)		(4 000)[11] k	(1 000)[11] l
	138 120		18 720	24 400[12] m

Workings: Analyis of equity

Working 1

64 000 Shares / 80 000 Shares × 100%

Note how we include a separate column for the non-controlling interest (NCI).

We use this column to establish the NCI's share of:

• S Ltd's AT acquisition equity; and
• the movement in S Ltd's equity POST acquisition date:
    ▪ to the beginning of the current year; and
    ▪ in the current year.

Explanatory notes: Analysis of equity

[1] This amount represents the non-controlling interest's share of the subsidiary, S Ltd's, at acquisition equity and equals the non-controlling interest's 20% proportionate share of S Ltd's identifiable net assets at acquisition date. As goodwill is measured using the partial goodwill method, no goodwill is attributable to the non-controlling interest.

[2] This amount is the parent, P Ltd's, 80% share of S Ltd's CU 10 750 growth in retained earnings from acquisition date to the beginning of the current year. This amount of CU 8 600 (10 750 × 80%) is added to the opening retained earnings balance of P Ltd to arrive at the group's opening retained earnings balance in the consolidated statement of changes in equity. See Part (c) below.

[3] This amount is the non-controlling interest's 20% share of the CU 10 750 post-acquisition retained earnings of S Ltd up to the beginning of the current year. This amount of CU 2 150 (10 750 × 20%) is added to the value of the non-controlling interest at acquisition date as part of determining the non-controlling interest balance at the beginning of the year (see note 6 below), which opening balance is reflected in the consolidated statement of changes in equity. See Part (c) below.

[4] This amount is P Ltd's 80% share in the CU 4 200 growth of S Ltd's revaluation surplus balance since acquisition date to the beginning of the current year. This amount of CU 3 360 (4 200 × 80%) is added to the opening revaluation surplus balance of P Ltd to arrive at the group's opening revaluation surplus balance, which balance is reflected in the consolidated statement of changes in equity, in Part (c) below.

[5] This amount is the non-controlling interest's 20% share in the CU 4 200 post-acquisition growth in the revaluation surplus of S Ltd up to the beginning of the current year. This amount of CU 840 (4 200 × 20%) is added to the value of the non-controlling interest at acquisition as part of determining the non-controlling interest balance at the beginning of the year (see note 6 below), which opening balance is reflected in the consolidated statement of changes in equity. See Part (c) below.

[6] This amount represents the share of the non-controlling interest in the net assets (equity) of S Ltd at the beginning of the reporting period (beginning of the current year) and comprises the following:

		CU
• AT ACQUISITION interest in S Ltd's equity (see note 1 above)		19 720
PLUS		
• 20% share of S Ltd's POST-ACQUISITION reserves to the beginning of the year:		
	CU	
▪ Retained earnings (see note 3 above)	2 150	
▪ Revaluation surplus (see note 5 above)	840	2 990
	Total	**22 710**

This amount is reported in the consolidated statement of changes in equity as the **opening balance** of the **non-controlling interest** (see consolidated statement of changes in equity in Part (c) below).

[7] This amount is P Ltd's 80% share of the CU 10 450 current year profit of S Ltd. This CU 8 360 (10 450 × 80%) profit of S Ltd, allocated to P Ltd, is added to P Ltd's current year profit (as adjusted for the intragroup dividend elimination) to determine the consolidated profit for the year attributable to the owners of P Ltd, as reflected in the consolidated statement of profit or loss and other comprehensive income, in Part (c) below.

[8] This amount is the non-controlling interest's 20% share of S Ltd's current year profit of CU 10 450. In the consolidated statement of profit or loss and other comprehensive income, this CU 2 090 (10 450 × 20%) amount is reflected as the consolidated profit for the year attributable to the non-controlling interest. (See consolidated statement of profit or loss and other comprehensive income in Part (c) below.)

9   This amount is P Ltd's 80% share of S Ltd's CU 3 000 other comprehensive income (i.e., S Ltd's revaluation gain on property, plant and equipment) for the current year. This amount of CU 2 400 (3 000 × 80%) when combined with P Ltd's CU 5 000 other comprehensive income and the consolidated profit attributable to P Ltd's owners (see note 7 above) results in the total comprehensive income for the year attributable to the owners of P Ltd, as reflected in the consolidated statement of profit or loss and other comprehensive income, in Part (c) below.

10 This amount is the non-controlling interest's 20% share of S Ltd's CU 3 000 other comprehensive income for the year. This amount of CU 600 (3 000 × 20%) is added to the CU 2 090 consolidated profit attributable to the non-controlling interest (see note 8 above) to obtain the CU 2 690 total comprehensive income for the year attributable to the non-controlling interest, as reflected in the consolidated statement of profit or loss and other comprehensive income, in Part (c) below.

11 The total dividend of CU 5 000 paid by S Ltd to P Ltd and to the non-controlling interest is eliminated in full on consolidation. The CU 4 000 represents the dividend received by P Ltd from S Ltd and is eliminated on consolidation as it is an intragroup transaction. The remaining CU 1 000 received by the non-controlling interest from S Ltd reduces the non-controlling interest equity balance at year end. This is because the non-controlling interest's share in the equity of S Ltd decreases by the CU 1 000 distribution of S Ltd's equity to it by way of a dividend. Consequently, this CU 1 000 dividend is reflected in the consolidated statement of changes in equity as a deduction in the non-controlling interest column. See consolidated statement of changes in equity in Part (c) below.

12 This amount is the closing non-controlling interest balance at reporting period end and represents the non-controlling interest's share of the subsidiary's total equity (both pre and post acquisition) at reporting period end. As a check, this amount must agree with the closing non-controlling interest balance as per the consolidated statement of changes in equity in Part (c) below.

Part (b): Pro forma journal entries for the 20x8 financial year
AT ACQUISITION

Pro forma journal 1 (J1)	Dr CU	Cr CU
Share capital (S Ltd) (SCIE) (given)	80 000	
Retained earnings (S Ltd) (SCIE) (given)	13 800	
Revaluation surplus (S Ltd) (SCIE) (given)	4 800	
Goodwill (SFP) (balancing figure)	16 120	
Investment in S Ltd (P Ltd) (SFP) (given)		95 000
Non-controlling interest – Equity (SFP)		Wkg1 19 720
Elimination of common items and recognition of non-controlling interest and goodwill		

Working: Pro forma journals
Working 1

(80 000 Share capital + 13 800 Retained earnings + 4 800 Revaluation surplus) × 20% NCI Share

Comments: Pro forma journal 1

- This pro forma journal is the 'usual' at acquisition elimination journal of common amounts, where any goodwill or gain on bargain purchase is recognised. Note that the at acquisition equity of the subsidiary, S Ltd, includes all the equity reserves of S Ltd. In this example, the revaluation surplus of S Ltd, which comprises a portion of S Ltd's at acquisition equity, is also eliminated together with S Ltd's retained earnings and share capital.

- As we are dealing with a partly held subsidiary we need to recognise the non-controlling interest's share of S Ltd's at acquisition equity. In this case the 'partial goodwill method' applies. Consequently, the non-controlling interest at acquisition date is recognised at its proportionate share of S Ltd's identifiable net assets, with no goodwill attributable to the non-controlling interest.

- Note that we are dealing with a reporting period after acquisition date (in fact two years thereafter). As pro forma journals are not recognised in the separate accounting records of S Ltd and P Ltd we are required to repeat this at acquisition elimination journal every reporting period that we prepare consolidated financial statements.

SINCE ACQUISITION TO BEGINNING OF THE YEAR

Pro forma journal 2 (J2)	Dr CU	Cr CU
Retained earnings (S Ltd) (SCIE)	Wkg2 2 150	
Non-controlling interest – Equity (SFP)		Wkg2 2 150
Allocating the non-controlling interest its share of S Ltd's post-acquisition retained earnings to the beginning of the year		

Workings: Pro forma journals

Working 2

(24 550 Balance BOY – 13 800 Balance at acquisition) × 20% NCI Share

Comments: Pro forma journal 2

- 20% of the CU 10 750 increase in S Ltd's retained earnings balance, from acquisition date to the beginning of the current year, is allocated to the non-controlling interest by:

  - debiting and so reducing S Ltd's post-acquisition retained earnings to the beginning of the year, attributable to P Ltd; and

  - crediting the non-controlling interest balance in the consolidated statement of financial position and so increasing the non-controlling interest's share of S Ltd's equity.

- S Ltd's retained earnings balance that remains after processing pro forma journal 1 (elimination of the at acquisition retained earnings of S Ltd) and pro forma journal 2 (allocation to the non-controlling interest of 20% of S Ltd's post-acquisition retained earnings to BOY), is P Ltd's 80% share of the increase in the retained earnings of S Ltd from acquisition to the beginning of the current year.

Pro forma journal 3 (J3)	Dr CU	Cr CU
Revaluation surplus (S Ltd) (SCIE)	Wkg3 840	
Non-controlling interest – Equity (SFP)		Wkg3 840
Allocating the non-controlling interest its share of S Ltd's post-acquisition revaluation surplus to the beginning of the year		

Working: Pro forma journals

Working 3

(9 000 Balance BOY – 4 800 Balance at acquisition) × 20% NCI Share

Comments: Pro forma journal 3

- The non-controlling interest shares in the post-acquisition movement of all the reserves of the subsidiary, not only retained earnings. Accordingly, and in similar manner to pro forma journal 2, the non-controlling interest must be allocated its 20% share of the CU 4 200 post-acquisition movement in S Ltd's revaluation surplus up to the beginning of the current year. This amount is allocated to the non-controlling interest by:

- debiting and so reducing S Ltd's post-acquisition revaluation surplus to the beginning of the year, which is attributable to P Ltd; and

- crediting the non-controlling interest balance in the consolidated statement of financial position and so increasing the non-controlling interest's share of S Ltd's equity.

- After processing pro forma journal 1 (elimination of S Ltd's at acquisition revaluation surplus) and pro forma journal 3 (allocation to the non-controlling interest of 20% of S Ltd's post-acquisition revaluation surplus to BOY), the revaluation surplus balance of S Ltd that remains is the 80% share of the increase in S Ltd's revaluation surplus since acquisition up to the beginning of the current year, which is attributable to P Ltd.

CURRENT YEAR

Pro forma journal 4 (J4)	Dr CU	Cr CU
NCI – Share of profit or loss (P/L)	Wkg42 090	
Non-controlling interest – Equity (SFP)		Wkg42 090
Allocating the non-controlling interest its share of S Ltd's current year profit		

Working: Pro forma journals

Working 4

10 450 Current year profit × 20% NCI Share

Comments: Pro forma journal 4

- For the current reporting period, the non-controlling interest must be allocated its 20% share of S Ltd's current year profit. After processing this journal the remaining 80% of S Ltd's current year profit is the amount attributable to P Ltd.

Pro forma journal 5 (J5)	Dr CU	Cr CU
NCI – Share of other comprehensive income (OCI)	Wkg5600	
Non-controlling interest – Equity (SFP)		Wkg5600
Allocating to the non-controlling interest of its share of S Ltd's other comprehensive income for the year		

Working: Pro forma journals

Working 5

3 000 × 20%

Comments: Pro forma journal 5

- For the current reporting period, the non-controlling interest must be allocated its 20% share of S Ltd's current year other comprehensive income (the revaluation gain). After processing this journal, the remaining 80% of S Ltd's current year other comprehensive income is the amount attributable to P Ltd.

Pro forma journal 6 (J6)	Dr CU	Cr CU
Dividend received (P Ltd) (P/L) (given)	4 000	
Non-controlling interest – Equity (SFP)	Wkg6 1 000	
Dividend paid (S Ltd) (SCIE) (given)		5 000
Elimination of intragroup dividend and recognition of non-controlling interest in dividend		

Working: Pro forma journals

Working 6

Balancing figure **OR** 5 000 × 20% NCI Share

Comments: Pro forma journal 6

- The credit entry eliminates the CU 5 000 total dividend paid by S Ltd (4 000 to P Ltd and 1 000 to the non-controlling interest) in its entirety.
- In the first debit entry, the portion of the dividend received by P Ltd from S Ltd, of CU 4 000, which is an intragroup transaction, is eliminated against the CU 4 000 dividend paid by S Ltd to P Ltd.
- In the second debit entry, the CU 1 000 dividend received by the non-controlling interest from S Ltd, which reduces the non-controlling interest's equity interest in S Ltd by CU 1 000, is set off against the CU 1000 dividend paid by S Ltd to the non-controlling interest.

The full effects of the preceding pro forma journals on the consolidated financial statements of the P Ltd group are shown in the following consolidation worksheet as at 31 December 20x8.

	P Ltd Dr/(Cr) CU	S Ltd Dr/(Cr) CU	Pro forma journals At acquisition Dr/(Cr) CU	Journal ref	Pro forma journals Since acquisition Dr/(Cr) CU	Journal ref	Consolidated Dr/(Cr) CU
Equity							
Share capital	(100 000)	(80 000)	80 000	J1			(100 000)
Retained earnings (BOY)	(42 020)	(24 550)	13 800	J1	2 150	J2	(50 620)
Profit: Individual entities	(11 480)	(10 450)					–
Consolidated profit attributable to owners of parent							†(15 840)
Dividend paid	8 500	5 000			(5 000)	J6	8 500
Retained earnings (EOY)	(45 000)	(30 000)					(57 960)
Revaluation surplus (BOY)	(13 000)	(9 000)	4 800	J1	840	J3	(16 360)
OCI: Individual entities	(5 000)	(3 000)					–
Consolidated OCI attributable to owners of parent							†(7 400)
Revaluation surplus (EOY)	(18 000)	(12 000)					(23 760)
NCI Equity	–	–	(19 720)	J1	(2 150)	J2	(24 400)
					(840)	J3	
					(2 090)	J4	
					(600)	J5	
					1 000	J6	
Total equity	**(163 000)**	**(122 000)**					**(206 120)**
Liabilities:							
Trade and other payables	(117 000)	(19 700)					(136 700)
Total liabilities	**(117 000)**	**(19 700)**					**(136 700)**
Total equity & liabilities	**(280 000)**	**(141 700)**					**(342 820)**

Explanatory notes

† This amount has been brought forward from the second part of the consolidation worksheet on page 175

	P Ltd Dr/(Cr) CU	S Ltd Dr/(Cr) CU	Pro forma journals At acquisition Dr/(Cr) CU	Journal ref	Pro forma journals Since acquisition Dr/(Cr) CU	Journal ref	Consolidated Dr/(Cr) CU
Assets:							
Property plant and equipment	41 500	70 000					111 500
Investment in S Ltd	95 000	–	(95 000)	J1			–
Trade and other receivables	143 500	71 700					215 200
Goodwill	–	–	16 120	J1			16 120
Total assets	**280 000**	**141 700**					**342 820**
Profit or loss							
Operating profit	(15 180)	(15 950)					(31 130)
Dividend received	(4 000)	–			4000	J6	–
Taxation	7 700	5 500					13 200
Net profit	(11 480)	(10 450)					(17 930)
NCI: Share of profit					2090	J4	2090
Consolidated profit attributable to owners of parent							‡(15 840)
Other comprehensive income (OCI)							
Fair value gain on PPE (OCI)	(5 000)	(3 000)					(8 000)
NCI: Share of OCI					600	J5	600
Consolidated OCI attributable to owners of parent	–	–					‡(7 400)

Explanatory notes

‡ This amount has been carried forward to the first part of the consolidation worksheet on page 174

Part (c): Consolidated financial statements for the year ended 31 December 20x8

P LTD GROUP: ABRIDGED CONSOLIDATED STATEMENT OF PROFIT OR LOSS AND OTHER COMPREHENSIVE INCOME FOR THE YEAR ENDED 31 DECEMBER 20X8	
	CU
Profit before tax	31 130
(P Ltd: 19 180 – 4 000 (see AOE **k OR** (J6) Elimination of intragroup dividend)	
Income tax expense (7 700 (P Ltd) + 5 500 (S Ltd))	(13 200)
PROFIT FOR THE YEAR	**17 930**
Other comprehensive income	
Revaluation gain – PPE (5 000 (P Ltd) + 3 000 (S Ltd))	8 000
Other comprehensive income for the year, net of tax	8 000
TOTAL COMPREHENSIVE INCOME FOR THE YEAR	**25 930**
Profit for the year attributable to:	
Owners of the parent (balancing figure)	15 840
Non-controlling interest (see AOE **h OR** (J4))	2 090
	17 930
Total comprehensive income for the year attributable to:	
Owners of the parent (balancing figure)	23 240
Non-controlling interest	2 690
(2 090 Net profit + 600 Revaluation gain (see AOE **j OR** (J5)))	
	25 930

P LTD GROUP: CONSOLIDATED STATEMENT OF CHANGES IN EQUITY FOR THE YEAR ENDED 31 DECEMBER 20x8						
	Parent equity holders' interest				Non-controlling interest	Total equity of the group
	Share capital	Retained earnings	Revaluation surplus	Total parent equity		
	CU	CU	CU	CU	CU	CU
Opening balance at 1 Jan 20x8	100 000	Wkg1 50 620	Wkg2 16 360	166 980	Wkg3 22 710	189 690
Total comprehensive income:						
Profit for the period (from CSOPL_OCI)	–	15 840	–	15 840	2090	17 930
Other comprehensive income			Wkg4 7 400	7 400	Wkg5 600	8 000
Dividends	–	(8 500)		(8 500)	Wkg6 (1 000)	(9 500)
Closing balance at 31 Dec 20x8	100 000	57 960	23 760	181 720	24 400	206 120

Workings: Consolidated statement of changes

Working 1

P Ltd: 42 020 + S Ltd: 8 600 (see AOE **b**) P Ltd's 80% Share of the post-acquisition retained earnings to BOY of S Ltd

OR

P Ltd: 42 020 + (S Ltd: 24 550 Balance BOY – 13 800 (J1) Balance at acquisition – 2 150 (J2) NCI 20% Share of post-acquisition retained earnings to BOY of S Ltd)

Working 2

P Ltd: 13 000 + S Ltd: 3 360 (see AOE **d**) P Ltd's 80% Share of post-acquisition revaluation surplus to BOY of S Ltd

OR

P Ltd: 13 000 + (S Ltd: 9 000 Balance BOY – 4 800 (J1) Balance at acquisition – 840 (J2) NCI 20% Share of post-acquisition revaluation surplus to BOY of S Ltd)

Working 3

S Ltd: 22 710 (see AOE **f**)

OR

S Ltd: 19 720 (J1) NCI 20% Share of S Ltd at acquisition equity + 2 150 (J2) NCI 20% Share of S Ltd's post-acquisition retained earnings to BOY + 840 (J3) NCI 20% Share of S Ltd's post-acquisition revaluation surplus to BOY

Working 4

P Ltd: 5 000 + S Ltd: 2 400 (see AOE **i**) P Ltd's 80% Share of revaluation gain (OCI) of S Ltd

OR

P Ltd: 5 000 + (S Ltd: 3 000 Revaluation gain (OCI) – 600 (J5) NCI 20% Share of revaluation gain (OCI) of S Ltd)

Working 5

S Ltd: 600 (see AOE **j OR** (J5)) NCI 20% Share of revaluation gain (OCI) of S Ltd

Working 6

S Ltd: 1 000 (see AOE **l OR** (J6)) S Ltd dividend paid to the NCI

P LTD GROUP: CONSOLIDATED STATEMENT OF FINANCIAL POSITION AS AT 31 DECEMBER 20x8	
	CU
Assets	
Non-current assets	
Property, plant and equipment (41 500 (P Ltd) + 70 000 (S Ltd))	111 500
Goodwill (see AOE **a OR** (J1))	16 120
Current assets	
Trade and other receivables (143 500 (P Ltd) + 71 700 (S Ltd))	215 200
Total assets	**324 820**
Equity and liabilities	
Equity attributable to owners of the parent	
Share capital (from CSCIE)	100 000
Retained earnings (from CSCIE)	57 960
Revaluation surplus (from CSCIE)	23 760
Equity attributable to owners of the parent	181 720

P LTD GROUP: CONSOLIDATED STATEMENT OF FINANCIAL POSITION AS AT 31 DECEMBER 20x8 (continued)	
	CU
Non-controlling interest (from CSCIE **OR** see AOE **m**)	24 400
Total equity	206 120
Current liabilities	
Trade and other payables (117 000 (P Ltd) + 19 700 (S Ltd))	136 700
Total equity and liabilities	**324 820**

Comments: Consolidated statement of financial position

- Note how the consolidated statement of financial position above includes **100% of the assets and liabilities** of S Ltd, which demonstrates that P Ltd has **control** over 100% of the net assets of its subsidiary, S Ltd.

- Note further the **split** of the total shareholder's equity between the **owners of the parent** and the **non-controlling interest**. This split reflects the fact that there are **two categories of owners** of the net assets (equity) of S Ltd, namely the **shareholders of the parent** and the **non-controlling interest.**

4.2.6 Subsequent impairment of goodwill in the consolidated financial statements

In Volume 1 Chapter 2 it was explained that subsequent to initial recognition, goodwill acquired in a business combination must be tested for possible impairment at least annually in accordance with IAS 36 *Impairment of Assets*.

Any goodwill that arises in a business combination that results in a **parent subsidiary relationship**, exists **only** in the **consolidated financial statements**. This is because such goodwill is recognised as part of the **at acquisition pro forma consolidation journal passed** in which common items are eliminated and a non-controlling interest is recognised if a partly owned subsidiary has been acquired.

In other words, the pro forma journal recognising goodwill is passed **only for consolidation purposes** and affects **neither** the separate financial statements of the parent nor the individual financial statements of the subsidiary. It follows that any **subsequent impairment of this goodwill** is accounted for only at the level of the **group**, that is, **only when preparing** the **consolidated financial statements.**

4.2.6.1 Testing goodwill for impairment

In accordance with IAS 36, goodwill acquired in a business combination must be allocated to each of the acquirer's **cash-generating units** that are **expected to benefit from the synergies of the business combination** (IAS 36.80). An **impairment loss** is recognised when the **carrying amount** of a **cash generating unit exceeds its recoverable amount.** In a **group scenario**, where the **subsidiary** is the **cash-generating unit**, both the carrying amount and the recoverable amount of the subsidiary must include the identifiable net assets of the subsidiary and the goodwill allocated thereto, this being the goodwill attributable to **both** the parent and the non-controlling interest.

If the non-controlling interest is measured at its proportionate share of the identifiable net assets of the subsidiary, rather than at its fair value, then the **goodwill attributable to the non-controlling interest will be included in the recoverable amount** of the cash-generating unit subsidiary, but will *not* have been included in the **carrying amount** of the cash-generating unit subsidiary as this goodwill will not have been recognised in the consolidated financial statements.

To be consistent, the carrying value of the assets of the cash-generating unit subsidiary, that is tested for impairment, must include the assets attributable to **100%** of the **shareholding** in the subsidiary. Accordingly, we must **gross up** the **carrying amount** of the **goodwill** to what it would be if the **non-controlling interest's share thereof** was **also recognised**, to determine the **adjusted carrying amount** of the cash-generating unit subsidiary. This adjusted carrying amount is then compared to the cash-generating unit subsidiary's recoverable amount. For example, if the consolidated statement of financial position reflects goodwill of CU 80 000, which is solely attributable to the parent's 80% interest in a subsidiary, the notional amount attributable to the non-controlling interest will be CU 20 000 (80 000 × 20% / 80%) and the total goodwill amount will be CU 100 000 (80 000 × 100% / 80%). This CU 100 000 goodwill is then added to the other assets of the cash-generating unit subsidiary to arrive at its carrying amount for the purposes of doing the impairment test.

If the non-controlling interest is measured at its **fair value**, then the consolidated financial statements already **include the total goodwill** (i.e., the goodwill attributable to the parent and the goodwill attributable to the non-controlling interest). Consequently, goodwill does *not* need to be grossed up before being included as part of the carrying amount of the cash-generating unit subsidiary.

4.2.6.2 Allocating the impairment loss

An **impairment loss** calculated in respect of a **cash-generating unit subsidiary** is (IAS 36 Appendix C.5):

- **first allocated** to **reduce** the carrying amount of the **goodwill** of the subsidiary; and
- thereafter, any **remainder** is **allocated** to the **other assets** of the subsidiary, **pro rata**, based on the **carrying amount** of each asset of the subsidiary.

In addition, the impairment loss is allocated **between** the **parent** and the **non-controlling interest** on the **same basis** as that on which **profit or loss is allocated**, which ordinarily is the **percentage ownership interest** in the **subsidiary** held by the **parent** and the **non-controlling interest** respectively (IAS 36 Appendix C.6).

When the non-controlling interest is measured at its **proportionate share** of the **identifiable net assets** of the **subsidiary**, only the impairment loss relating to goodwill that is **allocated to the parent** is recognised as a goodwill impairment loss in the consolidated financial statements (IAS 36 Appendix C.8). In other words, the goodwill impairment attributable to the non-controlling interest is **not** recognised. This makes sense as no goodwill was ever attributed to the non-controlling interest so any reduction in the value of this 'notional goodwill' cannot be included at group level. That is, goodwill is **only grossed up** for purposes of establishing if the cash-generating unit subsidiary was **impaired**, *not* for purposes of **quantifying** the **goodwill impairment expense to be recognised.**

Example 4.4: Impairment of goodwill: Partly owned subsidiary and partial goodwill method used

P Ltd acquired 80% and control over S Ltd for CU 1 700 000 on 1 January 20x5. At that date S Ltd's identifiable net assets had a fair value of CU 1 800 000. At reporting period end, 31 December 20x5, P Ltd determines that the recoverable amount of cash-generating unit S Ltd is CU 1 850 000. The carrying amount of the net assets of S Ltd, excluding goodwill, is CU 1 640 000 on 31 December 20x5.

P Ltd measures the non-controlling interest at its proportionate share of the identifiable net assets of S Ltd.

Required

(a) Calculate the amount of goodwill that arises in this business combination at acquisition date.

(b) Determine the amount of the impairment loss that should be recognised in the consolidated financial statements of the P Ltd group for the reporting period ended 31 December 20x5.

(c) Provide the pro forma journal entry to record the impairment loss in the consolidated financial statements of the P Ltd group for the reporting period ended 31 December 20x5.

(d) Provide the pro forma journal entries to record the impairment losses in the consolidated financial statements of the P Ltd group for the reporting period ended 31 December 20x6, assuming that goodwill was impaired by an additional amount of CU 50 000 in the 20x6 reporting period. Furthermore, assume that this CU 50 000 is attributable to the goodwill allocated to P Ltd, that is, it is the actual impairment expense recognised.

Solution 4.4: Impairment of goodwill: Partly owned subsidiary and partial goodwill method used

Part (a): Goodwill arising on acquisition date – partial goodwill method

	Total of S Ltd's equity 100%	P Ltd at acquisition 80%	Non-controlling interest 20%
At acquisition date (1 January 20x5)	CU	CU	CU
Fair value of net assets of S Ltd	1 800 000	1 440 000	360 000
Goodwill – Parent (balancing figure)	260 000	260 000	–
Consideration and non-controlling interest	2 060 000	1 700 000	360 000

At acquisition, goodwill recognised amounts to **CU 260 000** and is wholly attributable to P Ltd.

➠

Part (b): Determination of impairment loss for the reporting period ended 31 December 20x5

	Goodwill of subsidiary CU	Identifiable net assets CU	Total CU
Carrying amount	260 000	1 640 000	1 900 000
Unrecognised non-controlling interest: Notional goodwill (260 000 × 20% / 80%)	65 000	–	65 000
Adjusted carrying amount	325 000	1 640 000	1 965 000
Recoverable amount			(1 850 000)
Impairment			115 000

Note: As the recoverable amount of the subsidiary is below its carrying amount, an impairment loss arises. As discussed above, the impairment loss is first allocated to goodwill, with any excess amount remaining allocated to the subsidiary's identifiable net assets. In this case, as the impairment amount of CU 115 000 is less than total goodwill of CU 325 000, all of the impairment loss is allocated against the carrying amount of goodwill.

Furthermore, because goodwill is recognised in the consolidated financial statements only to the extent of P Ltd's ownership interest in S Ltd (i.e., the partial goodwill method applies), P Ltd, in the consolidated financial statements, recognises **only 80%** of the total goodwill impairment of CU 115 000. Consequently, a **CU 92 000** (115 000 × 80%) impairment loss is recognised as an expense in the consolidated financial statements, which relates only to P Ltd's goodwill (i.e., no impairment loss is recognised in respect of the CU 65 000 notional goodwill determined for the non-controlling interest).

Part (c): Pro forma journal entry recognising the impairment loss in the consolidated financial statements for the 20x5 reporting period

Pro forma journal CURRENT YEAR	Dr CU	Cr CU
Impairment loss (P/L) (see Part (b))	92 000	
Goodwill: Accumulated impairment loss (SFP)		92 000
Recognition of impairment of goodwill in the current period		

Part (d): Pro forma journal entry recognising the impairment losses in the consolidated financial statements for the 20x6 reporting period

Pro forma journal SINCE ACQUISITION TO BEGINNING OF YEAR/CURRENT YEAR	Dr CU	Cr CU
Retained earnings (SCIE) (see Part (b))	92 000	
Impairment loss (P/L) (given)	50 000	
Goodwill: Accumulated impairment loss (SFP) (balancing figure)		142 000
Recognition of impairment of goodwill in prior and current periods		

Comments: Pro forma journal

- In the prior year (i.e., the 20x5 year) on consolidation, the impairment loss of CU 92 000 was recognised, via a pro forma journal, in P Ltd's prior year profit or loss, which was closed off to retained earnings at prior year end. That is, the prior year closing consolidated retained earnings balance included (was reduced by) the prior year CU 92 000 impairment loss.

- However, because pro forma journals are not carried forward to subsequent reporting periods, P Ltd's opening retained earnings balance will not include the effects of (i.e., will not have been reduced by) the prior year impairment loss recognised for consolidation purposes.
- Consequently, for consolidation purposes in the current (i.e., the 20x6) financial year, P Ltd's opening retained earnings balance must be adjusted (decreased) to include the effects of the prior year impairment loss recognised on consolidation. This is achieved by debiting (and so reducing) P Ltd's opening retained earnings with the CU 92 000 prior year impairment loss. This ensures that the opening consolidated retained earnings balance of the current year agrees to the closing consolidated retained earnings of the prior year.

Example 4.5: Impairment of goodwill: Partly owned subsidiary and full goodwill method used

The facts are exactly the same as in Example 4.4, except that the parent elects to measure non-controlling interest at its fair value of CU 400 000 at acquisition date.

Required

(a) Calculate the amount of goodwill that arises in this business combination at acquisition date.

(b) Determine the amount of the impairment loss that should be recognised in the consolidated financial statements of the P Ltd group for the reporting period ended 31 December 20x5.

(c) Provide the pro forma journal entries to record the impairment loss in the consolidated financial statements of the P Ltd group for the reporting period ended 31 December 20x5.

(d) Provide the pro forma journal entries to record the impairment losses in the consolidated financial statements of the P Ltd group for the reporting period ended 31 December 20x6, assuming that goodwill was impaired by an additional amount of CU 50 000 in the 20x6 reporting period.

Solution 4.5: Impairment of goodwill: Partly owned subsidiary and full goodwill method used

Part (a): Goodwill arising on acquisition date – full goodwill method

	Total of S Ltd's equity 100%	P Ltd at acquisition 80%	Non-controlling interest 20%
At acquisition date (1 January 20x5)	CU	CU	CU
Fair value of net assets of S Ltd	1 800 000	1 440 000	360 000
Goodwill – Parent (balancing figure)	260 000	260 000	–
Goodwill – NCI (balancing figure)	40 000	–	40 000
Consideration and non-controlling interest	2 100 000	1 700 000	400 000

Total goodwill of **CU 300 000** (260 000 Goodwill parent + 40 000 Non-controlling interest) arises on acquisition.

Part (b): Determination of impairment loss for the reporting period ended 31 December 20x5

	Goodwill of subsidiary CU	Identifiable net assets CU	Total CU
Carrying amount	300 000	1 640 000	1 940 000
Recoverable amount			(1 850 000)
Impairment loss			90 000

Note: As the recoverable amount of the subsidiary is below its carrying amount, an impairment loss arises. The impairment loss of CU 90 000 is less than the total goodwill of CU 300 000; accordingly all of the impairment loss is allocated against the carrying amount of goodwill and none against the subsidiary's identifiable net assets.

The impairment loss is allocated based on the respective ownership interests in the subsidiary of the parent, P Ltd, and the non-controlling interest. Consequently the CU 90 000 impairment loss is allocated as follows:

- P Ltd: CU 90 000 × 80% = CU 72 000

- Non-controlling interest: CU 90 000 × 20% = CU 18 000

Part (c): Pro forma journal entries recognising the impairment loss in the consolidated financial statements for the 20x5 reporting period

Pro forma journal 1 (J1) CURRENT YEAR	Dr CU	Cr CU
Impairment loss (P/L) (see Part (b))	90 000	
Goodwill: Accumulated impairment loss (SFP)		90 000
Recognition of impairment of goodwill in the current period		

Pro forma journal 2 (J2) CURRENT YEAR	Dr CU	Cr CU
Non-controlling interest – Equity (SFP)	Wkg1 18 000	
Non-controlling interest – Share of profit or loss (P/L)		Wkg1 18 000
Allocating the non-controlling interest its share of the current period impairment loss		

Workings: Pro forma journals

Working 1
90 000 (J1) × 20% NCI Share

Part (d): Pro forma journal entries recognising the impairment losses in the consolidated financial statements for the 20x6 reporting period

Pro forma journal 1 (J1) SINCE ACQUISITION TO BEGINNING OF THE YEAR	Dr CU	Cr CU
Retained earnings (SCIE) (see Part (b))	90 000	
Goodwill: Accumulated impairment loss (SFP)		90 000
Recognition of impairment of goodwill in prior periods		

Pro forma journal 2 (J2) SINCE ACQUISITION TO BEGINNING OF THE YEAR	Dr CU	Cr CU
Non-controlling interest – Equity (SFP)	Wkg1 18 000	
Retained earnings (SCIE)		Wkg1 18 000
Allocating the non-controlling interest its share of the prior period impairment loss		

⟳➡

Workings: Pro forma journals

Working 1

90 000 (J1) × 20% NCI Share

Pro forma journal 3 (J3) CURRENT YEAR	Dr CU	Cr CU
Impairment loss (P/L) (given)	50 000	
Goodwill: Accumulated impairment loss (SFP)		50 000
Recognition of impairment of goodwill in current period		

Pro forma journal 4 (J4) CURRENT YEAR	Dr CU	Cr CU
Non-controlling interest – Equity (SFP)	^{Wkg2}10 000	
Non-controlling interest – Share of profit or loss (P/L)		^{Wkg2}10 000
Allocating the non-controlling interest its share of the current period impairment loss		

Working 2

50 000 (J2) × 20% NCI Share

4.2.7 Consolidation of loss-making subsidiaries

So far, the examples in this publication concerning wholly owned and partly owned subsidiaries have always dealt with subsidiaries that have **retained earnings** at **acquisition date** and that make **profits subsequently**. Situations do, however, arise where a subsidiary acquired has an **accumulated loss** (i.e., **negative retained earnings**) **at acquisition** and/or **makes losses subsequent to acquisition**. Nevertheless, the basic consolidation procedures and principles remain the same irrespective of whether we are dealing with a profit- or a loss-making subsidiary.

4.2.7.1 Insolvent subsidiary acquired

A subsidiary is technically insolvent at acquisition date in circumstances where it has an equity deficit (i.e., its accumulated loss exceeds its share capital and other reserves). If we apply the accounting equation Equity = Assets – Liabilities, then this equity deficit also means that the subsidiary's liabilities exceed its assets.

A parent would naturally need to have a good reason to acquire a controlling interest in an insolvent subsidiary. It could be that the parent believes that the adverse financial condition of the subsidiary is only temporary and that the subsidiary, with the resources and support of the group, could be transformed into a profitable enterprise. Another reason could be that the subsidiary has an assessed/calculated loss for tax purposes that could be taken advantage of to reduce/eliminate any tax liability of the subsidiary that may arise in future years. (The implications for consolidation of acquiring a subsidiary with a tax loss are dealt with in Section 4.2.7.2.)

At **acquisition date** the **parent's share** of the **equity deficit** of an insolvent subsidiary would be **eliminated** against its **investment in the subsidiary**. Additionally, the insolvent position of the subsidiary may result in a **negative (deficit)** balance being recognised for the **non-controlling interest** at **acquisition date**. Although the non-controlling interest would ordinarily not be responsible to make good any such deficit of a subsidiary, the fact that the non-controlling interest meets the definition of equity as per the *Conceptual Framework for Financial Reporting* means that the non-controlling interest participates proportionately in the risks and rewards of the investment in the subsidiary. Consequently, any **negative total comprehensive income** will be attributed to the **non-controlling interest,** even if it results in the non-controlling interest having a **deficit (negative) balance** (IFRS 10.B94).

As with any other acquisition, when an interest is acquired in an insolvent subsidiary we need to establish whether any difference in the consideration paid by the parent and the underlying net asset value of the subsidiary is attributable to any specific asset (which may be under- or overvalued in the subsidiary's records) or if it constitutes goodwill or a gain on bargain purchase.

The profits of an insolvent subsidiary earned after acquisition date will usually be treated as distributable profits in the consolidated financial statements.

Example 4.6: Consolidation of a partly owned subsidiary which is insolvent at acquisition date

The following are the condensed financial statements of P Ltd and its subsidiary S Ltd for the financial year ended 31 December 20x7:

STATEMENTS OF FINANCIAL POSITION AS AT 31 DECEMBER 20x7	P Ltd CU	S Ltd CU
Assets		
Property, plant and equipment	335 500	57 000
Investment in S Ltd: 48 000 Ordinary shares at cost	6 000	–
Trade and other receivables	104 000	34 000
Total assets	445 500	91 000
Equity and liabilities		
Share capital (100 000 P Ltd shares/60 000 S Ltd shares)	100 000	60 000
Retained earnings/(Accumulated loss)	285 000	(62 000)
Long-term liabilities	24 500	54 000
Trade and other payables	36 000	39 000
Total equity and liabilities	445 500	91 000

EXTRACT: STATEMENTS OF PROFIT OR LOSS AND OTHER COMPREHENSIVE INCOME FOR THE YEAR ENDED 31 DECEMBER 20x7	P Ltd CU	S Ltd CU
Profit for the year	9 500	6 000
Other comprehensive income	–	–
Total comprehensive income for the year	9 500	6 000

EXTRACT: STATEMENTS OF CHANGES IN EQUITY FOR THE YEAR ENDED 31 DECEMBER 20x7	Retained earnings/(Accumulated loss)	
	P Ltd CU	**S Ltd** CU
Balance at 1 Jan 20x7	280 500	(68 000)
Total comprehensive income:		
Profit for the year	9 500	6 000
Dividend paid	(5 000)	–
Balance at 31 Dec 20x7	285 000	(62 000)

Additional information

P Ltd acquired an 80% controlling interest in S Ltd on 1 January 20x6, on which date the accumulated loss of S Ltd amounted to CU 75 000. At acquisition date S Ltd's assets and liabilities were considered to be fairly valued.

P Ltd elected to measure the non-controlling interest of S Ltd at its proportionate share of S Ltd's identifiable net assets at acquisition date. Furthermore, goodwill was impaired by CU 13 000 at the end of the financial reporting period in which S Ltd was acquired. There was no further impairment of goodwill at the end of the 20x7 financial year.

P Ltd recognised its investment in S Ltd in its separate financial statements using the cost price method.

Required

(a) Prepare the analysis of equity of S Ltd as at 31 December 20x7.

(b) Provide all the pro forma journal entries necessary to prepare the consolidated financial statements of the P Ltd group for the financial year ended 31 December 20x7.

(c) Prepare the consolidated statement of profit or loss and other comprehensive income as well as the consolidated statement of changes in equity for the P Ltd group for the financial year ended 31 December 20x7.

Solution 4.6: Consolidation of a partially owned subsidiary which is insolvent at acquisition date

Part (a): Analysis of equity (AOE) of S Ltd as at 31 December 20x7

| | Total of S Ltd's equity 100% | P Ltd 80% | | Non-controlling interest 20% |
| | | At acquisition | Since acquisition | |
At acquisition date (1 January 20x6)	CU	CU	CU	CU
Share capital	60 000	48 000		12 000
Accumulated loss	(75 000)	(60 000)		(15 000)
Fair value of net assets of S Ltd	(15 000)	(12 000)		(3 000)
Goodwill – Parent (balancing)	18 000	18 000 **a**		–
Consideration and non-controlling interest	3 000	6 000		(3 000)
Since acquisition				
• To beginning of current year:				
Reduction in accumulated loss	Wkg1 7 000		5 600 **b**	1 400 **c**
				(1 600) **d**
• Profit for the year	6 000		4 800 **e**	1 200 **f**
	16 000		10 400	(400) **g**

Workings: Analysis of equity

Working 1

–68 000 Accumulated loss BOY – (–75 000 Accumulated loss at acquisition)

CHECK: IFRS 3.32 – Goodwill calculation

Consideration transferred	6 000
Add: Non-controlling interest	(3 000)
Subtotal	3 000
Minus: Identifiable net assets	–(15 000)
Goodwill	**18 000**

Part (b): Pro forma journal entries for the 20x7 financial year

AT ACQUISITION

	Dr	Cr
Pro forma journal 1 (J1)	CU	CU
Share capital (S Ltd) (SCIE) (given)	60 000	
Accumulated loss (S Ltd) (SCIE) (given)		75 000
Goodwill (SFP) (balancing figure)	18 000	
Investment in S Ltd (P Ltd) (SFP) (given)		6 000
Non-controlling interest – Equity (SFP)	Wkg1 3 000	
Elimination of common items and recognition of non-controlling interest and goodwill		

Workings: Pro forma journals

Working 1

(60 000 – 75 000) × 20% NCI Share

SINCE ACQUISITION TO BEGINNING OF THE YEAR

	Dr	Cr
Pro forma journal 2 (J2)	CU	CU
Accumulated loss (S Ltd) (SCIE)	Wkg2 1 400	
Non-controlling interest – Equity (SFP)		Wkg2 1 400
Allocating the non-controlling interest its share of the reduction in S Ltd's accumulated loss since acquisition to the beginning of the year		

Working 2

(–68 000 Balance BOY – (–75 000 Balance at acquisition)) × 20% NCI Share

	Dr	Cr
Pro forma journal 3 (J3)	CU	CU
Accumulated loss (SCIE) (given)	13 000	
Goodwill: Accumulated impairment loss (SFP)		13 000
Recognition of impairment of goodwill in respect of prior periods		

CURRENT YEAR

	Dr	Cr
Pro forma journal 4 (J4)	CU	CU
Non-controlling interest – Share of profit or loss (P/L)	Wkg3 1 200	
Non-controlling interest – Equity (SFP)		Wkg3 1 200
Allocating the non-controlling interest its share of S Ltd's profit for the year		

Working 3

6 000 × 20% NCI Share

The full effects of the preceding pro forma journals on the consolidated financial statements of the P Ltd group are shown in the following consolidation worksheet as at 31 December 20x7.

	P Ltd Dr/(Cr) CU	S Ltd Dr/(Cr) CU	Pro forma journals At acquisition Dr/(Cr) CU	Journal ref	Pro forma journals Since acquisition Dr/(Cr) CU	Journal ref	Consolidated Dr/(Cr) CU
Equity							
Share capital	(100 000)	(60 000)	60 000				(100 000)
Retained earnings (BOY)	(280 500)	68 000	(75 000)	J1	1 400	J2	†(273 100)
					13 000	J3	
Net profit: Individual entities	(9 500)	(6 000)					
Consolidated profit attributable to owners of parent							†(14 300)
Dividends paid	5 000	–					5 000
Retained earnings (EOY)	(285 000)	62 000					(282 400)
NCI Equity	–	–	3 000	J1	(1 400)	J2	400
	–	–			(1 200)	J4	
Total equity	(385 000)	2 000					(382 000)
Liabilities:							
Long-term liabilities	(24 500)	(54 000)					(78 500)
Trade and other payables	(36 000)	(39 000)					(75 000)
Total liabilities	(60 500)	(93 000)					(153 500)
Total equity & liabilities	(445 500)	(91 000)					(535 500)

Explanatory notes

† This amount has been brought forward from the second part of the consolidation worksheet on page 189

	P Ltd Dr/(Cr) CU	S Ltd Dr/(Cr) CU	Pro forma journals At acquisition Dr/(Cr) CU	Journal ref	Pro forma journals Since acquisition Dr/(Cr) CU	Journal ref	Con-solidated Dr/(Cr) CU
Assets:							
Property plant and equipment	335 500	57 000					392 500
Investment in S Ltd	6 000	–	(6 000)	J1			–
Trade and other receivables	104 000	34 000					138 000
Goodwill			18 000	J1			18 000
Accumulated impairment loss – Goodwill					(13 000)	J3	(13 000)
Total assets	**445 500**	**91 000**					**535 500**
Profit or loss							
Net profit	(9 500)	(6 000)					(15 500)
NCI: Share of profit					1200	J4	1200
Consolidated profit attributable to owners of parent							‡(14 300)

Explanatory notes

‡ This amount has been carried forward to the first part of the consolidation worksheet on page 188

Part (c): Consolidated financial statements for the 20x7 financial year

P LTD GROUP: ABRIDGED CONSOLIDATED STATEMENT OF PROFIT OR LOSS AND OTHER COMPREHENSIVE INCOME FOR THE YEAR ENDED 31 DECEMBER 20x3	
	CU
PROFIT FOR THE YEAR (9 500 (P Ltd) + 6 000 (S Ltd))	15 500
Other comprehensive income for the year	–
TOTAL COMPREHENSIVE INCOME FOR THE YEAR	**15 500**
Total comprehensive income for the year attributable to:	
Owners of the parent [(balancing figure) **OR** (9 500 (P Ltd) + S Ltd: 4 800 AOE **e**)]	14 300
Non-controlling interest (see AOE **f OR** (J4))	1 200
	15 500

P LTD GROUP: CONSOLIDATED STATEMENT OF CHANGES IN EQUITY FOR THE YEAR ENDED 31 DECEMBER 20x7					
	Parent equity holders' interest			Non-controlling interest	Total equity of the group
	Share capital	Retained earnings	Total parent equity		
	CU	CU	CU	CU	CU
Opening balance at 1 Jan 20x7	100 000	Wkg1 273 100	373 100	Wkg2 (1 600)	371 500
Total comprehensive income:					
Profit for the period (from CSOPL_OCI)	–	14 300	14 300	1 200	15 500
Dividend	–	(5 000)	(5 000)	–	(5 000)
Closing balance at 31 Dec 20x7	100 000	282 400	382 400	†(400)	382 000

Explanatory note

† Note that the non-controlling interest has a deficit balance at year end.

Workings: Consolidated statement of changes in equity

Working 1
(P Ltd: 280 500 – 13 000 (J3) Goodwill impairment) + (S Ltd: 5 600 (see AOE **b**) P Ltd share of S Ltd post-acquisition retained earnings to BOY (i.e., share of reduction in accumulated loss since acquisition to BOY of S Ltd))

OR

(P Ltd: 280 500 – 13 000 (J3) Goodwill impairment) + (S Ltd: –68 000 Balance BOY – (–75 000) (J1) Balance at acquisition + 1 400 (J2) NCI share of S Ltd post-acquisition retained earnings (i.e., share of reduction in S Ltd accumulated loss since acquisition to BOY))

Working 2
S Ltd: –1 600 (see AOE **d**)

OR

S Ltd: –3 000 (J1) NCI Share of S Ltd at acquisition equity + 1 400 (J2) NCI Share of S Ltd post-acquisition retained earnings (i.e., share of reduction in S Ltd accumulated loss since acquisition to BOY)

4.2.7.2 Subsidiary with accumulated loss acquired

A parent may acquire a **solvent** subsidiary, albeit that the subsidiary has an **accumulated loss** at **acquisition date**. That is, the value of share capital and other reserves of the subsidiary would exceed the accumulated loss. Accordingly, the subsidiary would have a positive equity value at acquisition, meaning that its assets would exceed its liabilities and it would be solvent.

Consolidating a subsidiary that has an accumulated loss at acquisition is no different to the situation where the subsidiary has retained income. That is, at acquisition we eliminate the subsidiary's equity against the cost of the investment in the subsidiary, with any difference recognised as goodwill or a bargain purchase gain. Given, however, that an accumulated loss has a **debit balance**, we would eliminate this component of equity by **crediting** the amount in the pro forma journal as opposed to the debit entry passed when eliminating at acquisition retained earnings (which has a credit balance).

An additional consideration when a subsidiary with an accumulated loss is acquired, is whether the subsidiary also has a **corresponding tax loss** in respect of which the **subsidiary** has recognised a **deferred tax asset**. An entity is required to recognise a **deferred tax asset at acquisition date** arising from the potential benefit of an **income tax loss carry forward** that the **subsidiary acquired** has, to the **extent** that it is **probable** that (IAS 12.44):

- this **temporary difference** will **reverse** in the **foreseeable future**; and
- **taxable profit** will be **available against which this temporary difference can be used.**

Simply put, only if it appears **likely** that the subsidiary will **generate future taxable income** against which it can **offset its tax loss**, do we **recognise** a **deferred tax asset** in respect of this tax loss.

It may well be that the subsidiary, in its own accounting records, does *not* recognise a deferred tax asset as it does not believe it probable that future taxable profits will be earned. The group, however, may believe that, due to the benefits of synergy arising from the business combination and – as was discussed in Section 4.2.7.1 – with the support of the group, the subsidiary will be returned to profitability. Consequently, in the consolidated financial statements a deferred tax asset is recognised at acquisition, which was *not* recognised by the subsidiary in its individual financial statements.

The effects in the consolidated financial statements of recognising at acquisition date, a deferred tax asset in respect of subsidiary's at acquisition tax loss, are as follows:

- **At acquisition date,** recognition of a deferred tax asset will **increase** the **net asset value (equity)** of the **subsidiary,** acquired which, in turn, will impact on the **amount of any goodwill** or **gain on bargain purchase** recognised by the group.
- **Subsequent to acquisition date,** each financial year as the subsidiary earns taxable profits against which the subsidiary's tax loss at acquisition is utilised, the **value of this deferred tax asset** will **reduce.** This **reduction** in the **subsidiary's deferred tax asset** each year will result in a **corresponding income tax expense** of the **subsidiary,** recognised each year in the **consolidated financial statements.**

Example 4.7: Recognition of deferred tax asset in respect of subsidiary's tax loss in the consolidated financial statements

P Ltd acquired an 80% controlling interest in S Ltd for CU 11 000 on 1 January 20x2. At acquisition date the equity of S Ltd consisted of share capital of CU 80 000 and an accumulated loss of CU 65 000. There was an equivalent tax loss of CU 65 000 in respect of which S Ltd had not recognised a deferred tax asset. P Ltd, however, believed that with the financial support of the group, S Ltd would in future be restored to profitability and accordingly recognised a deferred tax asset in respect of S Ltd's tax loss at acquisition of S Ltd.

P Ltd measured the non-controlling interest at its proportionate share of S Ltd's identifiable net assets, which, aside from the recognition of the deferred tax asset, were considered to be fairly valued. Furthermore, P Ltd recognised its investment in S Ltd in its separate financial statements using the cost price method.

The following are the condensed financial statements of P Ltd and its subsidiary S Ltd for the financial year ended 31 December 20x3:

STATEMENTS OF FINANCIAL POSITION AS AT 31 DECEMBER 20x3		
	P Ltd	**S Ltd**
	CU	CU
Assets		
Property, plant and equipment	335 500	57 000
Investment in S Ltd: 64 000 Ordinary shares	11 000	–
Trade and other receivables	104 000	38 000
Total assets	450 500	95 000
Equity and liabilities		
Share capital (100 000 P Ltd shares/80 000 S Ltd shares)	100 000	80 000
Retained earnings/(Accumulated loss)	285 000	(24 000)
Trade and other payables	65 500	39 000
Total equity and liabilities	450 500	95 000

EXTRACT: STATEMENTS OF CHANGES IN EQUITY FOR THE YEAR ENDED 31 DECEMBER 20x3		
	Retained earnings/(Accumulated loss)	
	P Ltd	**S Ltd**
	CU	CU
Balance at 1 Jan 20x3	280 500	(46 000)
Total comprehensive income:		
Profit for the year	9 500	22 000
Dividend paid	(5 000)	–
Balance at 31 Dec 20x3	285 000	(24 000)

Additional information

- Assume an income tax rate of 28% and that all accounting profit is fully taxable.
- Assume that there are no other temporary differences pertaining to S Ltd.

Required

(a) Prepare the analysis of equity of S Ltd as at 31 December 20x3.

(b) Provide all the pro forma journal entries necessary to prepare the consolidated financial statements of the P Ltd group for the financial year ended 31 December 20x3.

(c) Prepare the consolidated financial statements of the P Ltd group for the financial year ended 31 December 20x3.

 Solution 4.7: Recognition of deferred tax asset in respect of subsidiary's tax loss in the consolidated financial statements

Part (a): Analysis of equity (AOE) of S Ltd as at 31 December 20x3

| | Total of S Ltd's equity 100% | P Ltd 80% | | Non-controlling interest 20% |
| | | At acqui-sition | Since acqui-sition | |
At acquisition date (1 January 20x2)	CU	CU	CU	CU
Share capital	80 000	64 000		16 000
Accumulated loss	†(65 000)	(52 000)		(13 000)
Deferred tax asset (see Working 1)	†18 200 **a**	14 560		3 640
Fair value of net assets of S Ltd	33 200	26 560		6 640
Gain on bargain purchase (balancing figure)	(15 560)	(15 560) **b**		–
Consideration and non-controlling interest	17 640	11 000		6 640
Since acquisition				
• To beginning of current year:				
Adjusted accumulated loss:	13 680		10 944 **c**	2 736 **d**
Movement (see Working 2)	†19 000			
Prior year income tax expense: Deferred tax asset (DTA) utilised (see Working 3)	†(5 320) **i**			
				9 376 **e**
• Adjusted profit for the year	15 840		12 672 **f**	3 168 **g**
Profit before adjustments	†22 000			
Income tax expense (DTA utilised) (see Working 4)	†(6 160) **j**			
	47 160		23 616	12 544 **h**

Workings: Analysis of equity

Working 1
65 000 Tax loss × 28%

Working 2
–46 000 Balance BOY – (– 65 000 Balance at acquisition)

Working 3
19 000 Taxable profit × 28%

Working 4
22 000 Taxable profit × 28%

Explanatory notes

† Subsequent to acquisition, as S Ltd earns taxable profit each year, its at acquisition tax loss is offset against this taxable profit, which causes this tax loss to reduce in amount each year.

Explanatory notes (continued)

For group purposes, this causes a reversal each year – equal to the taxable profit for the year concerned – of a portion of the CU 65 000 deductible temporary difference that arose at acquisition in respect of S Ltd's CU 65 000 tax loss.

For consolidation purposes, this results in a reduction each year of a portion of S Ltd's CU 18 200 deferred tax asset recognised at acquisition in respect of S Ltd's tax loss. This reduction each year in S Ltd's CU 18 200 deferred tax asset, causes a corresponding income tax expense of S Ltd, recognised each year in the consolidated financial statements.

CHECK: IFRS 3.32 and IFRS 3.34 Bargain purchase gain calculation

Consideration transferred	11 000
Add: Non-controlling interest	6 640
Subtotal	17 640
Minus: Identifiable net assets	(33 200)
Gain on bargain purchase	**(15 560)**

Part (b): Pro forma journal entries for the 20x3 financial year

AT ACQUISITION

Pro forma journal 1 (J1)	Dr CU	Cr CU
Share capital (S Ltd) (SCIE) (given)	80 000	
Accumulated loss (S Ltd) (SCIE) (given)		65 000
Deferred tax asset (S Ltd) (SFP)	Wkg1 18 200	
Gain on bargain purchase (P Ltd) (P/L) (balancing figure)		15 560
Investment in S Ltd (P Ltd) (SFP) (given)		11 000
Non-controlling interest – Equity (SFP)		Wkg2 6 640
Elimination of common items, recognition of deferred tax asset, non-controlling interest, and gain on bargain purchase		

Workings: Pro forma journals

Working 1

65 000 Tax loss × 28%

Working 2

(80 000 – 65 000 + 18 200) × 20% NCI Share

Comments: Pro forma journal 1

- As S Ltd did not recognise a deferred tax asset in respect of its CU 65 000 tax loss in its individual financial statements, we need to recognise a deferred tax asset of S Ltd at acquisition date for consolidation purposes. This is achieved by debiting deferred tax in the statement of financial position with CU 18 200 (65 000 Tax loss × 28%). Recognition of this deferred tax asset for consolidation purposes results is an increase of CU 18 200 in the value of S Ltd's at acquisition identifiable net assets (equity).

SINCE ACQUISITION TO BEGINNING OF CURRENT YEAR

Pro forma journal 2 (J2)	Dr CU	Cr CU
Gain on bargain purchase (P Ltd) (P/L) (see (J1))	15 560	
Retained earnings (P Ltd) (SCIE)		15 560
Recognition of gain on bargain purchase at beginning of the year		

Comments: Pro forma journal 2

- In the at acquisition pro forma journal 1, we recognised a gain on bargain purchase in the current year profit or loss of P Ltd. However, since we are preparing consolidated financial statements for the next financial period (financial year ended 31 December 20x3) – and not for the financial period in which the acquisition took place (financial year ended 31 December 20x2) – we need to:

  - eliminate the bargain purchase gain from P Ltd's current year profit or loss by debiting the bargain purchase gain with CU 15 560; and

  - recognise the bargain purchase gain in the opening balance of P Ltd's retained earnings by crediting retained earnings with CU 15 560.

Pro forma journal 3 (J3)	Dr CU	Cr CU
Accumulated loss (S Ltd) (SCIE)	^{Wkg3}5 320	
Deferred tax (S Ltd) (SFP)		^{Wkg3}5 320
Recognition of tax expense arising from prior period reversal of deductible temporary difference in respect of at acquisition tax loss		

Workings: Pro forma journals

Working 3

19 000 Reversal of deductible temporary difference × 28%

Comments: Pro forma journal 3

- In the prior year, S Ltd earned CU 19 000 taxable profit, which reduced by CU 19 000, S Ltd's CU 65 000 tax loss at acquisition, in respect of which was recognised at acquisition a CU 18 200 (65 000 Deductible temporary difference × 28%) deferred tax asset. That is, in the prior year, CU 19 000 of the CU 65 000 at acquisition deductible temporary difference, arising in respect of S Ltd's CU 65 000 tax loss, was reversed for consolidation purposes.

- In the prior year consolidated financial statements, the effect of this prior year CU 19 000 deductible temporary difference reversal was:

  - to recognise a prior year tax expense of CU 5 320 (19 000 × 28%) for S Ltd, reducing S Ltd's prior year profit by CU 5 320, which profit was closed off to accumulated loss at prior financial year end; and

  - to reduce S Ltd's CU 18 200 deferred tax asset, recognised at acquisition, by CU 5 320.

- As we are preparing consolidated financial statements for the reporting period one year after the year of acquisition (i.e., for the following financial year), S Ltd's profit or loss for the current year cannot be adjusted. Rather, for purposes of the current year consolidation, S Ltd's opening accumulated loss balance must be adjusted (i.e., increased) to take into account the CU 5 320 prior year tax expense of S Ltd, recognised for consolidation purposes in the prior year.

- For this reason we debit (thus increasing) S Ltd's opening accumulated loss balance with CU 5 320 (19 000 × 28%), while the CU 5 320 contra credit to deferred tax asset of S Ltd reduces by CU 5 320, the CU 18 200 deferred tax asset recognised at acquisition (see pro forma journal 1), in respect of S Ltd's tax loss.

Pro forma journal (J4)	Dr CU	Cr CU
Accumulated loss (S Ltd) (SCIE)	Wkg4 2 736	
Non-controlling interest – Equity (SCIE)		Wkg4 2 736
Allocating the non-controlling interest its share of the adjusted reduction in S Ltd's accumulated loss since acquisition to the beginning of the year		

Working: Pro forma journals

Working 4

[(–46 000 Balance BOY) – (–65 000 (J1) Balance at acquisition) – (5 320 (J3) Tax expense adjustment)] × 20% NCI Share

Comments: Pro forma journal 4

- The non-controlling interest needs to be allocated its 20% share of S Ltd's CU 5 320 prior year tax expense attributable to the prior year reversal of CU 5 320 of S Ltd's CU 18 200 at acquisition deferred tax asset. Accordingly, when allocating the non-controlling interest its 20% share of S Ltd's post-acquisition earnings to the beginning of the current year, these earnings are first reduced by the full prior year tax expense adjustment of CU 5 320 (see pro forma journal 3), after which the non-controlling interest is allocated its 20% share.

CURRENT YEAR

Pro forma journal (J5)	Dr CU	Cr CU
Income tax expense (S Ltd) (P/L)	Wkg5 6 160	
Deferred tax asset (S Ltd) (SFP)		Wkg5 6 160
Recognition of tax expense arising from current year reversal of deductible temporary difference in respect at acquisition tax loss		

Working: Pro forma journals

Working 5

22 000 Reversal of deductible temporary difference × 28%

Comments: Pro forma journal 5

- As CU 22 000 taxable profit is earned by S Ltd in the current year, CU 22 000 of the CU 65 000 at acquisition deductible temporary difference, arising in respect of S Ltd's tax loss, reverses in the current year. In the current year consolidated financial statements, the effect of this CU 22 000 deductible temporary difference reversal is:

  - the recognition of a CU 6 160 (22 000 × 28%) tax expense for S Ltd; this is the debit to S Ltd's income tax expense of CU 6160; and

  - a corresponding CU 6 160 reduction in the deferred tax asset of S Ltd, recognised on acquisition; this is the CU 6 160 credit to S Ltd's deferred tax asset.

Pro forma journal 6 (J6)	Dr CU	Cr CU
NCI – Share of profit or loss (P/L)	Wkg6 3 168	
Non-controlling interest – Equity (SFP)		Wkg6 3 168
Allocating the non-controlling interest its share of S Ltd's adjusted profit for the current year		

Working: Pro forma journals

Working 6

(22 000 – 6 160 Tax expense adjustment (J5)) × 20% NCI Share

Comment: Pro forma journal 6

- The non-controlling interest needs to be allocated its share of any adjustments to S Ltd's current year profit. Accordingly, when allocating the non-controlling interest its share of S Ltd's current year profit, this profit is first reduced by the full tax expense adjustment of CU 6 160 (see pro forma journal 5), after which the non-controlling interest is allocated its 20% share thereof.

The full effects of the preceding pro forma journals on the consolidated financial statements of the P Ltd group are shown in the following consolidation worksheet as at 31 December 20x3.

	P Ltd Dr/(Cr) CU	S Ltd Dr/(Cr) CU	Pro forma journals At acquisition Dr/(Cr) CU	Journal ref	Pro forma journals Since acquisition Dr/(Cr) CU	Journal ref	Consolidated Dr/(Cr) CU
Equity							
Share capital	(100 000)	(80 000)	80 000	J1			(100 000)
Retained earnings (BOY)	(280 500)	46 000	(65 000) (15 560)	J1 J2	5 320 2 736	J3 J4	(307 004)
Net profit: Individual entities	(9 500)	(22 000)					–
Consolidated profit attributable to the owners of the parent							†(22 172)
Dividend paid	5 000						5 000
Retained earnings (EOY)	(285 000)	24 000	(6 640)	J1			(324 176)
NCI Equity	–	–			(2 736) (3 168)	J4 J6	(12 544)
Total equity	**(385 000)**	**(56 000)**					**(436 720)**
Liabilities:							
Trade and other payables	(65 500)	(39 000)					(104 500)
Total liabilities	**(65 500)**	**(39 000)**					**(104 500)**

Explanatory notes

† This amount has been brought forward from the second part of the consolidation worksheet on page 199

	P Ltd Dr/(Cr) CU	S Ltd Dr/(Cr) CU	Pro forma journals At acquisition Dr/(Cr) CU	Journal ref	Pro forma journals Since acquisition Dr/(Cr) CU	Journal ref	Consolidated Dr/(Cr) CU
Total equity and liabilities	(450 500)	(95 000)					(541 220)
Assets:							
Property, plant and equipment	335 500	57 000					392 500
Investment in S Ltd	11 000		(11 000)	J1			–
Trade and other receivables	104 000	38 000					142 000
Deferred tax			18 200	J1	(5 320)	J3	6 720
					(6 160)	J5	
Total assets	450 500	95 000					541 220
Profit or loss							
Profit before tax	(9 500)	(22 000)					(31 500)
Income tax expense					6 160	J5	6 160
Net profit							(25 340)
NCI: Share of profit					3 168	J6	3 168
Consolidated profit attributable to owners of parent							‡(22 172)

Explanatory notes

‡ This amount has been carried forward to the first part of the consolidation worksheet on page 198

Part (c): Consolidated financial statements for the 20x3 financial year

P LTD GROUP: ABRIDGED CONSOLIDATED STATEMENT OF PROFIT OR LOSS AND OTHER COMPREHENSIVE INCOME FOR THE YEAR ENDED 31 DECEMBER 20x3	
	CU
Profit before tax (9 500 (P Ltd) + 22 000 (S Ltd))	31 500
Income tax expense (see AOE **j OR** (J5))	(6 160)
PROFIT FOR THE YEAR	25 340
Other comprehensive income for the year	–
TOTAL COMPREHENSIVE INCOME FOR THE YEAR	**25 340**
Total comprehensive income for the year attributable to:	
Owners of the parent [(balancing figure) **OR** (9 500 (P Ltd) + 12 672 (see AOE f))]	22 172
Non-controlling interest (see AOE **g OR** (J6))	3 168
	25 340

P LTD GROUP: CONSOLIDATED STATEMENT OF CHANGES IN EQUITY FOR THE YEAR ENDED 31 DECEMBER 20x3					
	Parent equity holders' interest			**Non-controlling interest**	**Total equity of the group**
	Share capital	**Retained earnings**	**Total parent equity**		
	CU	CU	CU	CU	CU
Opening balance at 1 Jan 20x3	100 000	Wkg1 307 004	407 004	Wkg2 9 376	416 380
Total comprehensive income:					
Profit for the period (from CSOPL_OCI)	–	22 172	22 172	3 168	25 340
Dividends	–	(5 000)	(5 000)		(5 000)
Closing balance at 31 Dec 20x3	100 000	324 176	424 176	12 544	436 720

Workings: Consolidated statement of changes in equity

Working 1

(P Ltd: 280 500 + 15 560 (see AOE **b**) Bargain purchase gain) + (S Ltd: 10 944 (see AOE **c**) PLtd's Share of S Ltd post-acquisition retained earnings to BOY)

OR

(P Ltd: 280 500 + 15 560 (J2) Bargain purchase gain) + (S Ltd: –46 000 Balance BOY – (–65 000)(J1) Balance at acquisition – 5 320 (J3) Income tax expense – 2 736 (J4) NCI Share of post-acquisition earnings of S Ltd to BOY)

Working 2

S Ltd: 9 376 (see AOE **e**)

OR

S Ltd: 6 640 (J1) NCI Share of S Ltd at acquisition equity + 2 736 (J4) NCI Share of S Ltd post-acquisition retained earnings to BOY

P LTD GROUP: CONSOLIDATED STATEMENT OF FINANCIAL POSITION AS AT 31 DECEMBER 20x3	
	CU
Assets	
Non-current assets	
Property, plant and equipment (335 500 (P Ltd) + 57 000 (S Ltd))	392 500
Deferred tax (S Ltd: 18 200 (see AOE **a OR** (J1)) – 5 320 (see AOE **i OR** (J3)) – 6 160 (see AOE **j OR** (J5))	6 720
Current assets	
Trade and other receivables (104 000 (P Ltd) + 38 000 (S Ltd))	142 000
Total assets	541 220
Equity and liabilities	
Share capital (from CSCIE)	100 000
Retained earnings (from CSCIE)	324 176
Equity attributable to owners of the parent	424 176
Non-controlling interest (from CSCIE) **OR** (see AOE **h**)	12 544
Total equity	436 720
Current liabilities	
Trade and other payables (65 500 (P Ltd) + 39 000 (S Ltd))	104 500
Total equity and liabilities	541 220

4.2.7.3 Subsidiary with post-acquisition losses

In the situation where a subsidiary makes losses after acquisition date, such losses will be allocated – as is the case with post-acquisition profits – to the **parent** and to the **non-controlling interest** in accordance with their **respective ownership interests** (i.e., shareholdings).

The parent will include its proportionate share of subsidiary post-acquisition accumulated losses, split between losses incurred:

- from **acquisition date to the beginning of the current reporting period**, affecting the **opening balances of retained earnings** or **accumulated loss** in the **consolidated statement of changes in equity**; and
- in the **current period**, affecting the **consolidated statement of profit or loss and other comprehensive income**.

The non-controlling interest's share in subsidiary post-acquisition losses will reduce its:

- opening balance in the consolidated statement of changes in equity; and
- its closing balance in the consolidated statement of changes in equity.

In this regard, as was discussed in Section 4.2.7.1, any **negative total comprehensive income** will be **attributable to the non-controlling interest** even if this results in the **non-controlling interest** having a **negative (deficit) balance** (IFRS 10.B94).

In addition, when consolidating a subsidiary with post-acquisition losses we need to be aware of the possibility that the parent in its **separate financial statements** may have impaired its investment in the subsidiary in accordance with IAS 36. An impairment loss will be recognised by the parent if the carrying amount of the investment in the subsidiary exceeds the investment's recoverable amount. Such an impairment loss must be **reversed on consolidation**. This is because both the impairment loss recognised by the parent and the actual losses made by the subsidiary would be included in the consolidated financial statements were the impairment loss recognised by the parent, in its separate financial statements not eliminated on consolidation, thereby double counting the losses at group level.

Example 4.8: Partly owned subsidiary with post-acquisition losses

P Ltd acquired 90% of the ordinary shares of S Ltd on 1 January 20x5 for CU 333 000, thereby obtaining control over S Ltd. At that date S Ltd's equity was as follows:
- share capital CU 250 000; and
- retained earnings CU 120 000

The condensed trial balances for P Ltd and S Ltd on 31 December 20x7 are as follows:

Trial balances at 31 December 20x7	P Ltd Dr/(Cr) CU	S Ltd Dr/(Cr) CU
Share capital	(300 000)	(250 000)
Retained earnings (1 Jan 20x7)	(110 000)	(15 000)
(Profit)/loss	(120 000)	85 000
Trade and other payables	(274 000)	(73 000)
Trade and other receivables	340 000	193 000
Bank	181 000	60 000
Investment in S Ltd	283 000	–

Additional information
- P Ltd measures the non-controlling interest at it proportionate share of S Ltd's identifiable net assets.
- All identifiable assets and liabilities of S Ltd were considered to be fairly valued at acquisition date.
- P Ltd recognised an impairment loss of CU 50 000 in respect of its investment in S Ltd in its separate financial statements in the current financial year. The impairment loss was included in arriving at P Ltd's profit for the year. The investment in subsidiary is reflected in P Ltd's trial balance at its impaired value of CU 283 000.

Required
(a) Prepare the analysis of equity of S Ltd as at 31 December 20x7.
(b) Provide all the pro forma journal entries necessary to prepare the consolidated financial statements of the P Ltd group for the financial year ended 31 December 20x7.
(c) Prepare the consolidated statement of profit or loss and other comprehensive income and the consolidated statement of changes in equity of the P Ltd group for the financial year ended 31 December 20x7.

Solution 4.8: Partly owned subsidiary with post-acquisition losses

Part (a): Analysis of equity (AOE) of S Ltd as at 31 December 20x7

| | Total equity | P Ltd 90% | | NCI 10% |
| | | At acquisition | Since acquisition | |
At acquisition date (1 January 20x5)	CU	CU	CU	CU
Share capital	250 000	225 000	–	25 000
Retained earnings	120 000	108 000		12 000
Fair value of net assets of S Ltd	370 000	333 000		37 000
Goodwill/gain on bargain purchase	–	–		–
Consideration and non-controlling interest	370 000	333 000		37 000
Since acquisition				
• To beginning of current year:				
Retained earnings (15 000 Balance BOY – 120 000 Balance at acquisition)	(105 000)		(94 500) **a**	(10 500) **b**
				26 500 **c**
• Loss for the year	(85 000)		(76 500) **d**	(8 500) **e**
	180 000		(171 000)	18 000

Part (b): Pro forma journal entries for the 20x7 financial year

AT ACQUISITION

Pro forma journal 1 (J1)	Dr CU	Cr CU
Investment in S Ltd (P Ltd) (SFP)	ᵂᵏᵍ¹50 000	
Profit [impairment loss] (P Ltd) (P/L)		ᵂᵏᵍ¹50 000
Reversal of impairment loss recorded in separate records of P Ltd		

Workings: Pro forma journals

Working 1

333 000 Investment cost – 283 000 Impaired value

Comments: Pro forma journal 1

- P Ltd has recognised an impairment loss and written down the value of its investment in S Ltd by CU 50 000 in its separate financial statements. Accordingly, so as not to double count losses, when consolidating a loss-making subsidiary we need to reverse this impairment loss. This is achieved by crediting P Ltd's current year profit with CU 50 000.

- The other side of the pro forma entry (i.e., the debit to the investment of CU 50 000) restores the value of the investment in S Ltd to its original at acquisition date cost of CU 333 000. Thereafter we can process the normal at acquisition elimination entry as per pro forma journal 2.

Pro forma journal 2 (J2)	Dr CU	Cr CU
Share capital (S Ltd) (SCIE) (given)	250 000	
Retained earnings (S Ltd) (SCIE) (given)	120 000	
Investment in S Ltd (P Ltd) (SFP) (given)		333 000
Non-controlling interest – Equity (SFP)		Wkg2 37 000
Elimination of common items and recognition of non-controlling interest		

Workings: Pro forma journals

Working 2

Balance figure **OR** (250 000 + 120 000) × 10% NCI Share

SINCE ACQUISITION TO BEGINNING OF YEAR

Pro forma journal 3 (J3)	Dr CU	Cr CU
Non-controlling interest – Equity (SFP)	Wkg3 10 500	
Retained earnings (S Ltd) (SCIE)		Wkg3 10 500
Allocating the non-controlling interest its share in S Ltd's post-acquisition losses to the beginning of the year		

Workings: Pro forma journals

Working 3

(15 000 Balance BOY – 120 000 Balance at acquisition) × 10% NCI Share

Comments: Pro forma journal 3

- As the non-controlling interest is sharing in S Ltd's post-acquisition **losses** we reduce its equity interest in S Ltd with a debit entry.
- The credit leg of the entry reduces the amount of S Ltd's post-acquisition losses to the beginning of the current year that is allocated to P Ltd, by allocating 10% of these losses to the non-controlling interest.

CURRENT YEAR

Pro forma journal 4 (J4)	Dr CU	Cr CU
Non-controlling interest – Equity (SFP)	Wkg4 8 500	
NCI – Share of profit or loss (P/L)		Wkg4 8 500
Allocating the non-controlling interest its share of the current year loss of S Ltd		

Workings: Pro forma journals

Working 4

85 000 Current year loss × 10% NCI Share

Comments: Pro forma journal 4

- As was explained in pro forma journal entry 3, once again the non-controlling interest is sharing in S Ltd's post acquisition **losses so we reduce** its equity interest in S Ltd with a debit entry.
- The credit leg of the entry reduces the current year loss allocated to P Ltd, by allocating 10% of this loss to the non-controlling interest.

The full effects of the preceding pro forma journals on the consolidated financial statements of the P Ltd group are shown in the following consolidation worksheet as at 31 December 20x7.

	P Ltd Dr/(Cr) CU	S Ltd Dr/(Cr) CU	Pro forma journals At acquisition Dr/(Cr) CU	Journal ref	Pro forma journals Since acquisition Dr/(Cr) CU	Journal ref	Consolidated Dr/(Cr) CU
Equity							
Share capital	(300 000)	(250 000)	250 000				(300 000)
Retained earnings (BOY)	(110 000)	(15 000)	120 000	J2	(10 500)	J3	(15 500)
Net profit: Individual entities	(120 000)	85 000		J2			
Consolidated profit attributable to the owners of the parent							†(93 500)
Retained earnings (EOY)	(230 000)	70 000	(37 000)	J2			(109 000)
NCI Equity	–	–			10 500	J3	(18 000)
	–	–			8 500	J4	
Total equity	**(530 000)**	**(180 000)**					**(427 000)**
Liabilities:							
Trade and other payables	(274 000)	(73 000)					(347 000)
Total liabilities	**(274 000)**	**(73 000)**					**(347 000)**

Explanatory notes

† This amount has been brought forward from the second part of the consolidation worksheet on page 206

	P Ltd	S Ltd	Pro forma journals At acquisition		Pro forma journals Since acquisition		Con-solidated
	Dr/(Cr) CU	Dr/(Cr) CU	Dr/(Cr) CU	Journal ref	Dr/(Cr) CU	Journal ref	Dr/(Cr) CU
Total equity & liabilities	(804 000)	(253 000)					(774 000)
Assets:							
Investment in S Ltd	283 000		50 000 (333 000)	J1 J2			–
Trade and other receivables	340 000	193 000					533 000
Bank	181 000	60 000					241 000
Total assets	804 000	253 000					774 000
Profit or loss							
Profit	(120 000)	85 000	(50 000)	J1			(85 000)
NCI: Share of profit					(8 500)	J4	(8 500)
Consolidated profit attributable to owners of the parent							‡(93 500)

Explanatory notes

‡ This amount has been carried forward to the first part of the consolidation worksheet on page 205

Part (c): Consolidated financial statements for the year ended 31 December 20x7

P LTD GROUP: ABRIDGED CONSOLIDATED STATEMENT OF PROFIT OR LOSS AND OTHER COMPREHENSIVE INCOME FOR THE YEAR ENDED 31 DECEMBER 20x7	
	CU
PROFIT FOR THE YEAR ((P Ltd: 120 000 + 50 000 (J1) Impairment loss reversal) + (S Ltd: -85 000 Loss for the year))	85 000
Other comprehensive income for the year, net of tax	–
TOTAL COMPREHENSIVE INCOME FOR THE YEAR	**85 000**
Total comprehensive income for the year attributable to:	
Owners of the parent [(balancing figure) **OR** (P Ltd: 120 000 + 50 000 (J1)) + (S Ltd: -76 500 (see AOE **d**))]	93 500
Non-controlling interest (see AOE **e OR** (J6))	(8 500)
	85 000

P LTD GROUP: CONSOLIDATED STATEMENT OF CHANGES IN EQUITY FOR THE YEAR ENDED 31 DECEMBER 20x7					
	Parent equity holders' interest			Non-controlling interest	Total equity of the group
	Share capital	Retained earnings	Total parent equity		
	CU	CU	CU	CU	CU
Opening balance at 1 January 20x7	300 000	Wkg1 15 500	315 500	Wkg 2 26 500	342 000
Total comprehensive income:					
Profit for the period (from CSOPL_OCL)		93 500	93 500	(8 500)	85 000
Closing balance at 31 December 20x7	300 000	109 000	409 000	18 000	427 000

Workings: Consolidated statement of changes in equity

Working 1
P Ltd: 110 000 + (S Ltd: –94 500 (see AOE **a**) P Ltd share of S Ltd post-acquisition loss to BOY)

OR

P Ltd: 110 000 + (S Ltd: 15 000 Balance BOY – 120 000 (J2) Balance at acquisition + 10 500 (J3) NCI share of S Ltd post-acquisition loss to BOY)

Working 2
S Ltd: 26 500 (see AOE **c**)

OR

S Ltd: 37 000 (J2) NCI share of S Ltd at acquisition equity – CU 10 500 (J3) NCI share of S Ltd post-acquisition loss to BOY

4.2.8 Different reporting dates (IFRS 10.B92 –B93)

As was discussed in Volume 1 Chapter 1, the financial statements of a parent and its subsidiaries that are used to prepare consolidated financial statements must have the

same reporting date. Recall that when the reporting date of the subsidiary is different from that of its parent, the subsidiary is required to prepare additional information for consolidation purposes as of the same date as the financial statements of its parent. This enables the parent to consolidate the subsidiary's financial information, unless it is impracticable to do so (i.e., undue cost and effort is involved).

Should it be **impracticable** to do so, then, as was explained in Volume 1 Chapter 1, the parent must consolidate the financial information of the subsidiary using the **most recent financial statements** of the **subsidiary** that have been **adjusted** for:

- the effects of **significant transactions and events;** and/or
- that occur between the **date of those financial statements** and the **date of the consolidated financial statements.**

Volume 1 Chapter 1 also explained that the difference between the date of the subsidiary's financial statements and that of the consolidated financial statements may *not* exceed **three months.** Furthermore, the **reporting period length** and any difference in dates of the subsidiary and consolidated financial statements must be the **same** from **period to period.**

Example 4.9: Subsidiary with a different reporting date to that of its parent

Parent, which has a reporting date of 30 September, acquires Subsidiary, which has a reporting date of 30 June. The difference in reporting periods may be dealt with as follows:

- Subsidiary could change its reporting period to 30 September.
- The reporting period of Subsidiary could remain unchanged as 30 June, in which case Subsidiary will prepare financial statements for the twelve months ended 30 September for consolidation purposes. Note that these financial statements will be prepared by Subsidiary in addition to its annual financial statements with period end 30 June.
- If it is impracticable for Subsidiary to prepare twelve-month financial statements for the period ended 30 September, the financial statements for the twelve-month period ended 30 June would then be used each year for consolidation purposes. This is permitted as the difference in reporting periods is not greater than three months. Adjustments would then be made for the effects of significant transactions or events that occur between 1 July and 30 September of each financial year.

4.2.9 Uniform accounting policies (IFRS 10.B87)

As was discussed in Volume 1 Chapter 1, consolidated financial statements must be prepared using **uniform** (that is, the same) **accounting policies** for **like transactions** and **events in similar circumstances.** More particularly, when an entity within a group applies accounting policies that **differ** from those accounting policies applied in the consolidated financial statements for like events and transactions, that entity's financial statements must be adjusted as follows:

- the **parent will instruct the subsidiary to change its accounting policy** to be in accordance with the group's accounting policy **prior** to **preparing consolidated financial statements;** or
- the group accounting policy will be applied to the subsidiary **on consolidation** (that is, **pro forma journal entries** will be passed to align the accounting policy of the entity with that of the group).

Example 4.10: Partially owned subsidiary applies a different accounting policy from that of the group

This example illustrates the scenario where the subsidiary applies the cost model for owner-occupied land, while the group policy is to apply the revaluation model. When consolidating the subsidiary, pro forma journals are required to recognise the subsidiary's land at the revalued amount and to recognise the deferred tax effects of the revaluation in the consolidated financial statements.

P Ltd acquired an 80% controlling interest in S Ltd on 1 January 20x5. On 1 August 20x6, S Ltd acquired an owner occupied property (which comprised its new head office and a plot of land). At that date CU 1 000 000 was attributable to the land. S Ltd applies the cost model for property, plant and equipment and accordingly the land was reflected at its acquisition cost of CU 1 000 000 in S Ltd's accounting records at financial year end 31 December 20x6.

The group, however, applies the revaluation model for property, plant and equipment and obtained a valuation for the land of CU 1 500 000 at reporting period end 31 December 20x6.

Required
Prepare the pro forma journal entries necessary to recognise the revaluation of the land (including any tax effects) in the consolidated financial statements of the P Ltd group for the reporting period ended 31 December 20x6.

The income tax rate is 28% and the effective capital gains tax rate is 22.4%. Furthermore, S Ltd is not a land dealer for tax purposes.

 ## Solution 4.10: Partially owned subsidiary applies a different accounting policy from that of the group

Extracts of the consolidation worksheet are provided to illustrate how the amounts recognised in the subsidiary, S Ltd, are adjusted by the pro forma journal entries to arrive at the amounts in the consolidated financial statements, applying the revaluation model, as follows:

EXTRACT: CONSOLIDATION WORKSHEET

	S Ltd Dr/(Cr) CU	Pro forma journals Dr/(Cr) CU	Con-solidated Dr/(Cr) CU	Comments
Land	1 000 000	500 000	1 500 000	1.
Deferred tax liability (500 000 × 22.4%)	–	(112 000)	(112 000)	2.
Non-controlling interest – Equity ((500 000 × 77.6% After tax) × 20%)	–	(77 600)	(77 600)	3.
Revaluation gain (OCI)	–	(500 000)	(388 000)	4.
Income tax expense (OCI) (500 000 × 22.4%)		112 000		
NCI – After tax share of OCI [388 000 (500 000 × 77.6%) × 20%]	–	77 600	77 600	5.

Comments: Extract: consolidation worksheet
1. The value of S Ltd's land is increased to its fair value in the consolidated financial statements at reporting period end, in accordance with the group's accounting policy of revaluing property, plant and equipment.

2. When the land is revalued, its carrying amount increases without a corresponding change in its tax base as the taxing authority does not recognise the revaluation gain for tax purposes. At group level, this gives rise to a taxable temporary difference (i.e., carrying amount of land is greater than its tax base), and the recognition of a deferred tax liability in the consolidated financial statements. This deferred tax liability is calculated at the 22.4% effective capital gains tax rate as the carrying amount of land can only be recovered by sale.

3. As the non-controlling interest shares in, among other things, the other comprehensive income of the subsidiary, S Ltd, we need to allocate it its 20% share of S Ltd's current year revaluation gain on land, which gain is recognised in S Ltd's current year other comprehensive income. This allocation increases the non-controlling interest's equity interest in S Ltd. Note further that this other comprehensive income, allocated to the non-controlling interest, is a net of tax amount. That is, the non-controlling interest shares in 20% of the after tax increase in S Ltd's other comprehensive income.

4. The current year other comprehensive income of S Ltd that is recognised in the consolidated financial statements is the after tax amount of S Ltd's current year revaluation gain.

5. The non-controlling interest shares, on an after tax basis, in 20% of S Ltd's current year revaluation gain, which gain is recognised in S Ltd's other comprehensive income. The remaining 80% of S Ltd's revaluation gain after tax, recognised in S Ltd's other comprehensive income, is allocated to the parent, P Ltd.

Following from the above, the pro forma journals that are passed are as follows:

Pro forma journal 1 (J1)	Dr CU	Cr CU
Land (S Ltd) (SFP)	500 000	
Revaluation gain PPE (S Ltd) (OCI)		[Wkg1]388 000
Deferred tax (S Ltd) (SFP)		[Wkg2]112 000
Revaluation of subsidiary's land including deferred tax effects – applying uniform group accounting policy		

Workings: Pro forma journals

Working 1
500 000 × 77.6% After tax

Working 2
500 000 × 22.4% Effective capital gains tax rate

Pro forma journal 2 (J2)	Dr CU	Cr CU
NCI – Share of other comprehensive income (OCI)	[Wkg3]77 600	
Non-controlling interest – Equity (SFP)		[Wkg3]77 600
Allocating the non-controlling interest its share of S Ltd's revaluation gain – applying uniform group accounting policy		

Workings: Pro forma journals

Working 3
388 000 (J1) × 20% NCI Share

Summary

The first part of this chapter explained the process and procedures necessary to consolidate partly owned subsidiaries, first at acquisition date, and then in subsequent reporting periods. A partly owned subsidiary's **equity** is owned by **more than one entity** – the **parent**, being the entity that **controls** the subsidiary, and the **non-controlling interest,** being the **other investors** who do *not* control the subsidiary.

The basic consolidation procedures explained in the previous chapter, applicable to a wholly owned subsidiary, apply equally when consolidating a partly owned subsidiary. Additionally, when consolidating a partly owned subsidiary, we recognise the **non-controlling interest's share of the subsidiary's:**

- **at acquisition equity;**
- **post-acquisition movement in reserves** (e.g., retained earnings and revaluation surplus) to the **beginning of the current year;** and
- **current year profit or loss and other comprehensive income.**

The following key learning points are important:

- In the consolidated statement of profit or loss and other comprehensive income, the partly owned subsidiary's **profit or loss,** and each component of its **other comprehensive income,** is attributed to the **owners of the parent** and to the **non-controlling interest,** based on **present ownership interests** (i.e. shareholding).
- On the **face of the consolidated statement of profit or loss and other comprehensive income,** both the **parent owners' share,** and the **non-controlling interest's share** of the partly owned subsidiary's **consolidated profit or loss,** and **total consolidated comprehensive income,** are reported.
- In the consolidated statement of changes in equity:
  - The **consolidated reserve(s) opening balance(s)** reported consists of the **parent's opening reserve(s) balance(s) plus** the **parent's proportionate share** of the **movement** in the partly owned **subsidiary's reserve(s)** for the period **since acquisition to the beginning of the current year.**
  - The **non-controlling interest opening balance** reported consists of the **non-controlling interest's share** of the partly owned subsidiary's **at acquisition equity, plus its share** of the partly **owned subsidiary's since acquisition reserves to beginning of the current year.**
  - The **non-controlling interest equity balance is reduced** by any **dividends** paid/declared **to the non-controlling shareholders by the partly owned subsidiary.**
- In the consolidated statement of financial position of a partly owned subsidiary, *all* the assets and liabilities of the **partly owned subsidiary are added to those of the parent.** This reflects the fact that the **parent controls 100% of the subsidiary's net assets (equity).** Furthermore, the equity section on the face of the consolidated statement of financial position **discloses separately,** the equity held by the **owners of the parent,** and the equity held by the **non-controlling interest.** This disclosure reflects the fact that there are **different owners** of the **subsidiary's net assets (equity).**

The second part of the chapter addressed various sundry aspects of consolidations, most notably:

- where goodwill arising on the acquisition of a subsidiary is **impaired in the consolidated financial statements** subsequent to acquisition date;
- the recognition at group level of a **deferred tax asset of a subsidiary at acquisition date**; and
- the reversal on consolidation of **impairment losses recognised** in respect of an investment in a subsidiary in the **parent's separate financial statements.**

Under IAS 36, where a subsidiary acquired is a **cash-generating unit,** an **impairment loss** is subsequently recognised in the consolidated financial statements when the subsidiary cash-generating unit's **carrying amount exceeds its recoverable amount.** This impairment loss is:

- **first allocated** to reduce the carrying amount of the subsidiary's **goodwill;** and
- thereafter any remainder is allocated to the **other assets** of the subsidiary cash-generating unit, pro rata, based on the carrying amount of each asset in the cash-generating unit.

At group level, the recognition of a **deferred tax asset** at acquisition date, in respect of a **subsidiary's at acquisition tax loss,** which deferred tax asset was **not recognised by the subsidiary,** has the following effects in the consolidated financial statements:

- **At acquisition date,** recognition of this deferred tax asset will **increase the net asset value (equity)** of the subsidiary acquired, which in turn impacts on the amount of any goodwill or bargain purchase gain recognised.
- **After acquisition date,** as the subsidiary earns taxable profits each year, the value of this **deferred tax asset is reduced each year,** while recognising a corresponding **increase** in the **subsidiary's income tax expense each year.**

Where the parent of a subsidiary which has incurred post-acquisition losses has **impaired** its **investment in the subsidiary** in its **separate financial statements,** this impairment loss must be **reversed on consolidation.** This prevents the double counting of losses at group level.

In Volume 1 Chapter 5 we address the impact on the preparation of the consolidated financial statements of IFRS 3 at acquisition fair value adjustments to subsidiary assets.

QUESTIONS

Question 4.1

The abridged trial balances of P Ltd and its subsidiary S Ltd at 31 December 20x6 were as follows:

Abridged trial balances at 31 December 20x6	P Ltd Dr/(Cr) CU	S Ltd Dr/(Cr) CU
Share capital (P Ltd 450 000 shares / S Ltd 100 000 shares)	(450 000)	(100 000)
Retained earnings (1 Jan 20x6)	(455 000)	(475 000)
Dividends paid	120 000	65 000
Revaluation surplus (1 Jan 20x6)	(108 000)	(204 139)
Mark to market reserve (1 Jan 20x6)	(51 645)	(55 304)
Deferred tax	(75 238)	(96 003)
Trade and other payables	(19 240)	(25 650)
Financial assets at fair value through OCI	397 227	636 622
Land	275 000	354 850
Investment in S Ltd (at cost)	535 000	–
Trade and other receivables	169 896	117 762
Profit for period	(237 000)	(145 000)
After tax revaluation gain: Land (OCI)	(85 000)	(52 805)
After tax fair value gain: Financial assets (OCI)	(16 000)	(20 333)

Further information

1. On 1 January 20x5, P Ltd acquired an 80% controlling interest in S Ltd, for CU 535 000. At acquisition date the equity of S Ltd consisted of the following:
   - share capital CU 100 000;
   - retained earnings CU 360 000; and
   - revaluation surplus CU 126 875.

2. At acquisition date, P Ltd considered the carrying amount of the identifiable net assets of S Ltd to be equal to their at acquisition fair values. Furthermore, no additional assets, liabilities or contingent liabilities of S Ltd were identified at this date.

3. P Ltd measured the non-controlling interest at its at acquisition date fair value. On 1 January 20x5, the shares of S Ltd were trading at CU 5.25 per share.

4. In accordance with IAS 27.10(a), P Ltd recognised the investment in S Ltd at cost.

5. The income tax rate is 28% and an effective capital gains tax rate of 22.4% applies.

6. Neither P Ltd, nor S Ltd are sharedealers for income tax purposes.

Required

Prepare the consolidated financial statements of the P Ltd group for the financial year ended 31 December 20x6.

Question 4.2

P Ltd acquired a 70% controlling interest in S Ltd on 1 January 20x5 for CU 606 440. At acquisition date the equity of S Ltd consisted of the following:

- share capital CU 350 000;
- retained earnings CU 280 000; and
- revaluation surplus CU 115 200.

P Ltd considered the net assets of S Ltd to be fairly valued at acquisition date. Furthermore, no additional assets, liabilities or contingent liabilities of S Ltd were identified at this date. In addition, P Ltd measured the non-controlling interest at its proportionate share of the identifiable net assets of S Ltd. The abridged trial balances of P Ltd and its subsidiary S Ltd at 31 December 20x6 were as follows:

Abridged trial balances at 31 December 20x6	P Ltd Dr/(Cr) CU	S Ltd Dr/(Cr) CU
Share capital	(600 000)	(350 000)
Retained earnings (1 Jan 20x6)	(536 060)	(162 000)
Dividends declared	90 000	50 000
Revaluation surplus (1 Jan 20x6)	(86 400)	(169 200)
Deferred tax	(53 200)	(65 800)
Dividends payable	(90 000)	(50 000)
Equipment	742 120	588 850
Investment in S Ltd (at cost)	606 440	–
Trade and other receivables	144 000	100 550
(Profit)/loss for period	(166 500)	90 000
After tax revaluation gain: Equipment (OCI)	(50 400)	(32 400)

Note: The dividend receivable from S Ltd is included in trade and other receivables of P Ltd.

Required

PART 1

(a) Provide the pro forma journal entries required to prepare the consolidated financial statements of the P Ltd group for the year ended 31 December 20x6. Journal narrations are *not* required.

(b) Prepare the abridged consolidated statement of profit or loss and other comprehensive income of the P Ltd group for the year ended 31 December 20x6.

(c) Prepare the consolidated statement of changes in equity of the P Ltd group for the year ended 31 December 20x6.

PART 2

Assume that at financial year end 31 December 20x6, P Ltd determines that the recoverable amount of cash-generating unit S Ltd is CU 634 743.

(a) Calculate the goodwill impairment loss that would be recognised in the consolidated financial statements of the P Ltd group for the year ended 31 December 20x6. Note – as discussed above – that P Ltd measures the non-controlling interest at its proportionate share of the identifiable net assets of S Ltd.

(b) Calculate the amount by which goodwill would be impaired at 31 December 20x6 assuming that P Ltd measures the non-controlling interest at its fair value of CU 243 560 at acquisition date.

(c) Provide the pro forma journals necessary to recognise the goodwill impairment as calculated in (b) in the consolidated financial statements of the P Ltd group for the year ended 31 December 20x6.

References

The Conceptual Framework for Financial Reporting

IAS 1 *Presentation of Financial Statements*

IAS 12 *Income Taxes*

IAS 36 *Impairment of assets*

IFRS 3 *Business Combinations*

IFRS 10 *Consolidated Financial Statements*

CHAPTER 5

CONSOLIDATIONS: IFRS 3 FAIR VALUE ADJUSTMENTS TO SUBSIDIARY ASSETS AT ACQUISITION

LEARNING OBJECTIVES

After studying this chapter, you should be able to:

- understand that, subject to limited exceptions, under IFRS 3 assets and liabilities of a subsidiary acquired must be measured at their respective fair values at acquisition date in the consolidated financial statements;

- understand the implications at acquisition of a subsidiary revaluing its assets to fair value in its own records;

- know how to process pro forma journal entries at acquisition date in order to record subsidiary assets (both current and non-current) at fair value under IFRS 3, in the consolidated financial statements where a subsidiary does not revalue its assets to fair value in its own records;

- understand the deferred tax effects arising from at acquisition IFRS 3 fair value adjustments to subsidiary assets (both current and non-current) and be able to process pro forma journal entries to record such deferred tax effects at acquisition date in the consolidated financial statements;

- understand the effects of IFRS 3 at acquisition fair value adjustments to subsidiary assets (both current and non-current) and the related deferred tax effects thereof on the amount of goodwill or gain on bargain purchase recognised at acquisition date;

- process the pro forma journals required in the post-acquisition period in order to adjust, for group purposes, the subsequent depreciation and/or profit/(loss) on disposal of property, plant and equipment, recognised by a subsidiary, which assets were fair valued, under IFRS 3, at acquisition date;

- process the pro forma journals required in the post-acquisition period to adjust, for group purposes, the subsequent cost of sales recognised by a subsidiary, in respect of inventory sold that was re-measured to fair value under IFRS 3, at acquisition date;

- process the pro forma journals required to recognise the deferred tax implications in the consolidated financial statements at acquisition and in subsequent reporting periods, arising from IFRS 3 at acquisition fair value adjustments to subsidiary assets, both current and non-current;

- apply the correct accounting treatment in the consolidated financial statements when a subsidiary's property, plant and equipment is adjusted to its at acquisition fair values on consolidation, and the subsidiary then revalues these assets in its own records subsequent to acquisition date; and

- prepare consolidated financial statements that include the effects of IFRS 3 at acquisition fair value adjustments to subsidiary assets, both current and non-current.

TOPIC LIST

Introduction

In Volume 1 Chapter 2 you learnt that under IFRS 3 *Business Combinations*, subject to limited exceptions, an acquirer must, **at acquisition date**, measure the acquiree's identifiable assets acquired and liabilities assumed in a business combination at **fair value**. It was explained that when the at acquisition fair value of an acquiree's asset or liability differs from its carrying amount as recognised in the acquiree's records, such item's carrying amount must be **adjusted to fair value**. This enables the acquirer to determine the **fair net asset value** of the business acquired and consequently to recognise the **correct** amount of **goodwill or bargain purchase gain**.

In the context of a group[5], when IFRS 3 at acquisition fair value adjustments must be made to subsidiary assets[6], two approaches (discussed more fully below) may be taken:

- either the **subsidiary itself** adjusts the carrying amounts of its assets to their respective fair values, in its **own accounting records**; or
- the remeasurement to fair value of the subsidiary's assets is included in the at acquisition **pro forma elimination journal**. That is, the remeasurement to fair value occurs as **part of the consolidation process**.

IFRS 3 fair value adjustments to a subsidiary's assets at acquisition date have a number of implications in the consolidated financial statements, both at acquisition and in subsequent reporting periods. These implications will be discussed and explained in detail in this chapter.

5.1 At acquisition fair value adjustments to subsidiary's assets: Adjustments made in subsidiary's records

In circumstances where the subsidiary makes IFRS 3 fair value adjustments to its at acquisition date assets in its **own accounting records** in accordance with the values placed on these assets by the parent (acquirer), there will be the following implication upon consolidation of the subsidiary:

- The assets of the subsidiary will already have been revalued and will therefore reflect their underlying fair values; for example, the subsidiary will have recognised a revaluation surplus in respect of the revaluation of its property, plant and equipment to fair value, which revaluation surplus which will form part of its at acquisition equity.

- There will be *no* follow-on implications in subsequent reporting periods arising from the remeasurement of the assets to fair value (e.g., no additional depreciation to be recognised for consolidation purposes). This is because the subsidiary's own financial statements will reflect the remeasured assets at the same values as will be reflected in the consolidated financial statements.

---

5   The situation where fair value adjustments are made to assets in a business combination where the assets and liabilities of the acquiree are directly purchased (i.e., consolidated financial statements are not prepared) is dealt with in Volume 1 Chapter 3.

6   For purposes of this chapter, only at acquisition fair value adjustments in respect of assets of a subsidiary are considered. Fair value adjustments relating to a subsidiary's at acquisition liabilities are dealt with in Volume 2 Chapter 1.

Example 5.1: Subsidiary recognises at acquisition fair value adjustment to property, plant and equipment

P Ltd acquired 100% of the ordinary share capital, giving it control over S Ltd, for CU 510 000 on 1 January 20x5. At that date P Ltd considered the net assets of S Ltd to be fairly valued, with the exception of plant, which was undervalued by CU 40 000. The plant was acquired by S Ltd on acquisition date for CU 60 000. The useful life of the plant was five years with zero residual value.

The equity of S Ltd at acquisition date (before any fair value adjustments) comprised the following:
- share capital CU 150 000; and
- retained earnings CU 300 000.

Assume an income tax rate of 28%.

Required
Prepare the at acquisition pro forma journal to give effect to the above information assuming that S Ltd agreed to remeasure the plant to fair value in its own accounting records at acquisition date.

 Solution 5.1: Subsidiary recognises at acquisition fair value adjustment to property, plant and equipment

AT ACQUISITION

Pro forma journal	Dr CU	Cr CU
Share capital (S Ltd) (SCIE) (given)	150 000	
Retained earnings (S Ltd) (SCIE) (given)	300 000	
Revaluation surplus (S Ltd) (SCIE)	Wkg1 28 800	
Investment in S Ltd (P Ltd) (SFP) (given)		510 000
Goodwill (SFP) (balancing figure)	31 200	
Elimination of at acquisition equity and the cost of investment in subsidiary and recognition of goodwill		

Workings: Pro forma journals
Working 1
40 000 Revaluation: Plant × 72% (100% − 28%) After tax

Comments: Pro forma journal
- S Ltd would have put through the following journal in its own accounting records when remeasuring the plant to fair value:

  Dr Plant CU 40 000

      Cr Revaluation surplus CU 28 800

      Cr Deferred tax CU 11 200

- Accordingly, on consolidation, *no* pro forma entry is required to increase the value of the plant. The result of S Ltd's remeasurement of the plant to fair value is that S Ltd's at acquisition equity now includes a revaluation surplus that is eliminated on consolidation.

- The cost of the plant reported in S Ltd's individual financial statements of CU 100 000 (60 000 Original cost + 40 000 Revaluation) will be the same as that reflected in the consolidated financial statements. Consequently, no consolidation adjustment is required to increase plant depreciation for group purposes as S Ltd, in its individual financial statements, will calculate depreciation on the same depreciable amount for the plant, of CU 100 000, as the group does.

5.2 Remeasurement of subsidiary assets to at acquisition fair values: Adjusted upon consolidation

In this case, as *no* at acquisition fair value adjustment has been made in the subsidiary's own records, **on consolidation**, we need to adjust the subsidiary's assets to fair value at acquisition date by way of **pro forma journals** processed every reporting period for as long as the subsidiary is held by the parent. In addition, most often these at acquisition fair adjustments to subsidiary assets will have deferred tax implications in the consolidated financial statements, both at acquisition and subsequently (as discussed fully in Sections 5.2.8 and 5.2.10).

Under IFRS 10 *Consolidated Financial Statements*, the income and expenses of a subsidiary must be based on, among other things, the amounts of the assets recognised in the consolidated financial statements at the acquisition date (IFRS 10.B88). This implies that if any at acquisition fair value remeasurement adjustments are made to one or more of a subsidiary's assets at acquisition, further adjustments are required when consolidating the subsidiary's income and expenses after acquisition date, where such income and expenses relate to the remeasured assets concerned. That is, these income and expenses should be based on the **fair values** attributed to the subsidiary's assets at acquisition. Consequently, the **subsidiary's current year profit**, and **post-acquisition retained earnings** to the **beginning of the year**, must be **adjusted** to recognise the **knock-on effects** of remeasuring the **subsidiary's assets to fair value at acquisition**, where necessary.

This chapter deals with the post-acquisition consolidation adjustments to subsidiary income and expenses required where the asset that is remeasured on consolidation to its at acquisition fair value:

- is **non-depreciable** property, plant and equipment (e.g., land) that is **subsequently disposed of** to a party outside the group (discussed in Section 5.2.4);
- is **depreciable** property, plant and equipment (e.g., machinery) (discussed in Section 5.2.6);
- is **depreciable** property, plant and equipment that is subsequently disposed of to a party outside the group (discussed in Section 5.2.7); and
- is the **current asset inventory** that is **subsequently disposed of** to a party outside the group (discussed in Section 5.2.10).

Note: The knock on effects, in the post-acquisition consolidated financial statements, of at acquisition fair value adjustments to amortisable intangible assets, are dealt with in Volume 2 Chapter 1.

5.2.1 Effect on the non-controlling interest at acquisition date: At acquisition fair value adjustments to subsidiary assets

Remeasurements to fair value, made at acquisition date, to a subsidiary's assets will only affect the non-controlling interest recognised and measured at acquisition date if the non-controlling interest is measured at its **proportionate share** of the at acquisition date fair value of the subsidiary's identifiable net assets. This makes sense as any fair value adjustments to subsidiary assets at acquisition date will affect the subsidiary's net asset value (equity), a portion of which is then allocated to the non-controlling interest at acquisition date.

When the non-controlling interest is measured at **its fair value** at acquisition date, the non-controlling interest amount recognised at acquisition will be **unaffected** by **at acquisition fair value adjustments** to the **subsidiary's assets**. This is because this basis of measuring the non-controlling interest at acquisition date is **independent** of the at acquisition fair value of the subsidiary's net assets (i.e. it is based on **other factors,** such as the market price of the subsidiary's shares at acquisition date).

5.2.2 Effect on the non-controlling interest subsequent to acquisition date: Consequences of at acquisition date fair value adjustments to subsidiary assets in subsequent reporting periods

IFRS 10 requires that profit or loss and other comprehensive income (which combined makes up total comprehensive income) must be attributed to the owners of the parent and to the non-controlling interest (IFRS 10.B94). This implies that when a subsidiary's **since acquisition profit or loss or other comprehensive income** is **adjusted** because of the follow-on effects of at acquisition remeasurements of its assets to fair value, then the **non-controlling interest's share** of the **subsidiary's total comprehensive income post acquisition** must be its share of this **adjusted** total comprehensive income (i.e., the **adjusted** profit or loss and other comprehensive income of the subsidiary).

5.2.3 Fair value adjustments at acquisition date: Non-depreciable property, plant and equipment

When non-depreciable property, plant and equipment (e.g., land) of a subsidiary is remeasured to its at acquisition date fair value, the at acquisition pro forma elimination journal will include an **adjustment for this remeasurement**. This remeasurement will affect (either increase or decrease) the at acquisition net asset value (equity) of the subsidiary and consequently will have a bearing on the amount of any goodwill or bargain purchase gain recognised. Furthermore, the **at acquisition fair value** of the non-depreciable property, plant and equipment will be the **cost** of the asset to the **group.**

Example 5.2: Remeasurement of subsidiary asset to fair value at acquisition: Non-depreciable property, plant and equipment

P Ltd acquired 80% of the ordinary share capital, giving it control of S Ltd, on 31 December 20x5 for CU 270 000. P Ltd considered the net assets of S Ltd to be fairly valued, except for land, which had a fair value of CU 300 000 at acquisition date.

The trial balances for P Ltd and its subsidiary S Ltd at acquisition date are provided below.

Trial balances at 31 December 20x5	P Ltd Dr/(Cr) CU	S Ltd Dr/(Cr) CU
Share capital	(150 000)	(140 000)
Retained earnings (31 Dec 20x5)	(120 000)	(110 000)
Land: Cost	–	250 000
Investment in S Ltd: Cost	270 000	–

Required

(a) Prepare the at acquisition section of the analysis of equity of S Ltd as at 31 December 20x5, assuming that P Ltd measures the non-controlling interest at its proportionate share of S Ltd's identifiable net assets at acquisition.

(b) Prepare the pro forma journal entry as at 31 December 20x5, assuming that P Ltd measures the non-controlling interest at its proportionate share of S Ltd's identifiable net assets at acquisition.

(c) Prepare the at acquisition section of the analysis of equity of S Ltd as at 31 December 20x5, assuming that P Ltd measures the non-controlling interest at its fair value of CU 65 000.

(d) Prepare the pro forma journal entry as at 31 December 20x5, assuming that P Ltd measures the non-controlling interest at its fair value of CU 65 000.

Ignore tax implications of fair value adjustments.

Solution 5.2: Remeasurement of subsidiary asset to fair value at acquisition: Non-depreciable property, plant and equipment

Part (a): Analysis of equity at acquisition of S Ltd: Partial goodwill method applies

At acquisition date (31 December 20x5)	Total of S Ltd's equity 100% CU	P Ltd at acquisition 80% CU	Non-controlling interest 20% CU
Share capital	140 000	112 000	28 000
Retained earnings	110 000	88 000	22 000
Land (300 000 – 250 000)	50 000[1]	40 000[2]	10 000[2]
Fair value of net assets of S Ltd	300 000	240 000	60 000
Goodwill – Parent (balancing figure)	30 000	30 000	–
Consideration and non-controlling interest	330 000	270 000	60 000

Explanatory notes: Analysis of equity

[1]   The fair value adjustment to land must be included in the analysis of equity of S Ltd at acquisition date so that the fair value of S Ltd's net assets can be determined at acquisition date. This adjusted net asset value can then be compared to the consideration transferred (cost to P Ltd of its investment in S Ltd) to calculate the correct goodwill figure. If the CU 50 000 fair value adjustment to land is not recognised at acquisition date, then the true net asset value (equity) of the subsidiary will be understated by CU 50 000 and the goodwill recognised will be incorrectly overstated by CU 40 000 (50 000 × 80% P Ltd's interest).

[2]   Note that the effect of the at acquisition fair value adjustment to land, an increase in S Ltd's at acquisition equity of CU 50 000, is shared between the parent (40 000 increase in equity allocated) and the non-controlling interest (10 000 increase in equity allocated) based on each shareholder's respective ownership interest (i.e., 80% of fair value increase allocated to parent P Ltd and 20% to the non-controlling interest).

Part (b): Pro forma journal entry at acquisition date: Partial goodwill method

Pro forma journal 1 (J1)	Dr CU	Cr CU
Share capital (S Ltd) (SCIE) (given)	140 000[1]	
Retained earnings (S Ltd) (SCIE) (given)	110 000[2]	
Land (S Ltd) (SFP) (see Working 1)	50 000[3]	
Investment in S Ltd (P Ltd) (SFP) (given)		270 000[4]
Non-controlling interest – Equity (SCIE) (see Working 2)		60 000[5]
Goodwill (SFP) (balancing figure)	30 000[6]	
Elimination of common items at acquisition, recognition of fair value adjustment to land, recognition of non-controlling interest and goodwill		

Note: For purposes of this chapter, the numbers adjacent to the amounts in the pro forma journal cross-reference these amounts to the corresponding consolidation worksheet.

Workings: Pro forma journals

Working 1
300 000 – 250 000

Working 2
(140 000 + 110 000 + 50 000) × 20% NCI Share

Comments: Pro forma journal 1

- After processing the above pro forma journal, the group will correctly reflect the land at its at acquisition fair value of CU 300 000 in the consolidated statement of financial position.

- The above journal can be illustrated as per the following diagram:

	S Ltd's total (100%) fair value = CU 330 000				
	Goodwill	CU 30 000			
Identifiable net assets of S Ltd (equity of S Ltd) at **FAIR VALUE CU 300 000**	Fair value adjustment land (equity of S Ltd)	CU 50 000	CU 60 000	Non-controlling interest	
	Identifiable net assets of S Ltd at **CARRYING AMOUNT** (equity of S Ltd)	CU 250 000	CU 270 000	Investment in S Ltd	
	Dr			Cr	

The effects of the above pro forma entry are further illustrated in the consolidation worksheet below.

	P Ltd Dr/(Cr) CU	S Ltd Dr/(Cr) CU	Pro forma journals At acquisition Dr/(Cr) CU J1	Con- solidated Dr/(Cr) CU
Equity				
Share capital	(150 000)	(140 000)	140 000[1]	(150 000)
Retained earnings (at acquisition date)	(120 000)	(110 000)	110 000[2]	(120 000)
Non-controlling interest equity	–	–	(60 000)[5]	(60 000)
Total equity	**(270 000)**	**(250 000)**		**(330 000)**
Total liabilities	–	–		–
Total equity & liabilities	**(270 000)**	**(250 000)**		**(330 000)**
Assets				
Investment in S Ltd	270 000		(270 000)[4]	–
Land		250 000	50 000[3]	300 000
Goodwill	–	–	30 000[6]	30 000
Total assets	**270 000**	**250 000**		**330 000**

Part (c): Analysis of equity of S Ltd at acquisition: Full goodwill method applies

At acquisition date (31 December 20x5)	Total of S Ltd's equity 100% CU	P Ltd at acquisition 80% CU	Non-controlling interest 20% CU
Share capital	140 000	112 000	
Retained earnings	110 000	88 000	
Land (300 000 – 250 000)	50 000[1]	40 000	
Fair value of net assets of S Ltd	300 000	240 000	60 000
Goodwill – Parent (balancing figure)	30 000	30 000	–
Goodwill – Non-controlling interest (balancing figure)	5 000		5 000[2]
Consideration and non-controlling interest	335 000	270 000	65 000

Explanatory notes: Analysis of equity

[1] Unlike the scenario in Part (a), no portion of this fair value adjustment to the land is included in the recognition and measurement of the non-controlling interest at acquisition date as the non-controlling interest is measured at its fair value.

[2] The goodwill attributable to the non-controlling interest is calculated as the excess of the non-controlling interest's fair value over its proportionate share of the subsidiary's net asset value.

Part (d): Pro forma journal entry at acquisition date: Full goodwill method applies

Pro forma journal 1 (J1)	Dr CU	Cr CU
Share capital (S Ltd) (SCIE) (given)	140 000[1]	
Retained earnings (S Ltd) (SCIE) (given)	110 000[2]	
Land (S Ltd) (SFP) (300 000 – 250 000)	50 000[3]	
Investment in S Ltd (P Ltd) (SFP) (given)		270 000[4]
Non-controlling interest – Equity (SCIE) (given)		65 000[5]
Goodwill (SFP) (balancing figure)	35 000[6]	
Elimination of common items at acquisition, recognition of fair value adjustment to land, recognition of non-controlling interest and goodwill		

The above journal can be illustrated as per the following diagram:

S Ltd's total (100%) fair value = CU 335 000				
Identifiable net assets of S Ltd (equity of S Ltd) **at FAIR VALUE CU 300 000**	Goodwill	CU 35 000		
	Fair value adjustment land (equity of S Ltd)	CU 50 000	CU 65 000	Non-controlling interest
	Identifiable net assets of S Ltd at **CARRYING AMOUNT** (equity of S Ltd)	CU 250 000	CU 270 000	Investment in S Ltd

Dr △ Cr

The effects of the above pro forma entry are further illustrated in the consolidation worksheet below.

	P Ltd Dr/(Cr) CU	S Ltd Dr/(Cr) CU	Pro forma journals At acquisition Dr/(Cr) CU J1	Con- solidated Dr/(Cr) CU
Equity				
Share capital	(150 000)	(140 000)	140 000[1]	(150 000)
Retained earnings (at acquisition date)	(120 000)	(110 000)	110 000[2]	(120 000)
Non-controlling interest equity	–	–	(65 000)[5]	(65 000)
Total equity	**(270 000)**	**(250 000)**		**(335 000)**
Total liabilities	–	–		–
Total equity & liabilities	**(270 000)**	**(250 000)**		**(335 000)**
Assets				
Investment in S Ltd	270 000		(270 000)[4]	–
Land		250 000	50 000[3]	300 000
Goodwill	–	–	35 000[6]	35 000
Total assets	**270 000**	**250 000**		**335 000**

5.2.4 Consequences of at acquisition fair value adjustment to non-depreciable property, plant and equipment in subsequent reporting periods: Subsequent sale of non-depreciable, property, plant and equipment, remeasured at fair value at acquisition

If a non-depreciable property, plant and equipment asset that was remeasured to fair value at acquisition date is **subsequently sold**, it follows that the **gain or loss on disposal** of this asset as determined by the **subsidiary** in its **separate accounting records, will differ** to that as recognised by the **group**. More particularly, the amount of the consolidated gain or loss on disposal will differ to that as determined by the subsidiary, by the amount of the **at acquisition fair value adjustment** made to this asset. Therefore, on consolidation, a **pro forma journal** is required to **adjust** the **subsidiary's gain or loss on disposal** to the correct gain or loss **for group purposes**.

When the gain or loss on disposal of the non depreciable property, plant and equipment asset occurs in the **current reporting period**, the **profit or loss** of the subsidiary is adjusted on consolidation. On the other hand, the **subsidiary's retained earnings since acquisition to the beginning of the year** is adjusted on consolidation, when this asset has been disposed in a **previous financial year**. In addition, **irrespective** of whether the partial or full goodwill method is applied, the **non-controlling interest** will be attributed its **appropriate share** of the **consolidation adjustment** to the **subsidiary's profit or loss on disposal** of the non-depreciable property, plant and equipment.

Example 5.3: Subsequent sale of non depreciable property, plant and equipment that was adjusted to fair value at acquisition date

This example follows on from the previous Example 5.2. During the financial year ended 31 December 20x6 S Ltd disposed of its land to a third party for CU 320 000. The abridged trial balances of P Ltd and S Ltd were as follows for the 20x6 and 20x7 financial years:

Abridged trial balances at 31 December 20x6	P Ltd Dr/(Cr) CU	S Ltd Dr/(Cr) CU
Share capital	(150 000)	(140 000)
Retained earnings (1 Jan 20x6)	(120 000)	(110 000)
Trade and other payables	(32 000)	(15 000)
Land	70 000	–
Equipment	144 000	225 000
Trade and other receivables	98 000	155 000
Investment in S Ltd: Cost	270 000	–
Profit for the period	(280 000)	(115 000)

Abridged trial balances at 31 December 20x7	P Ltd Dr/(Cr) CU	S Ltd Dr/(Cr) CU
Share capital	(150 000)	(140 000)
Retained earnings (1 Jan 20x7)	(400 000)	(225 000)

➠

Abridged trial balances at 31 December 20x7 (continued)	P Ltd Dr/(Cr) CU	S Ltd Dr/(Cr) CU
Trade and other payables	(18 000)	(22 000)
Land	70 000	–
Equipment	244 000	305 000
Trade and other receivables	118 000	157 000
Investment in S Ltd: Cost	270 000	–
Profit for the period	(134 000)	(75 000)

Additional information

- Assume that the non-controlling interest is measured at its proportionate share of the identifiable net assets of the subsidiary.
- Ignore tax implications of fair value adjustments.

Required

(a) Prepare the analysis of equity of S Ltd and the pro forma journal entries for the year ended 31 December 20x6.

(b) Prepare the analysis of equity of S Ltd and the pro forma journal entries for the year ended 31 December 20x7.

(c) Prepare the consolidated financial statements of the P Ltd group for the year ended 31 December 20x7.

 Solution 5.3: Subsequent sale of non depreciable property, plant and equipment that was adjusted to fair value at acquisition date

Part (a): Analysis of equity (AOE) of S Ltd at 31 December 20x6

At acquisition date (31 December 20x5)	Total of S Ltd's equity 100% CU	P Ltd 80% At acquisition CU	P Ltd 80% Since acquisition CU	Non-controlling interest 20% CU
Share capital	140 000	112 000		28 000
Retained earnings	110 000	88 000		22 000
Land: Fair value adjustment (300 000 – 250 000)	50 000[1]	40 000		10 000
Fair value of net assets of S Ltd	300 000	240 000		60 000
Goodwill – Parent (balancing figure)	30 000	30 000		–
Consideration and non-controlling interest	330 000	270 000		60 000
Since acquisition				
• Current year:				
Adjusted profit for the year	65 000		52 000	13 000
Profit for the period (given)	115 000		92 000	23 000
Profit on sale of land adjustment	(50 000)[1]		(40 000)[2]	(10 000)[2]
	395 000		52 000	73 000

Explanatory notes: Analysis of equity

[1] The cost of the land to the group – due to the fair value at acquisition – was CU 50 000 more than the cost recognised in subsidiary S Ltd's own records. Accordingly, the group's profit on disposal of the land is CU 50 000 less than that recognised by S Ltd in its own records.

We therefore need to adjust (reduce) the current year profit of S Ltd – which includes the profit on disposal of the land – by CU 50 000 to arrive at the correct profit of S Ltd to be included in consolidated profit or loss.

[2] The effect of the consolidation adjustment to the current year profit of S Ltd is allocated to the parent, P Ltd, and to the non-controlling interest in accordance with each respective party's shareholding in S Ltd (i.e., 80% to P Ltd and 20% to the non-controlling interest).

Part (a): Pro forma journal entries for the financial year ended 31 December 20x6

AT ACQUISITION

Pro forma journal 1 (J1)	Dr CU	Cr CU
Share capital (S Ltd) (SCIE) (given)	140 000	
Retained earnings (S Ltd) (SCIE) (given)	110 000	
Land (S Ltd) (SFP)	Wkg1 50 000	
Investment in S Ltd (P Ltd) (SFP) (given)		270 000
Non-controlling interest – Equity (SCIE)		Wkg2 60 000
Goodwill (SFP) (balancing figure)	30 000	
Elimination of at acquisition equity and cost of investment, recognition of fair value adjustment to land and recognition of non-controlling interest and goodwill at acquisition		

Workings: Pro forma journals

Working 1

300 000 – 250 000

Working 2

(140 000 + 110 000 + 50 000) × 20% NCI Share

Comments: Pro forma journal 1

- As discussed previously, given that pro forma journals affect neither the accounting records of the subsidiary nor the parent, we are required to process the same at acquisition pro forma journal every year that we prepare consolidated financial statements.

- Although the land has been sold at year end and is no longer an asset of the group, we still process the at acquisition fair value adjustment thereto. This is done so that we reflect the correct at acquisition equity that is acquired by the parent, P Ltd, in order to calculate correctly the goodwill at acquisition. The at acquisition fair value adjustment to the land is then eliminated in a subsequent pro forma journal (see pro forma journal 2), where the profit on disposal of the land is reduced by the same amount.

CURRENT YEAR

Pro forma journal 2 (J2)	Dr CU	Cr CU
Profit on disposal of land (S Ltd) (P/L)	50 000	
Land (S Ltd) (SFP) (see (J1))		50 000
Elimination of at acquisition fair value remeasurement of land and adjustment to recognise reduced group profit on disposal of this land outside of the group		

Comments: Pro forma journal 2

- The debit entry adjusts, S Ltd's profit on disposal of the land to reflect the reduced consolidated profit on disposal given the at acquisition fair value remeasurement of this land for group purposes. The profit on disposal of land reflected in the consolidated financial statements is CU 50 000 less than that recognised by S Ltd. This is because the value of S Ltd's land at acquisition was increased by CU 50 000 on consolidation to reflect its at acquisition fair value. That is, the land disposed of by S Ltd in the current year has a cost to the group that is CU 50 000 more than its cost to S Ltd. It follows then that the consolidated profit on disposal of the land must be CU 50 000 less than that recognised by S Ltd.

- The contra credit in this pro forma journal is to land, which results in a NIL balance for land in the consolidated financial statements at financial reporting period end. This makes sense as the land has been sold and is no longer a group asset at financial reporting period end.

Pro forma journal 3 (J3)	Dr CU	Cr CU
NCI – Share of profit or loss (P/L)	Wkg3 13 000	
Non-controlling interest – Equity (SFP)		Wkg3 13 000
Allocating the non-controlling interest its share of S Ltd's adjusted profit for the year		

Workings: Pro forma journals

Working 3

(115 000 Current year profit: Given – 50 000 (J2) Reduction in profit on disposal: land) × 20% NCI Share

Comments: Pro forma journal 3

- It is important to understand that S Ltd's profit for the year that is allocated to the non-controlling interest is S Ltd's profit **after first adjusting** this profit to recognise the reduced group profit on disposal of S Ltd's land (see pro forma journal 2).

The effects of the three preceding pro forma journal entries are further illustrated in the following consolidation worksheet.

	P Ltd Dr/(Cr) CU	S Ltd Dr/(Cr) CU	Pro forma journals At acquisition Dr/(Cr) CU	Journal ref	Pro forma journals Since acquisition Dr/(Cr) CU	Journal ref	Consolidated Dr/(Cr) CU
Equity							
Share capital	(150 000)	(140 000)	140 000	J1			(150 000)
Retained earnings (BOY)	(120 000)	(110 000)	110 000	J1			(120 000)
Net profit: Individual entities	(280 000)	(115 000)					†(332 000)
Consolidated profit – attributable to owners of parent							
Retained earnings (EOY)	(400 000)	(225 000)					(452 000)
NCI Equity	–	–	(60 000)	J1	(13 000)	J3	(73 000)
Total equity	(550 000)	(365 000)					(675 000)
Liabilities:							
Trade and other payables	(32 000)	(15 000)					(47 000)
Total liabilities	(32 000)	(15 000)					(47 000)
Total equity & liabilities	(582 000)	(380 000)					(722 000)

Explanatory notes

† This amount has been brought forward from the second part of the consolidation worksheet on page 232

| | P Ltd | S Ltd | Pro forma journals At acquisition | | Pro forma journals Since acquisition | | Con-solidated |
	Dr/(Cr) CU	Dr/(Cr) CU	Dr/(Cr) CU	Journal ref	Dr/(Cr) CU	Journal ref	Dr/(Cr) CU
Assets:							
Land	70 000	–	50 000	J1	(50 000)	J2	70 000
Equipment	144 000	225 000					369 000
Trade and other receivables	98 000	155 000					253 000
Investment in S Ltd	270 000	–	(270 000)	J1			–
Goodwill			30 000	J1			30 000
Total assets	**582 000**	**380 000**					**722 000**
Profit or loss							
Profit	(280 000)	(115 000)			50 000	J2	(345 000)
NCI: Share of profit					13 000	J3	13 000
Consolidated profit attributable to owners of parent							‡(332 000)

Explanatory notes

‡ This amount has been carried forward to the first part of the consolidation worksheet on page 231

Part (b): Analysis of equity (AOE) of S Ltd at 31 December 20x7

		P Ltd 80%		
At acquisition date (31 December 20x5)	**Total of S Ltd's equity 100%** CU	**At acquisition** CU	**Since acquisition** CU	**Non-controlling interest 20%** CU
Share capital	140 000	112 000		28 000
Retained earnings	110 000	88 000		22 000
Land (300 000 – 250 000)	50 000	40 000		10 000
Fair value of net assets of S Ltd	300 000	240 000		60 000
Goodwill – parent (balancing figure)	30 000	30 000 a		–
Consideration and non-controlling interest	330 000	270 000		60 000
Since acquisition				
• To beginning of current year:				
Adjusted retained earnings	65 000		52 000 b	13 000
Retained earnings movement (225 000 Balance BOY – 110 000 Balance at acquisition)	115 000		92 000	23 000
Reduced profit on sale of land	(50 000)[1]		(40 000)[2]	(10 000)[2]
				73 000 c
• Current year:				
Profit for the year	75 000		60 000 d	15 000 e
	470 000		112 000	88 000 f

Explanatory notes: Analysis of equity

[1] The effects of the prior year consolidation adjustment, which reduced S Ltd's prior year profit on disposal of land by CU 50 000, were included in S Ltd's prior year profit or loss, which was closed off to retained earnings at prior year end. Therefore, for current year consolidation purposes, this CU 50 000 prior year consolidation adjustment to S Ltd's profit is recognised as a CU 50 000 reduction in S Ltd's opening retained earnings balance.

[2] As was the case in Part (a), the effect of the consolidation adjustment is allocated to the parent and to the non-controlling interest, according to their respective shareholdings in S Ltd. The only difference is that in this case the adjustment is processed to S Ltd's retained earnings rather than S Ltd's profit or loss.

Part (b): Pro forma journal entries for the financial year ended 31 December 20x7

AT ACQUISITION

Pro forma journal 1 (J1)	Dr CU	Cr CU
Share capital (S Ltd) (SCIE) (given)	140 000	
Retained earnings (S Ltd) (SCIE) (given)	110 000	
Land (S Ltd) (SFP)	Wkg1 50 000	
Investment in S Ltd (P Ltd) (SFP) (given)		270 000
Non-controlling interest – Equity (SCIE)		Wkg2 60 000
Goodwill (SFP) (balancing figure)	30 000	
Elimination of at acquisition equity and cost of investment, recognition of fair value adjustment to land, recognition of non-controlling interest and goodwill		

Workings: Pro forma journals

Working 1

300 000 – 250 000

Working 2

(140 000 + 110 000 + 50 000) × 20% NCI Share

SINCE ACQUISITION TO THE BEGINNING OF THE YEAR

Pro forma journal 2 (J2)	Dr CU	Cr CU
Retained earnings (S Ltd) (P/L)	50 000	
Land (S Ltd) (SFP) (see (J1))		50 000
Elimination of at acquisition fair value remeasurement of land and recognition of prior period's reduced group profit on disposal of land		

Comments: Pro forma journal 2

- In the prior year, S Ltd's profit on disposal of land was reduced by CU 50 000 for group purposes because of the CU 50 000 at acquisition fair value adjustment that was made to this land (see pro forma journal 1). Consequently, on consolidation, S Ltd's prior year profit was reduced by CU 50 000, which profit was closed off to retained earnings at prior financial year end.

- As we are preparing consolidated financial statements for the reporting period, one year after the year of acquisition (i.e., for the following financial year), S Ltd's current year profit or loss cannot be adjusted. Rather, on consolidation in the current year, S Ltd's opening retained earnings balance must be adjusted (i.e., reduced) to take into account the prior year CU 50 000 reduction in the profit on sale of S Ltd's land recognised for group purposes. This is achieved by debiting and so reducing S Ltd's opening retained earnings balance by CU 50 000.

- The CU 50 000 contra credit to land reverses the at acquisition entry debiting land with CU 50 000 in order to recognise land at its at acquisition fair value (see pro forma journal 1). The at acquisition fair value adjustment to land must be reversed because the land has been sold by S Ltd and is therefore no longer held by the group.

Pro forma journal 3 (J3)	Dr CU	Cr CU
Retained earnings(S Ltd) (SCIE)	Wkg3 13 000	
Non-controlling interest – Equity (SFP)		Wkg3 13 000
Allocating the non-controlling interest its share of S Ltd's adjusted post-acquisition retained earnings to the beginning of the year		

Workings: Pro forma journals

Working 3

(225 000 Balance BOY – 110 000 (J1) Balance at acquisition – 50 000 (J2) Prior year reduction in profit on disposal of land) × 20% NCI Share

Comments: Pro forma journal 3

- The non-controlling interest is allocated its 20% share of S Ltd's since acquisition retained earnings to the beginning of the year. This allocation is only made, however, once S Ltd's opening retained earnings balance has **first been reduced** by the CU 50 000 prior year reduction in S Ltd's profit on sale of land, recognised for group purposes.

CURRENT YEAR

Pro forma journal 4 (J4)	Dr CU	Cr CU
NCI – Share of profit or loss (P/L)	Wkg4 15 000	
Non-controlling interest – Equity (SFP)		Wkg4 15 000
Allocating the non-controlling interest its share of S Ltd's profit for the year		

Workings: Pro forma journals

Working 4

75 000 Current year profit × 20% NCI Share

The full effects of these four preceding pro forma journals are illustrated in the following consolidation worksheet.

	P Ltd Dr/(Cr) CU	S Ltd Dr/(Cr) CU	Pro forma journals At acquisition Dr/(Cr) CU	Journal ref	Pro forma journals Since acquisition Dr/(Cr) CU	Journal ref	Con-solidated Dr/(Cr) CU
Equity							
Share capital	(150 000)	(140 000)	140 000	J1			(150 000)
Retained earnings (BOY)	(400 000)	(225 000)	110 000	J1	50 000	J2	(452 000)
					13 000	J3	
Net profit: Individual entities	(134 000)	(75 000)					
Consolidated profit – attributable to owners of parent							†(194 000)
Retained earnings (EOY)	(534 000)	(300 000)	(60 000)	J1			(646 000)
NCI Equity	–	–			(13 000)	J3	(88 000)
					(15 000)	J4	
Total equity	**(684 000)**	**(440 000)**					**(884 000)**
Liabilities:							
Trade and other payables	(18 000)	(22 000)					(40 000)
Total liabilities	**(18 000)**	**(22 000)**					**(40 000)**
Total equity & liabilities	**(702 000)**	**(462 000)**					**(924 000)**

Explanatory notes

† This amount has been brought forward from the second part of the consolidation worksheet on page 237

	P Ltd Dr/(Cr) CU	S Ltd Dr/(Cr) CU	Pro forma journals At acquisition Dr/(Cr) CU	Journal ref	Pro forma journals Since acquisition Dr/(Cr) CU	Journal ref	Consolidated Dr/(Cr) CU
Assets:							
Land	70 000	–	50 000	J1	(50 000)	J2	70 000
Equipment	244 000	305 000					549 000
Trade and other receivables	118 000	157 000					275 000
Investment in S Ltd	270 000	–	(270 000)	J1			–
Goodwill			30 000	J1			30 000
Total assets	**702 000**	**462 000**					**924 000**
Profit or loss							
Profit	(134 000)	(75 000)					(209 000)
NCI: Share of profit					15 000	J4	15 000
Consolidated profit attributable to owners of parent							‡(194 000)

Explanatory notes

‡ This amount has been carried forward to the first part of the consolidation worksheet on page 236

Part (c): Consolidated financial statements for the year ended 31 December 20x7

P LTD GROUP: ABRIDGED CONSOLIDATED STATEMENT OF PROFIT OR LOSS AND OTHER COMPREHENSIVE INCOME FOR THE YEAR ENDED 31 DECEMBER 20X7	
	CU
PROFIT FOR THE YEAR (134 000 (P Ltd) + 75 000 (S Ltd))	209 000
Other comprehensive income for the year	–
TOTAL COMPREHENSIVE INCOME FOR THE YEAR	**209 000**
Total comprehensive income for the year attributable to:	
Owners of the parent (balancing figure) **OR** (134 000 (P Ltd) + S Ltd: 60 000 (see AOE **d**))	194 000
Non-controlling interest (see AOE **e OR** (J4))	15 000
	209 000

P LTD GROUP: CONSOLIDATED STATEMENT OF CHANGES IN EQUITY FOR THE YEAR ENDED 31 DECEMBER 20x7	Parent equity holders' interest			Non-controlling interest	Total equity of the group
	Share capital	Retained earnings	Total parent equity		
	CU	CU	CU	CU	CU
Opening balance at 1 Jan 20x7	150 000	Wkg1 452 000	602 000	Wkg2 73 000	675 000
Total comprehensive income:					
Profit for the period (from CSOPL_OCI)		194 000	194 000	15 000	209 000
Closing balance at 31 Dec 20x7	150 000	646 000	796 000	88 000	884 000

Workings: Consolidated statement of changes in equity

Working 1

P Ltd: 400 000 + S Ltd: 52 000 (see AOE **b**) P Ltd Share of S Ltd post-acquisition retained earnings to BOY

OR

P Ltd: 400 000 + (S Ltd: 225 000 Balance BOY – 110 000 (J1) Balance at acquisition – 50 000 (J2) Reduction in profit on disposal of land – 13 000 (J3) NCI share of S Ltd post-acquisition retained earnings to BOY)

Working 2

S Ltd: 73 000 (see AOE **c**)

OR

S Ltd: 60 000 (J1) NCI Share of S Ltd at acquisition equity + 13 000 (J3) NCI Share of S Ltd post-acquisition retained earnings to BOY

P LTD GROUP: CONSOLIDATED STATEMENT OF FINANCIAL POSITION AS AT 31 DECEMBER 20x7	
	CU
Assets	
Non-current assets	
Property, plant and equipment ((P Ltd: 70 000 Land + 244 000 Equipment) + 305 000 Equipment (S Ltd))	619 000
Goodwill 30 000 ((see AOE **a**) **OR** (J1))	30 000
Current assets	
Trade and other receivables (118 000 (P Ltd) + 157 000 (S Ltd))	275 000
Total assets	924 000
Equity and liabilities	
Share capital (from CSCIE)	150 000
Retained earnings (from CSCIE)	646 000
Equity attributable to owners of the parent	796 000
Non-controlling interest (from CSCIE) **OR** (see AOE **f**)	88 000
Total equity	884 000
Current liabilities	
Trade and other payables (18 000 (P Ltd) + 22 000 (S Ltd))	40 000
Total equity and liabilities	924 000

5.2.5 Fair value adjustments at acquisition date: Depreciable property, plant and equipment

The **fair value** of a **depreciable** property, plant and equipment **asset** at **acquisition date** is the **cost** of that asset to the **group**. The implications of this on consolidation are the following:

- At acquisition date, we must **eliminate** – via a pro forma journal – the **accumulated depreciation** processed by the subsidiary, **before the date of acquisition** of the subsidiary, against the **cost of the asset**. This is because the accumulated depreciation of the asset pre acquisition date reflects usage of the asset pre acquisition date. From the group's perspective, however, the asset acquired is unused and therefore its pre-acquisition accumulated depreciation must be reduced to **NIL** to reflect this. The result is that the carrying amount of the depreciable asset in the subsidiary's own accounting records will initially be the cost to the group.

- When the **carrying amount** (as discussed above) of the subsidiary's depreciable asset is **different** to its **fair value at acquisition**, an additional pro forma consolidation adjustment is required in order to reflect the asset at **fair value at acquisition date**. This **fair value** then becomes the **cost of the asset to the group**.

5.2.6 Consequences of at acquisition fair value adjustments to depreciable property, plant and equipment in subsequent reporting periods

When preparing consolidated financial statements for reporting periods subsequent to acquisition date, we need to process a **consolidation adjustment** to the **depreciation** of the subsidiary's property, plant and equipment asset that was remeasured to fair value at acquisition date. This is because the **group** will depreciate this asset based on its acquisition date **fair value** – which is the cost of this asset to the group – while the **subsidiary** will continue to depreciate this asset based on its **carrying amount** (assuming that the subsidiary does not revalue the depreciable asset at acquisition in its own records). Accordingly, the depreciation expense to be recognised for this subsidiary asset for consolidation purposes will differ from the depreciation expense recognised for this asset in the subsidiary's separate records. This means that on consolidation, this **difference in the depreciation expense recognised** will need to be **adjusted for.**

More particularly:

- If there is an upward remeasurement of the subsidiary's depreciable property, plant and equipment to fair value at acquisition date, additional depreciation on this property, plant and equipment will be recognised on consolidation.
- If there is a downward remeasurement of the subsidiary's depreciable property, plant and equipment to fair value at acquisition date, a reduction in the depreciation of this property, plant and equipment will be recognised on consolidation.

The post-acquisition consolidation adjustments to the depreciation of the subsidiary will require adjustments to:

- the **opening retained earnings balance** of the subsidiary in respect of the depreciation of **prior periods** (i.e., depreciation in the period from acquisition date to the beginning of the current period); and
- the **profit or loss** of the subsidiary in respect of depreciation in the **current reporting period.**

In addition, the **non-controlling interest** will be allocated **its share of any consolidation adjustments** to the **subsidiary's depreciation.**

Example 5.4: Remeasurement of subsidiary non-current asset to fair value at acquisition: Depreciable property, plant and equipment

P Ltd acquired 80% of the ordinary share capital of S Ltd on 31 December 20x5 for CU 350 000. P Ltd considered the net assets of S Ltd to be fairly valued, except for plant, which had a fair value of CU 385 000 at acquisition date.

P Ltd measured the non-controlling interest at its proportionate share of the fair value of S Ltd's identifiable net assets at acquisition date.

The trial balances for P Ltd and its subsidiary S Ltd at acquisition date are provided below.

Trial balances at 31 December 20x5	P Ltd Dr/(Cr) CU	S Ltd Dr/(Cr) CU
Share capital	(150 000)	(170 000)
Retained earnings (31 Dec 20x5)	(200 000)	(145 000)
Plant: Cost	–	420 000
Plant: Accumulated depreciation		(105 000)
Investment in S Ltd: Cost	350 000	–

Required
Prepare the analysis of equity for S Ltd and the pro forma journal entries required at acquisition date.

Ignore tax implications of fair value adjustments.

Solution 5.4: Remeasurement of subsidiary non-current asset to fair value at acquisition: Depreciable property, plant and equipment

Analysis of equity of S Ltd at acquisition date

At acquisition date (31 December 20x5)	Total of S Ltd's equity 100% CU	P Ltd 80% at acquisition CU	Non-controlling interest 20% CU
Share capital	170 000	136 000	34 000
Retained earnings	145 000	116 000	29 000
Plant (385 000 Fair value – (420 000 Carrying amount – 105 000 Accumulated depreciation))	70 000[1]	56 000	14 000
Fair value of net assets of S Ltd	385 000	308 000	77 000
Goodwill – Parent (balancing figure)	42 000	42 000	–
Consideration and non-controlling interest	427 000	350 000	77 000

Explanatory note: Analysis of equity

[1] The fair value adjustment to plant increases the net asset value (equity) of S Ltd at acquisition by CU 70 000. In arriving at the fair value adjustment, we compare the carrying amount of S Ltd's plant of CU 315 000 (420 000 – 105 000) to its CU 385 000 fair value at acquisition date.

Pro forma journal entries at acquisition date

Pro forma journal 1 (J1)	Dr CU	Cr CU
Plant: Accumulated depreciation (S Ltd) (SFP) (given)	105 000[1]	
Plant: Cost (S Ltd) (SFP)		105 000[2]
Elimination of at acquisition accumulated depreciation of plant		

Comments: Pro forma journal 1

- The accumulated depreciation of the plant recognised by S Ltd prior to acquisition date is reversed against the cost of the plant on consolidation as such depreciation relates to the use of the plant prior to its acquisition by the group.
- The result at group level is NIL accumulated depreciation for the plant at acquisition date, with the plant's at acquisition carrying amount recognised as its initial cost to the group.
- Thereafter, this carrying amount is compared to the plant's fair value to determine any fair value adjustments required at acquisition date.

Pro forma journal 2 (J2)	Dr CU	Cr CU
Share capital (S Ltd) (SCIE) (given)	170 000[3]	
Retained earnings (S Ltd) (SCIE) (given)	145 000[4]	
Plant (S Ltd) (SFP) (see Working 1)	70 000[5]	
Investment in S Ltd (P Ltd) (SFP) (given)		350 000[6]
NCI – Equity (SCIE) (see Working 2)		77 000[7]
Goodwill (SFP) (balancing figure)	42 000[8]	
Elimination of at acquisition equity and cost of investment, remeasurement of plant at fair value and recognition of non-controlling interest and goodwill at acquisition		

Workings: Pro forma journals

Working 1

385 000 Fair value – (420 000 Carrying amount – 105 000 Accumulated depreciation)

Working 2

(170 000 + 145 000 + 70 000) × 20% NCI Share

Comments: Pro forma journal 2

- This journal processes the required at acquisition adjustment to the value of plant to reflect the plant at its fair value of CU 385 000, which is its cost to the group.
- Note that the remeasurement of the plant to fair value increases the at acquisition equity of S Ltd, which in turn affects the amount of goodwill and non-controlling interest recognised at acquisition.

This journal can be illustrated as per the following diagram:

	S Ltd's total (100%) fair value = CU 427 000			
	Goodwill	CU 42 000		
Identifiable net assets of S Ltd (equity of S Ltd) at **FAIR VALUE CU 385 000**	Fair value adjustment plant (equity of S Ltd)	CU 70 000	CU 77 000	Non-controlling interest
	Identifiable net assets of S Ltd at **CARRYING AMOUNT** (equity of S Ltd)	CU 315 000	CU 350 000	Investment in S Ltd

Dr △ Cr

The effects of the two pro forma journal entries above are further illustrated in the consolidation worksheet below.

Consolidated worksheet: P Ltd group as at 31 December 20x5

	P Ltd Dr/(Cr) CU	S Ltd Dr/(Cr) CU	Pro forma journals At acquisition Dr/(Cr) CU	Jour- nal ref	Con- solidated Dr/(Cr) CU
Equity					
Share capital	(150 000)	(170 000)	170 000[3]	J2	(150 000)
Retained earnings (at acquisition date)	(200 000)	(145 000)	145 000[4]	J2	(200 000)
Non-controlling interest equity	–	–	(77 000)[7]	J2	(77 000)
Total equity	**(350 000)**	**(315 000)**			**(427 000)**
Total liabilities	–	–			–
Total equity & liabilities	**(350 000)**	**(315 000)**			**(427 000)**
Assets					
Investment in S Ltd	350 000	–	(350 000)[6]	J2	–
Plant: Cost	–	420 000	(105 000)[2] 70 000[5]	J1 J2	†385 000
Plant: Accumulated depreciation	–	(105 000)	105 000[1]	J1	‡–
Goodwill	–	–	42 000[8]	J2	42 000
Total assets	**350 000**	**315 000**			**427 000**

Explanatory notes

† Note how the plant is reflected at fair value at acquisition date, which equals the cost to the group.

‡ Note how accumulated depreciation plant has been eliminated at acquisition.

Example 5.5: Depreciable property, plant and equipment remeasured to fair value at acquisition date: Post-acquisition implications

This example is a continuation of Example 5.4. Additional information:

- At acquisition date the estimated remaining useful life of S Ltd's plant was seven years with no residual value. These estimates were confirmed at each reporting date.
- Ignore the tax effects of fair value adjustments both at acquisition, and subsequently.

The trial balances of P Ltd and S Ltd at 31 December 20x8 were as follows:

Trial balances at 31 December 20x8	P Ltd Dr/(Cr) CU	S Ltd Dr/(Cr) CU
Share capital	(150 000)	(170 000)
Retained earnings (1 Jan 20x8)	(310 000)	(250 000)
Trade and other payables	(32 000)	(15 000)
Plant: Cost	–	420 000
Plant: Accumulated depreciation	–	(195 000)
Trade and other receivables	208 000	245 000

Trial balances at 31 December 20x8 (continued)	P Ltd Dr/(Cr) CU	S Ltd Dr/(Cr) CU
Investment in S Ltd: Cost	350 000	–
Profit before depreciation and tax	(108 000)	(115 000)
Taxation	42 000	35 000
Depreciation	–	45 000

Required

(a) Prepare the analysis of equity of S Ltd as at 31 December 20x8.

(b) Provide the pro forma journal entries necessary to prepare the consolidated financial statements of the P Ltd Group for the year ended 31 December 20x8.

(c) Prepare the consolidated financial statements of the P Ltd Group for the year ended 31 December 20x8.

Solution 5.5: Depreciable property, plant and equipment remeasured to fair value at acquisition date: Post-acquisition implications

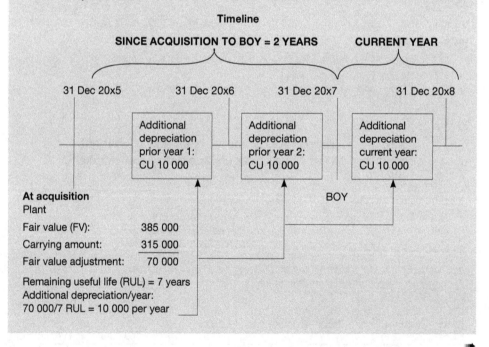

Depreciation table

	Plant carrying amount: S Ltd (i)	Plant carrying amount: Group (ii)	Plant carrying amount: Fair value adjustment (ii – i)	Pro forma journal	Period
Carrying amount 31 Dec 20x5	**315 000**	**315 000**	–		
Fair value adjustment 31 Dec 20x5	–	70 000	70 000 a	**Dr** Plant CU 70 000 (see pro forma journal 2 below)	At acquisition
Depreciation 1 Jan 20x6 – 31 Dec 20x7 (2 years)	Wkg1(90 000)	Wkg2(110 000)	(20 000) b	**Dr** Retained earnings CU 20 000; **Cr** Accumulated depreciation CU 20 000 (see pro forma journal 3 below)	Since acquisition to BOY
Carrying amount 1 Jan 20x8	**225 000**	**275 000**	**50 000**		**Balance BOY**
Depreciation year ended 31 Dec 20x8	Wkg3(45 000)	Wkg4(55 000)	(10 000) c	**Dr** Depreciation CU10 000; **Cr** Accumulated depreciation CU10 000 (see pro forma journal 5 below)	Current year
Carrying amount 31 Dec 20x8	**180 000**	**220 000**	**40 000**		**Balance EOY**

Workings: Depreciation table

Working 1

(315 000 Carrying amount of plant / 7 years RUL of plant at acquisition) × 2 Years since acquisition to BOY

Working 2

(315 000 Carrying amount of plant + 70 000 Fair value adjustment plant: at acquisition) / 7 years RUL of plant at acquisition) × 2 Years since acquisition to BOY

Working 3

(315 000 Carrying amount of plant / 7 years RUL of plant at acquisition)

Working 4

(315 000 Carrying amount of plant + 70 000 Fair value adjustment plant: at acquisition) / 7 years RUL of plant at acquisition

Comments: Timeline and depreciation table

- From the above timeline and depreciation table it is clear that the fair value of S Ltd's plant of CU 385 000 is CU 70 000 more than its CU 315 000 carrying amount at acquisition date.
- This fair value represents the cost of the plant to the group and is the value used in calculating the group depreciation charge for the plant. As the subsidiary, S Ltd, in its own records calculates depreciation based on the plant's lower carrying amount of CU 315 000, a consolidation adjustment increasing S Ltd's plant depreciation charge is required each year subsequent to acquisition for the plant's remaining useful life of seven years.
- More particularly, CU 10 000 of additional depreciation must be recognised each year on consolidation in respect of S Ltd's plant in order to reflect the correct group depreciation each year for S Ltd's plant in the consolidated financial statements.
- From the timeline and depreciation table it can be seen that this CU 10 000 additional depreciation in respect of S Ltd's plant, recognised on consolidation each year, represents:
    - the at acquisition fair value adjustment to S Ltd's plant, this being an increase of CU 70 000 in the plant's at acquisition carrying amount

    DIVIDED BY
    - the remaining useful life of the plant of seven years at acquisition date.
- As is evident from the depreciation table and the timeline, the period from acquisition date to the beginning of the current year is a two-year period and therefore CU 20 000 (10 000 annual depreciation × 2 years) of additional depreciation in respect of S Ltd's plant needs to be recognised on consolidation (see **b** in depreciation table). As this additional depreciation relates to prior periods, the consolidation adjustment required in the current year will be to the opening balance of S Ltd's retained earnings. More specifically, on consolidation, S Ltd's opening retained earnings balance will be reduced by CU 20 000 – see analysis of equity and pro forma journal 3.
- For the current period, a consolidation adjustment to recognise additional depreciation of CU 10 000 in respect of S Ltd's plant is required (see **c** in depreciation table), which will reduce S Ltd's current year profit, which is consolidated, by CU 10 000 – see analysis of equity and pro forma journal 5.

Part (a): Analysis of equity (AOE) of S Ltd for the financial year ended 31 December 20x8

At acquisition date (31 December 20x5)	Total of S Ltd's equity 100% CU	P Ltd 80% At acquisition CU	P Ltd 80% Since acquisition CU	Non-controlling interest 20% CU
Share capital	170 000	136 000		34 000
Retained earnings	145 000	116 000		29 000
Remeasurement plant [385 000 – (420 000 – 105 000)]	70 000	56 000		14 000[1]
Fair value of net assets of S Ltd	385 000	308 000		77 000
Goodwill – Parent (balancing figure)	42 000	42 000 **a**		–
Consideration and non-controlling interest	427 000	350 000		77 000
Since acquisition				
• To beginning of current year:				
Adjusted retained earnings	85 000		68 000 **b**	17 000
Retained earnings movement (250 000 Balance BOY – 145 000 Balancing acquisition)	105 000		84 000	21 000
Additional depreciation for 2 years ((70 000 / 7 RUL) × 2 Years)	(20 000)		(16 000)	(4 000)[1]
				94 000 **c**
• Current year:				
Adjusted profit for the year	25 000		20 000 **d**	5 000 **e**
Profit for the year (115 000 – 35 000 – 45 000)	35 000		28 000	7 000
Additional depreciation 1 year (70 000 / 7 RUL)	(10 000) **f**		(8 000)	(2 000)[1]
	537 000		**88 000**	**99 000 g**

Explanatory notes: Analysis of equity

[1] The fair value adjustment to S Ltd's plant at acquisition affects the non-controlling interest as follows:

• At acquisition date, the appropriate potion of the fair value adjustment relating to S Ltd's plant is attributed to the non-controlling interest, being an amount of CU 14 000 (70 000 × 20%).

• Subsequently, on consolidation, CU 10 000 of additional depreciation is recognised each year in respect of S Ltd's plant. An appropriate portion of this additional depreciation of S Ltd's plant, recognised for consolidation purposes, is allocated to the non-controlling interest as follows:

   ▪ CU 4 000 (20 000 × 20%) of S Ltd's CU 20 000 additional depreciation of plant, recognised on consolidation in respect of **prior years**, is allocated to the non-controlling interest, which allocation reduces the non-controlling interest's share of **S Ltd's post-acquisition retained earnings to the beginning of the current year**; and

   ▪ CU 2 000 (10 000 × 20%) of S Ltd's current year CU 10 000 additional depreciation of plant, recognised on consolidation, is allocated to the non-controlling interest, which allocation reduces the non-controlling interest's share of **S Ltd's current year profit**.

Part (b): Pro forma journal entries for the financial year ended 31 December 20x8

AT ACQUISITION

Pro forma journal (J1)	Dr CU	Cr CU
Plant: Accumulated depreciation (S Ltd) (SFP) (given)	105 000	
Plant: Cost (S Ltd) (SFP)		105 000
Elimination of at acquisition accumulated depreciation of plant		

Pro forma journal 2 (J2)	Dr CU	Cr CU
Share capital (S Ltd) (SCIE) (given)	170 000	
Retained earnings (S Ltd) (SCIE) (given)	145 000	
Plant (S Ltd) (SFP)	Wkg1 70 000	
Investment in S Ltd (P Ltd) (SFP) (given)		350 000
NCI – Equity (SCIE)		Wkg2 77 000
Goodwill (SFP) (balancing figure)	42 000	
Elimination of at acquisition equity and cost of investment, remeasurement of plant at fair value and recognition of non-controlling interest and goodwill at acquisition		

Workings: Pro forma journals

Working 1
385 000 Fair value – (420 000 Carrying amount – 105 000 Accumulated depreciation)

Working 2
(170 000 + 145 000 + 70 000) × 20% NCI Share

SINCE ACQUISITION TO THE BEGINNING OF THE YEAR

Pro forma journal 3 (J3)	Dr CU	Cr CU
Retained earnings (S Ltd) (SCIE)	Wkg3 20 000	
Plant: Accumulated depreciation (S Ltd) (SFP)		Wkg3 20 000
Recognition of prior years' additional depreciation in respect of plant of S Ltd		

Working 3
(70 000 Fair value adjustment plant / 7 Years RUL plant at acquisition) × 2 Years since acquisition to BOY

Pro forma journal 4 (J4)	Dr CU	Cr CU
Retained earnings (S Ltd) (SCIE)	Wkg4 17 000	
Non-controlling interest – Equity (SFP)		Wkg4 17 000
Allocating the non-controlling interest its share of S Ltd's adjusted post-acquisition retained earnings to the beginning of the year		

Working 4
(250 000 Balance BOY – 145 000 Balance at acquisition – 20 000 (J3) Additional depreciation: Plant since acquisition to BOY) × 20% NCI Share

CURRENT YEAR

Pro forma journal 5 (J5)	Dr CU	Cr CU
Depreciation (S Ltd) (P/L)	Wkg5 10 000	
Plant: Accumulated depreciation (S Ltd) (SFP)		Wkg5 10 000
Recognition of additional depreciation for the current year: Plant of S Ltd		

Working 5
(70 000 Fair value adjustment plant / 7 Years RUL plant at acquisition) × 1 Year

Pro forma journal 6 (J6)	Dr CU	Cr CU
NCI – Share of profit or loss (P/L)	Wkg6 5 000	
Non-controlling interest – Equity (SFP)		Wkg6 5 000
Allocating the non-controlling interest its share of S Ltd's adjusted profit for the year		

Workings: Pro forma journals

Working 6
(115 000 – 35 000 – 45 000 = 35 000 Current year profit – 10 000 (J5) Additional current year depreciation: Plant) × 20% NCI Share

The effects of the preceding six pro forma journals on the consolidated figures are illustrated in the following consolidation worksheet.

	P Ltd Dr/(Cr) CU	S Ltd Dr/(Cr) CU	Pro forma journals At acquisition Dr/(Cr) CU	Journal ref	Pro forma journals Since acquisition Dr/(Cr) CU	Journal ref	Consolidated Dr/(Cr) CU
Equity							
Share capital	(150 000)	(170 000)	170 000	J2			(150 000)
Retained earnings (BOY)	(310 000)	(250 000)	145 000	J2	20 000	J3	(378 000)
					17 000	J4	–
Net profit: Individual entities	(66 000)	(35 000)					–
Consolidated profit – attributable to owners of parent							†(86 000)
Retained earnings (EOY)	(376 000)	(285 000)	(77 000)	J2	(17 000)	J4	(464 000)
NCI Equity	–	–			(5 000)	J6	(99 000)
Total equity	(526 000)	(455 000)					(713 000)
Liabilities:							
Trade and other payables	(32 000)	(15 000)					(47 000)
Total liabilities	(32 000)	(15 000)					(47 000)
Total equity & liabilities	(558 000)	(470 000)					(760 000)

Explanatory notes

† This amount has been brought forward from the second part of the consolidation worksheet on page 251

	P Ltd Dr/(Cr) CU	S Ltd Dr/(Cr) CU	Pro forma journals At acquisition Dr/(Cr) CU	Journal ref	Pro forma journals Since acquisition Dr/(Cr) CU	Journal ref	Con-solidated Dr/(Cr) CU
Assets:							
Plant: Cost	–	420 000	(105 000) / 70 000	J1 / J2			385 000
Plant: Accumulated depreciation	–	(195 000)	105 000	J1	(20 000) / (10 000)	J3 / J5	(120 000)
Trade and other receivables	208 000	245 000					453 000
Investment in S Ltd	350 000	–	(350 000)	J2			–
Goodwill			42 000	J2			42 000
Total assets	**558 000**	**470 000**					**760 000**
Profit or loss							
Profit before tax and depreciation	(108 000)	(115 000)					(223 000)
Depreciation	–	45 000			10 000	J5	55 000
Taxation	42 000	35 000					77 000
Net profit for period	(66 000)	(35 000)					(91 000)
NCI: Share of profit					5 000	J6	5 000
Consolidated profit attributable to owners of parent							‡(86 000)

Explanatory notes

‡ This amount has been carried forward to the first part of the consolidation worksheet on page 250

Mastering Group Financial Statements Volume 1

Part (c): Consolidated financial statements for the financial year ended 31 December 20x8

P LTD GROUP: ABRIDGED CONSOLIDATED STATEMENT OF PROFIT OR LOSS AND OTHER COMPREHENSIVE INCOME FOR THE YEAR ENDED 31 DECEMBER 20X8	
	CU
Profit before taxation	168 000
(108 000 (P Ltd) + ((S Ltd: 115 000 – 45 000 Depreciation: Plant – 10 000 (see AOE **f OR** (J5)) Additional depreciation: Plant)	
Taxation (42 000 (P Ltd) + 35 000 (S Ltd))	(77 000)
PROFIT FOR THE YEAR	**91 000**
Other comprehensive income for the year	–
TOTAL COMPREHENSIVE INCOME FOR THE YEAR	**91 000**
Total comprehensive income for the year attributable to:	
Owners of the parent (balancing figure) **OR** (66 000 (P Ltd) + 20 000 (S Ltd) (see AOE **d**)	86 000
Non-controlling interest (see AOE **e OR** (J6))	5 000
	91 000

P LTD GROUP: CONSOLIDATED STATEMENT OF CHANGES IN EQUITY FOR THE YEAR ENDED 31 DECEMBER 20X8					
	Parent equity holders' interest			Non-controlling interest	Total equity of the group
	Share capital	Retained earnings	Total parent equity		
	CU	CU	CU	CU	CU
Opening balance at 1 Jan 20x8	150 000	Wkg1378 000	528 000	Wkg294 000	622 000
Total comprehensive income:					
Profit for the period (from CSOPL_OCI)		86 000	86 000	5 000	91 000
Closing balance at 31 Dec 20x8	150 000	464 000	614 000	99 000	713 000

Workings: Consolidated statement of changes in equity

Working 1
P Ltd: 310 000 + (S Ltd: 68 000 (see AOE **b**) P Ltd Share of S Ltd post-acquisition retained earnings to BOY)

OR

P Ltd: 310 000 + (S Ltd: 250 000 Balance BOY – 145 000 (J2) Balance at acquisition – 20 000 (J3) Additional depreciation: Plant – 17 000 (J4) NCI Share of S Ltd post-acquisition retained earnings to BOY)

Working 2
S Ltd: 94 000 (see AOE **c**)

OR

S Ltd: 77 000 (J2) NCI Share of S Ltd at acquisition equity + 17 000 (J4) NCI Share of S Ltd post-acquisition retained earnings to BOY

252

P LTD GROUP: CONSOLIDATED STATEMENT OF FINANCIAL POSITION AS AT 31 DECEMBER 20X8	
	CU
Assets	
Non-current assets	
Property, plant and equipment (S Ltd: 420 000 Cost: plant – 195 000 Accumulated depreciation: Plant + 70 000 (J2) Fair value adjustment: Plant – 20 000 (J3) Additional accumulated depreciation; Plant: Prior years – 10 000 (J5) Additional accumulated depreciation; Plant: Current year)	265 000
Goodwill (see AOE **a OR** (J2))	42 000
Current assets	
Trade and other receivables (208 000 (P Ltd) + 245 000 (S Ltd))	453 000
Total assets	**760 000**
Equity and liabilities	
Share capital (from CSCIE)	150 000
Retained earnings (from CSCIE)	464 000
Equity attributable to owners of the parent	614 000
Non-controlling interest (from CSCIE) **OR** (see AOE **g**)	99 000
Total equity	**713 000**
Current liabilities	
Trade and other payables (32 000 (P Ltd) + 15 000 (S Ltd))	47 000
Total equity and liabilities	**760 000**

5.2.7 Subsequent sale of depreciable property, plant and equipment remeasured at fair value at acquisition

Where a depreciable asset that was remeasured to fair value at acquisition date is subsequently sold, the profit or loss on sale recognised in the records of the subsidiary will *not* be the same as the profit or loss on sale recognised from a group perspective. This is because, at date of sale, the depreciable asset's **carrying amount** as recognised in the **consolidated financial statements** will **differ** from its **carrying amount** as per the **subsidiary's individual financial statements.**

Accordingly, a pro forma journal is required in order to adjust the **subsidiary's gain or loss on disposal** of the depreciable property, plant and equipment asset to the correct gain or loss on disposal to be recognised for **group purposes.** On consolidation, therefore, the amount by which the subsidiary's gain or loss on disposal of the depreciable asset will be reduced or increased, will be equal to:

- the **carrying amount**
- of the **at acquisition fair value adjustment** made to the subsidiary's depreciable asset,
- at **date of disposal** of this asset.

Where the depreciable property, plant and equipment asset was **remeasured upwards** to fair value at acquisition date, the **subsidiary's gain/(loss)** recognised on disposal of this asset will be **reduced/(increased)** for consolidation purposes. The carrying amount, at date of disposal of the asset, of this upwards remeasurement adjustment to fair value, is determined as:

- the **increase in the at acquisition carrying amount** of the subsidiary's depreciable asset, attributable to the asset's at acquisition remeasurement to fair value

  MINUS

- the **additional depreciation** on this asset, recognised on consolidation, for the period **since the subsidiary was acquired** up until the date of **disposal of this asset externally**, by the subsidiary.

Where the depreciable property, plant and equipment asset was **remeasured downwards** to fair value at acquisition date, the **subsidiary's gain/(loss)** recognised on disposal of this asset will be **increased/(reduced)** for consolidation purposes. The carrying amount, at date of disposal of the asset, of this downwards remeasurement adjustment to fair value, is determined as:

- the **decrease in the at acquisition carrying amount** of the subsidiary's depreciable asset, attributable to the asset's at acquisition remeasurement to fair value

  MINUS

- the **reduction in the depreciation** of this asset, recognised on consolidation, for the period **since the subsidiary was acquired** up until the date of **disposal of this asset externally**, by the subsidiary.

If the gain or loss on disposal of a subsidiary's depreciable asset occurs in the current reporting period, the **profit or loss** of the subsidiary is adjusted on consolidation, whereas the consolidation adjustment is made to the **subsidiary's opening retained earnings balance** should the subsidiary's depreciable asset have been disposed of in a previous financial year. In addition, the **non-controlling interest** will be attributed its **appropriate share** of these **consolidation adjustments** to the subsidiary's **profit or loss** or retained earnings, as the case may be.

Example 5.6: Subsequent disposal of depreciable property, plant and equipment that was remeasured to fair value at acquisition date

This example is a continuation of Example 5.5. Assume further that S Ltd disposed of its plant to a third party on 30 June 20x9 for CU 280 000.

The trial balances of P Ltd and S Ltd for the financial year ended 31 December 20x9 were as follows:

	P Ltd Dr/(Cr) CU	S Ltd Dr/(Cr) CU
Trial balances at 31 December 20x9		
Share capital	(150 000)	(170 000)
Retained earnings (1 Jan 20x9)	(376 000)	(285 000)
Trade and other payables	(100 000)	(200 000)
Trade and other receivables	398 000	792 500
Investment in S Ltd: Cost	350 000	–
Profit after tax for period	(122 000)	(137 500)

Required

(a) Prepare the analysis of equity of S Ltd as at 31 December 20x9.

(b) Provide all the pro forma journal entries necessary to prepare the consolidated financial statements of the P Ltd group for the financial year ended 31 December 20x9.

Ignore all tax effects relating to the fair value remeasurement of the plant.

⭢

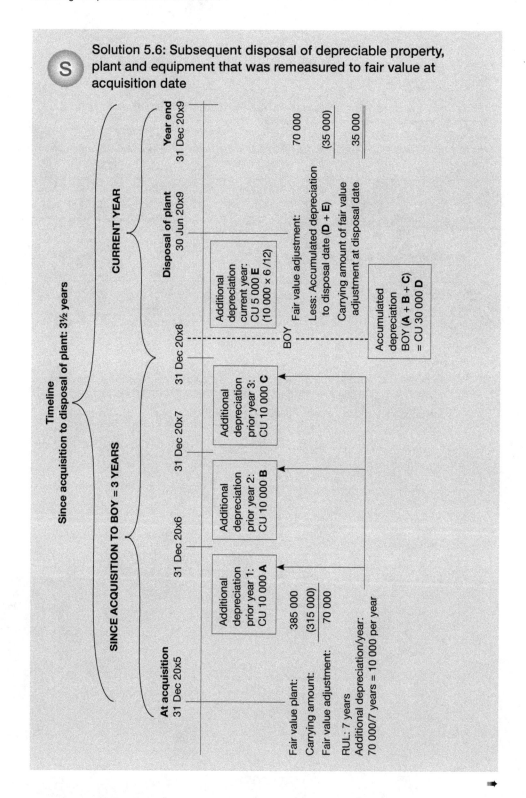

Solution 5.6: Subsequent disposal of depreciable property, plant and equipment that was remeasured to fair value at acquisition date

Comments: Timeline

- As can be seen from the timeline, the period since acquisition to the beginning of the year comprises three financial years, where, for consolidation purposes, additional depreciation of CU 10 000 is recognised each year in respect of S Ltd's plant. Therefore, at the beginning of the current year (i.e., financial year ended 31 December 20x9) a consolidation adjustment reducing S Ltd's opening retained earnings balance by CU 30 000 (10 000 annual depreciation × 3 years) must be made (see analysis of equity and pro forma journal 2 below).

- It is further apparent that the plant, which was remeasured to fair value at acquisition, increasing its carrying amount by CU 70 000 for group purposes (see pro forma journal 1), is sold midway through the current year. Therefore, on consolidation in the current year, we need to:

  - Adjust S Ltd's current year depreciation charge in respect of its plant by recognising additional depreciation on this plant of CU 5 000 (10 000 × 6/12) for six months, that is, until it is sold midway through the year (see analysis of equity and pro forma journal 4).

  - Eliminate the additional accumulated depreciation in respect of S Ltd's plant, recognised for group purposes, of CU 35 000 (30 000 in respect of prior years and 5 000 in respect of the current year) for the period from acquisition date to date of sale of the plant midway through the current year. This elimination is required as the plant no longer exists at year end (see pro forma journal 5).

  - Reduce the subsidiary's current year profit on disposal of the plant by the CU 35 000 carrying amount at date of disposal of the plant, of the at acquisition fair value adjustment to the plant (see analysis of equity and pro forma journal 5).

Part (a): Analysis of equity of S Ltd

At acquisition date (31 December 20x5)	Total of S Ltd's equity 100% CU	P Ltd 80% At acquisition CU	Since acquisition CU	Non-controlling interest 20% CU
Share capital	170 000	136 000		34 000
Retained earnings	145 000	116 000		29 000
Fair value adjustment: Plant (385 000 Fair value – (420 000 Carrying amount – 105 000 Accumulated depreciation))	70 000	56 000		14 000
Fair value of net assets of S Ltd	385 000	308 000		77 000
Goodwill – Parent (balancing figure)	42 000	42 000		–
Consideration and non-controlling interest	427 000	350 000		77 000
Since acquisition				
• To beginning of current year:				
Adjusted retained earnings	110 000		88 000	22 000
Retained earnings (285 000 – 145 000)	140 000		112 000	28 000
Additional plant depreciation for 3 years	Wkg1(30 000)		(24 000)	(6 000)
				99 000
• Current year:				
Adjusted profit for the year	97 500		78 000	19 500
Profit for the year	137 500		110 000	27 500
Additional depreciation plant for ½ a year	Wkg2(5 000)		(4 000)	(1 000)
Reduction: Profit on disposal of plant (70 000 – 30 000 – 5 000)	(35 000)		(28 000)	(7 000)
	634 500		**166 000**	**118 500**

Workings: Analysis of equity

Working 1

(70 000 Fair value adjustment / 7 Years RUL of plant at acquisition) × 3 Years from acquisition to BOY

Working 2

(70 000 Fair value adjustment / 7 Years RUL of plant at acquisition) × 6/12 Months

Part (b): Pro forma journal entries for the year ended 31 December 20x9

Note: Unlike Example 5.5, where we reversed the at acquisition accumulated depreciation of the plant against the cost of the plant on consolidation, that adjustment is *not* required in this example. This is because, in this example, the plant has been disposed of by period end. Accordingly, neither the plant nor its accumulated depreciation appears in S Ltd's records. It is therefore unnecessary to reverse any at acquisition accumulated depreciation relating to the plant.

AT ACQUISITION

Pro forma journal 1 (J1)	Dr CU	Cr CU
Share capital (S Ltd) (SCIE) (given)	170 000	
Retained earnings (S Ltd) (SCIE) (given)	145 000	
Plant (S Ltd) (SFP)	Wkg¹70 000	
Investment in S Ltd (P Ltd) (SFP) (given)		350 000
NCI – Equity (SCIE)		Wkg²70 000
Goodwill (SFP) (balancing figure)	42 000	
Elimination of at acquisition equity and cost of investment, remeasurement of plant at fair value and recognition of non-controlling interest and goodwill at acquisition		

Workings: Pro forma journals

Working 1

385 000 Fair value – (420 000 Carrying amount – 105 000 Accumulated depreciation)

Working 2

(170 000 + 145 000 + 70 000) × 20% NCI Share

Comments: Pro forma journal 1

- Although the plant has been sold during the current year and is no longer an asset of the group, we still process the at acquisition fair value adjustment thereto. This is done so that we reflect the correct at acquisition equity of S Ltd that P Ltd acquired in order to correctly calculate the goodwill at acquisition. The at acquisition fair value adjustment to S Ltd's plant is then eliminated in a subsequent pro forma journal (see pro forma journal 5).

SINCE ACQUISITION TO THE BEGINNING OF THE YEAR

Pro forma journal 2 (J2)	Dr CU	Cr CU
Retained earnings (S Ltd) (SCIE)	Wkg³30 000	
Plant: Accumulated depreciation (S Ltd) (SFP)		Wkg³30 000
Recognition of additional depreciation: Plant – Prior years		

Workings: Pro forma journals

Working 3

70 000 Fair value adjustment: Plant / 7 Years RUL of plant at acquisition × 3 Years since acquisition to BOY

Pro forma journal 3 (J3)	Dr CU	Cr CU
Retained earnings	Wkg⁴22 000	
Non-controlling interest – Equity (SFP)		Wkg⁴22 000
Allocating the non-controlling interest its share of S Ltd's adjusted post-acquisition retained earnings to the beginning of the year		

Workings: Pro forma journals

Working 4

(285 000 Balance BOY – 145 000 Balance at acquisition – 30 000 (J2) Additional depreciation: Plant) × 20% NCI Share

CURRENT YEAR

Pro forma journal 4 (J4)	Dr CU	Cr CU
Depreciation (S Ltd) (P/L)	[Wkg5]5 000	
Plant: Accumulated depreciation (S Ltd) (SFP)		[Wkg5]5 000
Recognition of additional depreciation: Plant for the current year		

Working 5

(70 000 Fair value adjustment: Plant / 7 Years RUL of plant at acquisition) × ½ Year until date of sale

Pro forma journal 5 (J5)	Dr CU	Cr CU
Profit on sale of plant (S Ltd) (P/L)	[Wkg6]35 000	
Plant: Accumulated depreciation (S Ltd) (SFP)	[Wkg7]35 000	
Plant (S Ltd) (SFP) (see (J1))		70 000
Recognition of reduction in S Ltd profit on disposal of plant, reversal of additional accumulated depreciation on plant, and reversal of at acquisition fair value remeasurement of plant due to disposal of plant in current year		

Workings: Pro forma journals

Working 6

	CU
Fair value (FV) adjustment: plant (see (J1))	70 000
Additional accumulated depreciation: FV adjustment, plant	(35 000)
Additional current year accumulated depreciation: Plant (see (J4))	(5 000)
Additional accumulated depreciation to BOY: Plant (see (J2))	(30 000)
Carrying amount FV adjustment, plant: at disposal date	35 000

OR

$$70\ 000\ \text{(J1) Fair value adjustment: Plant} \times \frac{3.5\ \text{Years (Plant RUL at disposal date)}}{7\ \text{Years (Plant RUL: Date of acquisition of subsidiary)}}$$

= 35 000 Carrying amount FV adjustment, plant: at disposal date

Working 7

Balancing figure

OR

30 000 (J2) Additional accumulated depreciation: Plant since acquisition to BOY + CU 5 000 (J4) Additional accumulated depreciation: Plant current year to date of disposal

Pro forma journal 5 is best explained with the aid of the following table:

	Plant carrying amount: S Ltd i	Plant carrying amount: Group ii	Plant carrying amount: Fair value adjustment ii – i	Period
Carrying amount 31 Dec 20x5	**315 000**	**315 000**	**–**	At
Fair value adjustment 31 Dec 20x5	–	70 000	70 000	acquisition
Depreciation 1 Jan 20x6 – 31 Dec 20x8 (3 Years)	Wkg1(135 000)	Wkg2(165 000)	(30 000)	Since acquisition to BOY
Depreciation 1 Jan 20x9 – 30 June 20x9	Wkg3(22 500)	Wkg4(27 500)	(5 000)	Current year
Carrying amount 30 June 20x9 (date of plant disposal)	**157 500**	**192 500**	**35 000**	Current year
Disposal proceeds	280 000	280 000	–	
Profit on disposal of plant	**122 500**	**87 500**	**(35 000)**	

Workings: Depreciation table

Working 1

(315 000 Carrying amount of plant / 7 years RUL of plant at acquisition) × 3 Years since acquisition to BOY

Working 2

[(315 000 Carrying amount of plant + 70 000 Fair value adjustment plant: at acquisition) / 7 years RUL of plant at acquisition] × 3 Years since acquisition to BOY

Working 3

(315 000 Carrying amount of plant / 7 years RUL of plant at acquisition) × 6/12 Months

Working 4

[(315 000 Carrying amount of plant + 70 000 Fair value adjustment plant: at acquisition) / 7 years RUL of plant at acquisition] × 6/12 Months

Comments: Pro forma journal 5

- As is clear from the table above, at the date of disposal of S Ltd's plant (30 June 20x9), the carrying amount of the CU 70 000 at acquisition fair value adjustment to this plant is CU 35 000 (70 000 Fair value adjustment – 35 000 Depreciation for 3½ years from acquisition to disposal date). Consequently – as is shown in the table above – at disposal date, the carrying amount of S Ltd's plant for group purposes is CU 35 000 more than its carrying amount as recorded in S Ltd's own records. It therefore follows that the consolidated profit to be recognised on disposal of S Ltd's plant must be CU 35 000 less than that recognised by S Ltd in its own records – see the table above. For this reason we debit and so reduce S Ltd's profit on sale of plant by CU 35 000, thereby recognising the correct reduced consolidated profit on sale of the plant of CU 87 500 – see the table above.

- As explained previously (see timeline), in the 3½-year period from acquisition to date of disposal of S Ltd's plant, the group recognised CU 35 000 more accumulated depreciation in respect of this plant than was recognised by S Ltd in its own records (see pro forma journal 2 and pro forma journal 4). However, because S Ltd disposed of this plant in the current year, the group no longer owns the plant. Consequently, this additional CU 35 000 accumulated depreciation recognised on plant for group purposes must be reversed in the current year. This is achieved by debiting accumulated depreciation: plant of S Ltd with CU 35 000.

- In pro forma journal 1, S Ltd's plant was debited with CU 70 000 in order to recognise the CU 70 000 at acquisition increase in its carrying amount, attributable to the plant's remeasurement to fair value at acquisition date. However, as S Ltd has now sold the plant in the current year, this at acquisition debit entry must be reversed in the current year. This is the reason why we credit S Ltd's plant with CU 70 000.

Pro forma journal 6 (J6)	Dr CU	Cr CU
NCI – Share of profit or loss (P/L)	Wkg8 19 500	
Non-controlling interest – Equity (SFP)		Wkg8 19 500
Allocating the non-controlling interest its share of S Ltd's adjusted profit for the year		

Workings: Pro forma journals

Working 8

(137 500 (given) Current year profit – 5 000 (J4) Additional current year depreciation: Plant – 35 000 (J5) Reduction in profit on disposal of plant) × 20% NCI Share

The effects of the six pro forma journal entries above, on the consolidated figures, are illustrated in the following consolidation worksheet.

	P Ltd Dr/(Cr) CU	S Ltd Dr/(Cr) CU	Pro forma journals At acquisition Dr/(Cr) CU	Journal ref	Pro forma journals Since acquisition Dr/(Cr) CU	Journal ref	Con-solidated Dr/(Cr) CU
Equity							
Share capital	(150 000)	(170 000)	170 000	J1			(150 000)
Retained earnings (BOY)	(376 000)	(285 000)	145 000	J1	30 000 / 22 000	J2 / J3	(464 000)
Net profit: Individual entities	(122 000)	(137 500)					–
Consolidated profit – attributable to owners of parent							†(200 000)
Retained earnings (EOY)	(498 000)	(422 500)			(22 000)	J3	(664 000)
NCI Equity	–	–	(77 000)	J1	(19 500)	J6	(118 500)
Total equity	**(648 000)**	**(592 500)**					**(932 500)**
Liabilities:							
Trade and other payables	(100 000)	(200 000)					(300 000)
Total liabilities	**(100 000)**	**(200 000)**					**(300 000)**
Total equity & liabilities	**(748 000)**	**(792 500)**					**(1 232 500)**

Explanatory notes

† This amount has been brought forward from the second part of the consolidation worksheet on page 264

	P Ltd Dr/(Cr) CU	S Ltd Dr/(Cr) CU	Pro forma journals At acquisition Dr/(Cr) CU	Journal ref	Pro forma journals Since acquisition Dr/(Cr) CU	Journal ref	Consolidated Dr/(Cr) CU
Assets:							
Plant: Cost	–	–	70 000	J1	(70 000)	J5	–
Plant: Accumulated depreciation	–	–			(30 000)	J2	–
					(5 000)	J4	
					35 000	J5	
Trade and other receivables	398 000	792 500					1 190 500
Investment in S Ltd	350 000	–	(350 000)	J1			–
Goodwill	–	–	42 000	J1			42 000
Total assets	**748 000**	**792 500**					**1 232 500**
Profit or loss							
Profit after tax for period	(122 000)	(137 500)			5 000	J4	(219 500)
					35 000	J5	
NCI: Share of profit					19 500	J6	19 500
Consolidated profit attributable to owners of parent							‡(200 000)

Explanatory notes

‡ This amount has been carried forward to the first part of the consolidation worksheet on page 263

5.2.8 Deferred tax effects: At acquisition fair value adjustments to property, plant and equipment of a subsidiary

At acquisition date, IFRS 3 fair value adjustments to a subsidiary's property, plant and equipment give rise to temporary differences, in terms of IAS 12 *Income Taxes* at group level, when the tax base of this property, plant and equipment is *not* affected by the business combination. In other words, temporary differences arise at group level when the carrying amount of a subsidiary's property, plant and equipment asset is adjusted to fair value at acquisition date under IFRS 3 for accounting purposes, while the corresponding tax base of this property, plant and equipment remains unchanged (as this accounting fair value adjustment is *not* recognised for tax purposes by the taxing authority).

On consolidation, these at acquisition temporary differences result in the recognition at group level of:

- A **deferred tax liability** of the subsidiary, at acquisition, when the subsidiary's property plant and equipment is remeasured **upwards** to fair value at acquisition. In these circumstances, the at acquisition carrying amount of the subsidiary's property, plant and equipment increases while its tax base remains unchanged. This gives rise to an at acquisition **taxable temporary difference** and the at acquisition recognition of a deferred tax liability.

- A **deferred tax asset** of the subsidiary, at acquisition, when the subsidiary's property, plant and equipment is remeasured **downwards** to fair value at acquisition. In these circumstances, the at acquisition carrying amount of the subsidiary's property, plant and equipment decreases while its tax base remains unchanged. This gives rise to an at acquisition **deductible** temporary difference and the at acquisition recognition of a deferred tax asset. Note that in accordance with IAS 12, a deferred tax asset may be recognised in respect of these deductible temporary differences **only to the extent** that it is **probable** that **taxable profit will be available** against which these **deductible temporary differences can be utilised** (IAS 12.24).

Recall from Volume 1 Chapters 1 and 2 that under IAS 12, the measurement of deferred tax assets and liabilities should reflect the tax consequences that would follow from the manner in which the entity expects to recover or settle the carrying amount of its assets and liabilities (IAS 12.51). Consequently, the appropriate tax rate used to measure the deferred tax effects of at acquisition fair value adjustments to subsidiary property, plant and equipment must be determined by establishing the manner in which the group expects – at acquisition date – to recover the carrying amount of this property, plant and equipment. In this regard:

- The carrying amount of the subsidiary's **depreciable** property plant and equipment is expected to be recovered **through use.** Recovery through use generates taxable income taxed at the income tax rate of 28%. Consequently, deferred tax in respect of at acquisition fair value adjustments to a subsidiary's **depreciable** property, plant and equipment must be calculated using the **income tax rate of 28%.**

- The carrying amount of a subsidiary's **non**-depreciable property plant and equipment is expected to be recovered **through sale.** Recovery through sale results in capital gains tax being levied at the effective rate of 22.4%. Consequently, deferred tax in respect of at acquisition fair value adjustments to a subsidiary's

non-depreciable property, plant and equipment must be calculated using the **effective capital gains tax rate of 22.4%**.

The recognition of a deferred tax asset or liability in respect of at acquisition fair value adjustments to a subsidiary's property, plant and equipment affects the at acquisition net asset value (equity) of the subsidiary. That is, the subsidiary's net asset value **increases** if a **deferred tax asset** is recognised and **decreases** if a **deferred tax liability is recognised**. This, in turn, impacts on the **amount of goodwill (or bargain purchase gain)** that is recognised.

Subsequent to acquisition date, the at acquisition fair value adjustment recognised in respect of the subsidiary property plant and equipment concerned, is reversed or realised each reporting period by way of depreciating, impairing or selling this property plant and equipment. These fair value reversals or realisations post acquisition, result in the temporary differences that originated at acquisition subsequently reversing. Reversal of these at acquisition temporary differences, in turn, causes the post-acquisition reversal each reporting period of the subsidiary's deferred tax asset or liability recognised at acquisition. More particularly, on consolidation:

- the subsequent reversal each reporting period of a subsidiary's at acquisition **deferred tax liability**, recognised in respect of **upward** at acquisition fair value adjustment to its property, plant and equipment, results in the recognition, each reporting period, of a corresponding **reduction** in the **subsidiary's income tax expense**, in the consolidated financial statements; and

- the subsequent reversal each reporting period of a subsidiary's at acquisition **deferred tax asset**, recognised in respect of at acquisition **downward** fair value adjustments to its property, plant and equipment, results in the recognition, each reporting period, of a corresponding **increase** in the **subsidiary's income tax expense**, in the consolidated financial statements.

Note that the **non-controlling interest** will be allocated its **share of the adjustments** to the **subsidiary's income tax expense post acquisition date** as discussed in the two bullet points immediately above.

The deferred tax effects of at acquisition fair value adjustments to subsidiary property, plant and equipment, both at acquisition and subsequently, are best illustrated in Examples 5.7 to 5.9 that follow.

Example 5.7: Fair value adjustments to property, plant and equipment at acquisition: Deferred tax implications at acquisition

P Ltd acquired an 80% controlling interest in subsidiary S Ltd on 1 January 20x5 for CU 1 050 000. On this date the equity of S Ltd consisted of share capital of CU 400 000 and retained earnings of CU 600 000. The net assets of S Ltd were considered to be fairly valued, with the exception of:

- land with a carrying amount of CU 180 000, which was undervalued by CU 100 000; and
- machinery with a carrying amount of CU 400 000 (cost CU 600 000, accumulated depreciation CU 200 000), which was undervalued by CU 250 000.

P Ltd measures the non-controlling interest at its proportionate share of the identifiable net assets of S Ltd, as fairly valued.

Required

(a) Prepare the analysis of equity of S Ltd at acquisition date.

(b) Prepare the at acquisition pro forma journal entries.

Assume an income tax rate of 28% and an effective capital gains tax rate of 22.4%. In addition, assume that the carrying amounts of the land and machinery equal the tax bases thereof.

 Solution 5.7: Fair value adjustments to property, plant and equipment at acquisition: Deferred tax implications at acquisition

Part (a): Analysis of equity of S Ltd at acquisition date

	Total of S Ltd's equity 100%	P Ltd 80% At acquisition	Non-controlling interest 20%
At acquisition date (31 December 20x5)	CU	CU	CU
Share capital	400 000	320 000	80 000
Retained earnings	600 000	480 000	120 000
Fair value adjustment: Land	100 000	80 000	20 000
Deferred tax liability: Land (100 000 × 22.4%)	(22 400)[1]	(17 920)	(4 480)
Fair value adjustment: Machinery	250 000	200 000	50 000
Deferred tax liability: Machinery (250 000 × 28%)	(70 000)[2]	(56 000)	(14 000)
Fair value of net assets of S Ltd	1 257 600	1 006 080	251 520
Goodwill – Parent (balancing figure)	43 920	43 920[3]	–
Consideration and non-controlling interest	1 301 520	1 050 000	251 520

Explanatory notes: Analysis of equity

[1] The IFRS 3 acquisition date fair value adjustment to land increases its carrying amount without any adjustment to its tax base. This results in a taxable temporary difference at acquisition equivalent to the fair value adjustment to the land, of CU 100 000. This is because the increased fair value of the land represents additional future taxable economic benefits of CU 100 000 that will arise upon recovery of the land (by way of sale), against which no additional amount will be deductible, as the land's tax base of CU 180 000 remains unchanged.

Further, as the asset will be recovered by way of sale, which will result in a capital gain, a deferred tax liability is recognised at the effective capital gains tax rate of 22.4% in respect of this CU 100 000 taxable temporary difference.

2 As was the case with the land, the IFRS 3 at acquisition fair value adjustment to S Ltd's machinery increases its carrying amount without any change in its tax base. Accordingly, the increased carrying amount represents additional future taxable economic benefits of CU 250 000 against which no additional tax allowances are claimable as the machinery's tax base remains unchanged at CU 400 000. This creates a taxable temporary difference at acquisition date, equal to the fair value adjustment of CU 250 000. A deferred tax liability is recognised in respect of this taxable temporary difference at the income tax rate of 28% as the carrying value of the machinery will be recovered through use.

3 The amount of goodwill recognised is affected by the recognition of the deferred tax effects of the fair value adjustments to the subsidiary's land and machinery at acquisition. More particularly, a total deferred tax liability of CU 92 400 (22 400 Deferred tax fair value adjustment: Land + 70 000 Deferred tax fair value adjustment: Machinery) is recognised in respect of a combined fair value adjustment of CU 350 000 (100 000 Land + 250 000 Machinery) at acquisition. Consequently, S Ltd's at acquisition net asset value (equity) is reduced by CU 92 400, the amount of this total deferred tax liability. This results in CU 73 920 (92 400 × 80% P Ltd's shareholding) more goodwill being recognised.

Part (b): Pro forma journal entries at acquisition date

Pro forma journal 1 (J1)	Dr CU	Cr CU
Machinery: Accumulated depreciation (S Ltd) (SFP) (given)	200 000	
Machinery: Cost (S Ltd) (SFP)		200 000
Elimination of at acquisition accumulated depreciation of machinery		

Pro forma journal 2 (J2)	Dr CU	Cr CU
Share capital (S Ltd) (SFP) (given)	400 000	
Retained earnings (S Ltd) (SFP) (given)	600 000	
Land (S Ltd) (SFP) (given: at fair value)	100 000	
Machinery (S Ltd) (SFP) (given: at fair value)	250 000	
Deferred tax liability (S Ltd) (SFP)		Wkg1 92 400
Investment in S Ltd (P Ltd) (SFP) (given)		1 050 000
NCI – Equity (SFP)		Wkg2 251 520
Goodwill (SFP) (balancing figure)	43 920	
Elimination of at acquisition equity and cost of investment, recognition of fair value adjustments in respect of land and machinery, including deferred tax effects, and recognition of non-controlling interest and goodwill		

Workings: Pro forma journals

Working 1

(100 000 × 22.4%) + (250 000 × 28%)

Working 2

(400 000 + 600 000 + 350 000 – 92 400) × 20% NCI Share

Example 5.8: Fair value adjustments to property, plant and equipment at acquisition: Deferred tax implications in subsequent reporting periods

In this example, the facts are the same as in Example 5.5, except that the deferred tax effects of the at acquisition fair value adjustment now need to be taken into account post acquisition date. The relevant facts are reproduced below.

P Ltd acquired an 80% controlling interest in S Ltd on 31 December 20x5 for CU 350 000. P Ltd considered the net assets of S Ltd to be fairly valued, except for plant, which had a fair value of CU 385 000 at acquisition date.

P Ltd measured the non-controlling interest at its proportionate share of the fair value of S Ltd's identifiable net assets at acquisition date.

Additional information:

Depreciation related-information
At acquisition date the estimated remaining useful life of S Ltd's plant was seven years with no residual value. These estimates were confirmed at each reporting date.

Tax-related information
- The tax base of the plant on acquisition date equalled its carrying amount of CU 315 000.
- The tax authority will allow S Ltd to deduct the remaining tax base of the plant over the remaining seven years on a straight line basis.
- The income tax rate is 28% and the subsidiary intends to continue using its plant.

The trial balances of P Ltd and S Ltd at 31 December 20x8 were as follows:

Trial balances at 31 December 20x8	P Ltd Dr/(Cr) CU	S Ltd Dr/(Cr) CU
Share capital	(150 000)	(170 000)
Retained earnings (1 Jan 20x8)	(310 000)	(250 000)
Trade and other payables	(32 000)	(15 000)
Plant: Cost	–	420 000
Plant: Accumulated depreciation	–	(195 000)
Trade and other receivables	208 000	245 000
Investment in S Ltd: Cost	350 000	–
Profit before depreciation and tax	(108 000)	(115 000)
Taxation	42 000	35 000
Depreciation	–	45 000

Required

(a) Prepare the analysis of equity of S Ltd as at 31 December 20x8.

(b) Provide all the pro forma journal entries necessary to prepare the consolidated financial statements of the P Ltd group for the year ended 31 December 20x8.

(c) Prepare the consolidated financial statements of the P Ltd Group for the year ended 31 December 20x8.

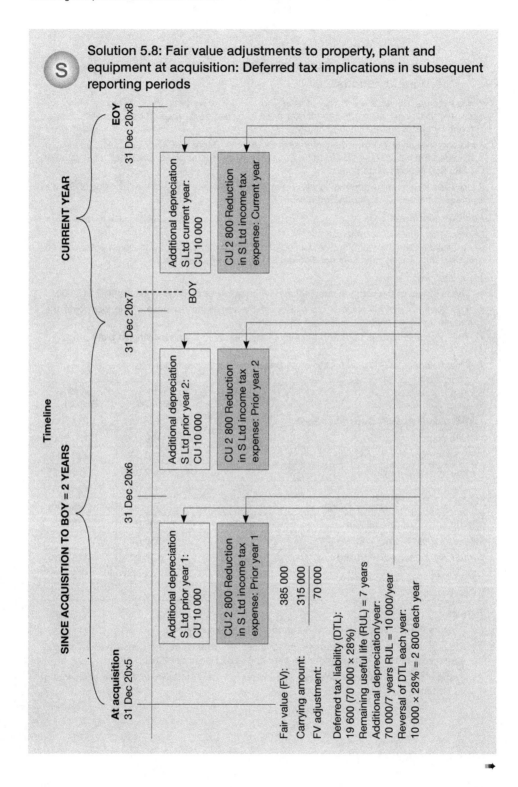

Solution 5.8: Fair value adjustments to property, plant and equipment at acquisition: Deferred tax implications in subsequent reporting periods

Comments: Timeline

- As can be seen from the timeline, the CU 19 600 at acquisition deferred tax liability, attributable to the CU 70 000 at acquisition fair value adjustment to S Ltd's plant, reduces every year as the group recognises CU 10 000 additional depreciation every year in respect of S Ltd's plant.

- More particularly, the CU 10 000 additional depreciation on S Ltd's plant, recognised each year on consolidation, causes the plant's carrying amount to reduce each year by CU 10 000 more than its tax base. This, in turn, causes the reversal each year of CU 10 000 of the CU 70 000 at acquisition fair value adjustment taxable temporary difference.

- This means that for consolidation purposes:

  - the CU 19 600 (70 000 Taxable temporary difference × 28%) at acquisition deferred tax liability, recognised on consolidation in respect of S Ltd's plant, must be reduced each year subsequent to acquisition, by CU 2 800 (10 000 Reversal of taxable temporary difference × 28%); and

  - a CU 2 800 corresponding reduction in S Ltd's income tax expense must be recognised each year on consolidation.

Deferred tax table: At acquisition fair value adjustment to S Ltd's plant

	Plant Carrying amount: S Ltd	Plant Carrying amount: Group	Plant Tax base: S Ltd & Group	(Taxable)/ deductible temporary difference: Group	Deferred tax (liability)/ asset: Group	Period	Pro forma journal
	A	B	C	C – B = D	D × 28%		
Balance 31 Dec 20x5	315 000	385 000	315 000	(70 000)	(19 600)a	At acquisition	**Cr** Deferred tax liability CU 19 000 (see pro forma journal 2 below)
Depreciation/tax allowance 1 Jan 20x6 – 31 Dec 20x7	Wkg1(90 000)	Wkg2(110 000)	Wkg1(90 000)	20 000	5 600**b**	Since acquisition to BOY	**Dr** Deferred tax liability CU 5600; **Cr** Retained earnings CU 5 600 (see pro forma journal 4 below)
Depreciation/tax allowance 20x8	Wkg3(45 000)	Wkg4(55 000)	Wkg3(45 000)	10 000	2 800**c**	Current year	**Dr** Deferred tax liability CU 2 800; **Cr** Income tax expense CU 2800 (see pro forma journal 7 below)
Balance 31 Dec 20x8	180 000	220 000	180 000	(40 000)	(11 200)**d**	**End of year**	

Workings: Deferred tax table

Working 1

(315 000 Carrying amount of plant / 7 years RUL of plant at acquisition) × 2 Years since acquisition to BOY

Working 2

(385 000 Fair value of plant / 7 years RUL of plant at acquisition) × 2 Years since acquisition to BOY

Working 3

(315 000 Carrying amount of plant / 7 years RUL of plant at acquisition)

Working 4

385 000 Fair value of plant / 7 years RUL of plant at acquisition

Comments: Deferred tax table

- At acquisition the carrying amount and cost of S Ltd's plant to the group is its fair value of CU 385 000. The tax authority, however, does not recognise the CU 70 000 accounting fair value adjustment for tax purposes, with the result that the at acquisition CU 315 000 tax base of S Ltd's plant, which equals the plant's at acquisition carrying amount in S Ltd's own records, remains unchanged (see the table above).

- For group purposes, as is shown in the table above, this causes a taxable temporary difference at acquisition, equivalent to the plant's at acquisition fair value increase of CU 70 000 (385 000 – 315 000) recognised. This at acquisition taxable temporary difference in respect of S Ltd's plant results in the recognition, for consolidation purposes, of a deferred tax liability of S Ltd of CU 19 600 (70 000 taxable temporary difference × 28%) at acquisition date (see **a** in the table).

- As the fair value of S Ltd's plant – which is the cost of the plant to the group – is CU 70 000 more than its carrying amount in S Ltd's own records, additional depreciation of CU 10 000 (70 000 Fair value adjustment: Plant / 7 years remaining useful life of plant) is recognised each year for this plant for group purposes – see the table above.

- As can be seen from the table above, this CU 10 000 additional plant depreciation, recognised on consolidation each year, reverses CU 10 000 each year of the CU 70 000 taxable temporary difference in respect of this plant, that arose on acquisition. This results in a reduction in the at acquisition deferred tax liability recognised in respect of S Ltd's plant, in subsequent reporting periods. More particularly, as can be seen from the table:

  - In the two-year period from acquisition date to the beginning of the current year, additional depreciation of CU 20 000 (10 000 × 2 years) in respect of S Ltd's plant is recognised for consolidation purposes, reversing CU 20 000 of the CU 70 000 at acquisition taxable temporary difference which arose in respect of plant. The result, on consolidation, is a CU 5 600 (20 000 Reversal of taxable temporary difference × 28%) post-acquisition reduction in S Ltd's at acquisition deferred tax liability (see **b** in table) and a corresponding CU 5 600 reduction in S Ltd's income tax expense, recognised in the consolidated financial statements over this two-year period. Because this reduction, for consolidation purposes, in S Ltd's income tax expense relates to prior years, in the current year, this CU 5 600 consolidation adjustment is made by increasing S Ltd's opening retained earnings balance by CU 5 600 (see analysis of equity and pro forma journal 4 that follow).

  - As can be seen in the table, the CU 10 000 (10 000 × 1 year) current year additional depreciation on S Ltd's plant, recognised for consolidation purposes, reverses in the current year an additional CU 10 000 of the CU 70 000 at acquisition taxable temporary difference that arose in respect of S Ltd's plant. The result, on consolidation, is a CU 2 800 (10 000 Reversal of taxable temporary difference × 28%) current year reduction in S Ltd's at acquisition deferred tax liability, (see **c** in table), with a corresponding CU 2 800 reduction in S Ltd's current year income tax expense, recognised in the consolidated financial statements (see analysis of equity and pro forma journal 7 that follow).

  - The deferred tax liability recognised in respect of the at acquisition fair value adjustment to S Ltd's plant will have a balance of CU 11 200 (see **d** in table) at financial year end 31 December 20x8, which will be reported in the consolidated statement of financial position at this reporting period end.

Part (a): Analysis of equity (AOE) of S Ltd as at 31 December 20x8

| | Total of S Ltd's equity 100% | P Ltd 80% | | Non-controlling interest 20% |
| | | At acquisi-tion | Since acquisi-tion | |
At acquisition date (31 December 20x5)	CU	CU	CU	CU
Share capital	170 000	136 000		34 000
Retained earnings	145 000	116 000		29 000
Fair value adjustment plant (385 000 Fair value – (420 000 Carrying amount – 105 000 Accumulated depreciation))	70 000	56 000		14 000
Deferred tax: Fair value adjustment plant (70 000 Fair value adjustment × 28%)	(19 600)	(15 680)		(3 920)[1]
Fair value of net assets of S Ltd	365 400	292 320		73 080
Goodwill – Parent (balancing figure)	57 680	57 680 a		–
Consideration and non-controlling interest	423 080	350 000		73 080
Since acquisition				
• To beginning of current year:				
Adjusted retained earnings	90 600		72 480 b	18 120
Retained earnings movement (250 000 – 145 000)	105 000		84 000	21 000
Additional depreciation plant 2 years [(70 000 / 7 year RUL) × 2 years]	(20 000)		(16 000)	(4 000)
Deferred tax: Additional depreciation plant (20 000 × 28%)	5 600		4 480	1 120[1]
				91 200 c
• Current year:				
Adjusted profit for the year	27 800		22 240 d	5 560 e
Profit for the year (115 000 – 35 000 – 45 000)	35 000		28 000	7 000
Additional depreciation plant 1 year (70 000 / 7 year RUL)	(10 000) f		(8 000)	(2 000)
Deferred tax: Additional depreciation plant (10 000 × 28%)	2 800 g		2 240	560[1]
	541 480		94 720	96 760 h

Explanatory note: Analysis of equity

[1] Note how the non-controlling interest is allocated its appropriate share of the deferred tax effects of the fair value adjustment to plant, both at acquisition and subsequently.

Part (b): Pro forma journal entries for the financial year ended 31 December 20x8

AT ACQUISITION

Pro forma journal 1 (J1)	Dr CU	Cr CU
Plant: Accumulated depreciation (S Ltd) (SFP) (given)	Wkg1105 000	
Plant: Cost (S Ltd) (SFP)		Wkg1105 000
Elimination of at acquisition accumulated depreciation of plant		

Workings: Pro forma journals

Working 1

420 000 Cost – 315 000 Carrying amount

Pro forma journal 2 (J2)	Dr CU	Cr CU
Share capital (S Ltd) (SCIE) (given)	170 000	
Retained earnings (S Ltd) (SCIE) (given)	145 000	
Plant (S Ltd) (SFP)	Wkg270 000	
Deferred tax (S Ltd) (SFP) [see **a** in deferred tax table above]		Wkg319 600
Investment in S Ltd (P Ltd) (SFP) (given)		350 000
NCI – Equity (SCIE)		Wkg473 080
Goodwill (SFP) (balancing figure)	57 680	
Elimination of at acquisition equity and cost of investment, recognition of fair value adjustment to plant and deferred tax effects, recognition of non-controlling interest and goodwill		

Working 2

385 000 Fair value – (420 000 Carrying amount – 105 000 Accumulated depreciation)

Working 3

70 000 Fair value adjustment × 28%

Working 4

(170 000 + 145 000 + 70 000 – 19 600) × 20% NCI Share

SINCE ACQUISITION TO THE BEGINNING OF THE YEAR

Pro forma journal 3 (J3)	Dr CU	Cr CU
Retained earnings (S Ltd) (SCIE)	Wkg520 000	
Plant: Accumulated depreciation (S Ltd) (SFP)		Wkg520 000
Recognition of additional depreciation on S Ltd plant in respect of prior years		

Working 5

(70 000 Fair value adjustment: Plant / 7 Years RUL plant at acquisition) × 2 Years since acquisition to BOY

Pro forma journal 4 (J4)	Dr CU	Cr CU
Deferred tax (S Ltd) (SFP) [see **b** in deferred tax table above]	Wkg65 600	
Retained earnings (S Ltd) (SCIE)		Wkg65 600
Recognition of tax effect of additional depreciation on S Ltd plant in respect of prior years		

Workings: Pro forma journals

Working 6

20 000 (J3) × 28%

Pro forma journal 5 (J5)	Dr CU	Cr CU
Retained earnings (S Ltd) (SCIE)	Wkg7 18 120	
Non-controlling interest – Equity (SFP)		Wkg7 18 120
Allocating the non-controlling interest its share of S Ltd adjusted retained earnings since acquisition to BOY		

Workings: Pro forma journals

Working 7

(250 000 Balance BOY – 145 000 Balance at acquisition – 20 000 (J3) Additional prior years' depreciation: Plant + 5 600 (J4) Tax effect: Additional prior years' depreciation: Plant) × 20% NCI Share

CURRENT YEAR

Pro forma journal 6 (J6)	Dr CU	Cr CU
Depreciation: Plant (S Ltd) (P/L))	Wkg8 10 000	
Plant: Accumulated depreciation (S Ltd) (SFP)		Wkg8 10 000
Recognition of additional depreciation plant of S Ltd for the current year		

Workings: Pro forma journals

Working 8

70 000 Fair value adjustment: Plant / 7 Years RUL plant × 1 Year

Pro forma journal 7 (J7)	Dr CU	Cr CU
Deferred tax (S Ltd) (SFP) [see **c** in deferred tax table above]	Wkg9 2 800	
Income tax expense (S Ltd) (P/L)		Wkg9 2 800
Recognition of tax effects of additional depreciation plant for the current year		

Workings: Pro forma journals

Working 9

10 000 (J6) × 28%

Pro forma journal 8 (J8)	Dr CU	Cr CU
NCI: Share of profit or loss (P/L)	Wkg10 5 560	
Non-controlling interest – Equity (SFP)		Wkg10 5 560
Allocating the non-controlling interest its share of S Ltd's adjusted profit for the year		

Workings: Pro forma journals

Working 10

(115 000 – 35 000 – 45 000 = 35 000 Current year profit – 10 000 (J6) Additional depreciation plant + 2 800 (J7) Tax effect: Additional depreciation plant) × 20% NCI Share

The effects of preceding pro forma journals 1 to 8 in arriving at the consolidated figures are illustrated in the following consolidation worksheet.

	P Ltd Dr/(Cr) CU	S Ltd Dr/(Cr) CU	Pro forma journals At acquisition Dr/(Cr) CU	Journal ref	Pro forma journals Since acquisition Dr/(Cr) CU	Journal ref	Consolidated Dr/(Cr) CU
Equity							
Share capital	(150 000)	(170 000)	170 000	J2			(150 000)
Retained earnings (BOY)	(310 000)	(250 000)	145 000	J2	20 000 / (5 600) / 18 120	J3 / J4 / J5	(382 480)
Net profit: Individual entities	(66 000)	(35 000)					
Consolidated profit – attributable to owners of parent							†(88 240)
Retained earnings (EOY)	(376 000)	(285 000)	(73 080)	J2	(18 120)	J5	(470 720)
NCI Equity	–	–			(5 560)	J8	(96 760)
Total equity	**(526 000)**	**(455 000)**					**(717 480)**
Liabilities:							
Trade and other payables	(32 000)	(15 000)					(47 000)
Deferred tax			(19 600)	J2	5 600 / 2 800	J4 / J7	(11 200)
Total liabilities	**(32 000)**	**(15 000)**					**(58 200)**

Explanatory notes

† This amount has been brought forward from the second part of the consolidation worksheet on page 278

	P Ltd Dr/(Cr) CU	S Ltd Dr/(Cr) CU	Pro forma journals At acquisition Dr/(Cr) CU	Journal ref	Pro forma journals Since acquisition Dr/(Cr) CU	Journal ref	Consolidated Dr/(Cr) CU
Total equity & liabilities	(558 000)	(470 000)					(775 680)
Assets:							
Plant: Cost	–	420 000	(105 000) 70 000	J1 J2			385 000
Plant: Accumulated depreciation	–	(195 000)	105 000	J1	(20 000) (10 000)	J3 J6	(120 000)
Trade and other receivables	208 000	245 000					453 000
Investment in S Ltd	350 000	–	(350 000)	J2			–
Goodwill			57 680	J2			57 680
Total assets	558 000	470 000					775 680
Profit or loss							
Profit before tax and depreciation	(108 000)	(115 000)					(223 000)
Depreciation	–	45 000			10 000	J6	55 000
Taxation	42 000	35 000			(2 800)	J7	74 200
Net profit for period	(66 000)	(35 000)					(93 800)
NCI: Share of profit					5 560	J8	5 560
Consolidated profit attributable to owners of parent							‡(88 240)

Explanatory notes

‡ This amount has been carried forward to the first part of the consolidation worksheet on page 277

Part (c): Consolidated financial statements for the financial year ended 31 December 20x8

P LTD GROUP: ABRIDGED CONSOLIDATED STATEMENT OF PROFIT OR LOSS AND OTHER COMPREHENSIVE INCOME FOR THE YEAR ENDED 31 DECEMBER 20X8	
	CU
Profit before taxation (108 000 (P Ltd) + (S Ltd: 115 000 – 45 000 Depreciation – 10 000 (see AOE **f OR** (J6)) Additional depreciation: Plant)	168 000
Taxation (42 000 (P Ltd) + (S Ltd: 35 000 – 2 800 (see AOE **g OR** (J7)) Tax effect: Additional depreciation plant))	(74 200)
PROFIT FOR THE YEAR	93 800
Other comprehensive income for the year	–
TOTAL COMPREHENSIVE INCOME FOR THE YEAR	**93 800**
Total comprehensive income for the year attributable to:	
Owners of parent (balancing figure) **OR** (66 000 (P Ltd) + S Ltd: 22 240 (see AOE **d**))	88 240
Non-controlling interest (see AOE **e OR** (J8))	5 560
	93 800

P LTD GROUP: CONSOLIDATED STATEMENT OF CHANGES IN EQUITY FOR THE YEAR ENDED 31 DECEMBER 20x8					
	Parent equity holders' interest			Non-control-ling interest	Total equity of the group
	Share capital CU	Retained earnings CU	Total parent equity CU	CU	CU
Opening balance at 1 Jan 20x8	150 000	Wkg1382 480	532 480	Wkg291 200	623 680
Total comprehensive income:					
Profit for the period (from CSOPL_OCI)	–	88 240	88 240	5 560	93 800
Closing balance at 31 Dec 20x8	150 000	470 720	620 720	96 760	717 480

Workings: Consolidated statement of changes in equity

Working 1
P Ltd: 310 000 + S Ltd: 72 480 (see AOE **b**) P Ltd share of S Ltd post-acquisition retained earnings to BOY

OR

P Ltd: 310 000 + (S Ltd: 250 000 Balance BOY – 145 000 (J2) Balance at acquisition – 20 000 (J3) Additional depreciation plant + 5 600 (J4) Tax effect: Additional depreciation plant – 18 120 (J5) NCI share of S Ltd post-acquisition retained earnings to BOY)

Working 2
S Ltd: 91 200 (see AOE **c**)

OR

S Ltd: 73 080 (J2) NCI Share of S Ltd at acquisition equity + 18 120 (J5) NCI Share of S Ltd post-acquisition retained earnings to BOY

P LTD GROUP: CONSOLIDATED STATEMENT OF FINANCIAL POSITION AS AT 31 DECEMBER 20X8	
	CU
Assets	
Non-current assets	
Property, plant and equipment	265 000
(S Ltd: 420 000 Cost: Plant – 195 000 Accumulated depreciation: Plant + 70 000 (J2) Fair value adjustment: Plant – 20 000 (J3) Additional accumulated depreciation; Plant: Prior years – 10 000 (J6) Additional accumulated depreciation; Plant: Current year)	
Goodwill (see AOE **a OR** (J2))	57 680
Current assets	
Trade and other receivables (208 000 (P Ltd) + 245 000 (S Ltd))	453 000
Total assets	**775 680**
Equity and liabilities	
Share capital (from CSCIE)	150 000
Retained earnings (from CSCIE)	470 720
Equity attributable to owners of the parent	620 720
Non-controlling interest (from CSCIE **OR** see AOE **h**)	96 760
Total equity	**717 480**
Non-current liabilities	
Deferred tax (see **d** in deferred tax table) **OR** (19 600 (J2) – 5 600 (J4) – 2 800 (J7))	11 200
Current liabilities	
Trade and other payables (32 000 (P Ltd) + 15 000 (S Ltd))	47 000
Total equity and liabilities	**775 680**

Example 5.9: Deferred tax implications: Subsequent disposal of depreciable property, plant and equipment which was remeasured to fair value at acquisition date

In this example, the facts are the same as in Example 5.6, except that the deferred tax effects of the fair value adjustment to, and subsequent disposal of, the plant now need to be taken into account for consolidation purposes. The relevant facts are reproduced below.

This example is a continuation of Example 5.5. Assume that S Ltd disposed of its plant to a third party on 30 June 20x9 for CU 280 000.

Additional information

Depreciation-related information

At acquisition date, the estimated remaining useful life of S Ltd's plant was seven years with no residual value. These estimates were confirmed at each reporting date.

Tax-related information

• The tax base of the plant on acquisition date equalled its carrying amount of CU 315 000.

• The tax authority will allow S Ltd to deduct the remaining tax base of the plant over the remaining seven years on a straight line basis.

• The income tax rate is 28% and the subsidiary intends to continue using its plant.

The abridged trial balances of P Ltd and S Ltd for the financial year ended 31 December 20x9 were as follows:

Abridged trial balances at 31 December 20x9	P Ltd Dr/(Cr) CU	S Ltd Dr/(Cr) CU
Share capital	(150 000)	(170 000)
Retained earnings (1 Jan 20x9)	(376 000)	(285 000)
Trade and other payables	(100 000)	(200 000)
Trade and other receivables	398 000	792 500
Investment in S Ltd: Cost	350 000	–
Profit before tax	(159 000)	(181 500)
Taxation expense	37 000	44 000

Required

(a) Prepare the analysis of equity of S Ltd for the financial year ended 31 December 20x9.

(b) Prepare all the pro forma journal entries for the financial year ended 31 December 20x9.

Solution 5.9: Deferred tax implications: Subsequent disposal of depreciable property, plant and equipment that was remeasured to fair value at acquisition

Draw up the following deferred tax table:

	Carrying amount: S Ltd A	Carrying amount: Group B	Tax base: S Ltd & Group C	(Taxable)/deductible temporary difference: Group C – B = D	Deferred tax (liability)/ asset: Group D × 28%	Pro forma journal	Period
Balance 31 Dec 20x5	315 000	385 000	315 000	(70 000)	(19 600)a	**Cr** Deferred tax liability CU 19 600 (see pro forma journal 1 below)	At acquisition
Depreciation/tax allowance 1 Jan 20x6 – 31 Dec 20x8 (3 Years)	Wkg1(135 000)	Wkg2(165 000)	Wkg1(135 000)	30 000	8 400b	**Dr** Deferred tax liability CU 8 400; **Cr** Retained earnings CU 8 400 (see pro forma journal 3 below)	Since acquisition to BOY
Balance 31 Dec 20x8	180 000	220 000	180 000	(40 000)	(11 200)		Beginning of year
Depreciation/tax allowance 20x9	Wkg3(22 500)	Wkg4(27 500)	Wkg3(22 500)	5 000	1 400c	**Dr** Deferred tax liability CU 1 400; **Cr** Income tax expense CU 1400 (see pro forma journal 6 below)	Current year (6 months)
Balance at date of disposal	157 500	192 500	157 500	(35 000)d	(9 800)		
Disposal of plant on 30 June 20x9	(157 500)	(192 500)	(157 500)	35 000e	9 800f	**Dr** Deferred tax liability CU 9 800; **Cr** Income tax expense CU 9 800 (see pro forma journal 8 below)	
Balance at 31 December 20x9	NIL	NIL	NIL	NIL	NILg		End of the year

Workings: Deferred tax table

Working 1
(315 000 Carrying amount of plant / 7 years RUL of plant at acquisition) × 3 Years since acquisition to BOY

Working 2
(385 000 Fair value of plant / 7 years RUL of plant at acquisition) × 3 Years since acquisition to BOY

Working 3
(315 000 Carrying amount of plant / 7 years RUL of plant at acquisition) × 6/12 Months

Working 4
(385 000 Fair value of plant / 7 years RUL of plant at acquisition) × 6/12 Months

Comments: Deferred tax table

- At acquisition, the carrying amount and cost of S Ltd's plant to the group is its fair value of CU 385 000. From a tax perspective, the tax authority does not recognise this IFRS3 fair value adjustment made to S Ltd's plant for accounting purposes, with the result that the at acquisition tax base of the plant remains unchanged at CU 315 000, which equals the plant's at acquisition carrying amount in S Ltd's separate records. A taxable temporary difference therefore arises at acquisition in respect of S Ltd's plant, equivalent to the plant's at acquisition fair value increase of CU 70 000, resulting in the recognition at group level of a deferred tax liability of S Ltd of CU 19 600 (70 000 Taxable temporary difference × 28%) at acquisition date (see **a** in the table).

- As the fair value of S Ltd's plant is CU 70 000 more than its carrying amount in S Ltd's own records, additional depreciation of CU 10 000 (70 000 Fair value adjustment plant / 7 year remaining useful life of plant at acquisition date) is recognised each year for group purposes. This additional depreciation each year on S Ltd's plant, recognised on consolidation, reverses the taxable temporary difference that arose in respect of this plant on acquisition, and results in a reduction in the at acquisition deferred tax liability, recognised for this plant, in subsequent reporting periods. More particularly, as can be seen from the table:

  - In the three-year period from acquisition date to the beginning of the current year, additional depreciation of CU 30 000 (10 000 × 3 years) on S Ltd's plant is recognised for group purposes, reversing CU 30 000 of the CU 70 000 at acquisition taxable temporary difference that arose in respect of this plant. The result on consolidation is a CU 8 400 (30 000 Reversal of taxable temporary difference × 28%) reduction in S Ltd's at acquisition deferred tax liability (see **b** in the table), and a corresponding CU 8 400 reduction in S Ltd's income tax expense in the consolidated financial statements over this three-year period. Because this CU 8 400 reduction, for consolidation purposes, in S Ltd's income tax expense relates to prior years (i.e., to the three-year period since acquisition to the beginning of the current year), in the current year this consolidation adjustment is made by increasing S Ltd's opening retained earnings balance by CU 8 400 (see analysis of equity and pro forma journal 3).

  - In the current year, additional depreciation of CU 5 000 (10 000 × 6/12 Months) on S Ltd's plant is recognised for consolidation purposes up until the plant is sold midway through the current year. This half a year of additional depreciation of S Ltd's plant, recognised on consolidation, reverses in the current year an additional CU 5 000 of the at acquisition taxable temporary difference that arose in respect of S Ltd's plant. On consolidation this results in a CU 1 400 (5 000 Reversal of taxable temporary differences × 28%) current year reduction in S Ltd's at acquisition deferred tax liability, (see **c** in the table), with a corresponding CU 1 400 current year reduction recognised in S Ltd's income tax expense (see analysis of equity and pro forma journal 6 below).

  - Of the at acquisition CU 70 000 taxable temporary difference that results from the acquisition fair value adjustment to S Ltd's plant, CU 35 000 of this taxable temporary difference remains just prior to S Ltd's disposal of the plant on 30 June 20x9 (see **d** in the table). Once the plant is sold by S Ltd to an external party, this remaining CU 35 000 taxable temporary difference also reverses for group purposes (see **e** in the table).

  - On consolidation, the current year reversal of this CU 35 000 remaining taxable temporary difference causes:

    - a further current year reduction of CU 9 800 (35 000 Reversal of remaining taxable temporary difference × 28%) in S Ltd's at acquisition deferred tax liability recognised in respect of this plant (see **f** in table above) bringing this deferred tax liability balance down to NIL (see **g** in table above); and

    - a corresponding further CU 9 800 reduction in S Ltd's current year income tax expense (see analysis of equity and pro forma journal 8).

➠

Part (a): Analysis of equity of S Ltd as at 31 December 20x9

| | Total of S Ltd's equity 100% | P Ltd 80% | | Non-controlling interest 20% |
| | | At acquisition | Since acquisition | |
At acquisition date (31 December 20x5)	CU	CU	CU	CU
Share capital	170 000	136 000		34 000
Retained earnings	145 000	116 000		29 000
Fair value adjustment plant [385 000 – (420 000 – 105 000)]	70 000	56 000		14 000
Deferred tax: Fair value adjustment plant (70 000 × 28%)	(19 600)[1]	(15 680)		(3 920)
Fair value of net assets of S Ltd	365 400	292 320		73 080
Goodwill – Parent (balancing figure)	57 680	57 680		–
Consideration and NCI	423 080	350 000		73 080
Since acquisition				
• To beginning of current year:				
Adjusted retained earnings	118 400		94 720	23 680
Retained earnings movement (285 000 Balance BOY – 145 000 Balance at acquisition)	140 000		112 000	28 000
Additional depreciation 3 years [(70 000/7 year RUL plant) × 3 years]	(30 000)		(24 000)	(6 000)
Tax effect: Additional depreciation plant (30 000 × 28%)	8 400[1]		6 720	1 680
				96 760
• Current year:				
Adjusted profit for the year	108 700		86 960	21 740
Profit for the year (181 500 – 44 000)	137 500		110 000	27 500
Additional depreciation plant for 1/2 year [(70 000 / 7 year RUL plant) × 6/12]	(5 000)		(4 000)	(1 000)
Tax effect: Additional depreciation plant (5 000 × 28%)	1 400[1]		1 120	280
Reduction in profit on disposal of plant (70 000 – 30 000 – 5000)	(35 000)		(28 000)	(7 000)
Tax effect: Disposal of plant (35 000 × 28%)	9 800[1]		7 840	1 960
	650 180		**181 680**	**118 500**

Explanatory notes: Analysis of equity

[1] Note how the total deferred tax liability of CU 19 600 recognised in respect of the at acquisition fair value adjustment to S Ltd's plant has reversed out completely by 20x9, after sale of the plant. Of this deferred tax liability:

- CU 9 800 (8 400 Since acquisition to BOY + 1 400 Current year) reversed due to additional depreciation in respect of S Ltd's plant of CU 35 000 recognised by the group in the 3½ years since acquisition to date of disposal of the plant; and
- CU 9 800 reversed upon disposal of the plant.

Part (b): Pro forma journal entries for the financial year ended 31 December 20x9

AT ACQUISITION

Pro forma journal 1 (J1)	Dr CU	Cr CU
Share capital (S Ltd) (SCIE) (given)	170 000	
Retained earnings (S Ltd) (SCIE) (given)	145 000	
Plant (S Ltd) (SFP)	Wkg1 70 000	
Deferred tax (S Ltd) (SFP) [see **a** in deferred tax table above]		Wkg2 19 600
Investment in S Ltd (P Ltd) (SFP) (given)		350 000
NCI – Equity (SCIE)		Wkg3 73 080
Goodwill (SFP) (balancing figure)	57 680	
Elimination of at acquisition equity and cost of investment, recognition of fair value adjustment in respect of plant and associated deferred tax effects, and recognition of non-controlling interest and goodwill at acquisition		

Workings: Pro forma journals

Working 1

385 000 Fair value – (420 000 Carrying amount – 105 000 Accumulated depreciation)

Working 2

70 000 Fair value adjustment: Plant × 28%

Working 3

(170 000 + 145 000 + 70 000 – 19 600) × 20% NCI Share

SINCE ACQUISITION TO THE BEGINNING OF THE YEAR

Pro forma journal 2 (J2)	Dr CU	Cr CU
Retained earnings (S Ltd) (SCIE)	Wkg4 30 000	
Plant: Accumulated depreciation (S Ltd) (SFP)		Wkg4 30 000
Recognition of additional depreciation plant – prior years		

Working 4

(70 000 Fair value adjustment plant / 7 Years RUL plant at acquisition) × 3 Years since acquisition to BOY

Pro forma journal 3 (J3)	Dr CU	Cr CU
Deferred tax (S Ltd) (SFP) [see **b** in deferred tax table above]	Wkg5 8 400	
Retained earnings (S Ltd) (SCIE)		Wkg5 8 400
Recognition of tax effects of additional depreciation plant – prior years		

Working 5

30 000 (J2) × 28%

Pro forma journal 4 (J4)	Dr CU	Cr CU
Retained earnings (S Ltd) (SCIE)	Wkg6 23 680	
Non-controlling interest – Equity (SFP)		Wkg6 23 680
Allocating the non-controlling interest its share of S Ltd's adjusted retained earnings since acquisition to the beginning of the year		

Working 6

(285 000 Balance BOY – 145 000 Balance at acquisition – 30 000 (J2) Additional prior years' depreciation: Plant + 8 400 (J3) Tax effect: Additional prior years' depreciation: Plant) × 20% NCI Share

CURRENT YEAR

Pro forma journal 5 (J5)	Dr CU	Cr CU
Depreciation: Plant (S Ltd) (P/L)	Wkg7 5 000	
Plant: Accumulated depreciation (S Ltd) (SFP)		Wkg7 5 000
Recognition of additional depreciation plant for the current year		

Workings: Pro forma journals

Working 7

(70 000 Fair value adjustment plant / 7 Years RUL plant) × 6/12 Months

Pro forma journal 6 (J6)	Dr CU	Cr CU
Deferred tax (S Ltd) (SFP) [see **c** in deferred tax table above]	Wkg8 1 400	
Income tax expense (S Ltd) (P/L)		Wkg8 1 400
Recognition of tax effects of additional depreciation plant for the current year		

Working 8

5 000 (J5) × 28%

Pro forma journal 7 (J7)	Dr CU	Cr CU
Profit on sale of plant (S Ltd) (P/L)	Wkg9 35 000	
Plant: Accumulated depreciation (S Ltd) (SFP)	Wkg10 35 000	
Plant (S Ltd) (SFP) (see (J1))		70 000
Recognition of current year reduction in S Ltd profit on disposal of plant, reversal of additional accumulated depreciation on plant to date of disposal, and reversal of at acquisition fair value adjustment to plant		

Workings: Pro forma journals

Working 9

	CU
Fair value (FV) adjustment: Plant (see (J1))	70 000
Additional depreciation: FV adjustment plant	(35 000)
Current year additional accumulated depreciation: Plant (see (J5))	(5 000)
Additional accumulated depreciation plant to BOY: Plant (see (J2))	(30 000)
Carrying amount FV adjustment plant: at disposal date	35 000

OR

70 000 (J1) Fair value adjustment: Plant × $\dfrac{\text{3.5 Years (Plant RUL at disposal date)}}{\text{7 Years (Plant RUL: date of acquisition of subsidiary)}}$

= 35 000 Carrying amount FV adjustment plant: at disposal date

Working 10

Balancing figure

OR

30 000 (J2) Additional accumulated depreciation: Plant since acquisition to BOY + CU 5 000 (J5) Additional accumulated depreciation: Plant current year to date of disposal

Pro forma journal 8 (J8)	Dr CU	Cr CU
Deferred tax (S Ltd) (SFP) [see **f** in deferred tax table above]	Wkg11 9 800	
Income tax expense (S Ltd) (P/L)		Wkg11 9 800
Recognition of tax effects of disposal of plant		

Working 11

35 000 (J7) × 28%

Pro forma journal 9 (J9)	Dr CU	Cr CU
NCI – Share of profit or loss (P/L)	Wkg12 21 740	
Non-controlling interest – Equity (SFP)		Wkg12 21 740
Allocating the non-controlling interest its share of S Ltd's adjusted profit for the year		

Working 12

181 500 – 44 000 = 137 500 Current year profit – 5 000 (J5) Additional depreciation plant + 1 400 (J6) Tax effect: Additional depreciation plant – 35 000 (J7) Reduction in profit on disposal of plant + 9 800 (J8) Tax effect: Disposal of plant) × 20% NCI Share

Mastering Group Financial Statements Volume 1

The effects of preceding pro forma journals 1 to 9 in arriving at the consolidated figures is illustrated in the following consolidation worksheet.

	P Ltd Dr/(Cr) CU	S Ltd Dr/(Cr) CU	Pro forma journals At acquisition Dr/(Cr) CU	Journal ref	Pro forma journals Since acquisition Dr/(Cr) CU	Journal ref	Consolidated Dr/(Cr) CU
Equity							
Share capital	(150 000)	(170 000)	170 000	J1			(150 000)
Retained earnings (BOY)	(376 000)	(285 000)	145 000	J1	30 000 (8 400) 23 680	J2 J3 J4	(470 720)
Net profit: Individual entities	(122 000)	(137 500)					
Consolidated profit – attributable to owners of parent							†(208 960)
Retained earnings (EOY)	(498 000)	(422 500)					(679 680)
NCI Equity	–	–	(73 080)	J1	(23 680) (21 740)	J4 J9	(118 500)
Total equity	**(648 000)**	**(592 500)**					**(948 180)**
Liabilities:							
Trade and other payables	(100 000)	(200 000)					(300 000)
Deferred tax			(19 600)	J1	8 400 1 400 9 800	J3 J6 J8	–
Total liabilities	**(100 000)**	**(200 000)**					**(300 000)**
Total equity & liabilities	**(748 000)**	**(792 500)**					**(1 248 180)**

Explanatory notes

† This amount has been brought forward from the second part of the consolidation worksheet on page 289

	P Ltd Dr/(Cr) CU	S Ltd Dr/(Cr) CU	Pro forma journals At acquisition Dr/(Cr) CU	Journal ref	Pro forma journals Since acquisition Dr/(Cr) CU	Journal ref	Con-solidated Dr/(Cr) CU
Assets							
Plant: Cost			70 000	J1	(70 000)	J7	–
Plant: Accumulated depreciation					(30 000) (5 000) 35 000	J2 J5 J7	–
Trade and other receivables	398 000	792 500					1 190 500
Investment in S Ltd	350 000	–	(350 000)	J1			–
Goodwill			57 680	J1			57 680
Total assets	**748 000**	**792 500**					**1 248 180**
Profit or loss							
Profit before tax	(159 000)	(181 500)			5 000 35 000	J5 J7	(300 500)
Taxation	37 000	44 000			(1 400) (9 800)	J6 J8	69 800
Net profit for the period	(122 000)	(137 500)					(230 700)
NCI: Share of profit					21 740	J9	21 740
Consolidated profit attributable to owners of parent							‡(208 960)

Explanatory notes

‡ This amount has been carried forward to the first part of the consolidation worksheet on page 288

5.2.9 At acquisition fair value adjustment to non-depreciable property, plant and equipment: Subsidiary subsequently revalues non-depreciable property, plant and equipment in its own books

It may happen that a subsidiary applies the revaluation model to its property, plant and equipment and accordingly revalues its property, plant and equipment at regular intervals. If the acquisition date, when the subsidiary's property, plant and equipment is remeasured to fair value under IFRS 3, does *not* coincide with the date that the subsidiary revalues this property, plant and equipment in its own records, **adjustments will be required on consolidation.**

This is because a portion of the after-tax revaluation gain, as recorded by the subsidiary, will already have been recognised under IFRS 3 at acquisition date, and consequently will represent pre-acquisition equity of the subsidiary, purchased by its parent.

When preparing the consolidated financial statements for the reporting period when the subsidiary revalues its non-depreciable property, plant and equipment, the following consolidation adjustments must be made:

- **Reduce** the subsidiary's **after-tax revaluation gain, recognised in other comprehensive income,** by the **after-tax effect of the remeasurement to fair value,** of the subsidiary's property, plant and equipment, recognised under IFRS 3 at acquisition date.
- Reduce the **revalued carrying amount** of the subsidiary's property, plant and equipment, by the amount of the **IFRS 3 remeasurement to fair value,** of this property, plant and equipment, recognised at **acquisition date.**
- Reduce the **deferred tax liability** recorded by the subsidiary in respect of its property, plant and equipment revaluation, by the **deferred tax liability amount recognised at acquisition date** because of the IFRS 3 fair value remeasurement of this property, plant and equipment, at acquisition date.

When preparing the current period consolidated financial statements, and the subsidiary has revalued its non-depreciable property, plant and equipment in its own records in a prior reporting period:

- Reduce the subsidiary's **opening revaluation surplus balance** by the amount of the **after-tax remeasurement** to fair value of the subsidiary's property, plant and equipment, recognised under IFRS 3 at acquisition date.
- The consolidation adjustments required in respect of (1) the revalued carrying amount of the subsidiary's property, plant and equipment, and (2) the deferred tax liability associated with the revaluation, are the same as those discussed in the second and third bullet points of the previous paragraph.

Note: For a discussion and illustration (by means of a worked example) of the accounting treatment in the consolidated financial statements, of the subsequent revaluation by a subsidiary of **depreciable** property, plant and equipment that was remeasured, under IFRS 3, to fair value at acquisition, see the Volume 1 Chapter 5 supplementary material which may be accessed online from Juta's website.

Example 5.10: At acquisition fair value adjustment to property, plant and equipment – subsidiary subsequently revalues property, plant and equipment in its own records

P Ltd acquired 80% of the ordinary share capital of S Ltd on 1 January 20x5 for CU 458 000 when S Ltd's equity comprised share capital of CU 170 000 and retained earnings of CU 325 000. P Ltd considered the net assets of S Ltd to be fairly valued, except for land, which had a carrying amount of CU 300 000 and a fair value of CU 350 000 at acquisition date. P Ltd measured the non-controlling interest at its proportionate share of S Ltd's identifiable net assets at acquisition.

S Ltd subsequently revalued its land in its own records as follows:

- Revaluation date 31 December 20x5: Land revalued to CU 420 000.
- Revaluation date 31 December 20x6: Land revalued to CU 460 000.

The abridged trial balances for P Ltd and its subsidiary S Ltd were as follows at 31 December 20x6:

Abridged trial balances at 31 December 20x6	P Ltd Dr/(Cr) CU	S Ltd Dr/(Cr) CU
Share capital	(250 000)	(170 000)
Revaluation surplus	–	(93 120)
Retained earnings (1 Jan 20x6)	(384 000)	(435 000)
Trade and other payables	(100 000)	(200 000)
Deferred tax	–	(35 840)
Land	–	460 000
Trade and other receivables	398 000	642 500
Investment in S Ltd: Cost	458 000	–
Profit after tax for period	(122 000)	(137 500)
Revaluation gain land (OCI)	–	(40 000)
Tax expense revaluation gain land (OCI)	–	8 960

Required

(a) Prepare the analysis of equity of S Ltd as at 31 December 20x6.

(b) Provide the pro forma journal entries required to prepare the consolidated financial statements of the P Ltd group for the year ended 31 December 20x6.

(c) Prepare the consolidated financial statements of the P Ltd group for the year ended 31 December 20x6.

Assume an income tax rate of 28% and an effective capital gains tax rate of 22.4%.

Solution 5.10: At acquisition fair value adjustment to property, plant and equipment – subsidiary subsequently revalues property, plant and equipment in its own records

Part (a): Analysis of equity (AOE) of S Ltd as at 31 December 20x6

| | Total of S Ltd's equity 100% | P Ltd 80% | | Non-controlling interest 20% |
| | | At acqui-sition | Since acquisi-tion | |
At acquisition date (1 January 20x5)	CU	CU	CU	CU
Share capital	170 000	136 000		34 000
Retained earnings	325 000	260 000		65 000
Fair value adjustment: Land (350 000 – 300 000)	50 000[1]a	40 000		10 000
Deferred tax: Fair value adjustment land (50 000 × 22.4%)	(11 200)[2]b	(8 960)		(2 240)
Fair value of net assets of S Ltd	533 800	427 040		106 760
Goodwill – Parent (balancing figure)	30 960	30 960c		–
Consideration and non-controlling interest	564 760	458 000		106 760
Since acquisition				
Retained earnings to BOY (435 000 – 325 000)	110 000		88 000d	22 000e
Adjusted revaluation surplus to BOY	54 320[3]		43 456[3]f	10 864[3]g
Post-acquisition revaluation surplus (given)	93 120[3]		74 496	18 624
Less: After tax revaluation at acquisition [50 000 × 77.6% (100% − 22.4%)]	(38 800)[3]		(31 040)	(7 760)
				139 624h
• Current year:				
Profit for the year (given)	137 500		110 000i	27 500j
Other comprehensive income for the year (40 000 Revaluation gain – 8 960 Tax)	31 040[4]		24 832[4]k	6 208[4]l
	897 620		**266 288**	**173 332 m**

Explanatory notes: Analysis of equity S Ltd

[1] As S Ltd did not revalue the land to fair value in its own records at acquisition, an IFRS 3 fair value adjustment, increasing S Ltd's land by CU 50 000, is required on consolidation in order to correctly reflect the fair value of the net assets (equity) of S Ltd at acquisition date. This at acquisition revaluation of land does not result in a revaluation surplus for the group at acquisition date. This is because the revaluation represents an increase in the pre acquisition equity of S Ltd, which was purchased by P Ltd and was not earned while S Ltd was part of the group.

[2] The IFRS 3 consolidation adjustment which increases the value of S Ltd's land to its fair value at acquisition results in a CU 50 000 increase in the land's carrying amount, while its tax base remains unchanged. This is because the taxing authority does not recognise this accounting fair value adjustment to the land for tax purposes. At group level, this causes a CU 50 000 taxable temporary difference at acquisition (i.e. the carrying amount of the asset land exceeds its tax base), and therefore the at acquisition recognition of a CU 11 200 deferred tax liability in respect of this land, measured at the effective capital gains tax rate since the land is recovered by way of sale.

[3]   Ordinarily, the full CU 93 120 (120 000 Gross revaluation surplus × 77.6% After tax) after tax revaluation surplus (i.e., net revaluation surplus) on S Ltd's land, arising in the period since acquisition up until the beginning of the year, would be included in the current year consolidated statement of changes in equity as follows:

- 80% of this revaluation surplus, the amount of CU 74 496 (93 120 × 80% P Ltd's shareholding) would constitute the opening consolidated revaluation surplus balance; and

- 20% of this revaluation surplus, the amount of CU 18 624 (93 120 × 20% NCI Share) would be included in the non-controlling interest opening balance.

However, this CU 93 120 net revaluation surplus, recognised by S Ltd for the period since acquisition up until the beginning of the year, includes the CU 38 500 (50 000 × 77.6% After tax) after tax IFRS 3 fair value adjustment to S Ltd's land, already recognised by the group at acquisition date. Consequently, the following adjustments are required in preparing the current year consolidated financial statements:

- Reduce S Ltd's CU 93 120 opening revaluation surplus balance by the above-mentioned CU 38 500 after-tax fair value adjustment to its land, recognised at acquisition – see Part (b): Pro forma journal 3. The net result of this consolidation adjustment is that the group now correctly recognises a CU 54 320 (93 120 – 38 800) after tax revaluation surplus in respect of S Ltd's land for the period since acquisition to the beginning of the year. This revaluation surplus is included in the current year consolidated statement of changes in equity -see Part (c) – as follows:

  - 80% of this revaluation surplus, the amount of CU 43 456 (54 320 × 80% P Ltd's shareholding) constitutes the opening consolidated revaluation surplus balance; and

  - 20% of this revaluation surplus, the amount of CU 10 864 (54 320 × 20% NCI Share) is included in the non-controlling interest opening balance.

- Reduce the CU 420 000 revalued carrying amount of S Ltd's land at the beginning of the year, by the CU 50 000 fair value adjustment to this land, recognised under IFRS 3 at acquisition date – see Part (b): Pro forma journal 3.

- Reduce the CU 26 880 ((420 000 Revalued carrying amount: Prior year end – 300 000 Carrying amount at acquisition) × 22.4%) deferred tax liability recorded by S Ltd in respect of its prior year revaluation of land, by the 11 200-deferred tax liability recognised at acquisition date as a result of the IFRS 3 fair value remeasurement of this land at acquisition date – see Part (b): Pro forma journal 3.

[4]   No consolidation adjustment is required for S Ltd's current year revaluation gain on land, an after-tax gain of CU 31 040, which constitutes S Ltd's other comprehensive income for the year. This is because the group is in agreement with the previous revalued carrying amount for land at prior year end and with the new revalued carrying amount for land at current year end.

Part (b): Pro forma journal entries for the financial year ended 31 December 20x6

AT ACQUISITION

Pro forma journal 1 (J1)	Dr CU	Cr CU
Share capital (S Ltd) (SCIE) (given)	170 000	
Retained earnings (S Ltd) (SCIE) (given)	325 000	
Land (S Ltd) (SFP)	Wkg1 50 000	
Deferred tax (S Ltd) (SFP)		Wkg2 11 200
Investment in S Ltd (P Ltd) (SFP) (given)		458 000
NCI – Equity (SCIE)		Wkg3 106 760
Goodwill (SFP) (balancing figure)	30 960	
Elimination of at acquisition equity and cost of investment, recognition of fair value adjustment to land and deferred tax effects, and recognition of non-controlling interest and goodwill at acquisition		

Workings: Pro forma journals

Working 1

350 000 – 300 000

Working 2

50 000 × 22.4%

Working 3

(170 000 + 325 000 + 50 000 – 11 200) × 20% NCI Share

SINCE ACQUISITION TO THE BEGINNING OF THE YEAR

Pro forma journal 2 (J2)	Dr CU	Cr CU
Retained earnings (S Ltd) (SCIE)	Wkg4 22 000	
Non-controlling interest – Equity (S Ltd) (SCIE)		Wkg4 22 000
Allocation of retained earnings since acquisition date to the non-controlling interest		

Workings: Pro forma journals

Working 4

(435 000 Balance BOY – 325 000 Balance at acquisition) × 20% NCI Share

Pro forma journal 3 (J3)	Dr CU	Cr CU
Revaluation surplus (S Ltd) (SCIE)	Wkg5 38 800	
Deferred tax (S Ltd) (SFP)	Wkg6 11 200	
Land (S Ltd) (SFP) (See (J1))		50 000
Reversal of revaluation surplus of subsidiary that constitutes pre-acquisition equity and reversal of fair value adjustment of land and associated tax effects at acquisition date, as subsidiary has since revalued its land		

Working 5

50 000 (J1) Fair value adjustment at acquisition × 77.6% After tax

Working 6

balancing figure **OR** 50 000 (J1) × 22.4%

Pro forma journal 4 (J4)	Dr CU	Cr CU
Revaluation surplus (S Ltd) (SCIE)	^{Wkg7}10 864	
Non-controlling interest – Equity (S Ltd) (SCIE)		^{Wkg7}10 864
Allocation of adjusted revaluation surplus of S Ltd since acquisition date beginning of year to the non-controlling interest		

Workings: Pro forma journals

Working 7

(93 120 Balance BOY – 38 800 (J3) At acquisition fair value remeasurement of land, after tax) × 20% NCI Share

CURRENT YEAR

Pro forma journal 5 (J5)	Dr CU	Cr CU
Non-controlling interest – Share of profit or loss (P/L)	^{Wkg8}27 500	
Non-controlling interest – Equity (SFP)		^{Wkg8}27 500
Allocating the non-controlling interest its share of S Ltd's profit for the year		

Workings: Pro forma journals

Working 8

137 500 × 20% NCI Share

Pro forma journal 6 (J6)	Dr CU	Cr CU
NCI – Share of other comprehensive income (OCI)	^{Wkg9}6 208	
Non-controlling interest – Equity (SFP)		^{Wkg9}6 208
Allocating the non-controlling interest its share of S Ltd's other comprehensive income for the year		

Workings: Pro forma journals

Working 9

(40 000 Revaluation gain – 8 960 Tax effect) × 20% NCI Share

The effects of preceding pro forma journals 1 to 6 in arriving at the consolidated figures are illustrated in the following consolidation worksheet.

	P Ltd Dr/(Cr) CU	S Ltd Dr/(Cr) CU	Pro forma journals At acquisition Dr/(Cr) CU	Journal ref	Pro forma journals Since acquisition Dr/(Cr) CU	Journal ref	Consolidated Dr/(Cr) CU
Equity							
Share capital	(250 000)	(170 000)	170 000	J1			(250 000)
Retained earnings (BOY)	(384 000)	(435 000)	325 000	J1	22 000	J2	(472 000)
Profit for period: Individual entities	(122 000)	(137 500)					†(232 000)
Consolidated profit – attributable to owners of parent							(704 000)
Retained earnings (EOY)	(506 000)	(572 500)			38 800	J3	(43 456)
Revaluation surplus (BOY)	–	(93 120)			10 864	J4	
OCI for the period: Individual entities	–	(31 040)					–
Consolidated other comprehensive income – owners of parent	–						†(24 832)
Revaluation surplus (EOY)	–	(124 160)					(68 288)
NCI Equity	–	–	(106 760)	J1	(22 000) J2 / (10 864) J4 / (27 500) J5 / (6 208) J6		(173 332)
Total equity	**(756 000)**	**(866 660)**					**(1 195 620)**
Liabilities:							
Trade and other payables	(100 000)	(200 000)					(300 000)
Deferred tax	–	(35 840)	(11 200)	J1	11 200	J3	(35 840)

Explanatory notes

† This amount has been brought forward from the second part of the consolidation worksheet on page 297

	P Ltd Dr/(Cr) CU	S Ltd Dr/(Cr) CU	Pro forma journals At acquisition Dr/(Cr) CU	Journal ref	Pro forma journals Since acquisition Dr/(Cr) CU	Journal ref	Consolidated Dr/(Cr) CU
Total liabilities	(100 000)	(235 840)					(335 840)
Total equity & liabilities	(856 000)	(1 102 500)					(1 531 460)
Assets:							
Land	–	460 000	50 000	J1	(50 000)	J3	460 000
Trade and other receivables	398 000	642 500					1 040 500
Investment in S Ltd	458 000	–	(458 000)	J1			–
Goodwill			30 960	J1			30 960
Total assets	856 000	1 102 500					1 531 460
Profit or loss							
Profit for the period	(122 000)	(137 500)					(259 500)
NCI: Share of profit					27 500	J5	27 500
Consolidated profit attributable to owners of parent							‡(232 000)
Other comprehensive income							
After tax fair value gain on PPE (OCI)	–	(31 040)					(31 040)
NCI: Share of OCI	–	–			6 208	J6	6 208
Consolidated other comprehensive income – owners of parent							‡(24 832)

Explanatory notes

‡ This amount has been carried forward to the first part of the consolidation worksheet on page 296

Part (c): Consolidated financial statements for the financial year ended 31 December 20x6

P LTD GROUP: ABRIDGED CONSOLIDATED STATEMENT OF PROFIT OR LOSS AND OTHER COMPREHENSIVE INCOME FOR THE YEAR ENDED 31 DECEMBER 20X6	
	CU
PROFIT FOR THE YEAR (122 000 (P Ltd) + 137 500 (S Ltd))	259 500
Other comprehensive income:	
Revaluation gain - Land (S Ltd: 40 000 – 8 960 Tax on gain)	31 040
TOTAL COMPREHENSIVE INCOME FOR THE YEAR	**290 540**
Profit attributable to:	
Owners of the parent [(balancing figure) **OR** (122 000 (P Ltd) + S Ltd: 110 000 (see AOE i)]	232 000
Non-controlling interest (see AOE **j OR** (J5))	27 500
	259 500
Total comprehensive income attributable to:	
Owners of the parent (balancing figure) **OR** (232 000 (P Ltd) + S Ltd: 24 832 (see AOE **k**))	256 832
Non-controlling interest (27 500 Profit + 6 208 Revaluation gain (see AOE **l**) **OR** (J6))	33 708
	290 540

P LTD GROUP: CONSOLIDATED STATEMENT OF CHANGES IN EQUITY FOR THE YEAR ENDED 31 DECEMBER 20x6

	Parent equity holders' interest				Non-controlling interest	Total equity of the group
	Share capital	Retained earnings	Revaluation surplus	Total parent equity		
	CU	CU	CU		CU	CU
Opening balance at 1 January 20x6	250 000	Wkg1472 000	Wkg243 456	765 456	Wkg3139 624	905 080
Total comprehensive income:						
Profit for the period (from CSOPL_OCI)		232 000	–	232 000	27 500	259 500
Other comprehensive income:			Wkg424 832	24 832	Wkg56 208	31 040
Closing balance at 31 December 20x6	250 000	704 000	†68 288	1 022 288	173 332	1 195 620

Explanatory notes: Consolidated statement of changes in equity

† This amount represents the 80% after tax post-acquisition revaluation surplus of S Ltd, attributable to P Ltd's owners at reporting period end.

It can also be calculated as follows:

	CU
S Ltd total after tax revaluation surplus EOY	124 160
Less: At acquisition after tax remeasurement	(38 800)
Less: non-controlling interest 20% share	(17 072)
= 80% attributable to owners of parent	68 288

Workings: Consolidated statement of changes in equity

Working 1

P Ltd: 384 000 + S Ltd: 88 000 (see AOE **d**) P Ltd Share of S Ltd post-acquisition retained earnings to BOY

OR

P Ltd: 384 000 + (S Ltd: 435 000 Balance BOY – 325 000 (J1) Balance at acquisition – 22 000 (J2) NCI Share of S Ltd post-acquisition retained earnings to BOY)

Working 2

S Ltd: 43 456 (see AOE **f**)

OR

S Ltd: 93 120 Balance BOY – 38 800 (J3) After tax fair value remeasurement at acquisition – 10 864 (J4) NCI Share of S Ltd post-acquisition revaluation surplus to BOY

Working 3

S Ltd: 139 624 (see AOE **h**)

OR

S Ltd: 106 760 (J1) NCI Share of S Ltd at acquisition equity + 22 000 (J2) NCI Share of S Ltd post-acquisition retained earnings to BOY + 10 864 (J4) NCI Share of S Ltd post-acquisition revaluation surplus to BOY

Working 4

S Ltd: 24 832 (see AOE **k**)

OR

S Ltd: 31 040 – 6 208 (J6) NCI Share of S Ltd other comprehensive income for the current year

Working 5

S Ltd: 6 208 (see AOE **l OR** (J6)) NCI Share of S Ltd other comprehensive income for the current year

P LTD GROUP: CONSOLIDATED STATEMENT OF FINANCIAL POSITION AS AT 31 DECEMBER 20x6	
	CU
Assets	
Non-current assets	
Land (S Ltd: 460 000 + 50 000 (J1) Fair value adjustment – (J3) 50 000 Reversal of fair value adjustment))	†460 000
Goodwill (see AOE **c OR** (J1))	30 960
Current assets	
Trade and other receivables (398 000 (P Ltd) + 642 500 (S Ltd))	1 040 500
Total assets	1 531 460
Equity and liabilities	
Share capital (from CSCIE)	250 000
Retained earnings (from CSCIE)	704 000
Revaluation surplus (from CSCIE)	68 288
Equity attributable to owners of the parent	1 022 288
Non-controlling interest (from CSCIE) **OR** (see AOE **m**)	173 332
Total equity	1 195 620
Non-current liabilities	
Deferred tax (S Ltd: 35 840 + 11 200 (J1) Tax effect fair value adjustment land – 11 200 (J3) Tax effect reversal fair value adjustment land)	35 840
Current liabilities	
Trade and other payables (100 000 (P Ltd) + 200 000 (S Ltd))	300 000
Total equity and liabilities	1 531 460

Explanatory note

† As the at acquisition fair value adjustment to land was reversed when the subsidiary revalued its land, the group carrying amount for land now equals the subsidiary's carrying amount for land.

5.2.10 Fair value adjustments at acquisition date: Current assets

The fair value of **all** the assets and liabilities of a subsidiary acquired should be reviewed by the parent and on consolidation appropriate at acquisition fair value adjustments should be made under IFRS 3 in order to determine accurately the goodwill or gain on bargain purchase to be recognised. This includes all the subsidiary's **current assets**. In the section that follows, the implications, in the consolidated financial statements at acquisition and subsequently, of remeasuring the current asset inventory of the subsidiary, to fair value at acquisition are dealt with.

5.2.10.1 Fair value adjustments to inventory at acquisition date

As this chapter has already explained, the at acquisition fair value of an asset represents that asset's cost to the group. Accordingly, at acquisition the **fair value of** the subsidiary's inventory is the **cost of the inventory to the group**, while the **cost of the inventory to the subsidiary** is the amount paid by the subsidiary to **purchase or manufacture the inventory**.

Consequently, when the inventory value at acquisition, as recorded by the subsidiary in its own records, differs from the inventory's at acquisition fair value, the following implications arise on consolidation:

- For as long as the subsidiary's inventory is still held by the group, a pro forma consolidation adjustment is required each reporting period to **adjust the value of the inventory to fair value** so that it is reflected at its cost to the group.

- When the subsidiary's inventory is sold **outside the group post acquisition date**, a pro forma consolidation adjustment needs to be made to the subsidiary's **cost of sales** to obtain the correct cost of sales and gross profit to be recognised in the consolidated financial statements. This is because the profit on sale of the subsidiary's inventory is the difference between proceeds on sale and the cost of the inventory sold, which cost is – as discussed above – different for the subsidiary compared to the group.

- **Temporary differences** will arise that will result in **deferred tax implications** for **group purposes**. This is because the carrying amount of the inventory changes when remeasured to fair value at acquisition date, while its at acquisition tax base remains the same as the taxing authority does not recognise IFRS 3 fair value adjustments to inventory for tax purposes. Furthermore, as inventory is a non-depreciable asset, it is recovered through sale. Deferred tax should therefore be calculated at the **income tax rate of 28%** as the gross profit resulting from the sale of inventory is taxed at 28%.

- The **non-controlling interest** – as was the case with property, plant and equipment – **will share in** the **effects** of any **at acquisition fair value adjustment to the subsidiary's inventory**:

  - **at acquisition date** if the non-controlling interest is measured at its **proportionate share** of the subsidiary's **identifiable net assets** as fairly valued; and
  - **subsequent to acquisition** – irrespective of the method used to measure the non-controlling interest – a portion of the **consolidation adjustment** to the **subsidiary's cost of sales**, which affects the subsidiary's profit or loss, as discussed above, when the inventory is sold outside the group, will be **allocated to the non-controlling interest**.

Example 5.11: Fair value adjustment to inventory at acquisition date

P Ltd acquired a 60% controlling interest in S Ltd on 1 January 20x5 for CU 175 000. On this date P Ltd considered the fair value of the inventory of S Ltd to be CU 20 000 higher than its carrying amount of CU 90 000 at acquisition date. Aside from inventory, the assets and liabilities of S Ltd were considered to be fairly valued at acquisition date.

S Ltd had sold all of its at acquisition inventory to a third party for CU 145 000 by financial year end 31 December 20x5.

P Ltd recognised the non-controlling interest at its proportionate share of the fair value of S Ltd's at acquisition identifiable net assets.

The trial balances of P Ltd and subsidiary S Ltd at 31 December 20x5 were as follows:

Trial balances at 31 December 20x5	P Ltd Dr/(Cr) CU	S Ltd Dr/(Cr) CU
Share capital	(150 000)	(140 000)
Retained earnings (1 Jan 20x5)	(220 000)	(110 000)
Inventory	108 000	–
Non-current assets	95 000	286 000
Investment in S Ltd: Cost	175 000	–
Sales	(117 000)	(145 000)
Cost of sales	85 000	90 000
Other expenses	16 000	8 000
Taxation	8 000	11 000

Required

(a) Prepare the analysis of equity for S Ltd as at 31 December 20x5.

(b) Provide all the pro forma journal entries required in order to prepare the consolidated financial statements of the P Ltd group for the year ended 31 December 20x5.

(c) Prepare the consolidated statement of profit or loss and other comprehensive income for the P Ltd group for the year ended 31 December 20x5.

Assume an income tax rate of 28%.

⟫

Solution 5.11: Fair value adjustment to inventory at acquisition date

Part (a): Analysis of equity (AOE) of S Ltd as at 31 December 20x5

| | Total of S Ltd's equity 100% CU | P Ltd 60% | | Non-controlling interest 40% CU |
		At acquisition CU	Since acquisition CU	
At acquisition date (1 January 20x5)				
Share capital	140 000	84 000		56 000
Retained earnings	110 000	66 000		44 000
Fair value adjustment: Inventory	20 000[1]	12 000		8 000
Deferred tax: Fair value adjustment inventory (20 000 × 28%)	(5 600)[2]	(3 360)		(2 240)
Fair value of net assets of S Ltd	264 400	158 640		105 760
Goodwill – Parent (balancing figure)	16 360	16 360[3]		–
Consideration and non-controlling interest	280 760	175 000		105 760
Since acquisition				
• Current year:				
Adjusted profit for the year	21 600		12 960 **a**	8 640 **b**
Profit for the year	Wkg1 36 000		21 600	14 400
Inventory sold: Increased cost of sales	(20 000)[4] **c**		(12 000)	(8 000)
Reduced income tax expense: Inventory sold (20 000 × 28%)	5 600[5] **d**		3 360	2 240
	302 360		12 960	114 400

Workings: Analysis of equity

Working 1

145 000 – 90 000 – 8 000 – 11 000

Explanatory notes: Analysis of equity S Ltd

[1] The inventory should be recognised at the cost of CU 110 000 (90 000 + 20 000) to the group at acquisition. Therefore, a fair value adjustment of CU 20 000 is required at acquisition date, which increases the net asset value (equity) of S Ltd by CU 20 000.

[2] The fair value remeasurement of S Ltd's inventory at acquisition increases its carrying amount by CU 20 000 while its at acquisition tax base of CU 90 000, which equals its cost to S Ltd, remains the same. This creates a taxable temporary difference on consolidation of CU 20 000 (as the carrying amount of the inventory asset exceeds its tax base) which results in an at acquisition deferred tax liability of CU 5 600 (20 000 taxable temporary difference × 28%) of S Ltd. This deferred tax liability reduces the at acquisition net asset value (equity) of S Ltd by CU 5 600.

[3] The after tax effect of the at acquisition fair value adjustment to S Ltd's inventory is a net increase in S Ltd's net asset value (equity) at acquisition of CU 14 400 (20 000 Fair value adjustment × 72% After tax). This results in CU 8 640 (14 400 × 60% Interest of P Ltd) less goodwill being recognised compared to a situation where no fair value adjustment to inventory is recognised.

4   The cost of S Ltd's inventory to the group – being its at acquisition fair value – is CU 20 000 more than the cost of the inventory to S Ltd. Accordingly, when S Ltd's inventory is sold in the current year it follows that the group cost of sales will be CU 20 000 more than that recorded by S Ltd in its own records. This, in turn, means that the group's gross profit on disposal of S Ltd's inventory will be CU 20 000 less than that recorded by S Ltd. Consequently, a consolidation adjustment is required to increase S Ltd's cost of sales for the current period so that the correct (reduced) group profit on disposal of the inventory is recognised in the consolidated financial statements.

5   For consolidation purposes, the taxable temporary difference of CU 20 000 that originated on acquisition when S Ltd's inventory was fair valued, reverses in the current year, when this inventory is sold outside the group. This causes the CU 5 600 at acquisition deferred tax liability raised in respect of the inventory to reverse, resulting in a corresponding CU 5 600 reduction in S Ltd's income tax expense at group level. This reduced income tax charge, in turn, increases S Ltd's profit by CU 5 600 on consolidation.

Part (b): Pro forma journal entries for the financial year ended 31 December 20x5

AT ACQUISITION

Pro forma Journal 1 (J1)	Dr CU	Cr CU
Share capital (S Ltd) (SCIE) (given)	140 000	
Retained earnings (S Ltd) (SCIE) (given)	110 000	
Inventory (S Ltd) (SFP) (given)	20 000	
Deferred tax (S Ltd) (SFP)		[Wkg1]5 600
Investment in S Ltd (P Ltd) (SFP) (given)		175 000
Non-controlling interest – Equity (SCIE)		[Wkg2]105 760
Goodwill (SFP) (balancing figure)	16 360	
Elimination of at acquisition equity and cost of investment, recognition of fair value adjustment to inventory and deferred tax effects and recognition of non-controlling interest and goodwill at acquisition		

Workings: Pro forma journal

Working 1

20 000 × 28%

Working 2

(140 000 Share capital + 110 000 Retained earnings + 20 000 Fair value adjustment inventory – 5 600 Deferred tax effect fair value adjustment inventory) × 40% NCI Share

CURRENT YEAR

Pro forma Journal 2 (J2)	Dr CU	Cr CU
Cost of sales (S Ltd) (P/L)	20 000	
Inventory (S Ltd) (SFP) (see (J1))		20 000
Recognition of effect of increase in inventory carrying amount at acquisition date, inventory subsequently sold		

Comments: Pro forma journal 2

• The credit in this pro-forma journal reverses the increase in the value of S Ltd's inventory, recognised at acquisition (see J1). This reversal makes sense as the inventory has now been sold by the group. The cost of sales for the group is increased with the contra debit entry.

Pro forma journal 3 (J3)	Dr CU	Cr CU
Deferred tax (S Ltd) (SFP)	Wkg35 600	
Income tax expense (S Ltd) (P/L)		Wkg35 600
Deferred tax implications relating to elimination of the effect of the increase in the carrying amount of inventory at acquisition date, inventory subsequently sold		

Workings: Pro forma journals

Working 3
20 000 (J2) × 28%

Comments: Pro forma journal 3

- The debit in this entry reverses the deferred tax liability recognised at acquisition date. This makes sense as the deferred tax liability should be reversed when the inventory is sold. The corresponding credit entry reduces S Ltd's and the group's income tax expense. This makes sense since the group recognises a greater cost of sales expense in the current year in respect of S Ltd's inventory sold (see pro forma journal 2), which reduces the group's current year profit. Reduced group profit should, in turn, result in a corresponding reduced group income tax expense.

Pro forma journal 4 (J4)	Dr CU	Cr CU
Non-controlling interest: Share of profit	Wkg48 640	
Non-controlling interest – Equity (SFP)		Wkg48 640
Allocating the non-controlling interest its share of S Ltd's adjusted current year profit		

Workings: Pro forma journals

Working 4
145 000 – 90 000 – 8 000 – 11 000 = 36 000 Profit – 20 000 (J2) Increase in cost of sales + 5 600 (J3) Reduction in income tax expense arising from increased cost of sales) × 40% NCI Share

Comments: Pro forma journal 4

- The effect of this entry is to allocate to the non-controlling interest the appropriate portion of the after tax profit of S Ltd as **adjusted** for the effects of S Ltd's increased cost of sales and the corresponding reduction in S Ltd's income tax expense, recognised on consolidation.

Part (c) Consolidated statement of profit or loss and other comprehensive income for the year ended 31 December 20x5

P LTD GROUP: CONSOLIDATED STATEMENT OF PROFIT OR LOSS AND OTHER COMPREHENSIVE INCOME FOR THE YEAR ENDED 31 DECEMBER 20X5	
	CU
Sales (117 000 (P Ltd) + 145 000 (S Ltd))	262 000
Cost of sales	(195 000)
(85 000 (P Ltd) + (S Ltd: 90 000 + 20 000 (see AOE **c OR** (J2))) Inventory sold that was remeasured to fair value at acquisition)	
Gross profit	67 000
Operating expenses (16 000 (P Ltd) + 8 000 (S Ltd))	(24 000)
Profit before taxation	43 000
Income tax expense	(13 400)
(8 000 (P Ltd) + (S Ltd: 11 000 – 5 600 (see AOE **d OR** (J3))) Tax effect: Inventory sold that was remeasured to fair value at acquisition)	
PROFIT FOR THE YEAR	**29 600**
Other comprehensive income for the year	–
TOTAL COMPREHENSIVE INCOME FOR THE YEAR	**29 600**
Total comprehensive income for the year attributable to: Owners of the parent (balancing figure)	20 960
OR (8000 (P Ltd) + S Ltd: 12 960 (see AOE **a**))	
Non-controlling interest (see AOE **b OR** (J4))	8 640
	29 600

Summary

This chapter addressed the consequences in the consolidated financial statements, both at acquisition and in subsequent reporting periods, when a subsidiary's assets are remeasured to fair value, under IFRS 3, at acquisition date.

One way in which a subsidiary's assets may be remeasured to their at acquisition fair values, is for the **subsidiary itself to adjust the carrying amount** of its assets to their respective fair values in **its own accounting records**. Where this is the case, *no* adjustments are required **on consolidation** as the subsidiary's **individual financial statements** will reflect the remeasured assets at **the same values** as will be reflected in **the consolidated financial statements**.

Alternatively, in cases where *no* at acquisition fair value remeasurement adjustments are made by the subsidiary itself, pro forma adjustments are required on consolidation, both at acquisition date, and subsequently.

When **at acquisition fair value adjustments** are made to subsidiary assets on **consolidation,** the following key learning points are important:

- The **upward/(downward) remeasurement** of subsidiary assets to fair value **increases/ (decreases)** the subsidiary's at **acquisition equity** and therefore the amount of any **goodwill or bargain purchase gain recognised.**

- Only when the non-controlling interest is measured at its **proportionate share** of the subsidiary's identifiable net assets, will it be **allocated a portion** of the at acquisition fair value adjustment to the subsidiary's assets.

- At acquisition remeasurement of the subsidiary's assets to fair value gives rise to **at acquisition deferred tax effects**, since these fair value remeasurements recognised for accounting purposes are *not* recognised for tax purposes. An **upward/(downward)** remeasurement of the subsidiary's asset(s) to fair value results in the at acquisition recognition of a **deferred tax liability/(asset)** of the subsidiary.

When fair value remeasurement adjustments are made to subsidiary assets at acquisition, further adjustments are required when consolidating the subsidiary's income and expenses after acquisition date, where such income and expenses relate to the remeasured assets concerned. Therefore:

- Where a subsidiary's property, plant and equipment asset that was remeasured to fair value at acquisition date is subsequently sold, the consolidated gain or loss will differ from that determined by the subsidiary. Consequently, a pro forma consolidation journal is required to adjust the subsidiary's gain or loss on disposal to the correct gain or loss for group purposes.

- Where a depreciable property, plant and equipment asset of a subsidiary was remeasured to fair value at acquisition date, the group will depreciate this asset based on its acquisition date fair value, while the subsidiary will continue to depreciate this asset based on its carrying amount. Consequently, the depreciation expense to be recognised in respect of this asset for consolidation purposes will differ from the depreciation recognised on this asset by the subsidiary, with this difference needing to be adjusted for on consolidation each reporting period.

- Where subsidiary inventory that was remeasured to fair value at acquisition date is subsequently sold, a pro forma consolidation adjustment needs to be made to the subsidiary's cost of sales to obtain the correct cost of sales and gross profit to be recognised in the consolidated financial statements.

After acquisition date, the at acquisition fair value adjustment recognised for a subsidiary's asset is **reversed or realised** by way of **depreciating, impairing or selling** this asset. Such fair value reversals or realisations cause a:

- post-acquisition reversal at group level of the at acquisition deferred tax asset or liability that arose upon remeasurement of the asset to its at acquisition fair value; and

- a corresponding increase (if a deferred tax asset reverses post acquisition date) or decrease (if a deferred tax liability reverses post acquisition date) in the group's income tax expense.

It may happen that a subsidiary's non-depreciable property, plant and equipment is adjusted to its at acquisition fair value on consolidation, and the **subsidiary in its own records** then **revalues this property, plant and equipment in a subsequent reporting period**. In such a case, a consolidation adjustment is required to **reduce** the subsidiary's **opening revaluation surplus balance** (for a prior period revaluation), or the subsidiary's **after-tax revaluation gain** (for a current period revaluation), by the amount of the after-tax remeasurement of the subsidiary's property, plant and equipment, to fair value, recognised at acquisition date.

When a subsidiary's since acquisition profit or loss and other comprehensive income (i.e., total comprehensive income) is adjusted because of the follow-on effects of the at acquisition remeasurements of its assets to fair value, the non-controlling interest's share of the subsidiary's post-acquisition total comprehensive income must be its share of this adjusted total comprehensive income.

Volume 1 Chapters 3, 4 and 5 taught you a good deal about many of the adjustments and eliminations required when performing a consolidation. Volume 1 Chapter 6 will further broaden your knowledge of consolidations by introducing you to the host of additional consolidation adjustments and eliminations required when dealing with intragroup transactions and balances.

QUESTIONS

Question 5.1

P Ltd acquired a controlling interest of 60% of the issued share capital of S Ltd on 1 January 20x3 for CU 390 000.

At the date of acquisition the equity of S Ltd was as follows:

- share capital CU 150 000; and
- retained earnings CU 320 000.

P Ltd measured the non-controlling interest at its proportionate share of the identifiable net assets of S Ltd (as fairly valued) on acquisition date.

All the assets and liabilities of S Ltd were considered to be fairly valued at acquisition date, with the exception of land and machinery:

- P Ltd considered the land to be undervalued by CU 60 000. S Ltd did not revalue the land in its own records at acquisition date. The land was sold to a third party on 31 August 20x5 for CU 210 000.
- The machinery was acquired by S Ltd on 1 January 20x2 at a cost of CU 180 000 and had an expected useful life of five years and a zero residual value. P Ltd considered the machinery to be undervalued by CU 75 000 at acquisition date, but agreed with the remaining four year useful life of the machine at acquisition date. S Ltd did not make any fair value adjustments to the carrying amount of the machinery in its own records at acquisition date.

Furthermore, the following information was obtained relating to the equity of each company as at 31 December 20x5:

	P Ltd	S Ltd
	CU	CU
Share capital	200 000	150 000
Retained earnings at 1 January 20x5	566 000	485 000
Profit after tax for 20x5	212 000	175 000
Dividend paid	–	(48 000)
Retained earnings at 31 December 20x5	778 000	612 000
Total equity at 31 December 20x5	978 000	762 000

The following is an extract from the statements of financial position of each company as at 31 December 20x5:

	P Ltd	S Ltd
	CU	CU
Non-current assets		
Equipment	84 000	36 000
	84 000	36 000
Non-current liabilities		
Loan	91 000	48 000
	91 000	48 000

Assume an income tax rate of 28% and an effective capital gains tax rate of 22.4%.

Required

(a) Calculate the amount that will be disclosed as **goodwill** in the consolidated statement of financial position of the P Ltd group as at 31 December 20x5.

(b) Calculate the amount that will be disclosed as **opening retained earnings** in the consolidated statement of changes in equity of the P Ltd group for the year ended 31 December 20x5.

(c) Calculate the **consolidated profit** of the P Ltd group for the year ended 31 December 20x5.

(d) Calculate the amount that will be disclosed as the **closing non-controlling interest balance** in the consolidated statement of changes in equity of the P Ltd group for the year ended 31 December 20x5.

(e) Prepare an extract from the **consolidated statement of financial position** reflecting *only* the **non-current assets** and **non-current liabilities** of the P Ltd group as at 31 December 20x5.

Question 5.2

P Ltd acquired a controlling interest of 80% of the issued share capital of S Ltd on 1 January 20x2 for CU 415 000.

At the date of acquisition, the equity of S Ltd was as follows:

- share capital CU 180 000;
- retained earnings CU 245 000.

P Ltd measured the non-controlling interest at its proportionate share of the identifiable net assets of S Ltd (as fairly valued) on acquisition date.

P Ltd considered all the assets and liabilities of S Ltd to be fairly valued at acquisition date, with the exception of the following items:

- Fair value of inventory CU 80 000; carrying amount CU 50 000. This inventory was sold during the 20x2 financial year to an external party.

- Equipment that was acquired by S Ltd on 1 January 20x0 at a cost of CU 135 000 had an expected useful life of seven years and a zero residual value at that date. P Ltd considered this equipment to be undervalued by CU 40 000 at acquisition date, but agreed with the remaining useful life of the equipment at acquisition date. S Ltd did not revalue the equipment in its own records at acquisition date. The equipment was sold by S Ltd to a third party on 31 October 20x4 for CU 120 000.

ABRIDGED STATEMENTS OF PROFIT OR LOSS AND OTHER COMPREHENSIVE INCOME FOR THE YEAR ENDED 31 DECEMBER 20x4	P Ltd CU	S Ltd CU
Profit before tax	165 450	95 400
Income tax expense	(41 350)	(22 000)
PROFIT FOR THE YEAR	124 100	73 400

EXTRACT FROM THE STATEMENTS OF CHANGES IN EQUITY FOR THE YEAR ENDED 31 DECEMBER 20x4	Retained earnings	
	P Ltd CU	S Ltd CU
Balance at 1 Jan 20x4	456 800	377 300
Total comprehensive income		
Profit for the year	124 100	73 400
Dividend paid	(85 000)	(45 000)
Balance at 31 Dec 20x4	495 000	405 700

Required

(a) Prepare the pro forma journal entries required to prepare the consolidated financial statements of the P Ltd group for the year ended 31 December 20x4.

(b) Prepare the abridged consolidated statement of profit or loss and other comprehensive income of the P Ltd group for the year ended 31 December 20x4.

(c) Prepare the following extracts from the consolidated statement of changes in equity income of the P Ltd group for the year ended 31 December 20x4:
   - the retained earnings column; and
   - the non-controlling interest column.

References

IAS 12 *Income Taxes*

IFRS 3 *Business Combinations*

IFRS 10 *Consolidated Financial Statements*

CHAPTER 6

INTRAGROUP TRANSACTIONS AND BALANCES

LEARNING OBJECTIVES

After studying this chapter, you should be able to:

- understand what intragroup transactions and balances are and how they arise;

- understand how and why we eliminate intragroup transactions and balances in the consolidated financial statements;

- explain and prepare pro forma journal entries to reverse intragroup transactions and balances arising from:

  - intragroup services rendered; and

  - intragroup loans.

- explain the concept of unrealised profits and losses in respect of intragroup transactions;

- know how to process pro forma journals to eliminate unrealised profits arising from intragroup sales of inventory when consolidated financial statements are prepared;

- know how to process pro forma journals to recognise the prior year unrealised intragroup profit on sale of inventories in the current period when the inventory is sold outside the group, when consolidated financial statements are prepared;

- prepare pro forma journal entries in order to recognise the deferred tax implications:

  - of the elimination of unrealised intragroup profits on sale of inventories; and

  - of the subsequent realisation of previously unrealised intragroup profit on sale of inventories.

- understand and process the effects of inventories written down to net realisable value on the reversal of unrealised intragroup profits in the consolidated financial statements;

- know how to eliminate unrealised profits arising from intragroup sales of both depreciable and non-depreciable property, plant and equipment, when preparing consolidated financial statements;

- know how to recognise intragroup profit in respect of intragroup sales of property, plant and equipment in the consolidated financial statements of subsequent reporting periods where the intragroup profit realises either by way of:
  - sale to a party outside the group; or
  - a reduction in the depreciation charge.
- prepare pro forma journal entries in order to recognise the deferred tax implications:
  - of the elimination of unrealised intragroup profit on sale of property, plant and equipment; and
  - of the subsequent realisation of previously unrealised intragroup profit on sale of property, plant and equipment whether realised by way of sale of the property, plant and equipment to external parties or by way of a reduction in the depreciation charge.
- know how to eliminate unrealised losses arising from intragroup sale of property, plant and equipment, including understanding the effects of impairments losses on the amount of the unrealised loss eliminated, when preparing consolidated financial statements;
- prepare pro forma journal entries in respect of the intragroup sale of assets where there is a change of use of the asset sold intragroup in the following scenarios:
  - inventories of the seller are classified as property, plant and equipment by the buyer; and
  - property, plant and equipment of the seller are classified as inventory by the buyer.
- prepare consolidated financial statements for a group where there are all manner of intragroup transactions and balances.

TOPIC LIST

Introduction

Entities within a group of companies often transact with each other by, among others:

- trading with each other;
- loaning funds to each other;
- providing services to each other; and
- selling and renting assets to each other.

The result of the above-mentioned activities is that there is often a host of internal transactions undertaken between the **separate entities** within **one economic entity**, which is the **group**. The effects of these transactions are recognised by each group entity in the assets, liabilities, income, expenses and profits or losses recorded.

As has been discussed in this publication, consolidated financial statements are prepared in order to reflect the results and financial position of the group as that of a **single economic entity**. Consequently, transactions **between entities within the group** (hereafter referred to as '**intragroup transactions**') and any resulting **intragroup balances**, must be **eliminated** in the preparation of the consolidated financial statements. More particularly, as explained in Volume 1 Chapter 1, IFRS 10 *Consolidated Financial Statements* requires that on **consolidation** we **eliminate in full**, *inter alia*, **intragroup assets and liabilities** as well as **income and expenses** relating to transactions **between entities of the group** (IFRS 10.B86(c). In this way the consolidated financial statements will show only transactions with **parties outside the group** (hereafter referred to as 'external parties').

In light of the above, this chapter will discuss and explain in detail the consolidation principles and procedures required to deal with the effects of intragroup transactions and balances, including the related tax effects, arising from:

- services rendered between group companies;
- funds lent intragroup;
- intragroup sales of inventory; and
- intragroup sales of property, plant and equipment, both depreciable (e.g., machinery) and non-depreciable (e.g., land).

See Volume 1 Chapters 3 and 4 for a discussion of the treatment of intragroup dividends in the consolidated financial statements.

6.1   Services rendered intragroup

Many a time, entities within a group will provide various services to other group entities, for example, where management competencies are situated within a particular group entity that then provides management services for a fee to other group entities.

The group entity that renders the services will recognise service fee income, while the recipient group entity of the services will recognise a service fee expense.

From a **group perspective**, such fees charged represent an **intragroup transaction** where internal charges are levied within the group. As the group **cannot transact with itself**, these fees charged must be **eliminated on consolidation** by passing pro forma journals as follows:

- **eliminate** the **fee earned** by the one group entity with a **debit entry**; and
- **eliminate** the **fee expense** of the other group entity with a **credit entry**.

Additionally, where the full amount due for services rendered has **not been settled** by the reporting period end, we must **eliminate** the **intragroup balances on consolidation.** More particularly, the **fee receivable asset** recognised by the one group entity is **eliminated** by passing a **pro forma journal credit,** while the corresponding **fee payable liability** of the other group entity is **eliminated** with **a pro forma journal debit.**

 Example 6.1: Intragroup services

P Ltd acquired a 100% interest in S Ltd, giving it control over S Ltd a number of years ago. Since acquisition P Ltd has charged S Ltd a monthly management fee of CU 100 000.

At financial reporting period end 31 December 20x5, CU 100 000 (the management fee for December) was still outstanding. P Ltd recognised a profit of CU 3 750 000 for the year ended 31 December 20x5, while S Ltd recognised a profit of CU 2 500 000 for the same period.

Required

(a) Show the journal entries in the records of both P Ltd and S Ltd to account for the management fee paid/received during the 20x5 financial year as well as for the management fee due at financial year ended 31 December 20x5.

(b) Provide the pro forma journal entries required to eliminate the management fee charged, for purposes of preparing the consolidated financial statements of the P Ltd group for the financial year ended 31 December 20x5.

(c) Calculate the consolidated profit for the financial year ended 31 December 20x5 and explain what effect the pro forma journals passed in Part (b) have on the consolidated profit for the year.

(d) Explain what the deferred tax effects are of the pro forma journals passed in Part (b).

(e) Discuss the effect of the pro forma journals passed in Part (b) on the consolidated financial statements prepared for the following financial year.

 Solution 6.1: Intragroup services

Part (a): Journal entries for management fees charged and due in the separate records of P Ltd and S Ltd

Journal entry in P Ltd	Dr CU	Cr CU
Management fee receivable [asset] (SFP) (given)	100 000	
Bank (SFP) (100 000 × 11 months)	1 100 000	
Management fee income (P/L) (balancing figure)		1 200 000
Recognising management fee income earned and management fee owing by subsidiary		

Journal entry in S Ltd	Dr CU	Cr CU
Management fee expense (P/L) (balancing figure)	1 200 000	
Management fee payable [liability] (SFP) (given)		100 000
Bank (SFP) (100 000 × 11 months)		1 100 000
Recognising management fee expense and management fee owing to parent		

CHAPTER 6 Intragroup Transactions and Balances

Part (b): Pro forma journal entries required to eliminate the management fee for purposes of preparing the consolidated financial statements

CURRENT YEAR

Pro forma journal 1	Dr CU	Cr CU
Management fee income (P Ltd) (P/L)	1 200 000	
Management fee expense (S Ltd) (P/L)		1 200 000
Elimination of intragroup management fee		

Pro forma journal 2	Dr CU	Cr CU
Management fee payable [Liability] (S Ltd) (SFP)	100 000	
Management fee receivable [Asset] (P Ltd) (SFP)		100 000
Elimination of intragroup balances		

The effect of the above two pro forma journal entries on the consolidated financial statements is shown in the following extract from the consolidation worksheet:

Dr/(Cr)	P Ltd CU	S Ltd CU	Pro forma journal 1 CU	Pro forma journal 2 CU	Consolidated CU
Profit or loss					
Management fee income	(1 200 000)	–	1 200 000		–
Management fee expense	–	1 200 000	(1 200 000)		–
Statement of financial position					
Current asset: Management fee receivable	100 000	–		(100 000)	–
Current liability: Management fee payable	–	(100 000)		100 000	–

Comments: Consolidation worksheet

- The effect of the pro forma journals is to eliminate both the management fee income and expense and the associated intragroup balances (i.e., the fee receivable asset in the records of P Ltd and the fee payable liability in the records of S Ltd).
- If these amounts were not eliminated, the group would overstate its management fee income and management fee expense as well as its current assets and current liabilities.

Part (c): Consolidated profit calculation

	CU
Profit for the year P Ltd (given)	3 750 000
Add: Profit for the year S Ltd (given)	2 500 000
Total profit before pro forma adjustments	6 250 000

317

Part (c): Consolidated profit calculation (continued)

Less: Reversal of intragroup management fee income	(1 200 000)	Pro forma journal 1
Add: Reversal of intragroup management fee expense	1 200 000	Pro forma journal 1
Consolidated profit for the year	**6 250 000**	

As is clear from the above calculation, pro forma journal 1 which eliminates the intragroup management fee has **no effect** on the consolidated profit. This is because this pro forma journal eliminates income and expense items of **equal amount**.

It is important to note, however, that although the consolidated profit is unaffected by the elimination of the management fee, this pro forma journal is nevertheless required for **disclosure** purposes. This is because it ensures that the **relevant income and expense line items** as disclosed in the consolidated statement of profit or loss and other comprehensive income are **not overstated**.

Part (d): Deferred tax effects of elimination of intragroup fee charge and elimination of associated intragroup balances

The effect of eliminating:

- management fee income against a management fee expense of the same amount; and
- an asset (management fee receivable) against a liability (management fee payable) of the same amount,

is that the amount of **group net assets** (i.e., Assets – Liabilities) remains **unchanged**. In addition, as each group entity is regarded as a separate taxpayer by the tax authority, the tax base of the group's net assets also remains unchanged. Accordingly, as the pro forma journals affect **neither the carrying amount nor the tax base** of the group's net assets, **no temporary differences arise** that would give rise to deferred tax effects at group level.

We can also say that the elimination of the fee income against a fee expense of equivalent amount has no effect on the group's total profit. Consequently, as group profit remains unchanged, so too must the group tax charge remain the same, meaning that no deferred tax adjustments are required.

In conclusion, therefore, the two pro forma journals discussed above have **no deferred tax consequences**.

Part (e): Effect of elimination of intragroup fee charge and elimination of associated intragroup balances on the consolidated financial statements for the following financial year

When preparing the consolidated financial statements for the next reporting period (i.e., for the financial year ended 31 December 20x6) the following will be the case:

- the prior year management fee income will be included in P Ltd's opening retained earnings balance, increasing this balance by CU 1 200 000; and
- the prior year management fee expense will be included in S Ltd's opening retained earnings balance, decreasing this balance by CU 1 200 000.

As you know, the consolidated opening retained earnings balance is determined by adding the subsidiary's post-acquisition retained earnings to the beginning of the year to the opening retained earnings balance of the parent. The consolidated opening retained earnings balance will therefore include the effects of both the management fee income of the parent and management fee expense of the subsidiary, which will **exactly offset each other**.

Consequently, the consolidated retained earnings balance at the beginning of the year will be **unaffected** by this intragroup charge. Unlike the prior year, where this intragroup charge affected the amounts of separately disclosed line items in the prior year statement of profit or loss and other comprehensive income, this is not the case with the opening consolidated retained earnings balance (i.e., the retained earnings balance does *not* have separately disclosable line items). It is therefore *not* necessary in the subsequent financial year to repeat the prior year's

⬛➡

pro forma journal eliminating the prior year's management fee as this would have no effect on the opening consolidated retained earnings balance reported in the subsequent financial year.

As regards the intragroup balances, because the management fee outstanding will presumably be settled in the subsequent financial year, these balances will no longer exist at the end of the subsequent financial year. Accordingly, there will be no need to eliminate them on consolidation in the subsequent financial year.

6.2 Borrowings intragroup

When one group entity provides loan funding to another, the group's cash resources are deployed **within one economic entity**; in essence funds are simply being moved from one part of the group to another. In the financial statements of the individual group entities:

- the lending group entity will record a loan asset (loan receivable) and the borrowing group entity will reflect a loan liability; and
- interest charged on the loan is interest income for the lender and interest expense for the borrower.

On consolidation, we must **eliminate** – via pro forma journals – the **loan receivable asset** against the **loan liability**, and the **interest income** against the **interest expense**, as the group entity (as a single economic entity) cannot lend money to itself, borrow money from itself, nor earn interest income and incur interest expense on a transaction with itself.

As is the case with intragroup services, elimination of the intragroup borrowing and the intragroup interest charge has no effect on either the net assets or the consolidated profit of the group. Furthermore, as discussed in Example 6.1, the pro forma journals that eliminate the intragroup charge and the intragroup balances are for disclosure purposes only, that is, to make certain that the individual line items presented in the consolidated financial statements are reflected at the correct amounts.

In this case, elimination of the intragroup borrowing ensures that the assets and liabilities of the group are not overstated, while elimination of the related interest charge ensures that the group interest income and interest expense are not overstated. In addition, as with intragroup services, because the intragroup eliminations have no effect on group net assets, or on group profits, there are no deferred tax consequences on consolidation arising from the pro forma elimination of intragroup borrowings and the related intragroup interest charge thereon.

 Example 6.2: Intragroup borrowings

P Ltd acquired an 80% controlling interest in S Ltd a number of years ago. At the beginning of the financial year ended 31 December 20x5, P Ltd granted S Ltd a long-term loan of CU 500 000, repayable in full on 31 December 20x8. Furthermore, CU 65 000 interest was incurred and paid in respect of the loan for the 20x5 financial year. P Ltd reported a profit for the financial year ended 31 December 20x5 of CU 750 000 while S Ltd reported a profit of CU 250 000 for the same period.

Required

(a) Provide the pro forma journal entries for the intragroup borrowings and related interest charge required for preparing the consolidated financial statements of the P Ltd group for the financial year ended 31 December 20x5.

(b) Prepare an extract of the consolidated statement of profit or loss and other comprehensive income for the 20x5 financial year, showing the consolidated profit for the period and the attribution thereof to the owners of the parent, and to the non-controlling interest.

(c) Discuss the effect of the pro forma journals passed in Part (b) on the consolidated financial statements prepared for the following reporting period.

 Solution 6.2: Intragroup borrowings

Part (a): Pro forma journal entries for the intragroup borrowings and related interest charge

CURRENT YEAR

Pro forma journal 1	Dr CU	Cr CU
Interest income (P Ltd) (P/L) (given)	65 000	
Interest expense (S Ltd) (P/L) (given)		65 000
Elimination of intragroup interest charge		

Pro forma journal 2	Dr CU	Cr CU
Loan liability (S Ltd) (SFP) (given)	500 000	
Loan receivable (P Ltd) (SFP) (given)		500 000
Elimination of intragroup balances		

Part (b): Extract of the consolidated statement of profit or loss and other comprehensive income for the 20x5 financial year

EXTRACT: P LTD GROUP CONSOLIDATED STATEMENT OF PROFIT OR LOSS AND OTHER COMPREHENSIVE INCOME FOR THE YEAR ENDED 31 DECEMBER 20x5	
	CU
PROFIT FOR THE YEAR ((P Ltd: 750 000 – 65 000 (J1) Elimination of intragroup interest income) + (S Ltd: 250 000 + 65 000 (J1) Elimination of intragroup interest expense))	1 000 000
Other comprehensive income	–
TOTAL COMPREHENSIVE INCOME FOR THE YEAR	**1 000 000**
Total comprehensive income attributable to:	
Owners of the parent (750 000 (P Ltd) + 200 000 (80% of 250 000 (S Ltd)))	950 000
Non-controlling interest (250 000 (S Ltd) × 20%)	50 000
	1 000 000

Comments: Consolidated statement of profit or loss and other comprehensive income

- The consolidated profit for the year is unaffected by the reversal of the intragroup interest income and expense. This makes sense as income and expense items of equal amount have been eliminated.

- Note that the elimination of the intragroup interest charge has no effect on the consolidated profit attributable to the non-controlling interest. In other words, the non-controlling interest is allocated its share of the subsidiary's **profit as is, that is, without first adjusting (increasing) the subsidiary's profit for the effects of the pro forma journal that eliminates the subsidiary's intragroup interest expense**. This is because the total group profit is unaffected by the elimination of the intragroup interest income and expense.

Part (c): Effect of the pro forma journals passed in Part (b) on the consolidated financial statements prepared for the following reporting period

As was discussed in the solution to Example 6.1, when we prepare the consolidated financial statements for the subsequent reporting period, the intragroup charges (in this case the interest income and interest expense) will both be included in the opening balance of consolidated retained earnings and will cancel each other out. Accordingly, when preparing the subsequent reporting period's consolidated financial statements, we do not need to repeat the prior period's pro forma journal eliminating the prior period's intragroup interest charge.

The intragroup balances – the loan receivable asset and the loan payable liability – will, however, be carried forward to the subsequent reporting period (recall that the loan amount due will only be settled in 20x8). Accordingly, we will need to repeat the pro forma journal eliminating these intragroup balances (see pro forma journal 2 Part (a)) when preparing the consolidated financial statements for the subsequent reporting period.

6.3 Sale of inventory intragroup

Frequently, entities within a group sell trading inventories to one another in what is called an intragroup sale of inventory.

6.3.1 Intragroup inventory sales: No unrealised profit

The following implications will arise on consolidation when *all* the inventory purchased by one group entity (the purchasing group entity) from another group entity (the selling group entity) during the financial year has been on sold to parties outside the group by the purchasing group entity during the financial year:

- There will be *no* unrealised profit to eliminate as all the inventory initially sold intragroup has been on sold to parties outside the group.

- When combining the financial statements of the purchasing and selling group entities:
  - the combined sales will include **intragroup sales,** which must be **eliminated on consolidation** to ensure that the group sales reported reflect sales made **only to external parties;** and
  - the combined cost of sales will include cost of sales based on the **intragroup cost price** of the inventory, which cost will include the selling group entity's intragroup profit. These cost of sales must also be **eliminated on consolidation.** This ensures that the group cost of sales reported is based on the cost of inventory when **first acquired by the group from external parties.**

Example 6.3: Intragroup sale of inventory by parent to wholly owned subsidiary: No unrealised profit

P Ltd owns 100% of subsidiary S Ltd. The following took place during the financial year ended 31 December 20x5:

- P Ltd purchased inventory from an external party for CU 80.
- P Ltd sold all this inventory to S Ltd for CU 100 (i.e., at a 25% mark-up on cost).
- S Ltd sold this entire inventory to an external party for CU 130.

Required

(a) Show the sequence of events in a diagram from the perspective of the individual group companies.

(b) Show the sequence of events in a diagram from the group's perspective.

(c) Prepare the 20x5 pro forma journal entries pertaining to the intragroup sale of inventory.

(d) Prepare an extract from the 20x5 consolidation worksheet showing the full effects of the pro forma journals in Part (c). Ensure that the consolidation worksheet includes a pre-adjustment trial balance column.

 Solution 6.3: Intragroup sale of inventory by parent to wholly owned subsidiary: No unrealised profit

Part (a): Perspective of the individual group entities

P Ltd buys inventory from external party for CU 80

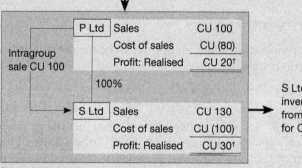

Explanatory note

† Combined profit of separate group entities is CU 50 (20 (P Ltd) + 30 (S Ltd))

Part (b): Perspective of the group

Group buys inventory from external party for CU 80

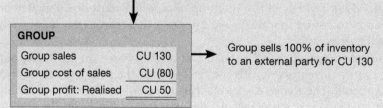

Part (c): Pro forma journal entry for intragroup sale of inventory
CURRENT YEAR

Pro forma journal 1 (J1)	Dr CU	Cr CU
Sales (P Ltd) (P/L) (given)	100	
Cost of sales (S Ltd) (P/L) (given)		100
Elimination of intragroup sale of inventory		

Part (d): Extract from consolidation worksheet for the year ended 31 December 20x5

Dr/(Cr)	P Ltd CU	S Ltd CU	Pre-adjust-ment trial balance (P Ltd + S Ltd) CU	Pro forma journal 1 CU	Con-solidated trial balance CU
Profit or loss					
Sales	(100)	(130)	(230)[1]	100[2]	(130)[3]
Cost of sales	80	100	180[4]	(100)[5]	80[6]
Gross profit	(20)	(30)	(50)[7]	–	(50)[7]
Statement of financial position					
Inventory	–	–	–	–	–

Explanatory notes: Extract from consolidation worksheet

[1] The combined sales of CU 230 are overstated by CU 100, which is the intragroup sale of inventory from P Ltd to S Ltd that does not constitute a sale for group purposes.

[2] In order to rectify the overstatement of sales discussed in 1 above, we reduce sales by debiting sales of P Ltd with CU 100 (see pro forma journal 1).

[3] The consolidated sales now correctly reflect the group sales of CU 130 made only to parties outside the group.

[4] The combined cost of sales is overstated by CU 100, which is the cost of sales based on the intragroup cost price of inventory purchased by S Ltd from P Ltd. This amount includes P Ltd's mark-up and does not constitute cost of sales for group purposes.

[5] To rectify the overstatement of cost of sales detailed in 4 above, we reduce cost of sales of S Ltd by crediting it with CU 100 (see pro forma journal 1).

[6] Consolidated cost of sales now correctly reflects the cost of sales made only to external parties based on the CU 80 cost of inventory purchased by the group from an external party.

[7] Both the pre-adjustment and the consolidated (or post-adjustment) trial balance reflect a profit of CU 50. The reason for this is that there was no unrealised profit in this scenario. There was no unrealised profit as there was no closing inventory on hand in S Ltd (the purchasing group entity) at financial year end. This means that P Ltd's entire intragroup profit of CU 20 (100 – 80) was realised when S Ltd sold all the inventory purchased intragroup from P Ltd onwards to an external party in the 20x5 financial year.

6.3.2 Intragroup inventory sales: Unrealised profit in closing inventory

In circumstances where one group entity sells inventory at a profit to another group entity, and the purchasing group entity has **all or part** of such inventory **still on hand at reporting period end:**

- The intragroup profit recognised by the selling group entity is **unrealised** from the group's perspective to the extent that this inventory sold intragroup has *not* been on sold to a party outside the group by reporting period end. Given that this intragroup profit is unrealised, it must be **eliminated in full** from the **selling group entity's profit or loss** on consolidation.

  More specifically, the pro forma journal passed to eliminate this unrealised intragroup profit from the selling group entity's profit or loss, must adjust the individual profit or loss line items making up this intragroup profit, namely **sales and cost of sales**. This ensures that the correct amounts are disclosed in the consolidated statement of profit or loss and other comprehensive income. In this regard, as discussed above:

  - group sales recorded must be only those sales made to **external parties;** and
  - group cost of sales must be the (1) cost of sales made only to **external parties;** and (2) measured at the cost of the inventory when **first acquired by the group from an external party/(parties).**

- The inventory on hand in the purchasing group entity at reporting period end is recognised by the purchasing group entity at the **intragroup cost price,** which cost **includes** the above-mentioned **unrealised intragroup profit** of the selling group entity. This implies that this inventory is recognised at an amount that is **different to the cost thereof to the group.** Consequently, on consolidation, this **unrealised intragroup profit** must be **eliminated** from the **cost of the purchasing group entity's inventory on hand at reporting period end.**

Example 6.4: Intragroup sale of inventory by parent to wholly owned subsidiary: Unrealised profit in closing inventory, with 100% of inventory on hand at year end

P Ltd owns 100% of subsidiary S Ltd. The following took place during the year ended 31 December 20x5:

- P Ltd purchased inventory from an external party for CU 80.
- P Ltd sold all this inventory to S Ltd for CU 100 (i.e., at a 25% mark-up on cost).
- S Ltd had not sold any of this inventory to external parties by year end.

Required

(a) Show the sequence of events in a diagram from the perspective of the individual group entities.

(b) Show the sequence of events in a diagram from the perspective of the group.

(c) Prepare an extract from the 20x5 consolidation worksheet showing the pre-adjustment trial balance.

(d) Prepare the 20x5 pro forma journal entry for the intragroup sale of inventory.

(e) Prepare an extract from the 20x5 consolidation worksheet showing the full effects of the pro forma journal in Part (d).

Ignore tax effects

Solution 6.4: Intragroup sale of inventory by parent to wholly owned subsidiary: Unrealised profit in closing inventory, with 100% of inventory on hand at year end

Part (a): Perspective of the individual group entities

P Ltd buys inventory from external party for CU 80

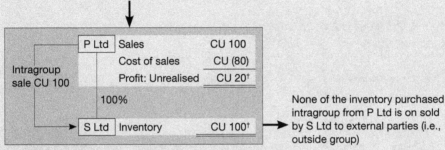

Explanatory note

† S Ltd's closing inventory is recorded at the inflated intragroup cost price of CU 100, which includes P Ltd's unrealised intragroup profit of CU 20

Part (b): Perspective of the group

Group buys inventory from external party for CU 80

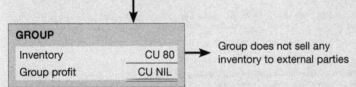

Part (c): Extract consolidation worksheet showing pre-adjustment trial balance

Dr/(Cr)	P Ltd CU	S Ltd CU	Pre-adjustment trial balance (P Ltd + S Ltd) CU
Profit or loss			
Sales	(100)	–	(100)[1]
Cost of sales	80	–	80[2]
Gross profit	(20)	–	(20)[3]
Statement of financial position			
Inventory	–	100	100[4]

Explanatory notes: Extract from consolidation worksheet

[1] The combined sales of CU 100 are all intragroup sales made by P Ltd to S Ltd and should not be recognised on consolidation as none were made to parties outside the group (i.e., group sales should be NIL).

[2] As the combined cost of sales of CU 80 is entirely in respect of intragroup sales, it does not constitute cost of sales from the group's perspective and must be eliminated (i.e., group cost of sales should also be NIL).

Explanatory notes: Extract from consolidation worksheet (continued)

3 The combined profit of CU 20 is unrealised as none of the inventory sold intragroup by P Ltd to S Ltd has been on sold to parties outside the group. Accordingly, this profit must be eliminated in full on consolidation (i.e., group profit should also be NIL).

4 The combined inventory is recorded at CU 100, which is overstated by P Ltd's unrealised intragroup profit of CU 20 included therein (i.e., the cost of the inventory to the group is only CU 80).

Part (d): Pro forma journal for intragroup sale of inventory
CURRENT YEAR

Pro forma journal 1 (J1)	Dr CU	Cr CU
Sales (P Ltd) (P/L) (given)	100	
Cost of sales (P Ltd) (P/L) (given)		80
Inventory (S Ltd) (SFP)		Wkg1 20
Elimination of intragroup sale, cost of sale and unrealised intragroup profit included in closing inventory		

Workings: Pro forma journals

Working 1
100 Closing inventory × 25/125 Unrealised profit element

Comments: Pro forma journal 1

- The debit entry eliminates the full intragroup sale while the credit to cost of sales eliminates the associated cost of sales (i.e., the intragroup transaction, being the sale of inventory from P Ltd to S Ltd, is eliminated in full as from the group's perspective no transaction has taken place).

- The credit to inventory of the purchasing group entity (S Ltd) reduces the inventory balance by the CU 20 unrealised intragroup profit. This is because S Ltd's inventory balance of CU 100 is measured based on the cost of S Ltd's intragroup inventory purchases from P Ltd instead of the original cost to the group of inventory purchased from external parties for an amount of only CU 80.

Part (e): Extract from the consolidation worksheet showing the full effects of the pro forma journal entry in respect of the intragroup sale of inventory

Dr/(Cr)	P Ltd CU	S Ltd CU	Pre-adjust-ment Trial balance (P Ltd + S Ltd) CU	Pro forma journal 1 CU	Con-solidated CU
Profit or loss					
Sales	(100)	–	(100)	100	0[1]
Cost of sales	80	–	80	(80)	0[2]
Gross profit	(20)	–	(20)	20	0[3]
Statement of financial position					
Inventory	–	100	100	(20)	80[4]

Explanatory notes: Extract from consolidation worksheet

1   P Ltd's sales for the year have been reduced to NIL, which is correct as there were no sales made to parties outside the group in this financial reporting period.

2   P Ltd's cost of sales has also been reduced to NIL. Because there were no sales recognised for group purposes, there can be no cost of sales recognised for group purposes.

3   P Ltd's profit of CU 20 has been reduced to NIL. This is correct as this amount is unrealised intragroup profit and consequently, it cannot be recognised by the group.

4   S Ltd's inventory, purchased intragroup from P Ltd, has been reduced to CU 80, which is correct as the inventory is now recognised at the cost to the group (i.e., the cost incurred when the group purchased inventory from an external party for CU 80).

Example 6.5: Intragroup sale of inventory by parent to wholly owned subsidiary: Unrealised profit in closing inventory; 40% of inventory on hand at year end

P Ltd owns 100% of subsidiary S Ltd. The following took place during the year ended 31 December 20x5:

- P Ltd purchased inventory from an external party for CU 100.
- P Ltd sold all this inventory to S Ltd for CU 120 (i.e., at a 20% mark-up on cost).
- S Ltd sold 60% of this inventory to external parties for CU 90 (i.e., at a 25% mark-up on cost).

Required

(a) Show the sequence of events in a diagram from the perspective of the individual group entities.

(b) Show the sequence of events in a diagram from the perspective of the group.

(c) Prepare an extract from the 20x5 consolidation worksheet showing the pre-adjustment trial balance.

(d) Prepare the 20x5 pro forma journal entry for the intragroup sale of inventory.

(e) Prepare an extract from the 20x5 consolidation worksheet showing the full effects of the pro forma journal in Part (d).

Ignore tax effects

Solution 6.5: Intragroup sale of inventory by parent to wholly owned subsidiary: Unrealised profit in closing inventory; 40% of inventory on hand at year end

Part (a): Perspective of the individual group entities

P Ltd buys inventory from external party for CU 100

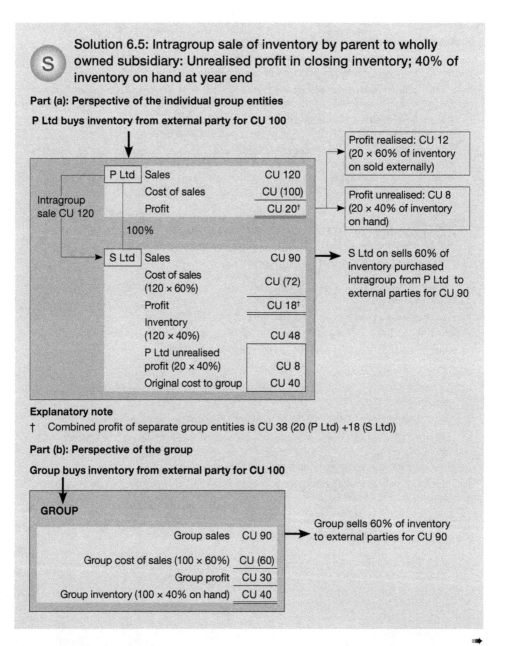

Profit realised: CU 12
(20 × 60% of inventory on sold externally)

Profit unrealised: CU 8
(20 × 40% of inventory on hand)

P Ltd	Sales	CU 120
	Cost of sales	CU (100)
	Profit	CU 20†

Intragroup sale CU 120

100%

S Ltd on sells 60% of inventory purchased intragroup from P Ltd to external parties for CU 90

S Ltd	Sales	CU 90
	Cost of sales (120 × 60%)	CU (72)
	Profit	CU 18†
	Inventory (120 × 40%)	CU 48
	P Ltd unrealised profit (20 × 40%)	CU 8
	Original cost to group	CU 40

Explanatory note

† Combined profit of separate group entities is CU 38 (20 (P Ltd) +18 (S Ltd))

Part (b): Perspective of the group

Group buys inventory from external party for CU 100

GROUP

Group sales	CU 90
Group cost of sales (100 × 60%)	CU (60)
Group profit	CU 30
Group inventory (100 × 40% on hand)	CU 40

Group sells 60% of inventory to external parties for CU 90

Part (c): Extract from the consolidation worksheet showing the pre-adjustment trial balance

Dr/(Cr)	P Ltd CU	S Ltd CU	Pre-adjustment trial balance (P Ltd + S Ltd) CU
Profit or loss			
Sales	(120)	(90)	(210)[1]
Cost of sales	100	72	172[2]
Gross profit	(20)	(18)	(38)[3]
Statement of financial position			
Inventory	–	48	48[4]

Explanatory notes: Extract from consolidation worksheet

[1] The combined sales are CU 210, when in fact the sales made to external parties to be recognised as group sales are only CU 90.

[2] The combined cost of sales are CU 172, when in fact the group cost of sales (being the cost of sales made only to external parties, and which must be measured based on the cost of inventory to the group) to be recognised is only CU 60 (60% × 100 Cost of inventory to group).

[3] The combined profit is CU 38, while the profit to be recognised for group purposes is that which arises in respect of inventory sold to external parties only, which amounts to CU 30 (Sales of CU 90 – Cost of sales CU 60). It follows that of the combined profit of CU 38, CU 8 (38 – 30) is unrealised. Furthermore, this unrealised profit of CU 8 is the 40% of P Ltd's total intragroup profit of CU 20 (120 – 100) that is included in S Ltd's year-end inventory on hand. This makes sense as 60% of the inventory sold intragroup by P Ltd was, in turn, on sold outside the group by S Ltd. Accordingly, 60% of P Ltd's intragroup profit of CU 20, an amount of CU 12, is realised. The remaining 40% of inventory sold intragroup is still on hand at year end and has therefore not been sold outside the group. This means that 40% of P Ltd's profit on intragroup inventory sales is unrealised and cannot be recognised as group profit for the current year.

[4] The combined inventory balance of CU 48 includes P Ltd's unrealised intragroup profit of CU 8 discussed in 3 above. The cost of the remaining inventory to the group must be the cost of the remaining inventory purchased from external parties, which cost must exclude this unrealised intragroup profit of CU 8. Accordingly, the remaining inventory balance must be reflected at a cost to the group of CU 40 (48 – 8 Unrealised intragroup profit).

Part (d): Pro forma journal for intragroup sale of inventory
CURRENT YEAR

Pro forma journal 1 (J1)	Dr CU	Cr CU
Sales (P Ltd) (P/L) (given)	120	
Cost of sales (P Ltd) (P/L) (given)		100
Cost of sales (P Ltd) (P/L)		[Wkg1]12
Inventory (S Ltd) (SFP)		[Wkg2]8
Elimination of intragroup sales, cost of sales and unrealised intragroup profit included in closing inventory		

Workings: Pro forma journals
Working 1
120 P Ltd Sales – 100 P Ltd Cost of Sales = 20 P Ltd intragroup profit × 60% of inventory sold intragroup by P Ltd that was sold externally by S Ltd.

Workings: Pro forma journals

Working 2

Balancing figure

OR

48 Closing inventory × 20/120 Unrealised profit element

Comments: Pro forma journal 1

- The CU 120 debit to sales reverses P Ltd's CU 120 intragroup sale of inventory to S Ltd, which cannot be recognised for group purposes as this inventory was not sold to a party outside the group.
- In respect of the two credits to cost of sales:
  - CU 100 is the elimination of the cost of sales recognised by P Ltd in respect of the intragroup sale of CU 120.
  - CU 12 is the reduction in S Ltd's cost of sales recognised, arising from sales to parties outside the group. S Ltd in its own records recognised cost of sales of CU 72, calculated as 60% × CU 120 Intragroup cost of inventory. However, for group purposes cost of sales should have been calculated based on the cost of inventory to the group of CU 60 (60% × 100). S Ltd's cost of sales is therefore overstated by CU 12, but we make the adjustment to **P Ltd's cost of sales** and **not to S Ltd's cost of sales**, because the original profit that was reversed (because it was unrealised) was **P Ltd's profit**. It follows that as and when S Ltd sells inventory to external parties, **P Ltd's profit** then becomes realised. There are accordingly two steps:
    - **Step 1**: The original unrealised intragroup profit of P Ltd is eliminated, calculated as follows:

	CU
Sales – Intragroup	120
Less: Cost of sales intragroup	(100)
Unrealised profit – Intragroup	20

      As per the pro forma journal above, it is apparent that we debited P Ltd's sales with CU 120 and credited P Ltd's cost of sales with CU 100, with the net result that P Ltd's profit is decreased by the unrealised profit of CU 20.

    - **Step 2**: Because S Ltd subsequently sold 60% of this inventory to external parties, 60% of P Ltd's unrealised intragroup profit of CU 20, an amount of CU 12, now becomes realised. We recognise this realised portion of P Ltd's originally unrealised profit by **crediting P Ltd's cost of sales** with CU 12, thus increasing P Ltd's profit by CU 12.

The pro forma journal above was provided in order to enable you to understand the journal fully. However, the simplest way of processing this journal (to be used for test and exam purposes) is as follows:

Pro forma journal 1 (J1)	Dr CU	Cr CU
Sales (P Ltd) (P/L) (given)	120	
Cost of sales (P Ltd) (P/L) (balancing figure)		112
Inventory (S Ltd) (SFP)		Wkg1 8
Elimination of intragroup sales, cost of sales and unrealised intragroup profit in closing inventory		

Workings: Pro forma journals

Working 1

48 Closing inventory × 20/120 Unrealised profit element

Part (e): Extract from the consolidation worksheet showing the full effects of the pro forma journal in respect of the intragroup sale of inventory

Dr/(Cr)	P Ltd CU	S Ltd CU	Pre-adjust- ment trial balance (P Ltd + S Ltd) CU	Pro forma journal 1 CU	Con- solidated CU
Profit or loss					
Sales	(120)	(90)	(210)	120	(90)[1]
Cost of sales	100	72	172	(112)	60[2]
Gross profit	(20)	(18)	(38)	8	(30)[3]
Statement of financial position					
Inventory	–	48	48	(8)	40[4]

Explanatory notes: Extract from consolidation worksheet

[1] The sales have been reduced to CU 90, which correctly reflects the sales made (by S Ltd) only to parties outside the group.

[2] The cost of sales have now been reduced to 60, which correctly reflects the cost of sales arising only from sales made (by S Ltd) to parties outside the group and which are measured based on the cost of inventory purchased (by P Ltd) from parties outside the group (60% Inventory sold outside group × CU 100 Cost of inventory to group).

[3] The group profit has now been reduced to CU 30, which correctly reflects the realised profit arising only from the sale of inventory to parties outside the group.

[4] The inventory of the group is now correctly reflected at CU 40, which is the remaining balance on hand based on the cost of inventories purchased by the group from external parties (40% of inventory remaining × CU 100 Cost of inventory to the group).

6.3.3 Intragroup inventory sales: Unrealised profit in opening inventories

Up to now we have dealt only with unrealised intragroup profit that is included in inventories on hand at reporting period end (i.e., unrealised intragroup profit included in closing inventory). When preparing the consolidated financial statements of the subsequent reporting period the following will apply:

- The **closing inventory** of the **prior reporting period**, which **includes** the selling group entity's **prior period unrealised intragroup profit**, becomes the **opening inventory** for the **current reporting period**.

- We assume that this **opening inventory** is **sold to parties outside the group** in the **current reporting period** such that the selling group entity's **prior period intragroup profit becomes realised**, and must therefore be **recognised**, in the **current reporting period**.

Accordingly, on consolidation in the current reporting period, we will need to pass a pro forma journal in order to:

- First, **reduce** the **selling group entity's opening retained earnings balance** for the **current period** by the amount of the **prior period unrealised intragroup profit** recognised, which profit was **eliminated on consolidation** in the **prior period**.

Since pro forma journals are *not* carried forward to subsequent reporting periods, the selling group entity's opening retained earnings balance, which is extracted in the current period, will *not* include the effects of (i.e., will not have been reduced by) this prior period intragroup profit elimination.

For this reason, in the current period, we **debit** the selling group entity's **opening retained earnings balance, reducing it** by the selling group entity's **prior period unrealised intragroup profit recognised** (note that we are ignoring any tax effects for the moment; these are dealt with in Sections 6.3.5 and 6.3.6).

- Second, **recognise** the selling group entity's **prior year unrealised intragroup profit** in the **current period.** This is because – as discussed above – the opening inventory, which includes the selling group entity's prior year unrealised intragroup profit, is assumed to have been sold to **parties outside the group** in the **current period.** This implies that this previously unrealised intragroup profit becomes realised and must therefore be recognised in the current period.

The purchasing group entity's current period cost of sales includes the cost of sales of its opening inventory. Since this **opening inventory sold includes** the selling group entity's **prior period unrealised intragroup profit,** the group's **cost of sales is overstated** and must be **reduced** accordingly. This **reduction in cost of sales** has the effect of **realising the selling group entity's prior period unrealised intragroup profit** in the **current year.** Consequently, we **recognise** this **prior period intragroup profit** in the **current period** by **crediting** and thereby **reducing the selling group entity's cost of sales.**

Accordingly, the following pro forma journal must be processed in the current reporting period:

	Dr CU	Cr CU
Retained earnings (selling group entity) (SCIE) [Elimination of prior year unrealised intragroup profit]	xxx	
Cost of sales (selling group entity) (P/L) [Current year recognition of prior year intragroup profit]		xxx

It should be noted that most often in any given financial year – aside from unrealised intragroup profit included in opening inventory – there will once again be unrealised intragroup profit included in **closing inventory,** arising from intragroup sales of inventory during that financial reporting period. In other words, for each reporting period, when preparing the consolidated financial statements of a group where there are intragroup inventory sales, we will typically be required to pass:

- A pro forma journal, as discussed above, to:
  - **eliminate** the selling group entity's **prior year unrealised intragroup profit,** included in the current year's opening inventory balance, by **reducing** the selling group entity's **opening retained earnings balance;** and
  - **recognise** this **formerly unrealised prior year intragroup profit** in the **current year** by **reducing** the selling group entity's current year **cost of sales expense** (i.e., the selling group entity's prior year unrealised intragroup profit which is included in the current year's opening inventory, becomes realised, and must be recognised on consolidation in the current year, upon the current year sale of this opening inventory outside the group).

- A pro forma journal, as discussed in Section 6.3.2:
  - to eliminate from profit or loss, the intragroup profit recognised by the selling group entity, arising from its current year intragroup inventory sales, to the extent that this inventory sold intragroup is still on hand as closing inventory of the group at current financial year end; and
  - to eliminate this unrealised intragroup profit from the cost of the purchasing group entity's inventory on hand at current financial year end.

Example 6.6: Intragroup sale of inventory by parent to wholly owned subsidiary: Unrealised profit in opening and closing inventory

P Ltd owns 100% of subsidiary S Ltd, which it acquired on 1 January 20x5.

- P Ltd sells all its inventory to S Ltd.
- S Ltd buys all its inventory from P Ltd and had no inventory on hand when it was acquired by P Ltd.

The following took place during the financial year ended 31 December 20x5:

- P Ltd sold inventory that had cost it CU 100 000 to S Ltd for CU 120 000 (i.e., at a 20% mark-up on cost).
- S Ltd sold 70% of this inventory to external parties during 20x5 for CU 105 000.
- S Ltd reflected a closing balance for inventory of CU 36 000 in its records as at 31 December 20x5.
- P Ltd had a NIL closing balance for inventory on hand in its records as at 31 December 20x5.

The following took place during the financial year ended 31 December 20x6:

- P Ltd sold inventory that had cost it CU 150 000 to S Ltd for CU 180 000 (i.e., at a 20% mark-up on cost).
- S Ltd sold all its opening inventory as well as 85% of inventory purchased during 20x6 to external parties for CU 235 000.
- S Ltd reflected a closing balance for inventory of CU 27 000 in its records as at 31 December 20x6.
- P Ltd had a NIL closing balance for inventory on hand in its records as at 31 December 20x6.

Required
In so far as the information allows:

(a) Prepare the since acquisition pro forma journal(s) for the financial year ended 31 December 20x5.

(b) Prepare the since acquisition pro forma journal(s) for the financial year ended 31 December 20x6.

Ignore tax effects

Solution 6.6: Intragroup sale of inventory by parent to wholly owned subsidiary: Unrealised profit in opening and closing inventory

Part (a): Since acquisition pro forma journal for the financial year ended 31 December 20x5

CURRENT YEAR

Pro forma journal 1 (J1)	Dr CU	Cr CU
Sales (P Ltd) (P/L) (given)	120 000	
Cost of sales (P Ltd) (P/L) (balancing figure)		114 000
Inventory (S Ltd) (SFP)		Wkg1 6 000
Elimination of intragroup sales, cost of sales and unrealised intragroup profit in closing inventory		

Workings: Pro forma journals

Working 1

36 000 Closing inventory × 20/120 Unrealised profit

The effects of the pro forma journal above on the consolidated financial statements are illustrated in the consolidation worksheet below as at 31 December 20x5.

	P Ltd CU	S Ltd CU	Pre-adjust-ment TB (P Ltd + S Ltd) CU	Pro forma journal 1 CU	Con-solidated CU
Retained earnings – BOY	–	–	–	–	–
Profit for the period	(20 000)	(21 000)	(41 000)		(35 000)
Retained earnings – EOY	(20 000)	(21 000)	(41 000)¹		(35 000)¹
Profit or loss					
Sales	(120 000)	(105 000)	(225 000)	120 000	(105 000)²
Cost of sales	100 000	84 000	184 000	(114 000)	70 000³
Gross profit	(20 000)	(21 000)	(41 000)		(35 000)
Statement of financial position					
Inventory	–	36 000	36 000	(6 000)	30 000⁴

Explanatory notes: Consolidation worksheet

¹ The consolidated retained earnings closing balance of CU 35 000 is CU 6 000 less than the combined (pre-adjusted) retained earnings closing balance of CU 41 000. This is because the pre-adjusted profit of P Ltd for the period, which is included in the combined (pre-adjusted) retained earnings balance at financial year end includes P Ltd's unrealised intragroup profit of CU 6 000, recognised in respect of inventory sales to S Ltd. As P Ltd's profit is adjusted on consolidation – via pro forma journal 1 – to eliminate this CU 6 000 unrealised intragroup profit, the closing consolidated retained earnings balance is accordingly CU 6 000 less than the closing combined (pre-adjusted) retained earnings balance.

² The sales are correctly reflected as being only the sales made to parties outside the group.

³ The cost of sales:
   - are correctly reflected as the cost of inventory sold only to parties outside the group;
   - are measured based on the cost of the inventory to the group; and
   - are calculated as: the 70% of inventories purchased intragroup in the current year that were sold outside the group in the current year × CU 100 000 Total current year inventory cost to group = CU 70 000.

⁴ The cost of inventory on hand is correctly reflected at the cost to the group, calculated as follows:

- 30% Remaining inventory × CU 100 000 Total current year inventory cost to group = CU 30 000

  OR

- CU 36 000 Combined inventory balance – CU 6 000 (36 000 × 20/120) Unrealised intragroup profit = CU 30 000

Part (b): Since acquisition pro forma journal(s) for the financial year ended 31 December 20x6

SINCE ACQUISITION TO THE BEGINNING OF THE YEAR/CURRENT YEAR

	Dr CU	Cr CU
Pro forma journal 1 (J1)		
Retained earnings (SCIE) (P Ltd)	Wkg1 6 000	
Cost of sales (P/L) (P Ltd)		Wkg2 6 000
Recognition of prior year elimination of unrealised intragroup profit on sale of inventory to ensure current year opening consolidated retained earnings balance agrees to prior year closing consolidated retained earnings balance, and recognition of prior year intragroup profit which realises in the current year		

Workings: Pro forma journals

Working 1
36 000 Prior year closing inventory × 20/120 Unrealised profit element

Working 2
36 000 Opening inventory × 20/120 Realised profit element

Comments: Pro forma journal 1

- In the prior financial year (20x5 financial year), P Ltd's CU 6 000 unrealised intragroup profit, recognised on sale of inventory to S Ltd, was eliminated on consolidation, via a pro forma journal. This elimination on consolidation reduced P Ltd's prior year profit by CU 6 000, which profit was closed off to retained earnings in the prior year consolidated financial statements.

  However, pro forma journals do not affect the accounting records of the individual group entities and are therefore not carried forward to subsequent reporting periods. Consequently, P Ltd's opening retained earnings balance for the current year (20x6 financial year), obtained from its separate financial statements, does not include the effects of (i.e., will not have been reduced by) the prior year pro forma elimination of P Ltd's CU 6 000 unrealised intragroup profit recognised. For this reason, on consolidation in the current year, we debit P Ltd's opening retained earnings balance with CU 6 000, reducing it by the prior year unrealised intragroup profit recognised by P Ltd. Consequently, the CU 6 000 debit to retained earnings ensures that the current year consolidated retained earnings opening balance equals the prior year consolidated retained earnings closing balance.

- In the current year, S Ltd on sells to parties outside the group, all its opening inventory, which inventory was purchased from P Ltd in the prior year. Consequently, P Ltd's CU 6 000 prior year intragroup profit becomes realised and must therefore be recognised in the current year consolidated financial statements. S Ltd's CU 84 000 current year cost of sales includes the cost of sales of S Ltd's opening inventory. Because the cost of this opening inventory sold includes P Ltd's CU 6 000 prior year unrealised intragroup profit (recall that the prior year pro forma journal eliminating this unrealised profit from inventory is not carried forward to the current year) cost of sales is overstated at group level and must be reduced by CU 6 000 on consolidation. This reduction in cost of sales has the effect of recognising P Ltd's prior year CU 6 000 intragroup profit in the current year. For this reason, we credit cost of sales of P Ltd with CU 6 000.

CURRENT YEAR

Pro forma journal 2 (J2)	Dr CU	Cr CU
Sales (P Ltd) (P/L) (given)	180 000	
Cost of sales (P Ltd) (P/L) (balancing figure)		175 500
Inventory (S Ltd) (SFP)		Wkg3 4 500
Elimination of intragroup sales, cost of sales and unrealised intragroup profit in closing inventory		

Workings: Pro forma journals

Working 3
27 000 Closing inventory × 20/120 Unrealised profit element

Comments: Pro forma journal 2

- As not all the inventory that was sold intragroup by P Ltd to S Ltd in the current year was on sold by S Ltd to parties outside the group, not all the profit recognised by P Ltd in respect of such sales was realised in the current financial year. Consequently, this unrealised profit portion must be eliminated on consolidation in the current year. This is achieved by debiting P Ltd's sales with CU 180 000 and crediting P Ltd's cost of sales with CU 175 500, the net effect of which is a CU 4 500 debit to P Ltd's current year profit . In this way, P Ltd's CU 4 500 current year unrealised intragroup profit recognised is eliminated on consolidation.

- In addition, the closing inventory of S Ltd (the purchasing group entity), which includes P Ltd's unrealised intragroup profit, is overstated by CU 4 500 and must be reduced in order to reflect the inventory on hand at its original cost to the group. For this reason we credit S Ltd's closing inventory with CU 4 500.

The effects of the pro forma journals above on the consolidated financial statements are illustrated in the consolidation worksheet below as at 31 December 20x6.

Dr/(Cr)	P Ltd CU	S Ltd CU	Pre-adjustment TB (P Ltd + S Ltd) CU	Pro forma journal 1 CU	Pro forma journal 2 CU	Con-solidated CU
Retained earnings – BOY	(20 000)	(21 000)	(41 000)	6 000[1]		(35 000)[1]
Profit for the period	(30 000)	(46 000)	(76 000)			(77 500)
Retained earnings – EOY	(50 000)	(67 000)	(117 000)			(112 500)
Profit or loss						
Sales	(180 000)	(235 000)	(415 000)		180 000	(235 000)[3]
Cost of sales	150 000	189 000	339 000	(6 000)[2]	(175 500)	157 500[4]
Gross profit	(30 000)	(46 000)	(112 000)			(77 500)
Retained						
Statement of financial position						
Inventory	–	27 000	27 000		(4 500)	22 500[5]

Explanatory notes: Consolidation worksheet

1. By reducing P Ltd's opening retained earnings with P Ltd's prior year CU 6 000 unrealised intragroup profit – as per pro forma journal 1 – the current year consolidated opening retained earnings balance now agrees with the prior year closing consolidated retained earnings (see consolidation worksheet in Part (a)).

2. The credit leg of pro forma journal 1, effectively reallocates the recognition of P Ltd's CU 6 000 intragroup profit on sale of inventory to S Ltd, from the prior year to the current year. This makes sense as S Ltd's opening inventory, which includes this CU 6 000 intragroup profit, is sold to parties outside the group in the current year. The implication is that P Ltd's formerly unrealised intragroup profit now becomes realised in the current year and accordingly must be recognised as current year income of the group.

3. The sales are correctly reflected as being only those sales made to parties outside the group.

4. The cost of sales:
   - are correctly reflected as the cost of inventory sold only to parties outside the group;
   - are measured based on the cost of the inventory to the group; and
   - are calculated as:
     - the 30% of inventories purchased intragroup in the prior year that were sold outside the group in the current year × CU 100 000 Prior year inventory cost to group = CU 30 000 **A**

     PLUS
     - the 85% of inventories purchased intragroup in the current year that were sold outside the group in the current year × CU150 000 Total current year inventory cost to group = CU 127 500 **B**

     SUM of **A** and **B** = CU 157 500 (30 000 + 127 500)

5. The cost of closing inventory on hand is correctly reflected at the cost to the group, calculated as follows:
   - 15% Remaining inventory × CU 150 000 Total current year cost of inventory to group = CU 22 500

   OR
   - CU 27 000 Combined inventory balance – CU 4 500 (27 000 × 20/120) Unrealised intragroup profit = CU 22 500

6.3.4 The effect of intragroup inventory sales on the non-controlling interest

So far we have dealt only with the sale of inventory intragroup by a **parent** to its **wholly owned subsidiary**. When dealing with a wholly owned subsidiary, the consolidated profit attributable to the owners of the parent will be adjusted for the **full effects** of the elimination of any unrealised profit and the subsequent recognition of this profit when it becomes realised in a subsequent year. This is **irrespective** of whether the inventory is sold by the **parent to the subsidiary** or by the **subsidiary to the parent,** given that there is *no* non-controlling interest.

Where a subsidiary is **partly owned,** whether or not the non-controlling interest is affected by the intragroup inventory sale is dependent upon **which group entity sold the inventory** to which other group entity, and therefore **recognised the unrealised intragroup profit**. Thus:

- If the parent sells inventory to the partly owned subsidiary – known as a **downstream sale** – then the **parent recognises the unrealised intragroup profit** in its own records. It follows that when the parent's unrealised intragroup profit recognised is eliminated on consolidation and is then recognised on consolidation in a subsequent reporting period when it becomes realised for group purposes, it is the **parent's profit** or loss, and **reserves** that are adjusted on consolidation. As the non-controlling interest does *not* participate in a share of the profits or reserves of the parent, there is therefore **no effect** on the non-controlling interest when there is a downstream sale of inventory from parent to partly owned subsidiary.

- If the partly owned subsidiary sells inventory **to the parent** – known as an **upstream sale** – or to a **fellow subsidiary**, then the **unrealised intragroup profit arises in the partly owned subsidiary**. In this instance, as the non-controlling interest **does share** in the profit or loss, and reserves of the subsidiary, it **will be allocated its appropriate share** of the consolidation adjustments:
  - **eliminating** the subsidiary's **unrealised intragroup profit**; and
  - **subsequently recognising** the subsidiary's **unrealised intragroup profit** as income when realised in a succeeding reporting period.

Example 6.7: Intragroup sale of inventory by partly owned subsidiary to parent: Unrealised profit in opening and closing inventory

The facts for this example are the same as Example 6.6, except that:

- S Ltd is now a 70% partly owned subsidiary of P Ltd; and
- S Ltd sells inventory to P Ltd.

The facts given in Example 6.6 are reproduced below with the changes highlighted in bold.

P Ltd owns 70% of subsidiary S Ltd, which it acquired on 1 January 20x5:

- **S Ltd** sells all its inventory to **P Ltd**.
- **P Ltd** buys all its inventory from **S Ltd**.

The following took place during the financial year ended 31 December 20x5:

- **S Ltd** sold inventory that had cost it CU 100 000 to P Ltd for CU 120 000 (i.e., at a 20% mark-up on cost).
- **P Ltd** sold 70% of this inventory to external parties during 20x5 for CU 105 000.
- **P Ltd** reflected a closing balance for inventory of CU 36 000 in its records as at 31 December 20x5.
- **S Ltd** had a NIL closing balance for inventory on hand in its records as at 31 December 20x5.

The following took place during the financial year ended 31 December 20x6:

- **S Ltd** sold inventory that had cost it CU 150 000, to P Ltd for CU 180 000 (i.e., at a 20% mark-up on cost).
- **P Ltd** sold all its opening inventory as well as 85% of inventory purchased during 20x6 to external parties for CU 235 000.
- **P Ltd** reflected a closing balance for inventory of CU 27 000 in its records as at 31 December 20x6.
- **S Ltd** had a NIL closing balance for inventory on hand in its records as at 31 December 20x6.

In addition, the statements of profit or loss and other comprehensive income for P Ltd and S Ltd were as follows for the 20x5 and 20x6 financial years:

STATEMENTS OF PROFIT OR LOSS AND OTHER COMPREHENSIVE INCOME FOR THE YEAR ENDED 31 DECEMBER 20x5		
	P Ltd	**S Ltd**
	CU	CU
Sales	105 000	120 000
Cost of sales	(84 000)	(100 000)
Gross profit	21 000	20 000
PROFIT FOR THE YEAR	**21 000**	**20 000**

STATEMENTS OF PROFIT OR LOSS AND OTHER COMPREHENSIVE INCOME FOR THE YEAR ENDED 31 DECEMBER 20x6		
	P Ltd	**S Ltd**
	CU	CU
Sales	235 000	180 000
Cost of sales	(189 000)	(150 000)
Gross profit	46 000	30 000
PROFIT FOR THE YEAR	**46 000**	**30 000**

Required

(a) Prepare the since acquisition pro forma consolidation journal(s) for the financial year ended 31 December 20x5.

(b) Prepare an extract of the analysis of equity of S Ltd as at 31 December 20x6, showing only the analysis of the post-acquisition equity of S Ltd.

(c) Prepare the since acquisition pro forma consolidation journal(s) for the financial year ended 31 December 20x6.

(d) Prepare the consolidated statement of profit or loss and other comprehensive income for the P Ltd group for the financial year ended 31 December 20x6.

(e) Assuming that the non-controlling interest balance that arose on acquisition of S Ltd was CU 10 000 and that the retained earnings balances of both P Ltd and S Ltd as at 1 December 20x5 were NIL, prepare an extract from the consolidated statement of changes in equity for the P Ltd group for the financial year ended 31 December 20x6, showing only the columns for retained earnings and for the non-controlling interest.

Ignore tax effects

Solution 6.7: Intragroup sale of inventory by partly owned subsidiary to parent: Unrealised profit in opening and closing inventory

Part (a): Since acquisition pro forma journal(s) for the financial year ended 31 December 20x5

CURRENT YEAR

	Dr	Cr
Pro forma journal 1 (J1)	CU	CU
Sales (S Ltd) (P/L) (given)	120 000	
Cost of sales (S Ltd) (P/L) (balancing figure)		114 000
Inventory (P Ltd) (SFP)		^{Wkg1}6 000
Elimination of intragroup sales, cost of sales and unrealised intragroup profit in closing inventory		

Workings: Pro forma journals

Working 1

36 000 Closing inventory × 20/120 Unrealised profit element

Pro forma journal 2 (J2)	Dr CU	Cr CU
NCI: Share of profit or loss (P/L)	Wkg2 4 200	
Non-controlling interest – Equity (SFP)		Wkg2 4 200
Allocating the non-controlling interest its share of S Ltd's adjusted profit for the year		

Workings: Pro forma journals

Working 2

(20 000 – 6 000 (J1) Unrealised intragroup profit) × 30% NCI Share

Comments: Pro forma journal 2

- Since the sale of inventory was upstream (i.e., subsidiary to parent), the unrealised intragroup profit of CU 6 000, which is eliminated on consolidation as per pro forma journal 1, arises in subsidiary S Ltd. Consequently, S Ltd's profit must first be adjusted (reduced) by this CU 6 000 unrealised intragroup profit before being allocated to the non-controlling interest. The non-controlling interest therefore shares in the unrealised intragroup profit elimination to the extent of CU 1800 (6 000 × 30%).

The effects of the preceding pro forma journals on the consolidated financial statements are illustrated in the following consolidation worksheet as at 31 December 20x5.

Dr/(Cr)	P Ltd CU	S Ltd CU	Pro forma journals CU	Journal ref	Con- solidated CU
Retained earnings (BOY)	–	–	–		–
Profit for period: Individual entities	(21 000)	(20 000)			–
Consolidated profit – attributable to owners of parent					(30 800) ◄
Retained earnings (EOY)	(21 000)	(20 000)			(30 800)
			(10 000)	(given)	(14 200)
NCI Equity			(4 200)	J2	
Profit or loss					
Sales	(105 000)	(120 000)	120 000	J1	(105 000)
Cost of sales	84 000	100 000	(114 000)	J1	70 000
Gross profit	(21 000)	(20 000)			(35 000)
NCI: Share of profit			4 200	J2	4 200
Consolidated profit attributable to owners of parent					(30 800) ┘
Statement of financial position					
Inventory	36 000	–	(6 000)	J1	30 000

Part (b): Post-acquisition analysis of equity (AOE) of S Ltd as at 31 December 20x6

	Total of S Ltd's equity 100%	P Ltd 70% Since acquisition	Non-controlling interest 30%
Since acquisition			
• To beginning of current year:			
Adjusted retained earnings to BOY	14 000[1]	9 800 **a**	4 200[1] **b**
Retained earnings movement	20 000		
Elimination prior year unrealised intragroup profit: Closing inventory (36 000 × 20/120)	(6 000)[1&2]		
• Current year:			
Adjusted profit for the year	31 500[1]	22 050 **c**	9 450[1] **d**
Profit for the year	30 000		
Recognition realised intragroup profit: Opening inventory: (36 000 × 20/120)	6 000[1&2]		
Elimination current year unrealised intragroup profit: Closing inventory: (27 000 × 20/120)	(4 500)[1]		

Explanatory notes: Analysis of equity

[1] Because there has been an upstream sale of inventory by S Ltd to P Ltd, the intragroup profit arises in S Ltd. Consequently, S Ltd's post-acquisition retained earnings and current year profit, allocated to the non-controlling interest, have been **adjusted** for the effects of S Ltd's intragroup profit included in prior year closing inventory and in current year opening inventory.

[2] Note how S Ltd's CU 6000 prior year unrealised intragroup profit becomes realised and is therefore recognised in the current year when this opening inventory – which includes S Ltd's prior year intragroup profit – is sold outside the group in the current year.

Part (c): Pro forma journal entries since acquisition for the 20x6 financial year

SINCE ACQUISITION TO BEGINNING OF THE YEAR/CURRENT YEAR

Pro forma journal 1 (J1)	Dr CU	Cr CU
Retained earnings (S Ltd) (SCIE)	[Wkg1]6 000	
Cost of sales (S Ltd) (P/L)		[Wkg2]6 000
Recognition of prior year elimination of unrealised intragroup profit on sale of inventory to ensure current year opening consolidated retained earnings balance agrees to prior year closing consolidated retained earnings balance, and recognition of prior year unrealised intragroup profit in the current year		

Workings: Pro forma journals

Working 1
36 000 Prior year closing inventory × 20/120 Unrealised profit element

Working 2
36 000 Opening inventory × 20/120 Realised profit element

Pro forma journal 2 (J2)	Dr CU	Cr CU
Retained earnings (S Ltd) (SCIE)	Wkg3 4 200	
Non-controlling interest – Equity (SFP)		Wkg3 4 200
Allocating the non-controlling interest its share of S Ltd's adjusted retained earnings since acquisition to the beginning of the year		

Workings: Pro forma journals

Working 3

(20 000 – 6 000 (J1) Prior year unrealised intragroup profit) × 30% NCI Share

CURRENT YEAR

Pro forma journal 3 (J3)	Dr CU	Cr CU
Sales (S Ltd) (P/L) (given)	180 000	
Cost of sales (S Ltd) (P/L) (balancing figure)		175 500
Inventory (P Ltd) (SFP)		Wkg4 4 500
Elimination of intragroup sales, cost of sales and unrealised intragroup profit in closing inventory		

Workings: Pro forma journals

Working 4

27 000 Closing inventory × 20/120 Unrealised profit

Pro forma journal 4 (J4)	Dr CU	Cr CU
NCI: Share of profit or loss	Wkg5 9 450	
Non-controlling interest – Equity (SFP)		Wkg5 9 450
Allocating the non-controlling interest its share of S Ltd's adjusted current year profit		

Workings: Pro forma journals

Working 5

30 000 Current year profit + 6 000 (J1) Recognition of S Ltd prior year intragroup profit – 4 500 (J3) Elimination of S Ltd current year unrealised intragroup profit) × 30% NCI Share

Comments: Pro forma journal 4

- The non-controlling interest is allocated its appropriate share of the profit of S Ltd, adjusted for the current year recognition of S Ltd's prior year unrealised intragroup profit (which increases S Ltd's profit – see pro forma journal 1) and the elimination of S Ltd's unrealised intragroup profit included closing inventory (which decreases S Ltd's profit – see pro forma journal 3).

The effects of the preceding pro forma journals on the consolidated financial statements are illustrated in the following consolidation worksheet as at 31 December 20x6.

Dr/(Cr)	P Ltd CU	S Ltd CU	Pro forma journals CU	Journal ref	Con-solidated CU
Retained earnings (BOY)	(21 000)	(20 000)	6 000	J1	(30 800)
			4 200	J2	
Profit: Individual entities	(46 000)	(30 000)			
Consolidated profit – attributable to owners of parent					(68 050)
Retained earnings (EOY)	(67 000)	(50 000)			(98 850)
NCI Equity			(10 000)	(given)	(23 650)
			(4 200)	J2	
			(9 450)	J4	
Profit or loss					
Sales	(235 000)	(180 000)	180 000	J3	(235 000)
Cost of sales	189 000	150 000	(6 000)	J1	157 500
			(175 500)	J3	
Gross profit	(46 000)	(30 000)			(77 500)
NCI: Share of profit			9 450	J4	9 450
Consolidated profit attributable to owners of parent					(68 050)
Statement of financial position					
Inventory	27 000	–	(4 500)	J3	22 500

Part (d): Consolidated statement of profit or loss and other comprehensive income for the 20x6 financial year

P LTD GROUP: CONSOLIDATED STATEMENT OF PROFIT OR LOSS AND OTHER COMPREHENSIVE INCOME FOR THE YEAR ENDED 31 DECEMBER 20x6	
	CU
Sales (235 000 (P Ltd) + (S Ltd: 180 000 – 180 000 (J3) Elimination of intragroup sales))	235 000
Cost of sales (189 000 (P Ltd) + (S Ltd: 150 000 – 175 500 (J3) Elimination of intragroup cost of sales – 6 000 (J1) Recognition of prior year intragroup profit))	(157 500)
Gross profit	77 500
PROFIT FOR THE YEAR	**77 500**
Other comprehensive income	–
TOTAL COMPREHENSIVE INCOME FOR THE YEAR	**77 500**
Total comprehensive income attributable to:	
Owners of the parent (balancing figure) **OR** (46 000 (P Ltd) + 22 050 (S Ltd) (see AOE **c**))	68 050
Non-controlling interest (see AOE **d OR** (J4))	9 450
	77 500

Part (e): Extract from the consolidated statement of changes in equity for the 20x6 financial year

EXTRACT: P LTD GROUP CONSOLIDATED STATEMENT OF CHANGES IN EQUITY FOR THE YEAR ENDED 31 DECEMBER 20x6		
	Retained earnings CU	Non-controlling interest CU
Opening balance at 1 Jan 20x6	[Wkg1]30 800	[Wkg2]14 200
Total comprehensive income:		
Profit for the period (from CSOPL_OCI)	68 050	9 450
Closing balance at 31 Dec 20x8	98 850	23 650

Workings: Consolidated statement of changes in equity

Working 1
P Ltd: 21 000 + S Ltd: 9 800 (see AOE a) P Ltd share of S Ltd post-acquisition retained earnings to BOY

OR

P Ltd: 21 000 + (S Ltd: 20 000 Post-acquisition retained earnings to BOY– 6 000 (J1) Elimination of S Ltd prior year unrealised intragroup profit – 4 200 (J2) NCI share of S Ltd post-acquisition retained earnings to BOY)

Working 2
S Ltd: 10 000 (given) NCI share of at acquisition equity + 4 200 (see AOE **b** OR (J2)) NCI share of S Ltd post-acquisition retained earnings to BOY

6.3.5 Tax effects: Elimination of unrealised intragroup profit in closing inventory

When for consolidation purposes, the selling group entity's **unrealised intragroup profit is eliminated** from the purchasing group entity's **closing inventory,** a pro forma **deferred tax adjustment** is required. This is because the elimination of this unrealised intragroup profit creates a deductible temporary difference in terms of IAS 12 *Income Taxes* since the carrying amount of this inventory is decreased, without a corresponding reduction in its base cost. The tax base of the inventory remains unchanged as the tax authority does not recognise the intragroup profit elimination from this inventory for tax purposes.

This deductible temporary difference results in the recognition, on consolidation, of:

- a **deferred tax asset** of the **purchasing group entity** – this is why we **debit** a **deferred tax asset** in the pro forma journal entry passed; and
- a corresponding **reduction** in the **income tax expense** of the **selling group entity** – this is why we **credit income tax expense** in the pro forma journal entry passed.

Another way of understanding the tax effects of the unrealised intragroup profit elimination is to consider its effects on the **group's profit or loss.** Because the **group profit reduces** when eliminating the unrealised intragroup profit of the selling group entity, so **too** must the **group tax expense be reduced** as it is based on this reduced profit. That is, we need to **match group tax expense** to **group profit** for the relevant financial year.

As the entities making up the group are regarded as separate taxpayers, the tax authority will tax an entity within a group on all its profits made on intragroup sales of inventory, including those profits that for group purposes are regarded as unrealised and in respect of which a tax charge is not recognised by the group until such profits are realised in a subsequent reporting period. Therefore, from the group's perspective, the **portion of the tax charge paid** by an **entity in a group** on **unrealised intragroup profit** represents a **prepayment of tax** and therefore a **deferred tax asset**. Consequently, we:

- **debit** a **deferred tax asset** of the purchasing group entity to **record this** prepayment of tax at group level; and
- **credit** the **income tax expense** of the selling group entity, thereby removing the tax charge, attributable to the unrealised intragroup profit that the group has not yet recognised, from the group's tax expense.

Where the selling group entity is a partly owned subsidiary, the non-controlling interest will be allocated its appropriate share of the consolidation adjustment reducing the subsidiary's current year income tax charge with the tax effect of the current year elimination of the subsidiary's intragroup profit.

6.3.6 Tax effects in the current year of the prior year unrealised intragroup profit

At group level, the prior year tax effect of the selling group entity's unrealised intragroup profit elimination is a reduction – by way of a pro forma journal – in the selling group entity's prior year income tax expense. This prior year tax charge reduction increases the selling group entity's prior year profit, which is closed off to consolidated retained earnings at prior year end.

Because pro forma journals are not carried forward to subsequent reporting periods, in the current year, the selling group entity's opening retained earnings balance, which is extracted from its own records, does not include the effects of (i.e., will not have been increased by) the prior year reduction in its income tax expense, recognised in the prior year's consolidation. For this reason, on consolidation in the current year, we need to **credit** the selling group entity's **opening retained earnings balance** in the pro forma journal passed, increasing this balance by the amount of the **prior year reduction** in this entity's **income tax expense**, recognised on consolidation in the prior year.

Furthermore, when the opening inventory acquired intragroup – which includes the selling group entity's prior year unrealised profit – is sold outside the group in the current year, the deductible temporary difference that arose at group level when the unrealised intragroup profit was eliminated from the cost of this inventory in the prior year, now reverses. This causes a current year reversal of the prior year deferred tax asset recognised in respect of this inventory, and results in the current year recognition, for consolidation purposes, of an increased income tax expense of the selling group entity. For this reason, in the current year, we **debit** the selling group entity's **income tax expense** in the pro forma journal passed.

More simply put, for group purposes we recognise the selling group entity's prior year intragroup profit in the current year, which increases the group profit in the current year. As the **group profit increases, so too must the group tax**

expense increase. In this way we recognise a group tax expense that is based on **group/consolidated profit** rather than the profits of the individual entities of the group.

Where the selling group entity is a partly owned subsidiary, the non-controlling interest will be allocated its appropriate share of:

- the consolidation adjustment increasing the subsidiary's opening retained earnings with the prior year tax effect of the prior year elimination of the subsidiary's intragroup profit; and

- the consolidation adjustment increasing the subsidiary's current year income tax charge with the current year tax effect of the current year recognition of the subsidiary's prior year intragroup profit.

Example 6.8: Intragroup sale of inventory by partly owned subsidiary to parent: Unrealised profit in opening and closing inventory and tax effects

The facts for this example are the same as Example 6.7, except that taxation now needs to be taken into account. The income tax rate is 28%.

The facts in Example 6.7 are reproduced below, with the addition of a tax expense line item for both P Ltd and S Ltd.

P Ltd owns 70% of subsidiary S Ltd, which it acquired on 1 January 20x5:

- **S Ltd** sells all its inventory to **P Ltd**.
- **P Ltd** buys all its inventory from **S Ltd**.

The following took place during the financial year ended 31 December 20x5:

- **S Ltd** sold inventory that had cost it CU 100 000 to P Ltd for CU 120 000 (i.e., at a 20% mark-up on cost).
- **P Ltd** sold 70% of this inventory to external parties during 20x5 for CU 105 000.
- **P Ltd** reflected a closing balance for inventory of CU 36 000 in its records as at 31 December 20x5.
- **S Ltd** had a NIL closing balance for inventory on hand in its records as at 31 December 20x5.

The following took place during the financial year ended 31 December 20x6:

- **S Ltd** sold inventory that had cost it CU 150 000, to P Ltd for CU 180 000 (i.e., at a 20% mark-up on cost).
- **P Ltd** sold all its opening inventory as well as 85% of inventory purchased during 20x6 to external parties for CU 235 000.
- **P Ltd** reflected a closing balance for inventory of CU 27 000 in its records as at 31 December 20x6.
- **S Ltd** had a NIL closing balance for inventory on hand in its records as at 31 December 20x6.

➥

In addition, the statements of profit or loss and other comprehensive income for P Ltd and S Ltd were as follows for the 20x5 and 20x6 financial years:

STATEMENTS OF PROFIT OR LOSS AND OTHER COMPREHENSIVE INCOME FOR THE YEAR ENDED 31 DECEMBER 20x5		
	P Ltd	**S Ltd**
	CU	CU
Sales	105 000	120 000
Cost of sales	(84 000)	(100 000)
Gross profit	21 000	20 000
Taxation	(5 880)	(5 600)
PROFIT FOR THE YEAR	**15 120**	**14 400**

STATEMENTS OF PROFIT OR LOSS AND OTHER COMPREHENSIVE INCOME FOR THE YEAR ENDED 31 DECEMBER 20x6		
	P Ltd	**S Ltd**
	CU	CU
Sales	235 000	180 000
Cost of sales	(189 000)	(150 000)
Gross profit	46 000	30 000
Taxation	(12 880)	(8 400)
PROFIT FOR THE YEAR	**33 120**	**21 600**

Required

(a) Prepare the since acquisition pro forma consolidation journal(s) for the financial year ended 31 December 20x5.

(b) Prepare an extract of the analysis of equity of S Ltd as at 31 December 20x6, showing only the analysis of the post-acquisition equity of S Ltd.

(c) Prepare the since acquisition pro forma consolidation journal(s) for the financial year ended 31 December 20x6.

(d) Prepare the consolidated statement of profit or loss and other comprehensive income for the P Ltd group for the financial year ended 31 December 20x6.

(e) Assuming that the non-controlling interest balance that arose on acquisition of S Ltd was CU 10 000, prepare an extract from the consolidated statement of changes in equity for the P Ltd group for the financial year ended 31 December 20x6, showing only the columns for retained earnings and for the non-controlling interest.

Solution 6.8: Intragroup sale of inventory by partly owned subsidiary to parent: Unrealised profit in opening and closing inventory and tax effects

Part (a): Pro forma journal entries since acquisition for the 20x5 financial year

CURRENT YEAR

Pro forma journal 1 (J1)	Dr CU	Cr CU
Sales (S Ltd) (P/L) (given)	120 000	
Cost of sales (S Ltd) (P/L) (balancing figure)		114 000
Inventory (P Ltd) (SFP)		Wkg1 6 000
Elimination of intragroup sales, cost of sales and unrealised intragroup profit in closing inventory		

Workings: Pro forma journals

Working 1

36 000 Closing inventory × 20/120 Unrealised profit element

Pro forma journal 2 (J2)	Dr CU	Cr CU
Deferred tax (P Ltd) (SFP)	Wkg2 1 680	
Income tax expense (S Ltd) (P/L)		Wkg2 1 680
Recognition of tax effect of the elimination of the unrealised intragroup profit		

Workings: Pro forma journals

Working 2

6 000 (J1) × 28%

Comments: Pro forma journal 2

- As CU 6 000 of S Ltd's profit recognised on sale of inventory to P Ltd is unrealised at year end, we eliminate this amount on consolidation as per pro forma journal 1. The effect of this unrealised intragroup profit elimination is to reduce the group profit by CU 6 000. As we calculate the group tax expense based on this group profit, which has been decreased, so too must the tax expense of the group be reduced. This is achieved by crediting S Ltd's income tax expense with CU 1 680 (6 000 Elimination of unrealised profit × 28% Tax rate).

- The debit to deferred tax asset of CU 1 680 recognises a prepayment of tax in respect of S Ltd's unrealised intragroup profit not yet recognised by the group, but which was taxed in the hands of the separate legal entity S Ltd.

- The deferred tax implications of the elimination of unrealised profit in closing inventory can also be explained based on the effect of this elimination on the carrying amount of inventory in the statement of financial position and its related tax base, as per the table below:

	Carrying amount (CA)	Tax base (TB)	Temporary difference (deductible)/ taxable	Deferred tax asset/ (liability) @ 28%
Closing inventory: CA and TB in records of P Ltd	36 000[1]	36 000[1]	–[1]	–[1]
Elimination of unrealised profit – Pro forma journals	(6 000)[2]	–[3]	(6 000)	1 680
Closing inventory: CA and TB for group purposes	30 000[4]	36 000[4]	(6 000)[4]	1 680[4]

Explanatory notes: Table

1. As is clear from the table, in the separate records of P Ltd, the group entity that purchases the inventory intragroup, the carrying amount of inventory on hand at period end of CU 36 000 equals its tax base and there is therefore no deferred tax.

2. From the group's perspective, however, the inventory on hand at period end must be carried at initial cost to the group and consequently, on consolidation, the intragroup profit is eliminated from the closing inventory balance (refer pro forma journal 1), reducing its carrying amount by CU 6 000.

3. As the tax authority does not regard the group as a taxable entity, the CU 6 000 pro forma elimination of S Ltd's unrealised intragroup profit, included in P Ltd's closing inventory, is disregarded for tax purposes, and the tax base of the inventory therefore remains unchanged at CU 36 000.

4. The tax base of the inventory of CU 36 000 is now CU 6 000 greater than its group carrying amount of CU 30 000, resulting in a deductible temporary difference of CU 6 000. This results in the recognition on consolidation in the current year of:
   - a deferred tax asset of P Ltd of CU 1 680, which is the debit entry in pro forma journal 2; and
   - a corresponding CU 1 680 reduction in S Ltd's income tax expense, which is the credit entry in pro forma journal 2.

Pro forma journal 3 (J3)	Dr CU	Cr CU
NCI: Share of profit or loss (P/L)	Wkg³3 024	
Non-controlling interest – Equity (SFP))		Wkg³3 024
Allocating the non-controlling interest its share of S Ltd's adjusted profit for the year		

Workings: Pro forma journals

Working 3

14 400 S Ltd profit (given) – 6 000 (J1) Elimination of S Ltd unrealised intragroup profit + 1 680 (J2) Tax effect: Elimination of S Ltd unrealised intragroup profit) × 30% NCI Share

The effects of the preceding pro forma journals on the consolidated financial statements are illustrated in the following consolidation worksheet as at 31 December 20x5.

Dr/(Cr)	P Ltd CU	S Ltd CU	Pro forma journals CU	Journal ref	Con- solidated CU
Retained earnings (BOY)	–	–	–		–
Profit: Individual entities	(15 120)	(14 400)			
Consolidated profit attributable to owners of parent					(22 176)
Retained earnings (EOY)	(15 120)	(14 400)			(22 176)
			(10 000)	(given)	(13 024)
NCI: Equity			(3 024)	J3	
Profit or loss					
Sales	(105 000)	(120 000)	120 000	J1	(105 000)
Cost of sales	84 000	100 000	(114 000)	J1	70 000
Gross profit	(21 000)	(20 000)			(35 000)
Taxation	5 880	5 600	(1 680)	J2	9 800
Net profit	(15 120)	(14 400)			(25 200)
NCI: Share of profit			3 024	J3	3 024
Consolidated profit attributable to owners of parent					(22 176)
Statement of financial position					
Inventory	36 000	–	(6 000)	J1	30 000
Deferred tax asset			1 680	J2	1 680

Part (b): Post-acquisition analysis of equity (AOE) of S Ltd as at 31 December 20x6

	Total of S Ltd's equity 100%	P Ltd 70% Since acquisition	Non- controlling interest 30%
Since acquisition			
• To beginning of current year:			
Adjusted retained earnings	10 080	7 056 a	3 024 b
Retained earnings movement since acquisition to BOY (given)	14 400	10 080	4 320
Closing inventory prior year: After tax effect of elimination of unrealised intragroup profit [(36 000 × 20/120) × 72%]	(4 320)	(3 024)	(1 296)
• Current year:			
Adjusted profit for the year	22 680	15 876 c	6 804 d
Profit for the year (given)	21 600	15 120	6 480
After tax effect of prior year intragroup profit recognised in current year [(36 000 × 20/120) × 72%]	4 320	3 024	1 296
Closing inventory current year: After tax effect of elimination of unrealised intragroup profit [(27 000 × 20/120) × 72%]	(3 240)	(2 268)	(972)

Part (c): Pro forma consolidation journal entries post acquisition for the 20x6 financial year

SINCE ACQUISITION TO BEGINNING OF THE YEAR/CURRENT YEAR

Pro forma journal 1 (J1)	Dr CU	Cr CU
Retained earnings (S Ltd) (SCIE)	Wkg1 6 000	
Cost of sales (S Ltd) (P/L)		Wkg2 6 000
Recognition of prior year elimination of unrealised intragroup profit on sale of inventory to ensure current year opening consolidated retained earnings balance agrees to prior year closing consolidated retained earnings balance, and current year recognition of prior year unrealised intragroup profit on sale of inventory		

Workings: Pro forma journals

Working 1

36 000 (given) Prior year closing inventory × 20/120 Unrealised profit element

Working 2

36 000 (given) Opening inventory × 20/120 Realised profit element

Pro forma journal 2 (J2)	Dr CU	Cr CU
Income tax expense (S Ltd) (P/L)	Wkg3 1 680	
Retained earnings (S Ltd) (SCIE)		Wkg4 1 680
Tax effect: Recognition of prior year elimination of unrealised intragroup profit on sale of inventory to ensure current year opening consolidated retained earnings balance agrees to prior year closing consolidated retained earnings balance, and recognition of tax effects of current year recognition of prior year unrealised intragroup profit on sale of inventory		

Workings: Pro forma journals

Working 3

6 000 (J1) Prior year intragroup profit recognised × 28%

Working 4

6 000 (J1) Elimination of prior year intragroup profit × 28%

Comments: Pro forma journal 2

- Because S Ltd's prior year unrealised intragroup profit of CU 6 000 is recognised as income of the group in the current year, this increases the group's current year profit (see pro forma journal 1). It makes sense then that the tax expense of the group should also be increased in the current year in line with this CU 6 000 increase in group profit. Accordingly, we debit S Ltd's income tax expense with CU 1 680 (6 000 × 28%) and so increase the group income tax expense by CU 1 680, with this amount being the tax effect of the CU 6 000 prior year intragroup profit which is recognised on consolidation in the current year.

- We can also say that the increase in the group income tax charge in the current year is because the deductible temporary difference that arose in the prior year – when S Ltd's unrealised intragroup profit was eliminated from P Ltd's prior year closing inventory balance – reverses in the current year with the current year sale of the opening inventory (the prior year's closing inventory) to parties outside of the group. This is shown in the following deferred tax table:

	Inventory carrying amount (CA): Group	Inventory Tax base (TB)	Temporary difference (deductible)/ taxable	Deferred tax asset/ (liability) @ 28%
Balance 31 December 20x5 (prior year end)	30 000	36 000	(6 000)	1 680
Sale of opening inventory outside group during 20x6	(30 000)	(36 000)	6 000	(1 680)
Balance 31 December 20x6 (current year end)	NIL	NIL	NIL	NIL

Comments: Pro forma journal 2 (Continued)

- In the prior year's consolidation, the prior year tax effect of eliminating S Ltd's prior year unrealised intragroup profit was a CU 1 680 (6 000 × 28%) prior year reduction in S Ltd's tax charge and therefore a CU 1 680 prior year increase in S Ltd's profit. This profit, in turn, was closed off retained earnings in the prior year consolidated financial statements.

- As we are preparing the consolidated financial statements for the following financial year (20x6 financial year), S Ltd's profit or loss for the current year cannot be adjusted. Rather, for purposes of the current year consolidation, S Ltd's opening retained earnings balance is adjusted (increased) to include the effect of the CU 1 680 prior year reduction, on consolidation, in S Ltd's income tax expense. For this reason we credit S Ltd's opening retained earnings balance with CU 1 680. This ensures that the current year opening consolidated retained earnings balance agrees to the prior year closing consolidated retained earnings balance.

Note: Pro forma journals 1 and 2 above may be combined into the following single pro forma journal shaded in dark grey:

Combined pro forma journal (J1 and J2)	Dr CU	Cr CU
Retained earnings (S Ltd) (SCIE)	Wkg1 4 320	
Income tax expense (S Ltd) (P/L)	Wkg2 1 680	
Cost of sales (P/L) (S Ltd) (balancing figure)		6 000
Recognition of after tax prior year elimination of unrealised intragroup profit on sale of inventory to ensure current year opening consolidated retained earnings balance agrees to prior year closing consolidated retained earnings balance, and recognition in the current year of prior year unrealised intragroup profit on sale of inventory, together with its associated tax effects		

Workings: Combined pro forma journal (CPFJ)

Working 1 CPFJ
36 000 Prior year closing inventory × 20 /120 Unrealised profit component × 72% After tax

Working 2 CPFJ
36 000 Opening inventory × 20 /120 Realised profit component × 28%

SINCE ACQUISITION TO BEGINNING OF THE YEAR

Pro forma journal 3 (J3)	Dr CU	Cr CU
Retained earnings (S Ltd) (SCIE)	Wkg5 3 024	
Non-controlling interest – Equity (SFP)		Wkg5 3 024
Allocating the non-controlling interest its share of S Ltd's adjusted retained earnings to BOY		

Workings: Pro forma journals

Working 5

14 400 (given) Balance since acquisition to BOY – 6 000 (J1) Elimination of S Ltd prior year unrealised intragroup profit + 1 680 (J2) Tax effect: Elimination of S Ltd prior year intragroup profit) × 30% NCI Share

CURRENT YEAR

Pro forma journal 4 (J4)	Dr CU	Cr CU
Sales (S Ltd) (P/L) (given)	180 000	
Cost of sales (S Ltd) (P/L) (balancing figure)		175 500
Inventory (P Ltd) (SFP)		Wkg6 4 500
Elimination of intragroup sales, cost of sales and unrealised intragroup profit in closing inventory		

Workings: Pro forma journals

Working 6

27 000 Closing inventory × 20/120 Unrealised profit

Pro forma journal 5 (J5)	Dr CU	Cr CU
Deferred tax (P Ltd) (SFP)	Wkg7 1 260	
Income tax expense (S Ltd) (P/L)		Wkg7 1 260
Recognition of tax effect of unrealised intragroup profit elimination in closing inventory		

Workings: Pro forma journals

Working 7

4 500 (J4) × 28%

Comments: Pro forma journal 5

- The current year elimination on consolidation of S Ltd's CU 4 500 unrealised intragroup profit (see pro forma journal 4) reduces the current year group profit by CU 4 500. Accordingly, as group profit decreases in the current year, so too must the group tax charge that is recognised be reduced. This is achieved by crediting S Ltd's income tax expense with CU 1 260 (4 500 × 28%) while recognising the corresponding prepayment of tax on the unrealised and therefore unrecognised intragroup profit, by debiting a deferred tax asset of P Ltd with CU 1 260.

- As discussed above, this pro forma journal entry can also be explained on the basis that the group carrying amount of inventory decreases when S Ltd's unrealised intragroup profit included therein is eliminated on consolidation, but the tax base remains unchanged. It will be recalled that this creates a CU 4 500 deductible temporary difference and therefore the recognition, on consolidation, of:

  - a deferred tax asset of P Ltd, the CU 1 260 debit entry; and

  - a corresponding reduction in S Ltd's income tax expense, the CU 1 260 credit entry.

Pro forma journal 6 (J6)	Dr CU	Cr CU
NCI: Share of profit or loss (P/L)	Wkg 8 6 804	
Non-controlling interest – Equity (SFP)		Wkg 8 6 804
Allocating the non-controlling interest its share of S Ltd's adjusted current year profit		

Workings: Pro forma journals

Working 8
(21 600 (given) S Ltd current year profit + 6 000 (J1) Recognition of S Ltd prior year intragroup profit – 1680 (J2) Tax effect: Recognition of S Ltd prior year intragroup profit – 4 500 (J4) Elimination of S Ltd current year unrealised intragroup profit + 1 260 (J5) Tax effect: Elimination of S Ltd current year unrealised intragroup profit) × 30% NCI Share

The effects of the preceding pro forma journals above on the consolidated financial statements are illustrated in the following consolidation worksheet as at 31 December 20x6.

Dr/(Cr)	P Ltd CU	S Ltd CU	Pro forma journals CU	Journal ref	Con-solidated CU
Retained earnings (BOY)	(15 120)	(14 400)	6 000	J1	(22 176)
			(1 680)	J2	
			3 024	J3	
Profit: Individual entities	(33 120)	(21 600)			
Consolidated profit – attributable to owners of parent					(48 996)
Retained earnings (EOY)	(48 240)	(36 000)			(71 172)
NCI: Equity			(10 000)	(given)	(19 828)
			(3 024)	J3	
			(6 804)	J6	
Profit or loss					
Sales	(235 000)	(180 000)	180 000	J4	(235 000)
Cost of sales	189 000	150 000	(6 000)	J1	157 500
			(175 500)	J4	
Taxation	12 880	8 400	1 680	J2	21 700
			(1 260)	J5	
Net profit	(33 120)	(21 600)			(55 800)
NCI: Share of profit			6 804	J6	6 804
Consolidated profit attributable to owners of parent					(48 996)
Statement of financial position					
Inventory	27 000	–	(4 500)	J4	22 500
Deferred tax asset			1 260	J5	1 260

Part (d): Consolidated statement of profit or loss and other comprehensive income 20x6 financial year

P LTD GROUP: CONSOLIDATED STATEMENT OF PROFIT OR LOSS AND OTHER COMPREHENSIVE INCOME FOR THE YEAR ENDED 31 DECEMBER 20x6	
	CU
Sales (235 000 (P Ltd) + (S Ltd: 180 000 – 180 000 (J4) Elimination of intragroup sales))	235 000
Cost of sales (189 000 (P Ltd) + (S Ltd: 150 000 – 175 500 (J4) Elimination of intragroup cost of sales – 6 000 (J1) Recognition of prior year intragroup profit))	(157 500)
Gross profit	77 500
Taxation (12 880 (P Ltd) + (S Ltd: 8 400 + 1 680 (J2) Tax effect: Recognition prior year intragroup profit – 1 260 (J5) Tax effect: Elimination current year unrealised intragroup profit))	(21 700)
PROFIT FOR THE YEAR	**55 800**
Other comprehensive income	–
TOTAL COMPREHENSIVE INCOME FOR THE YEAR	**55 800**
Total comprehensive income attributable to:	
Owners of the parent (balancing figure) **OR** (33 120 (P Ltd) + 15 876 (S Ltd) (see AOE **c**))	48 996
Non-controlling interest (see AOE **d OR** (J6))	6 804
	55 800

Part (e): Extract from the consolidated statement of changes in equity – 20x6 financial year

EXTRACT: P LTD GROUP CONSOLIDATED STATEMENT OF CHANGES IN EQUITY FOR THE YEAR ENDED 31 DECEMBER 20x6	Retained earnings	Non-controlling interest
	CU	CU
Opening balance at 1 January 20x6	Wkg1 22 176	Wkg2 13 024
Total comprehensive income: Profit for the period (from CSOPL_OCI)	48 996	6 804
Closing balance at 31 December 20x8	71 172	19 828

Workings: Consolidated statement of changes in equity

Working 1
P Ltd: 15 120 + S Ltd: 7 056 (see AOE **a**) P Ltd share of S Ltd post-acquisition retained earnings to BOY

OR

P Ltd: 15 120 + (S Ltd: 14 400 – 6 000 (J1) Elimination of S Ltd prior year unrealised intragroup profit + 1 680 (J2) Tax effect: Elimination of S Ltd prior year unrealised intragroup profit – 3 024 (J3) NCI share of S Ltd post-acquisition retained earnings to BOY)

Working 2
S Ltd: 10 000 (given) NCI share of S Ltd at acquisition equity + 3 024 (see AOE **b OR** (J3)) NCI share of S Ltd post-acquisition retained earnings to BOY)

6.3.7 Inventory sold intragroup written down to net realisable value

IAS 2 *Inventories* requires that inventory must be valued at the **lower of** (IAS 2.9):

- **cost**; and
- **net realisable value.**

Where the carrying amount of inventories purchased intragroup, which are on hand in the records of the purchasing group entity, is written down to net realisable value, there will be the following implications on consolidation:

- If the **net realisable value write-down** is **greater than the intragroup profit** that arose on sale, then the inventories will be recorded at a value **lower than cost price to the group.** This then means that **no elimination** of the unrealised intragroup profit on sale is required on consolidation. This is because the net realisable value at which the inventories are recorded in the individual financial statements of the purchasing group group entity is also the correct value for group purposes.
- To the extent that the **unrealised intragroup profit exceeds the write-down to net realisable value,** it must be **eliminated** on consolidation. This is because the carrying amount of the inventories after being written down to net realisable value will still exceed the initial cost of the inventories to the group.

Example 6.9: Inventory sold intragroup written down to net realisable value

During the financial year ended 31 December 20x6, P Ltd sold inventories to its subsidiary S Ltd for CU 80 000, applying a mark-up on cost of 30%. The closing inventories in the records of S Ltd at year end 31 December 20x6 were CU 80 000, which were all purchased from P Ltd. S Ltd did not have any opening inventories.

Required

(a) Determine the effect (if any) on the elimination of the unrealised intragroup profit in the consolidated financial statements if S Ltd writes the inventories down to net realisable value of CU 45 000 at 31 December 20x6.

(b) Determine the effect in the consolidated financial statements if the net realisable value of the inventories at 31 December 20x6 is CU 45 000 but S Ltd does not recognise the net realisable value write down in its own records.

(c) Determine the effect (if any) on the elimination of the unrealised intragroup profit in the consolidated financial statements if S Ltd writes the inventories down to net realisable value of CU 72 000 at 31 December 20x6.

Ignore any tax implications.

Solution 6.9: Inventory sold intragroup written down to net realisable value

Part (a): Effects (if any) on the elimination of the unrealised intragroup profit in the consolidated financial statements if S Ltd writes the inventories down to net realisable value of CU 45 000 at 31 December 20x6

As the write-down amount of CU 35 000 (80 000 Cost to S Ltd – 45 000 Net realisable value) is greater than the unrealised intragroup profit of CU 18 462 (80 000 Closing inventory × 30 / 130 Unrealised profit component), the net realisable value of the inventories of CU 45 000 is now **less than the original cost price of the inventories to the group** of CU 61 538 (80 000 × 100 / 130). Consequently, no further reduction in the value of these inventories is required. This means that *no* pro forma elimination journal is necessary to eliminate P Ltd's unrealised intragroup profit recognised.

Part (b): Effects in the consolidated financial statements if the net realisable value of the inventories at 31 December 20x6 is CU 45 000 but S Ltd does not recognise the net realisable value write down in its own records

As S Ltd has not recognised the write-down to net realisable value in its separate records:

- the unrealised intragroup profit would first need to be eliminated on consolidation; and
- thereafter, the net realisable value write-down would need to be recognised on consolidation by passing a pro forma journal entry.

The pro forma journals required would be as follows:

Pro forma journal 1 (J1)	Dr CU	Cr CU
Sales (S Ltd) (P/L) (given)	80 000	
Cost of sales (S Ltd) (P/L) (balancing figure)		61 538
Inventory (S Ltd) (SFP)		Wkg1 18 462
Elimination of intragroup sales, cost of sales and unrealised intragroup profit in closing inventories		

Workings: Pro forma journals

Working 1
80 000 Closing inventory × 30 / 130 Unrealised profit

Pro forma journal 2 (J2)	Dr CU	Cr CU
Cost of sales (P/L)	Wkg2 16 538	
Inventory (S Ltd) (SFP)		Wkg2 16 538
Inventories written down to net realisable value at reporting period end per IAS 2		

Workings: Pro forma journals

Working 2
80 000 – 18 462 (J1) Unrealised profit – 45 000 Net realisable value

Part (c): Effects (if any) on the elimination of the unrealised intragroup profit in the consolidated financial statements if S Ltd writes the inventories down to net realisable value of CU 72 000 at 31 December 20x6

The net realisable value of the inventories of CU 72 000 exceeds the original cost price to the group of CU 61 538 (80 000 × 100 / 130). Accordingly, the unrealised intragroup profit of CU 18 462 (80 000 closing inventory × 30 / 130 Unrealised profit component) needs to be eliminated on consolidation to the extent that it exceeds the net realisable value write down of CU 8 000 (80 000 – 72 000 Net realisable value). The pro forma journal to eliminate the unrealised intragroup profit will therefore be as follows:

Pro forma journal	Dr CU	Cr CU
Cost of sales (P Ltd) (P/L)	Wkg3 10 462	
Inventory (S Ltd) (SFP)		Wkg3 10 462
Elimination of unrealised intragroup profit in closing inventories		

Workings: Pro forma journal

Working 3
(18 462 Unrealised intragroup profit – 8 000 Net realisable value write-down) **OR** (72 000 Inventory at net realisable value – 61 538 Cost to group)

6.4 Disposals of property, plant and equipment within a group

Intragroup sales are not limited to the sale of inventory. It is common for property, plant and equipment also to be sold within a group. The sale of property, plant and equipment between group entities represents an **internal transaction**, which must be **eliminated** on consolidation as the group cannot sell an asset to itself. Consequently, any profit or loss made by a group entity on the sale of property, plant and equipment intragroup is, from the group's perspective, unrealised and cannot be recognised for group purposes. This means that on consolidation, among other things:

- the **intragroup profit or loss** on sale must be **eliminated**; and
- the **value of the property, plant and equipment** sold intragroup must be reinstated to its **original cost to the group**.

This previously unrealised intragroup profit or loss on disposal of property, plant and equipment does, however, become realised and will be recognised on consolidation:

- when the property, plant and equipment sold intragroup is subsequently **on sold to parties outside the group**; or
- by means of a **subsequent reduction** if sold at a profit, or increase, if sold at a loss, in the **depreciation charge**, recognised for group purposes, on the property, plant and equipment sold intragroup.

The additional consolidation procedures to be performed and pro forma journal entries to be passed will depend on whether the property, plant and equipment sold intragroup is depreciable or not. This, among other things, is dealt with below.

6.4.1 Profit on intragroup disposal of non-depreciable property, plant and equipment

When non-depreciable property, plant and equipment is sold intragroup at a profit, the selling group entity will record a profit on disposal of this property, plant and equipment, while the buying group entity will recognise the property, plant and equipment at its **intragroup cost price**, which cost will **include** the selling group entity's **profit on disposal**. This **full intragroup profit on disposal**, recognised by the selling group entity, must be **eliminated on consolidation** as such a profit will only be regarded as **realised** for group purposes when the non-depreciable asset is sold to a **third party outside the group**. In this regard, pro forma journal entries are passed:

- to **reverse** the **full amount** of the **unrealised intragroup profit** recognised by the selling group entity, thereby **reducing group profit**;
- to **eliminate** the selling group entity's **unrealised intragroup profit included** in the **cost** of the **property, plant and equipment** held by the **buying group entity**; and
- to **adjust (increase)** the **gain on disposal** (or **reduce the loss on disposal**) when the property, plant and equipment that was sold intragroup is eventually disposed of to a **party outside the group**.

As discussed in Section 6.3.4, profits made on the disposal of an asset intragroup will only impact the non-controlling interest when the disposal of the asset (in this case non-depreciable property, plant and equipment) is made by the **subsidiary to the parent** (i.e., an upstream sale) or to **another group entity**. As explained before, this is because the non-controlling interest shares only in the profits and reserves of the **subsidiary**, which profits and reserves are adjusted on consolidation by means of:

- a pro forma journal that eliminates the subsidiary's unrealised intragroup profit recognised on disposal of non-depreciable property, plant and equipment to another group entity; and
- a pro forma journal that recognises the subsidiary's previously unrealised intragroup profit on disposal of non-depreciable property, plant and equipment, in a subsequent reporting period, when the property, plant and equipment is sold outside the group.

 Example 6.10: Non depreciable property, plant and equipment sold intragroup

P Ltd acquired 80% and control of subsidiary S Ltd on 1 January 20x5, when S Ltd was incorporated. On 1 August 20x5 S Ltd sold land that it had purchased for CU 200 000 to P Ltd for CU 280 000. P Ltd sold the land for CU 350 000 to a third party on 31 May 20x6. The reporting period for the group ends on 31 December.

The following extracts from the statements of changes in equity of P Ltd and S Ltd for the 20x5 and 20x6 financial years are provided below:

EXTRACTS: STATEMENT OF CHANGES IN EQUITY FOR THE FINANCIAL YEAR ENDED 31 DECEMBER 20x5	Retained earnings	
	P Ltd	S Ltd
	CU	CU
Balance 1 Jan 20x5	520 000	–
Profit for the year	225 000	190 000
Balance 31 Dec 20x5	745 000	190 000

EXTRACT: STATEMENT OF CHANGES IN EQUITY FOR THE FINANCIAL YEAR ENDED 31 DECEMBER 20x6		
	Retained earnings	
	P Ltd	S Ltd
	CU	CU
Balance 1 Jan 20x6	745 000	190 000
Profit for the year	115 000	95 000
Balance 31 Dec 20x6	860 000	285 000

Required

(a) Prepare the since acquisition pro forma journals for the financial year ended 31 December 20x5.

(b) Prepare an extract of the analysis of equity of S Ltd as at 31 December 20x6, showing only the analysis of the post-acquisition equity of S Ltd.

(c) Prepare the since acquisition pro forma journals for the financial year ended 31 December 20x6.

(d) Prepare the consolidated statement of profit or loss and other comprehensive income for the P Ltd group for the financial year ended 31 December 20x6.

Ignore taxation.

 ## Solution 6.10: Non-depreciable property, plant and equipment sold intragroup

Part (a): Since acquisition Pro forma journal entries for the 20x5 financial year

CURRENT YEAR

Pro forma journal 1 (J1)	Dr CU	Cr CU
Other income [profit on disposal of land] (S Ltd) (P/L)	Wkg1 80 000	
Land (P Ltd) (SFP)		Wkg1 80 000
Elimination of unrealised intragroup profit on sale of land		

Workings: Pro forma journals

Working 1
280 000 – 200 000

Comments: Pro forma journal 1

- Because the land was sold intragroup, the CU 80 000 profit on sale that was recognised by S Ltd is unrealised for group purposes and accordingly must be eliminated on consolidation. For this reason we debit S Ltd's other income with the CU 80 000 unrealised intragroup profit amount. Note that the profit on disposal of the land will ordinarily be included in the line item 'other income' in the profit or loss section of the statement of profit or loss and other comprehensive income.

- P Ltd, the buying group entity, recognises the land purchased from S Ltd at its intragroup cost price of CU 280 000, which amount includes S Ltd's unrealised intragroup profit of CU 80 000. From the group's perspective, however, the carrying amount of the land remains at CU 200 000 (i.e., the cost of the land to the group based on the purchase thereof from an external party). We therefore credit land of P Ltd with the unrealised intragroup profit amount of CU 80 000 and so reinstate it to its original cost to the group of CU 200 000.

Pro forma journal 2 (J2)	Dr CU	Cr CU
NCI: Share of profit or loss (P/L)	Wkg2 22 000	
Non-controlling interest – Equity (SFP)		Wkg2 22 000
Allocating the non-controlling interest its share of S Ltd's adjusted current year profit		

Workings: Pro forma journals

Working 2
(190 000 (given) S Ltd Profit – 80 000 (J1) Unrealised intragroup profit) × 20% NCI Share

Comments: Pro forma journal 2

- As this example deals with an **upstream sale** of property, plant and equipment from subsidiary to parent, it is the **profit of the subsidiary S Ltd** that is affected (reduced) by the intragroup profit elimination (see pro forma journal 1) since it was S Ltd that disposed of the land and recognised the unrealised intragroup profit on sale thereof. Therefore, the non-controlling interest is allocated its appropriate share of S Ltd's profit as **adjusted (reduced)** by S Ltd's unrealised intragroup profit elimination.

The effects of the pro forma journals above on the consolidated financial statements are illustrated in the consolidation worksheet below as at 31 December 20x5.

Dr/(Cr)	P Ltd CU	S Ltd CU	Pro forma journals CU	Journal ref	Con- solidated CU
Retained earnings (BOY)	(520 000)	–			(520 000)
Profit: Individual entities	(225 000)	(190 000)			
Consolidated profit – attributable to owners of parent					(313 000) ←
Retained earnings (EOY)	(745 000)	(190 000)			(833 000)
NCI: Equity			(22 000)	J2	(22 000)
Profit or loss					
Profit on disposal of land	–	(80 000)	80 000	J1	NIL[1]
Profit for the period (excluding S Ltd profit on disposal of land)	(225 000)	(110 000)			(335 000)
Total profit for the period	(225 000)	(190 000)			(335 000)
NCI: Share of profit			22 000	J2	22 000[2]
Consolidated profit attributable to owners of parent					(313 000)
Statement of financial position					
Land	–	280 000	(80 000)	J1	200 000[3]

Explanatory notes: Consolidation worksheet

[1] S Ltd's intragroup profit on sale of the land has been eliminated. The result is that the group correctly reflects no profit on sale of the land as the land has not yet been sold to parties outside the group. That is, S Ltd's profit on sale of the land is unrealised from the group's perspective and accordingly cannot be recognised for group purposes.

[2] The non-controlling interest's share of S Ltd's profit is correctly calculated based on its 20% share of S Ltd's adjusted profit of CU 110 000 (190 000 – 80 000 Elimination of unrealised intragroup profit).

[3] The land is now correctly reflected at CU 200 000, which is its original cost of purchase from parties outside the group, and therefore the cost to the group.

Part (b): Extract of the analysis of equity (AOE) of S Ltd as at 31 December 20x6, showing only the analysis of the post-acquisition equity of S Ltd

Since acquisition	Total of S Ltd's equity 100%	P Ltd 80% Since acquisition	Non-controlling interest 20%
• To beginning of current year:			
Adjusted retained earnings	110 000	88 000	22 000
Retained earnings since acquisition to BOY (given)	190 000	152 000	38 000
Prior year elimination: Unrealised intragroup profit on disposal of land (280 000 – 200 000)	(80 000)[1]	(64 000)	(16 000)
• Current year:			
Adjusted profit for the year	175 000	140 000 **a**	35 000 **b**
Profit for the year (given)	95 000	76 000	19 000
Recognition intragroup profit: Land sold outside group (280 000 – 200 000)	80 000[2]	64 000	16 000

Explanatory notes: Analysis of equity

[1] S Ltd's CU 80 000 prior year intragroup profit, recognised on the sale of land to P Ltd, was unrealised, and was therefore eliminated on consolidation in the prior year, by means of a pro forma journal. This prior year pro forma elimination resulted in a CU 80 000 reduction in S Ltd's prior year profit, which profit was closed off to retained earnings in the prior year consolidated financial statements. Because this prior year pro forma adjustment is not carried forward to subsequent reporting periods, S Ltd's CU 80 000 prior year unrealised intragroup profit is automatically included in its opening retained earnings balance, extracted from its individual financial statements. Accordingly, we eliminate this unrealised prior year intragroup profit of S Ltd on consolidation in the current year by reducing S Ltd's opening retained earnings balance by CU 80 000.

[2] Because the land is sold to parties outside the group in the current year, S Ltd's CU 80 000 prior year unrealised intragroup profit on sale of this land becomes realised for group purposes in the current year. This results in the current year recognition, on consolidation, of this prior year intragroup profit, increasing S Ltd's current year profit by CU 80 000.

Part (c): Since acquisition pro forma journals for the financial year ended 31 December 20x6

SINCE ACQUISITION TO THE BEGINNING OF THE YEAR / CURRENT YEAR

Pro forma journal 1 (J1)	Dr CU	Cr CU
Retained earnings (S Ltd) (SCIE)	Wkg1 80 000	
Other income [profit on sale of land] (S Ltd) (P/L)		Wkg1 80 000
Recognition of prior year elimination of unrealised intragroup profit on disposal of land to ensure consolidated retained earnings balance beginning of the year agrees to balance at the end of the prior year, and recognition of prior year unrealised intragroup profit on sale of land in the current year when realised		

Workings: Pro forma journals

Working 1

280 000 – 200 000

Comments: Pro forma journal 1

- The CU 80 000 debit to S Ltd's opening retained earnings balance decreases this balance by the amount of S Ltd's CU 80 000 prior year unrealised intragroup profit on sale of land to P Ltd. This ensures that the current year opening consolidated retained earnings balance agrees to the prior year closing consolidated retained earnings balance. For further explanation, see the analysis of equity in Part (b) above.

- In the current year (i.e., the 20x6 financial year) when the land is sold to an external party (i.e., outside the group), the following applies:

  - P Ltd records a profit on sale of land in its own records of CU 70 000 (350 000 Selling price – 280 000 Price at which P Ltd purchased the land intragroup from S Ltd).

  - For group purposes, however, the profit should be CU 150 000 (350 000 Selling price – 200 000 Original cost to the group when land was purchased from an external party). By crediting S Ltd's other income (profit on sale of land) with the CU 80 000 prior year unrealised intragroup profit, we recognise the correct current year profit on sale of land of CU 150 000 (70 000 Profit recognised by P Ltd + 80 000 Prior year intragroup profit of S Ltd, per pro forma journal 1 above) in the consolidated financial statements.

Note that the credit passed in pro forma journal 1 increases the profit of the **subsidiary S Ltd, and not P Ltd**. Although P Ltd made the sale to the third party and recorded a profit thereon in its own records, it was S Ltd that sold the land initially. The intragroup profit arising in S Ltd's hands in respect of this sale was initially unrealised and therefore eliminated on consolidation as the land had not been sold outside the group. However, once P Ltd sold the land outside the group in the current year, **S Ltd's** intragroup profit **became realised** and accordingly must be recognised as a profit on sale of land **made by S Ltd.**

SINCE ACQUISITION TO THE BEGINNING OF THE YEAR

	Dr CU	Cr CU
Pro forma journal 2 (J2)		
Retained earnings (S Ltd) (SCIE)	Wkg2 22 000	
Non-controlling interest – Equity (SFP)		Wkg2 22 000
Allocating the non-controlling interest its share of S Ltd's adjusted retained earnings since acquisition to the beginning of the year		

Workings: Pro forma journals

Working 2
(190 000 (given) Post-acquisition retained earnings – 80 000 (J1) Prior year elimination of unrealised intragroup profit on sale of land) × 20% NCI Share

CURRENT YEAR

	Dr CU	Cr CU
Pro forma journal 3 (J3)		
NCI: Share of profit or loss	Wkg3 35 000	
Non-controlling interest – Equity (SFP)		Wkg3 35 000
Allocating the non-controlling interest its share of S Ltd's adjusted current year profit		

Workings: Pro forma journals

Working 3
(95 000 (given) Current year profit + 80 000 (J1) Recognition of prior year intragroup profit on sale of land) × 20% NCI Share

The effects of the preceding pro forma journals on the consolidated financial statements are illustrated in the following consolidation worksheet as at 31 December 20x6.

Dr/(Cr)	P Ltd CU	S Ltd CU	Pro forma journals CU	Journal ref	Con-solidated CU
Retained earnings (BOY)	(745 000)	(190 000)	80 000	J1	(833 000)
			22 000	J2	
Profit: Individual entities	(115 000)	(95 000)			
Consolidated profit attributable to owners of parent					(255 000) ◄
Retained earnings (EOY)	(860 000)	(285 000)			(1 088 000)
NCI: Equity			(22 000)	J2	(57 000)
			(35 000)	J3	
Profit or loss					
Profit on sale of land	(70 000)	–	(80 000)	J1	(150 000)
Profit for the period (excluding P Ltd profit on sale of land)	(45 000)	(95 000)			(140 000)
Total profit for the period	(115 000)	(95 000)			(290 000)
NCI: Share of profit			35 000	J3	35 000
Profit attributable to owners of parent					(255 000) ┘
Statement of financial position					
Land	–	–			–

Part (d): Consolidated statement of profit or loss and other comprehensive income – 20x6 financial year

P LTD GROUP: ABRIDGED CONSOLIDATED STATEMENT OF PROFIT OR LOSS AND OTHER COMPREHENSIVE INCOME FOR THE YEAR ENDED 31 DECEMBER 20x6	
	CU
Profit for the year [115 000 (P Ltd) + (S Ltd: 95 000 + 80 000 (J1) Recognition of prior year intragroup profit on sale of land)]	290 000
Other comprehensive income	–
TOTAL COMPREHENSIVE INCOME FOR THE YEAR	**290 000**
Total comprehensive income attributable to:	
Owners of the parent (balancing figure) **OR** (115 000 (P Ltd) + 140 000 (S Ltd) (see AOE **a**))	255 000
Non-controlling interest (see AOE **b OR** (J3))	35 000
	290 000

6.4.2 Profit on intragroup disposal of depreciable property, plant and equipment

The profit made on the intragroup sale of **depreciable** assets is treated in much the same way for consolidation purposes as non-depreciable assets. That is, the **profit** made by the **selling group entity** is **eliminated in full** and the **cost** of the **depreciable property, plant and equipment** asset purchased by the buying group entity is **reduced** by the **intragroup profit** so that it is reinstated to its carrying amount, immediately prior to its disposal intragroup, which carrying amount is based on its **original cost to the group**.

There are, however, additional implications that arise subsequently when dealing with depreciable assets sold intragroup at a profit, as follows:

- The buying group entity will calculate depreciation on the asset acquired intragroup based on this asset's **intragroup cost price**, which amount includes the selling group entity's unrealised intragroup profit. The intragroup cost price therefore **exceeds** the depreciable asset's **carrying amount**, based on its **original cost**, in the hands of the **selling group entity immediately prior** to this asset's **disposal intragroup**. Accordingly, the buying group entity, in its own records, will record a **higher** depreciation charge for this asset than should be recognised for group purposes (i.e., group depreciation should be based on the asset's original cost to the selling group entity). This means that on consolidation, an additional pro forma journal is required each year, to **reverse this excess depreciation charge** recognised by the buying group entity on the depreciable asset acquired intragroup.

- The selling group entity's unrealised intragroup profit, recognised on disposal of the depreciable asset to other group entities, is realised subsequently for group purposes through the process of depreciation, when the products or services produced by the use of the asset that was sold intragroup are sold to parties outside the group. To be more precise, the **selling group entity's unrealised intragroup profit** is **realised subsequently**, and therefore **recognised for group purposes**, by means of the **reversal on consolidation each year**, of the **excess depreciation** on the **depreciable asset acquired intragroup**, as discussed immediately above.

For example, suppose a parent sells new equipment at the beginning of the year which cost it CU 80 000, to its subsidiary for CU 100 000. The useful life of the equipment at date of sale is five years and the equipment has a NIL residual value. The subsidiary will calculate depreciation on the equipment based on the equipment's intragroup cost price of CU 100 000 and will recognise depreciation thereon of CU 20 000 (100 000 Intragroup cost price / 5-year RUL) per annum until the equipment has been fully depreciated by the end of the fifth year. For consolidation purposes, however, the parent's unrealised intragroup profit of CU 20 000 (100 000 – 80 000) is eliminated and a reduced annual depreciation charge on the equipment of CU 16 000 (80 000 Original cost to group / 5-year RUL) is subsequently recognised each year. Accordingly, on consolidation, one-fifth of the parent's unrealised intragroup profit, an amount of CU 4 000 (20 000 Intragroup profit / 5-year RUL of equipment sold intragroup) becomes realised annually by writing back the CU 4 000 (20 000 Annual depreciation based on intragroup cost – 16 000 Annual depreciation based on original cost to group) excess annual depreciation recognised by the subsidiary (the buying group entity) on the equipment that it acquired intragroup.

Note that the unrealised intragroup profit arising on the intragroup sale of a depreciable asset is also considered realised for group purposes when such asset is sold to **parties outside the group**. This means that there are two ways in which unrealised intragroup profits on depreciable assets may be realised subsequently, namely **through sale to parties outside the group**, or **through usage (i.e., depreciation)**.

Example 6.11: Parent sells depreciable property, plant and equipment to subsidiary

On 1 January 20x5 P Ltd sold a factory building to its subsidiary S Ltd for CU 700 000. P Ltd had purchased the factory building from an external party on 1 January 20x0 for CU 750 000. At that date the building was assessed to have a useful life of 15 years and a NIL residual value. On 1 January 20x5 the carrying amount of the building was CU 500 000 in P Ltd's own accounting records. The estimated remaining useful life of the building measured from 1 January 20x5 was 10 years and the residual value remained NIL. The method of depreciation adopted by all the entities in the group is straight line.

Required
Prepare the post-acquisition pro forma journal entries based on the above information for the financial year ended 31 December 20x5.

Ignore taxation.

Solution 6.11: Parent sells depreciable property, plant and equipment to subsidiary

CURRENT YEAR

Pro forma journal 1 (J1)	Dr CU	Cr CU
Other income [profit on sale of factory building] (P Ltd) (P/L)	Wkg1 200 000	
Factory building (S Ltd) (SFP)		Wkg1 200 000
Elimination of unrealised P Ltd intragroup profit on sale of factory building intragroup		

Workings: Pro forma journals

Working 1
700 000 Selling price – 500 000 Carrying amount

Comments: Pro forma journal 1

- From the group's perspective, as P Ltd's CU 200 000 profit recognised on sale of the factory building to S Ltd is intragroup, it is unrealised, and therefore cannot be recognised. Accordingly, this profit is eliminated on consolidation by debiting P Ltd's other income (profit on sale of factory building) with the CU 200 000 unrealised intragroup profit amount. Note that P Ltd's profit on disposal of the factory building will be included in the line item 'other income' in the profit or loss section of its statement of profit or loss and other comprehensive income.

- S Ltd recorded the cost of the factory building purchased intragroup from P Ltd on 1 January 20x5 at CU 700 000, which amount includes P Ltd's intragroup profit on sale of CU 200 000. However, at this date, the carrying amount of the factory building, based on its original cost to the group of CU 750 000 (that is, when P Ltd purchased the building for CU 750 000 from a party external to the group on 1 January 20x0) was only CU 500 000. We therefore credit factory building of S Ltd with P Ltd's unrealised intragroup profit of CU 200 000 and so reinstate it to its original carrying amount for group purposes of CU 500 000, which amount is based on the factory building's original cost to the group.

Pro forma journal 2 (J2)	**Dr** CU	**Cr** CU
Accumulated depreciation: Factory building (S Ltd) (SFP)	^{Wkg2}20 000	
Depreciation: Factory building (P Ltd) (P/L)		^{Wkg2}20 000
Recognition of realisation of P Ltd intragroup profit on sale of factory building through reduction in factory building depreciation charge		

Workings: Pro forma journals

Working 2

200 000 (J1) Unrealised intragroup profit: sale of factory building / 10 Years remaining useful life (RUL): factory building

Comments: Pro forma journal 2

- S Ltd's annual depreciation charge for the factory building is determined by dividing the factory building's CU 700 000 intragroup cost, by its 10-year remaining useful life at date of acquisition from P Ltd. For group purposes, however, the annual depreciation charge for the factory building must be determined based on its CU 500 000 carrying amount in the hands of P Ltd, just prior to this asset's disposal to S Ltd, divided by its remaining 10-year useful life at the date of its disposal to S Ltd. Accordingly, the excess depreciation recognised by S Ltd for the factory building, because its depreciable cost in S Ltd's hands includes P Ltd's CU 200 000 unrealised intragroup profit, must be eliminated on consolidation over the factory building's ten-year remaining useful life.

- On consolidation each year, the factory building's carrying amount must be increased, in line with the reduction each year in its depreciation expense, as discussed in the previous bulletpoint. This is achieved by debiting accumulated depreciation: factory building, with the excess depreciation expense that is written back each year; this is the debit to accumulated depreciation: factory building, of CU 20 000.

- The corresponding credit of CU 20 000 to depreciation: factory building, reverses the CU 20 000 excess annual depreciation charge recognised by S Ltd on the inflated intragroup cost of the factory building, as discussed in the first bulletpoint. This ensures that the group depreciation charge is based on the original cost of the factory building to the group.

- It is important to understand – as was discussed above – that the **selling group entity's** unrealised intragroup profit that is eliminated, subsequently realises, as the property, plant and equipment asset sold intragroup is used and therefore depreciated by the buying group entity. Applied to this example, on consolidation:

  - it is **P Ltd's unrealised intragroup profit** of CU 200 000 that is eliminated (see pro forma journal 1); and

  - it is **P Ltd's unrealised intragroup profit** that subsequently becomes realised and is recognised each year by means of an annual reduction in the factory building's depreciation charge, recognised over the period that S Ltd, the buying group entity, depreciates the factory building (see pro forma journal 2).

Accordingly, although S Ltd incurs the depreciation charge each year on the factory building, on consolidation:

- we **adjust (increase) P Ltd**, the **selling group entity's profit** each year via the **reversal each year** of the **excess depreciation** on the factory building; and

- we **increase the carrying amount of the factory building each year,** in the hands of **S Ltd,** the **buying group entity**, via a **reduction each year** in the factory building's **accumulated depreciation**.

The effects of the preceding pro forma journals on the consolidated financial statements are illustrated in the following consolidation worksheet as at 31 December 20x5.

Dr/(Cr)	P Ltd CU	S Ltd CU	Pro forma journals CU	Journal ref	Con-solidated CU
Profit or loss					
Profit on sale of factory building	(200 000)	–	200 000	J1	–[1]
Depreciation	–	70 000	(20 000)	J2	50 000[2]
Statement of financial position					
Factory building: Cost	–	700 000	(200 000)	J1	500 000
Factory building: Accumulated depreciation	–	(70 000)	20 000	J2	(50 000)
Factory building: Carrying amount		630 000			450 000[3]

Explanatory notes: Consolidation worksheet

[1] P Ltd's intragroup profit on disposal of the factory building to S Ltd is unrealised and has therefore been correctly eliminated in the consolidated financial statements

[2] The consolidated depreciation charge of CU 50 000 for the factory building correctly reflects a depreciation expense calculated on a carrying amount based on the original cost of the factory building to the group (i.e., 500 000 Carrying amount / 10-year remaining useful life at date of disposal to S Ltd = 50 000) **OR** (750 000 Cost to group / 15-year useful life at acquisition = 50 000).

[3] As the factory building cost the group CU 750 000 on 1 January 20x0 and had a useful life of 15 years at this date, as at 31 December 20x5, six years after its initial acquisition, CU 450 000 (750 000 × 9 / 15) is correctly reflected as the carrying amount of the factory building for group purposes at reporting period end.

6.4.2.1 Effect on the non-controlling interest: Intragroup profit on disposal of depreciable property, plant and equipment

As has been explained previously in this chapter, it is only when a partly owned subsidiary sells an asset to its **parent (an upstream sale)** – or to **another group entity** – that the unrealised intragroup profit on the sale arises in the **hands of the subsidiary**, with the result that the **non-controlling interest is affected** when the necessary consolidation adjustments are made in respect of this intragroup profit.

When an unrealised intragroup profit arises in a partly owned subsidiary in respect of its intragroup sale of depreciable property, plant and equipment to **its parent** or to **another group entity,** the following will occur on consolidation:

- The non-controlling interest will be allocated its appropriate share of the consolidation adjustment, which **eliminates** the **subsidiary's unrealised intragroup profit** on disposal of the depreciable property plant and equipment. This will mean that the subsidiary's profit or loss (or retained earnings, where the unrealised intragroup profit arose in a prior reporting period) will **first be adjusted** on consolidation to eliminate the unrealised intragroup profit included therein, before the non-controlling interest is allocated its appropriate share thereof.

- The non-controlling interest will also be allocated its appropriate share of the consolidation adjustment, which **recognises** the **subsidiary's unrealised intragroup profit in subsequent reporting periods,** when this profit becomes realised, whether by means of a reduction in the depreciation charge of the property, plant and equipment that was sold intragroup, or because of the subsequent disposal of this depreciable property, plant and equipment to parties external to the group.

 Example 6.12: Partly owned subsidiary sells depreciable property, plant and equipment to parent

On 1 January 20x5, when S Ltd was incorporated, P Ltd acquired control over S Ltd by acquiring an 80% shareholding in S Ltd. The share capital of S Ltd at acquisition date was CU 170 000. On 30 June 20x5, S Ltd purchased new plant from an external party for CU 350 000 and immediately sold the plant to P Ltd for CU 500 000. The plant is depreciated at 20% per annum on cost by P Ltd and a has a NIL residual value.

The trial balances of P Ltd and S Ltd for the financial years ended 31 December 20x5 and 20x6 are shown below:

Abridged trial balances at 31 December 20x5	P Ltd Dr/(Cr) CU	S Ltd Dr/(Cr) CU
Share capital	(450 000)	(170 000)
Retained earnings (1 Jan 20x5)	(414 000)	–
Trade and other payables	(100 000)	(25 000)
Plant: Cost	500 000	–
Plant: Accumulated depreciation	(50 000)	–
Trade and other receivables	398 000	406 000
Investment in S Ltd: Cost	176 000	–
Sales	(550 000)	(398 000)
Cost of sales	417 000	273 000
Other Income	–	(168 000)
Depreciation	50 000	–
Income tax expense	23 000	82 000

Abridged trial balances at 31 December 20x6	P Ltd Dr/(Cr) CU	S Ltd Dr/(Cr) CU
Share capital	(450 000)	(170 000)
Retained earnings (1 Jan 20x6)	(474 000)	(211 000)
Trade and other payables	(88 000)	(19 000)
Plant: Cost	500 000	–
Plant: Accumulated depreciation	(150 000)	–
Trade and other receivables	540 000	494 000
Investment in S Ltd: Cost	176 000	–
Sales	(520 000)	(379 000)
Cost of sales	350 000	260 000
Other income	–	(10 000)
Depreciation	100 000	–
Income tax expense	16 000	35 000

Additional information

- At acquisition date the net assets of S Ltd were considered to be fairly valued.
- P elected to measure the non-controlling interest at its proportionate share of S Ltd's identifiable net assets at acquisition date.
- P Ltd recognised its investment in S Ltd in its separate accounting records using the cost price method.
- Ignore tax implications of the intragroup disposal of plant.

Required

(a) Prepare the analysis of equity for S Ltd as at 31 December 20x5.

(b) Provide all the pro forma journal entries necessary to prepare consolidated financial statements for the P Ltd group for the financial year ended 31 December 20x5.

(c) Prepare the consolidated statement of profit or loss and other comprehensive income for the P Ltd group for the financial year ended 31 December 20x5.

(d) Prepare the analysis of equity for S Ltd as at 31 December 20x6.

(e) Provide all the pro forma journal entries necessary to prepare consolidated financial statements for the P Ltd group for the financial year ended 31 December 20x6.

(f) Prepare the consolidated financial statements of the P Ltd group for the financial year ended 31 December 20x6.

 Solution 6.12: Partly owned subsidiary sells depreciable property, plant and equipment to parent

Part (a): Analysis of equity (AOE) of S Ltd as at 31 December 20x5

| | Total of S Ltd's equity 100% | P Ltd 80% | | Non-controlling interest 20% |
		At acquisi-tion	Since acquisi-tion	
At acquisition date (1 January 20x5)	CU	CU	CU	CU
Share capital	170 000	136 000		34 000
Goodwill – Parent (balancing figure)	40 000	40 000 **a**		–
Consideration and non-controlling interest	210 000	176 000		34 000
Since acquisition				
• Current year:				
Adjusted profit for the year	76 000		60 800 **b**	15 200 **c**
Profit for the year (398 000 – 273 000 + 168 000 – 82 000)	211 000		168 800	42 200
Elimination: Unrealised intragroup profit plant (500 000 Selling price – 350 000 Original cost)	(150 000)[1] **d**		(120 000)	(30 000)
Write back of excess depreciation: Plant [(150 000 Unrealised intragroup profit: Plant / 5-year RUL plant) × 6/12]	15 000[2] **e**		12 000	3 000
	286 000		60 800	49 200

CHAPTER 6 Intragroup Transactions and Balances

Explanatory notes: Analysis of equity

[1] As S Ltd's CU 150 000 profit recognised on sale of the plant to P Ltd is intragroup, it is unrealised and consequently it is eliminated in full on consolidation, which reduces S Ltd's current year profit by CU 150 000.

[2] As the plant, which S Ltd sold intragroup at a profit to P Ltd, is used, it is depreciated to reflect such use. Of the total depreciation charge for this plant that is to be recognised in P Ltd's separate accounting records over the plant's remaining useful life of five years, the depreciation attributable to S Ltd's CU 150 000 unrealised intragroup profit, included in the plant's cost, must be reversed on consolidation over this five-year remaining useful life. In this way the group depreciation charge for this plant will be correctly determined, being based on the CU 350 000 initial cost of the plant to the group (i.e., excluding S Ltd's CU 150 000 intragroup profit on sale of plant).

This CU 15 000 is therefore the current year reduction, on consolidation, in the plant's depreciation charge, to ensure that the correct reduced group depreciation charge is recognised for this plant. As the plant was sold by S Ltd to P Ltd midway through the year, we reverse the excess depreciation recognised by P Ltd on this plant for half the year (i.e., for the period 30 June 20x5 to 31 December 20x5).

At group level, this CU 15 000 reversal of excess plant depreciation also represents the realisation, and therefore the recognition, in the current year, of CU 15 000 of S Ltd's CU 150 000 unrealised intragroup profit on sale of plant which was eliminated. Consequently, this CU 15 000 is added back to S Ltd's current year profit since it no longer constitutes an unrealised intragroup profit of S Ltd.

Part (b): Pro forma journal entries for the financial year ended 31 December 20x5

AT ACQUISITION

Pro forma journal 1 (J1)	Dr CU	Cr CU
Share capital (S Ltd) (SCIE) (given)	170 000	
Investment in S Ltd (P Ltd) (SFP) (given)		176 000
Non-controlling interest – Equity (SFP)		Wkg1 34 000
Goodwill (SFP) (balancing figure)	40 000	
Elimination of at acquisition equity and cost of investment and recognition of non-controlling interest and goodwill at acquisition of S Ltd		

Workings: Pro forma journals

Working 1
170 000 × 20% NCI Share

CURRENT YEAR

Pro forma journal 2 (J2)	Dr CU	Cr CU
Other income [profit on disposal of plant] (S Ltd) (P/L)	Wkg2 150 000	
Plant (P Ltd) (SFP)		Wkg2 150 000
Elimination of S Ltd unrealised intragroup profit on sale of plant		

Workings: Pro forma journals

Working 2
500 000 Selling price – 350 000 Cost

Pro forma journal 3 (J3)	Dr CU	Cr CU
Accumulated depreciation: Plant (P Ltd) (SFP)	Wkg3 15 000	
Depreciation: Plant (S Ltd) (P/L)		Wkg3 15 000
Recognition of S Ltd previously unrealised intragroup profit on sale of plant through reduction in plant depreciation charge		

Workings: Pro forma journals

Working 3

(150 000 (J2) Unrealised intragroup profit: Sale of plant / 5-year RUL of plant) × 6/12 Months

Pro forma journal 4 (J4)	Dr CU	Cr CU
NCI: Share of profit or loss (P/L)	Wkg4 15 200	
Non-controlling interest – Equity (SFP)		Wkg4 15 200
Allocating the non-controlling interest its share of S Ltd's adjusted current year profit		

Workings: Pro forma journals

Working 4

(398 000 – 273 000 + 168 000 – 82 000 = 211 000 Current year profit – 150 000 (J2) Elimination unrealised intragroup profit: Sale of plant + 15 000 (J3) Reversal of excess depreciation: Plant sold intragroup) × 20% NCI Share

The full effects of the preceding pro forma journals on the consolidated financial statements are shown in the following consolidation worksheet as at 31 December 20x5.

	P Ltd	S Ltd	Pro forma journals At acquisition		Pro forma journals Since acquisition		Con-solidated
	Dr/(Cr) CU	Dr/(Cr) CU	Dr/(Cr) CU	Journal ref	Dr/(Cr) CU	Journal ref	Dr/(Cr) CU
Equity							
Share capital	(450 000)	(170 000)	170 000	J1			(450 000)
Retained earnings (BOY)							
Profit: Individual entities	(414 000)	(211 000)					(414 000)
Consolidated profit attributable to owners of parent	(60 000)						†(120 800)
Retained earnings (EOY)	(474 000)	(211 000)	(34 000)	J1			(534 800)
NCI Equity	–	–			(15 200)	J4	(49 200)
Total equity	**(924 000)**	**(381 000)**					**(1 034 000)**
Liabilities:							
Trade and other payables	(100 000)	(25 000)					(125 000)
Total liabilities	**(100 000)**	**(25 000)**					**(125 000)**
Total equity & liabilities	**(1 024 000)**	**(406 000)**					**(1 159 000)**
Assets:							
Plant: Cost	500 000	–			(150 000)	J2	350 000
Plant: Accumulated depreciation	(50 000)	–			15 000	J3	(35 000)
Trade and other receivables	398 000	406 000					804 000
Investment in S Ltd	176 000	–	(176 000)	J1			–
Goodwill			40 000	J1			40 000
Total assets	**1 024 000**	**406 000**					**1 159 000**

Explanatory notes

† This amount has been brought forward from the second part of the consolidation worksheet on page 374

	P Ltd	S Ltd	Pro forma journals Since acquisition	Journal ref	Consolidated
	Dr/(Cr) CU	Dr/(Cr) CU	Dr/(Cr) CU		Dr/(Cr) CU
Profit or loss					
Sales	(550 000)	(398 000)			(948 000)
Cost of sales	417 000	273 000			690 000
Other income	–	(168 000)	150 000	J2	(18 000)
Depreciation	50 000	–	(15 000)	J3	35 000
Taxation	23 000	82 000			105 000
Profit for the period	(60 000)	(211 000)			(136 000)
NCI: Share of profit			15 200	J4	15 200
Consolidated profit attributable to owners of parent					‡(120 800)

Explanatory notes

‡ This amount has been carried forward to the first part of the consolidation worksheet on page 373

Part (c): Consolidated statement of profit or loss and other comprehensive income for the 20x5 financial year

P LTD GROUP: CONSOLIDATED STATEMENT OF PROFIT OR LOSS AND OTHER COMPREHENSIVE INCOME FOR THE YEAR ENDED 31 DECEMBER 20x5	
	CU
Sales (550 000 (P Ltd) + 398 000 (S Ltd))	948 000
Cost of sales (417 000 (P Ltd) + 273 000 (S Ltd))	(690 000)
Gross profit	258 000
Other income (S Ltd: 168 000 – 150 000 (see (J2) **OR** AOE **d**) Elimination intragroup profit: Plant)	18 000
Operating expenses (50 000 (P Ltd) – 15 000 (S Ltd) (see (J3) **OR** AOE **e**) Reversal excess depreciation: Plant)	(35 000)
Profit before tax	241 000
Income tax expense (23 000 (P Ltd) + 82 000 (S Ltd))	(105 000)
PROFIT FOR THE YEAR	**136 000**
Other comprehensive income	–
TOTAL COMPREHENSIVE INCOME FOR THE YEAR	**136 000**
Total comprehensive income attributable to:	
Owners of the parent (balancing figure) **OR** [60 000 (P Ltd) + (S Ltd: 60 800 (see AOE **b**))]	120 800
Non-controlling interest (see AOE **c OR** (J4))	15 200
	136 000

Part (d): Analysis of equity (AOE) of S Ltd as at 31 December 20x6

	Total of S Ltd's equity 100%	P Ltd 80%		Non-controlling interest 20%
		At acquisi-tion	Since acquisi-tion	
At acquisition date (1 January 20x5)	CU	CU	CU	CU
Share capital	170 000	136 000		34 000
Goodwill – Parent (balancing figure)	40 000	40 000 a		–
Consideration and non-controlling interest	210 000	176 000		34 000
Since acquisition				
• To the beginning of the year				
Adjusted retained earnings	76 000		60 800 b	15 200 c
Retained earnings since acquisition to BOY (given)	211 000		168 800	42 200
Prior year elimination of unrealised intragroup profit: Plant (500 000 Selling price – 350 000 Original cost)	(150 000)[1]		(120 000)	(30 000)
Prior year write back of excess depreciation: Plant [(150 000 Unrealised profit plant / 5-year RUL plant) × 6/12]	15 000[2]		12 000	3 000
				49 200 d

Part (d): Analysis of equity (AOE) of S Ltd as at 31 December 20x6 (Continued)

	Total of S Ltd's equity 100% CU	P Ltd 80%		Non-controlling interest 20% CU
		At acquisi-tion CU	Since acquisi-tion CU	
• Current year:				
Adjusted profit for the year	124 000		99 200 e	24 800 f
Profit for the year (379 000 – 260 000 + 10 000 – 35 000)	94 000		75 200	18 800
Write back of excess depreciation: Plant (150 000 Unrealised intragroup profit plant / 5-year RUL plant)	30 000³		24 000	6 000
	410 000		**160 000**	**74 000 g**

Explanatory notes: Analysis of equity

¹ S Ltd's CU 150 000 prior year intragroup profit, recognised on the sale of plant to P Ltd, was unrealised and was therefore eliminated on consolidation in the prior year by means of a pro forma journal. Because pro forma journals are not carried forward to subsequent reporting periods, S Ltd's CU 150 000 prior year unrealised intragroup profit is automatically included in its opening retained earnings balance, extracted from its individual financial statements. Accordingly, we eliminate this unrealised prior year intragroup profit of S Ltd, on consolidation in the current year, by reducing S Ltd's opening retained earnings balance by CU 150 000.

² In the prior year, CU 15 000 of S Ltd's CU 150 000 prior year unrealised intragroup profit on sale of plant became realised. This profit realisation occurred by means of a CU 15 000 prior year reduction in the plant's depreciation charge, recognised for group purposes, via a pro forma consolidation adjustment. Consequently, for consolidation purposes in the prior year, S Ltd's profit was increased by CU 15 000. Because pro forma journals are not carried forward to subsequent reporting periods, S Ltd's current year opening retained earnings, extracted from its individual financial statements, will not include this pro forma consolidation adjustment and will therefore be understated by CU 15 000. Accordingly, in the current year on consolidation, we recognise S Ltd's CU 15 000 intragroup profit realised in the prior year by increasing S Ltd's opening retained earnings balance by CU 15 000.

³ This amount is the reversal, on consolidation in the current year, of the CU 30 000 excess current year depreciation recognised in respect of the plant sold intragroup. This amount represents the current year realisation and recognition, for group purposes, of CU 30 000 of S Ltd's CU 150 000 prior year unrealised intragroup profit on sale of the plant to P Ltd. Consequently, this CU 30 000 realised profit is added back to S Ltd's current year profit as it must be recognised in the current year on consolidation, no longer forming part of S Ltd's prior year CU 150 000 unrealised intragroup profit on sale of plant.

Part (e): Pro forma journal entries for the financial year ended 31 December 20x6

AT ACQUISITION

Pro forma journal 1 (J1)	Dr CU	Cr CU
Share capital (S Ltd) (SCIE) (given)	170 000	
Investment in S Ltd (P Ltd) (SFP) (given)		176 000
Non-controlling interest – Equity (SFP)		Wkg1 34 000
Goodwill (SFP) (balancing figure)	40 000	
Elimination of at acquisition equity and cost of investment and recognition of non-controlling interest and goodwill at acquisition of S Ltd		

Workings: Pro forma journals

Working 1
170 000 × 20% NCI Share

SINCE ACQUISITION TO THE BEGINNING OF THE YEAR

Pro forma journal 2 (J2)	Dr CU	Cr CU
Retained earnings (S Ltd) (SCIE)	Wkg2 135 000	
Accumulated depreciation: Plant (P Ltd) (SFP)	Wkg3 15 000	
Plant (P Ltd) (SFP)		Wkg4 150 000
Prior year S Ltd intragroup profit adjustment: sale of plant, to ensure current year opening consolidated retained earnings balance agrees to prior year closing consolidated retained earnings balance, recognition of prior year reduction in accumulated depreciation of plant sold intragroup, and elimination of prior year unrealised S Ltd intragroup profit included in cost of plant acquired by P Ltd		

Workings: Pro forma journals

Working 2
Balancing figure

OR

	CU	
Elimination of S Ltd prior year unrealised intragroup profit: Plant	150 000	(Working 4)
Reversal prior year excess depreciation plant: Recognition of S Ltd prior year intragroup profit	(15 000)	(Working 3)
Balance of S Ltd unrealised intragroup profit plant: Unrecognised at BOY	135 000	

OR

$$150\ 000 \text{ (Working 4) S Ltd prior year unrealised intragroup profit: Plant} \times \frac{4.5 \text{ Years (Plant RUL at BOY)}}{5 \text{ Years (Plant RUL: Date of intragroup acquisition)}}$$

= 135 000 Balance of S Ltd unrealised intragroup profit plant: Unrecognised at BOY

Workings: Pro forma journals

Working 3

(150 000 (Working 4) S Ltd Prior year unrealised intragroup profit: Plant / 5-year RUL plant) × 6/12 Months = 15 000 Reversal prior year excess depreciation plant: Recognition of S Ltd prior year intragroup profit plant

Working 4

500 000 (given) Selling price – 350 000 (given) Original cost = 150 000 S Ltd Prior year unrealised intragroup profit: Plant

Pro forma journal 2 is best explained with the aid of the following table:

	Plant carrying amount: P Ltd	Plant carrying amount: Group	Plant unrealised intragroup profit: Carrying amount	Excess depreciation reversed/ S Ltd intragroup profit realised	Period
	A	B	A – B	A – B	
S Ltd sale of plant to P Ltd 30 June 20x5	500 000	350 000	150 000[1]	–	Since acquisition to BOY
Depreciation 20x5 (for 6 months)	Wkg1(50 000)	Wkg2(35 000)	(15 000)[2]	(15 000)[2]	
Balance 1 January 20x6	**450 000**	**315 000**	**135 000[3]**	**(15 000)[4]**	**Balance BOY**

Workings: Table

Working 1

500 000 (given) Intragroup cost price: Plant / 5-year RUL: Plant × 6/12 Months

Working 2

350 000 initial cost to group: Plant / 5-year RUL: Plant × 6/12 Months

Comments: Pro forma Journal 2

- The debit to retained earnings of CU 135 000 (see table[3] above) is the net adjustment recognised for purposes of the current year consolidation, in respect of:
  - the prior year CU 150 000 **reduction** in group profit (DR retained earnings CU 150 000), arising from the elimination on consolidation of S Ltd's prior year CU 150 000 unrealised intragroup profit recognised on sale of plant to P Ltd (see table[1] above); and
  - the prior year CU 15 000 **increase** in group profit (CR retained earnings CU 15 000), attributable to the prior year realisation and recognition of CU 15 000 of S Ltd's CU 150 000 unrealised intragroup profit on sale of the plant to P Ltd. At group level, this previously unrealised intragroup profit of S Ltd realises in the prior year by means of the CU 15 000 prior year reduction in the depreciation charge for this plant, recognised on consolidation (see table[2] above).

Note: As is clear from the above table, the CU 135 000 debit to retained earnings also represents the portion of S Ltd's CU 150 000 intragroup profit on disposal of the plant that is still unrealised, and that therefore remains unrecognised for group purposes, at the beginning of the current year.

Comments: Pro forma journal 2 (Continued)

- The amount of CU 15 000, debited to accumulated depreciation, is the contra entry to the reversal on consolidation of the CU 15 000 prior year excess depreciation on the plant sold intragroup, for the period since acquisition to the beginning of the current year (see table[4] above).

- The credit to plant of CU 150 000 reinstates the value of the plant to its original cost to the group of CU 350 000, by eliminating from the CU 500 000 cost of the plant recognised by P Ltd, S Ltd's unrealised intragroup profit of CU 150 000 (see table[1] above).

Pro forma journal 3 (J3)	Dr CU	Cr CU
Retained earnings (S Ltd) (SCIE)	[Wkg5]15 200	
Non-controlling interest – Equity (SFP)		[Wkg5]15 200
Allocating the non-controlling interest its share of S Ltd's adjusted post-acquisition retained earnings to the beginning of the year		

Workings: Pro forma journals

Working 5

211 000 (given) post-acquisition retained earnings to BOY – 135 000 (J2) Elimination balance of S Ltd prior year unrealised intragroup profit: plant at BOY) × 20% NCI Share

CURRENT YEAR

Pro forma journal 4 (J4)	Dr CU	Cr CU
Accumulated depreciation: Plant (P Ltd) (SFP)	[Wkg6]30 000	
Depreciation: Plant (S Ltd) (P/L)		[Wkg6]30 000
Recognition of S Ltd previously unrealised intragroup profit on sale of plant through reduction in plant depreciation charge		

Workings: Pro forma journals

Working 6

150 000 (J2) S Ltd Prior year unrealised intragroup profit: Plant / 5-year RUL plant × 1 Year

Pro forma journal 5 (J5)	Dr CU	Cr CU
NCI: Share of profit or loss (P/L)	[Wkg7]24 800	
Non-controlling interest – Equity (SFP)		[Wkg7]24 800
Allocating the non-controlling interest its share of S Ltd's adjusted current year profit		

Workings: Pro forma journals

Working 7

(379 000 – 260 000 + 10 000 – 35 000 = 94 000 Current year profit + 30 000 (J4) Reversal of excess depreciation: Plant) × 20% NCI Share

The full effects of the preceding pro forma journals on the 20x6 consolidated financial statements are shown in the following consolidation worksheet as at 31 December 20x6.

	P Ltd Dr/(Cr) CU	S Ltd Dr/(Cr) CU	Pro forma journals At acquisition Dr/(Cr) CU	Journal ref	Pro forma journals Since acquisition Dr/(Cr) CU	Journal ref	Con-solidated Dr/(Cr) CU
Equity							
Share capital	(450 000)	(170 000)	170 000	J1			(450 000)
Retained earnings (BOY)	(474 000)	(211 000)			135 000	J2	(534 800)
					15 200	J3	
Profit: Individual entities	(54 000)	(94 000)					
Consolidated profit attributable to owners of parent							†(153 200)
Retained earnings (EOY)	(528 000)	(305 000)					(688 000)
NCI Equity	–	–	(34 000)	J1	(15 200)	J3	(74 000)
					(24 800)	J5	
Total equity	(978 000)	(475 000)					(1 212 000)
Liabilities:							
Trade and other payables	(88 000)	(19 000)					(107 000)
Total liabilities	(88 000)	(19 000)					(107 000)
Total equity & liabilities	(1 066 000)	(494 000)					(1 319 000)

Explanatory notes

† This amount has been brought forward from the second part of the consolidation worksheet on page 381

	P Ltd Dr/(Cr) CU	S Ltd Dr/(Cr) CU	Pro forma journals At acquisition Dr/(Cr) CU	Journal ref	Pro forma journals Since acquisition Dr/(Cr) CU	Journal ref	Con-solidated Dr/(Cr) CU
Assets:							
Plant: Cost	500 000	–			(150 000)	J2	350 000
Plant: Accumulated depreciation	(150 000)	–			15 000	J2	(105 000)
					30 000	J4	
Trade and other receivables	540 000	494 000					1 034 000
Investment in S Ltd	176 000	–	(176 000)	J1			–
Goodwill			40 000	J1			40 000
Total assets	**1 066 000**	**494 000**					**1 319 000**
Profit or loss							
Sales	(520 000)	(379 000)					(899 000)
Cost of sales	350 000	260 000					610 000
Other income	–	(10 000)					(10 000)
Depreciation	100 000	–			(30 000)	J4	70 000
Taxation	16 000	35 000					51 000
Profit for the period	(54 000)	(94 000)					(178 000)
NCI: Share of profit					24 800	J5	24 800
Consolidated profit attributable to owners of parent							‡(153 200)

Explanatory notes

‡ This amount has been carried forward to the first part of the consolidation worksheet on page 380

Part (f): Consolidated financial statements for the 20x6 financial year

P LTD GROUP: CONSOLIDATED STATEMENT OF PROFIT OR LOSS AND OTHER COMPREHENSIVE INCOME FOR THE YEAR ENDED 31 DECEMBER 20x6	
	CU
Sales [520 000 (P Ltd) + 379 000 (S Ltd)]	899 000
Cost of sales [350 000 (P Ltd) + 260 000 (S Ltd)]	(610 000)
Gross profit	289 000
Other income (S Ltd)	10 000
Operating expenses	
[100 000 (P Ltd) – S Ltd: 30 000 (J4) Reversal excess depreciation: Plant]	(70 000)
Profit before tax	229 000
Income tax expense [16 000 (P Ltd) + 35 000 (S Ltd)]	(51 000)
PROFIT FOR THE YEAR	**178 000**
Other comprehensive income	–
TOTAL COMPREHENSIVE INCOME FOR THE YEAR	**178 000**
Total comprehensive income attributable to:	
Owners of the parent (balancing figure)	153 200
OR [54 000 (P Ltd) + (S Ltd: 99 200 (see AOE **e**))]	
Non-controlling interest (see AOE **f OR** (J5))	24 800
	178 000

P LTD GROUP: CONSOLIDATED STATEMENT OF CHANGES IN EQUITY FOR THE YEAR ENDED 31 DECEMBER 20x6					
	Parent equity holders' interest				
	Share capital CU	Retained earnings CU	Total parent equity CU	Non-controlling interest CU	Total equity of the group CU
Opening balance at 1 January 20x6	450 000	Wkg1 534 800	984 800	Wkg2 49 200	1 034 000
Total comprehensive income:					
Profit for the period (from CSOPL_OCI)		153 200	153 200	24 800	178 000
Closing balance at 31 December 20x6	450 000	688 000	1 138 000	74 000	1 212 000

Workings: Consolidated statement of changes in equity

Working 1

P Ltd: 474 000 + S Ltd: 60 800 (see AOE **b**) P Ltd share of S Ltd post-acquisition retained earnings to BOY

OR

P Ltd: CU 474 000 + (S Ltd: 211 000 (given) Post-acquisition retained earnings to BOY – 135 000 (J2) Elimination of balance of S Ltd prior year unrealised intragroup profit: Plant at BOY – 15 200 (J3) NCI share of S Ltd post-acquisition retained earnings to BOY)

Working 2

S Ltd: 49 200 (see AOE **d**)

OR

S Ltd: 34 000 (J1) NCI share of S Ltd at acquisition equity + 15 200 (J3) NCI share of S Ltd post-acquisition retained earnings to BOY

P LTD GROUP: CONSOLIDATED STATEMENT OF FINANCIAL POSITION AS AT 31 DECEMBER 20x6	
	CU
Assets	
Non-current assets	
Property, plant and equipment (P Ltd: 350 000 Carrying amount: Plant – 150 000 (J2) Prior year elimination of unrealised intragroup profit: Plant – 15 000 (J2) Prior year reversal of excess accumulated depreciation Plant – 30 000 (J4) Current year reversal of excess accumulated depreciation: Plant)	245 000
Goodwill (see AOE **a** OR (J1))	40 000
Current assets	
Trade and other receivables (540 000 (P Ltd) + 494 000 (S Ltd))	1 034 000
Total assets	**1 319 000**
Equity and liabilities	
Share capital (from CSCIE)	450 000
Retained earnings (from CSCIE)	688 000
Equity attributable to owners of the parent	1 138 000
Non-controlling interest (from CSCIE) **OR** (see AOE **g**)	74 000
Total equity	1 212 000
Current liabilities	
Trade and other payables (88 000 (P Ltd) + 19 000 (S Ltd))	107 000
Total equity and liabilities	**1 319 000**

6.4.3 Tax effects of intragroup disposal of property, plant and equipment: Elimination of unrealised intragroup profit

As you know, when property, plant and equipment is sold intragroup at a profit, the cost of such property, plant and equipment to the purchasing group entity includes the selling group entity's unrealised intragroup profit on sale. As this cost exceeds the initial cost of the property, plant and equipment to the group, on consolidation we **reduce** this cost, **reinstating** the property, plant and equipment to:

- its **original cost** to the group if the property, plant and equipment sold intragroup is **new** (i.e., is yet to be depreciated) or is a **non-depreciable** non-current asset;

- its **carrying amount** based on its **original cost to the group**, if the property, plant and equipment that is disposed of intragroup, has **already been depreciated** by the selling group entity. That is, the **carrying amount** of the property, plant and equipment in the hands of the **selling group entity, just prior** to its **disposal** to **another group entity**.

Even though we reduce the intragroup cost of the property, plant and equipment on consolidation, there is *no* corresponding reduction in the tax base of this property, plant and equipment. This is because the tax authority does not recognise this consolidation adjustment to the intragroup cost of property, plant and equipment, for tax purposes. The result is that on consolidation, a **deductible temporary difference** arises in terms of IAS 12, because the carrying amount of the property, plant and equipment for group purposes is less than its tax base. This, in turn, means that on consolidation we must recognise the associated deferred tax consequences, resulting from this deductible temporary difference. That is, we **debit a deferred tax asset** of the purchasing group entity and **reduce the group's tax charge** by **crediting** the **income tax expense** of the selling group entity.

Alternatively, we can also say that because, from the group's perspective, no profit on sale of the property, plant and equipment has been made on this intragroup sale, the related income tax expense of the separate legal and tax paying group entity that sold the property, plant and equipment intragroup, must be reversed on consolidation. This is done by:

- **crediting** the **income tax expense** of the selling group entity with the **tax effect** of the **elimination** of its **unrealised intragroup profit**; and
- **debiting a deferred tax asset** in order to recognise the tax paid by the selling group entity to the tax authority, on intragroup profit which has not yet been recognised at group level, as a **prepayment of tax** for group purposes.

When the selling group entity is a partly owned subsidiary, the non-controlling interest will be allocated its appropriate share of the consolidation adjustment reducing the subsidiary's current year income tax charge with the tax effect of the elimination of the subsidiary's intragroup profit.

As noted previously in this publication, deferred tax assets and liabilities must be measured in order to reflect the tax consequences that would follow from the manner in which the entity expects to recover or settle the carrying amount of its assets and liabilities (IAS 12.51):

- The carrying amount of **non**-depreciable property, plant and equipment sold intragroup will be recovered by **sale** of the property, plant and equipment, which will have **capital gains tax** consequences. Accordingly, we recognise deferred tax at the **effective capital gains tax rate of 22.4%** (80% × 28%).
- The carrying amount of depreciable property, plant and equipment sold intragroup will be recovered by generating economic benefits through use. Because these economic benefits will be subject to **income tax,** we recognise deferred tax at the **income tax rate of 28%.**

6.4.4 Tax effects: Intragroup profit on disposal of property, plant and equipment is subsequently recognised

As discussed in Section 6.4.1, the selling group entity's unrealised intragroup profit on disposal of **non**-depreciable property, plant and equipment becomes realised and is recognised subsequently for group purposes when this property, plant and equipment is **sold to parties outside the group**. In the period when this external sale occurs, the non-depreciable property, plant and equipment is **derecognised** from the statement of financial position of the group. This causes the **reversal** of the original deductible temporary difference that arose in respect of this non-depreciable property, plant and equipment. The reversal of this deductible temporary difference has the following deferred tax consequences on consolidation:

- We **credit** and so **reverse (derecognise)** the **deferred tax asset** that was recognised in respect of this deductable temporary difference.

- We **debit** the **income tax expense** of the selling group entity and so **increase** the group's tax charge.

Alternatively, we can also say that because the **group profit increases**, with the recognition of previously unrealised intragroup profit, upon sale of the non-depreciable asset externally, **so too** must the **group income tax expense be increased**, and the **deferred tax asset** previously recognised **be reversed**.

As was explained in Section 6.4.2, the previously unrealised intragroup profit in respect of **depreciable** property, plant and equipment sold intragroup, becomes realised, and is **recognised** for group purposes:

- when this depreciable property, plant and equipment is **sold to a third party outside the group**; or
- through a **reduction** in the subsequent **depreciation charge** for such depreciable property, plant and equipment sold intragroup, over its remaining useful life, at the date of its sale to another group entity.

The tax implications of subsequently recognising previously unrealised intragroup profit by subsequently selling depreciable property, plant and equipment to an external party are the same as for non-depreciable assets, as discussed above, and are therefore not repeated.

When the selling group entity's unrealised intragroup profit on sale of a **depreciable** asset is subsequently recognised for group purposes, through a **reduced depreciation charge**, the **deferred tax asset** that arose when the intragroup profit was initially eliminated from this depreciable asset's cost, will **reduce gradually** over this depreciable asset's **remaining useful life**. More particularly, the deductible temporary difference attributable to the unrealised intragroup profit elimination, will **reverse subsequently each reporting period** in line with the **reversal** on consolidation **each reporting period**, of the **excess depreciation** on the asset sold intragroup. This means that, on consolidation each reporting period, over the remaining useful life of the **depreciable** asset sold intragroup, we will need to:

- debit the **selling group entity's income tax expense**, thereby **increasing** the group's **tax charge**; and
- credit the **buying group entity's deferred tax asset**, thereby **reducing** the group's **deferred tax asset**.

We can also say that by **reducing** the **group depreciation charge** each financial year, we are **increasing** the **group profit each year** (profits previously not recognised are now realised each year by way of a reduced depreciation expense). As **group profit increases, so too** must the **group tax expense**. Accordingly, on consolidation, we must pass a pro forma journal each year:

- **debiting** the **selling group entity's income tax expense tax**, thereby recognising the income tax expense in the same period that the group recognises the selling group entity's previously unrealised intragroup profit; and
- **crediting** the **deferred tax asset** previously recognised on the basis of being a prepayment of tax, in line with the reduction of this prepaid tax asset, each successive reporting period that the group recognises the previously unrealised intragroup profit.

When the selling group entity is a partly owned subsidiary, the non-controlling interest will be allocated its appropriate share of the consolidation adjustment each year, increasing the subsidiary's income tax expense with the tax effect of the recognition of a portion of the subsidiary's intragroup profit, which profit realises and is recognised each year through a reduction in the depreciation charge on the property, plant and equipment sold intragroup.

Example 6.13: Partly owned subsidiary sells depreciable property, plant and equipment to parent; tax effects now included – year 1

The facts are the same as for Example 6.12, except that the tax effects of the intragroup profit elimination and subsequent recognition must now be taken into account.

The following additional information is thus provided:

- The tax authority grants an annual deduction, which is apportioned, of 20% of the cost of the plant to P Ltd.
- The income tax rate is 28%.

Also, in this example only the 20x5 financial year is dealt with.

Required

(a) Prepare the analysis of equity for S Ltd as at 31 December 20x5.

(b) Provide all the pro forma journal entries necessary to prepare consolidated financial statements for the P Ltd group for the financial year ended 31 December 20x5.

(c) Prepare the consolidated statement of profit or loss and other comprehensive income for the P Ltd group for the financial year ended 31 December 20x5.

Solution 6.13: Partly owned subsidiary sells depreciable property, plant and equipment to parent; tax effects now included – year 1

See the deferred tax table below and explanatory notes that follow for a detailed explanation of the deferred tax consequences arising on consolidation in the current year, in respect of:

- the current year elimination, on consolidation, of S Ltd's unrealised intragroup profit on sale of its plant to P Ltd; and
- the current year realisation and recognition, on consolidation, of a portion of this unrealised intragroup profit of S Ltd.

Deferred tax table

	Carrying amount plant: P Ltd	Carrying amount plant: Group	Tax base plant: P Ltd & Group	Deductible/(Taxable) temporary difference: Group	Deferred tax: Asset/(Liability): Group	Pro forma journal reference	Period
	A	B	C	C – B = D	D × 28%		
Cost 30 Jun 20x5	500 000[1]	350 000[2]	500 000[3]	150 000[4]	42 000[5]	J3	Current year
Depreciation/tax allowance 20x5 (30 Jun 20x5 – 31 Dec 20x5)	Wgk1(50 000)[6]	Wkg2(35 000)[7]	(50 000)[8]	(15 000)[9]	(4 200)[10]	J5	
Balance 31 Dec 20x5	**450 000**	**315 000**	**450 000**	**135 000**	**37 800[11]**		**End of year**

Workings: Deferred tax table

Working 1
500 000 / 5 Years RUL × 6/12 Months

Working 2
350 000 / 5 Years RUL × 6/12 Months

Explanatory notes: Deferred tax table

On consolidation, we eliminate from the CU 500 000 (see deferred tax table[1]) cost of the plant acquired intragroup by P Ltd, S Ltd's CU 150 000 unrealised intragroup profit. Consequently, for group purposes, the plant is recognised at its original cost to the group of CU 350 000 (see deferred tax table[2]). Because the tax authority does *not* recognise this accounting adjustment to the plant's cost for tax purposes, there is *no* corresponding reduction in the plant's CU 500 000 (see deferred tax table[3]) tax base. As the plant's unchanged tax base of CU 500 000 exceeds by CU 150 000 its CU 350 000 carrying amount for group purposes, this creates a CU 150 000 (see deferred tax table[4]) deductible temporary difference at group level. This CU 150 000 deductible temporary difference, in turn, results in the current year recognition, on consolidation of:

- a deferred tax asset of P Ltd of CU 42 000 (see deferred tax table[5]); and
- a corresponding CU 42 000 current year reduction in S Ltd's income tax expense.

P Ltd, the purchasing group entity, recognises depreciation based on the CU 500 000 intragroup cost of the plant, which cost includes the CU 150 000 unrealised intragroup profit of the selling group entity, namely S Ltd. The tax authority grants a tax deduction each year equivalent to P Ltd's depreciation charge. These amounts are equivalent as the cost of the plant for tax purposes is the same as the cost to P Ltd and because the annual tax deduction is also 20% per annum, pro-rated. Therefore, in P Ltd's separate financial statements, the carrying amount and tax base of the plant will be equal and accordingly no temporary difference will arise, which means that there are *no* deferred tax effects for P Ltd.

For group purposes, however, we depreciate the plant based on its original cost to the group of only CU 350 000, rather than its higher intragroup cost of CU 500 000. Therefore, on consolidation in the current year, we reverse the CU 15 000 excess depreciation on the plant, recognised by P Ltd in its separate financial statements. This means that the CU 50 000 (see deferred tax table[6]) current year tax deduction in respect of the plant is CU 15 000 more than the CU 35 000 (see deferred tax table[7]) current year group depreciation charge recognised for the plant. At group level, this causes a CU 15 000 (see deferred tax table[9]) current year reversal of the CU 150 000 deductible temporary difference that arose in respect of the plant sold intragroup. For consolidation purposes, this CU 15 000 deductible temporary difference reversal results in the current year:

- reversal, of CU 4 200 (see deferred tax table[10]) of the CU 42 000 deferred tax asset recognised in respect of the plant sold intragroup; and

- a corresponding CU 4 200 current year increase in S Ltd's income tax expense.

The net deferred tax effects in the current year, of:

- the elimination, on consolidation, of S Ltd's CU 150 000 unrealised intragroup profit on sale of plant to P Ltd; and

- the subsequent realisation and recognition, on consolidation, of CU 15 000 of this intragroup profit, by means of a CU 15 000 reduction in the plant depreciation charge are a CU 37 800 (42 000 – 4 200) net decrease in the group's current year income tax charge, and a corresponding CU 37 800 (see deferred tax table[11]) deferred tax asset of the group, recognised at reporting period end.

Part (a): Analysis of equity (AOE) of S Ltd as at 31 December 20x5

| | Total of S Ltd's equity 100% | P Ltd 80% | | Non-controlling interest 20% |
| | | At acquisi-tion | Since acquisi-tion | |
At acquisition date (1 January 20x5)	CU	CU	CU	CU
Share capital	170 000	136 000		34 000
Goodwill – Parent (balancing figure)	40 000	40 000a		–
Consideration and non-controlling interest	210 000	176 000		34 000
Since acquisition				
• Current year:				
Adjusted profit for the year	113 800		91 040b	22 760c
Profit for the year (398 000 – 273 000 + 168 000 – 82 000)	211 000		168 800	42 200
Elimination: Unrealised intragroup profit plant (500 000 – 350 000)	(150 000)		(120 000)	(30 000)
Tax effect: Elimination unrealised intragroup profit plant (150 000 × 28%)	42 000		33 600	8 400
Write back of excess depreciation: Plant [(150 000 Unrealised intragroup profit: Plant / 5-year RUL plant) × 6/12]	15 000		12 000	3 000
Tax effect: Write back of excess depreciation: Plant (15 000 × 28%)	(4 200)		(3 360)	(840)
	323 800		**91 040**	**56 760**

Part (b): Pro forma journal entries for the year ended 31 December 20x5

AT ACQUISITION

Pro forma journal 1 (J1)	Dr CU	Cr CU
Share capital (S Ltd) (SCIE) (given)	170 000	
Investment in S Ltd (P Ltd) (SFP) (given)		176 000
Non-controlling interest – Equity (SFP)		Wgk1 34 000
Goodwill (SFP) (balancing figure)	40 000	
Elimination of at acquisition equity and cost of investment, and recognition of non-controlling interest and goodwill, at acquisition of S Ltd		

Workings: Pro formal journals

Working 1
170 000 × 20% NCI Share

CURRENT YEAR

Pro forma journal 2 (J2)	Dr CU	Cr CU
Other income [profit on disposal of plant] (S Ltd) (P/L)	Wgk2 150 000	
Plant (P Ltd) (SFP)		Wgk2 150 000
Elimination of S Ltd unrealised intragroup profit on sale of plant		

Workings: Pro formal journals

Working 2
500 000 Selling price – 350 000 Original cost to group

Pro forma journal 3 (J3)	Dr CU	Cr CU
Deferred tax (P Ltd) (SFP) [see deferred tax table[5]]	Wgk3 42 000	
Income tax expense (S Ltd) (P/L)		Wgk3 42 000
Tax effects: Elimination of S Ltd unrealised intragroup profit on sale of plant		

Workings: Pro formal journals

Working 3
150 000 (J2) × 28%

Pro forma journal 4 (J4)	Dr CU	Cr CU
Accumulated depreciation: Plant (P Ltd) (SFP)	Wgk4 15 000	
Depreciation: Plant (S Ltd) (P/L)		Wgk4 15 000
Recognition of realisation of S Ltd intragroup profit plant through reduced group depreciation charge on plant		

Workings: Pro formal journals

Working 4
(150 000 (J2) Unrealised intragroup profit: Plant / 5-year RUL plant) × 6/12 Months

Pro forma journal 5 (J5)	Dr CU	Cr CU
Income tax expense (S Ltd) (P/L)	Wgk54 200	
Deferred tax (P Ltd) (SFP) [see deferred tax table[10]]		Wgk54 200
Tax effects: Recognition of realisation of S Ltd intragroup profit plant through reduced group depreciation charge on plant		

Workings: Pro formal journals

Working 5
15 000 (J4) × 28%

Pro forma journal 6 (J6)	Dr CU	Cr CU
NCI: Share of profit or loss (P/L)	Wkg622 760	
Non-controlling interest – Equity (SFP)		Wkg622 760
Allocating the non-controlling interest its share of current year profit of S Ltd		

Workings: Pro formal journals

Working 6
(398 000 – 273 000 + 168 000 – 82 000 = 211 000 Current year profit – 150 000 (J2) Elimination of unrealised intragroup profit: Plant + 42 000 (J3) Tax effect: Elimination of unrealised intragroup profit: Plant + 15 000 (J4) Reversal of excess depreciation: Plant – 4 200 (J5) Tax effect: Reversal of excess depreciation: Plant) × 20% NCI Share

The full effects of the preceding pro forma journals on the 20x5 consolidated financial statements are shown in the following consolidation worksheet as at 31 December 20x5.

	P Ltd Dr/(Cr) CU	S Ltd Dr/(Cr) CU	Pro forma journals At acquisition Dr/(Cr) CU	Journal ref	Pro forma journals Since acquisition Dr/(Cr) CU	Journal ref	Con-solidated Dr/(Cr) CU
Equity							
Share capital	(450 000)	(170 000)	170 000	J1			(450 000)
Retained earnings (BOY)	(414 000)	–					(414 000)
Profit: Individual entities	(60 000)	(211 000)					
Consolidated profit – attributable to owners of parent							†(151 040)
Retained earnings (EOY)	(474 000)	(211 000)					(565 040)
NCI Equity	–		(34 000)	J1	(22 760)	J6	(56 760)
Total equity	(924 000)	(381 000)					(1 071 800)
Liabilities:							
Trade and other payables	(100 000)	(25 000)					(125 000)
Total liabilities	(100 000)	(25 000)					(125 000)
Total equity & liabilities	(1 024 000)	(406 000)					(1 196 800)
Assets:							
Plant: Cost	500 000	–			(150 000)	J2	350 000
Plant: Accumulated depreciation	(50 000)	–			15 000	J4	(35 000)
Trade and other receivables	398 000	406 000					804 000
Investment in S Ltd	176 000	–	(176 000)	J1			–
Goodwill			40 000	J1			40 000
Deferred tax					42 000	J3	37 800
					(4 200)	J5	
Total assets	1 024 000	406 000					1 196 800

Explanatory notes

† This amount has been brought forward from the second part of the consolidation worksheet on page 392

	P Ltd Dr/(Cr) CU	S Ltd Dr/(Cr) CU	Pro forma journals At acquisition Dr/(Cr) CU	Journal ref	Pro forma journals Since acquisition Dr/(Cr) CU	Journal ref	Con-solidated Dr/(Cr) CU
Profit or loss							
Sales	(550 000)	(398 000)					(948 000)
Cost of sales	417 000	273 000					690 000
Other income	–	(168 000)			150 000	J2	(18 000)
Depreciation	50 000	–			(15 000)	J4	35 000
Taxation	23 000	82 000			(42 000)	J3	67 200
					4 200	J5	
Net profit for the period	(60 000)	(211 000)					(173 800)
NCI: Share of profit					22 760	J6	22 760
Consolidated profit attributable to owners of parent							‡(151 040)

Explanatory notes

‡ This amount has been carried forward to the first part of the consolidation worksheet on page 391

Part (c): Consolidated statement of profit or loss and other comprehensive income for the 20x5 financial year

P LTD GROUP CONSOLIDATED STATEMENT OF PROFIT OR LOSS AND OTHER COMPREHENSIVE INCOME FOR THE YEAR ENDED 31 DECEMBER 20X5	
	CU
Sales (550 000 (P Ltd) + 398 000 (S Ltd))	948 000
Cost of sales (417 000 (P Ltd) + 273 000 (S Ltd))	(690 000)
Gross profit	258 000
Other income	18 000
(S Ltd: 168 000 – 150 000 (J2) Elimination intragroup profit: Plant)	
Operating expenses	(35 000)
(50 000 (P Ltd) – (S Ltd: 15 000 (J3) Reversal excess depreciation: Plant))	
Profit before tax	241 000
Income tax expense	(67 200)
(23 000 (P Ltd) + (S Ltd: 82 000 – 42 000 (J3) Tax effect: Elimination of unrealised intragroup profit: Plant + 4 200 (J5) Tax effect: Recognition of intragroup profit: Plant))	
PROFIT FOR THE YEAR	**173 800**
Other comprehensive income	–
TOTAL COMPREHENSIVE INCOME FOR THE YEAR	**173 800**
Total comprehensive income attributable to:	
Owners of the parent (balancing figure)	151 040
OR (60 000 (P Ltd) + S Ltd: 91 040 (see AOE **b**))	
Non-controlling interest (see AOE **c OR** (J6))	22 760
	173 800

Example 6.14: Partly owned subsidiary sells depreciable property, plant and equipment to parent; tax effects now included – year 2

The facts are the same as for Example 6.12, except that the tax effects of the intragroup profit elimination and subsequent recognition must now be taken into account.

The following additional information is thus provided:

- The tax authority grants an annual deduction, which is apportioned, of 20% of the cost of the plant to P Ltd.
- The income tax rate is 28%.

Also, in this example, only the 20x6 financial year is dealt with.

Required

(a) Prepare the analysis of equity for S Ltd as at 31 December 20x6.

(b) Provide all the pro forma journal entries necessary to prepare consolidated financial statements for the P Ltd group for the financial year ended 31 December 20x6.

(c) Prepare the consolidated financial statements of the P Ltd group for the financial year ended 31 December 20x6.

Solution 6.14: Partly owned subsidiary sells depreciable property, plant and equipment to parent; tax effects now included – year 2

Part (a): Analysis of equity (AOE) of S Ltd as at 31 December 20x6

| | Total of S Ltd's equity 100% | P Ltd 80% | | Non-controlling interest 20% |
| | | At acquisi-tion | Since acquisi-tion | |
At acquisition date (1 January 20x5)	CU	CU	CU	CU
Share capital	170 000	136 000		34 000
Goodwill – Parent (balancing figure)	40 000	40 000a		–
Consideration and non-controlling interest	210 000	176 000		34 000
Since acquisition				
• To the beginning of the year				
Adjusted retained earnings	113 800		91 040b	22 760c
Retained earnings since acquisition to BOY (given)	211 000		168 800	42 200
Prior year elimination unrealised profit: Plant (500 000 – 350 000)	†(150 000)[1]		(120 000)	(30 000)
Tax effect: Prior year elimination unrealised profit: Plant (150 000 × 28%)	†42 000[1]		33 600	8 400
Prior year reversal excess depreciation: Plant [(150 000 / 5-year RUL) × 6/12]	‡15 000[2]		12 000	3 000
Tax effect: Prior year reversal excess depreciation: Plant (15 000 × 28%)	‡(4 200)[2]		(3 360)	(840)
				56 760d
• Current year:				
Adjusted profit for the year	115 600		92 480e	23 120f
Profit for the year (379 000 – 260 000 + 10 000 – 35 000)	94 000		75 200	18 800
Reversal excess depreciation: Plant (150 000 / 5-year RUL)	₮30 000[3]		24 000	6 000
Tax effect: Reversal excess depreciation plant (30 000 × 28%)	₮(8 400)[3]		(6 720)	(1 680)
	439 400		183 520	79 880g

† After tax net (reduction) of CU 108 000[1]

‡ After tax net increase of CU 10 800[2]

₮ After tax net increase of CU 21 600[3]

Explanatory notes: Analysis of equity

[1] The prior year after tax effect of the prior year elimination, on consolidation, of S Ltd's CU 150 000 unrealised intragroup profit on sale of plant to P Ltd, was a CU 108 000 (150 000 Unrealised intragroup profit × 72% After tax) decrease in S Ltd's prior year profit, which was closed off to retained earnings in the prior year consolidated financial statements. As this prior year consolidation adjustment, processed by means of a pro forma journal, is not

carried forward to subsequent reporting periods, S Ltd's opening retained earnings balance in the current year will not include this consolidation adjustment and will accordingly be overstated by CU 108 000 for group purposes. Consequently, we process this prior year after tax consolidation adjustment in the current year by decreasing S Ltd's opening retained earnings balance by CU 108 000.

2   The prior year after tax effect of the prior year recognition, on consolidation, of CU 15 000 of S Ltd's CU 150 000 unrealised intragroup profit on disposal of plant to P Ltd, was a CU 10 800 (15 000 Reversal of excess depreciation × 72% After tax) after tax increase in S Ltd's prior year profit, which was closed off to retained earnings in the prior year consolidated financial statements. As this prior year consolidation adjustment, processed by means of a pro forma journal, is not carried forward to subsequent reporting periods, S Ltd's opening retained earnings balance in the current year will not include this consolidation adjustment and will accordingly be understated by CU 10 800 for group purposes. Consequently, we process this prior year after tax consolidation adjustment in the current year by increasing S Ltd's opening retained earnings by CU 10 800.

3   The current year reversal, on consolidation, of CU 30 000 excess depreciation recognised by P Ltd on the plant acquired intragroup, results in the current year recognition, for group purposes, of CU 30 000 of S Ltd's previously unrealised intragroup profit, thereby increasing S Ltd' and the group's current year profit by CU 30 000. Because the group profit has increased, there must be a corresponding increase in the group tax expense recognised. This is achieved by increasing S Ltd's current year income tax expense by CU 8 400 (30 000 Recognised intragroup profit × 28%) on consolidation. Consequently, on consolidation, the after tax effect of the current year recognition of S Ltd's intragroup profit is a CU 21 600 (30 000 Reversal of excess depreciation × 72% After tax) current year increase in S Ltd's profit.

Part (b): Pro forma journal entries for the 20x6 financial year

AT ACQUISITION

Pro forma journal 1 (J1)	Dr CU	Cr CU
Share capital (S Ltd) (SCIE) (given)	170 000	
Investment in S Ltd (P Ltd) (SFP) (given)		176 000
Non-controlling interest – Equity (SFP)		Wkg134 000
Goodwill (SFP) (balancing figure)	40 000	
Elimination of at acquisition equity and cost of investment and recognition of non-controlling interest and goodwill at acquisition of S Ltd		

Workings: Pro forma journals

Working 1

170 000 × 20% NCI Share

SINCE ACQUISITION TO BEGINNING OF THE YEAR

Pro forma journal 2 (J2)	Dr CU	Cr CU
Retained earnings (S Ltd) (SCIE) (S Ltd)	Wkg2135 000	
Accumulated depreciation: Plant (P Ltd) (SFP)	Wkg315 000	
Plant (P Ltd) (SFP)		Wkg4150 000
Prior year S Ltd intragroup profit adjustment: Sale of plant, to ensure current year opening consolidated retained earnings balance agrees to prior year closing consolidated retained earnings balance, recognition of prior year reduction in accumulated depreciation of plant sold intragroup, and elimination of prior year unrealised S Ltd intragroup profit included in cost of plant acquired by P Ltd		

Workings: Pro forma journals

Working 2

Balancing figure

OR

	CU	
Elimination of S Ltd prior year unrealised intragroup profit: Plant	150 000	(Working 4)
Reversal prior year excess depreciation plant: recognition of S Ltd prior year intragroup profit, plant	(15 000)	(Working 3)
Balance of S Ltd unrealised intragroup profit plant: Unrecognised at BOY	135 000	

OR

150 000 (Working 4) S Ltd prior year unrealised intragroup profit: Plant × $\frac{\text{4.5 Years (Plant RUL at BOY)}}{\text{5 Years (Plant RUL: Date of intragroup acquisition)}}$

= 135 000 Balance of S Ltd unrealised intragroup profit plant: Unrecognised at BOY

Working 3

(150 000 (Working 4) S Ltd Prior year unrealised intragroup profit: Plant / 5-year RUL plant) × 6/12 Months = 15 000 Reversal prior year excess depreciation plant: recognition of S Ltd prior year intragroup profit, plant

Working 4

500 000 (given) Selling price – 350 000 (given) Original cost = 150 000 S Ltd Prior year unrealised intragroup profit: Plant

Pro forma journal 3 (J3)	Dr CU	Cr CU
Deferred tax (P Ltd) (SFP)	Wkg537 800	
Retained earnings (S Ltd) (SCIE)		Wkg537 800
Tax adjustments intragroup profit: Plant, to ensure current year opening consolidated retained earnings balance agrees to prior year closing consolidated retained earnings balance		

Workings: Pro forma journals

Working 5

135 000 (J2) Balance of S Ltd unrealised intragroup profit plant: Unrecognised at BOY × 28%

Pro forma journal 3 above is best explained with the aid of the following deferred tax table:

	Plant Carrying amount: P Ltd	Plant Carrying amount: Group	Plant Tax base: P Ltd & Group	Deductible/ (Taxable) temporary difference: Group	Deferred tax asset/ (Liability): Group	Period
	A	B	C	C – B = D	D × 28%	
Cost 30 June 20x5	500 000	350 000	500 000	150 000	42 000	Since acquisition to BOY
Depreciation /tax allowance 20x5	Wkg1(50 000)	Wkg2(35 000)	Wkg3(50 000)	(15 000)	(4 200)	
Balance 1 Jan 20x6	**450 000**	**315 000**[1]	**450 000**[2]	**135 000**[3]	**37 800**[4]	**Balance BOY**

Workings: Deferred tax table

Working 1
500 000 (given) Intragroup cost: Plant / 5-year RUL plant, at date of acquisition from S Ltd × 6/12 Months

Working 2
350 000 (given) Initial cost to group: Plant / 5-year RUL plant, at date of acquisition from S Ltd × 6/12 Months

Working 3
500 000 (given) Intragroup cost: Plant / 5-year write off period for tax, at date of acquisition from S Ltd × 6/12 Months

Comments: Pro forma journal 3

- At the beginning of the current year, of the CU 150 000 S Ltd prior year unrealised intragroup profit that arose on S Ltd's prior year disposal of plant to P Ltd, an amount of CU 135 000 is still unrealised, and has therefore been eliminated on consolidation from the carrying amount of this plant (see pro forma journal 2 above).

- This CU 135 000 unrealised intragroup profit elimination, in turn, means that at the beginning of the current year, a deductible temporary difference of CU 135 000 (see deferred tax table[3]) exists at group level in respect of the plant sold intragroup. That is, at the beginning of the current year, the plant's tax base of CU 450 000 (see deferred tax table[2]) exceeds by CU 135 000 its group carrying amount of CU 315 000 (see deferred tax table[1]), giving rise to this CU 135 000 deductible temporary difference at group level. Consequently, on consolidation in the current year, we debit a deferred tax asset with CU 37 800 (see deferred tax table[4]) in order to recognise the CU 37 800 (135 000 deductible temporary difference × 28%) deferred tax asset that exists at group level at the beginning of the current year, in connection with the plant sold intragroup.

- We pass the contra credit of CU 37 800 to S Ltd's opening retained earnings since we are preparing the consolidated financial statements for the following financial period and cannot therefore process the consolidation adjustment, which pertains to the prior period, to S Ltd's current year income tax expense.

Pro forma journal 4 (J4)	Dr CU	Cr CU
Retained earnings (S Ltd) (SCIE)	Wkg6 22 760	
Non-controlling interest – Equity (SFP)		Wkg6 22 760
Allocating the non-controlling interest its share of S Ltd's adjusted post-acquisition retained earnings to the beginning of the year		

Workings: Pro forma journals

Working 6

(211 000 (given) Post-acquisition retained earnings to BOY – 135 000 (J2) Elimination of balance of S Ltd unrealised intragroup profit plant at BOY + 37 800 (J3) Tax effect: Elimination of balance of S Ltd unrealised intragroup profit plant at BOY) × 20% NCI Share

CURRENT YEAR

Pro forma journal 5 (J5)	Dr CU	Cr CU
Accumulated depreciation: Plant (P Ltd) (SFP)	Wkg7 30 000	
Depreciation: Plant (S Ltd) (P/L)		Wkg7 30 000
Current year recognition of realisation of S Ltd intragroup profit: Plant through current year reduction in depreciation charge plant		

Workings: Pro forma journals

Working 7

150 000 (J2) S Ltd Prior year unrealised intragroup profit: Plant / 5-year RUL plant × 1 Year

Pro forma journal 6 (J6)	Dr CU	Cr CU
Income tax expense (S Ltd) (P/L)	Wkg8 8 400	
Deferred tax (P Ltd) (SFP)		Wkg8 8 400
Tax effect: Current year recognition of S Ltd intragroup profit: Plant, through current year reduction in depreciation charge plant		

Workings: Pro forma journals

Working 8
30 000 (J5) × 28%

Comments: Pro forma journal 6

- The reversal, on consolidation, of CU 30 000 current year excess depreciation recognised by P Ltd, on the plant acquired intragroup, results in the current year realisation and recognition, for group purposes, of CU 30 000 of S Ltd's previously unrealised intragroup profit, increasing group profit by CU 30 000.

- In line with this increase in the current year group profit, the group income tax expense must also be increased. This is achieved by debiting and so increasing S Ltd's, and therefore the group's, current year income tax expense by CU 8 400 (CU 30 000 Recognition of S Ltd intragroup profit × 28%).

- The contra credit entry of CU 8 400 to the deferred tax asset of P Ltd reduces, by a further CU 8 400, the prior year CU 42 000 deferred tax asset of the group that initially arose in respect of the prior year intragroup sale of the plant.

This pro forma journal can also be explained using the following deferred tax table:

	Carrying amount: P Ltd	Carrying amount: Group	Tax base: P Ltd & Group	Deductible/ (Taxable) temporary difference: Group	Deferred tax asset/ (Liability): Group	Period
	A	B	C	C − B = D	D × 28%	
Balance 1 Jan 20x6	450 000	315 000	450 000	135 000	37 800	Balance BOY
Depreciation/ tax allowance 20x6	Wkg1(100 000)	Wkg2(70 000)[1]	Wkg3(100 000)[2]	(30 000)[3]	(8 400)[4]	Current year
Balance 31 Dec 20x6	**350 000**	**245 000**	**350 000**	**105 000**	**29 400**	**Balance EOY**

Workings: Deferred tax table

Working 1
500 000 (given) Intragroup cost: Plant / 5-year RUL plant, at date of acquisition from S Ltd × 1 Year

Working 2
350 000 (given) Initial cost to group: Plant / 5-year RUL plant, at date of acquisition from S Ltd × 1 Year

Working 3
500 000 (given) Intragroup cost: Plant / 5-year write off period for tax, at date of acquisition from S Ltd × 1 Year

Comments: Pro forma journal 6 (continued)

- In the current year a further CU 30 000 (see deferred tax table[3]) of the deductible temporary difference that arose for group purposes in respect of the plant sold intragroup in the prior year, reverses out. This is because the current year tax deduction in respect of this plant, of CU 100 000 (see deferred tax table[2]) is CU 30 000 more than the CU 70 000 (see deferred tax table[1]) current year group depreciation charge recognised for this plant.

- The effect on consolidation of this current year CU 30 000 deductible temporary difference reversal is:

  - a CU 8 400 (deferred tax table[4]) current year reduction in the deferred tax asset that initially arose at group level in respect of the prior year intragroup sale of the plant. For this reason we credit P Ltd's deferred tax asset with CU 8 400, thereby reducing the group's deferred tax by CU 8 400; and

  - a corresponding CU 8 400 current year increase in the group's income charge. For this reason we debit the income tax expense of S Ltd with CU 8 400, thereby increasing the group's current year income tax charge by CU 8 400.

Pro forma journal 7 (J7)	Dr CU	Cr CU
NCI: Share of profit or loss (P/L)	Wkg9 23 120	
Non-controlling interest – Equity (SFP)		Wkg9 23 120
Allocating the non-controlling interest its share of S Ltd's adjusted current year profit		

Working 9
(379 000 − 260 000 + 10 000 − 35 000 = 94 000 Current year profit + 30 000 (J5) Reversal of excess depreciation: Plant − 8 400 (J6) Tax effect: Reversal of excess depreciation, plant) × 20% NCI Share

The full effects of the preceding pro forma journals on the 20x6 consolidated financial statements are shown in the following consolidation worksheet as at 31 December 20x6.

	P Ltd Dr/(Cr) CU	S Ltd Dr/(Cr) CU	Pro forma journals At acquisition Dr/(Cr) CU	Journal ref	Pro forma journals Since acquisition Dr/(Cr) CU	Journal ref	Consolidated Dr/(Cr) CU
Equity							
Share capital	(450 000)	(170 000)	170 000	J1			(450 000)
Retained earnings (BOY)	(474 000)	(211 000)			135 000 / (37 800) / 22 760	J2 / J3 / J4	(565 040)
Profit: Individual entities	(54 000)	(94 000)					
Consolidated profit attributable to owners of parent							†(146 480)
Retained earnings (EOY)	(528 000)	(305 000)					(711 520)
NCI Equity	–	–	(34 000)	J1	(22 760) / (23 120)	J4 / J7	(79 880)
Total equity	(978 000)	(475 000)					(1 241 400)
Liabilities:							
Trade and other payables	(88 000)	(19 000)					(107 000)
Total liabilities	(88 000)	(19 000)					(107 000)
Total equity & liabilities	(1 066 000)	(494 000)					(1 348 400)
Assets:							
Plant: Cost	500 000	–			(150 000)	J2	350 000
Plant: Accumulated depreciation	(150 000)	–			15 000 / 30 000	J2 / J5	(105 000)

Explanatory notes

† This amount has been brought forward from the second part of the consolidation worksheet on page 401

	P Ltd Dr/(Cr) CU	S Ltd Dr/(Cr) CU	Pro forma journals At acquisition Dr/(Cr) CU	Journal ref	Pro forma journals Since acquisition Dr/(Cr) CU	Journal ref	Con-solidated Dr/(Cr) CU
Trade and other receivables	540 000	494 000					1 034 000
Investment in S Ltd	176 000	–	(176 000)	J1			–
Goodwill			40 000	J1			40 000
Deferred tax					37 800	J3	29 400
					(8 400)	J6	
Total assets	**1 066 000**	**494 000**					**1 348 400**
Profit or loss							
Sales	(520 000)	(379 000)					(899 000)
Cost of sales	350 000	260 000					610 000
Other income	–	(10 000)					(10 000)
Depreciation	100 000	–			(30 000)	J5	70 000
Taxation	16 000	35 000			8 400	J6	59 400
Profit for the period	(54 000)	(94 000)					(169 600)
NCI: Share of profit					23 120	J7	23 120
Consolidated profit attributable to owners of parent							‡(146 480)

Explanatory notes

‡ This amount has been carried forward to the first part of the consolidation worksheet on page 400

Part (c): Consolidated financial statements for the 20x6 financial year

P LTD GROUP: CONSOLIDATED STATEMENT OF PROFIT OR LOSS AND OTHER COMPREHENSIVE INCOME FOR THE YEAR ENDED 31 DECEMBER 20x6	
	CU
Sales (520 000 (P Ltd) + 379 000 (S Ltd))	899 000
Cost of sales (350 000 (P Ltd) + 260 000 (S Ltd))	(610 000)
Gross profit	289 000
Other income (S Ltd)	10 000
Operating expenses (100 000 (P Ltd) – S Ltd: 30 000 (J4) Reversal excess depreciation: Plant)	(70 000)
Profit before tax	229 000
Income tax expense (16 000 (P Ltd) + (S Ltd: 35 000 + 8 400 (J6) Tax effect: Reversal excess depreciation: Plant)	(59 400)
PROFIT FOR THE YEAR	**169 600**
Other comprehensive income	**–**
TOTAL COMPREHENSIVE INCOME FOR THE YEAR	**169 600**
Total comprehensive income attributable to:	
Owners of the parent (balancing figure) OR (54 000 (P Ltd) + S Ltd: 92 480 (see AOE **e**))	146 480
Non-controlling interest (see AOE **f** OR (J7))	23 210
	169 600

P LTD GROUP: CONSOLIDATED STATEMENT OF CHANGES IN EQUITY FOR THE YEAR ENDED 31 DECEMBER 20x6					
	Parent equity holders' interest			Non-controlling interest	Total equity of the group
	Share capital CU	Retained earnings CU	Total parent equity CU	CU	CU
Opening balance at 1 Jan 20x6	450 000	Wkg1565 040	1 015 040	Wkg256 760	1 071 800
Total comprehensive income:					
Profit for the period (from CSOPL_OCI)		146 480	146 480	23 120	169 600
Closing balance at 31 Dec 20x6	450 000	711 520	1 161 520	79 880	1 241 400

Workings: Consolidated statement of changes in equity

Working 1
P Ltd: 474 000 + S Ltd: 91 040 (see AOE **b**) P Ltd's share of the post-acquisition retained earning to BOY of S Ltd

OR

P Ltd: 474 000 + (S Ltd: 211 000 (given) Post-acquisition retained earnings to BOY – 135 000 (J2) Elimination of balance of prior year unrealised intragroup profit, plant, at BOY + 37 800 (J3) Tax effect: Elimination of balance of prior year unrealised intragroup profit, plant, at BOY – 22 760 (J4) NCI share of post-acquisition retained earnings to BOY of S Ltd)

Working 2
S Ltd: 56 760 (see AOE **d**)

OR

S Ltd: 34 000 (J1) NCI share of S Ltd at acquisition equity + 22 760 (J4) NCI share of post-acquisition retained earnings to BOY of S Ltd

P LTD GROUP: CONSOLIDATED STATEMENT OF FINANCIAL POSITION AS AT 31 DECEMBER 20X6	
	CU
Assets	
Non-current assets	
Property, plant and equipment (P Ltd: 350 000 – 150 000 (J2) Elimination prior year unrealised intragroup profit: Plant + 15 000 (J2) Prior year reversal excess accumulated depreciation: Plant + 30 000 (J5) Current year reversal excess accumulated depreciation: Plant)	245 000
Goodwill (see AOE **a OR** (J1))	40 000
Deferred tax (P Ltd: 37 800 (J3) Balance BOY – 8 400 (J6) Tax effect: Current year reversal excess depreciation: Plant)	29 400
Current assets	
Trade and other receivables (540 000 (P Ltd) + 494 000 (S Ltd))	1 034 000
Total assets	1 348 400
Equity and liabilities	
Share capital (from CSCIE)	450 000
Retained earnings (from CSCIE)	711 520
Equity attributable to owners of the parent	1 161 520
Non-controlling interest (from CSCIE) **OR** (see AOE **g**)	79 880
Total equity	1 241 400
Current liabilities	
Trade and other payables (88 000 (P Ltd) + 19 000 (S Ltd))	107 000
Total equity and liabilities	1 348 400

6.4.5 Impairment of property, plant and equipment sold intragroup at a loss

IAS 36 *Impairment of Assets* requires that we test if certain assets (e.g., property, plant and equipment and intangible assets) are impaired if impairment indicators exist. The sale of property, plant and equipment intragroup at a **loss** is one such impairment indicator. This means that we need to test the property, plant and equipment sold intragroup at a loss for possible impairment by establishing its recoverable amount and comparing this to its carrying amount. IAS 36 explains that the recoverable amount of an asset is the **higher** of its (IAS 36.18):

- **fair value less cost of disposal**; and its
- **value in use.**

If the property, plant and equipment sold intragroup at a loss is in fact found to be impaired (i.e., its recoverable amount is less than its carrying amount), then this loss (or a part thereof) on the intragroup sale, recognised by the selling group entity:

- is **not** eliminated on consolidation; and
- is simply **reclassified** from 'loss on sale' to 'impairment loss'.

Should the sale of the property, plant and equipment intragroup at a loss *not* indicate that the asset is impaired, then the **full intragroup loss** recognised by the selling group entity will be unrealised for group purposes and will therefore be eliminated on consolidation. These concepts are best explained in the examples that follow.

 Example 6.15: Parent sells property, plant and equipment to subsidiary at a loss: No impairment

P Ltd acquired control over S Ltd a number of years ago. On 31 December 20x5, the financial year end of the group, P Ltd sold equipment to S Ltd for CU 75 when the equipment had:

- a carrying amount of CU 90;
- a fair value less cost of disposal of CU 70; and
- value in use of CU 110.

Required
Prepare the pro forma journal entry in light of the above information for the financial year ended 31 December 20x5.

Ignore taxation.

 Solution 6.15: Parent sells property, plant and equipment to subsidiary at a loss: No impairment

Pro forma journal	Dr CU	Cr CU
Equipment (S Ltd) (SFP)	Wkg1 15	
Loss on sale (P Ltd) (P/L)		Wkg1 15
Elimination of unrealised intragroup loss on sale of property, plant and equipment		

Workings: Pro forma journals
Working 1
90 Carrying amount – 75 Selling price

Comments: Pro forma journal
- The equipment sold intragroup at a loss is not impaired because its recoverable amount of CU 110 (which is the higher of its value in use of CU 110 and its fair value less cost of disposal of CU 70) is greater than its carrying amount of CU 90. Accordingly, no impairment of the equipment is required. This means that the loss on the intragroup sale must be eliminated in full on consolidation.
- Although S Ltd bought the equipment from P Ltd for CU 75, the asset's carrying amount from a group perspective must be based on its original cost to the group when P Ltd acquired the equipment from a party outside the group. Since this equipment was not impaired, on consolidation, it should be reinstated to its carrying amount of CU 90 in the hands of P Ltd just prior to its intragroup disposal to S Ltd. This is achieved by debiting equipment of S Ltd with CU 15.
- As the CU 15 intragroup loss on disposal of equipment, recognised by P Ltd, is unrealised, it does not represent an actual loss for group purposes and must therefore be eliminated on consolidation. This is achieved by crediting P Ltd's loss on disposal of the equipment with CU 15.

Example 6.16: Parent sells property, plant and equipment to subsidiary at a loss: Property, plant and equipment impaired

P Ltd acquired control over S Ltd a number of years ago. On 31 December 20x5, the financial year end of the group, P Ltd sold equipment to S Ltd for CU 75, when the equipment had:

- a carrying amount of CU 90;
- a fair value less cost of disposal of 75; and
- a value in use of CU 65.

Required
Prepare the pro forma journal entry in light of the above information for the financial year ended 31 December 20x5.

Ignore taxation.

 ## Solution 6.16: Parent sells property, plant and equipment to subsidiary at a loss: Property, plant and equipment impaired

Pro forma journal	Dr CU	Cr CU
Impairment loss (P Ltd) (P/L)	Wkg1 15	
Loss on sale (P Ltd) (P/L)		Wkg1 15
Reclassification of loss on sale of property, plant and equipment to impairment loss		

Workings: Pro forma journals
Working 1
90 Carrying amount – 75 Recoverable amount

Comments: Pro forma journal
- In this instance, the recoverable amount of the equipment is CU 75, this being the higher of its value in use of CU 65 and its fair value less cost of disposal of CU 75. Because the carrying amount of the equipment of CU 90 is greater than its recoverable amount of CU 75, the equipment is considered to be impaired by CU 15 (90 Carrying amount – 75 Recoverable amount).
- As the equipment is impaired, the intragroup loss on sale, recognised by P Ltd, is not eliminated but is recognised as an impairment loss instead. This is purely a classification issue for disclosure purposes and therefore has no effect on P Ltd's profit.
- Accordingly, on consolidation, the CU 15 intragroup loss on sale of equipment recognised by P Ltd is reallocated to an impairment loss account by crediting P Ltd's loss on sale of equipment with CU 15 and debiting an impairment loss with CU 15.

Example 6.17: Parent sells property, plant and equipment to subsidiary at a loss: Loss on disposal greater than impairment of property, plant and equipment

P Ltd acquired control over S Ltd a number of years ago. On 31 December 20x5, the financial year end of the group, P Ltd sold equipment to S Ltd for CU 75 when the equipment had:

- a carrying amount of CU 90;
- a fair value less costs of disposal of CU 70; and
- a value in use of CU 82.

Required

Prepare the pro forma journal entry in light of the above information for the financial year ended 31 December 20x5.

Ignore taxation.

Solution 6.17: Parent sells property, plant and equipment to subsidiary at a loss: Loss on disposal greater than impairment of property, plant and equipment

Pro forma journal	Dr CU	Cr CU
Impairment loss: (P Ltd) (P/L)	Wkg1 8	
Equipment (S Ltd) (SFP)	Wkg2 7	
Loss on sale (P Ltd) (P/L)		Wkg3 15
Elimination of unrealised intragroup loss on sale of equipment and reclassification of a portion of this loss as an impairment loss		

Workings: Pro forma journals

Working 1

90 Carrying amount – 82 Recoverable amount

Working 2

82 Recoverable amount – 75 Intragroup cost

Working 3

8 Reclassified as impairment + 7 Eliminated as unrealised

Comments: Pro forma journal

- In this instance, the recoverable amount of the equipment is CU 82, this being the higher of its value in use of CU 82 and its fair value less costs of disposal of CU 70. Because the carrying amount of the equipment of CU 90 is greater than its recoverable amount of CU 82, the equipment is considered to be impaired by CU 8 (90 Carrying amount – 82 Recoverable amount).

- Therefore, of the total CU 15 intragroup loss on sale of equipment, recognised by P Ltd, CU 8 is an impairment loss that must be recognised by the group. This is done by debiting an impairment loss of CU 8 and crediting P Ltd's loss on sale of equipment with CU 8, thereby reclassifying this loss as an impairment loss.

- Although S Ltd bought the equipment from P Ltd for CU 75, the group regards the value of the equipment as being CU 82, which is the equipment's recoverable amount. Accordingly, on consolidation, the cost of S Ltd's equipment must be increased by CU 7 (82 Recoverable amount – 75 Cost of acquisition intragroup from P Ltd) in order to recognise this equipment at its CU 82 recoverable amount. For this reason we debit S Ltd's cost of equipment with CU 7.

- We eliminate the remaining CU 7 (15 Total loss on sale – 8 Portion reclassified as an impairment loss) intragroup loss on sale of equipment, recognised by P Ltd, as this loss does not represent an impairment loss and is therefore unrealised for group purposes. For this reason we credit P Ltd's loss on sale of equipment with CU 7.

6.5 Change in use of assets when sold between group entities

Situations may arise where there is a **change in use** of an asset sold intragroup as follows:

- An asset that is regarded by one entity in the group as **inventory** is sold to another entity in the group that classifies it as **property, plant and equipment.**

- An asset that is regarded by one entity in the group as **property, plant and equipment** is sold to another entity in the group that classifies it as **inventory.**

6.5.1 Change in use of asset sold intragroup: Inventory of seller becomes property, plant and equipment of buyer

Where a subsidiary sells inventory at a profit to its parent that the parent will use as depreciable property, plant and equipment, then the following will apply in the separate accounting records of these two group entities:

- The subsidiary, in its own accounting records, will record the **sale of the inventory** and the associated **cost of sales**, and will recognise the resulting **intragroup profit** on sale of inventory.

- The parent will recognise the asset acquired as **property, plant and equipment** at its **intragroup acquisition cost** – which includes the subsidiary's intragroup profit – and will depreciate the property, plant and equipment based on this **intragroup acquisition cost.**

For group purposes, however, the following adjustments will be required on consolidation:

- The subsidiary's **profit on sale** of the inventory is intragroup and is therefore unrealised and must be **eliminated** on consolidation by reversing the intragroup transaction, that is, by **eliminating** the **inventory sale** and the **associated cost of sale.**

- The **cost to the group** of the asset must be the **original cost** when first acquired by the subsidiary, meaning that the **unrealised intragroup profit** of the subsidiary, included in the cost of the property, plant and equipment acquired by the parent, must be **removed.**

- The **group depreciation charge** on the property, plant and equipment acquired by the parent must be based on the **original cost** of the asset to the group. That is, based on the original cost when first acquired by the subsidiary, and not on the higher intragroup purchase price. This means that the **excess depreciation** recognised by the parent on the property, plant and equipment acquired intragroup must be **written back each year.**

- The unrealised intragroup profit of the subsidiary that was eliminated on consolidation will become realised, and therefore **recognised subsequently** for group purposes, by means of a **reduction** on consolidation, in the **depreciation charge** for the property, plant and equipment acquired intragroup.

- Given that the cost of the property, plant and equipment acquired intragroup is reduced for group purposes to the initial cost to the group, without a corresponding reduction in its tax base, a **deductible temporary difference will arise** (i.e., the asset's tax base will exceed its carrying amount for group purposes). This will give rise to a **deferred tax asset of the group** and a corresponding **decrease in** the **group tax charge**.

- The **subsidiary's unrealised intragroup profit** is subsequently recognised each reporting period, through a **reduction** in the **group depreciation charge** on the **asset sold intragroup**. This means that above-mentioned deductible temporary difference will reverse, **reducing** the **deferred tax asset initially recognised** and causing a corresponding **increase** in the **group tax expense each reporting period**.
- Because the unrealised intragroup profit arises **in the subsidiary**, the non-controlling interest's share of the profit and post-acquisition reserves of the subsidiary must be **adjusted** for the non-controlling interest's:
  - share of the after tax effect of the elimination from the subsidiary's profit or loss of its unrealised intragroup profit on sale of inventory; and
  - share of the after tax effect of the subsequent recognition each year of a portion of the subsidiary's previously unrealised intragroup profit, which realises each year through a reduction in the depreciation charge recognised for the asset sold intragroup.

It should be noted that if the **parent** sold inventory to its subsidiary (i.e., a downstream sale) that the subsidiary used as property, plant and equipment, the adjustments required on consolidation would be the **same as for an upstream sale**, as discussed in the points above, *except* that the non-controlling interest would *not* be allocated any share of the consolidation adjustments to the parent's profit and reserves.

 Example 6.18: Change in use from inventory to property, plant and equipment: Partly owned subsidiary sells to parent

P Ltd acquired an 80% controlling interest in S Ltd on 1 January 20x5, when S Ltd was incorporated. Assume that the non-controlling interest that arose on acquisition of the subsidiary was CU 25 000. S Ltd sold an item of inventory that it has manufactured at a cost of CU 100 000 to P Ltd for CU 160 000 on 1 July 20x5. S Ltd's profit of CU 60 000 was taxed by the revenue authority at 28% during the financial year ended 31 December 20x5. P Ltd intended to use the item as machinery with a useful life of five years and NIL residual value on 1 July 20x5. Tax deductions may be claimed by P Ltd on the machinery at 20% per annum, apportioned, based on the cost of the machinery to P Ltd of CU 160 000.

The abridged statements of profit or loss and extracts from the statements of changes in equity for P Ltd and its subsidiary S Ltd, for the 20x5 and 20x6 financial years, are shown below.

STATEMENTS OF PROFIT OR LOSS FOR THE YEAR ENDED 31 DECEMBER 20X5		
	P Ltd CU	S Ltd CU
Sales	350 000	380 000
Cost of sales	(240 000)	(237 500)
Gross profit	110 000	142 500
Depreciation	(16 000)	–
Profit before tax	94 000	142 500
Taxation	(26 320)	(39 900)
PROFIT FOR THE YEAR	**67 680**	**102 600**

STATEMENTS OF PROFIT OR LOSS FOR THE YEAR ENDED 31 DECEMBER 20X6

	P Ltd CU	S Ltd CU
Sales	235 000	180 000
Cost of sales	(189 000)	(150 000)
Gross profit	46 000	30 000
Depreciation	(32 000)	–
Profit before tax	14 000	30 000
Taxation	(3 920)	(8 400)
PROFIT FOR THE YEAR	**10 080**	**21 600**

EXTRACTS: STATEMENTS OF CHANGES IN EQUITY FOR THE YEAR ENDED 31 DECEMBER 20X5

	Retained earnings P Ltd CU	S Ltd CU
Balance 1 Jan 20x5	380 000	–
Profit for the year	67 680	102 600
Balance 31 Dec 20x5	**447 680**	**102 600**

EXTRACTS: STATEMENTS OF CHANGES IN EQUITY FOR THE YEAR ENDED 31 DECEMBER 20X6

	Retained earnings P Ltd CU	S Ltd CU
Balance 1 Jan 20x6	447 680	102 600
Profit for the year	10 080	21 600
Balance 31 Dec 20x6	**457 760**	**124 200**

Note: For both the 20x5 and 20x6 financial years, neither P Ltd nor S Ltd had any other comprehensive income. Furthermore, retained earnings was the only reserve of both P Ltd and S Ltd.

Required

(a) Prepare an extract of the analysis of equity of S Ltd as at 31 December 20x5, showing only the analysis of the post-acquisition equity of S Ltd.

(b) Prepare the since acquisition pro forma consolidation journals for the financial year ended 31 December 20x5.

(c) Prepare the consolidated statement of profit or loss and other comprehensive income for the P Ltd group for the financial year ended 31 December 20x5.

(d) Prepare an extract of the analysis of equity of S Ltd as at 31 December 20x6, showing only the analysis of the post-acquisition equity of S Ltd.

(e) Prepare the since acquisition pro forma consolidation journals for the financial year ended 31 December 20x6.

(f) Prepare the consolidated statement of profit or loss and other comprehensive income for the P Ltd group for the financial year ended 31 December 20x6.

(g) Prepare an extract from the consolidated statement of changes in equity for the P Ltd group for the financial year ended 31 December 20x6, showing only the columns for retained earnings and for the non-controlling interest.

Solution 6.18: Change in use from inventory to property plant and equipment: Partly owned subsidiary sells to parent

Part (a): Analysis of equity (AOE) of S Ltd as at 31 December 20x5, showing only the analysis of the post-acquisition equity of S Ltd.

	Total of S Ltd's equity 100% CU	P Ltd 80% Since acquisition CU	Non-controlling interest 20% CU
Since acquisition			
• Current year:			
Adjusted profit for the year	63 720	50 976**a**	12 744**b**
Profit for the year	102 600	82 080	20 520
Elimination unrealised intragroup profit: inventory (160 000 – 100 000)	(60 000)	(48 000)	(12 000)
Tax effect: Elimination unrealised intragroup profit: Inventory (60 000 × 28%)	16 800	13 440	3 360
Reversal excess depreciation: Machinery [(60 000 Unrealised profit / 5-year RUL machinery) × 6/12]	6 000	4 800	1 200
Tax effect: Reversal excess depreciation: Machinery (6 000 × 28%)	(1 680)	(1 344)	(336)

Part (b): Since acquisition pro forma journals for the financial year ended 31 December 20x5

CURRENT YEAR

Pro forma journal 1 (J1)	Dr CU	Cr CU
Sales (S Ltd) (P/L) (given)	160 000	
Cost of sales (S Ltd) (P/L) (given)		100 000
Machinery (P Ltd) (SFP) (balancing figure)		60 000
Elimination of intragroup sale, cost of sale and unrealised S Ltd intragroup profit included in the machinery acquired by P Ltd		

Comments: Pro forma journal 1

- Because S Ltd has sold an asset intragroup to P Ltd, the sale is unrealised for group purposes and accordingly is eliminated on consolidation by reversing the entire transaction. That is, S Ltd's CU 160 000 intragroup sale of inventory recognised is reversed by debiting S Ltd's sales with CU 160 000 while the associated CU 100 000 cost of sales recognised by S Ltd is reversed by crediting S Ltd's cost of sales with CU 100 000. The net effect on consolidation is the elimination of S Ltd's CU 60 000 (160 000 Sales – 100 000 Cost of sales), unrealised intragroup profit recognised on inventory sold to P Ltd.

- The cost of machinery as recognised in the separate records of the buying group entity, P Ltd, is overstated for group purposes as it includes the above-mentioned unrealised intragroup profit of S Ltd of CU 60 000. Accordingly, on consolidation we credit machinery of P Ltd with CU 60 000 so that it is recognised at its initial CU 100 000 cost to the group, which in this example is its cost of manufacture by S Ltd.

Pro forma journal 2 (J2)	Dr CU	Cr CU
Deferred tax (P Ltd) (SFP)	Wkg1 16 800	
Income tax expense (S Ltd) (P/L)		Wkg1 16 800
Tax effect of elimination of unrealised S Ltd intragroup profit included in the machinery acquired by P Ltd		

Workings: Pro forma journals

Working 1
60 000 (J1) Deductible temporary difference: elimination unrealised intragroup profit × 28%

Comments: Pro forma journal 2

- As the cost of the machinery purchased intragroup is reduced – as per pro forma journal 1 – by CU 60 000, without a corresponding change in its tax base (as the taxing authority does not recognise this consolidation adjustment for tax purposes), this gives rise to a CU 60 000 deductible temporary difference at group level. This is because the machinery's tax base of CU 160 000, which is its intragroup cost to P Ltd, exceeds by CU 60 000 its CU 100 000 group carrying amount. This deductible temporary difference of CU 60 000:

  - results in the recognition on consolidation of a CU 16 800 (60 000 Deductible temporary difference × 28%) deferred tax asset of P Ltd – this is the debit to deferred tax asset of P Ltd of CU 16 800; and
  - causes a corresponding CU 16 800 reduction on consolidation in S Ltd's income tax charge – this is the credit to income tax expense of S Ltd of CU 16 800.

- We can also say that the elimination of S Ltd's unrealised intragroup profit on consolidation reduces the profit of the group, meaning that we must also reduce the tax charge of the group, by crediting the income tax expense of S Ltd. In addition, we recognise what is essentially a prepayment of tax by the group on profit not yet recognised for group purposes by debiting a deferred tax asset of P Ltd.

Pro forma journal 3 (J3)	Dr CU	Cr CU
Accumulated depreciation: Machinery (P Ltd) (SFP)	Wkg2 6 000	
Depreciation: Machinery (S Ltd) (P/L)		Wkg2 6 000
Recognition of realisation of S Ltd intragroup profit through reduction in group depreciation charge: Machinery		

Working 2
(60 000 (J1) Unrealised intragroup profit / 5-year RUL machinery) × 6/12 Months

Comments: Pro forma journal 3

- P Ltd recognises depreciation on the machinery acquired intragroup, over its 5-year remaining useful life, based on its intragroup cost of CU 160 000. Therefore, P Ltd's depreciation expense on this machinery for the six months since it was acquired intragroup, (i.e., for the period 1 July 20x5 – 31 December 20x5) amounts to CU 16 000 [(160 000 Intragroup cost / 5-year RUL machinery) × 6/12]. From the group's perspective, however, the cost of the machinery is only CU 100 000, this being its initial cost of manufacture by S Ltd.

- Accordingly, group depreciation to be recognised on this machinery must be only CU 10 000 [(100 000 Original group cost of manufacture / 5 year RUL machinery) × 6/12]. This means that CU 6 000 (16 000 Depreciation P Ltd – 10 000 Depreciation group) of P Ltd's current year depreciation charge on this machinery is excessive for group purposes and must be reversed on consolidation. For this reason we credit Depreciation expense: Machinery with CU 6 000 and pass the corresponding debit to Accumulated depreciation: Machinery.

- In addition, the current year reversal, on consolidation, of the CU 6 000 excess depreciation on machinery constitutes the current year realisation and recognition, at group level, of CU 6 000 **of S Ltd's** CU 60 000 unrealised intragroup profit. For this reason the write back of this excess depreciation affects (increases) S Ltd's profit and *not* P Ltd's profit, despite P Ltd having incurred the depreciation expense on the machinery, the excessive portion of which is reversed on consolidation. Consequently, on consolidation we reverse the excess depreciation on machinery by crediting the depreciation expense of S Ltd, and *not* P Ltd.

Pro forma journal 4 (J4)	Dr CU	Cr CU
Income tax expense (S Ltd) (P/L)	Wkg3 1 680	
Deferred tax (P Ltd) (SFP)		Wkg3 1 680
Tax effect of recognition of realisation of S Ltd intragroup profit through reduction in group depreciation charge for machinery		

Workings: Pro forma journals

Working 3
6 000 (J3) Reversal of deductible temporary difference: recognition of intragroup profit × 28%

Comments: Pro forma journal 4

- The current year reversal on consolidation of CU 6 000 excess depreciation on the machinery acquired intragroup means that the current year tax deduction for this machinery exceeds by CU 6 000 the current year group depreciation charge for this machinery. This causes the current year reversal, for group purposes, of CU 6 000 of the CU 60 000 total deductible temporary difference, attributable to S Ltd's intragroup profit elimination.

- In the current year, this CU 6 000 deductible temporary difference reversal reduces by CU 1 680 (6 000 × 28%) the group deferred tax asset of CU 16 800, recognised, in respect of the CU 60 000 deductible temporary difference. For this reason we credit the deferred tax asset of P Ltd with CU 1 680, while the corresponding debit is to income tax expense of S Ltd, thereby increasing the current year income tax charge of the group by CU 1 680.

Pro forma journal 5 (J5)	Dr CU	Cr CU
NCI: Share of profit or loss (P/L)	Wkg4 12 744	
Non-controlling interest – Equity (SFP)		Wkg4 12 744
Allocating the non-controlling interest its share of S Ltd's adjusted current year profit		

Workings: Pro forma journals

Working 4
(102 600 (given) Current year profit – 60 000 (J1) Elimination of unrealised intragroup profit + 16 800 (J2) Tax effect: Elimination of unrealised intragroup profit + 6 000 (J3) Reversal excess depreciation: Machinery – 1 680 (J4) Tax effect: Reversal excess depreciation machinery) × 20% NCI Share

The full effects of the preceding pro forma journals on the 20x5 consolidated financial statements are shown in the following extract from the consolidation worksheet as at 31 December 20x5.

	P Ltd	S Ltd	Pro forma journals Since acquisition		Con- solidated
	Dr/(Cr) CU	Dr/(Cr) CU	Dr/(Cr) CU	Journal ref	Dr/(Cr) CU
Retained earnings (BOY)	(380 000)	–			(380 000)
Net profit: Individual entities	(67 680)	(102 600)			
Consolidated profit – attributable to owners of parent					(118 656)
Retained earnings (EOY)	(447 680)	(102 600)			(498 656)
Non-controlling interest: Equity	–	–	(25 000)	(given)	(37 744)
			(12 744)	J5	
Assets					
Machinery: Cost	160 000	–	(60 000)	J1	100 000
Machinery: Accumulated depreciation	(16 000)	–	6 000	J3	(10 000)
Deferred tax			16 800	J2	15 120
			(1 680)	J4	
Profit or loss					
Sales	(350 000)	(380 000)	160 000	J1	(570 000)
Cost of sales	240 000	237 500	(100 000)	J1	377 500
Depreciation	16 000	–	(6 000)	J3	10 000
Taxation	26 320	39 900	(16 800)	J2	51 100
			1 680	J4	
Net profit for the period	(67 680)	(102 600)			(131 400)
Non-controlling interest: Share of profit			12 744	J5	12 744
Consolidated profit attributable to owners of parent					(118 656)

Part (c): Consolidated financial statements

PLTD GROUP: CONSOLIDATED STATEMENT OF PROFIT OR LOSS AND OTHER COMPREHENSIVE INCOME FOR THE YEAR ENDED 31 DECEMBER 20x5	
	CU
Sales (350 000 (P Ltd) + (S Ltd: 380 000 – 160 000 (J1) Elimination: Intragroup sale))	570 000
Cost of sales	(377 500)
(240 000 (P Ltd) + (S Ltd: 237 500 – 100 000 (J1) Elimination: Intragroup cost of sales))	
Gross profit	192 500
Operating expenses	(10 000)
(16 000 (P Ltd) – 6 000 (S Ltd) (J3) Reversal: Excess depreciation: Machinery)	
Profit before tax	182 500
Income tax expense	(51 100)
(26 320 (P Ltd) + (S Ltd: 39 900 – 16 800 (J2) Tax effect: Elimination unrealised intragroup profit + 1 680 (J4) Tax effect: Recognition intragroup profit))	
PROFIT FOR THE YEAR	**131 400**
Other comprehensive income	**–**
TOTAL COMPREHENSIVE INCOME FOR THE YEAR	**131 400**
Total comprehensive income attributable to:	
Owners of the parent (balancing figure) **OR** (67 680 (P Ltd) + S Ltd: 50 976 (see AOE **a**))	118 656
Non-controlling interest (see AOE **b OR** (J5))	12 744
	131 400

Part (d): Extract of the analysis of equity (AOE) of S Ltd as at 31 December 20x6, showing only the analysis of the post-acquisition equity of S Ltd

	Total of S Ltd's equity 100% CU	P Ltd 80% Since acquisition CU	Non-controlling interest 20% CU
• **Since acquisition to BOY:**			
Adjusted retained earnings	63 720	50 976 **a**	12 744 **b**
Post-acquisition retained earnings to BOY (given)	102 600	82 080	20 520
Elimination prior year unrealised intragroup profit: Inventory (160 000 – 100 000)	(60 000)	(48 000)	(12 000)
Tax effect: Elimination prior year unrealised intragroup profit: Inventory (60 000 × 28%)	16 800	13 440	3 360
Prior year reversal excess depreciation: Machinery [(60 000 Unrealised profit / 5-year RUL machinery) × 6/12]	6 000	4 800	1 200
Prior year tax effect: Reversal excess depreciation: Machinery (6 000 × 28%)	(1 680)	(1 344)	(336)

AOE of S Ltd (continued)

	Total of S Ltd's equity 100%	P Ltd 80%	
		Since acquisition	Non-controlling interest 20%
	CU	CU	CU
• Current year:			
Adjusted profit for the year	30 240	24 192 **c**	6 048 **d**
Profit for the year (given)	21 600	17 280	4 320
Reversal excess depreciation: Machinery (60 000 Unrealised profit / 5-year RUL machinery)	12 000	9 600	2 400
Tax effect: Reversal excess depreciation: Machinery (12 000 × 28%)	(3 360)	(2 688)	(672)

Part (e): Since acquisition pro forma journal entries for the financial year ended 31 December 20x6

SINCE ACQUISITION TO THE BEGINNING OF THE YEAR

Pro forma journal 1 (J1)	Dr CU	Cr CU
Retained earnings (S Ltd) (SCIE)	Wkg1 54 000	
Accumulated depreciation: Machinery (P Ltd) (SFP)	Wkg2 6 000	
Machinery (P Ltd) (SFP)		Wkg3 60 000
Prior year S Ltd intragroup profit adjustment: sale of inventory, to ensure current year opening consolidated retained earnings balance agrees to prior year closing consolidated retained earnings balance, recognition of prior year reduction in accumulated depreciation of machinery (reclassified from inventory) acquired intragroup, and elimination of prior year unrealised S Ltd intragroup profit included in cost of machinery acquired intragroup		

Workings: Pro forma journals

Working 1
Balancing figure

OR

	CU	
Elimination of S Ltd prior year unrealised intragroup profit, machinery	60 000	(Working 3)
Minus: Reversal of prior year excess depreciation machinery: recognition of S Ltd prior year intragroup profit, machinery	(6 000)	(Working 2)
Balance of S Ltd unrealised intragroup profit: Unrecognised at BOY	54 000	

OR

$$60\ 000\ \text{(Working 3) S Ltd prior year unrealised intragroup profit:} \times \frac{\text{4.5 Years (Machinery RUL at BOY)}}{\text{5 Years (Machinery RUL: Date of intragroup acquisition)}}$$

= 54 000 Balance of S Ltd unrealised intragroup profit: Unrecognised at BOY

Working 2
(60 000 (Working 3) S Ltd Prior year unrealised intragroup profit / 5-year RUL machinery) × 6/12 Months = 6 000 Reversal of prior year excess depreciation machinery: recognition of S Ltd prior year intragroup profit, machinery

Working 3
160 000 (given) Selling price – 100 000 (given) Original cost = 60 000 S Ltd Prior year unrealised intragroup profit, machinery

Pro forma journal 2 (J2)	Dr CU	Cr CU
Deferred tax (P Ltd) (SFP)	Wkg4 15 120	
Retained earnings (S Ltd) (SCIE)		Wkg4 15 120
Tax adjustments prior year S Ltd intragroup profit, to ensure current year opening consolidated retained earnings balance agrees to prior year closing consolidated retained earnings balance		

Workings: Pro forma journals

Working 4
54 000 (J1) Elimination of balance of S Ltd unrealised intragroup profit, machinery at BOY × 28%

Pro forma journal 3 (J3)	Dr CU	Cr CU
Retained earnings (S Ltd) (SCIE)	Wkg5 12 744	
Non-controlling interest – Equity (SFP)		Wkg5 12 744
Allocating the non-controlling interest its share of S Ltd's adjusted post-acquisition retained earnings to the beginning of the year		

Workings: Pro forma journals

Working 5
(102 600 (given) Post-acquisition retained earnings to BOY – 54 000 (J1) Elimination of balance of S Ltd unrealised intragroup profit at BOY + 15 120 (J2) Tax effect: Elimination of balance of S Ltd unrealised intragroup profit at BOY) × 20% NCI Share

CURRENT YEAR

Pro forma journal 4 (J4)	Dr CU	Cr CU
Accumulated depreciation: machinery (P Ltd) (SFP)	Wkg6 12 000	
Depreciation: Machinery (S Ltd) (P/L)		Wkg6 12 000
Current year recognition of S Ltd intragroup profit through current year reduction in depreciation charge: Machinery		

Workings: Pro forma journals

Working 6
60 000 (J1) S Ltd Prior year unrealised intragroup profit / 5-year RUL machinery

Pro forma journal 5 (J5)	Dr CU	Cr CU
Income tax expense (S Ltd) (P/L)	Wkg7 3 360	
Deferred tax (P Ltd) (SFP)		Wkg7 3 360
Tax effect: Current year recognition of realisation of S Ltd intragroup profit, through current year reduction in depreciation charge: Machinery		

Workings: Pro forma journals

Working 7
12 000 (J4) Reversal deductible temporary difference machinery: recognition of S Ltd prior year intragroup profit × 28%

Pro forma journal 6 (J6)	Dr CU	Cr CU
NCI: Share of profit or loss (P/L)	^{Wkg8}6 048	
Non-controlling interest – Equity (SFP)		^{Wkg8}6 048
Allocating the non-controlling interest its share of S Ltd's adjusted current year profit		

Workings: Pro forma journals

Working 8

(21 600 (given) Current year profit + 12 000 (J4) Reversal of excess depreciation: Machinery – 3 360 (J5) Tax effect: Reversal of excess depreciation: machinery) × 20% NCI Share

The full effects of the preceding pro forma journals on the 20x6 consolidated financial statements are shown in the following extract from the consolidation worksheet as at 31 December 20x6.

	P Ltd Dr/(Cr) CU	S Ltd Dr/(Cr) CU	Pro forma journals Since acquisition Dr/(Cr) CU	Journal ref	Con-solidated Dr/(Cr) CU
Retained earnings (BOY)	(447 680)	(102 600)	54 000	J1	(498 656)
			(15 120)	J2	
			12 744	J3	
Profit: Individual entities	(10 080)	(21 600)			
Consolidated profit attributable to the owners of the parent					(34 272) ←
Retained earnings (EOY)	(457 760)	(124 200)			(532 928)
NCI Equity	–	–	(25 000)	(given)	(43 792)
			(12 744)	J3	
			(6 048)	J6	
Assets:					
Machinery: Cost	160 000	–	(60 000)	J1	100 000
Machinery: Accumulated depreciation	(48 000)	–	6 000	J1	(30 000)
			12 000	J4	
Deferred Tax			15 120	J2	11 760
			(3 360)	J5	
Profit or loss					
Sales	(235 000)	(180 000)			(415 000)
Cost of sales	189 000	150 000			339 000
Depreciation	32 000	–	(12 000)	J4	20 000
Taxation	3 920	8 400	3 360	J5	15 680
Profit for the period	(10 080)	(21 600)			(40 320)
NCI: Share of profit			6 048	J6	6 048
Consolidated profit attributable to owners of the parent					(34 272)

Part (f): Consolidated statement of profit or loss and other comprehensive income for the 20x6 year

P LTD GROUP: CONSOLIDATED STATEMENT OF PROFIT OR LOSS AND OTHER COMPREHENSIVE INCOME FOR THE YEAR ENDED 31 DECEMBER 20x6	
	CU
Sales (235 000 (P Ltd) + 180 000 (S Ltd))	415 000
Cost of sales (189 000 (P Ltd) + 150 000 (S Ltd))	(339 000)
Gross profit	76 000
Operating expenses (32 000 (P Ltd) – 12 000 (S Ltd) (J4) Reversal: Excess depreciation machinery)	(20 000)
Profit before tax	56 000
Income tax expense (3 920 (P Ltd) + (S Ltd: 8 400 + 3 360 (J2) Tax effect: Reversal excess depreciation machinery))	(15 680)
PROFIT FOR THE YEAR	**40 320**
Other comprehensive income	**–**
TOTAL COMPREHENSIVE INCOME FOR THE YEAR	**40 320**
Total comprehensive income attributable to:	
Owners of the parent (balancing figure) **OR** (10 080 (P Ltd) + S Ltd: 24 192 (see AOE **c**))	34 272
Non-controlling interest (see AOE **d OR** (J6))	6 048
	40 320

Part (g): Extract from the consolidated statement of changes in equity for the P Ltd group for the 20x6 year

EXTRACT: P LTD GROUP CONSOLIDATED STATEMENT OF CHANGES IN EQUITY FOR THE YEAR ENDED 31 DECEMBER 20x6	Retained earnings CU	Non-controlling interest CU
Opening balance at 1 Jan 20x6	Wkg1 498 656	Wkg2 37 744
Total comprehensive income: Profit for the period (from CSOPL_OCI)	34 272	6 048
Closing balance at 31 Dec 20x6	532 928	43 792

Workings: Consolidated statement of changes in equity

Working 1
P Ltd: 447 680 + S Ltd: 50 976 (see AOE **a**) P Ltd's share of the post-acquisition retained earning to BOY of S Ltd

OR

P Ltd: 474 680 + (S Ltd: 102 600 (given) Post-acquisition retained earnings to BOY – 54 000 (J1) Elimination of balance of prior year unrealised intragroup profit, machinery, at BOY + 15 120 (J2) Tax effect: Elimination of balance of prior year unrealised intragroup profit, machinery, at BOY – 12 744 (J3) NCI share of post-acquisition retained earnings to BOY of S Ltd)

Working 2
S Ltd: 25 000 (given) NCI share of S Ltd at acquisition equity + 12 744 (see AOE **b OR** (J3)) NCI share of post-acquisition retained earnings to BOY of S Ltd

6.5.2 Change in use of asset: Property, plant and equipment of seller becomes inventory of buyer

Where a **subsidiary** sells an asset that it **classifies as property, plant and equipment** at a **profit** to its **parent**, which classifies this asset **as inventory**, the following will apply:

- The **subsidiary** in its **own records** will record a **profit on sale of property, plant and equipment.**

- The **parent** in its **own records** will recognise the asset acquired as **inventory**, at its **intragroup cost price** – which includes the subsidiary's intragroup profit on sale – and no depreciation will be charged.

- For group purposes:

    - The **subsidiary's profit on sale of the property, plant and equipment** to its parent is intragroup and is therefore unrealised and must be **eliminated** on **consolidation.**

    - The **cost** to the **group** of the **inventory** must be the **carrying amount** of the **property, plant and equipment** at the **date when it is reclassified to inventory.** This means that the **unrealised intragroup profit of the subsidiary**, which is included in the cost of inventory purchased by the parent, must be **eliminated** on consolidation.

    - Because the cost of the inventory acquired intragroup by the parent is reduced for group purposes, without a corresponding reduction in its tax base, a deductible temporary difference arises (i.e., the tax base of the inventory will be greater than its carrying amount), which causes the recognition of a **deferred tax asset of the group** and a corresponding **reduction in the group's tax charge.**

    - The **subsidiary's unrealised intragroup profit** on sale of property, plant and equipment becomes **realised** and **is recognised subsequently on consolidation** when the **inventory** – which includes this unrealised intragroup profit of the subsidiary – is **sold by the parent** to **a party outside the group.**

    - The subsequent realisation and recognition, on consolidation, of the subsidiary's previously unrealised intragroup profit results in the **subsequent reversal** of the deductible temporary difference and therefore the **deferred tax asset of the group** that arose initially, when the subsidiary's unrealised intragroup profit was eliminated on consolidation. Furthermore, the reversal of this deferred tax asset causes a corresponding **increase in the group tax expense recognised.**

    - As the unrealised intragroup profit arose **in the subsidiary,** the non-controlling interest's share of the profit and post-acquisition reserves of the subsidiary must be **adjusted** for:
        - the after tax elimination of the **subsidiary's unrealised intragroup profit;** and
        - the after tax **subsequent recognition** of the subsidiary's previously unrealised intragroup profit, upon disposal by the parent of the inventory acquired intragroup, to parties outside the group.

Note that if the parent sold property, plant and equipment to its subsidiary (i.e., a downstream sale), which the subsidiary used as inventory, the adjustments on consolidation would be the same as an upstream sale, as described in the points above, except that the non-controlling interest would not be allocated any share of the consolidation adjustments to the parent's profit and reserves.

Example 6.19: Change in use from property, plant and equipment to inventory: Partly owned subsidiary sells to parent

P Ltd acquired an 80% controlling interest in S Ltd on 1 January 20x5, when S Ltd was incorporated. Assume that the non-controlling interest that arose on acquisition of the subsidiary was CU 25 000. S Ltd sold equipment to P Ltd for CU 160 000, on 31 December 20x5. The carrying amount of the equipment was CU 100 000 in S Ltd's records when it was disposed of to P Ltd on 31 December 20x5. P Ltd classified the asset purchased from S Ltd as inventory and sold this inventory to a party outside the group during the 20x6 financial year. The abridged statements of profit or loss and extracts from the statements of changes in equity for P Ltd and its subsidiary S Ltd for the 20x5 and 20x6 financial years are shown below.

STATEMENTS OF PROFIT OR LOSS FOR THE YEAR ENDED 31 DECEMBER 20X5		
	P Ltd	S Ltd
	CU	CU
Sales	350 000	380 000
Cost of sales	(240 000)	(237 500)
Gross profit	110 000	142 500
Other income	–	60 000
Depreciation	–	(10 000)
Profit before tax	110 000	192 500
Taxation	(21 840)	(53 900)
PROFIT FOR THE YEAR	**88 160**	**138 600**

STATEMENTS OF PROFIT OR LOSS FOR THE YEAR ENDED 31 DECEMBER 20x6		
	P Ltd	S Ltd
	CU	CU
Sales	335 000	180 000
Cost of sales	(289 000)	(150 000)
Gross profit	46 000	30 000
Taxation	(12 880)	(8 400)
PROFIT FOR THE YEAR	**33 120**	**21 600**

EXTRACTS STATEMENTS OF CHANGES IN EQUITY FOR THE YEAR ENDED 31 DECEMBER 20X5		
	Retained earnings	
	P Ltd	S Ltd
	CU	CU
Balance 1 Jan 20x5	380 000	–
Profit for the year	88 160	138 600
Balance 31 Dec 20x5	**468 160**	**138 600**

EXTRACTS STATEMENTS OF CHANGES IN EQUITY FOR THE YEAR ENDED 31 DECEMBER 20X6	Retained earnings	
	P Ltd	S Ltd
	CU	CU
Balance 1 Jan 20x6	468 160	138 600
Profit for the year	33 120	21 600
Balance 31 Dec 20x6	**501 280**	**160 200**

Note: For both the 20x5 and 20x6 financial years, neither P Ltd nor S Ltd had any other comprehensive income. Furthermore, retained earnings was the only reserve of both P Ltd and S Ltd.

Required

(a) Prepare an extract of the analysis of equity of S Ltd as at 31 December 20x5, showing only the analysis of the post-acquisition equity of S Ltd.

(b) Prepare the since acquisition pro forma journals for the financial year ended 31 December 20x5.

(c) Prepare the consolidated statement of profit or loss and other comprehensive income for the P Ltd group for the financial year ended 31 December 20x5.

(d) Prepare an extract of the analysis of equity of S Ltd as at 31 December 20x6, showing only the analysis of the post-acquisition equity of S Ltd.

(e) Prepare the since acquisition pro forma journals for the financial year ended 31 December 20x6.

(f) Prepare the consolidated statement of profit or loss and other comprehensive income for the P Ltd group for the financial year ended 31 December 20x6.

(g) Prepare an extract from the consolidated statement of changes in equity for the P Ltd group for the financial year ended 31 December 20x6, showing only the columns for retained earnings and for the non-controlling interest.

 Solution 6.19: Change in use from property, plant and equipment to inventory: Partly owned subsidiary sells to parent

Part (a): Extract of the analysis of equity (AOE) of S Ltd as at 31 December 20x5

Since acquisition	Total of S Ltd's equity 100%	P Ltd 80% Since acquisition	Non-controlling interest 20%
	CU	CU	CU
• Current year:			
Adjusted profit for the year	95 400	76 320 **a**	19 080 **b**
Profit for the year (given)	138 600	110 880	27 720
Elimination unrealised profit: Closing inventory (160 000 – 100 000)	(60 000)	(48 000)	(12 000)
Tax effect: Elimination unrealised profit – Closing inventory (60 000 × 28%)	16 800	13 440	3 360

Part (b): Since acquisition pro forma journal entries for the financial year ended 31 December 20x5

CURRENT YEAR

Pro forma journal 1 (J1)	Dr CU	Cr CU
Other income [profit on sale of equipment] (S Ltd) (P/L)	Wkg1 60 000	
Inventory (P Ltd) (SFP)		Wkg1 60 000
Elimination of S Ltd unrealised intragroup profit included in closing inventory of P Ltd		

Workings: Pro forma journals

Working 1

160 000 (given) Selling price – 100 000 (given) Carrying amount: Equipment

Comments: Pro forma journal 1

- On consolidation, we eliminate the CU 60 000 unrealised intragroup profit on disposal of equipment, recognised by S Ltd, by debiting S Ltd's other income with CU 60 000.
- The corresponding credit of CU 60 000 to P Ltd's inventory:
  - removes S Ltd's CU 60 000 unrealised intragroup profit from the cost of P Ltd's inventory purchased intragroup; and
  - reinstates such cost to the CU 100 000 carrying amount of the equipment at the date of its reclassification to inventory, which is the date it was sold by S Ltd to P Ltd.

Pro forma journal 2 (J2)	Dr CU	Cr CU
Deferred tax (P Ltd) (SFP)	Wkg2 16 800	
Income tax expense (S Ltd) (P/L)		Wkg2 16 800
Tax effect of elimination of S Ltd unrealised intragroup profit included in closing inventory of P Ltd		

Workings: Pro forma journals

Working 2

60 000 (J1) Origination of deductible temporary difference inventory: elimination of S Ltd unrealised intragroup profit × 28%

Comments: Pro forma journal 2

- The CU 60 000 elimination of S Ltd's unrealised intragroup profit from the cost of P Ltd's inventory (see pro forma journal 1 above), reduces the cost of P Ltd's inventory by CU 60 000. This CU 60 000 reduction in P Ltd's inventory cost is not matched by a corresponding reduction in the tax base of this inventory (since the taxing authority does not recognise S Ltd's intragroup profit elimination for tax purposes).
- This causes a CU 60 000 deductible temporary difference at group level since the CU 160 000 tax base of the inventory exceeds by CU 60 000, the inventory's CU 100 000 carrying amount for group purposes. This results in:
  - the recognition of a CU 16 800 (60 000 deductible temporary difference × 28%) deferred tax asset of the group – this is the CU 16 800 debit to deferred tax asset of P Ltd; and
  - a corresponding CU 16 800 decrease in the group tax charge – this is the CU 16 800 credit to the income tax expense of S Ltd.

- We can also say that the elimination of S Ltd's unrealised intragroup profit on consolidation reduces the profit of the group, meaning that we must also reduce the tax charge of the group, by crediting the income tax expense of S Ltd. In addition, we recognise what is essentially a prepayment of tax by the group on profits not yet recognised for group purposes by debiting a deferred tax asset of P Ltd.

Pro forma journal 3 (J3)	Dr CU	Cr CU
NCI: Share of profit or loss (P/L)	Wkg3 19 080	
Non-controlling interest – Equity (SFP)		Wkg3 19 080
Allocating the non-controlling interest its share of S Ltd's adjusted current year profit		

Workings: Pro forma journals

Working 3
(138 600 (given) Current year profit – 60 000 (J1) Elimination of S Ltd unrealised intragroup profit + 16 800 (J2) Tax effect: Elimination of S Ltd unrealised intragroup profit) × 20% NCI Share

The full effects of the preceding pro forma journals on the 20x5 consolidated financial statements are shown in the following extract from the consolidation worksheet as at 31 December 20x5.

	P Ltd Dr/(Cr) CU	S Ltd Dr/(Cr) CU	Pro forma journals Since acquisition Dr/(Cr) CU	Journal ref	Con-solidated Dr/(Cr) CU
Retained earnings (BOY)	(380 000)	–			(380 000)
Profit: Individual entities	(88 160)	(138 600)			
Consolidated profit attributable to owners of parent					(164 480)
Retained earnings (EOY)	(468 160)	(138 600)			(544 480)
Non-controlling interest: Equity	–	–	(25 000)	(given)	(44 080)
			(19 080)	J3	
Assets					
Inventory	160 000	–	(60 000)	J1	100 000
Deferred Tax			16 800	J2	16 800
Profit or loss					
Sales	(350 000)	(380 000)			(730 000)
Cost of sales	240 000	237 500			477 500
Profit on sale of equipment	–	(60 000)	60 000	J1	–
Depreciation	–	10 000			10 000
Taxation	21 840	53 900	(16 800)	J2	58 940
Net profit for the period	(88 160)	(138 600)			(183 560)
Non-controlling interest: Share of profit			19 080	J3	19 080
Consolidated profit attributable to owners of parent					(164 480)

Part (c): Consolidated statement of profit or loss and other comprehensive income for the 20x5 financial year

P LTD GROUP: CONSOLIDATED STATEMENT OF PROFIT OR LOSS AND OTHER COMPREHENSIVE INCOME FOR THE YEAR ENDED 31 DECEMBER 20x5	
	CU
Sales (350 000 (P Ltd) + 380 000 (S Ltd))	730 000
Cost of sales (240 000 (P Ltd) + 237 500 (S Ltd))	(477 500)
Gross profit	252 500
Other income (S Ltd: 60 000 – 60 000 (J1) Elimination unrealised intragroup profit)	–
Operating expenses (S Ltd)	(10 000)
Profit before tax	242 500
Income tax expense (21 840 (P Ltd) + (S Ltd: 53 900 – 16 800 (J2) Tax effect: Elimination unrealised intragroup profit))	(58 940)
PROFIT FOR THE YEAR	**183 560**
Other comprehensive income	–
TOTAL COMPREHENSIVE INCOME FOR THE YEAR	**183 560**
Total comprehensive income attributable to:	
Owners of the parent (balancing figure) **OR** (88 160 (P Ltd) + S Ltd: 76 320 (see AOE **a**))	164 480
Non-controlling interest (see AOE **b OR** (J3))	19 080
	183 560

Part (d): Extract of the analysis of equity (AOE) of S Ltd as at 31 December 20x6

Since acquisition	Total of S Ltd's equity 100% CU	P Ltd 80% Since acquisition CU	Non-controlling interest 20% CU
• To beginning of current year:			
Adjusted retained earnings	95 400	76 320 **a**	19 080 **b**
Retained earnings since acquisition to BOY (given)	138 600	110 880	27 720
Elimination prior year unrealised intragroup profit: Closing inventory (160 000 – 100 000)	(60 000)	(48 000)	(12 000)
Tax effect: Elimination prior year unrealised intragroup profit in closing inventory (60 000 × 28%)	16 800	13 440	3 360
• Current year:			
Adjusted profit for the year	64 800	51 840 **c**	12 960 **d**
Profit for the year (given)	21 600	17 280	4 320
Recognition of prior year unrealised intragroup profit (160 000 – 100 000)	60 000	48 000	12 000
Tax effect: Recognition of prior year unrealised intragroup profit (60 000 × 28%)	(16 800)	(13 440)	(3 360)

Part (e): Since acquisition pro forma journals for the financial year ended 31 December 20x6

SINCE ACQUISITION TO THE BEGINNING OF THE YEAR / CURRENT YEAR

Pro forma journal 1 (J1)	Dr CU	Cr CU
Retained earnings (S Ltd) (SCIE)	Wkg1 43 200	
Income tax expense (S Ltd) (P/L)	Wkg2 16 800	
Other income [profit on sale of equipment] (S Ltd) (P/L)		Wkg3 60 000
S Ltd Intragroup profit adjustment: Equipment, to ensure consolidated retained earnings balance beginning of the year agrees to the consolidated retained earnings balance at the end of the prior year, current year recognition of S Ltd prior year intragroup profit: equipment, and related tax effects		

Workings: Pro forma journals

Working 1
Balancing figure

OR

60 000 (Working 3) Elimination of S Ltd prior year unrealised intragroup profit: Equipment × 72% After tax

Working 2
60 000 (Working 3) Reversal of deductible temporary difference equipment: recognition of S Ltd prior year unrealised intragroup profit equipment × 28%

Working 3
160 000 Selling price (given) – 100 000 (given) Carrying amount of equipment = 60 000 S Ltd Prior year intragroup profit: Equipment

Comments: Pro forma journal 1

- The prior year pro forma journal elimination, of S Ltd's CU 60 000 prior year unrealised intragroup profit on sale of equipment to P Ltd, reduced S Ltd's prior year profit by an after tax amount of CU 43 200 (60 000 Unrealised intragroup profit × 72%). Because pro forma journals are not carried forward to subsequent reporting periods, S Ltd's CU 43 200 prior year after tax unrealised intragroup profit is automatically included in its opening retained earnings balance extracted from its individual financial statements. Consequently, S Ltd's current year opening retained earnings balance is overstated by CU 43 000 for group purposes.

- Accordingly, in the current year, on consolidation, we debit the opening balance of S Ltd's retained earnings with CU 43 200, which ensures that the current year opening consolidated retained earnings balance agrees to the prior year closing consolidated retained earnings balance.

- S Ltd's CU 60 000 prior year unrealised intragroup profit on sale of equipment becomes realised in the current year because of the current year sale of P Ltd's opening inventory – which includes this prior year unrealised intragroup profit of S Ltd – to parties outside the group. Consequently, in the current year on consolidation, we recognise this CU 60 000 previously unrealised intragroup profit of S Ltd by crediting S Ltd's other income with CU 60 000, thereby increasing the current year group profit by CU 60 000.

- Because the current year group profit has increased, a corresponding increase in the current year group tax charge must be recognised. This is achieved by debiting S Ltd's income tax expense with CU 16 800 (60 000 Increase in group profit × 28%).

- We can also say that the increase in the group income tax charge in the current period is because the deductible temporary difference and associated deferred tax asset that arose in the prior year – when S Ltd's prior year unrealised intragroup profit was eliminated from the prior year closing inventory balance – reverse in the current year, when the opening inventory (the prior year's closing inventory) is sold to parties outside of the group in the current year.

SINCE ACQUISITION TO THE BEGINNING OF THE YEAR

Pro forma journal 2 (J2)	Dr CU	Cr CU
Retained earnings (S Ltd) (SCIE)	Wkg4 19 080	
Non-controlling interest – Equity (SFP)		Wkg4 19 080
Allocating the non-controlling interest its share of S Ltd's adjusted post-acquisition retained earnings to the beginning of the year		

Workings: Pro forma journals

Working 4
(138 600 (given) Post-acquisition retained earnings to BOY – 43 200 (J1) After tax elimination of S Ltd prior year unrealised intragroup profit) × 20% NCI Share

CURRENT YEAR

Pro forma journal 3 (J3)	Dr CU	Cr CU
NCI: Share of profit or loss (P/L)	Wkg5 12 960	
Non-controlling interest – Equity (SFP)		Wkg5 12 960
Allocating the non-controlling interest its share of S Ltd's adjusted current year profit		

Working 5
(21 600 (given) Current year profit + 60 000 (J1) Recognition of S Ltd prior year unrealised intragroup profit: Equipment – 16 800 (J1) Tax effect: Recognition of S Ltd prior year unrealised intragroup profit: Equipment) × 20% NCI Share

The full effects of the pro forma journals on the 20x6 consolidated financial statements are shown in the following extract from the consolidation worksheet as at 31 December 20x6.

	P Ltd Dr/(Cr) CU	S Ltd Dr/(Cr) CU	Pro forma journals Since acquisition Dr/(Cr) CU	Journal ref	Con- solidated Dr/(Cr) CU
Retained earnings (BOY)	(468 160)	(138 600)	43 200	J1	(544 480)
			19 080	J2	
Profit: Individual entities	(33 120)	(21 600)			
Consolidated profit attributable to owners of parent					†(84 960)
Retained earnings (EOY)	(501 280)	(160 200)			(629 440)
Non-controlling interest: Equity	–	–	(25 000)	(given)	(57 040)
			(19 080)	J2	
			(12 960)	J3	

Explanatory notes

† This amount has been brought forward from the second part of the consolidation worksheet on page 427

	P Ltd	S Ltd	Pro forma journals		Con-solidated
			Since acquisition		
	Dr/(Cr)	Dr/(Cr)	Dr/(Cr)	Journal ref	Dr/(Cr)
	CU	CU	CU		CU
Profit or loss					
Sales	(335 000)	(180 000)			(515 000)
Cost of sales	289 000	150 000			439 000
Profit on sale of equipment	–	–	(60 000)	J1	(60 000)
Taxation	12 880	8 400	16 800	J1	38 080
Net profit for the period	(33 120)	(21 600)			(97 920)
Non-controlling interest: Share of profit			12 960	J3	12 960
Consolidated profit attributable to owners of parent					‡(84 960)

Explanatory notes

‡ This amount has been carried forward to the first part of the consolidation worksheet on page 426

Part (f): Consolidated statement of profit or loss and other comprehensive income for the 20x6 financial year

CONSOLIDATED STATEMENT OF PROFIT OR LOSS AND OTHER COMPREHENSIVE INCOME FOR THE P LTD GROUP FOR THE YEAR ENDED 31 DECEMBER 20x6	
	CU
Sales (335 000 (P Ltd) + 180 000 (S Ltd))	515 000
Cost of sales (289 000 (P Ltd) + 150 000 (S Ltd))	(439 000)
Gross profit	76 000
Other income (S Ltd: 60 000 (J1) Recognition of prior year unrealised intragroup profit, equipment)	60 000
Profit before tax	136 000
Income tax expense (12 880 (P Ltd) + (S Ltd: 8 400 + 16 800 (J2) Tax effect: Recognition prior year intragroup profit))	(38 080)
PROFIT FOR THE YEAR	**97 920**
Other comprehensive income	**–**
TOTAL COMPREHENSIVE INCOME FOR THE YEAR	**97 920**
Total comprehensive income attributable to:	
Owners of the parent (balancing figure) **OR** (33 120 (P Ltd) + S Ltd: 51 840 (see AOE **c**))	84 960
Non-controlling interest (see AOE **d OR** (J3))	12 960
	97 920

Part (g): Extract from the consolidated statement of changes in equity for the 20x6 financial year

EXTRACT: P LTD GROUP CONSOLIDATED STATEMENT OF CHANGES IN EQUITY FOR THE YEAR ENDED 31 DECEMBER 20x6		
	Retained earnings CU	Non-controlling interest CU
Opening balance at 1 Jan 20x6	Wkg1 544 480	Wkg2 44 080
Total comprehensive income: Profit for the period (from CSOPL_OCI)	84 960	12 960
Closing balance at 31 Dec 20x6	629 440	57 040

Workings: Consolidated statement of changes in equity

Working 1
P Ltd: 468 160 + S Ltd: 76 320 (see AOE **a**) P Ltd Share of S Ltd post-acquisition retained earnings to BOY

OR

P Ltd: 468 160 + (S Ltd: 138 600 (given) Post-acquisition retained earnings to BOY – 43 200 (J1) After tax elimination of prior year intragroup profit: Equipment – 19 080 (J2) NCI share of S Ltd post-acquisition retained earnings to BOY)

Working 2
S Ltd: 25 000 (given) NCI share of S Ltd at acquisition equity + 19 080 (see AOE **b OR** (J2)) NCI share of S Ltd post-acquisition retained earnings to BOY

Summary

This chapter considered how to account for intragroup transactions (except for intragroup dividends, covered in Volume 1 Chapters 3 and 4) within the consolidated financial statements. Intragroup transactions are those transactions undertaken between separate group entities. All **intragroup transactions** and **intragroup balances** must be **eliminated in full** in the preparation of the consolidated financial statements. In this way the consolidated financial statements will only reflect transactions with parties outside the group.

When inventory is sold intragroup at a profit, and all or part of these inventories are on hand in the group at year end, pro forma consolidation journals are passed:

- In the year of sale:
  - eliminating the unrealised intragroup profit recognised by the selling group entity, by adjusting the individual line items making up this profit, namely sales and cost of sales;
  - eliminating the unrealised intragroup profit included in the cost of closing inventory of the purchasing group entity; and

- recognising the tax effects of the intragroup profit elimination, namely the recognition of a deferred tax asset of the group and a corresponding reduction in the group's tax charge.
- In the following year:
  - reducing the opening retained earnings balance of the selling group entity by this entity's prior year after tax unrealised intragroup profit recognised;
  - recognising the selling group entity's prior year intragroup profit, which realises in the current period with the sale of the inventory – which includes the prior year unrealised intragroup profit – outside the group in the current year; and
  - recognising the tax expense associated with the current year recognition of the selling group entity's prior year intragroup profit.

When **non**-depreciable property, plant and equipment is sold intragroup at a profit, pro forma consolidation journals are passed:

- eliminating the selling group entity's unrealised intragroup profit;
- reducing the cost of the non-depreciable property, plant and equipment purchased intragroup, by the intragroup profit, thereby reinstating this property, plant and equipment to its original cost to the group;
- recognising the tax effects of the intragroup profit elimination, namely the recognition of a deferred tax asset of the group and a corresponding reduction in the group's tax charge, calculated using the effective capital gains tax rate;
- recognising the previously unrealised intragroup profit, upon sale of the non-depreciable property, plant and equipment outside the group; and
- recognising the tax effects of the intragroup profit recognition, namely the reversal of the deferred tax asset of the group and the corresponding increase in the group's tax charge, calculated using the effective capital gains tax rate.

The intragroup sale of **depreciable** property, plant and equipment at a profit has additional implications on consolidation.

First, the purchasing group entity will calculate the depreciation on the property, plant and equipment acquired based on its intragroup cost price, which includes the selling group entity's unrealised intragroup profit, and which therefore exceeds the depreciable property, plant and equipment's carrying amount based on its initial cost to the group. Accordingly, the purchasing group entity, in its own records, will record a higher depreciation charge for this property, plant and equipment than should be recognised for group purposes. Therefore, on consolidation, an additional pro forma journal is required each year to reverse the excess depreciation charge recognised by the purchasing group entity on the depreciable property, plant and equipment acquired.

Second, the selling group entity's unrealised intragroup profit realises subsequently, and is recognised for group purposes, by means of the reversal each year on consolidation, of the excess depreciation charge recognised by the purchasing group entity on the depreciable property, plant and equipment acquired.

Third, the deductible temporary difference attributable to the elimination of the intragroup profit on sale of the depreciable property, plant and equipment, reverses subsequently each reporting period. This reversal is in line with the reversal on consolidation each period, of the excess depreciation on the property, plant and equipment sold intragroup. This means that in each reporting period over the remaining useful life of this depreciable property, plant and equipment, a pro forma journal is passed (1) increasing the group's tax charge; and (2) reducing the group's deferred tax asset, initially recognised in respect of the depreciable property, plant and equipment sold intragroup.

It should be noted that the **intragroup profit** arising on the **intragroup sale of depreciable property, plant and equipment** is also considered **realised** for group purposes when this depreciable property, plant and equipment is **sold to parties outside the group.**

When dealing with partly owned subsidiaries, it is only when the **subsidiary sells inventory/property, plant and equipment to its parent** – known as an upstream sale – or to a **fellow subsidiary,** that the non-controlling interest is **affected** by such intragroup sales since the unrealised intragroup profit arises in the **subsidiary** in such cases. In this instance, as the non-controlling interest shares in the subsidiary's profit and reserves, it is allocated its appropriate share of the consolidation adjustments:

- eliminating the subsidiary's unrealised intragroup profit; and
- subsequently recognising the subsidiary's unrealised intragroup profit when realised in a future reporting period.

Your knowledge of the consolidation process is further expanded in Volume 1 Chapter 7, which addresses the consolidation of complex groups.

QUESTIONS

Question 6.1

On 1 January 20x0 P Ltd acquired an 80% controlling interest in S Ltd for CU 210 000. At that date S Ltd's equity consisted of the following:

- share capital – CU 150 000; and
- retained earnings – CU 110 000.

At acquisition date, S Ltd's identifiable net assets were considered to be fairly valued.

The abridged statements of profit or loss of P Ltd and its subsidiary S Ltd for the reporting period ended 31 December 20x5 are as follows:

	P Ltd	S Ltd
	CU	CU
Revenue	470 000	380 000
Cost of sales	(376 000)	(275 500)
Gross profit	94 000	104 500
Other income	97 000	30 000
Depreciation	(25 000)	(9 000)
Other expenses	(36 000)	(45 000)
Profit before taxation	130 000	80 500
Taxation	(56 000)	(17 000)
PROFIT FOR THE YEAR	**74 000**	**63 500**

Note: Neither P Ltd nor S Ltd had any other comprehensive income for the 20x5 financial year.

An extract from the abridged statements of changes in equity of the two entities for the reporting period ended 31 December 20x5 is as follows:

	Retained earnings	
	P Ltd	S Ltd
	CU	CU
Balance at 1 Jan 20x5	380 000	226 000
Profit for the year	74 000	63 500
Dividend paid	(65 000)	(28 000)
Balance at 31 Dec 20x5	389 000	261 500

Note: Retained earnings was the only reserve of both P Ltd and S Ltd.

At 31 December 20x5 the following items, among others, appeared in the two entities' statements of financial position:

	P Ltd	S Ltd
	CU	CU
Property, plant and equipment: Carrying amount	265 000	48 000
Inventory at cost	23 000	52 000

Further information

1. During the 20x5 reporting period S Ltd paid management fees of CU 25 000 to P Ltd.

2. Included in P Ltd's property, plant and equipment is a machine that was sold by S Ltd to P Ltd on 1 January 20x2. S Ltd recorded a profit on disposal of this machine of CU 50 000. This machinery has a remaining useful life of five years on date of disposal to P Ltd and a NIL residual value.

3. Since S Ltd was acquired by P Ltd it has always purchased all its inventory from P Ltd at the normal selling prices, determined by P Ltd as cost plus 35%. Total inventory sales from P Ltd to S Ltd for the reporting period ended 31 December 20x5 amounted to CU 180 000.

4. At the beginning of the reporting period, S Ltd had inventories on hand (all purchased from P Ltd) of CU 35 000.

5. On 2 February 20x5 S Ltd sold non-depreciable property that it had acquired at a cost of CU 100 000 on 14 June 20x3, to P Ltd for CU 130 000.

6. P Ltd elected to measure the non-controlling interest in S Ltd at its proportionate share of S Ltd's identifiable net assets at acquisition date.

7. Ignore tax implications.

8. P Ltd measured its investment in S Ltd at cost price, in accordance with IAS 27.10(a), in its separate financial statement.

Required

(a) Prepare the pro forma journal entries required to prepare the consolidated financial statements of the P Ltd group for the year ended 31 December 20x5.

(b) Prepare the abridged consolidated statement of profit or loss and other comprehensive income of the P Ltd group for the year ended 31 December 20x5.

(c) Prepare the following extracts from the consolidated statement of changes in equity of the P Ltd group for the year ended 31 December 20x5:
   - retained earnings column; and
   - non-controlling interest column.

(d) Present the following items as they would appear in the consolidated statement of financial position of the P Ltd group as at 31 December 20x5:
   - property, plant and equipment; and
   - inventories.

Question 6.2

The following balances appeared in the trial balances of P Ltd and its 80% owned subsidiary S Ltd for the year ended 28 February 20x6:

Abridged trial balances at 28 February 20x6	P Ltd Dr/(Cr) CU	S Ltd Dr/(Cr) CU
Share capital	(750 000)	(170 000)
Retained earnings (1 March 20x5)	(245 000)	(140 000)
Trade and other payables	(88 000)	(19 000)
Plant: Cost	450 000	210 000
Plant: Accumulated depreciation	(80 000)	(50 000)
Inventory	90 000	35 000
Trade and other receivables	540 000	212 000
Investment in S Ltd: Cost	205 000	–
Profit after tax	(122 000)	(78 000)

Further information

1. On 1 March 20x2 P Ltd acquired an 80% controlling interest in S Ltd. At acquisition date S Ltd's equity comprised share capital of CU 170 000 and retained earnings of CU 35 000 and S Ltd's net assets were considered to be fairly valued.

2. Since acquisition, S Ltd has sold inventory to P Ltd at a gross profit percentage of 25%. During the current financial year, S Ltd sold inventory to P Ltd amounting to CU 125 000. The closing inventory of P Ltd, purchased from S Ltd, was CU 60 000 on 28 February 20x6 (28 February 20x5: CU 45 000).

3. On 1 December 20x3 S Ltd sold equipment to P Ltd for an amount of CU 80 000. The carrying amount of the equipment on 1 December 20x3 was CU 60 000 with a remaining useful life of four years. The tax authority allowed P Ltd to write off the cost of the equipment purchased from S Ltd over four years, pro-rated.

4. On 31 October 20x4 P Ltd acquired land at a cost of CU 50 000, which it immediately sold to S Ltd for CU 85 000. S Ltd disposed of this land at a profit to a party outside the group on 1 February 20x6.

5. Assume an income tax rate of 28% and that 80% of capital gains are included in taxable income.

Required

(a) Calculate the amount that will be disclosed as opening retained earnings in the consolidated statement of changes in equity of the P Ltd group for the year ended 28 February 20x6.

(b) Calculate the amount that will be disclosed as profit for the period attributable to the non-controlling interest, in the consolidated statement of profit or loss and other comprehensive income of the P Ltd group, for the year ended 28 February 20x6.

(c) Calculate the amount that will be disclosed as profit for the period attributable to the owners of the parent, in the consolidated statement of profit or loss and other comprehensive income of the P Ltd group for the year ended 28 February 20x6.

(d) Calculate the amount that will be disclosed as deferred tax (indicating whether an asset or a liability) in the consolidated statement of financial position of the P Ltd group as at 28 February 20x6.

(e) Calculate the amount that will be disclosed as property, plant and equipment in the consolidated statement of financial position of P Ltd group as at 28 February 20x6.

(f) Provide the pro forma journal entries that would be passed in the 20x6 financial year, assuming P Ltd sells the equipment that it purchased intragroup from S Ltd to a party outside the group on 28 February 20x6.

References

IAS 2 *Inventories*

IAS 12 *Income Taxes*

IAS 36 *Impairment of Assets*

IFRS 10 *Consolidated Financial Statements*

CONSOLIDATION OF COMPLEX GROUPS

LEARNING OBJECTIVES

After studying this chapter, you should be able to:

- understand the differences between a simple group, a horizontal group, a vertical group and a mixed group;

- understand what a direct controlling interest and an indirect controlling interest in a subsidiary are;

- know what an effective interest in the profit and post-acquisition reserves of a subsidiary is;

- determine the effective interest of a parent in the profit and post-acquisition reserves of the subsidiaries making up a horizontal group, a vertical group and a mixed group;

- determine the effective interest of the non-controlling interest in the profit and post-acquisition reserves of the subsidiaries making up a horizontal group, a vertical group and a mixed group;

- prepare consolidated financial statements for a horizontal group;

- understand how to account for intragroup transactions in the consolidated financial statements of a vertical group and a mixed group;

- prepare consolidated financial statements for a vertical group in the following circumstances:

  - the parent acquires a controlling interest in a subsidiary on the same date that this subsidiary acquires a controlling interest in a sub-subsidiary;

  - the parent acquires a controlling interest in a subsidiary, after which this subsidiary acquires a controlling interest in a sub-subsidiary; and

  - a subsidiary acquires a controlling interest in a sub-subsidiary before the parent acquires a controlling interest in the subsidiary.

- prepare consolidated financial statements for a mixed group.

TOPIC LIST

Introduction

So far in this publication we have dealt only with the preparation of consolidated financial statements for a **parent** and its **wholly or partly owned subsidiary**. Such a group structure is called a **simple group** as it consists of **a parent** and **its single subsidiary**.

Group structures, however, may take many forms, for example, a parent may have a number of subsidiaries and each subsidiary may itself be a parent (i.e., control its own subsidiaries), which makes the consolidation process more complicated.

In this chapter we consider the implications of different types of group structure on the preparation of consolidated financial statements. In particular, we look at:

- a **horizontal group**, which has a single-level structure in which a parent has a direct controlling interest in two or more subsidiaries;

- a **vertical group**, where the parent has a subsidiary and this subsidiary in turn has a subsidiary of its own; and

- a **mixed group**, where the parent and its subsidiary each own equity interests in a third entity such that the combination of the parent's and its subsidiary's ownership interests result in the parent having a controlling interest in the third entity, which then becomes another subsidiary of the parent.

Note that complex group structures that **include associates and joint ventures** are dealt with in **Volume 2 Chapter 2.**

7.1   Consolidation of a horizontal group

As discussed above, in a horizontal group the parent holds a direct equity interest in two or more subsidiaries. In addition, these subsidiaries do *not* hold any interests in each other or in other subsidiaries, that is, they are *not* **parent entities themselves.** This group structure is presented in Figure 7.1.

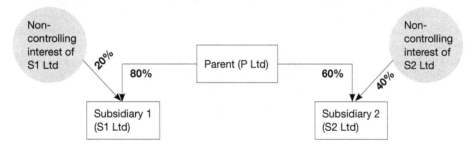

Figure 7.1: *Horizontal group structure*

Given that a horizontal group has a single-level shareholding structure, the consolidation process and procedures are essentially the same as those that apply to a simple group as dealt with in Volume 1 Chapters 3 to 6. The only difference is that for a horizontal group, these consolidation procedures now need to be applied to **more than one subsidiary**. This means that for **each subsidiary** in the horizontal group:

- a separate analysis of equity should be drawn up; and
- a set of pro forma journal entries must be processed.

The consolidated financial statements of a horizontal group will combine the assets, liabilities, income, expenses and equity of **multiple** subsidiaries (adjusted for the effects of subsidiary assets and liabilities remeasured to fair value at acquisition in terms of IFRS 3 Business Combinations, the elimination of common items, and the elimination of intragroup transactions and balances) with that of the parent. In addition, in a horizontal group where the subsidiaries are partly owned (see Figure 7.1) there will be **multiple non-controlling shareholders**, that is, non-controlling shareholders in **each partly owned subsidiary** of the group that will **share in the equity** of **each partly owned subsidiary** of the group.

 Example 7.1: Consolidation of a horizontal group

P Ltd acquired an 80% controlling interest in S1 Ltd on 1 January 20x1 for CU 178 000.

- On acquisition date, the share capital and retained earnings of S1 Ltd was CU 100 000 and CU 80 000 respectively. Furthermore, at this date, S1 Ltd's identifiable net assets were considered to be fairly valued.
- The non-controlling interest is measured at its fair value, which was CU 46 000 at acquisition date.
- Since its acquisition, S1 Ltd has sold inventories to P Ltd at cost plus 25%. S1 Ltd made inventory sales of CU 138 000 to P Ltd during the current year. In addition, P Ltd had opening inventory and closing inventory on hand, purchased from S1 Ltd, of CU 86 000 and CU 75 000 respectively.

P Ltd acquired a 60% controlling interest in S2 Ltd on 31 December 20x3 for CU 126 500.

- On acquisition date, the share capital and retained earnings of S2 Ltd was CU 120 000 and CU 35 000 respectively.
- The non-controlling interest is measured at its fair value, which was CU 76 200 at acquisition date.
- At acquisition date the net assets of S2 Ltd were considered to be fairly valued, with the exception of land, which was undervalued by CU 28 000.
- On 31 December 20x5 S2 Ltd sold plant at a profit of CU 45 000 to P Ltd.

P Ltd accounts for its investments in subsidiaries at cost price in accordance with IAS 27.10(a). In addition, an income tax rate of 28% and an effective capital gains tax rate of 22.4% apply.

The trial balances of P Ltd and its two subsidiaries for the financial year ended 31 December 20x5 appear below.

Trial balances at 31 December 20x5	P Ltd Dr/ (Cr) CU	S1 Ltd Dr/(Cr) CU	S2 Ltd Dr/(Cr) CU
Share capital	(350 000)	(100 000)	(120 000)
Retained earnings (1 Jan 20x5)	(490 000)	(260 000)	(115 600)
Dividend paid (31 Dec 20x5)	50 000	15 000	10 000
Trade and other payables	(126 000)	(68 300)	(128 000)
Plant	260 000	108 000	115 000
Land	–	–	75 000
Trade and other receivables	302 100	295 000	241 250
Inventory	117 900	96 000	57 350
Investment in S1 Ltd: Cost	178 000	–	–
Investment in S2 Ltd: Cost	126 500	–	–
Sales	(550 000)	(398 000)	(268 000)
Cost of sales	417 000	258 000	129 350
Other income	(22 000)	(13 270)	(52 000)
Other expenses	26 000	15 000	12 650
Income tax expense	60 500	52 570	43 000

Required

(a) Present a group diagram and a timeline.

(b) Prepare the relevant analyses of equity as at 31 December 20x5

(c) Provide the pro forma journals necessary to prepare consolidated financial statements for the P Ltd group for the financial year ended 31 December 20x5.

(d) Prepare the consolidated financial statements for the P Ltd group for the financial year ended 31 December 20x5.

 ## Solution 7.1: Consolidation of a horizontal group

Part (a): Group diagram and timeline

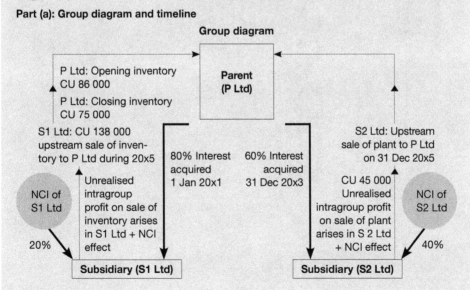

Group diagram

439

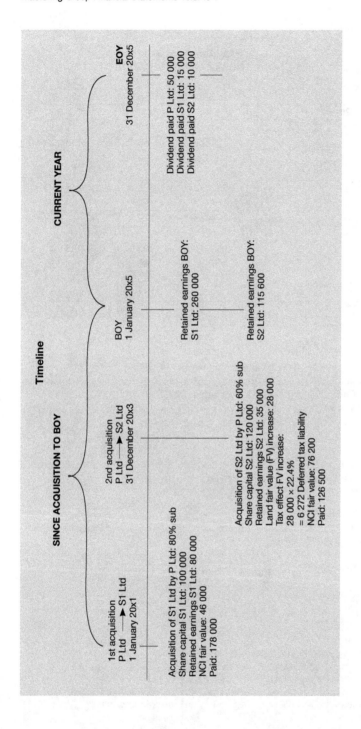

Timeline

SINCE ACQUISITION TO BOY

CURRENT YEAR

1st acquisition
P Ltd ➤ S1 Ltd
1 January 20x1

2nd acquisition
P Ltd ➤ S2 Ltd
31 December 20x3

BOY
1 January 20x5

EOY
31 December 20x5

Acquisition of S1 Ltd by P Ltd: 80% sub
Share capital S1 Ltd: 100 000
Retained earnings S1 Ltd: 80 000
NCI fair value: 46 000
Paid: 178 000

Acquisition of S2 Ltd by P Ltd: 60% sub
Share capital S2 Ltd: 120 000
Retained earnings S2 Ltd: 35 000
Land fair value (FV) increase: 28 000
Tax effect FV increase:
28 000 × 22.4%
= 6 272 Deferred tax liability
NCI fair value: 76 200
Paid: 126 500

Retained earnings BOY:
S1 Ltd: 260 000

Retained earnings BOY:
S2 Ltd: 115 600

Dividend paid P Ltd: 50 000
Dividend paid S1 Ltd: 15 000
Dividend paid S2 Ltd: 10 000

The preceding illustrations show a horizontal group with the following:

- A **parent: P Ltd – 100% of the assets** (except for P Ltd's investments in S1 Ltd and S2 Ltd, which are eliminated on consolidation), **liabilities, income** (as adjusted for the intragroup dividend eliminations) and **expenses** of which will be included in the consolidated financial statements.

- An **80% partly owned subsidiary** of P Ltd: **S1 Ltd** – 100% of the **assets, liabilities, income** and **expenses** (as adjusted for the effects of the intragroup sales of inventory) of which will be included in the consolidated financial statements. In addition, the non-controlling interest in S1 Ltd will be allocated 20% of the current year profit and post-acquisition reserves (i.e., post-acquisition equity) of S1 Ltd.

- A **60% partly owned subsidiary** of P Ltd: **S2 Ltd – 100% of the assets, liabilities, income** and **expenses** (as adjusted for the effects of the intragroup sale of plant) of which will be included in the consolidated financial statements. In addition, the **non-controlling interest in S2 Ltd** will be allocated **40%** of the **current year profit** and **post-acquisition reserves (i.e., post-acquisition equity) of S2 Ltd.**

Furthermore, the following is apparent:

- P Ltd acquires **two simple subsidiaries**, S1 Ltd and S2 Ltd, at different dates. Each acquisition by P Ltd is **a separate business combination** as per IFRS 3. This means that **two business combinations occur**, with the result that any **goodwill or gain on bargain purchase** that arises in respect of **each business combination** must be **recognised in the consolidated financial statements of the P Ltd group.**

- P Ltd obtains control of S1 Ltd on 1 January 20x1, with the result that S1 Ltd must be consolidated from this date. This implies the following regarding S1 Ltd's inclusion in the consolidated financial statements:

  - Both **S1 Ltd's at acquisition equity** of **CU 180 000** (100 000 Share capital + 80 000 Retained earnings) and **P Ltd's CU 178 000 investment in S1 Ltd**, must be **eliminated** on consolidation.

  - The **non-controlling interest in S1 Ltd's at acquisition equity** must be **recognised** at its **CU 46 000 fair value** at acquisition date.

  - **Goodwill** of **CU 44 000** [(178 000 Consideration paid + 46 000 NCI) – 180 000 At acquisition net asset value] arising on the acquisition of S1 Ltd must be **recognised**.

  - **S1 Ltd's current year profit**, and the **post-acquisition increase in its retained earnings**, form part of the P Ltd group's profit and post-acquisition reserves, and must be allocated **80% to P Ltd** and **20% to the non-controlling interest of S1 Ltd.**

- P Ltd obtains control of S2 Ltd on 31 December 20x3, with the result that S2 Ltd must be consolidated from this date. This implies the following regarding S2 Ltd's inclusion in the consolidated financial statements:

  - Both **S2 Ltd's at acquisition equity** of **CU 155 000** (120 000 Share capital + 35 000 Retained earnings) and **P Ltd's CU 126 500 investment in S2 Ltd**, must be **eliminated** on consolidation.

  - In accordance with IFRS 3, the at acquisition carrying amount of **S2 Ltd's land** must be **increased by CU 28 000** to its **at acquisition fair value.**

  - A **CU 6 272** (28 000 × 22.4%) **at acquisition deferred tax liability** must be recognised in respect of the at acquisition fair value remeasurement adjustment to S2 Ltd's land.

  - The **non-controlling interest in S2 Ltd's at acquisition equity** must be recognised at its **CU 76 200 fair value** at acquisition date.

  - **Goodwill of CU 25 972** [(126 500 Consideration paid + 76 200 NCI = 202 700) – (155 000 + 28 000 – 6 272 = 176 728 At acquisition net asset value)] arising on the acquisition of S2 Ltd must be **recognised.**

  - S2 Ltd's **current year profit,** and the **post-acquisition increase in its retained earnings**, form part of the P Ltd group's profit and post-acquisition reserves, and must be allocated **60% to P Ltd** and **40% to the non-controlling interest of S2 Ltd.**

In addition, there are several intragroup transactions within the P Ltd group. The effects of these intragroup transactions, on consolidation, are discussed below.

Current and prior year upstream sale of inventory by S1 Ltd to P Ltd

In the prior year, S1 Ltd sold inventory intragroup at a profit to P Ltd. CU 86 000 of this inventory sold intragroup was still on hand as closing inventory of P Ltd at prior year end. This prior year closing inventory became the current year's opening inventory that was sold outside the group in the current year. This implies the following:

- In the current year pro forma consolidation journal passed (see Part (c) Pro forma journal 3):
  - We **reduce S1 Ltd's opening retained earnings balance** by the **CU 12 384** (86 000 Prior year closing inventory x 25/125 Profit element = 17 200 Intragroup profit x 72%) **after tax effect** of the prior year elimination of S Ltd's CU 17 200 unrealised intragroup profit on sale of inventory.
  - We **reduce S1 Ltd's cost of sales by CU 17 200**, thereby recognising in the current year, S1 Ltd's CU 17 200 prior year intragroup profit on sale of inventory.
  - We **increase S1 Ltd's income tax expense by CU 4 816** (17 200 x 28%), thereby recognising the current year tax effect of recognising S1 Ltd's CU 17 200 prior year intragroup profit in the current year.
- Since the above-mentioned CU 17 200 prior year intragroup profit arose in **partly owned subsidiary S1 Ltd,** the **non-controlling interest of S1 Ltd** is allocated the following:
  - Its 20% share of the CU 12 384 after-tax prior year elimination of this prior year unrealised intragroup profit. This allocation reduces the non-controlling interest opening balance, as reported in the consolidated statement of changes in equity, by CU 2 476 (12 384 x 20%).
  - Its 20% share of the CU 12 384 after-tax current year recognition of this prior year intragroup profit. This allocation increases the profit attributable to the non-controlling interest, as reported in the consolidated statement of profit or loss and other comprehensive income, by CU 2 477 (12 384 x 20%).

In the current year, S1 Ltd sold inventory intragroup at a profit to P Ltd. CU 75 000 of this inventory sold intragroup was still on hand as closing inventory of P Ltd at current year end. This implies the following:

- In the current year pro forma consolidation journals passed (see Part (c) Pro forma journal 6 and 7):
  - We **eliminate from S1 Ltd's profit or loss its current year CU 15 000** (75 000 Current year closing inventory x 25/125 Profit element) **unrealised intragroup profit recognised** on inventory sold, thereby **reducing S1 Ltd's profit or loss by CU 15 000.**
  - We **decrease S1 Ltd's income tax expense by CU 4 200** (15 000 x 28%) and recognise a corresponding **CU 4 200 deferred tax asset of P Ltd**, thereby recognising the current year tax effects of eliminating S1 Ltd's CU 15 000 current year unrealised intragroup profit on inventory sold.
  - We **eliminate S1 Ltd's CU 15 000 unrealised intragroup profit** from the **CU 75 000 cost of P Ltd's closing inventory** on hand at current year end, purchased from S1 Ltd.
- Since the above-mentioned CU 15 000 current year unrealised intragroup profit arose in **partly owned subsidiary S1 Ltd**, the **non-controlling interest of S1 Ltd is allocated its 20% share of the CU 10 800** (15 000 x 72%) **after-tax elimination of this intragroup profit.** This allocation decreases the profit attributable to the non-controlling interest, as reported in the consolidated statement of profit or loss and other comprehensive income, by CU 2 160 (10 800 × 20%).

S2 Ltd's current year upstream sale of plant to P Ltd

At current year end, S2 Ltd sold plant intragroup to P Ltd and recognised a CU 45 000 profit on this sale. This implies the following:

- In the current year pro forma consolidation journals passed (see Part (c) Pro forma journals 9 and 10):

- ▪ We **eliminate S2 Ltd's current year CU 45 000 unrealised intragroup profit** recognised on plant sold to P Ltd, thereby **reducing S2 Ltd's profit or loss by CU 45 000**.

- ▪ We **decrease S2 Ltd's income tax expense by CU 12 600** (45 000 x 28%) and recognise a corresponding **CU 12 600 deferred tax asset** of P Ltd, thereby recognising the current year tax effects of eliminating S2 Ltd's CU 45 000 current year unrealised intragroup profit on plant sold to P Ltd.

- ▪ We **eliminate S2 Ltd's CU 45 000 unrealised intragroup profit** from the **cost of P Ltd's plant** acquired intragroup from S2 Ltd.

- • Since the above-mentioned CU 45 000 current year unrealised intragroup profit arose in **partly owned subsidiary S2 Ltd**, the **non-controlling interest of S2 Ltd is allocated its 40% share** of the **CU 32 400** (45 000 x 72%) **after-tax elimination of this intragroup profit**. This allocation decreases the profit attributable to the non-controlling interest, as reported in the consolidated statement of profit or loss and other comprehensive income, by CU 12 960 (32 400 x 40%).

Intragroup dividends

P Ltd as well as both S1 Ltd and S2 Ltd paid dividends in the current year. This has the following implications on consolidation:

- • Only the **CU 50 000 dividend paid by P Ltd to its owners** (i.e., shareholders) will be reported in the **retained earnings column** of the consolidated statement of changes in equity.

- • The **total** of **the dividends paid to the non-controlling shareholders of S1 Ltd and S2 Ltd**, amounting to **CU 7 000** [(15 000 x 20%) + (10 000 x 40%)], will be reflected as a **deduction** in the **non-controlling interest column** of the consolidated statement of changes in equity.

- • The **total** of the **intragroup dividends received** by **P Ltd from its subsidiaries** (S1 Ltd and S2 Ltd), **amounting to CU 18 000** [(15 000 x 80%) + (10 000 x 60%)], will be **eliminated from P Ltd's profit or loss** in arriving at the consolidated profit for the current year.

⫸

Part (b): Analyses of equity

Calculations: Analyses of equity as at 31 December 20x5

Calculation 1: Analysis of equity of S1 Ltd as at 31 December 20x5

Acquisition date (1 January 20x1)	Total of S1 Ltd's equity 100% CU	P Ltd 80% At acquisition CU	P Ltd 80% Since acquisition CU	Non-controlling interest 20% CU
Share capital	100 000			
Retained earnings	80 000			
Fair value of net assets of S Ltd	180 000	144 000		36 000
Goodwill (balancing figure)	44 000 **a**	34 000		10 000
Consideration and NCI	224 000	178 000		46 000
Since acquisition				
• To beginning of current year:				
Adjusted retained earnings	167 616		134 093 **b**	33 523
Retained earnings movement (260 000 Balance BOY – 80 000 Balance at acquisition)	180 000		144 000	36 000
Prior year after tax elimination of unrealised intragroup profit: Closing inventory [(86 000 × 25/125) × 72%]	(12 384)		(9 907)	(2 477)
				79 523 **c**
• Current year:				
Adjusted profit for the year	87 284		69 827 **d**	17 457 **e**
Profit for the year (398 000 – 258 000 + 13 270 – 15 000 – 52570)	85 700		68 560	17 140
After tax recognition of prior year intragroup profit realised: [(86 000 × 25/125) × 72%]	12 384		9 907	2 477
After tax elimination of unrealised intragroup profit: Closing inventory [(75 000 × 25/125) × 72%]	(10 800)		(8 640)	(2 160)
Dividend	(15 000)		(12 000) **f**	(3 000) **g**
	463 900		191 920	93 980 **h**

Calculation 2: Analysis of equity of S2 Ltd as at 31 December 20x5

| Acquisition date
(31 December 20x3) | Total of
S2 Ltd's
equity
100%
CU | P Ltd 60% | | Non-
controlling
interest
40%
CU |
		At acquisition CU	Since acquisition CU	
Share capital	120 000			
Retained earnings	35 000			
After tax fair value adjustment: Land (28 000 × 77.6% (100% – 22.4%))	21 728			
Fair value of net assets of S Ltd	176 728	106 037		70 691
Goodwill (balancing figure)	25 972 **A**	20 463		5 509
Consideration and NCI	202 700	126 500		76 200
Since acquisition				
• To beginning of current year:				
Retained earnings movement (115 600 Balance BOY – 35 000 Balance at acquisition)	80 600		48 360 **B**	32 240
				108 440 **C**
• Current year:				
Adjusted profit for the year	102 600		61 560 **D**	41 040 **E**
Profit for the year (268 000 – 129 350 + 52 000 – 12 650 – 43 000)	135 000		81 000	54 000
After tax elimination of unrealised intragroup profit: Plant (45 000 × 72%)	(32 400)		(19 440)	(12 960)
Dividend	(10 000)		(6 000) **F**	(4 000) **G**
	375 900		103 920	145 480 **H**

Part (c): Pro forma journal entries for the year ended 31 December 20x5

Note: A column has been included alongside the pro forma journal entries to keep track of the non-controlling interest balance. This is intended to save you time in tests and exams as the non-controlling interest balance at the beginning of the financial year, which is required in the consolidated statement of changes in equity, may be determined using this column. In addition, the non-controlling interest balance at financial year end, which is required in both the consolidated statements of changes in equity and in the consolidated statement of financial position, may also determined using this column.

AT ACQUISITION

Pro forma journal 1 (J1)	Dr CU	Cr CU	NCI Balance
Share capital (S1 Ltd) (SCIE) (given)	100 000		
Retained earnings (S1 Ltd) (SCIE) (given)	80 000		
Investment in S1 Ltd (P Ltd) (SFP) (given)		178 000	
NCI: S1 Ltd – Equity (SFP) (given – at fair value)		46 000	46 000
Goodwill (SFP) (balancing figure)	44 000		
Elimination of at acquisition equity of S1 Ltd and cost of investment, and recognition of non-controlling interest and goodwill at acquisition of S1 Ltd			

Pro forma journal 2 (J2)	Dr CU	Cr CU	NCI Balance
Share capital (S2 Ltd) (SCIE) (given)	120 000		
Retained earnings (S2 Ltd) (SCIE) (given)	35 000		
Land (S2 Ltd) (SFP) (given: fair value adjustment)	28 000		
Deferred tax (S2 Ltd) (SFP)		Wkg16 272	
Investment in S2 Ltd (P Ltd) (SFP) (given)		126 500	
NCI: S2 Ltd – Equity (SFP) (given – at fair value)		76 200	76 200
Goodwill (SFP) (balancing figure)	25 972		

Elimination of at acquisition equity of S2 Ltd and cost of investment, recognition of fair value adjustment to land and related tax effects thereof, and recognition of non-controlling interest in S2 Ltd and goodwill, at acquisition of S2 Ltd

Workings: Pro forma journals

Working 1
28 000 Fair value adjustment × 22.4% (80% × 28%)

SINCE ACQUISITION TO BEGINNING OF YEAR / CURRENT YEAR

Pro forma journal 3 (J3)	Dr CU	Cr CU
Retained earnings (S1 Ltd) (SCIE)	Wkg212 384	
Income tax expense (S1 Ltd) (P/L)	Wkg34 816	
Cost of sales (S1 Ltd) (P/L) (balancing figure)		17 200

After tax elimination of S1 Ltd prior year unrealised intragroup profit: inventory, to ensure current year opening consolidated retained earnings balance agrees to prior year closing consolidated retained earnings balance, and current year recognition of S1 Ltd prior year intragroup profit: inventory, and related income tax expense

Working 2
(86 000 Prior year closing inventory × 25/125 Unrealised profit component) × 72% After tax

Working 3
(86 000 Opening inventory sold externally × 25/125 Profit component realised) × 28%

Pro forma journal 4 (J4)	Dr CU	Cr CU	
Retained earnings (S1 Ltd) (SCIE)	Wkg433 523		
NCI: S1 Ltd – Equity (SFP)		Wkg433 523	33 523

Allocating the non-controlling interest in S1 Ltd its share of S 1 Ltd's adjusted post-acquisition retained earnings to the beginning of the year

Workings: Pro forma journals

Working 4
(260 000 Balance BOY – 80 000 (J1) Balance at acquisition – 12 384 (J3) After tax elimination of S1 Ltd prior year unrealised intragroup profit: Inventory) × 20% Effective interest of NCI of S 1 Ltd

Pro forma journal 5 (J5)	Dr CU	Cr CU	NCI Balance
Retained earnings (S2 Ltd) (SCIE)	Wkg5 32 240		
NCI: S2 Ltd – Equity (SFP)		Wkg5 32 240	32 240
Allocating the non-controlling interest in S2 Ltd its share of S 2 Ltd's post-acquisition retained earnings to the beginning of the year			**Balance 187 963 BOY (Calc 3)**

Workings: Pro forma journals

Working 5

(115 600 Balance BOY – 35 000 (J2) Balance at acquisition) × 40% Effective interest of NCI of S2 Ltd

CURRENT YEAR

Pro forma journal 6 (J6)	Dr CU	Cr CU
Sales (S1 Ltd) (P/L) (given)	138 000	
Cost of sales (S1 Ltd) (P/L) (balancing figure)		123 000
Inventory (P Ltd) (SFP)		Wkg6 15 000
Elimination of S1 Ltd intragroup sales, cost of sales and unrealised intragroup profit included in closing inventory of P Ltd		

Workings: Pro forma journals

Working 6

75 000 Closing inventory × 25/125 Unrealised profit component

Pro forma journal 7 (J7)	Dr CU	Cr CU
Deferred tax (P Ltd) (SFP)	Wkg7 4 200	
Income tax expense (S1 Ltd) (P/L)		Wkg7 4 200
Tax effect of elimination of S1 Ltd unrealised intragroup profit included in closing inventory of P Ltd		

Workings: Pro forma journals

Working 7

15 000 (J6) Elimination of S1 Ltd unrealised intragroup profit × 28%

Pro forma journal 8 (J8)	Dr CU	Cr CU	
NCI S1 Ltd: Share of S1 Ltd profit or loss (P/L)	Wkg8 17 457		
NCI S1 Ltd – Equity (SFP)		Wkg8 17 457	17 457
Allocating the non-controlling interest of S1 Ltd its share of S1 Ltd's adjusted current year profit			

Workings: Pro forma journals

Working 8

(398 000 – 258 000 + 13 270 – 15 000 – 52 570 = 85 700 Current year profit S1 Ltd + 12 284 (J3) After tax recognition of S1 Ltd prior year intragroup profit: Inventory – 15 000 (J6) Elimination current year unrealised S1 Ltd intragroup profit: Inventory + 4 200 (J7) Tax effect: Elimination current year unrealised S1 Ltd intragroup profit: Inventory) × 20% Effective interest of NCI of S 1 Ltd

Pro forma journal 9 (J9)	Dr CU	Cr CU	NCI Balance
Other income [profit on disposal of plant] (S2 Ltd) (P/L) (given)	45 000		
Plant (P Ltd) (SFP)		45 000	
Elimination of unrealised intragroup profit on sale of plant by S2 Ltd			

Pro forma journal 10 (J10)	Dr CU	Cr CU	
Deferred tax (P Ltd) (SFP)	Wkg9 12 600		
Income tax expense (S2 Ltd) (P/L)		Wkg9 12 600	
Tax effect of elimination of unrealised intragroup profit on sale of plant by S2 Ltd			

Workings: Pro forma journals

Working 9

45 000 (J9) Elimination of S2 Ltd unrealised intragroup profit: Plant × 28%

Pro forma journal 11 (J11)	Dr CU	Cr CU	
NCI S2 Ltd: Share of S2 Ltd profit or loss (P/L)	Wkg10 41 040		
NCI S2 Ltd – Equity (SFP)		Wkg10 41 040	41 040
Allocating the non-controlling interest of S2 Ltd its share of S2 Ltd's adjusted current year profit			

Working 10

(268 000 – 129 350 + 52 000 – 12 650 – 43 000 = 135 000 S2 Ltd Current year profit – 45 000 (J9) Elimination S2 Ltd unrealised intragroup profit: Plant + 12 600 (J10) Tax effect: Elimination S2 Ltd unrealised intragroup profit; Plant) × 40% Effective interest of NCI of S2 Ltd

Pro forma journal 12 (J12)	Dr CU	Cr CU	
Dividend received (P Ltd) (P/L)	Wkg11 12 000		
NCI: S1 Ltd – Equity (SFP) (balancing figure)	3 000		(3 000)
Dividend paid (S1 Ltd) (SCIE) (given)		15 000	
Elimination of intragroup dividend from S1 Ltd and recognition of non-controlling interest of S1 Ltd in the dividend			

Working 11

15 000 (given) Dividend × 80% P Ltd's shareholding

Pro forma journal 13 (J13)	Dr CU	Cr CU	
Dividend received (P Ltd) (P/L)	Wkg12 6 000		
NCI S2 Ltd – Equity (SFP) (balancing figure)	4 000		(4 000)
Dividend paid (S2 Ltd) (SCIE) (given)		10 000	
Elimination of intragroup dividend from S2 Ltd and recognition of non-controlling interest of S2 Ltd in the dividend			

Balance 239 460 EOY (Calc 4)

Working 12

10 000 (given) Dividend × 60% P Ltd's shareholding

The full effects of the preceding pro forma journals on the consolidated financial statements of the P Ltd group for the financial year ended 31 December 20x5 are illustrated in the following consolidation worksheet.

	P Ltd Dr/(Cr) CU	S1 Ltd Dr/(Cr) CU	S2 Ltd Dr/(Cr) CU	Pro forma journals At acquisition Dr/(Cr) CU	Jour-nal ref	Pro forma journals Since acquisition Dr/(Cr) CU	Journal ref	Con-solidated Dr/(Cr) CU
Equity								
Share capital	(350 000)	(100 000)	(120 000)	100 000 120 000	J1 J2			(350 000)
Retained earnings (BOY)	(490 000)	(260 000)	(115 600)	80 000 35 000	J1 J2	12 384 33 523 32 240	J3 J4 J5	(672 453)
Profit: Individual entities	(68 500)	(85 700)	(135 000)					
Consolidated profit attributable to owners of parent								†(181 887)
Dividends	50 000	15 000	10 000			(15 000) (10 000)	J12 J13	50 000
Retained earnings (EOY)	(508 500)	(330 700)	(240 600)					(804 340)
NCI Equity	–	–		(46 000) (76 200)	J1 J2	(33 523) (32 240) (17 457) (41 040) 3 000 4 000	J4 J5 J8 J11 J12 J13	(239 460)
Total equity	(858 500)	(430 700)	(360 600)					(1 393 800)

Explanatory notes

† This amount has been brought forward from the third part of the consolidation worksheet on page 451

	P Ltd Dr/(Cr) CU	S1 Ltd Dr/(Cr) CU	S2 Ltd Dr/(Cr) CU	Pro forma journals At acquisition Dr/(Cr) CU	Journal ref	Pro forma journals Since acquisition Dr/(Cr) CU	Journal ref	Consolidated Dr/(Cr) CU
Liabilities:								
Trade and other payables	(126 000)	(68 300)	(128 000)					(322 300)
Total liabilities	**(126 000)**	**(68 300)**	**(128 000)**					**(322 300)**
Total equity & liabilities	**(984 500)**	**(499 000)**	**(488 600)**					**(1 716 100)**
Assets:								
Plant	260 000	108 000	115 000			(45 000)	J9	438 000
Land	–	–	75 000	28 000	J2			103 000
Trade and other receivables	302 100	295 000	241 250					838 350
Inventory	117 900	96 000	57 350			(15 000)	J6	256 250
Investment in S1 Ltd	178 000	–	–	(178 000)	J1			–
Investment in S2 Ltd	126 500	–	–	(126 500)	J2			–
Goodwill				44 000	J1			69 972
				25 972	J2			
Deferred tax				(6 272)	J2	4 200	J7	10 528
						12 600	J10	
Total assets	**984 500**	**499 000**	**488 600**					**1 716 100**

	P Ltd Dr/(Cr) CU	S1 Ltd Dr/(Cr) CU	S2 Ltd Dr/(Cr) CU	Pro forma journals At acquisition Dr/(Cr) CU	Jour-nal ref	Pro forma journals Since acquisition Dr/(Cr) CU	Journal ref	Con-solidated Dr/(Cr) CU
Profit or loss								
Sales	(550 000)	(398 000)	(268 000)			138 000	J6	(1 078 000) J6
Cost of sales	417 000	258 000	129 350			(17 200)	J3	664 150 J3
						(123 000)	J6	
Other income	(22 000)	(13 270)	(52 000)			45 000	J9	(24 270)
						12 000	J12	
						6 000	J13	
Other expenses	26 000	15 000	12 650					53 650
Taxation	60 500	52 570	43 000			4 816	J3	144 086
						(4 200)	J7	
						(12 600)	J10	
Net profit for the period	(68 500)	(85 700)	(135 000)					(240 384)
NCI: Share of profit						17 457	J8	58 497 J8
						41 040	J11	
Consolidated profit attributable to owners of parent								‡(181 887)

Explanatory notes

‡ This amount has been carried forward to the first part of the consolidation worksheet on page 449

Part (d): Consolidated financial statements for the 20x5 year

P LTD GROUP: CONSOLIDATED STATEMENT OF PROFIT OR LOSS AND OTHER COMPREHENSIVE INCOME FOR THE YEAR ENDED 31 DECEMBER 20x5	
	CU
Revenue (550 000 (P Ltd) + (S1 Ltd: 398 000 – 138 000 (J6) Elimination intragroup sales) + 268 000 (S2 Ltd))	1 078 000
Cost of sales (417 000 (P Ltd) + (S1 Ltd: 258 000 – 17 200 (J3) Recognition prior year intragroup profit – 123 000 (J6) Elimination intragroup cost of sales) + 129 350 (S2 Ltd))	(664 150)
Gross profit	413 850
Other income (P Ltd: 22 000 – 12 000 (J12) Dividend from S1 Ltd – 6 000 (J13) Dividend from S2 Ltd) + 13 270 (S1 Ltd) + (S2 Ltd: 52 000 – 45 000 (J9) Elimination unrealised intragroup profit: Plant))	24 270
Operating expenses (26 000 (P Ltd) + 15 000 (S1 Ltd) + 12 650 (S2 Ltd))	(53 650)
Profit before tax	384 470
Income tax expense (60 500 (P Ltd) + (S1 Ltd: 52 570 + 4 816 (J3) Tax effect: Recognition prior year intragroup profit – 4 200 (J7) Tax effect: Elimination unrealised intragroup profit; Closing inventory) + (S2 Ltd: 43 000 – 12 600 (J10) Tax effect: Elimination unrealised intragroup profit; Plant))	(144 086)
PROFIT FOR THE YEAR	**240 384**
Other comprehensive income	**–**
TOTAL COMPREHENSIVE INCOME FOR THE YEAR	**240 384**
Total comprehensive income attributable to:	
Owners of the parent (balancing figure)	181 887
Non-controlling interest (NCI of S1 Ltd: 17 457 (see Calc 1 **e OR** (J8)) + NCI of S2 Ltd: 41 040 (see Calc 2 **E OR** (J11))	58 497
	240 384

P LTD GROUP: CONSOLIDATED STATEMENT OF CHANGES IN EQUITY FOR THE YEAR ENDED 31 DECEMBER 20x5					
	Parent equity holders' interest			Non-control-ling interest	Total equity of the group
	Share capital	Retained earnings	Total parent equity		
	CU	CU	CU	CU	CU
Opening balance at 1 January 20x5	350 000	Wkg1 672 453	1 022 453	Wkg2 187 963	1 210 416
Total comprehensive income:					
Profit for the period (from CSOPL_OCI)		181 887	181 887	58 497	240 384
Dividends	–	(50 000)	(50 000)	Wkg3 (7 000)	(57 000)
Closing balance at 31 December 20x5	**350 000**	**804 340**	**1 154 340**	**239 460**	**1 393 800**

Workings: Consolidated statement of changes in equity

Working 1

P Ltd: 490 000 + (S1 Ltd: 134 093 (see Calc 1 **b**) P Ltd Share of post-acquisition retained earnings to BOY of S1 Ltd) + (S2 Ltd: 48 360 (see Calc 2 **B**) P Ltd Share of post-acquisition retained earnings to BOY of S2 Ltd)

OR

P Ltd: 490 000 + (S1 Ltd: 260 000 Balance BOY – 80 000 (J1) Balance at acquisition – 12 384 (J3) After tax elimination of prior year unrealised intragroup profit: Inventory – 33 523 (J4) NCI of S1 Ltd: Share of S1 Ltd post-acquisition retained earnings to BOY) + (S2 Ltd: 115 600 Balance BOY – 35 000 (J2) Balance at acquisition – 32 240 (J5) NCI of S2 Ltd: Share of S2 Ltd post-acquisition retained earnings to BOY)

Working 2

NCI of S1 Ltd: 79 523 (see Calc 1 **c**) + NCI of S2 Ltd: 108 440 (see Calc 2 **C**)

OR

NCI of S1 Ltd and S2 Ltd: 187 963 (see pro forma journal entries: Calc 3)

Working 3

NCI share of S1 Ltd dividend: 3 000 (see Calc 1 **g OR** (J12)) + NCI share of S2 Ltd dividend: 4 000 (see Calc 2 **G OR** (J13))

P LTD GROUP: CONSOLIDATED STATEMENT OF FINANCIAL POSITION AS AT 31 DECEMBER 20x5	
	CU
Assets	
Non-current assets	
Property, plant and equipment (P Ltd: 260 000 – 45 000 (J9) Elimination unrealised intragroup profit: Plant) + 108 000 (S1 Ltd) + (S2 Ltd: 115 000 Plant + 75 000 Land + 28 000 (J2) At acquisition fair value adjustment: Land)	541 000
Goodwill (S1 Ltd: 44 000 (see Calc 1 **a OR** (J1)) + (S2 Ltd: 25 972 (see Calc 2 **A OR** (J2)))	69 972
Deferred tax (P Ltd: – 6 272 (J2) Deferred tax liability: Fair value adjustment land + 12 600 (J10) Deferred tax asset: Elimination unrealised intragroup profit plant + 4 200 (J7) Deferred tax asset: Elimination unrealised intragroup profit closing inventory)	10 528
Current assets	
Trade and other receivables (302 100 (P Ltd) + 295 000 (S1 Ltd) + 241 250 (S2 Ltd))	838 350
Inventory (P Ltd: 117 900 – 15 000 (J6) Elimination unrealised intragroup profit) + 96 000 (S1 Ltd) + 57 350 (S2 Ltd))	256 250
Total assets	1 716 100
Equity and liabilities	
Share capital (from CSCIE)	350 000
Retained earnings (from CSCIE)	804 340
Equity attributable to owners of the parent	1 154 340
Non-controlling interest (from CSCIE) **OR** (see pro forma journal entries: Calc 4) **OR** (93 980 (see Calc 1 **h**) + 145 480 (see Calc 2 **H**))	239 460
Total equity	1 393 800
Current liabilities	
Trade and other payables (126 000 (P Ltd) + 68 300 (S1 Ltd) + 128 000 (S2 Ltd))	322 300
Total equity and liabilities	1 716 100

7.2 Consolidation of a vertical group

7.2.1 Overview

As discussed in 7.1, a typical vertical group consists of a **parent company**, which **controls** a **subsidiary company**, which in turn has a **subsidiary of its own**, hereafter referred to as the sub-subsidiary. This group structure is presented in Figure 7.2. (Note that for purposes of this publication the principles and procedures explained for preparing consolidated financial statements for a vertical group will be for the type of vertical group as depicted in Figure 7.2. In this vertical group, control of an entity is always obtained by controlling the majority of the voting rights, by means of acquiring a majority shareholding in another entity.)

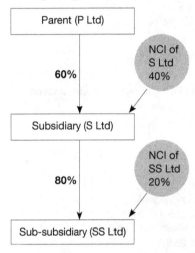

Figure 7.2: *Vertical group structure*

As is clear from Figure 7.2, unlike a simple group or a horizontal group, in a vertical group there are **multiple levels of shareholding** extending downwards from parent to subsidiary to sub-subsidiary (and may extend even further if the sub-subsidiary has subsidiaries of its own).

The consolidation procedures adopted for a vertical group are more complicated than those adopted for a simple group and a horizontal group. This increased complexity stems from the fact that control is exercised at **multiple levels**. The result is that it is **more difficult to determine the non-controlling interest** in a **vertical group** as we have **multiple non-controlling shareholders** at **different levels** within the vertical group structure.

Furthermore, when analysing the interest of P Ltd in S Ltd (see Figure 7.2) it must be remembered that this subsidiary has its own interest in SS Ltd, which needs to be brought to account in the consolidated financial statements of the P Ltd group. In addition, the specific consolidation procedures adopted are determined by the **dates** on which the acquisitions of **S Ltd by P Ltd** and **SS Ltd by S Ltd** occur.

7.2.2 General principles: Consolidation of a vertical group

Consider the vertical group as presented in Figure 7.3:

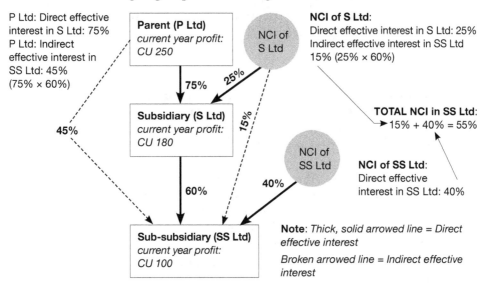

Figure 7.3: *Vertical group showing direct and indirect effective interests*

7.2.2.1 Control

In Volume 1 Chapter 1 we discussed the concepts of **direct** and **indirect controlling interests** in a **subsidiary**. To recap, when the shares of a subsidiary are **owned** by the **parent itself**, this is known as a **direct controlling interest**. An **indirect controlling interest** arises when a **subsidiary of a parent** in turn acquires an interest in **another entity**. If the **subsidiary** is able to **control this entity**, then this **controlled entity** becomes a **subsidiary** of the **parent's subsidiary**. Because the **parent controls the first subsidiary**, it is able to **control** its **subsidiary's shareholding and voting rights** in the **second subsidiary**. This means that the **second subsidiary**, in addition to being a subsidiary of the first subsidiary, is **also a subsidiary** of the **parent**. That is, the **parent** has an **indirect controlling interest** in the **second subsidiary**.

Figure 7.3 shows a vertical group where control of an entity is obtained by controlling the majority of the voting rights, by means of acquiring a majority shareholding in another entity. In the light of the principles discussed in the preceding paragraph, the following is evident in Figure 7.3:

- P Ltd controls S Ltd directly as it controls the majority (75%) of S Ltd's voting rights;
- S Ltd controls SS Ltd directly as it controls the majority (60%) of S Ltd's voting rights; and
- P Ltd controls SS Ltd indirectly as, via its control of S Ltd, it controls S Ltd's 60% majority shareholding and voting rights in SS Ltd. Accordingly, SS Ltd is a subsidiary of P Ltd in addition to being a subsidiary of S Ltd.

Consequently, in the vertical group depicted in Figure 7.3, P Ltd has two subsidiaries, namely S Ltd and SS Ltd, and must prepare consolidated financial statements for the P Ltd group that must include 100% of the assets and liabilities as well as the income and expenses of **both** these subsidiaries. It should also be noted that S Ltd in its own right would be required, unless the exception in IFRS 10.4 (a) applies, to prepare consolidated financial statements for the S Ltd group, which comprises S Ltd as parent and its single subsidiary SS Ltd.

7.2.2.2 Effective interest

A parent's **effective interest** in a subsidiary represents the **percentage** of the subsidiary's **profit or loss, other comprehensive income,** and **post-acquisition reserves allocated** to the **parent** in preparing consolidated financial statements. The effective interest in a subsidiary *not* held by the parent is attributable to **the non-controlling interest** in the subsidiary.

Subject to *one exception*, the **effective interest** in the **profit or loss and changes in equity (i.e., other comprehensive income and post-acquisition reserves)** of the subsidiary is determined solely based on **existing ownership interests.** That is, according to the **percentage shareholdings** in the subsidiary held by **the parent** and by **the non-controlling interest** respectively.

As discussed in Volume 1 Chapter 4, the exception applies to an entity that has **in substance** an existing ownership interest because of a transaction that currently gives the entity access to the returns associated with an ownership interest. In such a case, the proportion of the subsidiary's profit or loss and changes in equity allocated to the parent and non-controlling interest in preparing the consolidated financial statements is determined by taking into account the **eventual exercise of those potential voting rights** and **other derivatives** that currently give the entity access to the returns (IFRS 10.B90).

It should be noted that a **parent's effective interest** in a subsidiary may *not* equal the **percentage of voting rights controlled** (directly or indirectly) in the subsidiary.

As is shown in Figure 7.3, P Ltd shares in 75% of the post-acquisition profit and reserves of subsidiary S Ltd, which it controls **directly.** P Ltd therefore has a 75% **direct effective interest** in S Ltd's profit and post-acquisition reserves. Consequently, on consolidation, P Ltd is allocated CU 135 (180 × 75% Direct effective interest) of S Ltd's current year profit. Furthermore, P Ltd also shares in 75% of S Ltd's 60% share in the current year profit and post-acquisition reserves of sub-subsidiary SS Ltd. This means that P Ltd's actual share of the profit and post-acquisition reserves of SS Ltd, which it controls **indirectly,** via S Ltd, is 45% (75% × 60%). P Ltd therefore has a 45% **indirect effective interest** in SS Ltd's profit and post-acquisition reserves. Accordingly, on consolidation, P Ltd is allocated CU 45 (100 profit × 45% (75% × 60%) Indirect effective interest) of SS Ltd's current year profit.

Similarly, as indicated in Figure 7.3, the non-controlling shareholders in S Ltd have a direct effective interest of 25% in the post-acquisition profit and reserves of S Ltd and a 15% (25% × 60%) indirect effective interest in SS Ltd's profit and post- acquisition reserves. This means that the non-controlling interest of S Ltd will be attributed CU 45 (180 × 25% Direct effective interest) of S Ltd's current year profit and CU 15 (100 × 15% Indirect effective interest) of SS Ltd's current year profit. It is important also to remember that the non-controlling shareholders of SS Ltd will be attributed an appropriate share of SS Ltd's current year profit and post-acquisition reserves. These non-controlling shareholders have a direct effective interest of 40% in SS Ltd's current year profit and post-acquisition reserves. Accordingly, the non-controlling interest of SS Ltd will be allocated CU 40 (100 × 40% Direct effective interest) of SS Ltd's current year profit.

Based on the discussion in the paragraphs above, an extract of the consolidated statement of profit or loss for the P Ltd group, as depicted in Figure 7.3 would appear as follows:

EXTRACT: CONSOLIDATED STATEMENT OF PROFIT OR LOSS FOR THE P LTD GROUP	
	CU
Profit for the year (250 (P Ltd) + 180 (S Ltd) + 100 (SS Ltd))	530
Profit attributable to:	
Owners of the parent	[Wkg1]430
Non-controlling interest	[Wkg2]100
	530

Workings: Extract consolidated statement of profit or loss

Working 1

	CU
Profit P Ltd	250
P Ltd Share of profit of S Ltd (180 × 75% Direct effective interest)	135
P Ltd Share of profit of SS Ltd (100 × 45% (60% × 75%) Indirect effective interest)	45
	430

Working 2

	CU
NCI of SS Ltd: Share of profit of SS Ltd (100 ×40% Direct effective interest)	40
NCI of S Ltd: Share of profit of SS Ltd (100 × 15% (25% × 60%) Indirect effective interest)	15
NCI of S Ltd: Share of profit of S Ltd (180 × 25% Direct effective interest)	45
	100

It is also apparent from Figure 7.3 that the **non-controlling interest of S Ltd and SS Ltd together** have an **effective interest of 55%** (15% + 40%) in the post-acquisition profit and reserves of **SS Ltd**. In other words, the **total non-controlling interest** in SS Ltd's post-acquisition profit and reserves is **55%**. This makes sense as the parent has an effective interest of 45% (75% × 60%) in SS Ltd, so the remaining 55% interest in SS Ltd must be held by non-controlling shareholders of both SS Ltd and S Ltd.

7.2.3 Preparing consolidated financial statements of a vertical group

Given the additional complexity of consolidating a vertical group, particularly, in determining the correct non-controlling interest amounts as well as the profits and post-acquisition reserves of the subsidiaries of the group that are ultimately attributable to the parent (and by extension to the shareholders of the parent), it is recommended that analyses of equity be drawn up for **both** subsidiary **S Ltd** and sub-subsidiary **SS Ltd**. More specifically:

- **Start** by drawing up the analysis of equity of the **'bottom subsidiary'** SS Ltd in which SS Ltd's profit and post-acquisition reserves are analysed from the perspective of **S Ltd**, the 'middle subsidiary'. From this analysis you will be able to determine the share of profit and post-acquisition reserves of SS Ltd attributable to S Ltd and to the non-controlling interest of SS Ltd.

- **Thereafter,** compile the analysis of equity for **S Ltd** in which S Ltd's current year profit and post-acquisition reserves are analysed from the perspective of the ultimate parent in the group, **P Ltd**. In this analysis of equity it is important to include **S Ltd's share of SS Ltd's post-acquisition reserves and current year profit** – obtained from SS Ltd's analysis of equity. This will enable you to determine the appropriate share of the post-acquisition profit and reserves of SS Ltd attributable to P Ltd and to the non-controlling shareholders of S Ltd. Furthermore, as noted above, the sequence in which the direct controlling interest in S Ltd and SS Ltd is acquired by P Ltd and S Ltd respectively affects certain aspects of the consolidation process. Three different scenarios are dealt with below.

7.2.3.1 Simultaneous acquisitions

In this scenario P Ltd acquires a direct controlling interest in S Ltd on the **same date** that S Ltd acquires a controlling interest in SS Ltd. The consolidation process for this scenario is illustrated and explained by means of a comprehensive example included in the Volume 1 Chapter 7 supplementary material, which may be accessed online from the JUTA website.

7.2.3.2 Parent acquires subsidiary before subsidiary acquires sub-subsidiary

In a situation where the parent, P Ltd, acquires its direct controlling interest in subsidiary, S Ltd, **before** S Ltd acquires its direct controlling interest in the sub-subsidiary, SS Ltd, there are **two business combinations**, as follows:

- first, when P Ltd acquires its controlling interest in S Ltd; and
- second, when S Ltd acquires its controlling interest in SS Ltd at a later date.

This implies the following when preparing the consolidated financial statements of the P Ltd group:

- Any **goodwill (or bargain purchase gain)** arising upon **P Ltd's acquisition of S Ltd must be recognised in the consolidated financial statements of the P Ltd group.** Any such goodwill (or bargain purchase gain) recognised, must be calculated with reference to the at acquisition net asset value of **S Ltd only**. This is because S Ltd acquires SS Ltd in a **separate business combination** that occurs **after** the group reporting entity, P Ltd, has acquired S Ltd. Accordingly, P Ltd acquires the identifiable net assets of **S Ltd only** and *not* those of an existing group made up of S Ltd and its subsidiary SS Ltd.

- Any goodwill (or bargain purchase gain) that arises arising upon **S Ltd's acquisition of SS Ltd** must **also be recognised in the consolidated financial statements of the P Ltd group.**

- The **post-acquisition reserves** (e.g., retained earnings and revaluation surplus) of **S Ltd and of SS Ltd,** that are to be included in the consolidated financial statements of the P Ltd group, must be determined from the date of acquisition of **each respective subsidiary.**

Furthermore, when preparing the consolidated financial statements of the P Ltd group each reporting period, the following will apply:

- **100%** of the **assets**[7], **liabilities, income and expenses** of **P Ltd, S Ltd and SS Ltd** will be included in the consolidated financial statements of the P Ltd group.
- **S Ltd's current year profit or loss** and **post-acquisition reserves** will be allocated to **P Ltd** and to the **non-controlling interest in S Ltd** based on each respective party's **direct** effective interest in such profit or loss and post-acquisition reserves.
- **SS Ltd's current year profit or loss** and **post-acquisition reserves** will be allocated to **P Ltd** and to the **non-controlling interest in S Ltd** based on each respective party's **indirect** effective interest in such profit or loss and post-acquisition reserves.
- **SS Ltd's current year profit or loss** and **post-acquisition reserves** will be allocated to the **non-controlling interest in SS Ltd** based on its **direct** effective interest in such profit or loss and post-acquisition reserves.
- **Equity attributable to the owners of the parent each reporting date** will consist of the following:
  - **P Ltd's equity** at reporting period end; and
  - **P Ltd's share** of the **post-acquisition equity of S Ltd and of SS Ltd.**
- **The non-controlling interest each reporting date** will consist of the following:
  - **S Ltd's equity** attributable to the **non-controlling interest of S Ltd;** and
  - **SS Ltd's equity** attributable to the **non-controlling interest of both S Ltd and SS Ltd.**

---

7   Except for P Ltd's investment in S Ltd, and S Ltd's investment in SS Ltd, which are eliminated on consolidation.

Example 7.2: Consolidation of a vertical group: Parent acquires subsidiary before subsidiary acquires sub-subsidiary

P Ltd acquired an 80% controlling interest in S Ltd on 1 January 20x3 for CU 130 000, when S Ltd's retained earnings were CU 55 000 and its share capital was CU 80 000.

S Ltd acquired a 55% controlling interest in SS Ltd on 1 January 20x4 for CU 90 000, when SS Ltd's retained earnings were CU 86 000 and its share capital was CU 50 000.

The abridged trial balances of the three companies on 31 December 20x5 were as follows:

Abridged trial balances at 31 December 20x5	P Ltd Dr/(Cr) CU	S Ltd Dr/(Cr) CU	SS Ltd Dr/(Cr) CU
Share capital	(250 000)	(80 000)	(50 000)
Retained earnings (1 Jan 20x5)	(320 000)	(190 000)	(133 000)
Trade and other payables	(126 000)	(83 500)	(22 340)
Property, plant and equipment	409 600	248 000	170 590
Trade and other receivables	306 200	97 500	91 250
Investment in S Ltd: Cost	130 000	–	–
Investment in SS Ltd: Cost	–	90 000	–
Profit for the period	(149 800)	(82 000)	(56 500)

The group measures the non-controlling interest at its proportionate share of the identifiable net assets of the relevant subsidiary acquired.

All the assets and liabilities of the subsidiaries were considered to be fairly valued at acquisition date.

Both P Ltd and S Ltd measure their investments in subsidiaries at cost price.

Required

(a) Present a group diagram and a timeline.

(b) Prepare the relevant analyses of equity as at 31 December 20x5.

(c) Provide the pro forma journals necessary to prepare consolidated financial statements for the P Ltd group for the financial year ended 31 December 20x5.

(d) Prepare the consolidated financial statements for the P Ltd group for the financial year ended 31 December 20x5.

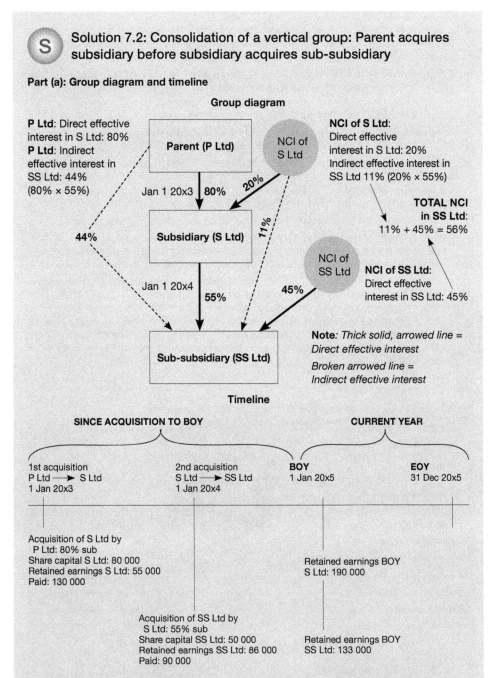

S **Solution 7.2: Consolidation of a vertical group: Parent acquires subsidiary before subsidiary acquires sub-subsidiary**

Part (a): Group diagram and timeline

Group diagram

P Ltd: Direct effective interest in S Ltd: 80%
P Ltd: Indirect effective interest in SS Ltd: 44% (80% × 55%)

NCI of S Ltd: Direct effective interest in S Ltd: 20% Indirect effective interest in SS Ltd 11% (20% × 55%)

Parent (P Ltd)

NCI of S Ltd

Jan 1 20x3 | 80% | 20%

44%

11%

Subsidiary (S Ltd)

TOTAL NCI in SS Ltd: 11% + 45% = 56%

NCI of SS Ltd

Jan 1 20x4 | 55% | 45%

NCI of SS Ltd: Direct effective interest in SS Ltd: 45%

Sub-subsidiary (SS Ltd)

Note: *Thick solid, arrowed line = Direct effective interest*

Broken arrowed line = Indirect effective interest

Timeline

SINCE ACQUISITION TO BOY | CURRENT YEAR

1st acquisition
P Ltd ➞ S Ltd
1 Jan 20x3

2nd acquisition
S Ltd ➞ SS Ltd
1 Jan 20x4

BOY
1 Jan 20x5

EOY
31 Dec 20x5

Acquisition of S Ltd by
 P Ltd: 80% sub
Share capital S Ltd: 80 000
Retained earnings S Ltd: 55 000
Paid: 130 000

Retained earnings BOY
S Ltd: 190 000

Acquisition of SS Ltd by
 S Ltd: 55% sub
Share capital SS Ltd: 50 000
Retained earnings SS Ltd: 86 000
Paid: 90 000

Retained earnings BOY
SS Ltd: 133 000

From the preceding illustrations we can see that we have a vertical group with the following:

- A **parent: P Ltd – 100%** of the **assets** (except for P Ltd's investment in S Ltd, which is eliminated on consolidation), **liabilities**, **income** and **expenses** of which will be included in the consolidated financial statements of the P Ltd group;

- A **subsidiary: S Ltd – 100%** of the **assets** (except for S Ltd's investment in SS Ltd, which is eliminated on consolidation), **liabilities, income and expenses** of which will be included in the consolidated financial statements of the P Ltd group; and

- A **sub-subsidiary: SS Ltd – 100%** of the **assets, liabilities, income and expenses** of which will be included in the consolidated financial statements of the P Ltd group.

In addition, the following is apparent:

- The parent, P Ltd, acquired its subsidiary, S Ltd, *before* S Ltd had acquired its sub-subsidiary SS Ltd; therefore, P Ltd acquired a **simple subsidiary**.

- Any goodwill or gain on bargain purchase arising from P Ltd's acquisition of S Ltd is based purely on S Ltd's net asset value and the consideration paid for it by P Ltd – P Ltd did *not* also acquire the net asset value of SS Ltd upon its acquisition of S Ltd (i.e., the S Ltd **group** was not acquired) because SS Ltd did not yet exist in the P Ltd group at date of acquisition of S Ltd.

- S Ltd was part of the P Ltd group when it acquired SS Ltd, which implies the following:

  ▪ **Any goodwill (or gain on bargain purchase)** arising on S Ltd's acquisition of SS Ltd, must be **recognised in the P Ltd group financial statements** as it arose in a separate business combination which occurred after S Ltd had already become part of the P Ltd group.

  ▪ All the **changes in equity of SS Ltd** that arose **after its acquisition by S Ltd** constitute **post-acquisition equity of the P Ltd group** and must therefore be included in the P Ltd group consolidated financial statements. More particularly, **SS Ltd's current year profit**, and the **increase in its retained earnings** from its **acquisition date, 1 January 20x4**, to the **beginning of the current year**, form **part of the P Ltd group's profit and reserves** and must be **allocated to P Ltd** as well as to the **non-controlling interest of both S Ltd and SS Ltd**.

Part (b): Analyses of equity

Calculation 1: Analysis of equity of SS Ltd as at 31 December 20x5

Acquisition date (1 January 20x4)	Total of SS Ltd's equity 100% CU	P Ltd 55% At acquisition CU	P Ltd 55% Since acquisition CU	Non-controlling interest 45% CU
Share capital	50 000			
Retained earnings	86 000			
Fair value of net assets of SS Ltd	136 000	74 800		61 200
Goodwill (balancing figure)	15 200 a	15 200		–
Consideration and NCI	151 200	90 000		61 200
Since acquisition				
• To beginning of current year:				
Retained earnings movement (133 000 Balance BOY – 86 000 Balance at acquisition)	47 000		25 850[1] b	21 150
				82 350[2] c
• Current year:				
Profit for the year (given)	56 500		31 075[1] d	25 425[3] e
				107 775 f

Explanatory notes: Analysis of equity of SS Ltd

1. Recall that these amounts, which represent **S Ltd's share in the post-acquisition reserves and current year profit of SS Ltd**, must be **included in the analysis of equity of S Ltd** so that they may be allocated to **P Ltd** and to the **non-controlling interest of S Ltd**.

    Therefore, be careful *not* to use these amounts as the SS Ltd post-acquisition reserves and current year profit attributable to P Ltd. Remember, we are preparing consolidated financial statements for the P **Ltd group** and *not* the S Ltd group.

2. This amount is the **SS Ltd non-controlling interest opening balance**, which is **added** to the **S Ltd non-controlling interest opening balance** (see analysis of equity of S Ltd, Calc 2 **C**) to determine the total **non-controlling interest opening balance** that is reported in the P Ltd group's consolidated statement of changes in equity (see Part (d)).

3. This amount is the 45% share in SS Ltd's current year profit that is attributable to the non-controlling interest of SS Ltd. This **amount is added** to the **share of the non-controlling interest of S Ltd in both SS Ltd's and S Ltd's current year profit** (see analysis of equity of S Ltd, Calc 2 **E**) to arrive at the **consolidated profit for the year attributable to the non-controlling interest,** which is reported in the P Ltd group's consolidated statement of profit or loss and other comprehensive income (see Part (d)).

Calculation 2: Analysis of equity of S Ltd as at 31 December 20x5

| | Total of S Ltd's equity 100% CU | P Ltd 80% | | Non-controlling interest 20% |
		At acquisition CU	Since acquisition CU	
At acquisition date (1 January 20x3)				CU
Share capital	80 000			
Retained earnings	55 000			
Fair value of net assets of S Ltd	135 000	108 000		27 000
Goodwill (balancing figure)	22 000 **A**	22 000		–
Consideration and NCI	157 000	130 000		27 000
Since acquisition				
• To beginning of current year:				
Retained earnings movement	160 850		128 680[1] **B**	32 170[2]
S Ltd (190 000 Balance BOY – 55 000 Balance at acquisition)	135 000		108 000	27 000
SS Ltd (Calc 1**b**)	25 850		20 680	5 170
				59 170[3] **C**
• Current year:				
Profit for the year	113 075		90 460[4] **D**	22 615[5] **E**
Profit S Ltd	82 000		65 600	16 400
Profit SS Ltd (see Calc 1**d**)	31 075		24 860	6 215
				81 785 **F**

Explanatory notes: Analysis of equity of S Ltd

[1] This amount is **P Ltd's share** of the **post-acquisition retained earnings** of both **S Ltd** and **SS Ltd** to the **beginning of the year**. This **amount** is **added** to **P Ltd's opening retained earnings balance** to determine the **consolidated opening retained earnings balance** of the P Ltd group, reported in the consolidated statement of changes in equity of the P Ltd group (see Part (d)).

Check:
P Ltd share of S Ltd post-acquisition retained earnings to BOY:
CU 108 000 (135 000 × 80% direct effective interest)

PLUS
P Ltd share of SS Ltd post-acquisition retained earnings to BOY:
CU 20 680 (47 000 × 44% (80% × 55%) indirect effective interest)

EQUALS: CU 128 680

[2] This amount is the share of the **non-controlling interest of S Ltd** in the **post-acquisition retained earnings up until the beginning of the year** of both **S Ltd** (20% Share / Direct effective interest) and **SS Ltd** (11% (20% × 55%) Share / Indirect effective interest).

Check:
NCI of S Ltd, share of S Ltd post-acquisition retained earnings to BOY:
CU 27 000 (135 000 × 20% Direct effective interest)

PLUS
NCI of S Ltd, share of SS Ltd post-acquisition retained earnings to BOY:
CU 5 170 (47 000 × 11% (20% × 55%) Indirect effective interest)

EQUALS: CU 32 170

[3] This amount is the **S Ltd non-controlling interest opening balance**, which is **added to the SS Ltd non-controlling interest opening balance** (see analysis of equity of SS Ltd, Calc 1 **c**) to determine the **non-controlling interest opening balance**, reported in the consolidated statement of changes in equity of the P Ltd group (see part (d)).

[4] This amount represents **P Ltd's share** of the **current year profit** of both **S Ltd and SS Ltd**. This **amount is added** to the **profit of P Ltd** to determine the **total consolidated profit for the year attributable to the owners of P Ltd**, reported in the consolidated statement of profit or loss and other comprehensive income of the P Ltd group (see part (d)).

Check:
P Ltd share of S Ltd profit for the year: CU 65 600 (82 000 × 80% Direct effective interest)
PLUS
P Ltd share of SS Ltd profit for the year: CU 24 860 (56 500 × 44% (80% × 55%) Indirect effective interest)

EQUALS: CU 90 460

[5] This amount is the share of the **non-controlling interest of S Ltd** in the **current year profit** of both **S Ltd** (20% Share / Direct effective interest) and **SS Ltd** (11% (20% × 55%) Share/ Indirect effective interest). **This amount is added** to the **45% share of SS Ltd's current year profit, attributable to the non-controlling interest of SS Ltd** (see analysis of equity of SS Ltd, Calc 1 **e** above), to determine the **consolidated profit for the year attributable to the non-controlling interest**, reported in the consolidated statement of profit or loss and other comprehensive income of the P Ltd group (see part (d)).

Check:
NCI of S Ltd, share of S Ltd profit for the year: CU 16 400 (82 000 × 20% Direct effective interest)
PLUS
NCI of S Ltd, share of SS Ltd profit for the year: CU 6 215 (56 500 × 11% (20% × 55%) Indirect effective interest)

EQUALS: CU 22 615

Part (c): Pro forma journal entries for the 20x5 financial year

AT ACQUISITION

Pro forma journal 1 (J1)	Dr CU	Cr CU	NCI Balance
Share capital (SS Ltd) (SCIE) (given)	50 000		
Retained earnings (SS Ltd) (SCIE) (given)	86 000		
Investment in SS Ltd (S Ltd) (SFP) (given)		90 000	
NCI: SS Ltd – Equity (SFP)		Wkg161 200	61 200
Goodwill (SFP) (balancing figure)	15 200		
Elimination of at acquisition equity of SS Ltd and cost of investment in SS Ltd and recognition of non-controlling interest and goodwill upon acquisition of SS Ltd			

Workings: Pro forma journals

Working 1
(50 000 + 86 000) × 45% Effective interest of NCI of SS Ltd

Pro forma journal 2 (J2)	Dr CU	Cr CU	
Share capital (S Ltd) (SCIE) (given)	80 000		
Retained earnings (S Ltd) (SCIE) (given)	55 000		
Investment in S Ltd (P Ltd) (SFP) (given)		130 000	
NCI: S Ltd – Equity (SFP)		Wkg227 000	27 000
Goodwill (SFP) (balancing figure)	22 000		
Elimination of at acquisition equity of S Ltd and cost of investment in S Ltd, and recognition of non-controlling interest and goodwill at acquisition of S Ltd			

Workings: Pro forma journals

Working 2
(80 000 + 55 000) × 20% Effective interest of NCI of S Ltd

SINCE ACQUISITION TO BEGINNING OF THE YEAR

Pro forma journal 3 (J3)	Dr CU	Cr CU	
Retained earnings (SS Ltd) (SCIE)	Wkg321 150		
NCI: SS Ltd – Equity (SFP)		Wkg321 150	21 150
Allocating the non-controlling interest in SS Ltd its share of SS Ltd's post-acquisition retained earnings to the beginning of the year			

Workings: Pro forma journals

Working 3
(133 000 SS Ltd Balance BOY – 86 000 SS Ltd Balance at acquisition) × 45% Effective interest of NCI of SS Ltd

Pro forma journal 4 (J4)	Dr CU	Cr CU	NCI Balance
Retained earnings (SS Ltd) (SCIE)	[Wkg4]5 170		
Retained earnings (S Ltd) (SCIE)	[Wkg5]27 000		
NCI: S Ltd – Equity (SFP) (balancing figure)		32 170	32 170
Allocating the non-controlling interest in S Ltd its share of SS Ltd's and S Ltd's post-acquisition retained earnings to the beginning of the year			

Workings: Pro forma journals

Working 4
(133 000 SS Ltd Balance BOY – 86 000 SS Ltd Balance at acquisition) ×
11% (20% × 55%) Effective interest of NCI of S Ltd

Working 5
(190 000 S Ltd Balance BOY – 55 000 S Ltd Balance at acquisition) ×
20% Effective interest of NCI of S Ltd

**Balance 141 520
BOY (Calc 3)**

CURRENT YEAR

Pro forma journal 5 (J5)	Dr CU	Cr CU	NCI Balance
NCI of SS Ltd: Share of SS Ltd profit or loss (P/L)	[Wkg6]25 425		
NCI: SS Ltd – Equity (SFP)		[Wkg6]25 425	25 425
Allocating the non-controlling interest of SS Ltd its share of SS Ltd's current year profit			

Workings: Pro forma journals

Working 6
56 500 Profit of SS Ltd × 45% Effective interest of NCI of SS Ltd

Pro forma journal 6 (J6)	Dr CU	Cr CU	NCI Balance
NCI of S Ltd: Share of SS Ltd profit or loss (P/L)	[Wkg7]6 215		
NCI of S Ltd: Share of S Ltd profit or loss (P/L)	[Wkg8]16 400		
NCI: S Ltd – Equity (SFP)		22 615	22 615
Allocating the non-controlling interest of S Ltd its share of SS Ltd's and S Ltd's current year profit			

Workings: Pro forma journals

Working 7
56 500 Profit of SS Ltd × 11% Effective interest of NCI of S Ltd

Working 8
82 000 Profit of S Ltd × 20% Effective interest of NCI of S Ltd

**Balance 189 560
EOY (Calc 4)**

The full effects of the preceding pro forma journals on the consolidated financial statements of the P Ltd group for the financial year ended 31 December 20x5 are illustrated in the following consolidation worksheet.

	P Ltd Dr/(Cr) CU	S Ltd Dr/(Cr) CU	SS Ltd Dr/(Cr) CU	Pro forma journals At acquisition Dr/(Cr) CU	Journal ref	Pro forma journals Since acquisition Dr/(Cr) CU	Journal ref	Consolidated Dr/(Cr) CU
Equity								
Share capital	(250 000)	(80 000)	(50 000)	50 000 / 80 000	J1 / J2			(250 000)
Retained earnings (BOY)	(320 000)	(190 000)	(133 000)	86 000 / 55 000	J1 / J2	21 150 / 5 170 / 27 000	J3 / J4 / J4	(448 680)
Profit: Individual entities	(149 800)	(82 000)	(56 500)					
Consolidated profit attributable to owners of parent		–						†(240 260)
Retained earnings (EOY)	(469 800)	(272 000)	(189 500)					(688 940)
NCI Equity	–			(61 200) / (27 000)	J1 / J2	(21 150) / (32 170) / (25 425) / (22 615)	J3 / J4 / J5 / J6	(189 560)
Total equity	(719 800)	(352 000)	(239 500)					(1 128 500)
Liabilities:								
Trade and other payables	(126 000)	(83 500)	(22 340)					(231 840)
Total liabilities	(126 000)	(83 500)	(22 340)					(231 840)
Total equity & liabilities	(845 800)	(435 500)	(261 840)					(1 360 340)

Explanatory notes

† This amount has been brought forward from the second part of the consolidation worksheet on page 468

	P Ltd Dr/(Cr) CU	S Ltd Dr/(Cr) CU	SS Ltd Dr/(Cr) CU	Pro forma journals At acquisition Dr/(Cr) CU	Journal ref	Pro forma journals Since acquisition Dr/(Cr) CU	Journal ref	Consolidated Dr/(Cr) CU
Assets:								
Property, plant and equipment	409 600	248 000	170 590					828 190
Trade and other receivables	306 200	97 500	91 250					494 950
Investment in S Ltd	130 000	–	–	(130 000)	J2			–
Investment in SS Ltd	–	90 000	–	(90 000)	J1			–
Goodwill				15 200	J1			37 200
				22 000	J2			
Total assets	845 800	435 500	261 840					1 360 340
Profit or loss								
Profit for the period	(149 800)	(82 000)	(56 500)					(288 300)
NCI: Share of profit						25 425	J5	48 040
						6 215	J6	
						16 400	J6	
Consolidated profit attributable to owners of parent								‡(240 260)

Explanatory notes

‡ This amount has been carried forward to the first part of the consolidation worksheet on page 467

Part (d): Consolidated financial statements for the 20x5 financial year

P LTD GROUP: ABRIDGED CONSOLIDATED STATEMENT OF PROFIT OR LOSS AND OTHER COMPREHENSIVE INCOME FOR THE YEAR ENDED 31 DECEMBER 20x5	
	CU
PROFIT FOR THE YEAR (149 800 (P Ltd) + 82 000 (S Ltd) + 56 500 (SS Ltd))	288 300
Other comprehensive income	–
TOTAL COMPREHENSIVE INCOME	288 300
Total comprehensive income attributable to:	
Owners of the parent (balancing figure) **OR** (149 800 (P Ltd) + 90 460 (S Ltd) (see Calc 2 **D**))	240 260
Non-controlling interest (NCI of SS Ltd: 25 425 (see Calc 1 **e OR** (J5)) + NCI of S Ltd: 22 615 (see Calc 2 **E OR** (J6))	48 040
	288 300

P LTD GROUP: CONSOLIDATED STATEMENT OF CHANGES IN EQUITY FOR THE YEAR ENDED 31 DECEMBER 20X5					
	Parent equity holders' interest			**Non-controlling interest**	**Total equity of the group**
	Share capital	**Retained earnings**	**Total parent equity**		
	CU	CU	CU	CU	CU
Opening balance at 1 January 20x5	250 000	Wkg1448 680	698 680	Wkg2141 520	840 200
Total comprehensive income:					
Profit for the period (from CSOPL_OCI)		240 260	240 260	48 040	288 300
Closing balance at 31 December 20x5	250 000	688 940	938 940	189 560	1 128 500

Workings: Consolidated statement of changes in equity

Working 1
P Ltd: 320 000 + S Ltd: 128 680 (see Calc 2 **B**) P Ltd Share of the post-acquisition retained earnings of S Ltd and SS Ltd to BOY

OR

P Ltd: 320 000 + (S Ltd: 190 000 Balance BOY – 55 000 (J2) Balance at acquisition – 27 000 (J4) NCI of S Ltd: Share of post-acquisition retained earnings of S Ltd to BOY) + (SS Ltd: 133 000 Balance BOY – 86 000 (J1) Balance at acquisition – 21 150 (J3) NCI of SS Ltd: Share of post-acquisition retained earnings of SS Ltd to BOY – 5 170 (J4) NCI of S Ltd: Share of post-acquisition retained earnings of SS Ltd to BOY)

Working 2
NCI of S Ltd: 59 170 (see Calc 2 **C**) + NCI of SS Ltd: 82 350 (see Calc 1 **c**)

OR

NCI of S Ltd and SS Ltd: 141 520 (see pro forma journal entries: Calc 3)

P LTD GROUP: CONSOLIDATED STATEMENT OF FINANCIAL POSITION AS AT 31 DECEMBER 20x5	
	CU
Assets	
Non-current assets	
Property, plant and equipment (409 600 (P Ltd) + 248 000 (S Ltd) + 170 590 (SS Ltd))	828 190
Goodwill (S Ltd: 22 000 (see Calc 2 **A OR** (J2)) + (SS Ltd: 15 200 (see Calc 1 **a OR** (J1))	37 200
Current assets	
Trade and other receivables (306 200 (P Ltd) + 97 500 (S Ltd) + 91 250 (SS Ltd))	494 950
Total assets	1 360 340
Equity and liabilities	
Share capital (from CSCIE)	250 000
Retained earnings (from CSCIE)	688 940
Equity attributable to owners of the parent	938 940
Non-controlling interest (from CSCIE) **OR** (see pro forma journal entries: Calc 4) **OR** (107 775 (see Calc 2 **f**) + 81 785 (see Calc 2 **F**))	189 560
Total equity	1 128 500
Current liabilities	
Trade and other payables (126 000 (P Ltd) + 83 500 (S Ltd) + 22 340 (SS Ltd))	231 840
Total equity and liabilities	1 360 340

7.2.3.3 Parent acquires subsidiary after subsidiary acquires sub-subsidiary

Where a parent, P Ltd, acquires an interest in its subsidiary, S Ltd, **after** that subsidiary has acquired its own interest in sub-subsidiary, SS Ltd, P Ltd has acquired a **group**. More precisely, the S Ltd group is acquired, which comprises S Ltd as the parent entity and its single, directly held subsidiary, S Ltd.

The implications of P Ltd acquiring the **S Ltd group** when preparing the consolidated financial statements of the P Ltd group (i.e., P Ltd as parent and its two subsidiaries, S Ltd and SS Ltd) are as follows:

- The **acquisition date**, from the perspective of the **P Ltd group**, of **both subsidiaries** S Ltd and SS Ltd, is the **acquisition date of S Ltd by P Ltd**. This means that any changes in the reserves (and therefore the equity) of SS Ltd from acquisition date of SS Ltd by S Ltd to date of acquisition of S Ltd by P Ltd must, from the **P Ltd group's perspective**, form part of **at acquisition reserves (and equity)**. In other words, the equity acquired by P Ltd at acquisition date of S Ltd (and the S Ltd group) is a **combination** of the equity of **S Ltd itself** and the equity of **SS Ltd that has accrued to S Ltd since it acquired SS Ltd.**

- Consequently, it is the equity of SS Ltd **on date of acquisition of the S Ltd group by P Ltd** that needs to be determined, and then included in the at acquisition section of the analysis of equity of SS Ltd. It is then **this at acquisition equity** of SS Ltd that is compared to the consideration paid by S Ltd for SS Ltd in order to calculate any goodwill or gain on bargain purchase that is initially determined to have arisen.

- When completing the at acquisition section of the analysis of equity of **S Ltd**, any **goodwill** or **gain on bargain purchase** calculated in respect of **S Ltd's acquisition of SS Ltd** – as discussed immediately above – must be **reversed**. This is because P Ltd, when acquiring the **S Ltd group**, is paying for the goodwill (or obtaining a bargain purchase) in respect of **both S Ltd and SS Ltd**. By reversing the goodwill or gain on bargain purchase arising from S Ltd's acquisition of SS Ltd, we are therefore preventing the goodwill or bargain purchase gain from being double counted in the P Ltd group's consolidated financial statements. We can also say that from the **P Ltd group's perspective** there is only **one business combination** that takes place (i.e., acquisition of S Ltd by P Ltd) and therefore there should only be one goodwill or gain on bargain purchase figure recognised for this **single business combination**.

- The post-acquisition equity of both S Ltd and SS Ltd that forms part of the P Ltd group's equity is then determined by establishing the movement in the reserves of both these subsidiaries **from the acquisition date of S Ltd by P Ltd** to the end of the current reporting period.

Furthermore, when preparing the consolidated financial statements of the P Ltd group each reporting period, the following will apply:

- **100%** of the **assets**[8], **liabilities, income and expenses** of **P Ltd, S Ltd and SS Ltd** will be included in the consolidated financial statements of the P Ltd group.

- **S Ltd's current year profit or loss and post-acquisition reserves** will be allocated to **P Ltd** and to the **non-controlling interest in S Ltd** based on each respective party's **direct** effective interest in such profit or loss, and post-acquisition reserves.

- **SS Ltd's current year profit or loss and post-acquisition reserves** will be allocated to **P Ltd** and to the **non-controlling interest in S Ltd** based on each respective party's **indirect** effective interest in such profit or loss and post-acquisition reserves.

- **SS Ltd's current year profit or loss and post-acquisition reserves** will be allocated to the **non-controlling interest in SS Ltd** based on its **direct** effective interest in such profit or loss and post-acquisition reserves.

- **Equity attributable to the owners of the parent each reporting date** will consist of the following:
  - **P Ltd's equity** at reporting period end; and
  - **P Ltd's share of the post-acquisition equity of S Ltd and of SS Ltd**.

- **The non-controlling interest each reporting date** will consist of the following:
  - **S Ltd's equity** attributable to the **non-controlling interest of S Ltd**; and
  - **SS Ltd's equity** attributable to the **non-controlling interest** of both **S Ltd and SS Ltd**.

---

8   Except for P Ltd's investment in S Ltd, and S Ltd's investment in SS Ltd, which are eliminated on consolidation.

Example 7.3: Consolidation of a vertical group: Subsidiary acquires sub-subsidiary before parent acquires subsidiary

S Ltd acquired a 55% controlling interest in SS Ltd on 1 January 20x3 for CU 90 000, when SS Ltd's retained earnings were CU 39 000 and its share capital was CU 50 000.

P Ltd acquired an 80% controlling interest in S Ltd on 1 January 20x4 for CU 130 000, when:

- S Ltd's retained earnings were CU 55 000 and its share capital was CU 80 000; and
- SS Ltd's retained earnings were CU 79 000 and its share capital was CU 50 000.

The abridged trial balances of the three companies on 31 December 20x5 were as follows:

Abridged trial balances at 31 December 20x5	P Ltd Dr/(Cr) CU	S Ltd Dr/(Cr) CU	SS Ltd Dr/(Cr) CU
Share capital	(250 000)	(80 000)	(50 000)
Retained earnings (1 Jan 20x5)	(320 000)	(190 000)	(133 000)
Trade and other payables	(126 000)	(83 500)	(22 340)
Property, plant and equipment	409 600	248 000	170 590
Trade and other receivables	306 200	97 500	91 250
Investment in S Ltd: Cost	130 000	–	–
Investment in SS Ltd: Cost	–	90 000	–
Profit for the period	(149 800)	(82 000)	(56 500)

The group measures the non-controlling interest at its proportionate share of the identifiable net assets of the relevant subsidiary acquired.

All the assets and liabilities of the subsidiaries were considered to be fairly valued at acquisition date.

Both P Ltd and S Ltd measure their investments in subsidiaries at cost price.

Required

(a) Present a group diagram and a timeline.

(b) Prepare the relevant analyses of equity as at 31 December 20x5.

(c) Provide the pro forma journals necessary to prepare consolidated financial statements for the P Ltd group for the financial year ended 31 December 20x5.

(d) Prepare the consolidated financial statements for the P Ltd group for the financial year ended 31 December 20x5.

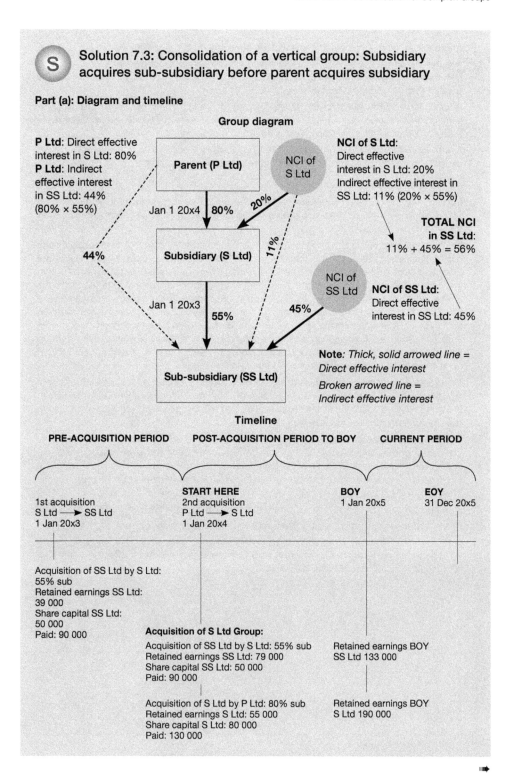

Solution 7.3: Consolidation of a vertical group: Subsidiary acquires sub-subsidiary before parent acquires subsidiary

Part (a): Diagram and timeline

From the above illustrations we can see that we have a vertical group with the following:

- A parent: P Ltd – 100% of the assets (Except for P Ltd's investment in S Ltd, which is elimination on consolidation), liabilities, income and expenses of which will be included in the consolidated financial statements of the P Ltd group;
- A subsidiary: S Ltd – 100% of the assets (Except for S Ltd's investment in SS Ltd, which is elimination on consolidation), liabilities, income and expenses of which will be included in the consolidated financial statements of the P Ltd group; and
- A sub-subsidiary: SS Ltd – 100% of the assets, liabilities, income and expenses of which will be included in the consolidated financial statements of the P Ltd group.

In addition the following is apparent:

- Parent, P Ltd, acquired its subsidiary, S Ltd, after S Ltd had acquired its sub-subsidiary, SS Ltd. Therefore, P Ltd acquired an **existing group** (comprising S Ltd as parent and SS Ltd as subsidiary) on 1 January 20x4.
- For purposes of preparing the consolidated financial statements of the P Ltd group, only **one** acquisition date is relevant, this being the **acquisition date of the S Ltd group** on **1 January 20x4 by P Ltd** as this is the date when the P Ltd group came into being. Therefore, the at acquisition equity of both S Ltd and SS Ltd must be determined on this date. As far as the analysis of the at acquisition equity of SS Ltd is concerned, the retained earnings amount of CU 79 000 of SS Ltd on acquisition date of S Ltd by P Ltd, 1 January 20x4, must be used. SS Ltd's retained earnings balance of CU 39 000 when it was acquired by S Ltd on 1 January 20x3 represents pre acquisition equity at a point in the past when the P Ltd group had not yet come into existence, and is therefore not relevant in the analysis of SS Ltd's at acquisition equity from the P Ltd group's perspective.
- Any **goodwill or gain on bargain purchase** calculated in respect of S Ltd's acquisition of SS Ltd, using the P Ltd group acquisition date of 1 January 20x4, must be **eliminated** when P Ltd analyses **S Ltd's at acquisition equity** and a **new goodwill (or gain on bargain purchase)** amount must be determined.
- The movement in post-acquisition equity of both S Ltd and SS Ltd must be determined for the period from **acquisition date of S Ltd on 1 January 20x4** to the end of the reporting period, on 31 December 20x5. More particularly, SS Ltd's current year profit, and the increase in its retained earnings from 1 January 20x4 to the beginning of the current year, form part of the P Ltd group's profit and reserves and must be allocated:
  - **44% to P Ltd** based on **P Ltd's indirect** effective interest of **44%** (80% × 55%) **in SS Ltd**;
  - **45% to the non-controlling interest of SS Ltd** based on its **45% direct** effective interest in **SS Ltd**; and
  - **11% to the non-controlling interest of S Ltd** based on its **indirect** effective interest of **11%** (20% × 55%) in **SS Ltd**.

Part (b): Analyses of equity as at 31 December 20x5

Calculation 1: Analysis of equity SS Ltd as at 31 December 20x5

Acquisition date (1 January 20x4: when P Ltd acquired S Ltd)	Total of SS Ltd's equity 100% CU	P Ltd 55%		Non-controlling interest 45% CU
		At acquisition CU	Since acquisition CU	
Share capital	50 000			
Retained earnings	79 000			
Fair value of net assets of SS Ltd	136 000	70 950		58 050
Goodwill (balancing figure)	19 050**a**	19 050		–
Consideration and NCI	151 200	90 000		58 050
Since acquisition				
• To beginning of current year:				
Retained earnings movement (133 000 Balance BOY – 79 000 Balance at acquisition)	54 000		29 700**b**	24 300
				82 350[1]**c**
• Current year:				
Profit for the year (given)	56 500		31 075**d**	25 425[2]**e**
				107 775**f**

Explanatory notes: Analysis of equity of SS Ltd

[1]   This amount is the **SS Ltd non-controlling interest opening balance**, which is **added to the S Ltd non-controlling interest opening balance** (see analysis of equity of S Ltd, Calc 2 **C**) to determine the total **non-controlling interest opening balance**, reported in the P Ltd group consolidated statement of changes in equity (see Part (d)).

[2]   This amount is the **45% share in the current year profit of SS Ltd** that is attributable to the **non-controlling interest of SS Ltd**. This **amount is added** to the **share of the non-controlling interest of S Ltd** in the **current year profit of both SS Ltd and S Ltd** (see analysis of equity of S Ltd, Calc 2 **E**) to determine the **consolidated profit for the year attributable to the non-controlling interest**, reported in the P Ltd group consolidated statement of profit or loss and other comprehensive income (see Part (d)).

Additional comments

• Notice how the **at acquisition equity of SS Ltd** is analysed at the date that the **P Ltd group comes into being**, which is the date of acquisition of **S Ltd by P Ltd on 1 January 20x4**. This means that SS Ltd's retained earnings balance of **CU 79 000 on this date is used** and *not* its retained earnings balance of CU 39 000 upon its acquisition by S Ltd on 1 January 20x3.

• Consequently, from the P Ltd group's perspective, it is only the post-acquisition growth in SS Ltd's retained earnings from **1 January 20x4** to the beginning of the current year – amounting to CU 54 000 – that forms part of the P Ltd group's reserves.

Calculation 2: Analysis of equity of S Ltd as at 31 December 20x5

Acquisition date (1 January 20x4)	Total of S Ltd's equity 100% CU	P Ltd 80%		Non-controlling interest 20% CU
		At acquisition CU	Since acquisition CU	
Share capital	80 000			
Retained earnings	55 000			
Goodwill: Acquisition of SS Ltd (see Calc 1 **a**)	(19 050)[1]			
Fair value of net assets of S Ltd	115 950	92 760		23 190
Goodwill (balancing figure)	37 240[1] **A**	37 240		–
Consideration and NCI	153 190	130 000		23 190
Since acquisition				
• To beginning of current year:				
Retained earnings movement	164 700		131 760[2] **B**	32 940[3]
S Ltd (190 000 Balance BOY – 55 000 Balance at acquisition)	135 000		108 000	27 000
SS Ltd (see Calc 1 **b**)	29 700		23 760	5 940
				56 130[4] **C**
• Current year:				
Profit for the year	113 075		90 460[5] **D**	22 615[6] **E**
Profit S Ltd	82 000		65 600	16 400
Profit SS Ltd (see Calc 1 **d**)	31 075		24 860	6 215
				78 745 **F**

Explanatory notes: Analysis of equity of S Ltd

[1] For purposes of preparing consolidated financial statements for the P Ltd group, there is only **one** business combination that occurs, this being the **acquisition by P Ltd of the S Ltd group**, comprising S Ltd and its subsidiary, SS Ltd. Accordingly, goodwill can be calculated only **once**, and must be determined based on the **combined equity** of the **S Ltd group**, that is, the equity of both S Ltd and SS Ltd on acquisition date of S Ltd by P Ltd.

For this reason, **we eliminate the CU 19 050 goodwill** calculated in **respect of S Ltd's earlier acquisition of SS Ltd** (see analysis of equity of S Ltd, Calc 1 **a**) and replace it with an amount of **CU 37 240**, that represents the **goodwill paid by P Ltd** for the **combined equity** of the **two subsidiaries acquired** (S Ltd and SS Ltd), making up the S Ltd group.

[2] This amount is **P Ltd's share** of the **post-acquisition retained earnings of both S Ltd and SS Ltd** to the **beginning of the year**. This **amount** is **added to P Ltd's opening retained earnings balance** to determine the **consolidated opening retained earnings balance of the P Ltd group**, reported in the consolidated statement of changes in equity of the P Ltd group (see Part (d)).

Check:
P Ltd share of S Ltd post-acquisition retained earnings to BOY:
CU 108 000 (135 000 × 80% Direct effective interest)

PLUS
P Ltd share of SS Ltd post-acquisition retained earnings to BOY:
CU 23 760 (54 000 × 44% (80% × 55%) Indirect effective interest)

EQUALS: CU 131 760

³ This amount is the share of the **non-controlling interest of S Ltd** in the **post-acquisition retained earnings up until the beginning of the year** of **both S Ltd** (20% Share / Direct effective interest) and **SS Ltd** (11% (20% × 55%) Share / Indirect effective interest).

Check:
NCI of S Ltd, share of S Ltd post-acquisition retained earnings to BOY:
CU 27 000 (135 000 × 20% direct effective interest)

PLUS
NCI of S Ltd, share of SS Ltd post-acquisition retained earnings to BOY:
CU 5 940 (54 000 × 11% (20% × 55%) indirect effective interest)

EQUALS: CU 32 940

⁴ This amount is the **S Ltd non-controlling interest opening balance,** which is **added to the SS Ltd non-controlling interest opening balance** (see analysis of equity of SS Ltd, Calc 1 **c**) to determine the **non-controlling interest opening balance**, reported in the consolidated statement of changes in equity of the P Ltd group (see Part (d)).

⁵ This amount is **P Ltd's share** of the **current year profit** of both **S Ltd and SS Ltd. This amount is added** to the **profit of P Ltd** to determine the **total consolidated profit for the year attributable to the owners of P Ltd**, reported in the consolidated statement of profit or loss and other comprehensive income of the P Ltd group (see Part (d)).

Check:
P Ltd share of S Ltd profit for the year: CU 65 600 (82 000 × 80% Direct effective interest)

PLUS
P Ltd share of SS Ltd profit for the year: CU 24 860 (56 500 × 44% (80% × 55%) Indirect effective interest)

EQUALS: CU 90 460

⁶ This amount represents the share of the **non-controlling interest of S Ltd** in the **current year profit** of both **S Ltd** (20% Share / Direct effective interest) and **SS Ltd** (11% (20% × 55%) Share/ Indirect effective interest). **This amount is added** to the **45% share of SS Ltd's current year profit, attributable to the non-controlling interest of SS Ltd** (see analysis of equity of SS Ltd, Calc 1 **e**), to determine the **consolidated profit for the year attributable to the non-controlling interest**, reported in the consolidated statement of profit or loss and other comprehensive income of the P Ltd group (see Part (d)).

Check:
NCI of S Ltd, share of S Ltd profit for the year: CU 16 400 (82 000 × 20% Direct effective interest)

PLUS
NCI of S Ltd, share of SS Ltd profit for the year: CU 6 215 (56 500 × 11% (20% × 55%) Indirect effective interest)

EQUALS: CU 22 615

Part (c): Pro forma journal entries for the 20x5 financial year

AT ACQUISITION

Pro forma journal 1 (J1)	Dr CU	Cr CU	NCI Balance
Share capital (SS Ltd) (SCIE) (given)	50 000		
Retained earnings (SS Ltd) (SCIE) (given)	79 000		
Investment in SS Ltd (S Ltd) (SFP) (given)		90 000	
NCI: SS Ltd – Equity (SFP)		Wkg1 58 050	58 050
Goodwill (SFP) (balancing figure)	19 050		
Elimination of at acquisition equity SS Ltd and cost of investment in SS Ltd and recognition of non-controlling interest and goodwill upon acquisition of SS Ltd			

Workings: Pro forma journals

Working 1
(50 000 + 79 000) × 45% Effective interest of NCI of SS Ltd

Pro forma journal 2 (J2)	Dr CU	Cr CU	
Share capital (S Ltd) (SCIE) (given)	80 000		
Retained earnings (S Ltd) (SCIE) (given)	55 000		
Goodwill (S Ltd) (SFP) (J1)		19 050	
Investment in S Ltd (P Ltd) (SFP) (given)		130 000	
NCI: S Ltd – Equity (SFP)		Wkg2 23 190	23 190
Goodwill (SFP) (balancing figure)	37 240		
Elimination of at acquisition equity of S Ltd, cost of investment in S Ltd, goodwill arising on acquisition of SS Ltd, and recognition of non-controlling interest and goodwill at acquisition of S Ltd			

Workings: Pro forma journals

Working 2
(80 000 + 55 000 – 19 050) × 20% Effective interest of NCI of S Ltd

SINCE ACQUISITION TO BEGINNING OF THE YEAR

Pro forma journal 3 (J3)	Dr CU	Cr CU	
Retained earnings (SS Ltd) (SCIE)	Wkg3 24 300		
NCI: SS Ltd – Equity (SFP)		Wkg3 24 300	24 300
Allocating the non-controlling interest in SS Ltd its share of SS Ltd's post-acquisition retained earnings to the beginning of the year			

Workings: Pro forma journals

Working 3
(133 000 SS Ltd Balance BOY – 79 000 SS Ltd Balance at acquisition) × 45% Effective interest of NCI of SS Ltd

Pro forma journal 4 (J4)	Dr CU	Cr CU	NCI Balance
Retained earnings (SS Ltd) (SCIE)	[Wkg4]5 940		
Retained earnings (S Ltd) (SCIE)	[Wkg5]27 000		
NCI: S Ltd – Equity (SFP) (balancing figure)		32 940	32 940
Allocating the non-controlling interest in S Ltd its share of SS Ltd's and S Ltd's post-acquisition retained earnings to the beginning of the year			**Balance 138 480 BOY (Calc 3)**

Workings: Pro forma journals

Working 4
(133 000 SS Ltd Balance BOY – 79 000 SS Ltd Balance at acquisition) × 11% (20% × 55%) effective interest of NCI of S Ltd

Working 5
(190 000 S Ltd Balance BOY – 55 000 S Ltd Balance at acquisition) × 20% Effective interest of NCI of S Ltd

CURRENT YEAR

Pro forma journal 5 (J5)	Dr CU	Cr CU	NCI Balance
NCI of SS Ltd: Share of SS Ltd profit or loss (P/L)	[Wkg6]25 425		
NCI: SS Ltd – Equity (SFP)		[Wkg6]25 425	25 425
Allocating the non-controlling interest of SS Ltd its share of SS Ltd's current year profit			

Workings: Pro forma journals

Working 6
56 500 Profit of SS Ltd × 45% Effective interest of NCI of SS Ltd

Pro forma journal 6 (J6)	Dr CU	Cr CU	NCI Balance
NCI of S Ltd: Share of SS Ltd profit or loss (P/L)	[Wkg7]6 215		
NCI of S Ltd: Share of S Ltd profit or loss (P/L)	[Wkg8]16 400		
NCI S Ltd – Equity (SFP) (balancing figure)		22 615	22 615
Allocating the non-controlling interest of S Ltd its share of SS Ltd's and S Ltd's current year profit			**Balance 186 520 EOY (Calc 4)**

Workings: Pro forma journals

Working 7
56 500 Profit of SS Ltd × 11% Effective interest of NCI of S Ltd

Working 8
82 000 Profit of S Ltd × 20% Effective interest of NCI of S Ltd

Comments: Pro forma journals

Comments: Pro forma journal 2

- Goodwill of CU 19 050 arose on acquisition of SS Ltd by S Ltd, and was recognised in pro forma journal 1. This goodwill existed before P Ltd acquired the existing S Ltd group. In order to avoid the double counting of goodwill in the P Ltd group financial statements, it is necessary to reverse out this CU 19 050 goodwill. For this reason, the CU 19 050 goodwill recognised in pro forma journal 1 is credited, and thereby eliminated, in this pro forma journal entry.

The full effects of the preceding pro forma journals on the consolidated financial statements of the P Ltd group for the financial year ended 31 December 20x5 are illustrated in the following consolidation worksheet.

	P Ltd Dr/(Cr) CU	S Ltd Dr/(Cr) CU	SS Ltd Dr/(Cr) CU	Pro forma journals At acquisition Dr/(Cr) CU	Journal ref	Pro forma journals Since acquisition Dr/(Cr) CU	Journal ref	Consolidated Dr/(Cr) CU
Equity								
Share capital	(250 000)	(80 000)	(50 000)	50 000 / 80 000	J1 / J2			(250 000)
Retained earnings (BOY)	(320 000)	(190 000)	(133 000)	79 000 / 55 000	J1 / J2	24 300 / 5 940 / 27 000	J3 / J4 / J4	(451 760)
Profit: Individual entities	(149 800)	(82 000)	(56 500)					
Consolidated profit – attributable to owners of parent								†(240 260)
Retained earnings (EOY)	(469 800)	(272 000)	(189 500)					(692 020)
NCI Equity	–	–		(58 050) / (23 190)	J1 / J2	(24 300) / (32 940) / (25 425) / (22 615)	J3 / J4 / J5 / J6	(186 520)
Total equity	**(719 800)**	**(352 000)**	**(239 500)**					**(1 128 540)**
Liabilities:								
Trade and other payables	(126 000)	(83 500)	(22 340)					(231 840)
Total liabilities	**(126 000)**	**(83 500)**	**(22 340)**					**(231 840)**
Total equity & liabilities	**(845 800)**	**(435 500)**	**(261 840)**					**(1 360 380)**

Explanatory notes

† This amount has been brought forward from the second part of the consolidation worksheet on page 481

	P Ltd Dr/(Cr) CU	S Ltd Dr/(Cr) CU	SS Ltd Dr/(Cr) CU	Pro forma journals At acquisition Dr/(Cr) CU	Journal ref	Pro forma journals Since acquisition Dr/(Cr) CU	Journal ref	Con-solidated Dr/(Cr) CU
Assets:								
Property, plant and equipment	409 600	248 000	170 590					828 190
Trade and other receivables	306 200	97 500	91 250					494 950
Investment in S Ltd	130 000	–	–	(130 000)	J2			–
Investment in SS Ltd	–	90 000	–	(90 000)	J1			–
Goodwill				19 050	J1			37 240
				(19 050)	J2			
				37 240	J2			
Total assets	845 800	435 500	261 840					1 360 380
Profit of loss								
Profit for the period	(149 800)	(82 000)	(56 500)					(288 300)
NCI: Share of profit						25 425	J5	48 040
						6 215	J6	
						16 400	J6	
Consolidated profit attributable to owners of parent								‡(240 260)

Explanatory notes

‡ This amount has been carried forward to the first part of the consolidation worksheet on page 480

Part (d): Consolidated financial statements for the 20x5 financial year

P LTD GROUP: ABRIDGED CONSOLIDATED STATEMENT OF PROFIT OR LOSS AND OTHER COMPREHENSIVE INCOME FOR THE YEAR ENDED 31 DECEMBER 20x5	
	CU
PROFIT FOR THE YEAR (149 800 (P Ltd) + 82 000 (S Ltd) + 56 500 (SS Ltd))	288 300
Other comprehensive income	–
TOTAL COMPREHENSIVE INCOME	**288 300**
Total comprehensive income attributable to:	
Owners of the parent (balancing figure) **OR** (149 800 (P Ltd) + 90 460 (S Ltd) (see Calc 2 **D**))	240 260
Non-controlling interest (NCI of SS Ltd: 25 425 (see Calc 1 **e OR** (J5)) + NCI of S Ltd: 22 615 (see Calc 2 **E OR** (J6)))	48 040
	288 300

P LTD GROUP: CONSOLIDATED STATEMENT OF CHANGES IN EQUITY FOR THE YEAR ENDED 31 DECEMBER 20x5					
	Parent equity holders' interest			Non-controlling interest	Total equity of the group
	Share capital	Retained earnings	Total parent equity		
	CU	CU	CU	CU	CU
Opening balance at 1 Jan 20x5	250 000	Wkg1451 760	701 760	Wkg2138 480	840 240
Total comprehensive income:					
Profit for the period (from CSOPL_OCI)		240 260	240 260	48 040	288 300
Closing balance at 31 Dec 20x5	250 000	692 020	942 020	186 520	1 128 540

Workings: Consolidated statement of changes in equity

Working 1
(P Ltd: 320 000 + S Ltd: 131 760 (see Calc 2 **B**)) P Ltd Share of post-acquisition retained earnings of S Ltd and SS Ltd to BOY

OR

P Ltd: 320 000 + (S Ltd: 190 000 Balance BOY – 55 000 (J2) Balance at acquisition – 27 000 (J4) NCI of S Ltd: Share of post-acquisition retained earnings of S Ltd to BOY) + (SS Ltd: 133 000 Balance BOY – 79 000 (J1) Balance at acquisition – 24 300 (J3) NCI of SS Ltd: Share of post-acquisition retained earnings of SS Ltd to BOY – 5 940 (J4) NCI of S Ltd: Share of post-acquisition retained earnings of SS Ltd to BOY)

Working 2
NCI of S Ltd: 56 130 (see Calc 2 **C**) + NCI of SS Ltd: 82 350 (see Calc 1 **c**)

OR

NCI of S Ltd and SS Ltd: 138 480 (see pro forma journal entries: Calc 3)

P LTD GROUP: CONSOLIDATED STATEMENT OF FINANCIAL POSITION AS AT 31 DECEMBER 20x5	
	CU
Assets	
Non-current assets	
Property, plant and equipment (409 600 (P Ltd) + 248 000 (S Ltd) + 170 590 (SS Ltd))	828 190
Goodwill (see Calc 2 **A**) **OR** (19 050 (J1) – 19 050 (J2) + 37 240 (J2))	37 240
Current assets	
Trade and other receivables (306 200 (P Ltd) + 97 500 (S Ltd) + 91 250 (SS Ltd))	494 950
Total assets	1 360 380
Equity and liabilities	
Share capital (from CSCIE)	250 000
Retained earnings (from CSCIE)	692 020
Equity attributable to owners of the parent	942 020
Non-controlling interest (from CSCIE) **OR** (see pro forma journal entries: Calc 4) **OR** (107 775 (see Calc 1 **f**) + 78 745 (see Calc 2 **F**))	186 520
Total equity	1 128 540
Current liabilities	
Trade and other payables (126 000 (P Ltd) + 83 500 (S Ltd) + 22 340 (SS Ltd))	231 840
Total equity and liabilities	1 360 380

7.2.3.4 *Intragroup transactions and balances in vertical groups*

The consolidation principles and procedures pertaining to intragroup transactions and balances as covered in detail in Volume 1 Chapter 6 *do not change* when we are dealing with a vertical group. This is because, irrespective of the particular group structure that we are dealing with, when preparing consolidated financial statements we are always preparing the financial statements of a **single economic entity**.

To recap, on consolidation we are required to **eliminate** in **full all intragroup transactions** and **balances,** including the **unrealised profit or loss** arising from the **intragroup sale of inventory, property, plant and equipment** and other assets.

In addition, as was explained in Volume 1 Chapter 6, the non-controlling interest will bear its share of the elimination and then the subsequent recognition of previously unrealised intragroup profits or losses when the **initial intragroup profit or loss,** on disposal of inventory or property, plant and equipment, **arises in the partly owned subsidiary** concerned.

Applied to the typical vertical group that we have looked at in this chapter (that consists of parent, P Ltd, partly owned subsidiary, S Ltd, and partly owned sub-subsidiary, SS Ltd), the non-controlling interest concerned will be affected by consolidation adjustments in respect of profits or losses on the intragroup sale of inventory and property, plant and equipment, as follows:

- where SS Ltd sells inventory or property, plant and equipment intragroup to S Ltd;
- where SS Ltd sells inventory or property, plant and equipment intragroup to P Ltd;
- where S Ltd sells inventory or property, plant and equipment intragroup to SS Ltd; and
- where S Ltd sells inventory or property, plant and equipment intragroup to P Ltd.

 Example 7.4: Consolidation of a vertical group with intragroup transactions and balances

P Ltd acquired an 85% controlling interest in S Ltd on 1 January 20x3 for CU 172 000.

- On acquisition date, the share capital and retained earnings of S Ltd was CU 100 000 and CU 80 000 respectively.
- The non-controlling interest is measured at its fair value, which was CU 33 000 at acquisition date.
- On 30 June 20x4 S Ltd sold plant at a profit of CU 45 000 to P Ltd. The remaining useful life of the plant at date of sale to P Ltd was three years and the plant had a NIL residual value.

S Ltd acquired a 60% controlling interest in SS Ltd on 1 January 20x4 for CU 115 600.

- On acquisition date, the share capital and retained earnings of SS Ltd was CU 120 000 and CU 35 000 respectively.
- The non-controlling interest is measured at its fair value, which was CU 67 200 at acquisition date.
- Since its acquisition, SS Ltd has sold inventories to P Ltd at cost plus 25%. In this regard, SS Ltd made inventory sales of CU 145 000 to P Ltd during the current year. In addition, P Ltd had opening inventory and closing inventory on hand purchased from SS Ltd of CU 72 000 and CU 91 000 respectively.

All the assets and liabilities of the subsidiaries were considered to be fairly valued at acquisition date.

Both P Ltd and S Ltd measure their investments in subsidiaries at cost price.

In addition, an income tax rate of 28% and an effective capital gains tax rate of 22.4% apply.

The trial balances of P Ltd and its two subsidiaries for the financial year ended 31 December 20x5 appear below.

Trial balances at 31 December 20x5	P Ltd Dr/(Cr) CU	S Ltd Dr/(Cr) CU	SS Ltd Dr/(Cr) CU
Share capital	(350 000)	(100 000)	(120 000)
Retained earnings (1 Jan 20x5)	(345 000)	(133 000)	(190 000)
Dividend paid (31 Dec 20x5)	50 000	15 000	10 000
Trade and other payables	(126 300)	(168 300)	(38 000)
Plant	260 000	123 050	95 000
Trade and other receivables	317 980	177 350	300 750
Inventory	117 900	69 000	57 350
Investment in S Ltd: Cost	172 000	–	–
Investment in SS Ltd: Cost	–	115 600	–
Sales	(450 000)	(398 000)	(268 000)
Cost of sales	290 000	258 000	129 200
Other income	(15 880)	(12 450)	(5 000)
Depreciation	48 000	25 000	8 800
Income tax expense	31 300	28 750	19 900

Required

(a) Present a group diagram and a timeline.

(b) Prepare the relevant analyses of equity as at 31 December 20x5.

(c) Provide the pro forma journals necessary to prepare consolidated financial statements for the P Ltd group for the financial year ended 31 December 20x5.

(d) Prepare the consolidated financial statements for the P Ltd group for the financial year ended 31 December 20x5.

Solution 7.4: Consolidation of a vertical group with intragroup transactions and balances

Part (a): Diagram and timeline

Group diagram

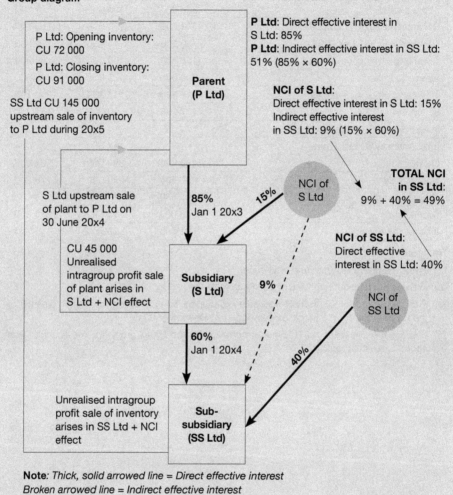

P Ltd: Opening inventory: CU 72 000

P Ltd: Closing inventory: CU 91 000

SS Ltd CU 145 000 upstream sale of inventory to P Ltd during 20x5

Parent (P Ltd)

P Ltd: Direct effective interest in S Ltd: 85%
P Ltd: Indirect effective interest in SS Ltd: 51% (85% × 60%)

NCI of S Ltd:
Direct effective interest in S Ltd: 15%
Indirect effective interest in SS Ltd: 9% (15% × 60%)

TOTAL NCI in SS Ltd:
9% + 40% = 49%

NCI of S Ltd

S Ltd upstream sale of plant to P Ltd on 30 June 20x4

85% Jan 1 20x3

15%

CU 45 000 Unrealised intragroup profit sale of plant arises in S Ltd + NCI effect

NCI of SS Ltd:
Direct effective interest in SS Ltd: 40%

Subsidiary (S Ltd)

9%

NCI of SS Ltd

60% Jan 1 20x4

40%

Unrealised intragroup profit sale of inventory arises in SS Ltd + NCI effect

Sub-subsidiary (SS Ltd)

Note: *Thick, solid arrowed line = Direct effective interest*
Broken arrowed line = Indirect effective interest

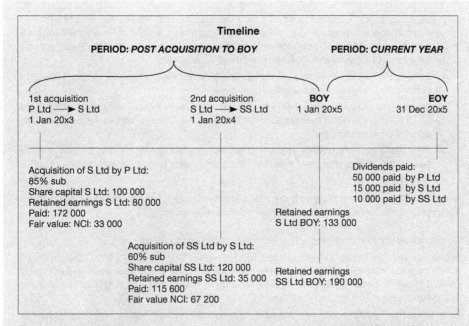

From the above illustrations we can see that we have a **vertical group** with the following:

- A **parent: P Ltd – 100%** of the **assets** (except for P Ltd's investments in S Ltd, which is eliminated on consolidation), **liabilities, income** (as adjusted for the intragroup dividend) and **expenses** of which will be included in the consolidated financial statements of the P Ltd group.

- A **subsidiary: S Ltd – 100%** of the **assets** (except for S Ltd's investment in SS Ltd, which is eliminated on consolidation), **liabilities, income** (as adjusted for the intragroup transactions) and **expenses** of which will be included in the consolidated financial statements of the P Ltd group.

- A **sub-subsidiary: SS Ltd – 100%** of the **assets, liabilities, income** (as adjusted for the intragroup transactions) and **expenses** of which will be included in the consolidated financial statements. of the P Ltd group.

In addition, the following is apparent:

- Parent P Ltd acquires its subsidiary, S Ltd, **before** S Ltd acquires sub-subsidiary, SS Ltd. Therefore, P Ltd acquires a **simple subsidiary**, after which S Ltd also acquires a **simple subsidiary** of its own. This means that **two business combinations** occur, with the result that any **goodwill or gain on bargain purchase** that arises in respect of **each business combination** must be **recognised** in the consolidated financial statements of the P Ltd group.

- S Ltd becomes part of the P Ltd group upon its acquisition by P Ltd on 1 January 20x3. Consequently, **S Ltd's current year profit**, and the **increase in its retained earnings** from **1 January 20x3 to the beginning of the current year**, form part of the **P Ltd group's profit and post-acquisition reserves,** and must be allocated:

  - **85% to P Ltd** (i.e., P Ltd has an 85% **direct** effective interest in S Ltd's current year profit and post-acquisition reserves); and

  - **15%** to the **non-controlling interest of S Ltd** (i.e., the non-controlling interest of S Ltd has a 15% **direct** effective interest in S Ltd's current year profit and post-acquisition reserves).

- S Ltd is part of the P Ltd group when it acquires SS Ltd. This implies that SS Ltd's current year profit, and the increase in its retained earnings from the date of its **acquisition by S Ltd**, on **1 January 20x4**, to the beginning of the current year, form part of the **P Ltd group's profit and post-acquisition reserves**, and must be allocated:

  - **51%** to **P Ltd** (i.e., P Ltd has a 51% (85% x 60%) **indirect** effective interest in SS Ltd's current year profit and post-acquisition reserves);

  - **9%** to the **non-controlling interest of S Ltd** (i.e., the non-controlling interest of S Ltd has a 9% (15% x 60%) **indirect** effective interest in SS Ltd's current year profit and post-acquisition reserves); and

  - **40%** to the **non-controlling interest of SS Ltd** (i.e., the non-controlling interest of S Ltd has a **40% direct** effective interest in SS Ltd's current year profit and post-acquisition reserves).

In addition, there are several intragroup transactions within the P Ltd group. The effects of these intragroup transactions, on consolidation, are discussed below.

Current and prior year upstream sale of inventory by SS Ltd to P Ltd

In the prior year, SS Ltd sold inventory intragroup at a profit to P Ltd. CU 72 000 of this inventory sold intragroup was still on hand as closing inventory of P Ltd at prior year end. This prior year closing inventory became the current year's opening inventory that was sold outside the group in the current year. This implies the following:

- In the current year pro forma consolidation journal passed (see Part (c) Pro forma journal 3):

  - We **reduce SS Ltd's opening retained earnings balance** by the **CU 10 368** (72 000 Prior year closing inventory x 25/125 Profit element = 14 400 Intragroup profit x 72%) **after tax effect** of the prior year elimination of S Ltd's CU 14 400 unrealised intragroup profit on sale of inventory.

  - We **reduce SS Ltd's cost of sales** by **CU 14 400**, thereby recognising in the current year, SS Ltd's CU 14 400 prior year intragroup profit on sale of inventory.

  - We **increase SS Ltd's income tax expense by CU 4 032** (14 400 x 28%), thereby recognising the current year tax effect of recognising SS Ltd's CU 14 400 prior year intragroup profit in the current year.

In the current year, SS Ltd sold inventory intragroup at a profit to P Ltd. CU 91 000 of this inventory sold intragroup was still on hand as closing inventory of P Ltd at current year end. This implies the following:

- In the current year pro forma consolidation journals passed (see Part (c) Pro forma journals 8 and 9):

  - We **eliminate SS Ltd's current year CU 18 200** (91 000 Current year closing inventory x 25/125 Profit element) **unrealised intragroup profit recognised** on inventory sold to P Ltd, thereby reducing SS Ltd's profit or loss by CU 18 200.

  - We **decrease SS Ltd's income tax expense by CU 5 096** (18 200 x 28%) and recognise a corresponding **CU 5 096 deferred tax asset** of P Ltd, thereby recognising the current year tax effects of eliminating SS Ltd's CU 18 200 current year unrealised intragroup profit on inventory sold.

  - We **eliminate SS Ltd's CU 18 200 unrealised intragroup profit** from the **CU 91 000 intragroup cost of P Ltd's closing inventory** on hand at current year end, purchased from SS Ltd.

S Ltd's prior year upstream sale of plant to P Ltd

Midway through the prior year (i.e., 30 June 20x4), S Ltd sold plant intragroup to P Ltd and recognised a CU 45 000 profit on this sale. This implies the following:

- In the current year pro forma consolidation journals passed (see Part (d) Pro forma journals 5, 6, 12 and 13):

  - We **reduce S Ltd's opening retained earnings balance by CU 27 000** (45 000 x 2.5 Years RUL plant BOY / 3 Years RUL plant = 37 500 Unrealised intragroup profit EOY x 72%). This amount is the **prior year after-tax effect** of **eliminating**, at prior year end, the **CU 37 500 unrealised balance of S Ltd's intragroup profit on sale of plant to P Ltd.**

  - We **recognise** a **CU 10 500** (37 500 x 28%) **deferred tax asset of P Ltd at the beginning of the current year**, in respect of the above-mentioned prior year end elimination of S Ltd's CU 37 500 unrealised intragroup profit on plant sold.

  - We **reduce by CU 7 500** (45 000 / 3 Years RUL plant x 6/12 Months) the **accumulated depreciation at the beginning of the current year**, recognised by **P Ltd on the plant acquired intragroup.** This represents the prior year recognition of CU 7 500 of S Ltd's prior year intragroup profit on plant sold, which profit realised in the prior year through a CU 7 500 prior year reduction in this plant's depreciation charge.

  - We **eliminate S Ltd's CU 45 000 prior year unrealised intragroup profit** from the **intragroup cost of the plant** acquired by P Ltd from S Ltd on 30 June 20x4.

  - We **reduce by CU 15 000** (45 000 / 3 Years RUL plant x 1 Year) **both** the **current year depreciation** and the **current year accumulated depreciation** recognised on the **plant sold intragroup.** This represents the current year recognition of a further CU 15 000 of S Ltd's prior year intragroup profit on plant sold, which profit realises in the current year through a CU 15 000 current year reduction in the plant's depreciation charge.

  - We **increase S Ltd's income tax expense by CU 4 200** (15 000 x 28%) and recognise a **corresponding CU 4 200 reduction in P Ltd's CU 10 500 deferred tax asset at the beginning of the current year**. These are current year tax effects of recognising in the current year, the realisation of CU 15 000 of S Ltd's prior year intragroup profit on plant sold, which profit realises through a CU 15 000 current year reduction in the plant's depreciation charge.

Intragroup dividends

P Ltd as well as both S Ltd and SS Ltd paid dividends in the current year. This has the following implications on consolidation:

- Only the **CU 50 000 dividend paid by P Ltd** to its **owners** will be reported in the **retained earnings column** of the consolidated statement of changes in equity.

- The **total** of the **dividends paid to the non-controlling shareholders** of **S Ltd and SS Ltd**, amounting to **CU 6 250** [(15 000 x 15%) + (10 000 x 40%)], will be reflected as a **deduction in the non-controlling interest column** of the consolidated statement of changes in equity.

- The **CU 12 750** (15 000 x 85%) **dividend received by P Ltd from S Ltd** will be **eliminated** from **P Ltd's profit or loss** in arriving at the consolidated profit for the current year.

- The **CU 6 000** (10 000 x 60%) **dividend received by S Ltd** from **SS Ltd** will be **eliminated from S Ltd's profit or loss** in arriving at the consolidated profit for the current year. Furthermore, in S Ltd's analysis of equity (see Part (b)), its current year profit must be reduced by the CU 6 000 dividend received from SS Ltd. Not to do so would result in the group profit attributable to the owners of the parent, and to the non-controlling interest of S Ltd, being overstated.

Part (b) Analyses of equity as at 31 December 20x5

Calculation 1: Analysis of equity of SS Ltd as at 31 December 20x5

Acquisition date (1 January 20x4)	Total of SS Ltd's equity 100% CU	S Ltd 60%		Non-controlling interest 40% CU
		At acquisition CU	Since acquisition CU	
Share capital	120 000			
Retained earnings	35 000			
Fair value of net assets of SS Ltd	155 000	93 000		62 000
Goodwill (balancing figure)	27 800 **a**	22 600		5 200
Consideration and NCI	182 800	115 600		67 200
Since acquisition				
• To beginning of current year:				
Adjusted retained earnings	144 632		86 779 **b**	57 853 **c**
Retained earnings movement (190 000 Balance BOY – 35 000 Balance at acquisition)	155 000		93 000	62 000
After tax elimination of prior year unrealised intragroup profit: Closing inventory [(72 000 × 25/125) × 72%]	(10 368)		(6 221)	(4 147)
				125 053 **d**
• Current year:				
Adjusted profit for the year	112 364		67 418 **e**	44 946 **f**
Profit for the year (268 000 – 129 200 – 8 800 – 19 900 + 5 000)	115 100		69 060	46 040
After tax recognition of prior year intragroup profit inventory [(72 000 × 25/125) × 72%]	10 368		6 221	4 147
After tax elimination of current year unrealised intragroup profit: Closing inventory [(91 000 × 25/125) × 72%]	(13 104)		(7 862)	(5 242)
Dividend paid	(10 000)		(6 000) **g**	(4 000) **h**
	429 796		148 197	165 999 **i**

Calculation 2: Analysis of equity of S Ltd as at 31 December 20x5

Acquisition date (1 January 20x3)	Total of S Ltd's equity 100% CU	P Ltd 85%		Non-controlling interest 15% CU
		At acquisition CU	Since acquisition CU	
Share capital	100 000			
Retained earnings	80 000			
Fair value of net assets of S Ltd	180 000	153 000		27 000
Goodwill (balancing figure)	25 000 **A**	19 000		6 000
Consideration and NCI	205 000	172 000		33 000
Since acquisition				
• To beginning of current year:				
Adjusted retained earnings	112 779		95 862 **B**	16 917 **C**
Retained earnings movement (133 000 Balance BOY – 80 000 Balance at acquisition)	53 000		45 050	7 950
After tax elimination of prior year unrealised intragroup profit: Plant (45 000 × 72%)	(32 400)		(27 540)	(4 860)
After tax reversal of prior year excess depreciation: Plant [(45 000 Unrealised intragroup profit / 3-years RUL × 6/12) × 72%]	5 400		4 590	810
Retained earnings SS Ltd (Calc 1**b**)	86 779		73 762	13 017
				49 917 **D**
• Current year:				
Adjusted profit for the year	170 918		145 280 **E**	25 638 **F**
Profit for the year (398 000 – 258 000 – 25 000 – 28 750 + 12 450)	98 700		83 895	14 805
Dividend from SS Ltd (Calc 1**g**) OR (10 000 × 60%)	(6 000)[1]		(5 100)	(900)
After tax reversal of current year excess depreciation: Plant [(45 000 Unrealised intragroup profit / 3-years RUL) × 72%]	10 800		9 180	1 620
Profit SS Ltd (Calc 1**e**)	67 418		57 305	10 113
Dividend	(15 000)		(12 750) **G**	(2 250) **H**
	473 697		228 392	73 305 **I**

Explanatory notes: Analysis of equity of S Ltd

[1] This amount is the dividend received by S Ltd from its 60% owned subsidiary SS Ltd, which paid a total dividend of CU 10 000, CU 4 000 of which was paid to the non-controlling interest of SS Ltd. As this is an intragroup dividend, it must be eliminated on consolidation. Accordingly, we reduce S Ltd's current year profit by this dividend received as it is not income from the group's perspective.

Part (c): Pro forma journal entries for the 20x5 financial year

AT ACQUISITION

Pro forma journal 1 (J1)	Dr CU	Cr CU	NCI Balance
Share capital (SS Ltd) (SCIE) (given)	120 000		
Retained earnings (SS Ltd) (SCIE) (given)	35 000		
Investment in SS Ltd (S Ltd) (SFP) (given)		115 600	
NCI: SS Ltd – Equity (SFP) (given – at fair value)		67 200	67 200
Goodwill (SFP) (balancing figure)	27 800		
Elimination of at acquisition equity SS Ltd and cost of investment in SS Ltd, and recognition of non-controlling interest and goodwill on acquisition of SS Ltd			

Pro forma journal 2 (J2)	Dr CU	Cr CU	
Share capital (S Ltd) (SCIE) (given)	100 000		
Retained earnings (S Ltd) (SCIE) (given)	80 000		
Investment in S Ltd (P Ltd) (SFP) (given)		172 000	
NCI: S Ltd – Equity (SFP) (given – at fair value)		33 000	33 000
Goodwill (SFP) (balancing figure)	25 000		
Elimination of at acquisition equity S Ltd and cost of investment in S Ltd, and recognition of non-controlling interest and goodwill on acquisition of S Ltd			

SINCE ACQUISITION TO BEGINNING OF THE YEAR / CURRENT YEAR

Pro forma journal 3 (J3)	Dr CU	Cr CU
Retained earnings (SS Ltd) (SCIE)	[Wkg1]10 368	
Income tax expense (SS Ltd) (P/L) (balancing figure)	4 032	
Cost of sales (SS Ltd) (P/L)		[Wkg2]14 400
After tax SS Ltd prior year intragroup profit adjustment in respect of inventory to ensure current year opening consolidated retained earnings balance agrees to prior year closing consolidated retained earnings balance, and current year recognition of prior year SS Ltd unrealised intragroup profit on sale of inventory, together with associated current year tax effects		

Workings: Pro forma journals

Working 1
(72 000 (given) Prior year closing inventory × 25/125 Unrealised profit component) × 72% After tax

Working 2
72 000 (given) Opening inventory sold externally × 25/125 Profit component realised

SINCE ACQUISITION TO BEGINNING OF THE YEAR

Pro forma journal 4 (J4)	Dr CU	Cr CU		NCI Balance
Retained earnings (SS Ltd) (SCIE)	Wkg3 57 853			
NCI: SS Ltd – Equity (SFP) (SS Ltd)		Wkg3 57 853		57 853
Allocating the non-controlling interest in SS Ltd its share of SS Ltd's adjusted retained earnings since acquisition to the beginning of the year				

Workings: Pro forma journals

Working 3

	CU
SS Ltd Balance BOY (given)	190 000
SS Ltd Balance at acquisition (given)	(35 000)
After tax elimination of prior year unrealised intragroup profit: Inventory (J3)	(10 368)
Adjusted post-acquisition retained earnings of SS Ltd	144 632
40% Effective interest of NCI of SS Ltd (144 632 × 40%)	57 853

Pro forma journal 5 (J5)	Dr CU	Cr CU
Retained earnings (S Ltd) (SCIE) (balancing figure)	37 500	
Accumulated depreciation: Plant (P Ltd) (SFP)	Wkg4 7 500	
Plant (P Ltd) (SFP) (given: Unrealised intragroup profit: Plant)		45 000
Prior year S Ltd intragroup profit adjustment in respect of plant to ensure that the current year opening consolidated retained earnings balance agrees to the prior year closing consolidated retained earnings balance, recognition of prior year reduction in accumulated depreciation plant, and elimination of prior year S Ltd unrealised intragroup profit from cost of plant		

Workings: Pro forma journals

Working 4
(45 000 (given) Unrealised intragroup profit: Plant / 3-years RUL plant) × 6/12 Months

Pro forma journal 6 (J6)	Dr CU	Cr CU
Deferred tax (P Ltd) (SFP)	Wkg5 10 500	
Retained earnings (S Ltd) (SCIE)		Wkg5 10 500
Recognising tax effects of S Ltd unrealised Intragroup profit adjustment in respect of plant to ensure consolidated retained earnings balance beginning of the year agrees to the consolidated retained earnings balance at the end of the prior year		

Workings: Pro forma journals

Working 5
37 500 (J5) Elimination of balance of S Ltd unrealised intragroup profit plant, at beginning of year × 28%

Pro forma journal 7 (J7)	Dr CU	Cr CU	NCI Balance
Retained earnings (SS Ltd) (SCIE)	Wkg6 13 017		
Retained earnings (S Ltd) (SCIE)	Wkg7 3 900		
NCI S Ltd – Equity (SFP) (balancing figure)		16 917	16 917
Allocating the non-controlling interest in S Ltd its share of SS Ltd's and S Ltd's adjusted post-acquisition retained earnings to the beginning of the year			**Balance 174 970 BOY (Calc 3)**

Workings: Pro forma journals

Working 6
144 632 (Working 3) Adjusted post-acquisition retained earnings of SS Ltd × 9% (15% × 60%) Effective interest of NCI of S Ltd

Working 7
(133 000 S Ltd Balance BOY – 80 000 S Ltd Balance at acquisition – 37 500 (J5) Elimination of balance of S Ltd unrealised intragroup profit plant at BOY + 10 500 (J6) Tax effect: Elimination of balance of S Ltd unrealised intragroup profit plant at BOY) × 15% Effective interest of NCI of S Ltd

CURRENT YEAR

Pro forma journal 8 (J8)	Dr CU	Cr CU
Sales (SS Ltd) (P/L) (given)	145 000	
Cost of sales (SS Ltd) (P/L) (balancing figure)		126 800
Inventory (P Ltd) (SFP)		Wkg8 18 200
Elimination of SS Ltd intragroup sales, cost of sales and unrealised intragroup profit included in closing inventory of P Ltd		

Workings: Pro forma journals

Working 8
91 000 (given) Closing inventory × 25/125 Unrealised profit element

Pro forma journal 9 (J9)	Dr CU	Cr CU
Deferred tax (P Ltd) (SFP)	Wkg9 5 096	
Income tax expense (SS Ltd) (P/L)		Wkg9 5 096
Tax effects: Elimination of SS Ltd intragroup sales, cost of sales and unrealised intragroup profit included in closing inventory of P Ltd		

Workings: Pro forma journals

Working 9
18 200 (J8) Elimination unrealised intragroup profit: Inventory × 28%

Pro forma journal 10 (J10)	Dr CU	Cr CU	NCI Balance
NCI of SS Ltd: Share of SS Ltd profit (P/L)	Wkg10 44 946		
NCI: SS Ltd – Equity (SFP)		Wkg10 44 946	44 946
Allocating the non-controlling interest of SS Ltd its share of SS Ltd's adjusted current year profit			

Workings: Pro forma journals

Working 10

	CU
SS Ltd current year profit (268 000 – 129 200 + 5 000 – 8 800 – 19 900)	115 100
After tax recognition of SS Ltd prior year intragroup profit: Inventory (J3)	10 368
Elimination of SS Ltd intragroup profit: Closing inventory (J8)	(18 200)
Tax effect: Elimination of SS Ltd intragroup profit, closing inventory (J9)	5 096
SS Ltd adjusted current year profit	112 364
40% Effective interest of NCI of SS Ltd (112 364 × 40%)	44 946

Pro forma journal 11 (J11)	Dr CU	Cr CU	
Dividend received (S Ltd) (P/L)	Wkg11 6 000		
NCI: SS Ltd – Equity (SFP) (balancing figure)	4 000		(4 000)
Dividend paid (SS Ltd) (SCIE) (given)		10 000	
Elimination of intragroup dividend received from SS Ltd, and recognition of non-controlling interest of SS Ltd in the dividend			

Working 11
10 000 × 60% P Ltd effective interest

Pro forma journal 12 (J12)	Dr CU	Cr CU	
Accumulated depreciation: Plant (P Ltd) (SFP)	Wkg12 15 000		
Depreciation: Plant (S Ltd) (P/L)		Wkg12 15 000	
Recognition of realisation of S Ltd prior year intragroup profit plant through reduction in depreciation charge on plant			

Working 12
45 000 (given) Unrealised intragroup profit: Plant / 3-year RUL plant

Pro forma journal 13 (J13)	Dr CU	Cr CU	
Income tax expense (S Ltd) (P/L)	Wkg13 4 200		
Deferred tax (P Ltd) (SFP)		Wkg13 4 200	
Tax effect: Recognition of realisation of S Ltd prior year intragroup profit plant			

Workings: Pro forma journals

Working 13
15 000 (J12) Recognition of intragroup profit: Plant × 28%

Pro forma journal 14 (J14)	Dr CU	Cr CU	NCI Balance
NCI of S Ltd: Share of SS Ltd profit or loss (P/L)	Wkg14 10 113		
NCI of S Ltd: Share of S Ltd profit or loss (P/L)	Wkg15 15 525		
NCI: S Ltd – Equity (SFP) (balancing figure)		25 638	25 638
Allocating the non-controlling interest in S Ltd its share of SS Ltd's and S Ltd's adjusted current year profit			

Workings: Pro forma journals

Working 14
112 364 (Working 10) Adjusted SS Ltd profit × 9% Effective interest of NCI of S Ltd

Working 15

	CU
S Ltd current year profit (398 000 – 258 000 – 25 000 – 28 750 +12 450)	98 700
Intragroup dividend from SS Ltd (J11)	(6 000)
Reversal excess depreciation: Plant (J12)	15 000
Tax effect: Reversal excess depreciation: Plant (J13)	(4 200)
S Ltd adjusted current year profit	103 500
15% Effective interest of NCI of S Ltd (103 500 × 15%)	15 525

Pro forma journal 15 (J15)	Dr CU	Cr CU	
Dividend received (P Ltd)	Wkg16 12 750		
NCI: S Ltd – Equity (SFP) (balancing figure)	2 250		(2 250)
Dividend paid (S Ltd) (SCIE) (given)		15 000	
Elimination of intragroup dividend received from S Ltd, and recognition of non-controlling interest of S Ltd in the dividend			**Balance 239 304 EOY (Calc 4)**

Workings: Pro forma journals

Working 16
15 000 (given) Dividend × 85% P Ltd effective interest

The full effects of the preceding pro forma journals on the consolidated financial statements of the P Ltd group for the financial year ended 31 December 20x5 are illustrated in the following consolidation worksheet.

	P Ltd Dr/(Cr) CU	S Ltd Dr/(Cr) CU	SS Ltd Dr/(Cr) CU	Pro forma journals At acquisition Dr/(Cr) CU	Journal ref	Pro forma journals Since acquisition Dr/(Cr) CU	Journal ref	Consolidated Dr/(Cr) CU
Equity								
Share capital	(350 000)	(100 000)	(120 000)	120 000 / 100 000	J1 / J2			(350 000)
Retained earnings (BOY)	(345 000)	(133 000)	(190 000)	35 000 / 80 000	J1 / J2	10 368 / 57 853 / 37 500 / (10 500) / 13 017 / 3 900	J3 / J4 / J5 / J6 / J7 / J7	(440 862)
Dividends	50 000	15 000	10 000			(10 000) / (15 000)	J11 / J15	50 000
Profit: Individual entities	(96 580)	(98 700)	(115 100)					†(229 110)
Consolidated profit attributable to owners of parent								
Retained earnings (EOY)	(391 580)	(216 700)	(295 100)	(67 200) / (33 000)	J1 / J2	(57 853) / (16 917) / (44 946) / 4 000 / (25 638) / 2 250	J4 / J7 / J10 / J11 / J14 / J15	(619 972)
NCI Equity	–	–						(239 304)

Explanatory notes

† This amount has been brought forward from the third part of the consolidation worksheet on page 499

	P Ltd Dr/(Cr) CU	S Ltd Dr/(Cr) CU	SS Ltd Dr/(Cr) CU	Pro forma journals At acquisition Dr/(Cr) CU	Journal ref	Pro forma journals Since acquisition Dr/(Cr) CU	Journal ref	Consolidated Dr/(Cr) CU
Total equity	**(741 580)**	**(316 700)**	**(415 100)**					**(1 209 276)**
Liabilities:								
Trade and other payables	(126 300)	(168 300)	(38 000)					(332 600)
Total liabilities	**(126 300)**	**(168 300)**	**(38 000)**					**(332 600)**
Total equity & liabilities	**(867 880)**	**(485 000)**	**(453 100)**					**(1 541 876)**
Assets:								
Property, plant and equipment: Plant	260 000	123 050	95 000			7 500 / (45 000) / 15 000	J5 / J5 / J12	455 550
Trade and other receivables	317 980	177 350	300 750					796 080
Inventory	117 900	69 000	57 350		J2	(18 200)	J8	226 050
Investment in S Ltd	172 000	–	–	(172 000)	J1			–
Investment in SS Ltd	–	115 600	–	(115 600)	J1			–
Goodwill				27 800 / 25 000	J2			52 800
Deferred tax						10 500 / 5 096 / (4 200)	J6 / J9 / J13	11 396
Total assets	**867 880**	**485 000**	**453 100**					**1 541 876**

	P Ltd Dr/(Cr) CU	S Ltd Dr/(Cr) CU	SS Ltd Dr/(Cr) CU	Pro forma journals At acquisition Dr/(Cr) CU	Journal ref	Pro forma journals Since acquisition Dr/(Cr) CU	Journal ref	Consolidated Dr/(Cr) CU
Profit or loss								
Sales	(450 000)	(398 000)	(268 000)			145 000	J8	(971 000)
Cost of sales	290 000	258 000	129 200			(14 400)	J3	536 000
						(126 800)	J8	
Other income	(15 880)	(12 450)	(5 000)			6 000	J11	(14 580)
						12 750	J15	
Depreciation	48 000	25 000	8 800			(15 000)	J12	66 800
Income tax expense	31 300	28 750	19 900			4 032	J3	83 086
						(5 096)	J9	
						4 200	J13	
Profit for the period	(96 580)	(98 700)	(115 100)					(299 694)
NCI: Share of profit						44 946	J10	70 584
						10 113	J14	
						15 525	J14	
Consolidated profit attributable to owners of parent								‡(229 110)

Explanatory notes

‡ This amount has been carried forward to the first part of the consolidation worksheet on page 497

Part (d): Consolidated financial statements for the 20x5 financial year

P LTD GROUP: CONSOLIDATED STATEMENT OF PROFIT OR LOSS AND OTHER COMPREHENSIVE INCOME FOR THE YEAR ENDED 31 DECEMBER 20x5	
	CU
Sales (450 000 (P Ltd) + 398 000 (S Ltd) + (SS Ltd: 268 000 – 145 000 (J8) Elimination intragroup sales))	971 000
Cost of sales (290 000 (P Ltd) + 258 000 (S Ltd) + (SS Ltd: 129 200 – 14 400 (J3) Recognition prior year intragroup profit: Inventory – 126 800 (J8) Elimination intragroup cost of sales))	(536 000)
Gross profit	435 000
Other income (P Ltd: 15 880 – 12 750 (J15) Dividend from S Ltd) + (S Ltd: 12 450 – 6 000 (J11) Dividend from SS Ltd) + 5 000 (SS Ltd))	14 580
Operating expenses (48 000 (P Ltd) + (S Ltd: 25 000 – 15 000 (J12) Reversal excess depreciation: Plant) + 8 800 (SS Ltd))	(66 800)
Profit before tax	382 780
Income tax expense (31 300 (P Ltd) + (S Ltd: 28 750 + 4 200 (J13) Tax effect: Reversal excess depreciation, plant) + (SS Ltd: 19 900+ 4 032 (J3) Tax effect: Recognition prior year intragroup profit, inventory – 5 096 (J9) Tax effect: Elimination unrealised intragroup profit, closing inventory)	(83 086)
PROFIT FOR THE YEAR	299 694
Other comprehensive income	–
TOTAL COMPREHENSIVE INCOME	299 694
Attributable to:	
Owners of the parent (balancing figure) **OR** [(P Ltd: 96 580 – 12 750 (J15) Dividend from S Ltd) + (S Ltd: 145 280 (see Calc 2 **E**))]	229 110
Non-controlling interest (NCI of SS Ltd: 44 946 (see Calc 1 **f OR** (J10)) + NCI of S Ltd: 25 638 (see Calc 2 **F OR** (J14))	70 584
	299 694

P LTD GROUP: CONSOLIDATED STATEMENT OF CHANGES IN EQUITY FOR THE YEAR ENDED 31 DECEMBER 20x5					
	Parent equity holders' interest				
	Share capital CU	Retained earnings CU	Total parent equity CU	Non-controlling interest CU	Total equity of the group CU
Opening balance at 1 Jan 20x5	350 000	Wkg1440 862	790 862	Wkg2174 970	965 832
Total comprehensive income:					
Profit for the period (from CSOPL_OCI)		229 110	229 110	70 584	299 694
Dividends		(50 000)	(50 000)	Wkg3(6 250)	(56 250)
Closing balance at 31 Dec 20x5	**350 000**	**619 972**	**969 972**	**239 304**	**1 209 276**

Workings: Consolidated statement of changes in equity

Working 1

P Ltd: 345 000 + S Ltd: 95 862 (see Calc 2 **B**) P Ltd Share of post-acquisition retained earnings of S Ltd and SS Ltd to BOY

OR

P Ltd: 345 000 + (S Ltd: 133 000 Balance BOY − 80 000 (J2) Balance at acquisition − 37 500 (J5) Elimination of remaining unrealised intragroup profit: Plant at BOY + 10 500 (J6) Tax effect: elimination of remaining unrealised intragroup profit: Plant at BOY − 3 900 (J7) NCI of S Ltd: Share of post-acquisition retained earnings of S Ltd to BOY) + (SS Ltd: 190 000 Balance BOY − 35 000 (J1) Balance at acquisition − 10 368 (J3) After tax elimination of prior year unrealised intragroup profit: inventory − 57 853 (J4) NCI of SS Ltd: Share of post-acquisition retained earnings of SS Ltd to BOY − 13 017 (J7) NCI of S Ltd: Share of post-acquisition retained earnings of SS Ltd to BOY)

Working 2

NCI of SS Ltd: 125 053 (see Calc 1 **d**) + NCI of S Ltd: 49 917 (see Calc 2 **D**)

OR

NCI of S Ltd and SS Ltd: 174 970 (see pro forma journal entries: Calc 3)

Working 3

NCI share of SS Ltd dividend: 4 000 (see Calc 1 **h OR** (J11)) + NCI share of S Ltd dividend: 2 250 (see Calc 2 **H OR** (J15))

P LTD GROUP: CONSOLIDATED STATEMENT OF FINANCIAL POSITION AS AT 31 DECEMBER 20x5	
	CU
Assets	
Non-current assets	
Property, plant and equipment (P Ltd: 260 000 − 45 000 (J5) Elimination prior year unrealised intragroup profit: Plant + 7 500 (J5) Reversal prior year excess accumulated depreciation: Plant + 15 000 (J12) Reversal current year excess accumulated depreciation: Plant) + 123 050 (S Ltd) + 95 000 (SS Ltd))	455 550
Goodwill (27 800 (see Calc 1 **a OR** (J1)) + 25 000 (see Calc 2 **A OR** (J2))	52 800
Deferred tax (P Ltd: 10 500 (J6) Tax effect: Elimination of remaining unrealised intragroup profit, plant, BOY − 4 200 (J13) Tax effect: Reversal of current year excess depreciation, plant + 5 096 (J9) Tax effect: Elimination unrealised intragroup profit, closing inventory)	11 396
Current assets	
Trade and other receivables (317 980 (P Ltd) + 177 350 (S Ltd) + 300 750 (SS Ltd))	796 080
Inventory (P Ltd: 117 900 − 18 200 (J8) Elimination of unrealised intragroup profit: Closing inventory) + 69 000 (S Ltd) + 57 350 (SS Ltd))	226 050
Total assets	1 541 876
Equity and liabilities	
Share capital (from CSCIE)	350 000
Retained earnings (from CSCIE)	619 972
Equity attributable to owners of the parent	969 972
Non-controlling interest (from CSCIE) **OR** (see pro formal journal entries: Calc 4) **OR** (165 999 (see Calc 1 i) + 73 305 (see Calc 2 l))	239 304
Total equity	1 209 276
Current liabilities	
Trade and other payables (126 300 (P Ltd) + 168 300 (S Ltd) + 38 000 (SS Ltd))	332 600
Total equity and liabilities	1 541 876

7.3 Consolidation of a mixed group

As was discussed in the introduction, in its simplest form, a mixed group consists of a **parent, P Ltd,** that owns a **controlling interest** in a **subsidiary, S Ltd,** and **both P Ltd and S Ltd** each own **direct equity interests** in a **third entity, SS Ltd,** such that **P Ltd and S Ltd together** own **sufficient equity interests in SS Ltd** to make **SS Ltd** a **subsidiary of P Ltd as well.** A basic mixed group structure is presented in Figure 7.4.

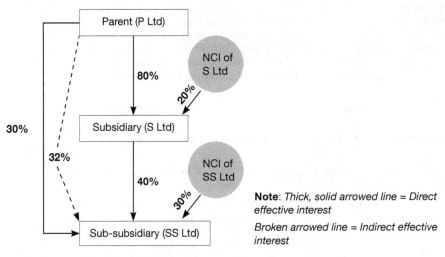

Figure 7.4: *A basic mixed group*

Figure 7.4 shows that P Ltd acquired 30% of SS Ltd, and S Ltd acquired 40% of SS Ltd. Since P Ltd controls S Ltd, P Ltd also controls the 40% interest that S Ltd holds in SS Ltd. P Ltd therefore controls SS Ltd by virtue of the fact that it controls 30% + 40% = 70% of SS Ltd's voting rights, which constitutes a majority of the voting rights in SS Ltd. Accordingly, SS Ltd is also a subsidiary of P Ltd.

Note that P Ltd's **share** in **SS Ltd's post-acquisition reserves** and **current year profit differs** from the **percentage of voting rights** (70% of voting rights) that it **controls** in SS Ltd. This is because P Ltd's effective interest in SS Ltd is determined by adding its direct effective interest in SS Ltd of 30% to its 80% share of S Ltd's 40% share of SS Ltd post-acquisition reserves and current year profit. Therefore, P Ltd will be attributed 30% direct effective interest + 32% (80% × 40%) indirect effective interest = 62% of SS Ltd's post-acquisition reserves and current year profit, in this scenario.

The consolidation of a mixed group follows the **same process** as for a **vertical group** (including the procedures to deal with intragroup transactions and balances), but with the **insertion of an additional column** in **SS Ltd's analysis of equity** in order to **analyse P Ltd's direct effective interest in SS Ltd.** The consolidation procedures when dealing with a simple mixed group are comprehensively illustrated in the example that follows.

Example 7.5: Consolidation of a mixed group

P Ltd acquired a 60% controlling interest in S Ltd on 1 January 20x3 for CU 65 000, when S Ltd's retained earnings were CU 55 000 and its share capital was CU 80 000.

On 1 January 20x4 P Ltd acquired 40% of SS Ltd for CU 75 000 and S Ltd acquired 25% of SS Ltd for CU 43 000, when SS Ltd's retained earnings were CU 86 000 and its share capital was CU 50 000.

The abridged trial balances of the three companies on 31 December 20x5 were as follows:

Abridged trial balances at 31 December 20x5	P Ltd Dr/(Cr) CU	S Ltd Dr/(Cr) CU	SS Ltd Dr/(Cr) CU
Share capital	(250 000)	(80 000)	(50 000)
Retained earnings (1 Jan 20x5)	(320 000)	(190 000)	(133 000)
Dividend paid (31 December 20x5)	35 000	18 000	8 000
Trade and other payables	(171 000)	(83 500)	(30 340)
Property, plant and equipment	409 600	277 000	170 590
Trade and other receivables	306 200	97 500	91 250
Investment in S Ltd: Cost	65 000	–	–
Investment in SS Ltd: Cost	75 000	43 000	–
Profit for the period	(149 800)	(82 000)	(56 500)

The group measures the non-controlling interest at its proportionate share of the identifiable net assets of the relevant subsidiary acquired.

All the assets and liabilities of the subsidiaries were considered to be fairly valued at acquisition date.

Both P Ltd and S Ltd measure their investments in subsidiaries at cost price.

Required

(a) Present a group diagram and a timeline.

(b) Prepare the relevant analyses of equity as at 31 December 20x5.

(c) Provide the pro forma journals necessary to prepare consolidated financial statements for the P Ltd group for the financial year ended 31 December 20x5.

(d) Prepare the consolidated financial statements for the P Ltd group for the financial year ended 31 December 20x5.

S Solution 7.5: Consolidation of a mixed group

Part (a): Group diagram and timeline

Group diagram

P Ltd: Direct effective interest in S Ltd: 60%
P Ltd: Direct effective interest in SS Ltd: 40%
P Ltd: Indirect effective interest in SS Ltd:
15% (60% × 25%):

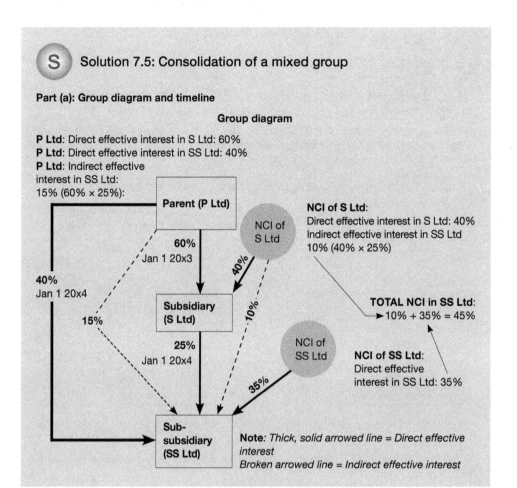

NCI of S Ltd:
Direct effective interest in S Ltd: 40%
Indirect effective interest in SS Ltd
10% (40% × 25%)

TOTAL NCI in SS Ltd:
10% + 35% = 45%

NCI of SS Ltd:
Direct effective interest in SS Ltd: 35%

Note: *Thick, solid arrowed line = Direct effective interest*
Broken arrowed line = Indirect effective interest

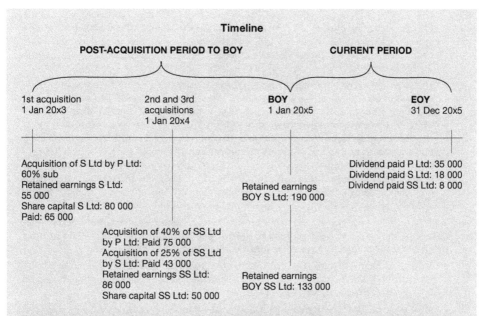

From the above illustrations we can see that we have a mixed group with the following:

- A **parent: P Ltd – 100%** of the **assets** (except for P Ltd's investment in S Ltd and SS Ltd, which are eliminated on consolidation), **liabilities**, **income** (adjusted for intragroup dividends) and **expenses** of which will be included in the consolidated financial statements of the P Ltd group;

- A **subsidiary: S Ltd – 100%** of the **assets** (except for S Ltd's investment in SS Ltd, which is eliminated on consolidation), **liabilities**, **income** (adjusted for intragroup dividends) and **expenses** of which will be included in the consolidated financial statements of the P Ltd group; and

- A **sub-subsidiary: SS Ltd – 100%** of the **assets, liabilities, income** and **expenses** of which will be included in the consolidated financial statements of the P Ltd group.

In addition, the following is apparent: P Ltd acquires its subsidiary, S Ltd, **before** SS Ltd also becomes a subsidiary of P Ltd. Therefore, P Ltd acquires **two subsidiaries**, each on a **separate date**. This means that **two business combinations** occur, with the result that any **goodwill or gain on bargain purchase** that arises in **respect of each business combination must be recognised** in the consolidated financial statements of the P Ltd group.

S Ltd is already part of the P Ltd group when it acquires its interest in SS Ltd. In addition, P Ltd acquires a direct equity interest in SS Ltd on the same date that S Ltd acquires its equity interest in SS Ltd. This is the date when SS Ltd also becomes a subsidiary of P Ltd.

The above-mentioned acquisitions have the following implications when preparing the consolidated financial statements of the P Ltd group for the financial year end 31 December 20x5:

- **SS Ltd's current year profit**, and the **increase** in its **retained earnings** from **acquisition date 1 January 20x4** to the **beginning of the current year**, form **part of the P Ltd group's profit** and **post-acquisition reserves** and are allocated as follows:

  - **40% of SS Ltd's post-acquisition retained earnings** and **current year profit** is allocated to **P Ltd** based on P Ltd's **direct** shareholding of **40%** in SS Ltd (i.e., based on **P Ltd's 40% direct effective interest** in SS Ltd).

  - An **additional 15% of SS Ltd's post-acquisition retained earnings** and **current year profit** will also be allocated to **P Ltd**. This 15% constitutes P Ltd's **indirect effective interest** in **SS Ltd**, which is P Ltd's 60% share of S Ltd's 25% share of SS Ltd's current year profit and post-acquisition reserves (i.e., 60% × 25% = 15% indirect effective interest of P Ltd in SS Ltd via S Ltd).

- Consequently, **in total**, **P Ltd** will share in **55%** (40% direct effective interest + 15% Indirect effective interest) of **SS Ltd's post-acquisition reserves and current year profit** from acquisition date 1 January 20x4 to the end of the current financial year on 31 December 20x5.

- The total non-controlling interest in the P Ltd group is made up of the **non-controlling interest in SS Ltd**, which has a **35% direct effective interest** in **SS Ltd's current year profit** and **post-acquisition reserves**, as well as the **non-controlling interest in S Ltd**, which has a **direct effective interest of 40%** in **S Ltd's current year profit and post-acquisition reserves** and an **indirect effective interest** of **10%** (40% × 25%) in **SS Ltd's current year profit** and **post-acquisition reserves**. This implies that the **total interest** of the **non-controlling shareholders** of the P Ltd group in the **current year profit** and **post-acquisition reserves** of **SS Ltd** is **45%** (35% Direct effective interest of the non-controlling interest of SS Ltd + 10% Indirect effective interest of the non-controlling interest of S Ltd OR 100% – 55% Total effective interest of P Ltd in SS Ltd).

- **S Ltd's current year profit**, and the **increase** in its **retained earnings** from **acquisition date 1 January 20x3** to the **beginning of the current year**, form **part of the P Ltd group's profit** and **post-acquisition reserves** and must be allocated as follows:

  - **60% of S Ltd's current year profit** and **post-acquisition retained earnings** will be allocated to **P Ltd** based on P Ltd's **direct** shareholding of **60% in S Ltd** (i.e., based on P Ltd's direct effective interest in S Ltd); and

  - **40% of S Ltd's current year profit** and **post-acquisition retained earnings** will be allocated to the **non-controlling interest of S Ltd**, which has a direct shareholding of **40%** in S Ltd (i.e., based on the 40% direct effective interest in S Ltd of the non-controlling interest of S Ltd).

Furthermore, there are intragroup dividends within the P Ltd group as follows:

- P Ltd receives a dividend from both of its subsidiaries, CU 3 200 (8 000 × 40%) from SS Ltd and CU 10 800 (18 000 × 60%) from S Ltd, and pays a dividend to its shareholders of CU 35 000. In this regard:

  - only **P Ltd's CU 35 000 dividend paid** to its **shareholders** is reported in the **retained earnings** column of the consolidated statement of changes in equity; and

  - the **total dividend received by P Ltd** from its **subsidiaries of CU 14 000** (3 200 + 10 800) must be **eliminated** from **P Ltd's profit** on consolidation.

- **S Ltd** receives a **dividend of CU 2 000** (8 000 × 25%) from **SS Ltd**, which must be **eliminated** from **S Ltd's profit** on consolidation. Recall, as was discussed in Example 7.4, that we must ensure that in S Ltd's analysis of equity, its current year profit is reduced by this CU 2 000 dividend received from SS Ltd.

- The **non-controlling interest of SS Ltd** receives a **dividend** of **CU 2 800** (8 000 × 35%) from **SS Ltd**, while the **non-controlling interest of S Ltd** receives a **dividend of CU 7 200** (18 000 × 40%) from **S Ltd**. The **total dividend amount received by the non-controlling interest** of the P Ltd group of **CU 10 000** (2 800 + 7 200) must be reflected as a **deduction** in the **non-controlling interest column** of the consolidated statement of changes in equity.

Part (b): Analyses of equity as at 31 December 20x5

Calculation 1: Analysis of equity of SS Ltd as at 31 December 20x5

> Note how we insert additional columns in SS Ltd's analysis of equity to keep track of P Ltd's DIRECT INTEREST in the equity of SS Ltd.

Acquisition date (1 January 20x4)	Total of SS Ltd's equity 100% CU	P Ltd 40%		S Ltd 25%		Non-controlling interest 35% CU
		At acquisition CU	Since acquisition CU	At acquisition	Since acquisition CU	
Share capital	50 000					
Retained earnings	86 000					
Fair value of net assets of S Ltd	136 000	54 400		34 000		47 600
Goodwill (balancing figure)	29 600 a	20 600		9 000		–
Consideration and NCI	165 600	75 000		43 000		47 600
Since acquisition						
• To beginning of current year:						
Retained earnings movement (133 000 Balance BOY – 86 000 Balance at acquisition)	47 000		18 800¹ b		11 750² c	16 450
						64 050³ d
• Current year:						
Profit for the year	56 500		22 600⁴ e		14 125² f	19 775⁵ g
Dividend	(8 000)		(3 200)		(2 000)	(2 800) h
	261 100		**38 200**		**23 875**	**81 025 i**

Explanatory notes: Analysis of equity of SS Ltd

1. This amount is **P Ltd's 40% share** (a 40% DIRECT effective interest) in the **post-acquisition retained earnings of SS Ltd** to the **beginning of the year**. This amount is **included** in the calculation of the **opening consolidated retained earnings balance** of the P Ltd group.

2. These are the amounts in which P Ltd and the non-controlling interest of S Ltd have an INDIRECT effective interest. Accordingly, we must ensure that such amounts are **carried forward to the analysis of equity of S Ltd** (see Calc 2) in order to allocate them appropriately to **P Ltd** and to the **non-controlling interest of S Ltd**.

3. This amount is the **SS Ltd non-controlling interest opening balance**, which is **added** to the **S Ltd non-controlling interest opening balance** (see analysis of equity of S Ltd, Calc 2 **D**) to determine the total **non-controlling interest opening balance** that is reported in the consolidated statement of changes in equity of the P Ltd group (see Part (d)).

4. This amount is **P Ltd's 40% share** (a 40% DIRECT effective interest) in **SS Ltd's current year profit**. This amount is **included** in the calculation of the **consolidated profit for the year that is attributable to the owners of the parent**, reported in the consolidated statement of profit or loss and other comprehensive income of the P Ltd group (see Part (d)).

[5] This amount is the **35% share** (a 35% DIRECT effective interest) in the **current year profit** of **SS Ltd** that is attributable to the **non-controlling interest of SS Ltd**. This amount is **added** to the **share of the non-controlling interest of S Ltd** in the **current year profit of both SS Ltd** and **S Ltd** (see analysis of equity of S Ltd, Calc 2 **F** below) to determine the **consolidated profit for the year attributable to the non-controlling interest**, reported in the consolidated statement of profit or loss and other comprehensive income of the P Ltd group (see Part (d)).

Calculation 2: Analysis of equity of S Ltd as at 31 December 20x5

		P Ltd 60%		
Acquisition date (1 January 20x3)	Total of S Ltd's equity 100% CU	At acquisition CU	Since acquisition CU	Non-controlling interest 40% CU
Share capital	80 000			
Retained earnings	55 000			
Fair value of net assets of S Ltd	135 000	81 000		54 000
Gain on bargain purchase (balancing figure)	(16 000) **A**	(16 000)		–
Consideration and NCI	119 000	65 000		54 000
Since acquisition				
• To beginning of current year:				
Retained earnings movement	146 750		88 050[1] **B**	58 700 **C**
S Ltd (190 000 Balance BOY – 55 000 Balance at acquisition)	135 000		81 000	54 000
SS Ltd (Calc 1**c**)	11 750		7 050	4 700
				112 700[2] **D**
• Current year:				
Profit for the year	94 125		56 475[3] **E**	37 650[4] **F**
Profit S Ltd	82 000		49 200	32 800
Dividend received from SS Ltd (8 000 × 25%)	(2 000)		(1 200)	(800)
Profit SS Ltd (Calc 1**f**)	14 125		8 475	5 650
Dividend	(18 000)		(10 800)	(7 200) **G**
	341 875		133 725	143 150 **H**

Explanatory notes: Analysis of equity of SS Ltd

[1] This amount comprises the following:

- **P Ltd's 60% share** (a 60% direct effective interest) of **S Ltd's post-acquisition retained earnings to the beginning of the year**

  PLUS
- **P Ltd's 15% share** (a 15% (60% × 25%) indirect effective interest) **of SS Ltd's post-acquisition retained earnings to the beginning of the year**.

Furthermore, this amount is **added to P Ltd's 40% share** (a 40% direct effective interest) of **SS Ltd's post-acquisition retained earnings to the beginning of the year** (see analysis of equity of SS Ltd, Calc 1 **b**), and to **P Ltd's opening retained earnings balance**, to determine the **consolidated opening retained earnings balance** which is reported in the consolidated statement of changes in equity of the P Ltd group (see Part (d)).

² This amount is **S Ltd's non-controlling interest opening balance**, which is **added** to **SS Ltd's non-controlling interest opening balance** (see analysis of equity of SS Ltd, Calc 1 **d**) to determine the total **non-controlling interest opening balance**, which is reported in the consolidated statement of changes in equity of the P Ltd group (see Part (d)).

³ This amount is comprised as follows:

- **P Ltd's 60% share** (a 60% direct effective interest) of **S Ltd's current year profit** (reduced by the intragroup dividend)
  PLUS
- **P Ltd's 15% share** (a 15% (60% × 25%) indirect effective interest) of **SS Ltd's current year profit**.

Furthermore, this amount is **added** to **P Ltd's 40% share** (a 40% direct effective interest) of **SS Ltd's current year profit** (see analysis of equity of SS Ltd, Calc 1 **e**), and to the **current year profit of P Ltd** (adjusted for the intragroup dividends), to determine the **consolidated profit for the year attributable to the owners of the parent**, reported in the consolidated statement of profit or loss and other comprehensive income of the P Ltd group (see Part (d)).

⁴ This amount represents the share of the **non-controlling interest of S Ltd** in the **current year profit** of **both S Ltd** (40% direct effective interest) and **SS Ltd** (10% (40% × 25%) indirect effective interest). This amount is **added** to the **35% share of SS Ltd's current year profit, attributable to the non-controlling interest of SS Ltd**, (see analysis of equity of SS Ltd, Calc 1 **g**) to determine the **consolidated profit for the year attributable to the non-controlling interest**, reported in the consolidated statement of profit or loss and other comprehensive income of the P Ltd group (see Part (d)).

Part (c): Pro forma journal entities for the 20x5 financial year

AT ACQUISITION

Pro forma journal 1 (J1)	Dr CU	Cr CU	NCI Balance
Share capital (SS Ltd) (SCIE) (given)	50 000		
Retained earnings (SS Ltd) (SCIE) (given)	86 000		
Investment in SS Ltd (SFP)		Wkg1 118 000	
NCI: SS Ltd – Equity (SFP)		Wkg2 47 600	47 600
Goodwill (SFP) (balancing figure)	29 600		

Elimination of at acquisition equity SS Ltd and cost of investment in SS Ltd by P Ltd and by S Ltd, and recognition of the non-controlling interest and goodwill upon acquisition of SS Ltd

Workings: Pro forma journals

Working 1
75 000 (given) Cost of P Ltd's investment in SS Ltd + 43 000 (given) Cost of S Ltd's investment in SS Ltd

Working 2
(50 000 + 86 000) × 35% Effective interest of NCI of SS Ltd

Pro forma journal 2 (J2)	Dr CU	Cr CU	NCI Balance
Share capital (S Ltd) (SCIE) (given)	80 000		
Retained earnings (S Ltd) (SCIE) (given)	55 000		
Investment in S Ltd (P Ltd) (SFP) (given)		65 000	
NCI: S Ltd – Equity (SFP)		Wkg3 54 000	54 000
Retained earnings (P Ltd) [bargain purchase gain] (balancing figure)		16 000	
Elimination of at acquisition equity of S Ltd and cost of investment in S Ltd, and recognition of the non-controlling interest and gain on bargain purchase at acquisition of S Ltd			

Workings: Pro forma journals

Working 3
(80 000 + 55 000) × 40% Effective interest of NCI of S Ltd

SINCE ACQUISITION TO BEGINNING OF THE YEAR

Pro forma journal 3 (J3)	Dr CU	Cr CU	
Retained earnings (SS Ltd) (SCIE)	Wkg4 16 450		
NCI: SS Ltd – Equity (SFP)		Wkg4 16 450	16 450
Allocating the non-controlling interest in SS Ltd its share of SS Ltd's post-acquisition retained earnings to the beginning of the year			

Workings: Pro forma journals

Working 4
(133 000 SS Ltd Balance BOY – 86 000 SS Ltd Balance at acquisition) × 35% Effective interest of NCI of SS Ltd

Pro forma journal 4 (J4)	Dr CU	Cr CU	
Retained earnings (SS Ltd) (SCIE)	Wkg5 4 700		
Retained earnings (S Ltd) (SCIE)	Wkg6 54 000		
NCI: S Ltd – Equity (SFP) (balancing figure)		58 700	58 700
Allocating the non-controlling interest in S Ltd its share of SS Ltd's and S Ltd's post-acquisition retained earnings to the beginning of the year			**Balance 176 750 BOY (Calc 3)**

Workings: Pro forma journals

Working 5
(133 000 SS Ltd Balance BOY – 86 000 SS Ltd Balance at acquisition) × 10% (40% × 25%) Effective interest of NCI of S Ltd

Working 6
(190 000 S Ltd Balance BOY – 55 000 S Ltd Balance at acquisition) × 40% Effective interest of NCI of S Ltd

CURRENT YEAR

Pro forma journal 5 (J5)	Dr CU	Cr CU	NCI Balance
NCI of SS Ltd: Share of SS Ltd profit or loss (P/L)	Wkg7 19 775		
NCI: SS Ltd – Equity (SFP)		Wkg7 19 775	19 775
Allocating the non-controlling interest of SS Ltd its share of SS Ltd's current year profit			

Workings: Pro forma journals

Working 7
56 500 Profit of SS Ltd × 35% Effective interest of NCI of SS Ltd

Pro forma journal 6 (J6)	Dr CU	Cr CU	
NCI of S Ltd: Share of SS Ltd profit or loss (P/L)	Wkg8 5 650		
NCI of S Ltd: Share of S Ltd profit or loss (P/L)	Wkg9 32 000		
NCI S Ltd – Equity (SFP) (balancing figure)		37 650	37 650
Allocating the non-controlling interest of S Ltd its share of SS Ltd's and S Ltd's current year profit			

Workings: Pro forma journals

Working 8
56 500 Profit of SS Ltd × 10% Effective interest of NCI of S Ltd

Working 9
(82 000 Profit of S Ltd – 2 000 (8 000 × 25%) Intragroup dividend) × 40% Effective interest of NCI of S Ltd

Pro forma journal 7 (J7)	Dr CU	Cr CU	
Dividend received (P Ltd) (P/L)	Wkg10 3 200		
Dividend received (S Ltd) (P/L)	Wkg11 2 000		
NCI: SS Ltd – Equity (SFP) (balancing figure)	2 800		
Dividend paid (SS Ltd) (SCIE) (given)		8 000	(2 800)
Elimination of intragroup dividends received by P Ltd and S Ltd from SS Ltd, and recognition of the non-controlling interest of SS Ltd in the dividend			

Workings: Pro forma journals

Working 10
8 000 (given) Dividend × 40% Effective interest of P Ltd

Working 11
8 000 (given) Dividend × 25% Effective interest of S Ltd

Pro forma journal 8 (J8)	Dr CU	Cr CU	NCI Balance
Dividend received (P Ltd) (P/L)	Wkg12 10 800		
NCI: S Ltd – Equity (SFP) (balancing figure)	7 200		(7 200)
Dividend paid (S Ltd) (SCIE) (given)		18 000	
Elimination of intragroup dividend received by P Ltd from S Ltd, and recognition of the non-controlling interest of S Ltd in the dividend			**Balance 224 175 BOY (Calc 4)**

Workings: Pro forma journals

Working 12
18 000 (given) Dividend × 60% Effective interest of P Ltd

Comments: Pro forma journals

Comments: Pro forma journal 2

- The acquisition of S Ltd took place in a prior year. This means that the gain on bargain purchase arising from this acquisition was included in that prior year's consolidated profit, which profit was closed off to retained earnings in that prior year's consolidated financial statements.

- Consequently, when preparing the current year consolidated financial statements, this gain on bargain purchase must be recognised in the current year opening consolidated retained earnings balance. For this reason, retained earnings is credited with the CU 16 000 prior year's bargain purchase gain.

The full effects of the preceding pro forma journals on the consolidated financial statements of the P Ltd group for the financial year ended 31 December 20x5 are illustrated in the following consolidation worksheet.

	P Ltd Dr/(Cr) CU	S Ltd Dr/(Cr) CU	SS Ltd Dr/(Cr) CU	Pro forma journals At acquisition Dr/(Cr) CU	Journal ref	Pro forma journals Since acquisition Dr/(Cr) CU	Journal ref	Consolidated Dr/(Cr) CU
Equity								
Share capital	(250 000)	(80 000)	(50 000)	50 000 80 000	J1 J2			(250 000)
Retained earnings (BOY)	(320 000)	(190 000)	(133 000)	86 000 55 000 (16 000)	J1 J2 J2	16 450 4 700 54 000	J3 J4 J4	(442 850)
Dividends	35 000	18 000	8 000			(8 000) (18 000)	J7 J8	35 000
Profit: Individual entities	(149 800)	(82 000)	(56 500)					
Consolidated profit attributable to owners of parent								†(214 875)
Retained earnings (EOY)	(434 800)	(254 000)	(181 500)					(622 725)
NCI Equity	–	–		(47 600) (54 000)	J1 J2	(16 450) (58 700) (19 775) (37 650) 2 800 7 200	J3 J4 J5 J6 J7 J8	(224 175)
Total equity	(684 800)	(334 000)	(231 500)					(1 096 900)

Explanatory notes

† This amount has been brought forward from the second part of the consolidation worksheet on page 514

	P Ltd Dr/(Cr) CU	S Ltd Dr/(Cr) CU	SS Ltd Dr/(Cr) CU	Pro forma journals At acquisition Dr/(Cr) CU	Journal ref	Pro forma journals Since acquisition Dr/(Cr) CU	Journal ref	Con-solidated Dr/(Cr) CU
Liabilities:								
Trade and other payables	(171 000)	(83 500)	(30 340)					(284 840)
Total liabilities	(171 000)	(83 500)	(30 340)					(284 840)
Total equity & liabilities	(855 800)	(417 500)	(261 840)					(1 381 740)
Assets:								
Property, plant and equipment	409 600	277 000	170 590					857 190
Trade and other receivables	306 200	97 500	91 250					494 950
Investment in S Ltd	65 000	–	–	(65 000)	J2			–
Investment in SS Ltd	75 000	43 000	–	(118 000)	J1			–
Goodwill				29 600	J1			29 600
Total assets	855 800	417 500	261 840					1 381 740
Profit or loss								
Net profit for the period	(149 800)	(82 000)	(56 500)			3 200	J7	(272 300)
						2 000	J7	
						10 800	J8	
NCI: Share of profit						19 775	J5	57 425
						5 650	J6	
						32 000	J6	
Consolidated profit attributable to owners of parent								‡(214 875)

Explanatory notes

‡ This amount has been carried forward to the first part of the consolidation worksheet on page 513

514

Part (d): Consolidated financial statements for the 20x5 financial year

P LTD GROUP: ABRIDGED CONSOLIDATED STATEMENT OF PROFIT OR LOSS AND OTHER COMPREHENSIVE INCOME FOR THE YEAR ENDED 31 DECEMBER 20x5	
	CU
PROFIT FOR THE YEAR ((P Ltd: 149 800 – 3 200 (J7) Dividend from SS Ltd – 10 800 (J8) Dividend from S Ltd) + (S Ltd: 82 000 – 2 000 (J7) Dividend from SS Ltd) + 56 500 (SS Ltd))	272 300
Other comprehensive income	–
TOTAL COMPREHENSIVE INCOME	**272 300**
Total comprehensive income attributable to:	
Owners of the parent (balancing figure) **OR** (P Ltd: 149 800 – 14 000 (J7 & J8) Dividends from SS Ltd & S Ltd) + S Ltd: 22 600 (see Calc 1 **e**) + 56 475 (see Calc 2 **E**))	†214 875
Non-controlling interest (NCI of SS Ltd: 19 775 (see Calc 1 **g OR** (J5)) + NCI of S Ltd: 37 650 (see Calc 2**F OR** (J6))	‡57 425
	272 300

† **Check:**

	CU
Profit P Ltd: (149 800 – 14 000 dividends)	135 800
Share of profit S Ltd [(82 000 – 2000 Dividends) × 60%]	48 000
Share of profit of SS Ltd [56 500 × 55% (15% + 40%)]	31 075
	214 875

‡ **Check:**

	CU
NCI of SS Ltd: Share of profit of SS Ltd (56 500 × 35%)	19 775
NCI of S Ltd: Share of profit of SS Ltd (56 500 × 10%)	5 650
NCI of S Ltd: Share of profit of S Ltd [(82 000 – 2 000 Dividend) × 40%]	32 000
	57 425

P LTD GROUP: CONSOLIDATED STATEMENT OF CHANGES IN EQUITY FOR THE YEAR ENDED 31 DECEMBER 20x5					
	Parent equity holders' interest			Non-controlling interest	Total equity of the group
	Share capital	Retained earnings	Total parent equity		
	CU	CU	CU	CU	CU
Opening balance at 1 Jan 20x5	250 000	Wkg1442 850	692 850	Wkg2176 750	869 600
Total comprehensive income:					
Profit for the period (from CSOPL_OCI)		214 875	214 875	57 425	272 300
Dividends		(35 000)	(35 000)	Wkg3(10 000)	(45 000)
Closing balance at 31 Dec 20x5	250 000	622 725	872 725	224 175	1 096 900

Workings: Consolidated statement of changes in equity

Working 1

(P Ltd: 320 000 + 16 000 (see Calc 2 **A**) Gain on bargain purchase) + (S Ltd: 18 800 (see Calc 1 **b**) + 88 050 (see Calc 2 **B**))

OR

(P Ltd: 320 000 + 16 000 (J2) Gain on bargain purchase) + (S Ltd: 190 000 Balance BOY – 55 000 (J2) Balance at acquisition – 54 000 (J4) NCI of S Ltd: Share of post-acquisition retained earnings of S Ltd to BOY) + (SS Ltd: 133 000 Balance BOY – 86 000 (J1) Balance at acquisition – 16 450 (J3) NCI of SS Ltd: Share of post-acquisition retained earnings of SS Ltd to BOY – 4 700 (J4) NCI of S Ltd: Share of post-acquisition retained earnings of SS Ltd to BOY)

Note: This amount represents P Ltd's opening retained earnings balance (adjusted for the 16 000 bargain purchase gain) plus:

• P Ltd's 60% share (a 60% direct effective interest) of S Ltd's post-acquisition retained earnings to the beginning of the current year;

• P Ltd's 40% share (a 40% direct effective interest) of SS Ltd's post-acquisition retained earnings to the beginning of the current year; and

• P Ltd's 15% share (a 15% (60% x25%) indirect effective interest) of SS Ltd's post-acquisition retained earnings to the beginning of the current year.

Working 2

(NCI of SS Ltd: 64 050 (see Calc 1 **d**)) + (NCI of SS Ltd: 112 700 (see Calc 2 **D**))

OR

(NCI of S Ltd and SS Ltd BOY: 176 750 (see pro forma journal entries: Calc 3))

Note: This amount represents the sum of the opening non-controlling interest balances of both S Ltd and SS Ltd.

In this regard:

• The non-controlling interest of S Ltd shares in 40% (40% direct effective interest) of S Ltd's equity and in 10% (10% (40% × 25% Indirect effective interest) of SS Ltd' post-acquisition equity (i.e., post-acquisition retained earnings and current year profit).

• The non-controlling interest of SS Ltd shares in 35% (35% direct effective interest) of SS Ltd's equity.

Working 3

NCI share of SS Ltd dividend: 2 800 (see (J7) **OR** Calc 1 **h**) + NCI share of S Ltd dividend: 7 200 (see (J8) **OR** Calc 2 **G**)

P LTD GROUP: CONSOLIDATED STATEMENT OF FINANCIAL POSITION AS AT 31 DECEMBER 20x5	
	CU
Assets	
Non-current assets	
Property, plant and equipment (409 600 (P Ltd) + 277 000 (S Ltd) + 170 590 (SS Ltd))	857 190
Goodwill (see Calc 1 **a OR** (J1))	29 600
Current assets	
Trade and other receivables (306 200 (P Ltd) + 97 500 (S Ltd) + 91 250 (SS Ltd))	494 950
Total assets	1 381 740
Equity and liabilities	
Share capital (from CSCIE)	250 000
Retained earnings (from CSCIE)	622 725
Equity attributable to owners of the parent	872 725
Non-controlling interest (from SCIE) **OR** (see pro forma journal entries: Calc 4) **OR** (81 025 (see Calc 1 **i**) + 143 150 (see Calc 2 **H**))	224 175
Total equity	1 096 900
Current liabilities	
Trade and other payables (171 000 (P Ltd) + 83 500 (S Ltd) + 30 340 (SS Ltd))	284 840
Total equity and liabilities	1 381 740

Summary

This chapter considered the implications of the following group structures on the preparation of consolidated financial statements: a horizontal group, a vertical group and a mixed group.

Because a horizontal group has a **single-level shareholding structure,** the consolidation process and procedures are essentially the **same** as those that apply to a **simple group,** dealt with in Volume 1 Chapters 3 to 6. The only difference is that for a horizontal group these consolidation procedures need to be applied to **more than one subsidiary.**

A typical vertical group consists of a parent P Ltd, which controls a subsidiary S Ltd, which in turn has a subsidiary of its own, referred to as the sub-subsidiary, SS Ltd. As was the case with a horizontal group, in a vertical group the assets, liabilities, income and expenses of the **multiple** subsidiaries are combined with those of the parent. The consolidation procedures for a vertical group are, however, more complicated than for a simple and a horizontal group since control is exercised at **multiple levels.**

When consolidating a vertical group, the following key learning points are important:

- P Ltd's total share of its subsidiaries' profits and post-acquisition reserves consists of its indirect effective interest and its direct effective interest in the profit and post-acquisition reserves of SS Ltd and S Ltd respectively.

- The non-controlling interest's total share of group profit and post-acquisition reserves consists of the non-controlling interest of SS Ltd's direct effective interest in SS Ltd's current year profit and post-acquisition reserves plus the non-controlling interest of S Ltd's indirect effective interest and its direct effective interest in the profit and post-acquisition reserves of SS Ltd and S Ltd respectively.

The sequence in which the direct controlling interest in S Ltd and SS Ltd is acquired by P Ltd and S Ltd respectively, affects certain aspects of the consolidation process. Three different scenarios arise.

The first scenario is a **simultaneous acquisition,** where P Ltd acquires a direct controlling interest in S Ltd on the **same date** that S Ltd acquires a controlling interest in SS Ltd. Here, **SS Ltd's post-acquisition reserves** form **part of the P Ltd group from acquisition date of SS Ltd by S Ltd,** when the P Ltd group comes into existence with the acquisition of S Ltd by P Ltd on the same date.

In the second scenario, P Ltd acquires its direct controlling interest in S Ltd **before** S Ltd acquires its direct controlling interest in SS Ltd. In this instance:

- The goodwill/bargain purchase gain arising from each of the two business combinations must be recognised in the consolidated financial statement of the P Ltd group.
- The post-acquisition reserves of both S Ltd and SS Ltd, to be included in the consolidated financial statements of the P Ltd group, are determined from the **date of acquisition of each respective subsidiary,** and are allocated to P Ltd and to the **non-controlling interest of both SS Ltd and S Ltd.**

In the third scenario, where P Ltd acquires an interest in S Ltd **after** that subsidiary has acquired its own interest in SS Ltd, P Ltd has acquired **the S Ltd group,** comprising **S Ltd as the parent entity** and its single, **directly held subsidiary, SS Ltd.** In this instance:

- The **acquisition date** of both subsidiaries S Ltd and SS Ltd, from the perspective of the **P Ltd group,** is the **acquisition date of S Ltd by P Ltd.** This means that any changes in the reserves (and therefore the equity) of SS Ltd from acquisition date of SS Ltd by S Ltd to date of acquisition of S Ltd by P Ltd must, from the P Ltd group's perspective, form part of **at acquisition reserves (and equity).**
- Any goodwill or bargain purchase gain calculated in respect of **S Ltd's acquisition of SS Ltd** – determined at acquisition date of **S Ltd by P Ltd** – must be **reversed.**
- The post-acquisition equity of both S Ltd and SS Ltd is then determined for the P Ltd group by establishing the movement in the reserves of both these subsidiaries **from the acquisition date of S Ltd by P Ltd to the end of the current reporting period,** and is allocated to P Ltd and to the non-controlling interest of both SS Ltd and S Ltd.

In a **mixed group,** the parent, P Ltd and its subsidiary S Ltd **each own equity interests in a third entity, SS Ltd,** such that the combination of P Ltd's and S Ltd's ownership interests result in the **P Ltd having a controlling interest in the third entity, SS Ltd,** which then becomes **another subsidiary of P Ltd.** The consolidation for a mixed group follows the same process as for a vertical group but with the need to **include the effects of P Ltd's direct shareholding in SS Ltd** when compiling the consolidated financial statements of the P Ltd group.

The focus of Volume 1 Chapter 8 is on the consolidation of a subsidiary with preference shares.

QUESTIONS

Question 7.1

The following are the trial balances of the companies within the P Ltd group for the year ended 31 December 20x5:

Trial balances at 31 December 20x5	P Ltd Dr/(Cr) CU	S Ltd Dr/(Cr) CU	SS Ltd Dr/(Cr) CU
Share capital	(480 000)	(250 000)	(100 000)
Retained earnings (1 Jan 20x5)	(345 000)	(95 000)	(210 000)
Revaluation surplus (1 Jan 20x5)	–	–	(142 000)
Mark to market reserve (1 Jan 20x5)	–	(17 460)	–
Dividend paid (31 December 20x5)	50 000	4 000	–
Trade and other payables	(127 020)	(161 820)	(38 000)
Deferred tax	(5 850)	(11 429)	(65 000)
Plant	260 000	125 000	250 140
Land	126 980	87 800	–
Trade and other receivables	197 980	149 350	300 750
Inventory	117 900	69 000	57 350
Investment in S Ltd: at fair value	337 100	–	–
Investment in SS Ltd: at fair value	–	238 300	–
Sales	(450 000)	(398 000)	(268 000)
Cost of sales	290 000	231 220	199 200
Other income	(42 000)	(12 450)	–
Depreciation	48 000	25 000	8 800
Income tax expense	31 300	28 750	19 900
Fair value gain on equity investment (OCI)	(12 100)	(15 800)	–
Tax on fair value gain (OCI)	2 710	3 539	–
Revaluation gain: Plant (OCI)	–	–	(18 250)
Tax on revaluation gain: Plant (OCI)	–	–	5 110

- S Ltd acquired a 65% controlling interest in SS Ltd on 1 July 20x3 for CU 200 000, when SS Ltd had retained earnings of CU 120 000, a revaluation surplus of 85 000 and share capital of CU 100 000. At acquisition date, all of SS Ltd's assets and liabilities were considered to be fairly valued.

- P Ltd acquired a 75% controlling interest in S Ltd on 1 January 20x5 for CU 325 000, when:
  - S Ltd's retained earnings were CU 95 000 and its share capital was CU 250 000; and
  - SS Ltd's retained earnings were CU 210 000, its revaluation surplus was CU 142 000 and its share capital was CU 100 000.

- On date of acquisition of S Ltd, the inventory of S Ltd had a fair value of CU 14 000 more than its carrying amount. This inventory was sold outside the group during the current financial year. In addition, at acquisition, S Ltd's plant was determined to be undervalued by CU 56 210. The remaining useful life of the plant at that date was five years with a zero residual value. S Ltd did not revalue the plant in its own records. All the assets and liabilities of SS Ltd were considered to be fairly valued on 1 January 20x5.

- The following intragroup transactions occurred within the P Ltd group:
  - In the current financial year, S Ltd began selling inventory to SS Ltd at cost plus 35%. In this regard, S Ltd made inventory sales of CU 138 000 to SS Ltd during the current financial year. In addition, SS Ltd had closing inventory on hand at financial year end purchased from S Ltd of CU 21 500.
  - On 1 October 20x5, P Ltd sold owner-occupied land at a profit of CU 36 000 to S Ltd.
- Both P Ltd and S Ltd accounted for their investments in subsidiaries at fair value through other comprehensive income, in accordance with IFRS 9, in their separate financial statements.
- The non-controlling interest is measured at its proportionate share of the identifiable net assets of the subsidiary acquired.
- An income tax rate of 28% applies and 80% of capital gains are included in taxable income thereof.
- Neither P Ltd, nor S Ltd are sharedealers for income tax purposes.

Required

(a) Provide the pro forma journals necessary to prepare consolidated financial statements for the P Ltd group for the financial year ended 31 December 20x5.

(b) Prepare the consolidated statement of profit or loss and other comprehensive income for the P Ltd group for the financial year ended 31 December 20x5.

(c) Prepare **only the assets and liabilities sections** of consolidated statement of financial position for the P Ltd group as at 31 December 20x5.

Question 7.2

- P Ltd acquired an 80% controlling interest in S1 Ltd on 1 January 20x3 for CU 272 800 when S1 Ltd's share capital was CU 200 000 and its retained earnings were CU 110 000.
- P Ltd also acquired a 60% controlling interest in S3 Ltd on 1 January 20x3 for CU 69 000. Furthermore:
  - On acquisition date, S3 Ltd had share capital of CU 150 000 as well as an accumulated loss of CU 60 000.
  - Since its acquisition, P Ltd has sold inventories to S3 Ltd at cost plus 25%. In this regard, P Ltd made inventory sales of CU 122 000 to S3 Ltd during the current year. In addition, S3 Ltd had opening inventory and closing inventory on hand purchased from P Ltd of CU 68 000 and CU 81 000 respectively.
- S1 Ltd acquired a 70% controlling interest in S2 Ltd on 1 January 20x4 for CU 201 000. In addition:
  - On acquisition date, the share capital and retained earnings of S2 Ltd was CU 100 000 and CU 160 000 respectively.

- On 31 March 20x4, S2 Ltd sold machinery with a carrying amount of CU 46 000 to S3 Ltd for CU 70 000. On this date, the estimated useful life of the machinery sold was three years and the machinery had a NIL residual value. The group policy is to provide for depreciation over the expected useful life of machinery using the straight line method, which is consistent with the tax allowances granted by the tax authority

Further information

1. At the end of the current financial year, it was assessed that goodwill recognised in respect of the acquisition of S3 Ltd was impaired by CU 12 000. Goodwill recognised in respect of the acquisition of the other group entities was not considered to be impaired at financial year end. The group elected to measure any non-controlling interest in an acquiree at its proportional share of the acquiree's identifiable net assets at acquisition date.

2. All the assets and liabilities of the P Ltd group subsidiaries were considered to be fairly valued at acquisition date.

3. Both P Ltd and S1 Ltd measure their investments in subsidiaries at cost price in accordance with IAS 27.10.

4. The income tax rate is 28% and in all the entities, each share carries one vote. Furthermore, 80% of capital gains are included in taxable income.

The abridged trial balances of P Ltd and its subsidiaries for the financial year ended 31 December 20x5 appear below.

Abridged trial balances at 31 December 20x5	P Ltd Dr/(Cr) CU	S1 Ltd Dr/(Cr) CU	S2 Ltd Dr/(Cr) CU	S3 Ltd Dr/(Cr) CU
Share capital	(250 000)	(200 000)	(100 000)	(150 000)
(Retained earnings)/Accumulated loss (1 Jan 20x5)	(300 000)	(226 750)	(279 000)	140 000
Trade and other payables	(120 680)	(52 700)	(58 000)	(323 250)
Machinery	–	–	226 150	124 900
Trade and other receivables	317 980	365 450	300 750	15 750
Inventory	167 900	–	–	134 600
Investment in S1 Ltd: 80 000	272 800	–	–	–
Investment in S2 Ltd: 56 000	–	201 000	–	–
Investment in S3 Ltd: 30 000	69 000	–	–	–
(Profit)/Loss for the period	(157 000)	(87 000)	(89 900)	58 000

Required

(a) Prepare only the **EQUITY** section of the consolidated statement of financial position of the P Ltd Group as at 31 December 20x5

(b) Calculate the following amounts that will be disclosed in the consolidated statement of financial position of the P Ltd Group as at 31 December 20x5:
- goodwill;
- machinery; and
- deferred tax (specify if the amount is a deferred tax asset or liability).

References

IFRS 3 *Business Combinations*

IFRS 10 *Consolidated Financial Statements*

CONSOLIDATING A SUBSIDIARY WITH PREFERENCE SHARES

LEARNING OBJECTIVES

After studying this chapter, you should be able to:

- understand the differences between the rights attached to preference shares and ordinary shares;

- explain the implications of consolidating a subsidiary with preference shares at acquisition both when the preference shares are classified as equity and when classified as a liability of the issuing subsidiary;

- understand how to allocate profits of the subsidiary between the ordinary and preference shareholders on consolidation when the preference dividend is non-cumulative and when it is cumulative;

- prepare consolidated financial statements where the subsidiary has issued preference shares classified as equity and the parent has acquired some, all, or none of the preference shares;

- prepare consolidated financial statements where the preference dividend is in arrears at the date of acquisition and after that date; and

- prepare consolidated financial statements where the subsidiary has issued preference shares classified as a liability and the parent has acquired some, all, or none of the preference shares.

TOPIC LIST

Introduction

When we prepare consolidated financial statements it is important to establish the nature of the shares that have been issued by the subsidiary that has been acquired. This is because the subsidiary may have issued more than one class of shares. More particularly, it is common in many jurisdictions for a subsidiary to issue **another class of shares** known as **preference shares** in addition to ordinary shares.

Preference shares, as the name implies, typically have **preferential rights attached to them** compared to ordinary shares as regards, among others, **dividends** and the **return of share capital** to investors. Most notably, **preference shares** grant their holders **first entitlement** to the **payment of dividends.** That is, the company must first pay its preference shareholders their preference dividend before any dividends are paid to the ordinary shareholders. Preference shares usually carry a fixed percentage dividend. For example, if a shareholder owns a 100 8% preference shares of CU 10 each, the shareholder will be entitled to a preference dividend of CU 80 (100 shares × 10 × 8%).

Furthermore, preference shares ordinarily do *not* have voting rights, subject to the exception that preference shares will normally carry voting rights if the preference dividend is in arrears, in which case voting rights will be limited to issues affecting their rights as preference shareholders.

Preference shares may also be **cumulative,** where broadly speaking, the **right** to the **preference dividend** is **carried forward to a subsequent period** should no preference dividend be declared in the current reporting period. Conversely, preference shares may be **non-cumulative,** which means that **no right** to the **preference dividend** is **carried forward** in the event that the company fails to declare a preference dividend in any given period. These concepts are explained in detail together with the effects on consolidation in the sections below.

Additionally, preference shares may be **classified** as **equity** or as a **liability** of the **issuing company,** with such a classification being very much dependent on whether the preference shares are **redeemable or not.** This is discussed in depth in Section 8.1.

8.1 Classification of preference shares as equity or as a liability of the issuing company

As noted above, whether preference shares are classified as equity or as a liability of the issuing company is primarily based on whether or not they are redeemable, that is, whether the preference share capital will be repaid to the preference shareholders at some point in the future.

Preference shares will be classified as a **liability** of the **issuing company** if:

- it is **compulsory** for the **issuing company** to redeem them at a **future date;** or
- the **preference shareholders may elect** that the **issuing company must redeem their preference shares.**

In addition, when preference shares are classified as a **liability,** the related **preference dividend** will be classified as a **finance charge** of the **issuing company** and will be reflected as such in the statement of profit or loss and other comprehensive income of the issuing company.

Preference shares will be classified as **equity** of the **issuing company** if:

- **redemption** of the preference shares is *not* compulsory, but may be made at the **election** of the **issuing entity;** or
- the preference shares are *not* redeemable.

8.1.1 At acquisition: Consolidation of a subsidiary with preference shares classified as a liability

To the extent that the parent has an interest in the subsidiary's preference shares (i.e., has subscribed for any of the subsidiary's preference share capital) we must **eliminate** such interest, being the parent's **investment in the subsidiary's preference share capital,** against the **portion** of the **subsidiary's preference share capital,** classified as a **liability.** This is because these two items are **intragroup balances** that must be set off against one another on consolidation.

In addition, in circumstances where the parent has remeasured its investment in the subsidiary's preference share capital to fair value (through profit or loss or through other comprehensive income) in terms of IFRS 9 *Financial Instruments,* such remeasurement (together with the related tax effects) must **first be reversed** so that the investment is restated to its original cost, before eliminating it against the subsidiary's preference share liability.

Furthermore, to the extent that any **non-controlling shareholders** own **preference shares in the subsidiary** that are classified as a **liability,** such liability will *not* be eliminated on consolidation as it is regarded as an **external liability of the group** and *not* an intragroup balance (i.e., it will remain a group liability and will accordingly be included in the consolidated financial statements).

Example 8.1: At acquisition: Consolidation of a partly owned subsidiary with preference shares classified as a liability

On 31 December 20x5 P Ltd acquired:

- 80% (a controlling interest) of the ordinary shares of S Ltd; and
- 30% of the preference shares of S Ltd.

Additional information

- S Ltd's net assets were considered to be fairly valued at acquisition date.
- P Ltd measures the non-controlling interest at its proportionate share of the identifiable net assets of S Ltd.
- P Ltd measures both its investment in S Ltd's ordinary shares and in S Ltd's preference shares at cost price.

The abridged trial balances of P Ltd and its subsidiary S Ltd on 31 December 20x5 were as follows:

Abridged trial balances at 31 December 20x5	P Ltd Dr/(Cr) CU	S Ltd Dr/(Cr) CU
Ordinary share capital	(450 000)	(100 000)
Preference share capital (Liability)	–	(70 000)
Retained earnings (31 Dec 20x5)	(160 000)	(40 000)
Trade and other payables	(88 000)	(19 000)
Plant	200 000	86 000
Trade and other receivables	335 000	143 000
Investment in S Ltd: Ordinary shares	142 000	–
Investment in S Ltd: Preference shares	21 000	–

Required

(a) Provide the at acquisition pro forma journal entries.

(b) Prepare the consolidation worksheet at 31 December 20x5.

 Solution 8.1: At acquisition: Consolidation of a partly owned subsidiary with preference shares classified as a liability

Part (a): Pro forma journal entries at acquisition

Pro forma journal 1 (J1)	Dr CU	Cr CU
Share capital (S Ltd) (SCIE) (given)	100 000	
Retained earnings (S Ltd) (SCIE) (given)	40 000	
Investment: S Ltd ordinary shares (P Ltd) (SFP) (given)		142 000
NCI – Equity (SCIE)		Wkg1 28 000
Goodwill (SFP) (balancing figure)	30 000	
Elimination of at acquisition ordinary owners equity of S Ltd and cost of investment, and recognition of the non-controlling interest and goodwill at acquisition of S Ltd's ordinary shares		

Workings: Pro forma journals

Workings 1
(100 000 + 40 000) × 20% NCI Share

Pro forma journal 2 (J2)	Dr CU	Cr CU
Preference share liability (S Ltd) (SCIE) (balancing figure)	21 000	
Investment: S Ltd preference shares (P Ltd) (SFP) (given)		21 000
Elimination of intragroup balances, offsetting S Ltd preference share liability against P Ltd investment in S Ltd preference shares		

Comments: Pro forma journal 2

- S Ltd's preference share liability is offset to the extent of P Ltd's investment in S Ltd's preference shares as these are intragroup balances that require elimination on consolidation. The result is that the remaining preference shares, owned by the non-controlling interest, are reflected as a liability in the consolidated financial statements.

Part (b): Consolidation worksheet for the P Ltd group as at 31 December 20x5

	P Ltd Dr/(Cr) CU	S Ltd Dr/(Cr) CU	Pro forma journals Dr/(Cr) CU	Journal ref	Con- solidated Dr/(Cr) CU
Equity					
Share capital	(450 000)	(100 000)	100 000	J1	(450 000)
Retained earnings (EOY)	(160 000)	(40 000)	40 000	J1	(160 000)
NCI – Equity			(28 000)	J1	(28 000)[1]
Total equity	(610 000)	(140 000)			(638 000)
Liabilities					
Preference shares	–	(70 000)	21 000	J2	(49 000)[2]
Trade and other payables	(88 000)	(19 000)			(107 000)
Total liabilities	(88 000)	(89 000)			(156 000)
Total equity & liabilities	(698 000)	(229 000)			(794 000)
Assets					
Plant	200 000	86 000			286 000
Trade and other receivables	335 000	143 000			478 000
Investment in S Ltd: Ordinary shares	142 000	–	(142 000)	J1	–
Investment in S Ltd: Preference shares	21 000	–	(21 000)	J2	–
Goodwill	–	–	30 000	J1	30 000
Total assets	**698 000**	**229 000**			**794 000**

Comments: Consolidation worksheet

[1]   The NCI – Equity balance reflects the non-controlling interest's share of S Ltd's ordinary equity (i.e., ordinary share capital and retained earnings). That is, it does *not* include the non-controlling interest's share of S Ltd's preference equity, given that S Ltd's preference shares are *not* classified as equity.

[2]   The portion of S Ltd's preference shares classified as a liability, which is owned by P Ltd, an amount of CU 21 000 (70 000 S Ltd's total preference shares × 30% Percentage owned by P Ltd), is an intragroup balance, which is eliminated on consolidation. This leaves the portion of S Ltd's preference shares owned by the non-controlling interest, an amount of CU 49 000 (70 000 S Ltd's total preference shares × 70% Percentage owned by the non-controlling interest), which is *not* intragroup and is therefore included as a group liability.

8.1.2 At acquisition: Consolidation of subsidiary with preference shares classified as equity

Preference shares of a subsidiary classified as equity are consolidated in the same manner as ordinary shares at acquisition, that is:

* the **parent's at acquisition share** of the subsidiary's **preference share capital** is **eliminated** against the **parent's investment** in the **subsidiary's preference share equity** and any **difference** between these two items is recognised either as **goodwill** or as a **gain on bargain purchase;** and
* any **non-controlling interest** in the **preference shares** of the subsidiary is **recognised.**

As you know from Volume 1 Chapter 2, in terms of IFRS 3 *Business Combinations*, if the non-controlling interests concerned are **present ownership interests** that entitle their holders to a **proportionate share** of the subsidiary's net assets in the event of liquidation of the subsidiary, the acquirer (i.e., the parent) has a **choice**, available for **each business combination**, to **measure** the **non-controlling interest at acquisition date**, either (IFRS 3.19):

- at its **fair value**; or
- at its **proportionate share of the subsidiary's identifiable net assets**, which have been fairly valued in terms of IFRS 3.

Conversely – as was explained in Volume 1 Chapter 2 – components of non-controlling interests that are *not* present ownership interests and which *do not* entitle their holders to a proportionate share of the subsidiary's net assets upon liquidation of the subsidiary, must be measured at **fair value** at acquisition date (IFRS 3.19).

The implications of the IFRS 3 measurement requirements, as discussed above, when measuring the non-controlling interest in the subsidiary's preference share equity at acquisition are therefore as follows:

- The non-controlling interest may **only be measured at its fair value** at acquisition, where the preference shares grant the holders thereof:
  - the right to receive their preference dividends before the payment of an ordinary dividend; and
  - the right to a receive a **repayment of the nominal value** of their preference shares upon liquidation of the subsidiary (more simply put, the preference shareholders will get back the preference share capital that they initially subscribed for).
- The non-controlling interest may be measured at acquisition **either at its proportionate share in the subsidiary's identifiable net assets or at its fair value**, where the preference shareholders:
  - have the right to receive their preference dividends before the payment of an ordinary dividend; and
  - have the right to receive a **proportionate share of the subsidiary's net assets** upon liquidation of the subsidiary.

Example 8.2: Consolidation of partly owned subsidiary at acquisition: Preference shares classified as equity and with rights to proportionate share of subsidiary net assets upon liquidation

On 31 December 20x5 P Ltd acquired 80% (being a controlling interest) of the ordinary shares of S Ltd for CU142 000.

Additional information

- S Ltd's net assets were considered to be fairly valued at acquisition date.
- S Ltd's preference shares were classified as equity.
- P Ltd does not own any of S Ltd's preference shares.
- P Ltd uses the partial goodwill method to measure the non-controlling interest where this is allowed.

- P Ltd measures its investment in S Ltd's ordinary shares at cost price.
- The preference shareholders have the following rights:
  - Their dividend payment has priority over that of the ordinary shareholders.
  - They will receive a proportionate share of the net assets of S Ltd should this entity be liquidated.

The abridged trial balances of P Ltd and its subsidiary S Ltd on 31 December 20x5 were as follows:

Abridged trial balances at 31 December 20x5	P Ltd Dr/(Cr) CU	S Ltd Dr/(Cr) CU
Ordinary share capital	(450 000)	(100 000)
Preference share capital	–	(70 000)
Retained earnings (31 Dec 20x5)	(160 000)	(40 000)
Trade and other payables	(88 000)	(19 000)
Plant	200 000	86 000
Trade and other receivables	356 000	143 000
Investment in S Ltd: Ordinary shares at cost	142 000	–
Investment in S Ltd: Preference shares	–	–

Required

(a) Prepare the at acquisition analyses of equity.

(b) Provide the at acquisition pro forma journal entries.

(c) Prepare the consolidation worksheet as at 31 December 20x5.

Solution 8.2: Consolidation of partly owned subsidiary at acquisition: Preference shares classified as equity and with rights to proportionate share of subsidiary net assets upon liquidation

Part (a): Analyses of equity of S Ltd at acquisition date

Note: When preparing the consolidated financial statements of a subsidiary with preference share capital classified as equity, the shareholders' interest in the subsidiary's equity must be determined with reference to the **two classes** of share capital in issue – the ordinary share capital and the preference share capital of the subsidiary. To this end it is recommended that an **analysis of the subsidiary's ordinary owners' equity** is prepared, followed by the compilation of an **analysis of the subsidiary's preference owners' equity**, as illustrated below.

Analysis of S Ltd's ordinary equity – at acquisition

At acquisition date (31 December 20x5)	Total of S Ltd's ordinary equity 100% CU	P Ltd 80% At acquisition CU	Non-controlling interest 20% CU
Share capital – Ordinary	100 000		
Retained earnings	40 000		
Fair value of net assets of S Ltd	140 000	112 000	28 000
Goodwill (balancing figure)	30 000	30 000	–
Consideration and NCI	170 000	142 000	28 000

Analysis of S Ltd's preference equity – at acquisition

	Total of S Ltd's preference equity 100%	P Ltd 0% At acquisition	Non-controlling interest 100%
At acquisition date (31 December 20x5)	CU	CU	CU
Share capital – preference	70 000	–	70 000
Goodwill (balancing figure)	–	–	–
Consideration and NCI	70 000	–	70 000

Part (b): Pro forma journal entries at acquisition date

Pro forma journal 1 (J1)	Dr CU	Cr CU
Ordinary share capital (S Ltd) (SCIE) (given)	100 000	
Retained earnings (S Ltd) (SCIE) (given)	40 000	
Investment: S Ltd ordinary shares (P Ltd) (SFP) (given)		142 000
NCI – Equity (SCIE)		[Wkg1]28 000
Goodwill (SFP) (balancing figure)	30 000	

Elimination of at acquisition ordinary owners' equity of S Ltd and cost of investment, and recognition of non-controlling interest and goodwill at acquisition of ordinary shares of S Ltd

Workings: Pro forma journal

Working 1
(100 000 + 40 000) × 20% NCI Share

Pro forma journal 2 (J2)	Dr CU	Cr CU
Preference share capital (S Ltd) (SCIE) (given)	70 000	
NCI – Equity (SCIE) (balancing figure)		70 000

Elimination of at acquisition preference owners' equity by allocating it to the non-controlling interest

Comments: Pro forma journal 2

- Because S Ltd's preference shares acquired are classified as equity, this preference equity must be eliminated on consolidation. This is the CU 70 000 debit to *preference share capital* of S Ltd at acquisition date.

- On consolidation, we recognise the CU 70 000 equity interest of the non-controlling interest in all of S Ltd's preference shares issued by crediting CU 70 000 to the *NCI – Equity* account.

- Since these preference shares grant the preference shareholders a proportionate share of the net assets of S Ltd should this entity be liquidated, the non-controlling interest's share of S Ltd's preference shares (which is 100%) may be measured using the partial goodwill method (i.e., at the non-controlling interest's proportionate share of S Ltd's preference share equity).

Part (c): Consolidation worksheet for the P Ltd Group as at 31 December 20x5

	P Ltd Dr/(Cr) CU	S Ltd Dr/(Cr) CU	Pro forma journals Dr/(Cr) CU	Journal ref	Con-solidated Dr/(Cr) CU
Equity					
Ordinary share capital	(450 000)	(100 000)	100 000	J1	(450 000)
Preference share capital	–	(70 000)	70 000	J2	–
Retained earnings (EOY)	(160 000)	(40 000)	40 000	J1	(160 000)
NCI – Equity			(28 000)	J1	(98 000)[1]
			(70 000)	J2	
Total equity	(610 000)	(210 000)			(708 000)
Liabilities					
Trade and other payables	(88 000)	(19 000)			(107 000)
Total liabilities	**(88 000)**	**(19 000)**			**(107 000)**
Total equity & liabilities	**(698 000)**	**(229 000)**			**(815 000)**
Assets					
Plant	200 000	86 000			286 000
Trade and other receivables	356 000	143 000			499 000
Investment in S Ltd: Ordinary shares	142 000	–	(142 000)	J1	–
Goodwill	–	–	30 000	J1	30 000[2]
Total assets	**698 000**	**229 000**			**815 000**

Comments: Consolidation worksheet

[1] This amount represents the non-controlling interest's total share of S Ltd's equity (both ordinary and preference share equity) at acquisition date, which consists of:

- the non-controlling interest's 20% share of S Ltd's at acquisition ordinary equity, which comprises ordinary share capital and retained earnings, measured using the partial goodwill method, giving an amount of CU 28 000 [(100 000 ordinary share capital + 40 000 retained earnings) × 20%]

PLUS

- the non-controlling interest's 100% share of S Ltd's at acquisition preference share equity, measured using the partial goodwill method, giving an amount of CU 70 000.

[2] This amount is the goodwill attributable to P Ltd arising from P Ltd's acquisition of S Ltd's ordinary equity. As the at acquisition non-controlling interest in both the ordinary and preference equity of S Ltd is measured using the partial goodwill method, any goodwill that arises will not be attributable to the non-controlling interest (i.e., the only goodwill recognised on consolidation pertains to the parent's acquisition of the subsidiary's ordinary shares).

Example 8.3: Consolidation of partly owned subsidiary at acquisition: Preference shares classified as equity and with limited rights on liquidation of subsidiary

The facts are the same as for Example 8.2, except that now S Ltd's preference shareholders are only granted the right to receive a return of their preference share investment upon liquidation.

Additional information

The fair value of the preference shares on acquisition date was CU 82 000.

Required

(a) Prepare the at acquisition analyses of equity.

(b) Provide the at acquisition pro forma journal entries.

(c) Prepare the consolidation worksheet as at 31 December 20x5.

Solution 8.3: Consolidation of partly owned subsidiary at acquisition: Preference shares classified as equity and with limited rights on liquidation of subsidiary

Part (a): Analyses of equity of S Ltd at acquisition date

Analysis of S Ltd's ordinary equity – at acquisition

| | Total of S Ltd's ordinary equity 100% | P Ltd 80% | |
		At acquisition	Non-controlling interest 20%
At acquisition date (31 December 20x5)	CU	CU	CU
Share capital – Ordinary	100 000		
Retained earnings	40 000		
Fair value of net assets of S Ltd	140 000	112 000	28 000
Goodwill (balancing figure)	30 000	30 000	–
Consideration and NCI	170 000	142 000	28 000

Analysis of S Ltd's preference equity – at acquisition

| | Total of S Ltd's preference equity 100% | P Ltd 0% | |
		At acquisition	Non-controlling interest 100%
At acquisition date (31 December 20x5)	CU	CU	CU
Share capital – Preference	70 000	–	70 000
Goodwill (balancing figure)	12 000	–	12 000[1]
Consideration and NCI	82 000	–	82 000

Explanatory note: Analysis of S Ltd's at acquisition preference equity

[1] As the non-controlling interest is measured at its fair value of CU 82 000, the amount by which this fair value exceeds the non-controlling interest's proportionate share of S Ltd's preference equity at acquisition, of CU 70 000, represents goodwill attributable to the non-controlling interest of CU 12 000.

Part (b): Pro forma journal entries at acquisition date

Pro forma journal 1 (J1)	Dr CU	Cr CU
Ordinary share capital (S Ltd) (SCIE) (given)	100 000	
Retained earnings (S Ltd) (SCIE) (given)	40 000	
Investment: S Ltd ordinary shares (P Ltd) (SFP) (given)		142 000
NCI – Equity (SCIE)		Wkg1 28 000
Goodwill (SFP) (balancing figure)	30 000	
Elimination of at acquisition ordinary owners' equity of S Ltd and cost of investment, and recognition of the non-controlling interest and goodwill at acquisition of S Ltd's ordinary shares		

Workings: Pro forma journal

Working 1
(100 000 + 40 000) × 20% NCI Share

Pro forma journal 2 (J2)	Dr CU	Cr CU
Preference share capital (S Ltd) (SCIE) (given)	70 000	
Goodwill (SFP) (balancing figure)	12 000	
NCI – Equity (SCIE) (given: at fair value)		82 000
Elimination of at acquisition preference owners' equity of S Ltd by allocating it to the non-controlling interest, measured at acquisition date fair value and the recognition of related goodwill		

Comments: Pro forma journal 2

- As the preference shares have limited rights in this example (i.e., the preference shareholders are entitled only to a return of their initial investment on liquidation), the non-controlling interest's at acquisition share of the subsidiary's preference equity may only be measured at its fair value (i.e., the partial goodwill method may *not* be used). This results in goodwill being attributable to the non-controlling interest arising from its acquisition of S Ltd's preference shares, which is recognised by the CU 12 000 debit to goodwill.

Part (c): Consolidation worksheet for the P Ltd Group as at 31 December 20x5

	P Ltd Dr/(Cr) CU	S Ltd Dr/(Cr) CU	Pro forma journals Dr/(Cr) CU	Journal ref	Con-solidated Dr/(Cr) CU
Equity					
Ordinary share capital	(450 000)	(100 000)	100 000	J1	(450 000)
Preference share capital	–	(70 000)	70 000	J2	–
Retained earnings (EOY)	(160 000)	(40 000)	40 000	J1	(160 000)
NCI equity			(28 000)	J1	(110 000)[1]
			(82 000)	J2	
Total equity	(610 000)	(210 000)			(720 000)
Liabilities					
Trade and other payables	(88 000)	(19 000)			(107 000)
Total liabilities	(88 000)	(19 000)			(107 000)
Total equity & liabilities	(698 000)	(229 000)			(827 000)
Assets					
Plant	200 000	86 000			286 000
Trade and other receivables	356 000	143 000			499 000
Investment in S Ltd: Ordinary shares	142 000	–	(142 000)	J1	–
Goodwill	–	–	30 000	J1	42 000[2]
			12 000	J2	
Total assets	698 000	229 000			827 000

Comments: Consolidation worksheet

[1] This amount represents the non-controlling interest's total share of S Ltd's equity (both ordinary and preference share equity) at acquisition date, which consists of:

- the non-controlling interest's 20% share of S Ltd's at acquisition ordinary equity, which consists of ordinary share capital and retained earnings, measured using the partial goodwill method, giving an amount of CU 28 000 [(100 000 Ordinary share capital + 40 000 Retained earnings) × 20%]

  PLUS

- the non-controlling interest's 100% share of S Ltd's at acquisition preference share equity, measured at fair value (using the full goodwill method), giving an amount of CU 82 000.

[2] This amount is the sum of the following two goodwill figures:

- CU 30 000 attributable to P Ltd arising from P Ltd's acquisition of S Ltd's ordinary equity. As the non-controlling interest in S Ltd's ordinary equity at acquisition is measured using the partial goodwill method, no goodwill pertaining to the acquisition of S Ltd's ordinary shares is attributable to the non-controlling interest.

- CU 12 000 attributable to the non-controlling interest, arising from the acquisition of S Ltd's preference share capital by the non-controlling interest. The non-controlling interest's share of this at acquisition preference share equity of S Ltd is measured using the full goodwill method, that is, it is measured at its fair value. Because the parent P Ltd did not acquire any of S Ltd's preference shares, all the goodwill relating to the acquisition of these preference shares is attributable to the non-controlling interest in S Ltd's preference share equity.

Example 8.4: At acquisition consolidation of a partly owned subsidiary with preference shares owned by the parent and by the non-controlling interest

On 31 December 20x5 P Ltd acquired:

- 80% (a controlling interest) of the ordinary shares of S Ltd; and
- 30% of the preference shares of S Ltd.

Additional information

- S Ltd's net assets were considered to be fairly valued at acquisition date.
- P Ltd measures the non-controlling interest at its proportionate share of the identifiable net assets of S Ltd.
- P Ltd measures both its investment in S Ltd's ordinary shares and in S Ltd's preference shares at cost price.
- The preference shareholders have the following rights:
  - their dividend payment has priority over that of the ordinary shareholders; and
  - they will receive a proportionate share of the net assets of S Ltd should this entity be liquidated.

The abridged trial balances of P Ltd and its subsidiary S Ltd on 31 December 20x5 were as follows:

Abridged trial balances at 31 December 20x5	P Ltd Dr/(Cr) CU	S Ltd Dr/(Cr) CU
Ordinary share capital	(450 000)	(100 000)
Preference share capital	–	(70 000)
Retained earnings (31 Dec 20x5)	(160 000)	(40 000)
Trade and other payables	(88 000)	(19 000)
Plant	200 000	86 000
Trade and other receivables	320 000	143 000
Investment in S Ltd: Ordinary shares	142 000	–
Investment in S Ltd: Preference shares	36 000	–

Required

(a) Prepare the at acquisition analyses of equity.

(b) Provide the at acquisition pro forma journal entries.

(c) Prepare the consolidation worksheet as at 31 December 20x5.

Solution 8.4: At acquisition consolidation of a partly owned subsidiary with preference shares owned by the parent and by the non-controlling interest

Part (a): Analyses of equity of S Ltd at acquisition date

Analysis of S Ltd's ordinary equity – at acquisition

	Total of S Ltd's ordinary equity 100%	P Ltd 80% At acquisition	Non-controlling interest 20%
At acquisition date (31 December 20x5)	CU	CU	CU
Share capital – Ordinary	100 000		
Retained earnings	40 000		
Fair value of net assets of S Ltd	140 000	112 000	28 000
Goodwill (balancing figure)	30 000	30 000	–
Consideration and NCI	170 000	142 000	28 000

Analysis of S Ltd's preference equity – at acquisition

	Total of S Ltd's preference equity 100%	P Ltd 30% At acquisition	Non-controlling interest 70%
At acquisition date (31 December 20x5)	CU	CU	CU
Share capital – Preference	70 000	21 000	49 000
Goodwill (balancing figure)	15 000	15 000	–
Consideration and NCI	85 000	36 000	49 000

Part (b): Pro forma journal entries at acquisition date

	Dr	Cr
Pro forma journal 1 (J1)	CU	CU
Ordinary share capital (S Ltd) (SCIE) (given)	100 000	
Retained earnings (S Ltd) (SCIE) (given)	40 000	
Investment: S Ltd ordinary shares (P Ltd) (SFP) (given)		142 000
NCI – Equity (SCIE)		^{Wkg1}28 000
Goodwill (SFP) (balancing figure)	30 000	
Elimination of at acquisition ordinary owners' equity of S Ltd and cost of investment, and recognition of the non-controlling interest and goodwill at acquisition of S Ltd's ordinary shares		

Workings: Pro forma journals
Working 1
(100 000 + 40 000) × 20% NCI Share

Pro forma journal 2 (J2)	Dr CU	Cr CU
Preference share capital (S Ltd) (SCIE) (given)	70 000	
Investment: S Ltd preference shares (P Ltd) (SFP) (given)		36 000
NCI – Equity (SCIE)		^{Wkg2}49 000
Goodwill (SFP) (balancing figure)	15 000	
Elimination of at acquisition preference owners' equity of S Ltd and cost of investment and recognition of the non-controlling interest and goodwill at acquisition of S Ltd's preference shares		

Workings: Pro forma journals

Working 2
70 000 Preference share capital × 70% NCI Share

Comments: Pro forma journal 2

- The debit of CU 70 000 to S Ltd's *Preference share capital* eliminates S Ltd's remaining equity – with S Ltd's ordinary equity already having been eliminated in pro forma journal 1 above – which consists of preference shares. In this regard:

  - 30% of the CU 70 000 at acquisition preference share capital of S Ltd that was acquired by P Ltd, the amount of CU 21 000 (70 000 × 30%), is eliminated as a common item on consolidation against P Ltd's CU 36 000 investment in the preference share capital of S Ltd. This is achieved by debiting S Ltd's preference share capital with CU 21 000, with the corresponding credit of CU 36 000 being passed to investment in S Ltd preference shares.

  - The extent to which the CU 36 000 consideration paid by P Ltd for S Ltd's preference shares exceeds P Ltd's 30% share of S Ltd's preference share equity acquired of CU 21 000, is recognised as goodwill by debiting *Goodwill* with CU 15 000 (36 000 – 21 000).

  - 70% of the CU 70 000 at acquisition preference share capital of S Ltd that was acquired by the non-controlling interest, the amount of CU 49 000 (70 000 × 70%), is eliminated on consolidation by allocating it to the non-controlling interest; hence the credit of CU 49 000 to *NCI – Equity* with the corresponding CU 49 000 debit to S Ltd's preference share capital.

  - The CU 21 000 debit required to S Ltd's preference share capital, discussed above, together with the CU 49 000 debit required to S Ltd's preference share capital, discussed above, are processed in this pro forma journal by means of the single CU 70 000 debit to S Ltd's preference share capital.

Part (c): Consolidation worksheet of P Ltd group as at 31 December 20x5

	P Ltd Dr/(Cr) CU	S Ltd Dr/(Cr) CU	Pro forma journals Dr/(Cr) CU	Journal ref	Con- solidated Dr/(Cr) CU
Equity					
Ordinary share capital	(450 000)	(100 000)	100 000	J1	(450 000)
Preference share capital	–	(70 000)	70 000	J2	–
Retained earnings (EOY)	(160 000)	(40 000)	40 000	J1	(160 000)
NCI Equity			(28 000)	J1	(77 000)[1]
			(49 000)	J2	
Total equity	(610 000)	(210 000)			(687 000)
Liabilities					
Trade and other payables	(88 000)	(19 000)			(107 000)
Total liabilities	(88 000)	(19 000)			(107 000)
Total equity & liabilities	(698 000)	(229 000)			(794 000)
Assets					
Plant	200 000	86 000			286 000
Trade and other receivables	320 000	143 000			463 000
Investment in S Ltd: Ordinary shares	142 000	–	(142 000)	J1	–
Investment in S Ltd: Preference shares	36 000	–	(36 000)	J2	–
Goodwill	–	–	30 000	J1	45 000[2]
			15 000	J2	
Total assets	698 000	229 000			794 000

Comments: Consolidation worksheet

[1] This amount represents the non-controlling interest's total share of S Ltd's equity at acquisition date (both ordinary and preference share equity), which consists of:

- the non-controlling interest's 20% share of S Ltd's at acquisition ordinary equity, which comprises ordinary share capital and retained earnings, measured using the partial goodwill method, giving an amount of CU 28 000 [(100 000 Ordinary share capital + 40 000 Retained earnings) × 20%]

  PLUS

- the non-controlling interest's 70% share of S Ltd's at acquisition preference share equity, measured using the partial goodwill method, giving an amount of CU 49 000 (70 000 × 70%).

[2] This amount is the sum of the following two goodwill figures:

- CU 30 000 attributable to P Ltd arising from P Ltd's acquisition of S Ltd's ordinary equity. As the non-controlling interest in S Ltd's ordinary equity at acquisition is measured using the partial goodwill method, no goodwill pertaining to the acquisition of S Ltd's ordinary shares is attributable to the non-controlling interest.

- CU 15 000 that arises from P Ltd's acquisition of S Ltd's preference equity (preference share capital). No goodwill arises in respect of the portion of S Ltd's preference equity acquired by the non-controlling interest because the non-controlling interest's share of the preference equity acquired is measured using the partial goodwill method.

8.2 Allocation and attribution of subsidiary profit and post-acquisition reserves: Subsidiary with preference shares

8.2.1 Overview

Preference shares issued by a subsidiary have a favoured entitlement to the profit of the subsidiary for the relevant reporting period. More precisely, this entitlement is limited to the fixed preference dividend each year (for a detailed discussion of the nature of the preference dividend entitlement as regards cumulative and non-cumulative preference shares, see Sections 8.2.2.1 and 8.2.2.2).

The profit of a subsidiary that is attributable to the subsidiary's ordinary shareholders (i.e., the parent and, in the case of a partly owned subsidiary, the non-controlling interest) for the current reporting period must accordingly be determined **after taking into account** the profit that belongs to the **preference shareholders**, that is, the **preference dividend**.

Where the preference shares are classified as equity, the related preference dividends represent an equity distribution and will be included in the subsidiary's statement of changes in equity as a deduction from retained earnings. This implies that the preference dividend will *not* have been deducted from the subsidiary's current year profit. Consequently, we must **first deduct the preference dividend** in calculating how much of the subsidiary's current year profit must be allocated to the **subsidiary's ordinary shareholders**.

Where the preference shares are classified as a liability of the issuing entity (the subsidiary), then – as discussed in Section 8.1.1 – the related preference dividend will be included in the subsidiary's statement of profit or loss and other comprehensive income as a finance charge. This means that the preference dividends **will already have been deducted** from the subsidiary's current year profit. It then follows that **no further adjustments** are required before attributing the subsidiary's current year profit between the parent and the non-controlling interest ordinary shareholders of the subsidiary.

8.2.2 Steps to follow: Allocation and attribution of post-acquisition profits – subsidiary preference shares classified as equity

In allocating the profit of a subsidiary for the reporting period to its ordinary and preference shareholders and in determining the profit attributable to the parent and to the non-controlling interest on consolidation, the following steps should be applied:

Step 1: Deduct the **preference dividend** (also referred to as 'the preference profit') from the **current year profit of the subsidiary** to get the subsidiary's current year profit **attributable to its ordinary shareholders** (hereafter referred to as 'the ordinary profit' of the subsidiary). **Allocate** the **subsidiary's ordinary profit** between the **parent ordinary shareholders** and the **non-controlling investors** who are **ordinary shareholders** of the subsidiary. This allocation of the subsidiary's ordinary profit is made by passing a pro forma journal in which we:

- debit the *Non-controlling interest: Share of profit* account; and
- credit the *Non-controlling interest: Equity* account

with the **share of the subsidiary's ordinary profit** that is **attributable to the non-controlling ordinary shareholders**.

The amount of the **subsidiary's ordinary profit** that **remains** after passing this pro forma journal is then the **amount attributed to the parent** and, by extension, to the owners of the parent.

Step 2: Allocate the **preference dividend/profit**, deducted in Step 1, to the **parent** and to the **non-controlling preference shareholders** of the subsidiary in proportion to their **respective ownership interests in the preference shares** of the subsidiary. This allocation of the subsidiary's preference dividend/profit is made by passing a pro forma journal in which we:

- debit the *Non-controlling interest: Share of profit* account; and
- credit the *Non-controlling interest: Equity* account

 with the appropriate portion of the **subsidiary's preference dividend/profit attributable** to the **non-controlling preference shareholders.**

The amount of the **subsidiary's preference dividend/profit remaining** after passing this pro forma journal is then the **amount attributed to the parent** and, by extension, to the owners of the parent.

Step 3: Account for the effects, on consolidation, of the **declaration and/or payment** of the **preference dividend** by the **subsidiary to the parent** and **to the non-controlling shareholders.** To this end, a pro forma journal is required in which we:

- Debit the *Preference dividend income* recognised by the parent in its separate financial statements. As with ordinary dividends, this represents an intragroup transaction that must be eliminated on consolidation.

- Debit the *Non-controlling interest: Equity* account with the amount of the preference dividend declared/paid to the non-controlling preference shareholders. As with ordinary dividends, this treatment reflects a reduction in the non-controlling interest's share of the subsidiary's equity because the subsidiary's equity is reduced by declaring/paying the preference dividend to the non-controlling interest.

- Credit *Preference dividend declared/paid* by the subsidiary, thereby eliminating in full the total preference dividend declared/paid by the subsidiary. This is the same treatment which applies on consolidation when an ordinary dividend is declared/paid to the parent and to the non-controlling interest.

In addition, if there are any **unpaid preference dividends outstanding** at the reporting period end, the **unpaid portion relating to the non-controlling interest** does *not* constitute an intragroup balance that must be eliminated. Instead it represents an **external obligation** of the group to be **disclosed as a liability** on the **consolidated statement of financial position at reporting period end.** Stated differently, of the total preference dividend payable recorded by the subsidiary, only the **portion that is due to the parent** is **eliminated** against the **dividend receivable as recorded by the parent.** This leaves the **remaining dividend payable to the non-controlling interest** to be presented as a **liability** of the group at reporting period end. To this end, a pro forma journal is required in which we.

- Debit the *Preference dividend receivable* asset recognised by the parent in its separate financial statements. As with ordinary dividends receivable, this represents an **intragroup balance** that must be **eliminated on consolidation.**

• Credit the *Preference dividend payable* liability, recognised by the subsidiary in its individual financial statements, with the amount of the preference dividend owing to the **parent**. As with ordinary dividends payable, this represents an **intragroup balance** that must be **eliminated on consolidation**.

8.2.2.1 Non-cumulative preference shares

As explained above, preference shares may be **non**-cumulative, which means that the shareholders do *not* have any entitlement to the payment of arrear preference dividends. To explain further: If a preference dividend is not declared in any particular year, the preference shareholders have no right to claim payment of that preference dividend in a subsequent period. In other words, the preference shareholders are entitled to a preference dividend in any given year only once the preference dividend for that year has **been declared**.

The implication, on consolidation, is that a preference dividend in respect of non-cumulative preference shares is only deducted from the subsidiary's current year profit in determining the relevant amounts attributable to ordinary and preference shareholders – as discussed above – when the preference dividend for the period concerned **has been declared or paid**.

8.2.2.2 Cumulative preference shares

Preference shares may also be **cumulative**, in which case the holders are **entitled** to some **specified dividend every period**. The result is that if the company fails to declare a dividend in a specific reporting period, the preference shareholders have a right of preference to the arrear and current preference dividends before a dividend may be declared in respect of the ordinary (or any other class) of shares, upon the first subsequent dividend declaration.

IFR10 *Consolidated Financial Statements* stipulates that where a subsidiary has **cumulative preference shares** classified as **equity** that are held by **non-controlling interests**, the entity must determine its share of profit or loss **after adjusting** for the **preference dividend, whether or not** such dividend has been **declared** (IFRS 10. B95). More simply put, this means that the holders of cumulative preference shares in a subsidiary are entitled to a stipulated amount of subsidiary profits, equal to the specified preference dividend, every period **even** if a dividend has *not* been declared.

Consequently, in the case of cumulative preference shares on consolidation, the allocation of the subsidiary's profit every reporting period between the parent and the non-controlling ordinary shareholders must always be determined **after** deducting the **specified preference dividend** to which the preference shareholders are entitled for the reporting period concerned, **even if such profits have *not* yet been declared as a dividend**.

Example 8.5: Consolidation of partly owned subsidiary with non-cumulative preference shares: After acquisition date

On 1 January 20x4 P Ltd acquired 80% (a controlling interest) of the ordinary shares of S Ltd for CU 142 000 and 30% of S Ltd's preference shares for CU 49 000. The equity of S Ltd at acquisition date consisted of the following:
- ordinary share capital CU 100 000;
- preference share capital CU 125 000;
- retained earnings CU 40 000.

Additional information
- S Ltd issued 500 non-redeemable, non-cumulative preference shares on 1 January 20x4 at CU 250 per share with a dividend rate of 15%. No preference dividend was declared in respect of the 20x4 financial year.
- The preference shareholders have the following rights:
  - their dividend payment has priority over that of the ordinary shareholders; and
  - they will receive a proportionate share of the net assets of S Ltd should this entity be liquidated.
- P Ltd measured the non-controlling interest at its fair value and in this regard:
  - the fair value of the non-controlling interest in the ordinary shares on acquisition date was CU 35 000; and
  - the fair value of the non-controlling interest in the preference shares on acquisition date was CU 93 800.
- The net assets of S Ltd were considered to be fairly valued at acquisition date.
- P Ltd measured both its investment in S Ltd's ordinary shares and in S Ltd's preference shares at cost price.

The abridged trial balances of P Ltd and its subsidiary S Ltd on 31 December 20x5 were as follows:

Abridged trial balances at 31 December 20x5	P Ltd Dr/(Cr) CU	S Ltd Dr/(Cr) CU
Ordinary share capital	(450 000)	(100 000)
Preference share capital	–	(125 000)
Retained earnings (1 Jan 20x5)	(160 000)	(117 650)
Ordinary dividend paid	38 000	15 000
Preference dividend paid	–	18 750
Trade and other payables	(101 000)	(19 000)
Plant	352 000	299 900
Trade and other receivables	320 000	143 000
Investment in S Ltd: Ordinary shares at cost	142 000	–
Investment in S Ltd: Preference shares at cost	49 000	–
Profit for the year	(190 000)	(115 000)

Required

(a) Prepare the relevant analyses of equity as at 31 December 20x5.

(b) Provide the pro forma journals necessary to prepare consolidated financial statements for the P Ltd group for the financial year ended 31 December 20x5.

(c) Prepare the consolidated financial statements for the P Ltd group for the financial year ended 31 December 20x5.

Solution 8.5: Consolidation of partly owned subsidiary with non-cumulative preference shares: After acquisition date

Part (a): Analyses of equity of S Ltd as at 31 December 20x5

Calculation 1: Analysis of ordinary equity of S Ltd as at 31 December 20x5

| Acquisition date (1 January 20x4) | Total of S Ltd's ordinary equity 100% CU | S Ltd 80% | | Non-controlling interest 20% CU |
		At acquisition CU	Since acquisition CU	
Ordinary share capital	100 000			
Retained earnings	40 000			
Fair value of net assets of S Ltd	140 000	112 000		28 000
Goodwill (balancing figure)	37 000 **A**	30 000		7 000
Consideration and NCI	177 000	142 000		35 000
Since acquisition				
• To beginning of current year:				
Retained earnings movement (117 650 Balance BOY – 40 000 Balance at acquisition)	77 650[1]		62 120 **B**	15 530
				50 530 **C**
• Current year:				
Profit for the year attributable to ordinary shareholders (115 000 – 18 750 preference dividend)	96 250[2]		77 000 **D**	19 250 **E**
Ordinary dividend	(15 000)		(12 000) **F**	(3 000) **G**
	335 900		127 120	66 780 **H**

Explanatory notes: Analysis of ordinary equity of S Ltd

[1] In determining the **prior year** profit attributable to the ordinary shareholders of S Ltd, the specified dividend of CU 18 750 is *not* deducted as it was *not* declared in the prior year and the preference shares are *non-cumulative*.

[2] The preference dividend of the **current year** is deducted in determining S Ltd's current year profit attributable to its ordinary shareholders. This is because the preference shares are *non-cumulative* and the preference dividend was *declared* (and paid) for the current year.

Calculation 2: Analysis of preference equity of S Ltd as at 31 December 20x5

Acquisition date (1 January 20x4)	Total of S Ltd's preference equity 100% CU	P Ltd 30% At acquisition CU	P Ltd 30% Since acquisition CU	Non-controlling interest 70% CU
Preference share capital	125 000	37 500		87 500
Goodwill (balancing figure)	17 800 a	11 500		6 300
Consideration and NCI	142 800	49 000		93 800 b
Since acquisition				
• Current year:				
Profit attributable to preference shareholders	18 750		5 625 c	13 125 d
Preference dividend (given)	(18 750)		(5 625) e	(13 125) f
	142 800		**–**	**93 800 g**

Part (b): Pro forma journal entries for the 20x5 financial year

AT ACQUISITION

Pro forma journal 1 (J1)	Dr CU	Cr CU	NCI balance
Ordinary share capital (S Ltd) (SCIE) (given)	100 000		
Retained earnings (S Ltd) (SCIE) (given)	40 000		
Investment: S Ltd ordinary shares (P Ltd) (SFP) (given)		142 000	
NCI – Equity (SCIE) (given – at fair value)		35 000	35 000
Goodwill (SFP) (balancing figure)	37 000		

Elimination of at acquisition ordinary owners' equity of S Ltd and cost of investment, and recognition of the non-controlling interest and goodwill at acquisition of S Ltd's ordinary shares

Pro forma journal 2 (J2)	Dr CU	Cr CU	NCI balance
Preference share capital (S Ltd) (SCIE) (given)	125 000		
Investment: S Ltd preference shares (P Ltd) (SFP) (given)		49 000	
NCI – Equity (SCIE) (given – at fair value)		93 800	93 800
Goodwill (SFP) (balancing figure)	17 800		

Elimination of at acquisition preference owners' equity of S Ltd and cost of investment, and recognition of the non-controlling interest and goodwill at acquisition of S Ltd's preference shares

SINCE ACQUISITION TO BEGINNING OF THE YEAR

Pro forma journal 3 (J3)	Dr CU	Cr CU		NCI balance
Retained earnings (S Ltd) (SCIE)	Wkg1 15 530			
NCI – Equity (SFP)		Wkg1 15 530		15 530
Allocating the non-controlling interest in S Ltd's ordinary equity its share of S Ltd's post-acquisition retained earnings to the beginning of the year				**Balance 144 330 BOY (Calc 3)**

Workings: Pro forma journals

Working 1
(117 650 Balance BOY – 40 000 Balance at acquisition) × 20% NCI Share

CURRENT YEAR

Pro forma journal 4 (J4)	Dr CU	Cr CU		
NCI: Share of profit or loss (P/L)	Wkg2 19 250			
NCI – Equity (SFP)		Wkg2 19 250		19 250
Allocating the non-controlling interest in S Ltd's ordinary equity its share of S Ltd's current year profit after deducting the preference dividend				

Workings: Pro forma journals

Working 2
(115 000 Current year profit – 18 750 Preference dividend) × 20% NCI Share

Pro forma journal 5 (J5)	Dr CU	Cr CU		
NCI: Share of profit or loss (P/L)	Wkg3 13 125			
NCI – Equity (SFP)		Wkg3 13 125		13 125
Allocating the non-controlling interest in S Ltd's preference share equity its share of S Ltd's current year preference dividend				

Workings: Pro forma journals

Working 3
18 750 Preference dividend × 70% NCI Share

Pro forma journal 6 (J6)	Dr CU	Cr CU		
Ordinary dividend received (P Ltd) (P/L)	Wkg4 12 000			
NCI – Equity (SFP) (balancing figure)	3 000			
Ordinary dividend paid (S Ltd) (SCIE) (given)		15 000		(3 000)
Elimination of intragroup ordinary dividend from S Ltd and recognition of non-controlling interest in the dividend				

Workings: Pro forma journals

Working 4
15 000 × 80% P Ltd Share

Pro forma journal 7 (J7)	Dr CU	Cr CU		NCI balance:
Preference dividend received (P Ltd) (P/L)	Wkg5 5 625			
NCI – Equity (SFP) (balancing figure)	13 125			(13 125)
Preference dividend paid (S Ltd) (SCIE) (given)		18 750		
Elimination of intra-group preference dividend from S Ltd and recognition of non-controlling interest in the dividend				

Workings: Pro forma journals

Working 5
18 750 × 30% P Ltd Share

Balance 160 580 EOY (Calc 4)	

⟶

The full effects of the preceding pro forma journals on the consolidated financial statements of the P Ltd group for the financial year ended 31 December 20x5 are illustrated in the following consolidation worksheet.

	P Ltd Dr/(Cr) CU	S Ltd Dr/(Cr) CU	Pro forma journals At acquisition Dr/(Cr) CU	Journal ref	Pro forma journals Since acquisition Dr/(Cr) CU	Journal ref	Con-solidated Dr/(Cr) CU
Equity							
Ordinary share capital	(450 000)	(100 000)	100 000	J1			(450 000)
Preference share capital	–	(125 000)	125 000	J2			–
Retained earnings (BOY)	(160 000)	(117 650)	40 000	J1	15 530	J3	(222 120)
Profit: Individual entities	(190 000)	(115 000)					–
Consolidated profit attributable to owners of parent	–	–					†(255 000)
Ordinary dividends	38 000	15 000			(15 000)	J6	38 000
Preference dividends	–	18 750			(18 750)	J7	–
Retained earnings (EOY)	(312 000)	(198 900)					(439 120)
NCI Equity	–	–	(35 000)	J1	(15 530)	J3	(160 580)
			(93 800)	J2	(19 250)	J4	
					(13 125)	J5	
					3 000	J6	
					13 125	J7	
Total equity	**(762 000)**	**(423 900)**					**(1 049 700)**

Explanatory notes

† This amount has been brought forward from the second part of the consolidation worksheet on page 549.

	P Ltd Dr/(Cr) CU	S Ltd Dr/(Cr) CU	Pro forma journals At acquisition Dr/(Cr) CU	Journal ref	Pro forma journals Since acquisition Dr/(Cr) CU	Journal ref	Consolidated Dr/(Cr) CU
Liabilities							
Trade and other payables	(101 000)	(19 000)					(120 000)
Total liabilities	(101 000)	(19 000)					(120 000)
Total equity & liabilities	**(863 000)**	**(442 900)**					**(1 169 700)**
Assets:							
Plant	352 000	299 900					651 900
Trade and other receivables	320 000	143 000					463 000
Investment in S Ltd: Ordinary shares	142 000	–	(142 000)	J1			–
Investment in S Ltd: Preference shares	49 000	–	(49 000)	J2			–
Goodwill			37 000 17 800	J1 J2			54 800
Total assets	**863 000**	**442 900**					**1 169 700**
Profit or loss							
Profit for the year	(190 000)	(115 000)			12 000 5 625	J6 J7	(287 375)
NCI: Share of profit					19 250 13 125	J4 J5	32 375
Consolidated profit attributable to owners of parent							‡(255 000)

Explanatory notes

‡ This amount has been carried forward to the first part of the consolidation worksheet on page 548

549

Part (c): Consolidated financial statements for the 20x5 financial yaer

P LTD GROUP: ABRIDGED CONSOLIDATED STATEMENT OF PROFIT OR LOSS AND OTHER COMPREHENSIVE INCOME FOR THE YEAR ENDED 31 DECEMBER 20x5	
	CU
PROFIT FOR THE YEAR (P Ltd: 190 000 – 12 000 (see Calc 1 **F OR** (J6)) Ordinary dividend from S Ltd – 5 625 (see Calc 2 **e OR** (J7)) Preference dividend from S Ltd) + 115 000 (S Ltd))	287 375
Other comprehensive income	–
TOTAL COMPREHENSIVE INCOME	**287 375**
Total comprehensive income attributable to:	
Owners of the parent	Wkg1255 000
Non-controlling interest (Ordinary NCI[1]: 19 250 (see Calc 1 **E OR** (J4)) + Preference NCI[2]: 13 125 (see Calc 2 **d OR** (J5))	32 375
	287 375

Workings: Abridged consolidated statement of profit or loss and other comprehensive income

Working 1
(P Ltd: 190 000 – 12 000 (J6) Ordinary dividend – 5 625 (J7) Preference dividend) + (S Ltd: 77 000 (see Calc 1 **D**) + 5 625 (see Calc 2 **c**)) **OR** Balancing figure

Explanatory notes

[1] Ordinary NCI refers to the non-controlling interest that acquired a portion of S Ltd's ordinary share capital.
[2] Preference NCI refers to the non-controlling interest that acquired a portion of S Ltd's preference share capital.

P LTD GROUP: CONSOLIDATED STATEMENT OF CHANGES IN EQUITY FOR THE YEAR ENDED 31 DECEMBER 20x5					
	Parent equity holders' interest			Non-controlling interest	Total equity of the group
	Ordinary share capital	Retained earnings	Total parent equity		
	CU	CU	CU	CU	CU
Opening balance at 1 Jan 20x5	450 000	Wkg1222 120	672 120	Wkg2144 330	816 450
Total comprehensive income:					
Profit for the period (from CSOPL_OCI)		255 000	255 000	32 375	287 375
Dividends		(38 000)	(38 000)	Wkg3(16 125)	(54 125)
Closing balance at 31 Dec 20x5	450 000	439 120	889 120	160 580	1 049 700

Workings: Consolidated statement of changes in equity

Working 1
P Ltd: 160 000 + S Ltd: 62 120 (see Calc 1 **B**) P Ltd Share of post-acquisition retained earnings of S Ltd to BOY

OR
P Ltd: 160 000 + (S Ltd: 117 650 Balance BOY – 40 000 (J1) Balance at acquisition – 15 530 (J3) Ordinary NCI of S Ltd: Share of post-acquisition retained earnings of S Ltd to BOY)

Workings: Consolidated statement of changes in equity

Working 2

Ordinary NCI of S Ltd: 50 530 (see Calc 1 **C**) + Preference NCI of S Ltd: 93 800 (see Calc 2 **b**)

OR

NCI of S Ltd (both ordinary and preference): 144 330 (see pro forma journal entries: Calc 3)

Working 3

NCI share of S Ltd ordinary dividend: 3 000 (see (J6) **OR** Calc 1 **G**) + NCI share of S Ltd preference dividend: 13 125 (see (J7) **OR** Calc 2 **f**)

P LTD GROUP: CONSOLIDATED STATEMENT OF FINANCIAL POSITION AS AT 31 DECEMBER 20x5	
	CU
Assets	
Non-current assets	
Property, plant and equipment (352 000 (P Ltd) + 299 900 (S Ltd))	651 900
Goodwill (37 000 (see Calc 1 **A OR** (J1)) Acquisition of ordinary shares + 17 800 (see Calc 2 **a OR** (J2)) Acquisition of preference shares)	54 800
Current assets	
Trade and other receivables (320 000 (P Ltd) + 143 000 (S Ltd))	463 000
Total assets	1 169 700
Equity and liabilities	
Share capital (from CSCIE)	450 000
Retained earnings (from CSCIE)	439 120
Equity attributable to owners of the parent	889 120
Non-controlling interest (from CSCIE) **OR** (see pro forma journal entries: Calc 4) **OR** (66 780 (see Calc 1 **H**) + 93 800 (see Calc 2 **g**))	160 580
Total equity	1 049 700
Current liabilities	
Trade and other payables (101 000 (P Ltd) + 19 000 (S Ltd))	120 000
Total equity and liabilities	1 169 700

 ## Example 8.6: Consolidation of a partly owned subsidiary with cumulative preference shares: After acquisition date

On 1 January 20x4 P Ltd acquired 80% (a controlling interest) of the ordinary shares of S Ltd for CU 142 000. The equity of S Ltd at acquisition date consisted of the following:

- ordinary share capital CU 100 000; and
- retained earnings CU 40 000.

On 1 January 20x5 S Ltd issued non-redeemable, cumulative preference shares at CU 50 per share. The preference shares entitle the holder to an annual dividend of 15% (on 31 December). P Ltd acquired 30% of the preference shares on 1 January 20x5 for CU 49 000.

Additional information

- No preference dividend was declared for the reporting period ended 31 December 20x5. The arrear preference dividend for the 20x5 financial year and the current preference dividend for the financial year ended 31 December 20x6 was paid on 31 December 20x6.

- The preference shareholders have the following rights:
  - their dividend payment has priority over that of the ordinary shareholders; and
  - they will receive a proportionate share of the net assets of S Ltd should this entity be liquidated.
- P Ltd measured the non-controlling interest at its proportionate share of S Ltd's identifiable net assets.
- The net assets of S Ltd were considered to be fairly valued at acquisition date.
- P Ltd measured both its investment in S Ltd's ordinary shares and in S Ltd's preference shares at cost price.

The abridged trial balances of P Ltd and its subsidiary S Ltd on 31 December 20x6 were as follows:

Abridged trial balances at 31 December 20x6	P Ltd Dr/(Cr) CU	S Ltd Dr/(Cr) CU
Ordinary share capital	(450 000)	(100 000)
Preference share capital	–	(125 000)
Retained earnings (1 Jan 20x6)	(160 000)	(117 650)
Preference dividend paid	–	37 500
Trade and other payables	(101 000)	(19 000)
Plant	390 000	296 150
Trade and other receivables	320 000	143 000
Investment in S Ltd: Ordinary shares at cost	142 000	–
Investment in S Ltd: Preference shares at cost	49 000	–
Profit for the year	(190 000)	(115 000)

Required

(a) Prepare the relevant analyses of equity as at 31 December 20x6.

(b) Provide the pro forma journals necessary to prepare consolidated financial statements for the P Ltd group for the financial year ended 31 December 20x6.

(c) Prepare the consolidated financial statements for the P Ltd group for the financial year ended 31 December 20x6.

Solution 8.6: Consolidation of a partly owned subsidiary with cumulative preference shares: After acquisition date

Part (a): Analyses of equity of S Ltd as at 31 December 20x6

Calculation 1: Analysis of ordinary equity of S Ltd as at 31 December 20x6

Acquisition date (1 January 20x4)	Total of S Ltd's ordinary equity 100% CU	S Ltd 80% At acquisition CU	S Ltd 80% Since acquisition CU	Non-controlling interest 20% CU
Ordinary share capital	100 000			
Retained earnings	40 000			
Fair value of net assets of S Ltd	140 000	112 000		28 000
Goodwill (balancing figure)	30 000 **A**	30 000		–
Consideration and NCI	170 000	142 000		28 000
Since acquisition				
• To beginning of current year:				
Retained earnings attributable to ordinary shareholders	58 900		47 120 **B**	11 780
Retained earnings movement (117 650 Balance BOY – 40 000 Balance at acquisition)	77 650		62 120	15 530
Arrear preference dividend for 20x5 (125 000 × 15%)	(18 750)[1]		(15 000)	(3 750)
				39 780 **C**
• Current year:				
Profit for the year attributable to ordinary shareholders (115 000 – 18 750 (125 000 × 15%) Preference dividend)	96 250		77 000 **D**	19 250 **E**
	325 150		124 120	59 030 **F**

Explanatory notes: Analysis of ordinary equity of S Ltd

[1] As the preference dividends are cumulative, the preference shareholders are entitled to receive the specified dividend of CU 18 750 each year even if no dividend has been declared, as is the case in the 20x5 financial year.

Consequently, we deduct the arrear 20x5 preference dividend from the retained earnings of S Ltd as it relates to preference profit of the prior year that must be allocated to S Ltd's preference shareholders, and such profits are included in S Ltd's opening balance of retained earnings in the current year.

Calculation 2: Analysis of preference equity of S Ltd as at 31 December 20x6

| Acquisition date (1 January 20x5) | Total of S Ltd's preference equity 100% CU | P Ltd 30% | | Non-controlling interest 70% CU |
		At acquisition CU	Since acquisition CU	
Preference share capital	125 000	37 500		87 500
Goodwill (balancing figure)	11 500 a	11 500		–
Consideration and NCI	136 500	49 000		87 500
Since acquisition				
• To beginning of current year:				
Arrear preference dividend 20x5 (125 000 × 15%)	18 750		5 625[1] b	13 125[1]
				100 625 c
• Current year:				
Profit attributable to preference shareholders (125 000 × 15%)	18 750		5 625[2] d	13 125[2] e
Preference dividend paid (given)	(37 500)[3]		(11 250) f	(26 250) g
	136 500		–	87 500 h

Explanatory notes: Analysis of preference equity of S Ltd

[1] These amounts are the allocation of S Ltd's prior year preference profits (equal to the specified preference dividend of CU 18 750 that was not declared in the prior year) to the parent and to the non-controlling interest preference shareholders according to their respective ownership interests in the preference shares.

[2] These amounts are the allocation of S Ltd's current year preference profit (equal to the specified preference dividend of CU 18 750) to the parent and to the non-controlling interest preference shareholders, according to their respective ownership interests in the preference shares.

[3] This amount represents the payment by S Ltd in the current year of two years' worth of preference dividends, namely:
- the 20x5 arrear preference dividend of CU 18 750; and
- the current year (20x6) preference dividend of CU 18 750.

Of this total preference dividend paid:
- CU 11 250 is eliminated against the dividend income recognised by P Ltd; and
- CU 26 250 is eliminated against the non-controlling interest's equity balance.

Part (b): Pro forma journal entries for the 20x6 financial year

AT ACQUISITION

Pro forma journal 1 (J1)	Dr CU	Cr CU	NCI Balance
Ordinary share capital (S Ltd) (SCIE) (given)	100 000		
Retained earnings (S Ltd) (SCIE) (given)	40 000		
Investment: S Ltd ordinary shares (P Ltd) (SFP) (given)		142 000	
NCI – Equity (SCIE)		Wkg1 28 000	28 000
Goodwill (SFP) (balancing figure)	30 000		
Elimination of at acquisition ordinary owners equity of S Ltd and cost of ordinary share investment in S Ltd and recognition of the non-controlling interest and goodwill upon acquisition of S Ltd's ordinary shares			

Workings: Pro forma journals

Working 1
(100 000 + 40 000) × 20% NCI Share

Pro forma journal 2 (J2)	Dr CU	Cr CU	
Preference share capital (S Ltd) (SCIE) (given)	125 000		
Investment: S Ltd preference shares (P Ltd) (SFP) (given)		49 000	
NCI – Equity (SCIE)		Wkg2 87 500	87 500
Goodwill (SFP) (balancing figure)	11 500		
Elimination of at acquisition preference owners equity of S Ltd and cost of preference share investment in S Ltd, and recognition of non-controlling interest and goodwill upon acquisition of S Ltd's preference shares			

Workings: Pro forma journals

Working 2
125 000 × 70% NCI Share

SINCE ACQUISITION TO BEGINNING OF THE YEAR

Pro forma journal 3 (J3)	Dr CU	Cr CU	
Retained earnings (S Ltd) (SCIE)	Wkg3 11 780		
NCI – Equity (SFP)		Wkg3 11 780	11 780
Allocating the non-controlling interest in S Ltd's ordinary shares its share of S Ltd's post-acquisition retained earnings to the beginning of the year			

Working 3
(117 650 Balance BOY – 40 000 Balance at acquisition – 18 750 Arrear preference dividend) × 20% NCI Share

Pro forma journal 4 (J4)	Dr CU	Cr CU	NCI Balance
Retained earnings (S Ltd) (SCIE)	Wkg4 13 125		
NCI – Equity (SFP)		Wkg4 13 125	13 125
Allocating the non-controlling interest in S Ltd's preference share capital its share of S Ltd's post-acquisition retained earnings to the beginning of the year			**Balance 140 405 BOY (Calc 3)**

Working 4
125 000 (given) Preference share capital × 15% Dividend rate × 70%
= 13 125 20x5 Arrear preference dividend attributable to the NCI of S Ltd

CURRENT YEAR

Pro forma journal 5 (J5)	Dr CU	Cr CU	
NCI share of profit or loss (P/L)	Wkg5 19 250		
NCI – Equity (SFP)		Wkg5 19 250	19 250
Allocating the non-controlling interest in S Ltd's ordinary equity its share of S Ltd's current year profit after deducting the current year preference dividend			

Working 5
(115 000 (given) S Ltd current year profit – 18 750 (125 000 × 15%) Current year preference dividend) × 20% NCI Share

Pro forma journal 6 (J6)	Dr CU	Cr CU	
NCI share of profit or loss (P/L)	Wkg6 13 125		
NCI – Equity (SFP)		Wkg6 13 125	13 125
Allocating the non-controlling interest in S Ltd's preference share capital its share of S Ltd's current year preference dividend			

Workings: Pro forma journals

Working 6
18 750 (Working 5) Current year preference dividend × 70% NCI Share

Pro forma journal 7 (J7)	Dr CU	Cr CU	
Preference dividend received (P Ltd) (P/L)	Wkg7 11 250		
NCI – Equity (SFP) (balancing figure)	26 250		(26 250)
Preference dividend paid (S Ltd) (SCIE) (given)		37 500	
Elimination of intragroup preference dividend received from S Ltd, and recognition of non-controlling interest in the dividend			

Workings: Pro forma journals

Working 7
37 500 (given) Preference dividend paid × 30% P Ltd share

Balance 146 530 EOY (Calc 4)

The full effects of the preceding pro forma journals on the consolidated financial statements of the P Ltd group for the financial year ended 31 December 20x6 are illustrated in the following consolidation worksheet.

	P Ltd Dr/(Cr) CU	S Ltd Dr/(Cr) CU	Pro forma journals At acquisition Dr/(Cr) CU	Journal ref	Pro forma journals Since acquisition Dr/(Cr) CU	Journal ref	Con-solidated Dr/(Cr) CU
Equity							
Ordinary Share capital	(450 000)	(100 000)	100 000	J1			(450 000)
Preference Share capital	–	(125 000)	125 000	J2			–
Retained earnings (BOY)	(160 000)	(117 650)	40 000	J1	11 780	J3	(212 745)
					13 125	J4	
Profit: Individual entities	(190 000)	(115 000)					
Consolidated profit attributable to owners of parent							†(261 375)
Preference dividend		37 500			(37 500)	J7	–
Retained earnings (EOY)	(350 000)	(195 150)					(474 120)
NCI Equity			(28 000)	J1	(11 780)	J3	(146 530)
			(87 500)	J2	(13 125)	J4	
					(19 250)	J5	
					(13 125)	J6	
					26 250	J7	
Total equity	**(800 000)**	**(420 150)**					**(1 070 650)**

Explanatory notes

† This amount has been brought forward from the second part of the consolidation worksheet on page 558

	P Ltd Dr/(Cr) CU	S Ltd Dr/(Cr) CU	Pro forma journals At acquisition Dr/(Cr) CU	Journal ref	Pro forma journals Since acquisition Dr/(Cr) CU	Journal ref	Con- solidated Dr/(Cr) CU
Liabilities:							
Trade and other payables	(101 000)	(19 000)					(120 000)
Total liabilities	**(101 000)**	**(19 000)**					**(120 000)**
Total equity & liabilities	**(901 000)**	**(439 150)**					**(1 190 650)**
Assets:							
Plant	390 000	296 150					686 150
Trade and other receivables	320 000	143 000					463 000
Investment in S Ltd: Ordinary shares	142 000	–	(142 000)	J1			–
Investment in S Ltd: Preference shares	49 000	–	(49 000)	J2			–
Goodwill			30 000	J1			41 500
			11 500	J2			
Total Assets	**901 000**	**439 150**					**1 190 650**
Profit or loss							
Profit for the year	(190 000)	(115 000)			11 250	J7	(293 750)
NCI: share of profit					19 250	J5	32 375
					13 125	J6	
Consolidated profit attributable to owners of parent							‡(261 375)

Explanatory notes

‡ This amount has been carried forward to the first part of the consolidation worksheet on page 557

Part (c): Consolidated financial statements for the 20x6 financial year

P LTD GROUP: ABRIDGED CONSOLIDATED STATEMENT OF PROFIT OR LOSS AND OTHER COMPREHENSIVE INCOME FOR THE YEAR ENDED 31 DECEMBER 20x6	
	CU
PROFIT FOR THE YEAR (P Ltd: 190 000 – 11 250 (see Calc 2 **f OR** (J7)) Preference dividend + 115 000 (S Ltd)	293 750
Other comprehensive income	–
TOTAL COMPREHENSIVE INCOME	**293 750**
Attributable to:	
Owners of the parent	Wkg1261 375
Non-controlling interest (Ordinary NCI: 19 250 (Calc 1 **E OR** (J5)) + Preference NCI: 13 125 (see Calc 2 **e OR** (J6))	32 375
	293 750

Workings: Consolidated statement of profit or loss and other comprehensive income

Working 1
(P Ltd: 190 000 – 11 250 (see Calc 2f **OR** (J7)) Preference dividend) + (S Ltd: 77 000 (see Calc 1 **D**) + 5 625 (see Calc 2 **d**)) **OR** Balancing figure

P LTD GROUP: CONSOLIDATED STATEMENT OF CHANGES IN EQUITY FOR THE YEAR ENDED 31 DECEMBER 20x6					
	Parent equity holders' interest			Non-controlling interest	Total equity of the group
	Ordinary Share capital	Retained earnings	Total parent equity		
	CU	CU	CU	CU	CU
Opening balance at 1 Jan 20x6	450 000	Wkg1212 745	662 745	Wkg2140 405	803 150
Total comprehensive income:					
Profit for the period (from CSOPL_OCI)		261 375	261 375	32 375	293 750
Dividend				Wkg3(26 250)	(26 250)
Closing balance at 31 Dec 20x6	450 000	474 120	924 120	146 530	1 070 650

Workings: Consolidated statement of changes in equity

Working 1
P Ltd: 160 000 + (S Ltd: 47 120 (see Calc 1 **B**) P Ltd Share of S Ltd post-acquisition retained earnings to BOY + 5 625 (see Calc 2 **b**)) P Ltd Share of arrear preference dividend of S Ltd)

OR

P Ltd: 160 000 + (S Ltd: 117 650 Balance BOY – 40 000 (J1) Balance at acquisition – 11 780 (J3) Ordinary NCI of S Ltd: Share of post-acquisition retained earnings of S Ltd to BOY – 13 125 (J4) Peference NCI of S Ltd: Share of arrear preference dividend of S Ltd)

Working 2
Ordinary NCI of S Ltd: 39 780 (see Calc 1 **C**) + Preference NCI of S Ltd: 100 625 (see Calc 2 **c**)

OR

NCI of S Ltd (both ordinary and preference): 140 405 (see pro forma journal entries: Calc 3)

Working 3
NCI share of S Ltd preference dividend: 26 250 (see (J7) **OR** Calc 2 **g**)

P LTD GROUP: CONSOLIDATED STATEMENT OF FINANCIAL POSITION AS AT 31 DECEMBER 20x6	
	CU
Assets	
Non-current assets	
Property, plant and equipment (390 000 (P Ltd) + 296 150 (S Ltd))	686 150
Goodwill (30 000 (see Calc 1 **A OR** (J1)) Acquisition of ordinary shares + 11 500 (see Calc 2 **a OR** (J2)) Acquisition of preference shares)	41 500
Current assets	
Trade and other receivables (320 000 (P Ltd) + 143 000 (S Ltd))	463 000
Total assets	1 190 650
Equity and liabilities	
Share capital (from CSCIE)	450 000
Retained earnings (from CSCIE)	474 120
Equity attributable to owners of the parent	924 120
Non-controlling interest (from CSCIE) **OR** (see pro forma journal entries: Calc 4) **OR** (59 030 (see Calc 1 **F**) + 87 500 (see Calc 2 **h**))	146 530
Total equity	1 070 560
Current liabilities	
Trade and other payables (101 000 (P Ltd) + 19 000 (S Ltd))	120 000
Total equity and liabilities	1 190 650

Example 8.7: Consolidation of a partly owned subsidiary with cumulative preference shares and preference dividend in arrear at acquisition

On 1 January 20x5 P Ltd acquired 80% (a controlling interest) of the ordinary shares of S Ltd for CU 142 000. The equity of S Ltd at acquisition date consisted of the following:

- ordinary share capital CU 100 000; and
- retained earnings CU 40 000.

P Ltd acquired 30% of the non-redeemable, cumulative preference shares of S Ltd on 1 January 20x5 for CU 55 000. The preference shares entitle the holder to an annual dividend of 15% (on 31 December). In addition, at 1 January 20x5 the preference dividend for the previous two years was in arrears.

Additional information

- The preference shareholders have the following rights:
  - their dividend payment has priority over that of the ordinary shareholders; and
  - they will receive a proportionate share of the net assets of S Ltd should this entity be liquidated.
- P Ltd measured the non-controlling interest at its proportionate share of S Ltd's identifiable net assets.
- The net assets of S Ltd were considered to be fairly valued at acquisition date.
- P Ltd measured both its investment in S Ltd's ordinary shares and in S Ltd's preference shares at cost price.

The abridged trial balances of P Ltd and its subsidiary S Ltd on 31 December 20x5 were as follows:

Abridged trial balances at 31 December 20x5	P Ltd Dr/(Cr) CU	S Ltd Dr/(Cr) CU
Ordinary share capital	(450 000)	(100 000)
Preference share capital	–	(125 000)
Retained earnings (1 Jan 20x5)	(160 000)	(40 000)
Preference dividend paid	–	56 250
Trade and other payables	(107 000)	(115 400)
Plant	390 000	296 150
Trade and other receivables	320 000	143 000
Investment in S Ltd: Ordinary shares at cost	142 000	–
Investment in S Ltd: Preference shares at cost	55 000	–
Profit for the year	(190 000)	(115 000)

Required

(a) Prepare the relevant analyses of equity as at 31 December 20x5.

(b) Provide the pro forma journals necessary to prepare consolidated financial statements for the P Ltd group for the financial year ended 31 December 20x5.

(c) Prepare the abridged consolidated statement of profit or loss and other comprehensive income of the P Ltd group for the financial year ended 31 December 20x5.

(d) Prepare the consolidated statement of changes in equity of the P Ltd group for the financial year ended 31 December 20x5.

Solution 8.7: Consolidation of partly owned subsidiary with cumulative preference shares and preference dividend in arrear at acquisition

Part (a): Analyses of equity of S Ltd as at 31 December 20x5

Calculation 1: Analysis of ordinary equity of S Ltd as at 31 December 20x5

| | Total of S Ltd's ordinary equity 100% CU | S Ltd 80% | | Non-controlling interest 20% CU |
| | | At acquisition CU | Since acquisition CU | |
Acquisition date (1 January 20x5)				
Ordinary share capital	100 000			
Retained earnings	40 000			
Arrear preference dividend (125 000 × 15% × 2 years)	(37 500)			
Fair value of net assets of S Ltd	102 500	82 000		20 500
Goodwill (balancing figure)	60 000 **A**	60 000		–
Consideration and NCI	162 500	142 000		20 500 **B**
Since acquisition				
• Current year:				
Profit for the year attributable to ordinary shareholders (115 000 – 18 750 (125 000 × 15%) Preference dividend)	96 250		77 000 **C**	19 250 **D**
	258 750		77 000	39 750

Explanatory notes: Analysis of ordinary equity of S Ltd

- Because the subsidiary acquired has preference dividends in arrears at acquisition date, a portion of S Ltd's at acquisition retained earnings (equal to the preference dividend in arrears of CU 37 500) belongs to the preference shareholders of S Ltd. Accordingly, we need to subtract this arrear preference dividend when analysing the at acquisition ordinary equity of S Ltd acquired so that we can obtain the correct goodwill figure as well as determine the correct non-controlling interest in S Ltd's ordinary equity. This is because the consideration paid by P Ltd for the ordinary equity of S Ltd, and the non-controlling interest's share of the at acquisition ordinary equity of S Ltd are based on the retained earnings of S Ltd attributable to its **ordinary shareholders**, which amount excludes any portion of S Ltd's retained earnings attributable to S Ltd's preference shareholders in the form of arrear preference dividends.

- Were this adjustment (reducing at acquisition retained earnings by the arrear preference dividend) not processed, then the ordinary equity of S Ltd acquired would be overstated, which would result in the understatement of goodwill and the overstatement of the non-controlling interest in S Ltd's ordinary equity at acquisition.

Calculation 2: Analysis of preference equity of S Ltd as at 31 December 20x5

| Acquisition date
(1 January 20x5) | Total of
S Ltd's
preference
equity 100%
CU | P Ltd 30% | | Non-
controlling
interest
70%
CU |
		At acquisition CU	Since acquisition CU	
Preference share capital	125 000			
Arrear preference dividend (125 000 × 15% × 2 years)	37 500			
	162 500	48 750		113 750
Goodwill (balancing figure)	6 250 a	6 250		–
Consideration and NCI	168 750	55 000		113 750 b
Since acquisition				
• Current year:				
Profit attributable to preference shareholders (125 000 × 15%)	18 750		5 625 c	13 125 d
Preference dividend paid (given)	(56 250)		(16 875) e	(39 375) f
	131 250		(11 250)	87 500

Explanatory notes: Analysis of preference equity of S Ltd

- S Ltd's preference share equity acquired at acquisition date must **include the arrear preference dividend** owing to its preference shareholders. In this regard:
  - The amount paid by P Ltd for the preference shares of S Ltd, and therefore the goodwill that arises, is determined by taking into account the preference dividend of prior years that will be paid in a future period. That is, S Ltd's preference equity acquired at acquisition date includes preference profits (the arrear preference dividend) in addition to the preference share capital.
  - The non-controlling interest's share of the at acquisition preference equity of S Ltd is similarly calculated based on an amount that includes S Ltd's arrear preference dividends in addition to the preference share capital itself.
- Were this adjustment (increasing the at acquisition preference equity by the arrear preference dividend) not processed, then the preference equity of S Ltd acquired would be understated, which would result in the overstatement of goodwill and the understatement of the non-controlling interest in S Ltd's at acquisition preference equity.

Part (b): Pro forma journal entries for the 20x5 financial year

Pro forma journal 1 (J1)	Dr CU	Cr CU	NCI Balance
Ordinary share capital (S Ltd) (SCIE) (given)	100 000		
Retained earnings (S Ltd) (SCIE)	Wkg1 2 500		
Investment: S Ltd ordinary shares (P Ltd) (SFP) (given)		142 000	
NCI – Equity (SCIE)		Wkg2 20 500	20 500
Goodwill (SFP) (balancing figure)	60 000		
Elimination of at acquisition ordinary owners equity of S Ltd and cost of ordinary share investment in S Ltd and recognition of the non-controlling interest and goodwill upon acquisition of S Ltd's ordinary shares			

Workings: Pro forma journals

Working 1
40 000 (given) – 37 500 Arrear preference dividend at acquisition
(125 000 Preference share capital × 15% Dividend rate × 2 years)

Working 2
(100 000 + 2 500) × 20% NCI Share

Pro forma journal 2 (J2)	Dr CU	Cr CU	
Preference share capital (S Ltd) (SCIE) (given)	125 000		
Retained earnings (S Ltd) (SCIE) (see Working 1: Arrear preference dividend) Investment in S Ltd preference shares (P Ltd)	37 500		
(SFP) (given)		55 000	
NCI – Equity (SCIE)		Wkg3 113 750	113 750
Goodwill (SFP) (balancing figure)	6 250		
Elimination of at acquisition preference owners equity of S Ltd and cost of preference share investment in S Ltd, and recognition of non-controlling interest and goodwill, upon acquisition of S Ltd's preference shares			

Workings: Pro forma journals

Working 3
(125 000 + 37 500) × 70% NCI Share

Balance 134 250 at acquisition (Calc 3)

CURRENT YEAR

Pro forma journal 3 (J3)	Dr CU	Cr CU	
NCI share of profit or loss (P/L)	Wkg4 19 250		
NCI – Equity (SFP)		Wkg4 19 250	19 250
Allocating the non-controlling interest in S Ltd's ordinary equity its share of S Ltd's current year profit after deducting the current year preference dividend			

Workings: Pro forma journals

Working 4
(115 000 (given) Current year profit of S Ltd – 18 750 (125 000 × 15%)
Current year preference dividend) × 20% NCI Share

Pro forma journal 4 (J4)	Dr CU	Cr CU	NCI Balance
NCI share of profit or loss (P/L)	Wkg5 13 125		
NCI – Equity (SFP)		Wkg5 13 125	13 125
Allocating the non-controlling interest in S Ltd's preference share equity its share of S Ltd's current year preference dividend			

Workings: Pro forma journals

Working 5
18 750 (Working 4) Current year preference dividend × 70% NCI Share

Pro forma journal 5 (J5)	Dr CU	Cr CU	
Preference dividend received (P Ltd) (P/L)	Wkg6 16 875		
NCI – Equity (SFP) (balancing figure)	39 375		(39 375)
Preference dividend paid (S Ltd) (SCIE) (given)		56 250	
Elimination of intragroup preference dividend received from S Ltd, and recognition of non-controlling interest in the dividend			

Workings: Pro forma journals

Working 6
56 250 (given) Preference dividend paid × 30% P Ltd Share

Balance 127 250 EOY (Calc 4)

The full effects of the preceding pro forma journals on the consolidated financial statements of the P Ltd group for the financial year ended 31 December 20x5 are illustrated in the following consolidation worksheet.

	P Ltd Dr/(Cr) CU	S Ltd Dr/(Cr) CU	Pro forma journals At acquisition Dr/(Cr) CU	Journal ref	Pro forma journals Since acquisition Dr/(Cr) CU	Journal ref	Consolidated Dr/(Cr) CU
Equity							
Ordinary share capital	(450 000)	(100 000)	100 000	J1			(450 000)
Preference share capital		(125 000)	125 000	J2			
Retained earnings (BOY)	(160 000)	(40 000)	2 500 / 37 500	J1 / J2			(160 000)
Profit: Individual entities	(190 000)	(115 000)					
Consolidated profit attributable to owners of parent							†(255 750)
Preference dividend	–	56 250			(56 250)	J5	
Retained earnings (EOY)	(350 000)	(98 750)					(415 750)
NCI Equity			(20 500) / (113 750)	J1 / J2	(19 250) / (13 125) / 39 375	J3 / J4 / J5	(127 250)
Total equity	(800 000)	(323 750)					(993 000)
Liabilities:							
Trade and other payables	(107 000)	(115 400)					(222 400)
Total liabilities	(107 000)	(115 400)					(222 400)
Total equity & liabilities	(907 000)	(439 150)					(1 215 400)

Explanatory notes

† This amount has been brought forward from the second part of the consolidation worksheet on page 567

	P Ltd	S Ltd	Pro forma journals At acquisition		Pro forma journals Since acquisition		Con-solidated
	Dr/(Cr) CU	Dr/(Cr) CU	Dr/(Cr) CU	Journal ref	Dr/(Cr) CU	Journal ref	Dr/(Cr) CU
Assets:							
Plant	390 000	296 150					686 150
Trade and other receivables	320 000	143 000					463 000
Investment in S Ltd: Ordinary shares	142 000	–	(142 000)	J1			–
Investment in S Ltd: Preference shares	55 000	–	(55 000)	J2			–
Goodwill			60 000	J1			66 250
			6 250	J2			
Total assets	907 000	439 150					1 215 400
Profit or loss							
Profit for the year	(190 000)	(115 000)			16 875	J5	(288 125)
NCI: Share of profit					19 250	J3	32 375
					13 125	J4	
Consolidated profit attributable to owners of parent							‡(255 750)

Explanatory notes

‡ This amount has been carried forward to the first part of the consolidation worksheet on page 566

Part (c): Consolidated financial statements for the 20x5 financial year

P LTD GROUP: ABRIDGED CONSOLIDATED STATEMENT OF PROFIT OR LOSS AND OTHER COMPREHENSIVE INCOME FOR THE YEAR ENDED 31 DECEMBER 20x5	
	CU
PROFIT FOR THE YEAR (P Ltd: 190 000 – 16 875 (see Calc 2 **e OR** (J5)) Preference dividend) + 115 000 (S Ltd))	288 125
Other comprehensive income	–
TOTAL COMPREHENSIVE INCOME	288 125
Attributable to:	
Owners of the parent	Wkg1255 750
Non-controlling interest (Ordinary NCI: 19 250 (see Calc 1 **D OR** (J3)) + Preference NCI: 13 125 (see Calc 2 **d OR** (J4)))	32 375
	288 125

Workings: Abridged consolidated statement of profit or loss and other comprehensive income

Working 1

(P Ltd: 190 000 – 16 875 (see Calc 2 **e OR** (J5)) Preference dividend) + (S Ltd: 77 000 (see Calc 1 **C**) + 5 625 (see Calc 2 **c**)) **OR** Balancing figure

P LTD GROUP: CONSOLIDATED STATEMENT OF CHANGES IN EQUITY FOR THE YEAR ENDED 31 DECEMBER 20x5					
	Parent equity holders' interest			Non-controlling interest	Total equity of the group
	Ordinary Share capital	Retained earnings	Total parent equity		
	CU	CU	CU	CU	CU
Opening balance at 1 Jan 20x5	450 000	160 000	610 000	–	610 000
Acquisition of subsidiary				Wkg1134 250	134 250
Total comprehensive income:					
Profit for the period (from CSOPL_OCI)		255 750	255 750	32 375	288 125
Dividend				Wkg2(39 375)	(39 375)
Closing balance at 31 Dec 20x5	450 000	415 750	865 750	127 250	993 000

Workings: Consolidated statement of changes in equity

Working 1

Ordinary NCI of S Ltd: 20 500 (see Calc 1 **B**) + Preference NCI of S Ltd: 113 750 (see Calc 2 **b**)

OR

NCI of S Ltd (both ordinary and preference): 134 250 (see pro forma journal entries: Calc 3)

Working 2

NCI share of S Ltd preference dividend: 39 375 (see (J5) **OR** Calc 2 f)

8.2.3 Attribution and allocation of post-acquisition profits – subsidiary preference shares classified as a liability

As was discussed in Section 8.1.1, when preference shares are classified as a **liability** (i.e., **redemption is compulsory** or **redemption** is at the **election of the holder** of the preference shares), then the associated preference dividend will be included in the subsidiary's statement of **profit or loss and other comprehensive income** as a **finance charge**. The implication of this accounting treatment is that the preference dividend will **already have been deducted** in arriving at the subsidiary's after tax profit. This means **that no adjustment is required** (i.e., the preference dividend must not be deducted) to the subsidiary's profit before allocating such profit between the parent and the non-controlling interest, which are ordinary shareholders of the subsidiary.

In addition, to the extent that the parent holds subsidiary preference shares, the parent's share of the subsidiary's preference dividend declared/paid – which is accounted for as a finance charge of the subsidiary – is eliminated against the preference dividend recognised as income in the separate financial statements of the parent. The net result is that the **non-controlling interest's share of the subsidiary's preference dividend** declared/paid then becomes **the finance charge recognised for group purposes.**

 Example 8.8: Consolidation of partly owned subsidiary with cumulative preference shares classified as a liability

On 1 January 20x4 P Ltd acquired 80% (a controlling interest) of the ordinary shares of S Ltd for CU 170 000 and 30% of S Ltd's preference shares for CU 33 000. The equity of S Ltd at acquisition date consisted of the following:

- ordinary share capital CU 100 000; and
- retained earnings CU 40 000.

Additional information

- S Ltd issued 500 compulsory redeemable, cumulative preference shares on 1 January 20x4 at CU 220 per share with a dividend rate of 15%. The preference shares are classified as a financial liability.
- No preference dividends were in arrears in the 20x4 and 20x5 financial reporting periods.
- P Ltd measures the non-controlling interest at its fair value and the fair value of the non-controlling interest in the ordinary shares on acquisition date was CU 45 000.
- The net assets of S Ltd were considered to be fairly valued at acquisition date
- P Ltd measured both its investment in S Ltd's ordinary shares and in S Ltd's preference shares at cost price.

➥

The abridged trial balances of P Ltd and its subsidiary S Ltd on 31 December 20x5 were as follows:

Abridged trial balances at 31 December 20x5	P Ltd Dr/(Cr) CU	S Ltd Dr/(Cr) CU
Ordinary share capital	(450 000)	(100 000)
Preference share liability	–	(110 000)
Retained earnings (1 Jan 20x5)	(160 000)	(108 000)
Trade and other payables	(181 950)	(60 150)
Plant	390 000	296 150
Trade and other receivables	324 500	201 150
Investment in S Ltd: Ordinary shares at cost	170 000	–
Investment in S Ltd: Preference shares at cost	33 000	–
Gross profit	(320 000)	(280 000)
Other income (including preference dividend)	(10 800)	–
Operating expenses	160 000	105 000
Finance charges	–	16 500
Taxation	45 250	39 350

Note: During the 20x5 financial reporting period S Ltd declared and paid a preference dividend of CU 16 500, which was classified as a finance charge by S Ltd.

Required

(a) Provide the pro forma journals necessary to prepare consolidated financial statements for the P Ltd group for the financial year ended 31 December 20x5.

(b) Prepare the abridged consolidated statement of profit or loss and other comprehensive income for the P Ltd group for the financial year ended 31 December 20x5.

(c) Determine the preference share liability that will be disclosed in the consolidated statement of financial position of the P Ltd group as at 31 December 20x5.

 Solution 8.8: Consolidation of a partly owned subsidiary with cumulative preference shares classified as a liability

Part (a): Pro forma journal entries for the 20x5 financial year

AT ACQUISITION

Pro forma journal 1 (J1)	Dr CU	Cr CU
Share capital (S Ltd) (SCIE) (given)	100 000	
Retained earnings (S Ltd) (SCIE) (given)	40 000	
Investment: S Ltd ordinary shares (P Ltd) (SFP) (given)		170 000
NCI – Equity (SCIE) (given – at fair value)		45 000
Goodwill (SFP) (balancing figure)	75 000	
Elimination of at acquisition ordinary equity and cost of investment, and recognition of non-controlling interest and goodwill at acquisition of ordinary shares of S Ltd		

Pro forma journal 2 (J2)	Dr CU	Cr CU
Preference share liability (S Ltd) (SCIE) (balancing figure)	33 000	
Investment: S Ltd ordinary shares (P Ltd) (SFP) (given)		33 000
Elimination of intra-group balances, setting off S Ltd preference share liability against P Ltd investment in S Ltd preference shares		

Comments: Pro forma journal 2

- S Ltd's preference share liability is eliminated to the extent of P Ltd's investment in S Ltd's preference shares as these are intragroup balances that require elimination on consolidation. The result is that the remaining preference shares of S Ltd, owned by the non-controlling interest, are reflected as a liability in the consolidated financial statements.

SINCE ACQUISITION TO THE BEGINNING OF THE YEAR

Pro forma journal 3 (J3)	Dr CU	Cr CU
Retained earnings (S Ltd) (SCIE)	Wkg1 13 600	
NCI – Equity (SFP)		Wkg1 13 600
Allocating the non-controlling interest in S Ltd's ordinary equity its share of S Ltd's post-acquisition retained earnings to the beginning of the year		

Workings: Pro forma journals

Working 1
(108 000 Balance BOY – 40 000 Balance at acquisition) × 20% NCI Share

CURRENT YEAR

Pro forma journal 4 (J4)	Dr CU	Cr CU
NCI: Share of profit or loss (P/L)	Wkg2 23 830	
NCI – Equity (SFP)		Wkg2 23 830
Allocating the non-controlling interest in S Ltd's ordinary entity, its share of S Ltd's current year profit		

Workings: Pro forma journals

Working 2
(280 000 – 105 000 – 16 500 – 39 350) × 20% NCI Share

Comments: Pro forma journal 4

- Note that as the preference dividend paid of CU 16 500 is classified as a finance charge, it has already been deducted in arriving at S Ltd's profit after tax. Consequently, it is not deducted again in determining S Ltd's profit attributable to the non-controlling ordinary shareholders.

Pro forma journal 5 (J5)	Dr CU	Cr CU
Other income [Preference dividend received] (P Ltd) (P/L)	Wkg3 4 950	
Finance charge (S Ltd) (P/L)		Wkg3 4 950
Elimination of intragroup preference dividend		

Workings: Pro forma journals

Working 3
16 500 (given) S Ltd Total finance charge × 30% P Ltd Share

Part (b): Abridged consolidated statement of profit or loss and other comprehensive income for the 20x5 financial year

P LTD GROUP: ABRIDGED CONSOLIDATED STATEMENT OF PROFIT OR LOSS AND OTHER COMPREHENSIVE INCOME FOR THE YEAR ENDED 31 DECEMBER 20x5	
	CU
Gross profit (320 000 (P Ltd) + 280 000 (S Ltd))	600 000
Other income (P Ltd: 10 800 – 4 950 (J5) Intragroup preference dividend)	5 850
Operating expenses (160 000 (P Ltd) + 105 000 (S Ltd))	(265 000)
Finance charges (S Ltd: 16 500 – 4 950 (J5) Intragroup finance charge)	†(11 550)
Profit before tax	329 300
Income tax expense (45 250 (P Ltd) + 39 350 (S Ltd))	(84 600)
PROFIT FOR THE YEAR	**244 700**
Other comprehensive income	–
TOTAL COMPREHENSIVE INCOME	**244 700**
Total comprehensive income attributable to:	
Owners of the parent (balancing figure)	220 870
Non-controlling interest (see (J4))	23 830
	244 700

Explanatory notes

† This is the finance charge after eliminating the portion that is intragroup (i.e., S Ltd's preference dividend attributable to P Ltd).

This results in only the non-controlling interest's share of the subsidiary's preference dividend being recognised as the finance charge of the group.

Part (c): Preference share liability disclosed in the consolidated statement of financial position as at 31 December 20x5

	CU
Preference liability per separate records of S Ltd:	110 000
Less: Intragroup portion (see (J2))	(33 000)
Preference liability disclosed in the consolidated statement of financial position	77 000

Summary

Volume 1 Chapter 8 addressed the consolidation both at acquisition, and then in subsequent reporting periods, of a subsidiary that has preference shares in issue. The main difference between preference shares and ordinary shares is the preferential right of the former to dividends as well as the fact that, most often, the preference dividend is fixed in percentage terms.

Importantly, the subsidiary's preference shares may be classified either as equity or as a liability, with each classification having different consolidation implications. Preference shares are classified as equity when the preference shares are non-redeemable, or redemption is at the option of the issuing company. Conversely, preference shares are classified as a liability when the preference shares are compulsory redeemable, or redemption is at the option of the holder.

At the **acquisition date,** when consolidating a subsidiary with preference shares classified as **equity,** the key learnings are as follows:

- The cost of the parent's investment in the subsidiary's preference shares is eliminated against the parent's share of the subsidiary's at acquisition preference equity, and any difference that arises is recognised as goodwill or a bargain purchase gain.
- The non-controlling interest in the subsidiary's at acquisition preference equity is recognised and may be measured:
  - **only at fair value** if the preference shares are **entitled only** to the return of their **preference capital** upon **liquidation** of the subsidiary; and
  - **either at fair value or** at its **proportionate share in the subsidiary's identifiable net assets** where it is entitled to a **proportionate share of the subsidiary's net assets on liquidation** of the subsidiary.
- Where the subsidiary's preference dividend is in **arrears at acquisition date,** the subsidiary's at acquisition **ordinary equity** is **reduced** by such **arrear preference dividends** (at acquisition retained earnings is reduced). These arrear preference dividends then form part of the **at acquisition preference equity** acquired by the **parent** and by the **non-controlling shareholders** who hold the subsidiary's **preference shares.**

After acquisition date, when a subsidiary with preference shares classified as equity is consolidated, it is important to understand the following:

- The subsidiary's post-acquisition profit is allocated to the parent and to the non-controlling interest, which are ordinary shareholders of the subsidiary, after **first deducting** the **preference dividend** due to the preference shareholders, more specifically:
  - when the preference dividend is **non-cumulative,** it is deducted only when it has **been declared;** and
  - when the preference dividend is **cumulative,** the **specified dividend is deducted each year** even if the preference dividend has *not* been declared.
- The preference dividend deducted is allocated to the non-controlling interest and to the parent preference shareholders based on their respective ownership interests in the subsidiary's preference equity.

Any **preference dividend** received/receivable by **the parent from its subsidiary** is an **intragroup item** that requires elimination on consolidation. The portion of the **subsidiary's preference dividend declared/paid to the parent** is eliminated against the **dividend income** recognised by the **parent in its separate financial statements.** Furthermore, the portion of the **subsidiary's preference dividend declared/paid to the non-controlling interest** is **eliminated against the non-controlling interest's equity balance,** reducing its interest in the subsidiary's preference equity.

Where preference shares issued by a subsidiary are classified as a liability, then on consolidation:

- At acquisition, the cost of the parent's investment in the subsidiary's preference shares is eliminated against the parent's share of the subsidiary's preference share capital (classified as a liability). The result is that any non-controlling interest in the subsidiary's preference shares is then recognised as a liability of the group.

- After acquisition, the parent's share of the subsidiary's preference dividend declared/paid (which is classified as a finance charge in the subsidiary's financial statements) is eliminated against the preference dividend income of the parent. Accordingly, any non-controlling share of the subsidiary's preference dividend declared/paid will be recognised as a finance charge in the consolidated financial statements.

In Volume 2 Chapter 1, we delve into the advanced aspects of IFRS 3 business combinations.

QUESTIONS

Question 8.1

The following are the abridged trial balances of P Ltd and its subsidiary S Ltd for the year ended 31 December 20x5:

Abridged trial balances at 31 December 20x5	P Ltd Dr/(Cr) CU	S Ltd Dr/(Cr) CU
Ordinary share capital	(150 000)	(100 000)
Preference share capital	–	(80 000)
Retained earnings (1 January 20x5)	(300 000)	(288 000)
Ordinary dividend paid (31 December 20x5)	35 000	15 000
Preference dividend paid (31 December 20x5)	–	19 200
Trade and other payables	(120 680)	(52 700)
Equipment	145 200	214 810
Trade and other receivables	317 980	365 450
Investment in S Ltd: Ordinary shares at cost	210 000	–
Investment in S Ltd: Preference shares at cost	19 500	–
Profit for the period	(157 000)	(93 760)

Further information

1. P Ltd acquired a 70% controlling interest in the ordinary share capital of S Ltd on 1 January 20x4 for CU 210 000, when S Ltd had share capital of CU 100 000 and retained earnings of CU 180 000. At acquisition date the identifiable net assets of S Ltd were considered to be fairly valued.

2. On 1 January 20x4 S Ltd issued non-redeemable, cumulative, preference shares at CU 50 per share. The preference shares entitle the holder to an annual dividend of 12% (on 31 December). P Ltd acquired 40% of the preference shares on 1 January 20x4 for CU 19 500.

3. The preference shareholders have the following rights:
   - their dividend payment has priority over that of the ordinary shareholders; and
   - they will receive a proportionate share of the net assets of S Ltd should this entity be liquidated.

4. On 1 January 20x4 S Ltd sold equipment with a carrying amount of CU 52 000 to P Ltd for CU 77 000. On this date the estimated useful life of the equipment sold was five years and the equipment had a NIL residual value. The group policy is to provide for depreciation over the expected useful life of machinery using the straightline method, which is consistent with the tax allowances granted by the tax authority.

5. The group elected to measure any non-controlling interest in an acquiree at its proportionate share of the acquiree's identifiable net assets at acquisition date.

6. P Ltd measured both its investment in S Ltd's ordinary shares and in S Ltd's preference shares at cost price.

7. The income tax rate is 28% and in all the entities each share carries one vote. Furthermore, 80% of capital gains are included in taxable income.

Required

Prepare the abridged consolidated statement of profit or loss and other comprehensive income and the consolidated statement of changes in equity for the P Ltd group for the financial year ended 31 December 20x5.

Question 8.2

The following are the abridged trial balances of P Ltd and its subsidiary S Ltd for the year ended 30 June 20x5:

Abridged trial balances at 30 June 20x5	P Ltd Dr/(Cr) CU	S Ltd Dr/(Cr) CU
Ordinary share capital	(250 000)	(100 000)
Preference share capital	–	(75 000)
Retained earnings (1 July 20x4)	(290 000)	(268 000)
Ordinary dividend declared	–	17 800
Preference dividend declared	–	10 125
10% loan from P Ltd	–	(83 000)
Trade and other payables	(120 680)	(52 700)
Shareholders for dividends: Ordinary shares	–	(17 800)
Shareholders for dividends: Preference shares	–	(10 125)
10% loan to S Ltd	83 000	–
Equipment	177 300	298 400
Trade and other receivables	317 980	356 200
Dividends receivable	17 906	–
Investment in S Ltd: Ordinary shares at cost	147 000	–
Investment in S Ltd: Preference shares at cost	41 500	–
Profit before dividend, interest and tax	(137 000)	(106 100)
Dividend income	(17 906)	–
Interest income	(8 300)	–
Interest expense	–	8 300
Taxation	39 200	21 900

Further information

1. P Ltd acquired a 75% controlling interest in the ordinary share capital of S Ltd on 1 July 20x2 for CU 147 000, when S Ltd had share capital of CU 100 000 and retained earnings of CU 35 000. At acquisition date the identifiable net assets of S Ltd were considered to be fairly valued with the exception of plant, which had a fair value of CU 230 000 and a carrying amount of CU 180 000. The remaining useful life of the plant at that date was four years with a NIL residual value.

2. On 1 July 20x4 S Ltd issued non-redeemable, cumulative, preference shares at CU 50 per share. The preference shares entitle the holder to an annual dividend of 13.5% (on 1 July). P Ltd acquired 45% of the preference shares on 1 July 20x4 for CU 41 500.

3. The preference shareholders have the following rights:
   - their dividend payment has priority over that of the ordinary shareholders; and
   - they will receive a proportionate share of the net assets of S Ltd should this entity be liquidated.

4. The group elected to measure any non-controlling interest in an acquiree at its fair value at acquisition date, which was CU 49 000 for the non-controlling interest in the ordinary shares and CU 45 500 for the non-controlling interest in the preference shares.

5. P Ltd measured both its investment in S Ltd's ordinary shares and in S Ltd's preference shares at cost price.

6. The income tax rate is 28% and in all the entities each share carries one vote. Furthermore, 80% of capital gains are included in taxable income.

Required

Provide the pro forma journals necessary to prepare consolidated financial statements for the P Ltd group for the financial year ended 30 June 20x5.

References

IFRS 3 *Business Combinations*

IFRS 9 *Financial Instruments*

IFRS 10 *Consolidated Financial Statements*

CPSIA information can be obtained
at www.ICGtesting.com
Printed in the USA
LVHW021929190822
726388LV00007B/430